Cardinal Isidore, c. 1390–1462

A member of the imperial Palaiologan family, albeit most probably illegitimate, Isidore became a scholar at a young age and began his rise in the Byzantine ecclesiastical ranks. He was an active advocate of the union of the Orthodox and Catholic churches in Constantinople. His military exploits, including his participation in the defense of Constantinople in 1453, provide us with eyewitness accounts. Without doubt he traveled widely, perhaps more so than any other individual in the annals of Byzantine history: Greece, Asia Minor, Sicily, Russia, Poland, Lithuania, and Italy. His roles included diplomat, high ecclesiastic in both the Orthodox and Catholic churches, theologian, soldier, papal emissary to the Constantinopolitan court, delegate to the Council of Florence, advisor to the last Byzantine emperors, metropolitan of Kiev and all Russia, and member of the Vatican *curia*.

This is an original work based on new archival research and the first monograph to study Cardinal Isidore in his many diverse roles. His contributions to the events of the first six decades of the *quattrocento* are important for the study of major Church councils and the fall of Constantinople to the Ottoman Turks. Isidore played a crucial role in each of these events.

Marios Philippides is Professor of Classics, Emeritus at the University of Massachusetts, Amherst, USA. He has published numerous articles on the fall of Constantinople, 1453, on late Byzantine and early post-Byzantine historiography, and on the Palaiologan era. He has authored numerous books and two books with Walter K. Hanak.

Walter K. Hanak was Professor of History, Emeritus at Shepherd University, Shepherdstown, West Virginia, USA. He was the editor and publisher of the scholarly journal *Byzantine Studies/Etudes Byzantines* for many decades. He has published numerous articles on medieval Greece, Russia, and the Slavonic word. He was the author of a number of books and collaborated with Marios Philippides in the publication of two books.

Cardinal Isidore, c. 1390–1462

A Late Byzantine Scholar, Warlord, and Prelate

Marios Philippides and
Walter K. Hanak†

LONDON AND NEW YORK

First published 2018
by Routledge
2 Park Square, Milton Park, Abingdon, Oxon OX14 4RN

and by Routledge
711 Third Avenue, New York, NY 10017

Routledge is an imprint of the Taylor & Francis Group, an informa business

© 2018 Marios Philippides and the Estate of Walter K. Hanak

The right of Marios Philippides and the Estate of Walter K. Hanak to be identified as authors of this work has been asserted by them in accordance with sections 77 and 78 of the Copyright, Designs and Patents Act 1988.

All rights reserved. No part of this book may be reprinted or reproduced or utilised in any form or by any electronic, mechanical, or other means, now known or hereafter invented, including photocopying and recording, or in any information storage or retrieval system, without permission in writing from the publishers.

Trademark notice: Product or corporate names may be trademarks or registered trademarks, and are used only for identification and explanation without intent to infringe.

British Library Cataloguing-in-Publication Data
A catalogue record for this book is available from the British Library

Library of Congress Cataloging-in-Publication Data
Names: Philippides, Marios, 1950– author.
Title: Cardinal Isidore (c. 1390–1462) : a late Byzantine scholar, warlord, and prelate / Marios Philippides.
Description: New York : Routledge, 2018. | Includes bibliographical references and index.
Identifiers: LCCN 2017046381 | ISBN 9780815379829 (hardback : alk. paper) | ISBN 9781351214902 (ebook)
Subjects: LCSH: Isidore, of Kiev, approximately 1385–1463. | Cardinals—Ukraine—Kiev–Biography. | Kiev (Ukraine)—Church history. | Church history—Middle Ages, 600-1500.
Classification: LCC BX4705.I793 P45 2018 | DDC 282.092 [B]—dc23
LC record available at https://lccn.loc.gov/2017046381

ISBN: 978-0-8153-7982-9 (hbk)
ISBN: 978-1-351-21490-2 (ebk)

Typeset in Bembo
by Apex CoVantage, LLC

Contents

Preface	vii
Acknowledgements	x
Abbreviations	xi

1 The rise of Isidore   1
    1 *The early years 1*
    2 *The sojourn in the Morea and the letters of Isidore 8*

2 Isidore and the Council of Basle   38
    1 *Prelude to Basle 38*
    2 *At Basle 40*
    3 *Byzantine issues resulting from Basle 64*
    4 *The Muscovite reaction 69*

3 The rise of Isidore and the Council of Ferrara-Florence   79
    1 *Metropolitan of Kiev and of All Rus' 79*
    2 *The Council of Ferrara-Florence 89*
    3 *The return to Muscovy and the aftermath of Florence 99*

4 The papal emissary   122
    1 *The first mission to Constantinople: a failure 122*
    2 *The second mission to Constantinople: warlord and gift-bearer 124*
    3 *Disputations 135*
    4 *Isidore and the declaration of church union 150*

5 Defender, humanist, and survivor   189
    1 *Imperial councilor and legate 189*
    2 *Warrior and reporter 194*
    3 *Two letters of Isidore 198*
    4 *The escape of Isidore 212*

6 Cretan interlude 243
1 Early propagandist 243
2 Two major themes in Isidore's letters from Candia 248
3 Religious propaganda and military strategy 259

7 Il Cardinal Greco Vecchio: The last years 290

8 Conclusions: *Damnatio memoriae?* 329

Appendix 348
1 Isidore the historian 348
2 Selections from Isidore's Panegyric to Manuel II and John VIII 349
3 English translation of selections from Isidore's Panegyric to Manuel II and John VIII 360

Bibliography 376
Index Nominum 408
Index Locorum 415
Index Rerum Antiquarum 420

Preface

In contemporary academic scholarship, the field of history is often viewed as a branch of literary studies. To a certain degree, this is true. However, our approach in this study is to treat each of these disciplines as co-partners, for both disciplines are dependent upon original source materials that we employ extensively in our research topic. It is true that each of the fields of study scrutinizes the materials, one from the perspective of literary analysis, and the other from a search for internal evidence illuminating the role of individuals in diverse encounters and revealing evidentiary information for its historical significance. To cite the importance of the historical process, we quote James Howard-Johnston, who elaborates:[1]

> History is not a social science. Historians handle data – gathering, sorting, patterning – rather than constructing theories. They deal with a bewildering array of particulars – individuals and groups, places of every conceivable sort (from the smallest of localities to whole continents), times, actions and processes (slow- or fast-moving, gentle or violent), structures (whether the built environment in town and country or the institutions developed by human societies for the ordering of life), thoughts passing in and out of minds (only to be grasped if articulated in words), thought worlds (the immaterial structures of minds linked together in social networks) *etc. etc.* There is no question of exactitude in history. If calculation of the effects of a single wave in the sea or a slight breadth of wind in the air is beyond the capacity of the swiftest and most capacious of computers, it is inconceivable that useful general laws of human behavior in social aggregates can ever be formulated, when thoughts are continually bubbling to the surface in billions of minds, when gestures and actions are continually setting in motion causal chains which have no end. No, the historian is, first and foremost, a sleuth, seeking out data and clues to data, trying to understand the surrounding world.

It is in this context that we approach the study of a significant individual, Cardinal Isidore, who contributed much to his age, but also added to the inconclusive circumspections of that period. And yet, we employ throughout this work literary analysis in our examination of original texts, without which there would exist a vacuum in this study.

Isidore over a span of a half century demonstrated that he was a complex individual, involving himself in sundry activities (literary happenings, writing, textual transmission, and manuscript copying; diplomat, high ecclesiastic, theologian, and soldier, among other undertakings) and significant historical events (to cite at this moment but two from among many, especially the Council of Ferrara-Florence and the fall of Constantinople in 1453). It is not our intention to evaluate his personality from the perspective of psychohistory, for this would lead us through endless mazes from which we could not extricate ourselves. Rather, we see Isidore from the perspective of his actions and accomplishments, his successes and failures, and numerous other activities. To say that he was an enigmatic figure with a strange personality would be a misstatement of the evidence at hand. He did influence prominent people, both lay and ecclesiastic, and was involved, even if minimally, in the main intellectual movement of his age – the Renaissance. We have attempted, then, to reconstruct a picture of him that exemplifies all his strengths, accomplishments, and even shortcomings.

This study is based upon extracting significant information from primary sources, since the extant secondary literature is at time erroneous, lacks meticulousness in providing historical information, and advances interpretations that cannot be supported by the primary sources. This is not to say that the primary sources themselves do not also contain erroneous and contradictory information, for indeed they do. Our approach has been to carefully weigh all source materials for relevancy, historical accuracy, and literary achievement. The primary sources were obtained from leading depositories, whose archival holdings are extensive. Our leading source for manuscripts was the Vatican Library, which provided us reproductions of countless materials, including documents and letters, among other texts. We were fortunate to avail ourselves of printed sources, some of questionable editorial quality, but nonetheless useful. As our bibliography demonstrates, our secondary source list is extensive. We had to garner every conceivable tidbit of information to understand the role that Isidore, in his many capacities, played in his time that indeed was an eventful age. To support our study of this high churchman, we have provided quotations from the primary source materials in their original languages with accompanying English translation. What emerges in our study is a fresh and perhaps a new critical understanding of the contributions of Cardinal Isidore to the historical record and the literary world of the fifteenth century.

Walter K. Hanak and Marios Philippides

†Walter K. Hanak, a close friend and a scholarly collaborator for over three decades, died on January 28, 2016. By that time we had compiled an early draft of this study. It fell upon me to complete the research, the text of the book, and

see it through publication. Our project could not have been completed without his detailed knowledge and command of Slavonic material. He is greatly missed by his family, by his former students, and by the scholarly community.

Marios Philippides

Note

1 J. Howard-Johnston, *Historical Writing in Byzantium* (Heidelberg, 2014), p. 11.

Acknowledgements

In our research and writing of *The Siege and the Fall of Constantinople in 1453: Historiography, Topography and Military Studies* (Farnham: Ashgate, 2011), we came to the realization that no comprehensive study exists of the life and times of Cardinal Isidore, a participant in so many significant events of the *quattrocento*. We also recognized that our research would rely extensively upon primary source materials, since the secondary literature provides an incomplete picture of this churchman and his accomplishments in the historical and literary events of his time. Our work required us to obtain and to peruse a significant number of original texts that are available through various depositories. The list of institutions is extensive, but in the main we requested and received reproductions of documents from the Vatican Library (Rome). We are grateful to their staff for furnishing us this valuable material. Next, we should be grateful to the librarians in charge of the Vatican microfilm collection at Saint Louis University (Missouri), who pointed us in the right direction. Additional original source materials in printed form and secondary works were made available to us at the Dumbarton Oaks Center for Byzantine Studies. We are particularly appreciative of our respective university libraries – Shepherd University and the University of Massachusetts at Amherst – which obtained microfilm collections and printed materials, mainly through the interlibrary loan process. We are especially grateful to Professor Julie Hayes, the Dean of the College of Humanities and Fine Arts of the University of Massachusetts, for a Faculty Research Grant that allowed us to purchase digital images of Isidore's manuscripts housed in the Library of the Vatican Archives. If we have overlooked other depositories that contributed significantly to our study, we are duly apologetic.

Abbreviations

AG	Joseph Gill, ed. *Quae supersunt Actorum Graecorum Concilii Florentini*, 2 parts
BS	*Byzantinoslavica*
Byz	*Byzantion*
BZ	*Byzantinische Zeitschrift*
CBB	Peter Schreiner, ed. *Die byzantinischen Kleinchroniken, Chronica Byzantina Breviora*
CC	Agostino Pertusi, ed. *La Caduta di Costantinopoli. Vol. 1: Le Testimonianze del Contemporanei. Vol. 2: L'Eco nel Mondo*
CF	Joseph Gill, *The Council of Florence*
CFDS	*Concilium Florentinum. Documenta et Scriptores. Series A and B*
CFHB	*Corpus Fontium Historiae Byzantinae*
CSHB	*Corpus Scriptorum Historiae Byzantinae*
CW	*The Classical World*
DOP	*Dumbarton Oaks Papers*
DOS	*Dumbarton Oaks Studies*
FC	Steven Runciman, *The Fall of Constantinople*
JWarb	*Journal of the Warburg and Courtauld Institutes*
LCB	Donald M. Nicol, *The Last Centuries of Byzantium, 1261–1453*
MCT	Franz Babinger, *Mehmed the Conqueror and His Time*
MHH	Philippe A. Déthier and Carl [Karl] Hopf, eds. *Monumenta Hungariae Historica Ser. Scriptores. Vol. 22.1*
MP	John W. Barker, *Manuel II Palaeologus (1391–1425): A Study in Late Byzantine Statesmanship*
NE	Nicolai Iorga, *Notes et Extraits pour servir à l'histoire des Croisades au XVe Siècle*, 6 vols.
NH	*Νέος Ἑλληνομνήμων*
N-I	Nestor-Iskander, *The Tale of Constantinople (Of Its Origin and Capture by the Turks in the Year 1453). (From the Early Sixteenth-Century Manuscript of the Troitse-Sergieva Lavra, No. 773)*. Trans. and Annotated by Walter K. Hanak and Marios Philippides
OCP	*Orientalia Christiana Periodica*

ODB	Alexander P. Kazhdan, et al., eds., The Oxford Dictionary of Byzantium, 3 vols.
PaL	Kenneth M. Setton, The Papacy and the Levant (1204–1571). Vol. 2: The Fifteenth Century
PG	Jacques-Paul Migne, ed. Patrologia Cursus Completus, Series Graeco-Latina
ПкΠ	Spyridon P. Lampros, Παλαιολόγεια καὶ Πελοποννησιακά. 4 vols.
PLP	Erich Trapp, et al., eds. Prosopographisches Lexikon der Palaiologenzeit. 7 vols.
ПСРЛ	Полное Собраніе Русскихъ Лѣтописей.
RdD	Freddy Thiriet, Régestes des déliberations du Sénat de Venise concernant la Romanie. 3 vols.
REB	Revue des etudes byzantines
РИБ	Русская историческая Библиотека
RKOR	Franz Dölger, ed. Regesten der Kaiserurkunden des oströmischen Reiches
SF	Marios Philippides and Walter K. Hanak, The Siege and Fall of Constantinople in 1453: Historiography, Topography, and Military Studies
TIePN	Agostino Pertusi and Antonio Carile, eds. Testi Inediti e Poco Noti sulla Caduta di Costantinopoli
ТОДРЛ	Труды Отдела Древне Русской Литературы
ВВ	Византийский Временник
ЗРВИ	Зборник радова Византлошког Института

1 The rise of Isidore

1 The early years

The career of Isidore (Ἰσίδωρος, Isidorus, Исидоръ, Сидоръ)[1] spans a number of decades, but he is largely known for his later years after he had assumed a leadership role in the affairs of the Orthodox Church, and then in the Roman Church following the union of churches that had been proclaimed at Florence. Thus the latter part of his life is well documented and can be reconstructed with a certain degree of certainty and confidence. Less documented is the middle phase from about 1420 to his rise to the metropolitan seat of Kiev and of All Rus'. Lamentably documented are his early years, his childhood and youth, which an investigator faces with a certain degree of uncertainty, if not despair, and often speculation must be, as it always has been, evoked when we are dealing with insurmountable obstacles created by *lacunae* in the primary sources, lack of information and erroneous citations in the secondary works, and considerable scholarly controversy in all works relative to him. We have often encountered challenging notions of who he was and what he had accomplished. Generally speaking, the early life of churchmen is often shrouded from public view, perhaps viewed as a period of little consequence, and thus adds to the mystery of who that person might be or had been. This has proven to be a rather common practice. As Isidore's career was spent in the late medieval Greek world, in the early Italian Renaissance, and in the northern Slavic area, one would anticipate a wealth of documents addressing all phases of his life.[2] The Greek sources, however, are reticent about his childhood years as are the Italian-Latin works, which become numerous after his elevation to cardinal in the later stages of his life. We should anticipate that Muscovite sources would provide us with additional factual information about Isidore's birth, life, and significant accomplishments prior to his designation as the metropolitan of Kiev and of All Rus', but no such *vita* exists by his hand; additionally, there is no biographical information compiled by his associates and by contemporaneous ecclesiastical scribes to enlighten us. Given the controversial issues associated with his rise to the metropolitan seat at Moscow, his initial role at the Council of Basle (Bâle, Basil, Basel) in favor of the union of the churches and then his major role in the Council of Ferrara-Florence to subject the Greek and the

Russian Church to the pope, the absence of a *vita* is understandably reasonable, if in fact it is not to be attributed to the vicissitudes of times. Its absence is an unfortunate circumstance and has led to substantial controversy and speculation among scholars. Thus we know of no Greek or Slavic sources that precisely identify his family, provide us with any familial associations, or supply concrete knowledge about his background, considerable education, and ecclesiastical connections. The sources, particularly the secondary works, present a confusing and puzzled picture. Isidore then remains in many respects a mysterious figure to scholarship, as he did to the Muscovite Rus', to the Roman *curia*, and even to the Byzantine Greeks themselves. As we shall have occasion to observe, he emerges as an enigmatic figure who appeared upon the scene at a crucial phase in both the history of the rise of Muscovite Rus' and then later participated in and witnessed the end of the Byzantine Empire. For Muscovy, this was their attempt to consolidate authority and dominion under the grand prince Vasilii II Vasil'evich, and for the Byzantines and their last two emperors, John VIII and Constantine XI, this was their eleventh-hour struggle to salvage remnants of their rapidly disintegrating, declining, and territorially receding "empire," whose lands were being consumed through the onslaughts of the Ottoman Turks under the sultans Murad II and Mehmed II.

To begin with, there survive no authoritative sources to establish his origins.[3] Was he a Moreot, from Monemvasia perhaps as he seems to have been rather attached to this Peloponnesian town, or was he born in Constantinople and eventually found his way to the Morea? Early views by scholars suggest that he had been born either in Constantinople or in Thessalonike, or perhaps even in Dalmatia.[4] On the other hand, A.W. Ziegler, citing an unknown and unpublished *curriculum vitae* of Isidore, states:[5] "d'origine grecque, il était vraisemblablement né entre 1380 et 1390 dans la ville commerçante de Monembasia en Péloponèse." Generally speaking, the Muscovite Rus' scribes tend to favor Thessalonike as his place of origin,[6] apparently intending to link him with the venerable monks Saints Constantine-Cyril and Methodios and their role in the mid-ninth century conversion and Christianization of the Slavs.[7] Beyond this meager information, the Slavic sources stress either his Greek roots[8] or identify him as a Greco-Slav without providing additional information.[9] The Greek sources as well lack specificity and remain at variance with Slavic accounts. Isidore, according to one version popular with modern scholars who stress his Constantinopolitan links and his assumed noble birth[10] without directly linking him to a particular family,[11] was born c. 1385 or perhaps c. 1390 in Monemvasia or elsewhere in the Morea,[12] and expired in Rome on Wednesday, the 27th of April (the dates often cited as the 23rd or the 29th of April 1463 are erroneous).[13] Addressing his lineage, Haris A. Kalligas has drawn an interesting supposition that merits comment. She advances the unsubstantiated notion that Isidore was the illegitimate son of the despot Theodoros I of the Morea, the fourth son of the emperor John V Palaiologos and Helena Kantakouzene, and the brother of the reigning emperor Manuel II.[14] Kalligas adds further:[15] "It is certain that he came from the Peloponnese and that he had a special attachment and constant interest in Monemvasia." However, the sources are persistently silent concerning his origin and this silence has led to a number of widely differing opinions on it – e.g., that he came from Thessalonike or that he was of Slav descent. This silence seems very strange regarding a person whose activities during a half century covered an area from Crete and the Peloponnese to Russia [Muscovite Rus'], and from Constantinople to Rome, who mixed and corresponded with the important people of his time in Byzantium and the West, and about whom much has been written.[16] The only firm conclusion in this labyrinth of suppositions that can be made is that Isidore, from early on in his childhood, was well connected and had the patronage of the imperial family. A lowly social status would not have afforded him the education that he received and the attention that was lavished upon him by the imperial family. A connection with the Palaiologan family cannot be ruled out, for such an advantage assisted in his rise to become an important ecclesiastical leader.[17]

Similarly, one may not be certain as to the year of his birth, but we can only surmise and make general inferences that may lead to further complications. If we assume that he was born c. 1385 or c. 1390, this would imply that when he was assigned a defensive military role during the siege of Constantinople in 1453 he was already advanced in age, in his sixties, and perhaps too aged to participate in the military operations and direct combat, with perhaps one exception. We know from the sources that on the day of the fall and sack of the imperial city he was riding a horse and received a wound during a skirmish. Yet we know that he had been assigned an important military sector to defend,[18] the area in the northwest of the city near the juncture of the sea walls along the Golden Horn with the Wall of Herakleios.[19] He was familiar with the sector, for he had been both a monk and *hegoumenos* (abbot) of the monastery of Saint Demetrios[20] (Δημητρίου [Μονὴ τοῦ ἁγ.] τῶν Παλαιολόγων, Ἅγιος Δημήτριος εἰς Ξυλόπορταν, Ἅγ. Δημήτριος ὁ Κανάβης [Καναβοῦ]).[21] At that time he would have been 68 if 1385 is the actual year of his birth (or 63 if 1390 is his year of birth). Thereafter, he managed to have an active life for another decade until he fell victim to a stroke and eventual death. If all this were true he would have enjoyed a remarkable constitution and would have been in command of exceptional physical strength and prowess in his advanced years. If, on the other hand, we adjust the year of his birth to c. 1390, then we encounter another challenging problem when we consider that Isidore was entrusted by Emperor Manuel II to pronounce the eulogy for his brother, Theodoros I, on an unspecified anniversary date commemorating his death. On this occasion, Isidore would have been a young man and one may ask whether the emperor would have entrusted such a serious and demanding task to a youth, unless he was an immediate descendant of Theodoros, as was custom.[22] If indeed that is the case and the youthful Isidore was entrusted with such a task, is it possible that he had very close ties with the imperial family; perhaps he was even a close blood relative of Theodoros I, an illegitimate son, and a nephew of Manuel II.[23] Or does this occasion imply that he was a child prodigy in public speaking and that was the reason why he was chosen to pronounce the eulogy? His participation in the operations of the siege of Constantinople in 1453 and his active role in the defense suggest that, at the time of the siege, he was perhaps in his fifties, but even that age would make him too young to pronounce a speech composed by the emperor in the second decade of the fifteenth century. Conversely, if he had been approaching his twentieth year when he gave this oratorical recital, then he was too old to actively participate in the defense of Constantinople, escape with a head wound, and survive another ten years. His actions on the fateful day of 29 May 1453, may have been occasioned by a momentary urge to defend Santa Sophia, perhaps to earn a martyr's death in doing so, in spite of his advanced age. Given the chronological constraints combined with the lack of evidence, a tentative conclusion may be reached that would suggest that Isidore was born c. 1390. That date concurs with the years of his education, the rudiments of which could not antedate 1400, with the recitation he provided as a talented young man while still in his teens, and would not preclude his limited combat experience, perhaps directing his troops from the safety of the walls or limited and light military activity during the actual operations in the defense of Constantinople in 1453. Moreover, this date would also allow him another decade to recover from the wound that he had received on the day of the fall and sack and his subsequent debilitating adventures, only to fall victim to a stroke in the next decade and die soon thereafter when he was in his seventies. That Isidore died in Rome on Wednesday, 27 April 1463, has now become an indisputable fact,[24] contrary to the earlier given dates.

We may state with some degree of certainty that Isidore received a significant portion of his education in the Greek imperial capital,[25] whether he was a native of that city or was a recently arrived émigré from the Morea. If he had actually been born in Constantinople, his early years would have been marked by the traumatic and intermittent land blockade conducted by the Ottoman Emir Bayezid I, which began in 1394 and lasted, on and off, until 1402 and the monumental battle of Ankara.[26] During the years of the prolonged blockade the population of Constantinople suffered greatly, along with the institutions that had been traditionally supervised by the court and the church. The terrible economic conditions, the inclination of its citizens to abandon their traditional homes, the acute spread of the plague within confined quarters,[27] and the general dissolution of society robbed the imperial capital of its numerous institutions that must have included the educational as well, which had to be revived after the elimination of Bayezid and the return of the emperor Manuel Palaiologos to his capital following his long absence in the West in a vain search for aid.[28] It has been implied that Isidore traveled to Constantinople in the retinue of Manuel upon his return from the West in 1403.[29] Manuel had slowly made his way to Italy and had departed Venice for the Morea in mid-April 1403. There, Manuel was reunited with his wife and family. While in the Morea he also took considerable time to resolve a number of problems and finally reached his imperial city in June of 1403.

When still in Venice, Manuel II was joined by his friend, the famous intellectual and teacher of ancient Greek, Manuel Chrysoloras, who then accompanied the emperor on his return voyage to Constantinople.[30] Is it possible that Manuel II recalled his friend from the West in order to revive the state of education in his imperial capital, which obviously had suffered during the long Ottoman blockade? The education system in Constantinople had to be restored. For Manuel, its revitalization was of immense interest for he himself was an intellectual[31] and clearly he had an intense concern for education.[32] Exactly who taught Isidore, where he studied, and what subjects he excelled in cannot be established with certainty.[33] Given the literary interests that he later exhibited in his own writings, letters, and essays, he received training in the scriptures, in the Church Fathers, and in laws governing the different dioceses and ecclesiastical jurisdictions. In addition, a prerequisite would have been solid training in ancient Greek and specifically in the Attic dialect favored by the intellectuals of the period. He was certainly comfortable in corresponding with the other humanists in Italy in Attic. In Constantinople he had studied in the company of notable Italian humanists, including the famous Guarino dei Guarini of Verona (1374–1460).[34] Isidore's association with Guarino provides us with the possibility of identifying a probable teacher. Guarino, we know, followed Chrysoloras to the imperial city and became one of his disciples in the summer of 1404.[35] Can we then conclude that Isidore received instruction, together with his friend Guarino, under the direction of one of the most famous teachers of Greek, Manuel Chrysoloras? Isidore's training must have included calligraphy and the transcription of ancient manuscripts. It is not generally known that numerous manuscripts copied by the hand of Isidore survive and are of the highest quality.[36] Isidore's career shows that he had received a considerable education under a great master, who could have been the famous Chrysoloras.[37] In his later years after the fall of Constantinople, Isidore borrowed books from the Vatican Library that reveal an intellectual bent with a keen interest in antiquity, ethnography, astronomy, and the occult.[38] The rudiments, if not actual advanced study, for his considerable command of literature must have their roots at this early stage in his career. However, his instruction under Chrysoloras had frequent interruptions. In 1404 and again in 1405–1406, Chrysoloras traveled to Italy.[39] If in fact Isidore had been under the tutelage of Chrysoloras, his studies must have come to an end in 1407, when Manuel II dispatched Chrysoloras to western courts in an endless search for military aid. His travels took him as far away as Spain. This was the great teacher's last voyage to the West[40] and he never returned to Constantinople.[41] But by the time of his departure, Isidore must have been quite an accomplished pupil, for he emerges in history soon thereafter.

The earliest work associated with Isidore is in fact the funeral oration that Emperor Manuel II composed for his brother, Theodoros I of the Morea,[42] which has created considerable confusion among scholars[43] concerning the actual date of its composition and the occasion or perhaps the occasions at which it was pronounced by Manuel II and/or Isidore himself.[44] At a later date,[45] Isidore composed a speech in honor of Emperors Manuel II and John VIII, and spoke of the circumstances that led to the composition of Manuel II's eulogy for his dead brother. This lengthy and in many aspects tedious speech required substantial time to reach its final form. The emperor sought scholarly advice on its style and composition.[46] It is known that Manuel forwarded several advanced copies of his composition to at least three scholars, whose advice he sought and evidently whose opinions he respected. To improve it, he requested comments on the text's style. Thus Georgios Gemistos Plethon, Isidore, and Manuel Chrysoloras were recipients of advanced copies.[47] Plethon submitted a few observations that survive;[48] whether Isidore replied we do not know, but the probability remains high that he did. Chrysoloras's long reply has survived, has been edited, and printed recently.[49] This rediscovery of Chrysoloras's text[50] has important chronological implications. The speech had yet to be pronounced in the summer of 1414 when Chrysoloras was still writing his response.[51] This is to say that the oration must have been pronounced *after* 1414.[52] In addition, we may perhaps suggest that the speech was delivered before 1417. In the summer of 1417,[53] Manuel II wrote a letter to Guarino and asked him to translate the Greek text into Latin or into Italian.[54] Manuel must have been proud of his accomplishment and elated upon its reception by the audience at Mistra. The conclusion that we may reach suggests that the speech was pronounced after 1414, but before 1417.

Isidore himself writes of the circumstances of his delivery of Manuel II's funeral oration in the letter that he addressed to the emperor, which in fact is a report of his arrival in the Morea.[55] We would place this letter as the first surviving letter that Isidore composed when he took up residence in the Morea, for it was written soon after he pronounced half of the speech at the ceremony, that is, soon after his arrival in the Morea.[56] It is in fact more than a letter. It constitutes a report on his voyage and the opening passages address the situation and the conditions that he encountered in the Morea. He apologizes for not immediately writing and excuses himself for his lack of education (ἀμουσία) and his inability to express himself (τὸ μὴ σὺν ὥρᾳ δύνασθαι λέγειν ... καὶ τὴν σιωπὴν ἀσπάζεσθαι ἔπειθεν), which forced him into a temporary silence. These are *topoi* within the genre of epistolography and indicate the literary "humility" that declares the writer's pretended lack of education.[57] Isidore highlights this point by declaring his familiarity with Attic Greek and with the style and language of Plato and Demosthenes, as he humbly states that only these authors could speak it properly.[58] After a few more formalities, Isidore states that he intends to give a brief statement of his experiences, which he asserts are in sore need of a much more sophisticated literary talent than his own.[59]

He appears to be astonished at the local customs of the inhabitants of the Morea and expresses surprise at their character, which he judges to be rather primitive and barbaric, especially since their cruelty "surpassed that of the Scythians."[60] Once he arrives in Mistra, the capital of the Morea, his tone changes. He has found a haven of civilization. There he maintains a watchful eye over his manuscript and reveals nothing of its contents, suggesting in a classical reference that he retained a silence befitting an initiate into the Eleusinian mysteries.[61] He does not wish his audience to gain an "advanced look" at the emperor's speech before the appointed day, even though his arrival and the impending address apparently and speedily became "the talk of the town" ("winged rumor was faster than a bird").[62] Isidore describes the ceremony in the same letter, which also reveals that it was on an unspecified anniversary of Theodoros's death:[63]

> ἀλλ᾽ ἐπεὶ τοίνυν ἧκεν ἡ προθεσμία καὶ ἡ ἡμέρα τοῦ ἔτους, καθ᾽ ἣν ὁ εὐφημούμενος μετέστη τῶν ὧδε, τελευτὴ δὲ ἐπὶ τῇδε γίγνεται, ἔδει δὲ ἐν ταύτῃ καὶ τὸ βιβλίον [Ἐπιτάφιος τοῦ Μανουὴλ] ἀναγινώσκεσθαι, παρῆν μὲν ὁ πάντα ἄριστος καὶ λαμπρότατος δεσπότης [Θεόδωρος Βʹ], παρῆν δὲ καὶ ὁ ἀρχιερεὺς καὶ ἡ γερουσία δὲ καὶ πᾶν ὅσον ἔκκριτόν τε καὶ καθαρὸν τοῦ ἱερατικοῦ καταλόγου. καὶ τοῦ δήμου δὲ οὐδεὶς ἀπῆν. συνέρρεον γὰρ ἅπαντες ἐπὶ τὴν ἀκρόασιν μᾶλλον ἢ τῶν Ὀλυμπίασιν ἀγώνων οἱ θεαταί. καλὸν τοιγαροῦν ἐδόκει καὶ προσῆκον πρὸ τῆς τελετῆς τὸν Ἐπιτάφιον ἀναγινώσκεσθαι, καὶ ὁ τοῦ βιβλίου διακομιστὴς [Ἰσίδωρος] ἐπὶ τοῦτο προεκαλεῖτο. ὁ δὲ οὐχ ὑπήκουεν, ἑτέροις τοῦτο φάσκων προσήκειν. καὶ οἱ μὲν ἐνέκειντο, ὁ δὲ οὐκ ἐνεδίδου, ὡς καὶ ὁ δεσπότης παρεκελεύετο, εἶξε τῷ ἐκείνου προστάγματι, καὶ ἀνεγίνωσκε μὲν ἐξαναστάς, ἠκροῶντο δὲ ἅπαντες ... διεξῄει δὲ τοῦ βιβλίου τὸ ἥμισυ. ἐπ᾽ ἐκείνῃ δὲ Γαζῆς ὁ καλὸς ἀνεγίνωσκε, τὸ μὲν πρῶτον ἠρέμα καὶ ὁμαλῶς τὴν ἠχὼ πέμπων, κατὰ μικρὸν δ᾽ ἔτι τὴν φωνὴν ὑπεραίρων ἐς διάτορόν τι καὶ γεγωνὸς ὅσον τε ἐχρῆν καὶ ἡ τάξις ἀπῄτει τοῦ λόγου ... εἶπεν ἄν τις μουσικός ... τούτοις [τοῖς ἀκροαταῖς] δὲ τὸ δάκρυον ἔρρει κρουνηδὸν καὶ τὸ ἆσθμα συνεχὲς ἐξῄει κεραννύμενον τῷ τῆς λύπης χρώματι. ὁ δὴ δῆμος ἐκπεπληγμένοις ἐῴκεισαν....

The appointed day came and the day of the year, which marked the anniversary to the eulogized man's death, arrived. A ceremony was held, during which the book [the speech of Manuel] had to be read aloud. Present were His Excellency, the most illustrious despot [Theodoros II Palaiologos of the Morea], the chief priest [bishop/metropolitan], the senate, and all the prominent individuals and the holy members of the ecclesiastical hierarchy. No citizen stayed away. All crowded to the recital; their number surpassed the number of fans in the Olympic games. So it seemed that it was the appropriate and the respected time for the Funeral Speech to be read aloud, before the formal ceremony, and they urged the bearer of the book [Isidore] to proceed. But he would not obey and kept saying that this task should be given to others. They persisted, but he would not yield. Finally the despot himself urged him and he had to obey that order. So he rose and began reading aloud. All listened ... and he went through half of the book. ... From that point on the good man Gazes began reading. At first he did so calmly and smoothly with a resounding voice, which, in a short time, he raised to the high level that was required by the arrangement of the speech. ... One might think of him as a musician ... the audience cried rivers and poured out sighs mixed with the colors of grief. The people appeared thunderstruck.

It is understandable that Isidore could not finish the reading of the speech. It was too long[64] and if indeed Theodoros had been his near relative or even his father, he may have been overcome by emotion. Gazes's first name is not provided but it appears almost certain that he was the person who went on to become a famous humanist, Theodoros Gazes.[65] It has been also suspected that he may have been Demetrios Gazes, a minor personality of the period.[66] Moreover, we wonder whether the audience could actually be moved to tears, for it is certain that the vast majority of them would have been unable to comprehend the difficult and tortuous text of Manuel, couched in classical Attic, an idiom that was no longer immediately nor easily understood by the average Greek, excepting the intellectuals, who had received serious training in classical Greek.[67] Thus, in terms of chronology, this letter of Isidore, recounting the recitation of the emperor's oration, amounts to his first definitive public appearance. After his description of the ceremony, Isidore reverts to comparisons of similar speeches in antiquity and concludes his letter to the emperor.[68]

It is also noteworthy that the "book," as Isidore labels his manuscript that contained the address,[69] has survived and is a masterpiece, both in terms of calligraphy and of art history. Isidore himself thus reveals two important talents – that of a manuscript copyist and an exceptional calligrapher. There survive seven other manuscripts that contain the speech of the emperor, but none are of the same quality nor contain a portrait. The exquisite nature of this particular manuscript would explain why numerous individuals in Mistra wished to examine the text, but Isidore would not grant permission to anyone to peruse it before he delivered the speech.[70] The enclosed portrait of Manuel II in tempera, gold, and ink on parchment bears an inscription in red ink, which duplicates the formal signature of the emperor in official documents: Μανουὴλ ἐν Χ<ριστ>ῷ τῷ Θ<ε>ῷ πιστὸς βασιλεὺς καὶ αὐτοκράτωρ Ῥωμαίων ὁ Παλαιολόγος, "Manuel in Christ the God the faithful king and emperor of the Romans [Greeks] Palaiologos." The illuminated portrait depicts the emperor in formal attire with crown and *prependulia*, a scepter crowned with a cross, and the *akakia*, a silk pouch filled with earth. He is clad in the σάκκος μέλας, the imperial black tunic decorated with the gold *loros*, the medieval Greek descendant of the Roman *trabea triumphalis* that was draped about the shoulder and around the waist.[71]

2 The sojourn in the Morea and the letters of Isidore

In his letters, composed after his arrival, Isidore does not appear to have been enamored with his Peloponnesian surroundings, but appears rather disappointed. He leaves the impression that he longed for Constantinople and its literary environment. Perhaps he was not impressed with the local conditions, as he makes clear in his letter to the emperor.[72] The letters to his friends are more explicit in details and his complaints seem to multiply with each written communication. Even though he seems to suggest that he misses his friends with whom he is corresponding, we form the impression that a great deal more is at stake than just the friends that he longs for. We wonder whether his departure for the Morea had been forced upon him; thus, he was an unwilling traveler to the despotate and had been ordered there by the emperor himself for unspecified reasons. In the final analysis, he seems to have found the new environment rather objectionable. As a consequence, his complaints about life in the Morea to his friend in Letter 3, judging from the letter's tone, are striking; the friend must have been aware of his feeling, since he had accompanied him when he boarded the ship for the Morea. At that moment, Isidore had promised his friend that he would send frequent letters:[73] οἶσθα δέ, ὅτε προσειπόντες ὑμᾶς ἐνεβαίνομεν τῇ νηΐ, ὅτι σὺ μὲν παρεκελεύου καὶ πέμπειν καὶ πυκνά [γράμματα], ἡμεῖς δὲ χρῆσθαι σε τοῖς ἴσοις ἀξιοῦμεν, ἀπηγόρευες δὲ αὐτὸς οὐδαμῶς. ποίει τοίνυν τουτί, "you know that when I was about to board the ship, that you, in our conversation, asked me to send many [letters] and often, and that I demanded the same of you and you accepted this condition readily. So please do it." The letter demonstrates that Isidore really desired to leave the peninsula and to return to Constantinople and to his circle of scholarly friends. He expresses this wish in classical terms:[74] πολλάκις ἠράσθην τῆς Δαιδάλου τέχνης, ἐζήτησα δὲ καὶ τὸ πτηνὸν Διὸς ἅρμα, ὅπως ἀφικοίμην τάχιστα παρὰ σοί. ἐπέτυχον δὲ οὐδέποτε, "how greatly did I miss the craft of Daedalus! I even looked for the winged chariot of Zeus to bring me to you as speedily as possible! I ended up in perpetual frustration." He furnishes a list of items that he was missing, which his friend in Constantinople was enjoying; this listing implies that Isidore was sorely lacking such amenities in the despotate: Constantinople's handsome porticoes, beautiful churches, elegant houses, and the quality and abundance of various edible items whose superiority was unsurpassed.[75]

Some time after his arrival in the Morea, Isidore became a victim to the plague. He survived as one of his early letters to Guarino attests:[76] ἄρτι τοῦ μετοπώρου τὴν τοῦ θέρους ὥραν διαδεξαμένου νοσοῦντι νόσον μακρὰν καὶ βαρεῖαν, τὴν λοιμώδη, "it was in the fall, right after summer, that I endured a long and difficult illness that was related to the plague." Perhaps the year can be established with some degree of certainty. In the so-called "Short/Brief Chronicles," we encounter mention of the plague affecting the Peloponnese and two possible dates can be reconstructed for this affliction. One records the year as 1409,[77] which is enumerated as the seventh visitation, and the second for the year 1417. Thus again we encounter the same chronological discrepancies for the early career of Isidore. Since in 1407 Isidore was still resident in Constantinople, under the new chronology through a process of elimination the year 1417 must be the date when Isidore suffered his bout with the plague. It further makes sense that he survived the epidemic of 1417, as he had probably developed some immunity to the affliction during his crucial childhood years. Had he been younger, that is during the first appearance of the plague in 1407, he would have been more susceptible to the extremes of the disease. The appearance of the pestilence in 1417 is counted as the eighth attack in a brief chronicle:[78] ἔτους ͵ϛϠκϛ' ἐγέγονεν τὸ ὄγδοον θανατικόν, "in the year 6926

10 *The rise of Isidore*

[*anno mundi*, that is 1417] the eighth attack of the deadly disease occurred." Unlike the seventh visitation, the eighth was more serious as notice of it is made in the literature of the period. Thus Sphrantzes states that Lady Anna of Muscovite Rus', the child-wife of Manuel's son, John VIII, died in August, a victim of the plague.[79] He further adds that the outbreak began in the winter of 1416/1417 in the Black Sea region and then progressed to Constantinople.[80] He elaborates that the plague had affected other areas, in addition to the imperial city.[81] Moreover, he assigns the outbreak in Constantinople to the "spring and summer,"[82] perhaps with the climax, which took away Lady Anna of Muscovite Rus', occurring in August. The death of Anna is also cited by Doukas who agrees with the statements of Sphrantzes.[83] Doukas further adds that it was the bubonic plague.[84] These dates are in agreement with the period that Isidore was also afflicted.[85] Isidore emerges as one of the few fortunate individuals to escape the consequences of this epidemic and to recover, even though the sources note that this wave of bubonic plague claimed numerous victims.[86]

Isidore continues by expressing his best wishes for his friend's health and then mentions their "old friendship," undoubtedly referring to the days when they were students together in Constantinople. He then adds in simile that old friendships can be cultivated to become even stronger with the passage of time before he moves on to hint that he expects more letters from his friends, voicing a complaint that we encounter in all his letters at this stage.[87] The next important section of the letter to Guarino informs us of the classical interests of Isidore. He clearly had undertaken the task of supplying ancient works (copied by himself perhaps) to his Italian friend:[88]

> δέχου τοίνυν ἅμα τούτοις τοῖς γράμμασι τήν τε Ξενοφῶντος Κύρου Ἀνάβασιν τόν τε Οἰκονομικόν, καὶ σὺν αὐτοῖς τὸν οὕτω πως Ἱέρωνα ἢ Τυραννικὸν ἐπιγραφόμενον, ἀρίστου ῥήτορος ἄριστα συγγράμματα, ἃ δὴ σοι πάντα δεικνύειν μέλλει τό τε τῶν γραμμάτων κάλλος τήν τε περὶ ταῦτα μετὰ σπουδῆς ὀρθότητα. ἕξεις δὲ ἅμα ἦρι, σύν γε τῇ τοῦ Θεοῦ βοηθείᾳ. Καὶ τὰ τοῦ Σύρου Σαμοσατέως. εἰ δὴ οἷον θ᾽ ἡμῖν γένοιτο, λήψῃ καὶ τὰ τοῦ συγγραφέως ᾽Αθηναίου κατ᾽αὐτὴν τὴν τοῦ ἦρος ὥραν.

Together with this letter accept Xenophon's *Anabasis* and *Oeconomicus*, in addition to the work normally entitled *Hiero* or *Tyrannikos*, the outstanding writings of an excellent rhetorician, which will demonstrate literary beauty and accurate style. You will have, by spring, with God's help, the works of the Syrian from Samosata [Lucian]. If I can manage it at the same time next spring you will also receive the works [*Deipnosophistai*] of the author Athenaeus.

It is unclear whether Isidore sent ancient manuscripts to Guarino or copies that he had made from ancient manuscripts. Most probably, they were his own transcriptions and had been copied by Isidore himself, who was involved in this activity throughout his lifetime. Thus he was quite accomplished in calligraphy and was an avid copyist of ancient works even in his later years.[89] After all, the beautiful manuscript of Manuel's address had been copied in Isidore's calligraphy.[90] Moreover, the promise that he would send by springtime Lucian's and Athenaeus's works suggests that at the time he transmitted his letter he was engaged in copying the voluminous works of these authors and that he needed time to finish this task. It is plausible that he was already at work transcribing these works, but had to stop when he became ill. He was by the fall prepared to resume the task. The despotate of Morea and its capital, Mistra, at the time, had been centers of ancient learning and had attracted a number of intellectuals who were interested in antiquity, including the famous Georgios Gemistos Plethon.[91] Less prominent were other individuals and scholars, some of whom were in fact members of Plethon's circle, if not actual disciples, and who regularly transcribed ancient works.[92] If one had need of a classical work, one might have had good fortune in the Morea, for it possessed a number of well-stocked libraries.[93]

At the conclusion of this letter, Isidore reveals another interesting aspect of his personality. He had an unquestionable interest in the occult. He complains to Guarino that the horoscopes that he had requested had not reached him. This was for him a vexing matter, which he couches in a witty yet rather forceful way:[94]

ἃ γὰρ πάλαι μὲν αὐτὸς ὑπισχνοῦ, ἤλπιζον δὲ ἐγὼ λαβεῖν. λέγω δὴ τοὺς ἀπὸ τῶν ὀΐων κώδικας, ἵνα σὲ καὶ αὖθις ἐκείνων ἀναμνήσω, οὔπω παρ' ἡμῖν ἐγένοντο, ἀλλ' οὐδὲ τὰ ὡροσκόπεια. ἢ τοίνυν θᾶττον αὐτὰ πέμπε, κἂν τούτῳ πολλὴν ἔξω σοι χάριν, ἢ βραδύνοντα περὶ τὰς ὑποσχέσεις ἐν τοῖς ὀφείλουσιν ἔξω, καὶ ἀντὶ τοῦ χάριν εἰδέναι ἐγκαλεῖν σοι μᾶλλον ἀναγκασθήσομαι.

I was hoping to receive what you had promised me: I mean the sheep [= parchment] *codices* (so I may refresh your memory). Neither they nor the horoscopes have reached me. Either send them soon so I may be in your debt or you may delay to fulfill your promises and I will count you among my debtors and, in fact, instead of owing you a favor, I will be forced to place a charge against you.

Isidore remained a believer in horoscopes to the end of his life. In 1453, he was convinced that the final assault against Constantinople was launched by the sultan on the day and at the hour that had been suggested to Mehmed II by his group of astrologers, as he declared to his friend Bessarion in a letter dated *in Creta, die sexta Iulii anno Domini M°CCCC°LIII°*, "in Crete, July 6, 1453 A.D.":[95]

inter haec quinquaginta et tres dies Turcus consumpsit Constantinopolim obsidens nec quicquam perfecit. Sed cum omnis cognitionis illud difficilimum est quod futurum est, nobis oculos mentis occecavit, illi vero ita aperuit, ut Martem potentissimum ac diem et horam accuratissime observaverit; habet enim diligentissimos astrologos persas, quorum consiliis ac iudicio fretus summa quaeque ac maxima sese consecuturum sperat.

> The Turk [Sultan Mehmed II Fatih] wore down Constantinople in fifty-three days of siege, but was unable to prevail. Prediction of the future is a very difficult task and our mind's eyes become blind. Yet, the future was revealed to him so that he reserved the mightiest attack for a specific day and hour. He has, after all, very energetic Persian astrologers on whose advice and judgment he relies when he is about to pursue the most difficult and worthiest operations.[96]

In his second letter to Guarino,[97] Isidore first praises his friend's talent for Greek, and expresses admiration about his ability to learn the language and to be bilingual. He first cites that he could not control his joy when he read Guarino's letter to his circle of friends and, in a classical mode that would be so dear to a humanist, states that he was so captivated by the letter as if he were a member of Odysseus's crew charmed by the song of the Sirens.[98] He then praises Guarino for glorifying his city and Italy with his scholarship, as he has also decorated Greece with scholarship.[99] Because of his ties to Greece and a deep command of classical scholarship, Guarino is, according to Isidore, a "Panhellene" (Πανελλήνιος). Isidore suggests, in what he thinks is a flattering comment, that Guarino has less in common with Cicero and more in common with Aelius Aristides and Demosthenes. Then Isidore adds that "as yet the horoscopes have not arrived," οὔπω γὰρ ἧκε παρ' ἡμῖν τὰ ὡροσκοπεῖα. Perhaps it is best to assume that this letter, Regel's Letter 2, precedes his Letter 1. It appears that Guarino dispatched his epistle in the spring. Isidore then replied (Regel's Letter 2) and requested horoscopes, which had not arrived. Isidore after that went through his illness and in the fall wrote a stronger letter (Regel's Letter 1) emphasizing his previous request and adding as an incentive his copies of ancient works.

This examination of the early letters brings into question the old assumption that the manuscript presents the letters in a chronological order. This assumption can no longer be considered valid, as the chronology has changed. The impression was that all these letters were written soon after the arrival of Isidore in the Morea, which scholars used to date to c. 1407. Because of the circumstances of the delivery of the emperor's speech we now know that this event took place one decade later, and this new chronology affects the date of the composition of the letters also. Probably the earliest letter is the one addressed to Manuel II, as it contains the fresh impressions of Isidore with regard to the Peloponnese, along with his account of his voyage, and his report on the recital of Manuel's *Funeral Speech*. Yet in the manuscript, this letter appears as the fifth epistle, as it was published in this order by Regel. Moreover, there is reason to believe that the letter addressed to Khortasmenos is an early letter by Isidore, while he was still longing for the amenities of Constantinople. While this letter appears as the fourth, it seems to have been written after the fifth. The first and second letter to Guarino come after Isidore's illness, that is, after the letters to the emperor and to Khortasmenos, and the second letter to Guarino, we believe, is the first epistle that Isidore wrote. In conclusion, we have to observe that the order of the letters in the manuscript compilation does not preserve the actual chronology and the logical sequence, contrary to what scholars have assumed thus far.[100]

Further, a group of eight early letters were published long after Regel's edition.[101] These eight letters are included in the same manuscript compilation,[102] but they are not as informative about Isidore's personal life as the Regel letters. They are more concerned with Isidore as an ecclesiastic and as a public figure. The first letter in this group is addressed to someone who was a close relative/friend of Isidore, of whom it has been noted[103] that nothing more can be gathered from the correspondence. He appears to have been a resident of Patras,[104] and Isidore labels him an "Achaean,"[105] as he, in his archaizing language, so styles the *quattrocento* Patrenses:[106]

> ἐπέστελλες γὰρ καὶ ὡς φίλος ἀληθὴς πρὸς φιλεῖν εἰδότα καὶ ὡς ἐξ ἐκείνης ἕλκων τὴν σειρὰν τοῦ γένους ἧσπερ καὶ ἡμεῖς. τὸ γένος τε ἐφίλεις τὴν συγγένειάν τε ἠσπάζω καὶ μετὰ θάρρους ἔγραφες. ἐν δὲ μόνον ἡμίασεν, σφόδρα δέ μ' ἠνίασεν. ἦν δὲ ἐκεῖνο ποῖον; ἔφασκες ἐν τούτοις ὡς ἢ πόρρω τοῦ γένους ἡμῶν αὐτὸς ἢ μή γε τοῦτο ἀλλ' ἐγγύς, ὥσπερ οὖν ὑπεροπτικοί τινες ἡμεῖς καὶ ἀλαζόνες καὶ οὐχ οὕτω λογιζόμεθα. ἀλλ' ὦ ποῖόν σε ἔπος ἕρκος φύγεν ὀδόντων,[107] ἀνδρῶν βέλτιστε. ἐπὶ τίνι γὰρ ἡμεῖς ἑτέρῳ μᾶλλον αὐχοῦμεν ἢ σοί; τί δ' ἄλλο βέλτιον ἡγούμεθα τῆς τε συγγενείας τῆς σῆς τῆς τε φιλίας; τίνος δ' ἂν προὐκρίναμεν ἑταιρίαν τῆς σῆς μᾶλλον;

> Indeed you sent [the letter] as a true friend to one who knows what love is and who also shares the same descent with you. One matter bothered me, and it bothered me a great deal. What is it? You said, among other things, that either you were far removed from our family or, if this is not the case, and you are close, then I was looking upon you in some form of snobbery when I failed to take it into account. My best friend: what word escaped the barrier of your teeth? Can I boast of a better friend than you? What is dearer to me than our family relationship and your friendship? Whose company would I choose over yours?

The only hint of a date for this short letter comes near its conclusion:[108] ὅθεν δὴ συναιρουμένου θεοῦ οὐκέτι πόρρω τῶν ἰαννουαρίων καλανδῶν, ἀλλ' ἐγγύττερον ἐλπὶς ἡμᾶς ἀφικνεῖσθαι παρ' ὑμᾶς τοὺς Ἀχαιούς, "so, with God's will, no later than the kalends of January, I hope to come to you Achaeans." The year is not mentioned but it is clear that Isidore's health is strong and he can travel, so the least that may be said is that he had totally recovered from his bout with the plague. Therefore, the position of this letter within the correspondence corpus must follow Isidore's letters to Guarino, and the cited dispatch cannot be earlier than January 1420.[109]

The remaining letters, as they stand, cannot be placed in chronological order. The first of those letters[110] is addressed, according to the opinion of one scholar,[111] to the despot of the Morea, Theodoros II Palaiologos. Of interest are the opening statements, for they indicate that Isidore had a deep interest in ancient Persia:[112]

τῷ μὲν οὖν βασιλεῖ τῶν Περσῶν Ἀρταξέρξῃ σφόδρα καταθύμιον ἐδόκει, ἄν τις αὐτῷ δῶρα ϖροσάγων, κἂν ᾖ ϖάνυ σμικρά, μετὰ ϖολλῆς εἰσεκόμιζε εὐνοίας. ᾧ δὴ καί ϖοτε ϖερὶ τὰς τοῦ Ὑδάσϖου ὄχθας ϖαριόντι τῶν γεωργούντων ἐκεῖσέ τις, μάλα ϖένης, ἀλλὰ καὶ μηδὲν ἕτερον ἔχων, ᾧ τὸν βασιλέα δεξιώσεται τῆς εὐνοίας καὶ μόνης χωρίς, ἀϖὸ τοῦ ϖαρατυχόντος ϖοταμίου ῥεύματος ϖλήσας τὰς χεῖρας τούτῳ σοι δεξιοῦμαι, φησί, λαμϖρότατε βασιλέων. καὶ ὃς μάλα μὲν ἡσθεὶς ἐϖὶ τῇ τοῦ ϖροσάγοντος εὐνοίᾳ, σφόδρα δὲ καὶ ἑαυτὸν οἷος ἦν ἐϖιδεῖξαι βουλόμενος, μεγάλης τὸν γεωργὸν ἐκεῖνον ἠξίωσε τῆς κηδεμονίας. χιλίους γὰρ χρυσίνους ἐδωρήσατο καὶ τὴν ἀϖορίαν ἔλυσε τῷ ϖένητι. ἀλλὰ τοιαῦτα μὲν ϖερὶ ἐκείνου καὶ ϖολὺς τῶν ξυγγραφέων ὁ λόγος.

The Persian king Artaxerxes found it extremely moving when someone brought him gifts, even though they were of very small value, since they were brought with good will. At one time, there was a very poor farmer who lived near the banks of the Hydaspes River and had nothing other than his good will alone to bring to his king. So he filled his hands with water from a river stream that happened to be there and said: "Most illustrious king: I bring this as my gift." The king was very pleased with the bearer's good will and, wishing to match the good will, he took great care of that farmer. He gave him one thousand gold pieces and erased his poverty. There are many such stories and many authors have told them.

What is of importance here is the manifest interest of Isidore in ancient Persia and *Perserei*, in general. He must have acquired this inquisitiveness about ancient Persia and its great kings while reading classical literature, an interest that remained with him throughout his lifetime. Later he attempted to contrast an "ancient oracle" supposedly dating from the time of Xerxes's invasion of Greece in 480 BC; again in 1453, when Constantinople was under Ottoman attack he remembered the ancient attempt of the Persian king. Isidore and his learned friend Leonardo of Chios found time in 1453 to compare Mehmed II to Xerxes and to associate the sultan's operations to those of the great king.[113] Clearly, Isidore's attention to the classical era developed at an early age. Isidore probably wrote the next two letters to the despot of the Morea as well. They are composed in a witty style and, like the first letter, underscore the poverty of the Moreots.[114]

In the years from 1420 to 1430 we find Isidore in the Morea, during which period the Palaiologoi launched an offensive against the remaining local Latin lords. Three Palaiologan brothers, Theodoros II, Constantine XI, and the emperor himself, John VIII, conducted the offensive. Their primary target was the Latin lord Carlo Tocco, who had directed raids deep into Greek territory. The focal point of the Greeks was their concern about Tocco's control of the stronghold of Glarentza, which provided him with a secure and fortified base for operations within the despotate. From Glarentza Tocco extended his attacks into Elis, as far as River Alpheios. For the time being, Theodoros did not attack Tocco directly, as he was busy with a campaign against Centurione and the Venetians. Tocco then furnished a *casus belli* in 1427. Matters now reached a turning point.[115] In the fall of that year some Albanian groups under the protection of Theodoros brought their herds to the valleys of Elis, their customary winter grazing quarters. During the winter months, Tocco's men, confronted with a scarcity of food, raided the camps of the Albanians in search of foodstuffs. The ensuing Palaiologan land operations against his raids were indecisive and the result was inconclusive at best, even though some modern historians would have us believe that this Greek campaign resulted in total success.[116] Nevertheless, their offensive culminated in a Palaiologan naval victory. This sea engagement took place near Actium, the site of Octavian's victory against Mark Anthony, and in the area where later the monumental battle of Lepanto was fought, that is, in the vicinity of the Ekhinades (Curzolari) islands in the Ionian Sea. The "fleet" that John VIII had earlier assembled was placed under the command of Leontaris[117] and was dispatched to confront the enemy armada. Tocco had summoned ships from the Ionian Islands and from Epiros as well as reinforcements from Marseilles. Tocco's admiral was his own son, Turnus/Turno. The battle resulted in a decisive victory for the Greeks. The Latin armada suffered heavy losses and Tocco's own nephew was captured during the course of the battle while Turnus, the commanding admiral, barely escaped with his life.

The reason we know of this engagement is that Isidore took up the pen and composed a very long *Panegyric*. The work is important, even though formally speaking it is intended to be a communication. Within this oratorical text there is embedded a substantial amount of history. In a number of sections, Isidore plays the role of a historian who has preserved for us an account of this campaign.[118] It was indeed a major victory for the Byzantines, the last at sea to be won by a Greek fleet until the nineteenth century. Sphrantzes, Khalkokondyles, and the short chronicles maintain a strange silence concerning the naval engagement. Perhaps their failure to record the event suggests that it was not viewed as a triumph at that time. Yet Isidore, the supposed author of the *Panegyric*, had no reservations, for he fully realized the importance of the battle. It further seems safe to assume that Carlo Tocco viewed this encounter and its outcome as a major setback for his cause, because soon thereafter he displayed a willingness to negotiate with the Greeks.[119] He retreated from the Morea under an arrangement that removed the stigma of humiliation and became a relative of the imperial family through marriage.

It is possible that Isidore was attached in some capacity to the headquarters of the brothers during this period. Not long afterward he returned to Constantinople. Is it possible that he returned with John VIII to the capital in 1428 and that his *Panegyric* was the triumphal announcement of his return? Near the end of the summer of 1428, John, in the company of his brothers, Constantine, Thomas, and Theodoros, rode from Mistra to Corinth. At Kenkhreai, the port of Corinth, the emperor embarked and left for the capital. Sphrantzes furnishes details on his voyage:[120]

> οἱ δὲ ἀδελφοί . . . ἐκαβαλλίκευσαν ὁμοῦ καὶ ἀπῆλθον μέχρι καὶ τῆς Κορίνθου. καὶ ὁ μὲν βασιλεὺς ἐμβὰς εἰς τὰ κάτεργα ἀπέπλευσεν εἰς τὴν Κωνσταντινούπολιν, ὁ δὲ δεσπότης κῦρ Θεόδωρος ἀπῆλθεν ὄπισθεν τὴν αὐτὴν ὁδὸν τὴν φέρουσαν εἰς τὸν Μυζηθρᾶν.
>
> The brothers . . . traveled on horseback to Corinth. There the emperor embarked and sailed to Constantinople. Lord Theodoros, the despot, returned to Mistra by the same road.

Was Isidore a member of the emperor's retinue on the return journey? The answer to this question is difficult to expound upon, for the evidence is inconclusive and is subject to speculation at best.

We do not know what activities occupied Isidore upon his return to Constantinople, perhaps as a member of the imperial retinue. It is possible that he did not remain in Constantinople for long, as there exists a manuscript, an autograph, that suggests that soon after his arrival in the imperial city, Isidore embarked on a journey, probably to the Morea, but his ship encountered a storm, was blown off course, and made landfall in Sicily.[121] The note penned by Isidore does not state the year of this journey. It is a journal entry that, nevertheless, furnishes the day-by-day progress of the ship. Since the days of the week and the month are mentioned, we can make a simple calculation based upon the Julian calendar that was then employed. The year of the journey is 1429 and this is the only year in which the days coincide with the month cited in the note.

If indeed Isidore is the author of this note and not simply the copyist of another individual's journal, we can then conclude that he had not remained in Constantinople for an extended stay upon his return with the imperial train. Further, if the note refers to Isidore himself, then this was the first notice that he had traveled abroad and only through the chance of adverse weather conditions. His later travels would carry him through various parts of Europe. The text of this unintended voyage and a translation follow:

> τῇ ιε[η] τοῦ Σεπτεμβρίου ἡμέρα Πέμπτῃ μεσούσῃ ἀνήλθομεν εἰς τὴν ναῦν, καὶ τῇ αὐτῇ ἑσπέρας, τοῦ ὁρίζοντος οὔπω τοῦ δυτικοῦ ἐπιβαίνοντος τοῦ ἡλίου, ἄραντες τὰ ἱστία, εὐκραεῖ τῷ ἀνέμῳ δι' ὅλης πλέοντες τῆς νυκτὸς ἅμα ἕω περὶ τὴν Προικόννησον ἐγενόμεθα, εἶτα τῇ ις[η] τοῦ ἀνέμου ἐνδόντος πάντῃ, πανημέριοι μικρὸν παρήλθομεν τῆς Προικοννήσου. τῆς αὐτῆς δὲ ἡμέρας περὶ δείλην ὀψίαν ἐγείρεται βορρᾶς εὐκρατής, καὶ πλέοντες μέχρι τοῦ μεσονυκτίου καὶ ἐπέκεινα, περὶ τὴν Λάμψακον ἐγενόμεθα, ἔνθα αἱ τριήρεις νοήσασαι τῶν Βενετίκων, ἐκεῖσε ναυλοχοῦσαι προσυπήντων ἡμᾶς καὶ τὰ ἱστία καταίρειν ἐκέλευον. ὃ δὴ καὶ γεγονός, ἄγκυράν τε προσωρνίσαμεν μέχρι τῆς ἕω. εἶτα ἄραντες τὰ ἱστία πανημέριοι διεκπλεύσαμεν τόν τε Ἑλλήσποντον καὶ τὴν Τένεδον παρημείψαμεν καὶ

καθ' ἑσπέραν ἐγενόμεθα τοῦ Σιγρί<ου> κατ' ἰσότητα τῇ ιζ^η τοῦ αὐτοῦ. τὴν δὲ νύκτα ἐνδόντος τοῦ πνεύματος μόλις ἐγενόμεθα κατὰ τὴν Σκῦρον, ἐν δεξιᾷ ταύτην ἔχοντες.

τῇ ιη^η δὲ ἡμέρᾳ Κυριακῇ, ὀλίγου ὄντος τοῦ πνεύματος, Εὔ<β>οιάν τε παρεδράμαμεν ἐν δεξιᾷ καὶ τὴν Μακρόννησον, ἡ Μῆλος τε ἡμῖν ἀνεφαίνετο, σχεδὸν οὐδὲ τῶν ἱστίων ἐγκειμένων, ἅμα ἕῳ περὶ τὰ Κύθηρα γενόμενοι, ἐπὶ μᾶλλον ἐξηγρίαινε τὸ πέλαγος ὁ ἀπαρκτίας καὶ οὐκέτι Κυθήροις προσχεῖν ἠδυνήθημεν. ἀλλὰ ἡ φορὰ καὶ ἡ βία τοῦ ἀνέμου παραμείνασα<ι> μέχρις ὅλης τῆς ιθ^ης, ἐξωκείλαμεν περὶ τὸ Λιβυκὸν πέλαγος, μόλις ὁρῶντες τὰς κατὰ Μεθώνην ἀκρωρείας τῆς Πελοποννήσου, ἀφιστάμενοι ὡς πρὸς Λιβύην στάδιά που περίπου τὰ ψ'. τοῦτο μὲν ἐκτοπισθέντες τῷ ἀπαρκτίᾳ, τοῦτο δὲ καὶ τῶν ἐμπόρων τῶν Σικελῶν ἀνθισταμένων καὶ οὐκ ἐώντων ὅλως προσχεῖν τῇ Μεθώνῃ διὰ τὴν πειρατικὴν ναῦν, ἣν ἔφασκε ὁ ναύαρχος τῶν ἐν Ἑλλησπόντῳ νηῶν ἱσταμένην ἐκεῖσε σκυλεύειν πᾶσαν ναῦν.

ἔρις οὖν ἐγίνετο, τῶν μὲν ἐξαγαγεῖν ἡμᾶς ἐν Μεθώνῃ σπευδόντων, τῶν δὲ μηδόλως προσχεῖν ὑποφερόντων. νικᾷ τοίνυν αὐτῶν ἡ ἔνστασις. ἡμῖν συνεπιτιθεμένου τοῦ καιροῦ, καὶ τὴν νύκτα πᾶσαν εὐθὺς Σικελίας ἐπλέομεν. τὴν δὲ κ^ην ἡμέραν μέτριον γίνεται τὸ πνεῦμα ὡς μόλις κινεῖν τὰ ἱστία. τῇ δὲ κα^η ἡμέρᾳ τετράδι ἐπλέομεν πανημέριοι ἀνέμῳ βορρᾷ εὐκραεῖ οὐχ ὁρῶντες γῆν μετὰ τὴν ἑσπέραν τῆς ιθ^ης (ἤγουν τὴν Δευτέραν). περὶ δὲ τὰς ἀρχὰς τῆς νυκτὸς ἐξαίφνης μεταβάλλεται ὁ ἀὴρ καὶ γίνεται ταραχὴ μεγάλη. καὶ ἀστραπῶν καὶ βροντῶν πλῆθος κατέλαβεν ἡμᾶς καὶ ὑετὸς συχνός. τρίς τε τῆς νυκτὸς ταύτης κατεβάλλομεν τὰ ἱστία σὺν βίᾳ καὶ ἀνάγκῃ πολλῇ καὶ σχεδὸν ἐκινδυνεύομεν ὁλονύκτιοι. ἅμα δ' ἕῳ ἐλόφησε τὰ δεινά. καὶ περὶ ε^ην ὥραν τῆς ἡμέρας πάλιν ταραχαὶ καὶ νεφῶν κύκλωθεν ἐπισωρεύσεις καὶ ὑετοὶ καὶ οἱ ὀνομαζόμενοι σίφωνες πρὸς αὐτοῖς. καὶ πάλιν τρὶς τὰ ἱστία κατήραμεν καὶ τὴν κβ^αν πᾶσαν περὶ κινδύνους ἐτελοῦμεν, ἀλλ' ἡ νὺξ ἐπισελθοῦσα ἐλόφησε τὰ δεινὰ καὶ ταύτην διεδράμομεν ἡσύχῳ τῷ πνεύματι καὶ τὴν κγ^ην ὁμοίως καὶ τὴν κδ^ην.

τῇ δὲ κε^ην ἅμα ἕῳ γῆν τε ἑωρῶμεν (ἥδ' ἦν ἡ Καλαβρῶν) καὶ κατανοήσαντες ἐν οἷς ἐσμεν, ἔτι καὶ τοῦ πνεύματος αἰρομένου, τὴν Σικελῶν πανημέριοι παραπλέοντες ἐς Συρρακούσας δεκαταῖοι κατήχθημεν περὶ τὸ τέλος τῆς κης ἡμέρας τοῦ Σεπτεμβρίου. ἀλλ' οὔπω φθασάντων ἐλλιμενίσαι καλῶς καὶ πρότονα δῆσαι, οἱ τῶν Συρρακοσίων ἄρχοντες πέμψαντες αἴρουσι τὰ ἱστία καὶ τὸ πηδάλιον καὶ τὸν ναύκληρον ἐξελθεῖν ἐκέλευον λέγοντες ὅτι Λιβυκὸς τὴν Μελίτην πολιορκεῖ νῆσον καὶ τὴν Γόζαν. ἑξήκοντα δὲ τριήρεις ἔλεγον εἶναι καὶ ναῦς τὸν στόλον, καὶ τετρακοσίους ἱππεῖς. ψ' δὲ στάδια τὸ μεταξὺ Συρρακουσῶν ἐστι καὶ τοῦ Λιβυκοῦ στόλου. εὕρομεν δὲ καὶ ἑτέρας ναῦς δύο πρὸς ταῖς δέκα κεκρατημένας. ἠβούλοντο δὲ κινηθῆναι κατὰ τῶν Καρχηδονίων. ἀλλὰ καὶ λοιμὸς ἐπίεζε Συρρακουσίους καὶ ἡμᾶς πᾶν ἐπεῖχε δεινόν, νόσος κυνάγχης μετὰ πυρετοῦ, φόβοι τῶν ἔξωθεν, στεναχωρίαι τῶν ἔνδοθεν καὶ πᾶν ἄλλο κακοῦ γένος, καὶ τὸ ἐπελθὸν καθ' ἑκάστην ἡμῖν ὅτι μὴ δεινόν.

ἀλλ' ὅμως τὸν ἐν Συρρακούσαις λοιμὸν ἡγησάμενοι βέλτιον τοῦ τῶν βαρβάρων δεσμοῦ καὶ φόνου, ϖερὶ τὴν κϛην τοῦ αὐτοῦ μηνὸς ἐξήλθομεν τῆς νηὼς καὶ ϖαρά τινι διγλώσσῳ Σικελῷ ϖροσεξενώθημεν.

Voyage to Sicily (Sept. 15–26, 1429)

1 On September 15, a Thursday, at high noon, we boarded the ship and during the evening of the same day, as the sun was about to reach the western horizon, we made sail and with a favorable strong wind we sailed through the night. It was dawn when we found ourselves about Proikonnesos. Then on the 16th the wind failed and died. After a whole day had passed we were still close to Proikonnesos. Late at sunset of the same day a favorable steady north wind arose and we were able to sail until midnight and beyond, and we reached the neighborhood of Lampsakos. The *triremes* [galleys] of the Venetians had put about in anticipation of our arrival. They came to meet us and urged us to lower our sails. We did so, dropped anchor, and waited for daylight. At dawn, we made sail and in one day we sailed through the Hellespont, passed by Tenedos, and on a straight course reached Sigrion that evening. It was the 17th of the month. During the night the wind dropped and we just made it to the neighborhood of Skyros, which we kept to our right.

2 On the 18th, a Sunday, propelled by a weak wind, we passed on our right Euboea and Makronnesos; by evening we could just see Melos. Then there arose a mighty wind from the north and all night long without sails we were pushed on and by dawn we reached the vicinity of Kythera, where the wind turned the sea ugly. We were unable to reach Kythera. The force and violence of the wind persisted throughout the day of the 19th and we were pushed toward the Libyan Sea, barely making out the tip of the Peloponnese by Methone. We were about 700 *stades* from Libya [= Africa]. We had been brought so far by the mighty wind and by the Sicilian merchants who resisted any attempt to approach Methone because a pirate ship that lurked there bent on preying on any vessel that happened to come by, as the admiral of the ships at the Hellespont had reported.

3 An argument thus arose on board. Some urged that we reach Methone and others argued an opposite course. The persistence of the latter won the day (as they were also assisted by the tempest) and we sailed all night long toward Sicily. On the 20th the force of the wind dropped and became so moderate that it hardly filled the sails. On the 21st we sailed all day long under a favorable strong north wind. From the evening of the 19th, that is Monday, we were out of sight of land. It was almost evening when the atmosphere suddenly changed and a great storm arose. Numerous thunderclaps and a downpour overtook us. Three times we were compelled and forced to lower our sails that night. We were in terrible danger all night long, but at dawn our woes found some relief. But then again about the fifth hour of the day there was a storm and the clouds all around sent sheets

of rain. In addition, there were storms called "tempests" and again we were forced to lower our sails three times. Thus we spent all of the 22nd in danger. But relief came at nightfall that we spent under a mild wind and similar was the situation all day long on the 23rd and on the 24th.

4 On the 25th we saw land at dawn. It was the region of Calabria. We realized where we were and, as the wind all day long guided us toward Sicily, we at last reached Syracuse on the 25th of September. The voyage had taken, ten days. But we were not permitted to enter the harbor in peace. We put out our stern cables, since the Syracusan authorities hastened to take up our sails and our steering oar. They asked the captain to disembark. They disclosed that a Libyan armada had laid siege to the island of Melite and to Goza. They said that there were sixty *triremes* [galleys] and ships that were transporting four hundred horsemen. The Libyan armada was 700 *stades* from Syracuse. We discovered that another twelve vessels had been detained and that they wished to move against the Carthaginians. However, the plague was creating difficulties for the Syracusans. We too had our own woes, for we had been infected with sore throats and fevers. The external situation scared us, but we had our own problems on board and encountered all sorts of daily woes.

5 We concluded that the plague in Syracuse presented less of a threat than captivity or death at the hands of the barbarians [Muslims]. Thus, on the 26th of the same month, we disembarked and became guests in the house that belonged to a bilingual Sicilian.

Notes

1 It is unclear from all relevant and extant sources whether the name Isidoros (hereafter the more familiar and commonly used Isidore will be cited in this study) was his baptismal name or whether he took this name upon being tonsured a monk. He regularly uses the name Isidoros and does not allude to another, although we may suspect that, if given another name, perhaps baptismal, it too began with an *iota* as was common Greek practice. The question is further complicated by the account of Nestor-Iskander, which more often than not simply makes reference to an unidentified patriarch. Nestor-Iskander provides only two citations for purposes of identification, one shortly prior to and then another soon after the fall of the imperial city in late May 1453. He identifies the cardinal as Patriarch Anastasios and later as Athanasios. It is known that Isidore received the appointment from the pope (*without* the specification of a place name for his ecclesiastical jurisdiction, a situation that will be reviewed more fully in Chapter 4); thus he had no ecclesiastical authority over the imperial city, but only over the outlying territories. It is probable that upon being elevated to Latin Patriarch he assumed another name: perhaps Anastasios or Athanasios, hence the confusion of the sources. For the account of Nestor-Iskander, cf. N-I: for patriarch: pars. 28, 29 ff., and 81, 82; and for Anastasios and Athanasios: pars. 68 and 81. For further commentary cf. ibid., pp. 116, 117 and n. 33; 131 n. 87; and 150, 151, and 156 n. 27. There survives a letter from a member of Isidore's household to Cardinal Domenico Capranica, dated 15 July 1453, that was dispatched from Candia. The document does not identify him by name and only refers to him as "Lord Cardinal." Cf. *CC* 1: 112–119; *The Cambridge History of the Byzantine Empire, c. 500–1492*, ed. J. Shepard (Cambridge, 2008), Table 3, *Patriarchs*, p. 911, which lists an Athanasios II for the year 1450 without further comment in the text; and *ODB*

1, which discusses neither an Athanasios II nor an Anastasios as patriarch of Constantinople for that year or the years of 1452–1453. The matter of the existence of a Patriarch Athanasios was examined from the archival point of view and the conclusion was that such a patriarch had never existed. On this, cf. Gennadios, Metropolitan of Heliopolis, "Ὑπῆρξεν ἢ ὄχι Πατριάρχης Ἀθανάσιος Ὀλίγον πρὸ τῆς Ἁλώσεως," Ὀρθοδοξία 18 (1943): pp. 117–123.

2 Attention is directed to a highly generalized and undocumented account about Isidore's life, albeit written by a modern cleric and notable scholar, Joseph Gill, SJ. Cf. his *Personalities of the Council of Florence and Other Essays* (New York, 1964), pp. 65–78.

3 The situation is succinctly summarized by W. Regel, who edited and published the earliest surviving letters of Isidore, *Analecta Byzantino-Russia* (Petropoli [St. Petersburg], 1891), p. xli of the "Introduction/*Proœmium*": "Nous ne savons rien de certain sur l'origine d'Isidore." A.M. Bandini, *De Bessarionis vita, rebus gestis, scriptis commentarius* (Rome, 1777), col. 904, was the first scholar to provide us with a list of the surviving compositions of Isidore. More recently, cf. Erika Elia, "Un restauro di erudite: Isidoro di Kiev e il conduce Peyron 11 della Biblioteca Nazionale Universitaria di Torino," *Medioevo Greco. Rivista di storia e filologia bizantina* 12 (2012): pp. 71–85; and esp. M. Manfredini, "Inventario dei codici scritti da Isidoro di Kiev," *Studi Classici e Orientali*, 46/2 (1997): pp. 611–624.

4 Bandini: "Sa ville natale paraît avoir été Constantinople ou Thessalonique." The identification of these cities as Isidore's birthplace is cited in several studies: A. Chacón [Ciaconi], *et al.*, *Vitae et res gestae pontificum romanorum et S.R.E. Cardinalium ab initio nascentis ecclesiae usque ad Urbanum VIII*, 1 (Rome, 1630): col. 903: *Isidorus Thessalonicensis monachus S. Basilii, et abbas S. Demetrii Constantinopolitani, Archiepiscopus Ruthenorum. . .* ; Bandini, ch. 8, *addendum* 15, states with a hint of preference that Isidore's birthplace was Thessalonike, but concedes that "others" favor Constantinople instead: *Isidorus patriam habuit Thessalonicam vel Constantinopolim, ut alii tradunt*; and J.-P. Migne, *PG* 161 (Paris, 1866), p. iii f. Migne was perhaps the earliest scholar to make this association when he edited *PG* 159 (Paris, 1866), cols. 943–944, and in the introduction to one Latin letter that Isidore addressed to Christendom on the fall of Constantinople. Migne cites: *Isidorus Thessalonicensis, monachus Sancti Blasii* [correctly *Basilii?*], *et abbas Sancti Demetrii Constantinopolitani, archiepiscopus Ruthenorum, cum ad concilium Florentinum in consortio Bessarionis venisset . . . Isidorus quidem sub titulo presbyteri cardinalis SS. Petri et Marcellini. . . .* Concerning a monastery of Saint Blaise (Ἅγ. Βλάσιος) two are identified from the sources: one in the vicinity of the cistern of Mokios in the area of the Golden Gate and a second, perhaps misidentified or misstated by Joannes Dominicus Mansi in his *Sacra Conciliorum. Nova, et Amplissima Collectio, in qua præter ea, quæ Phil. Labbeus, et Gabr. Cossartius. . .* 31 (Venice, 1793), 1040 C, that reads: ὅ ποτε ἡγούμενος τοῦ ἁγίου Βλασίου Γερμανός. Cf. R. Janin, *La géographie ecclésiastique de l'empire Byzantin*. Part 1: *Le siège de Constantinople et le patriarcat œcuménique*, 3: *Les églises et les monastères* (2nd ed., Paris, 1969), pp. 64, 65.

5 "Isidore de Kiev, apôtre de l'Union Florentine," *Irénikon* 13/4 (1936): p. 395. Cf. idem, *Die Union des Konzils von Florenz in der russischen Kirche*, Das östlichen Christentum 4/5 (Würzburg, 1938), pp. 56, 57, for an expanded discussion of Isidore's roots. A Latin rendition of this *curriculum vitae* appears in *Isidorus Arch. Kioviensis et Totius Russiae, Sermones inter Concilium Florentinum Conscripti. . .* , eds. G. Hofmann, E. Candal, and Cardinal Julian Cesarini, CFDS, series A, 10/1 (Rome, 1971), pp. vii, viii. It is apparent that Ziegler, Hofmann, and Candal had utilized the same *curriculum vita* that may be included in Isidore's papers that were donated to the Vatican Library in 1928.

6 Among the prominent Muscovite Rus', Russian, and Slavic sources, G. Vernadsky, *The Mongols and Russia*, A History of Russia 3 (New Haven and London, 1953), p. 308, identifies Isidore as a "Greek" or "Hellenized Slav"; whereas in *idem, Russia at the Dawn of the Modern Age* 4 (New Haven and London, 1959), p. 12, Vernadsky states that Isidore was a Greek born in Salonika (Thessalonike). H. Paszkiewicz, *The Making of the Russian Nation* (London, 1963), pp. 47 n. 187, and 56, concurs with Vernadsky concerning Isidore's roots. An older eighteenth-century Russian historiographical tradition states

that Isidore was a Greek born to a noble family in Dalmatia. On this cf. V. N. Tatishchev, *История Российская* [= *A History of Russia*], 5 (Moscow-Leningrad, 1965), pp. 242 and 244. Beyond this meager information, little is added in Slavic works. There is no firm evidence that Isidore was fluent in Old Slavonic, Medieval Rus', Bulgarian, or other Slavic languages, nor have any documents survived demonstrating his skills at writing in Old Slavonic or medieval Bulgarian that would explain his roots. He may have had an elementary training in these languages and possessed a reading knowledge of them, but did not feel comfortable to demonstrate a written skill. This is illustrated in *Codex Vat. sl. 14*, a Slavonic breviary, a Mass-book, perhaps dating to the period of 1453–1463, which was transcribed by an unnamed scribe familiar with Church Slavonic and the theological formulations of the Council of Ferrara-Florence. Isidore appended a Greek notation of his acceptance of the transcription. On this cf. I. Dujãev, "Un fragment des »Notitiae Episcopatuum Russiae«, Copié par Isidore Ruthenus," *ЗРВИ* 11 (1968): pp. 235–240, esp. 236. Haris A. Kalligas, *Byzantine Monemvasia: The Sources* (Monemvasia, 1990), p. 160, advances the plausible notion that Isidore may have received training under the metropolitan of Monemvasia, Akakios the Elder, who maintained a monastery school (presumably at Kontostephanos), where Slavonic languages were taught. The school became notable for producing several candidates who later became metropolitans of Kiev and of All Rus' or played other leading roles in Byzantine-Rus' ecclesiastical and cultural relations. Cf. A-E. Tachiaos, "The Testament of Photius Monembasiotes, Metropolitan of Russia (1408–1431): Byzantine Ideology in XVth-Century Muscovy," *Cyrillomethodianum* 8–9 (1984–1985): pp. 77–109; repr. in *idem, Greeks and Slavs: Cultural, Ecclesiastical and Literary Relations* (Thessalonike, 1997), pp. 365–397. The claim that he was somehow a Hellenized Slav from Thessalonike appears purely speculative, although it is a topic that requires more substantive scholarly scrutiny. The poem of Ubertino Pusculo, who wrote in Vergilian hexameters, is an eyewitness account of the siege of Constantinople in 1453. He states that Isidore was from the "city," that is, Constantinople. But Pusculo could have been misinformed, as he did not have access to the imperial court or the Constantinopolitan leadership; he probably had no personal contact with Isidore before the fall of 1453. Cf. Ubertino Pusculo, *Constantinopolis libri IV*, in *Miscellanea di varie operette*, ed. G. Bregantini, 1 (Venice, 1740), II.216: *Nam genus is [sc. Isidorus] magna Danaum ducebat ab urbe*. Also *SF*, ch. 1, no. I.7.

7 Two notable studies on the Cyril-Methodian tradition and its continuing legacy command attention: F. Dvornik, *Byzantine Missions among the Slavs: SS. Constantine-Cyril and Methodius*, Rutgers Byzantine Series (New Brunswick, 1970), esp. chs. 4–6 and 9; and A. P. Vlasto, *The Entry of the Slavs into Christendom: An Introduction to the Medieval History of the Slavs* (Cambridge, 1970), chs. 2 and 5.

8 Cf. *infra*, ch. 3, n. 13, and the associated text from the *Patriarchal or Nikon Annal*, that identifies Isidore as a Greek; modern Russian/Slavic scholars, cited *supra*, n. 6, have either overlooked or have ignored this citation of ethnic identification.

9 According to one opinion, but common among nineteenth-century Russian church historians, Isidore had Slavic origins, or was perhaps a Bulgarian "by descent." Cf. Regel, p. xli, n. 3. Among the Russian church historians, Filaret, archbishop of Chernigov, *Виз. История русской церкви. Періодъ Третнй, отъ раздѣлінія мнтрополій до учрежденія патріаршесва (1410–1588 г.)* [= *The History of the Russian Church. The Third Period: From the Division of the Metropolitanate to the Establishment of the Patriarchate (1410–1588)*], 3 (4th ed., Chernigov, 1862), p. 68 n. 154, relates: Ватиканское извѣст'е объ ун'и (слав. Рук. N° 12) называетъ Исидора словакомъ; это, вѣроятно, по его знан'ю славян. языка [= Vatican information concerning the Union (of Churches) (*Slav. ms. no. 12*) identifies Isidore as a Slav; this is probable by his knowledge of the Slavic language]. Further, Makarii, archbishop of Kharkov, *Istor`q russkoj cerkvi въ періодъ монгольскій* (= *A History of the Russian Church in the Mongol Period*) 4, Book 1 (St. Petersburg, 1866), p. 106, states: поспѣшили назначить иа каѳедру русской митрополіи Исидора, родом Болгарина [= Isidore of Bulgarian stock hastened to settle upon the Russian seat of metropolitan]. Of course, such views of ethnicity must be

rejected, as Regel realized, through the unambiguous statement of (Michael) Doukas, *Βυζαντινοτουρκικὴ Ἱστορία*, trans. B. Karales, Κείμενα Βυζαντινῆς Ἱστοριογραφίας 7 (Athens, 1997), that Isidore was "Roman [Greek] by descent," 36.1 (pp. 480–483): τόν ποτε ἀρχιεπίσκοπον Ῥωσίας Ἰσίδωρον . . . Ῥωμαῖον τὸ γένος, and 40.5: αὐτοῦ τοῦ γένους [Γραικοῦ] ὤν. Cf. Doukas, *Decline and Fall of Byzantium to the Ottoman Turks: An Annotated Translation of "Historia Turco-Byzantina,"* trans. H.J. Magoulias (Detroit, 1975), 36.1 (p. 203). Further, in this citation Doukas perhaps incorrectly identifies Isidore as "Cardinal of Poland"; the correct form from the Latin is "Cardinal of Ruthenia." Doukas may have been aware that Isidore, following the Council of Ferrara-Florence, had been awarded high episcopal authority by the papacy, that is, jurisdiction over the Rus' residing within the Polish-Lithuanian realm. This may have prompted Doukas to provide the designation of "Cardinal of Poland," albeit incorrectly.

In the "*Praefatio*" of the volume dedicated to Isidore, *Analecta Ordinis S. Basilii Magni. Miscellanea in Honorem Cardinalis Isidori (1463–1963)*, 4 (10), fasc. 1–2 (Rome, 1963), pp. vii, viii, Athanasius G. Welykyj/Welykyi summarizes the Slavic position:

> *Isidorus Thessalonicensis, vel rectius Moreus (in Peloponneso) secundum alios, immo et Bulgarus vel Constantinopolitanus ad mentem aliorum, natus est inter annum 1380–1390 (J. Mercati). Urbs vero Constantini ei, ut videtur, natalis fuit in spiritualibus, forsan in ipsis initiis saec. XV. Variis vicibus in patriam redux (1407, 1417, 1430), ibi etiam curriculum monasticum ingressus est in monasterio S. Michaelis in Monembasia. Mox tamen aërem natalem cum illo Constantinopolitano permutavit, ubi, post exant lata opera et onera, in monasterio S. Demetrii hegumenus conspicitur et ut talis actor historiae temporis devenit.*

This citation raises several questions. First, unless Janin, 3: 337–350, has overlooked a monastic institution bearing the name of Saint Michael at or near Monemvasia, none is so identified. No monastic foundation charters could be found to clarify the matter. The only monastery in the vicinity of Monemvasia is Kontostephanos, which we address *infra*, n. 13. For a resolution of the statement that "a monastic institution [bore] the name of Saint Michael," Kalligas, *Byzantine Monemvasia*, p. 176, makes an interesting observation concerning the monastery of Saint Michael and writes:

> It is known that after Manuel's visit to the Peloponnese in 1415–16 a tax was levied for the defence of the Isthmus of Corinth. . . . It has been assumed that it is from this tax that Isidore tried to relieve the Helikovounites and his interest arose from the fact that their town had been ceded a few years earlier to the metropolitan of Monemvasia in whose services Isidore was. He himself resided in the monastery of Kontostephanos nearby and had even composed a mass for the Archangel Michael to whom the monastery was dedicated.

Cf. ibid., n. 128.

Giovanni Mercati, however, in his *Scritti d'Isidoro il Cardinale Ruteno e Codici a lui Appartenuti che si conservano nella Biblioteca Apostolica Vaticana*, Studi e Testi 46 (Rome, 1926), pp. 12, 13, furnishes a somewhat different interpretation of Isidore's birthplace, date of birth, and familial association, and other evidence. He, citing *Codex Vat. gr. 914* and contrasting the information with *Palatino gr. 226*, writes:

> in alter parole, viene a meno la ragione di distinguere i due Isidori, monaci e scrittori entrambi, ed entrambi originarii, come sembra, della Morea e del pari interessatisi per Monembasia – probabilmente la patria – nello stesso giro abbastanza ristretto di tempo che corrisponde presso a poco all'episcopato di Fozio in Russia. Perchè – si badi – 1° il Ruteno vienne detto senz'altro « natione graecus ex Peloponneso» dall'autore dell'*Andreis* e da Pio II, quasi che fosse una cosa notoria, sicura, in Roma circa il 1462; e l'Isidoro del Vatic. Gr. 914 ci si dimostra non solo vissuto parecchio tempo nel Peloponneso, come già osservarono il Regel e il Pierling, ma imparentato con un letterato di colà, e quindi non difficilmente di famiglia peloponnesiaca ach'egli.

Perchè 2° come il Ruteno nel 1429 c. – sia che stesse ancora in Morea (appresso le navigò nel settembre di quell'anno, v. p. 58 sg., e là trovavasi circa il 1430), sia che fosse a S. Demetrio in Costantinopoli... – ... ch'era stata concessa dal despota Teodoro Paleologo e confermata nel 1405 dall'imperatore Manuele al metropolita Acacio, affinchè si celebrassero due messe settimanali per i due figli di Teodoro colà sepolti; terra nella quale penso che Isidoro allora abitasse.

Cf. ibid., p. 12 n. 2, and p. 13 nn. 1–6.

In the fourteenth and fifteenth centuries there were a number of Slavic pockets or settlements throughout the Morea and Thessaly. Cf. D.A. Zakythinos, *Οἱ Σλάβοι ἐν Ἑλλάδι. Συμβολαὶ εἰς τὴν Ἱστορίαν τοῦ Μεσαιωνικοῦ Ἑλληνισμοῦ* (Athens, 1945), pp. 61–66 and *passim*. In addition, cf. N. Nicoloudis, *Laonikos Chalkokondyles. A Translation and Commentary of the "Demonstrations of Histories" (Books I–III)*, Historical Monographs 16 (Athens, 1996), pp. 126, 127, 170 n. 90, 288, 289, and 342 n. 40; and H. Ditten, *Der Russland-Exkurs des Laonikos Chalkokondyles*, Berliner Byzantinistische Arbeiten Band 39 (Berlin, 1968), pp. 26, 27; 68, 69; 114–116 n. 148; 135 n. 225; and *passim*.

10 Cf., e.g., P. Pierling, *La Russie et le Saint-Siège. Etudes diplomatiques* (Paris, 1896), p. 7 and *passim*. He is deferential toward Isidore, because of his role as an imperial representative at the Council of Basle and then the leading Muscovite ecclesiastic at the Council of Ferrara-Florence, and often writes of him in glowing terms without providing documentary evidence to substantiate his statements.

11 *Ibid.*, p. 7. Pierling, herein, associates him with a nameless *famille illustre*. It is unclear whether the author is linking by implication the metropolitan of Rus' with the Palaiologan family or another notable noble family.

12 J. Gill, "Isidoros, Metropolit v. Kiew u. ganz Rußland (1437)," *Lexikon für Theologie und Kirche* 5 (Freiburg, 1960), pp. 788–789, more generally ascribes his birth either to the 1380s or 1390s in Monemvasia.

13 Cf. *infra*, ch. 7, n. 122.

14 Kalligas, *Byzantine Monemvasia*, p. 170. On Helena Kantakouzene Palaiologina, cf. D.M. Nicol, *The Byzantine Family of Kantakouzenos (Cantacuzenus) c. 1100–1460. A Genealogical and Prosopographical Study*, DOS 11 (Washington, DC, 1968), esp. 135–138 and *passim*. For sources on the Palaiologos family, cf. the works of Dölger and Papadop[o]ulos/Baloglou cited below. Theodoros had been married once, to Cleopa, by whom he had a daughter Helena. After Cleopa's death Theodoros never remarried. On this, cf. S. Runciman, "The Marriages of the Sons of the Emperor Manuel II," in *Rivista di Studi Bizantini e Slavi: Miscellanea Agostino Pertusi*, 1 (Bologna, 1981), pp. 279, 280 and n. 18 for the documentation. Further, Kalligas, *Byzantine Monemvasia*, p. 170 n. 98, states: "It is tempting to speculate on a possible identification of Isidore with one of the mysterious bastard sons of Theodore I, whose traces cannot be found anywhere." Barker in *MP*, p. 272, stresses that Theodore "had no legitimate male heir." M. Philippides, "The Fall of Constantinople 1453: Classical Comparisons and the Circle of Cardinal Isidore," *Viator: Medieval and Renaissance Studies* 38/1 (2007): p. 378 n. 123, also emphasizes Isidore's close ties to the imperial family, who "was forced, at an early age, to become a monk in order to eliminate any possible claim he might have to the throne of Constantinople." Cf. Alice-Mary Talbot, "Theodore I Palaiologos," *ODB* 3: 2040. In the final analysis, the hypothesis that Isidore had some imperial blood in his veins will remain an inference at best. Essentially, we lack any solid information in the literature of the period or soon thereafter. On Theodoros I, cf. also the brief comments of Averkios Th. Papadopoulos's fundamental ("cum laude") dissertation under Franz Dölger, titled *Versuch einer Genealogie der Palaiologen, 1259–1453*, published under the name A. Papadopulos [= Papadopoulos] in Munich, 1938; and the modern edition of the same work by C.P. Baloglou, *Γενεαλογία τῶν Παλαιολόγων: 1259–1453* (Athens, 2007), esp. p. 130, Τμ. Στ´, Κεφ. 2, No. 2.1, who refers to Theodoros's illegitimate children in a general manner: Ὁ Θεόδωρος εἶχε καὶ μὴ νόμιμα παιδία. Haris Kalligas does not repeat the speculation

that Isidore may have been an illegitimate son of Theodoros in her latest study, *Monemvasia: A Byzantine City State* (London and New York, 2010), but only states that Isidore was Emperor Manuel II's "protégé and had been offered by him his excellent education." It is probable that initially, after he departed Constantinople where he had received some preliminary education, perhaps prior to 1403, Isidore was dispatched to the Morea and specifically sent to the monastery of Kontostephanos, that bears the name of the founding family, the Kontostephanoi, but had imperial and patriarchal associations. Cf. *PaL* 2: 3, 4 n. 5. The monastery was situated by Monemvasia, at Helikovounon, and this may furnish a clue to why Isidore remained attached to the region. On this family and its intermarriage with other prominent Byzantine noble families, cf. C. Barzos, Ἡ Γενεαλογία τῶν Κομνηνῶν, 1. Κέντρον Βυζαντινῶν Ἐρευνῶν. Βυζαντινὰ Κείμενα καὶ Μελέται 20a 6 (Thessalonike, 1984), pp. 262, 263. For the monastery and the documentation associated with the metropolitan of Monemvasia and Isidore's role, cf. Kalligas, *Byzantine Monemvasia*, pp. 69, 159, 160, 176, 180, and 183. Cf. *Cod. Vat. gr. 914* and *Palatinus gr. 226*; S.P. Lampros, "Δύο Ἀναφοραὶ Μητροπολίτου Μονεμβασίας πρὸς τὸν Πατριάρχην," *NH* 12 (1915): pp. 255–318; Mercati, pp. 9; 12, 13; and K.M. Setton, "The Bulgars in the Balkans and the Occupation of Corinth in the Seventh Century," *Speculum* 25 (1950): pp. 502 and 525, 526 n. 1.

15 There exists in his own writings indirect corroboration that he was a Moreot by birth. Thus, e.g., it is evident that he had a special attachment to the Morea by various statements in one of his works, the *Encomium/Panegyric* to Emperors Manuel II and John VIII (cf. *infra*, nn. 16 and 44, and Appendix for the abridged text), as Mercati, p. 7 n. 1, astutely realized: "La larga parte datavi ala Grecie meglio si comprende e si apprezza, ove tengasi presente l'origine d'Isidoro 'ex Peloponneso'." In addition, the *Andreis* (complete title: *Andreis, id est Hystoria de receptione capitis Sancti Andreae*, authored by Pope Pius II, who had a long association with Isidore, cites him as a Moreot. Cf. the edition of the Latin text by S.P. Lampros, "Ἡ ἐκ Πατρῶν Ἀνακομιδὴ τῆς Κάρας τοῦ Ἁγίου Ἀνδρέου," *NH* 10 (1913): pp. 3–112 (Latin text: pp. 80–112), wherein Lampros on p. 103 cites: *Anno qui praecesserat proximus percusserat apoplexies Isidorum episcopum Sabinensem, sanctae Romanae ecclesiae Cardinalem, natione Graecum ex Peloponneso, qui olim Rossanis, borealis genti, praefuerat*. Following tradition, Lampros ascribed authorship of the *Andreis* to Alexander of Clusium, but with some reservations. Cf. *infra*, ch. 7, n. 115. Nowadays it has become increasingly clear, on stylistic grounds, that this work can be attributed to the pen of Pope Pius II. Cf. *PaL* 2: 229 n. 103, who further investigates the mysterious circumstances of the suppression of the true authorship of this interesting work. Also cf. further comments, *infra* ch. 7, n. 128.

16 Kalligas, *Byzantine Monemvasia*, pp. 169–178 and n. 97.

17 Moreover, we may suppose that in his early years he had links with Manuel II, for he is the only Greek author in his *Encomium* to Manuel II and John VIII to supply us details of the emperor's long voyage to the West that had taken him as far away as England. Is his knowledge of the imperial journey the direct result of his association with the emperor? At the very least, it implies some familiarity with the Constantinopolitan court and with the emperor's immediate retinue that had accompanied him to the West; on this work, cf. *infra*, n. 44.

18 This is reported by Heinrich of Soemmern who composed an account of the adventures of the cardinal during the sack of Constantinople and of his adventures and escape to Crete. For this account, cf. the new edition with English translation in M. Philippides, ed., trans. and annotated, *Mehmed II the Conqueror and the Fall of the Franco-Byzantine Levant to the Ottoman Turks: Some Western Views and Testimonies*, Medieval and Renaissance Texts and Studies 302 (Tempe, 2007), pp. 121–133, esp. 128, wherein it is stated that during the sack the cardinal was trying to rally the troops and to fight back, perhaps attempting to make a last stand in the vicinity of the Great Church, Santa Sophia: *per hunc Machometam [Mehmed II] capta quidem urbe, prope ecclesiam Sanctae Sophiae accessit, putans illic esse armatos aliquot qui Turcis resisterent*. In his letter to his friend Bessarion,

Isidore also alludes to these critical hours, mentions his wounds, and reveals himself to be an active defender in possession of considerable strength; cf. his testimony in *CC* 1: 66:

> *et per immortalem Deum . . . saepius et saepius illum execratus sum ac maledixi crudelem ex Turcis qui me sagitta fixit atque in sinistra capitis parte vulneravit ante ianuam cuiusdam monasterii [Sanctae Sophiae], non tam acriter tamen ut eadem hora mihi vitam eripuerit, propterea eques et attonitus et spiculum ipsum magna in parte vires amiserat.*

19 His military role is emphasized by his close friend, his *familiaris* and admirer, Archbishop Leonardo Giustiniani; for their association and conversations during the siege, which are echoed in their accounts of those fateful days, cf. Philippides, "The Fall of Constantinople 1453: Classical Comparisons and the Circle of Cardinal Isidore," pp. 366, 367. Leonardo stresses the role of the cardinal in the defense of the city in no uncertain terms. Cf. *CC* 1: 150: *Cardinalis [Isidorus], a consilio nunquam absens, Sancti Demetri regionem ad mare defensabat.*

20 The founder of the monastery is identified as Georgios Palaiologos, a general during the Komnenan dynasty. The initial date of foundation is given as the early twelfth century and appropriately the founder selected Saint Demetrios, an early Christian martyr-saint notable for his military accomplishments, as the patron for the new establishment. Cf. J. Thomas and Angela Constantinidis Hero, eds., *Byzantine Monastic Foundation Documents: A Complete Translation of the Surviving Founders' Typika and Testaments*, DOS 35/3 (Washington, DC, 2000), p. 1238. Saint Demetrios is also the patron of the city of Thessalonike where a church, but no monastery, was dedicated to him. Isidore is also associated with the Monastery of Prodromos ([μονὴ τοῦ Προδρόμου] ἐν τῇ Πέτρᾳ) in Constantinople. On this, cf. *Codex Monac. gr. 186*, fol. 298ᵛ; *Catalogus codicum manu scriptorium Bibliothecae Monacensis, 2/4: Codices Graecos 181–265 Continens/Katalog der griechischen Handschriften der Bayerischen Staatsbibliothek München*, 4: *Codices graeci Monacenses 181–265*, ed. Kerstin Hajdú (Wiesbaden, 2012), p. 53; and accompanying literature. Also on the monastery, cf. Janin, *La géographie ecclésiastique de l'empire Byzantin*, 3, pp. 421–429.

21 To fix a locale for this monastery within the imperial city is problematic. George Majeska identifies the site as mid-way along the southern sea walls, "between the port of Contoscalion harbor and the Jewish Gate at Vlanga, near the old port of Eleutherius]." He dismisses the localization of Alexander Van Millingen, Raymond Janin (who, he states, misread the travelers' accounts, especially that of Steven of Novgorod), and Wolfgang Müller-Wiener. Cf. G.P. Majeska, *Russian Travelers to Constantinople in the Fourteenth and Fifteenth Centuries*, DOS 19 (Washington, DC, 1984), p. 267. Although Van Millingen's testimony in part is to be questioned relative to the information that he furnishes, he does place the monastery of Saint Demetrios very near the modern-day mosque of Atik Mustafa Pasha, which is within the sea walls along the Golden Horn and is in close proximity to the juncture of the sea walls with the Wall of Herakleios. A. Van Millingen, *Byzantine Constantinople: The Walls of the City and Adjoining Historical Sites* (London, 1899), pp. 197, 198; further, he makes no reference to this monastery and perhaps a church associated with it in his later study, *Byzantine Churches in Constantinople: Their History and Architecture* (London, 1912), leading us to the conclusion that no church was attached to this monastic facility. Janin, *La géographie ecclésiastique de l'empire Byzantin* 3, pp. 92–94; idem, "Les sanctuaries byzantines des saints militaries," *Echos d'Orient* 33 (1934): pp. 163–180 and 331–342; *ibid.*, 34 (1935): pp. 56–70; and W. Müller-Wiener, *Bildlexikon zur Topographie Istanbuls. Byzantion – Konstantinupolis – Istanbul bis zum Beginn des 17. Jahrhunderts* (Tübingen, 1977), pp. 27, 32, 110, and 301 ff., concur with Van Millingen, and each provides substantial information regarding the location of this institution. Later, in 1452–1453, before and during the defense of Constantinople against Mehmed II, Isidore contributed funds, perhaps his own private funds, for the reinforcement of the walls and gates in this area. Further, there exists confusion in modern scholarship whether the monastery of Saint Demetrios was a male or female institution. Father Vitalien Laurent,

"Isidore de Kiev et la Métropole de Monembasie," *REB* 17 (1959): p. 154, notes his assignment to a convent or nunnery (couvent), hence the female monastery of Saint Demetrios, which is improbable. Earlier, Father Paul Pierling, p. 7, does not qualify whether it was a male or female institution. The issue has been recently resolved: an early fourteenth-century text, "Kellibara I: Typikon of Andronikos II Palaiologos for the Monastery of St. Demetrios-Kellibara in Constantinople," in Thomas and Hero, 3: pp. 1237–1253 (no. 38), and 4: pp. 1505–1511 (no. 56), establishes that from its very foundation the Constantinopolitan institution like its counterpart at Kellibara in southwestern Asia Minor was a male institution.

22 As we shall observe, *infra*, nn. 43 and 50, Isidore would have been a very young man, in his teens, if he delivered the speech in 1409. The modern chronological evidence indicates that Isidore could not have pronounced that speech before 1414, when he was in his twenties. The new evidence revises the chronology upwards. The shift in dates makes the role of Isidore as an orator easier to accept.

23 While delivering the eulogy, Isidore seems to have been greatly moved and proved unable to complete the reading. Another person had to continue the recitation. Is it possible that a torrent of emotion overcame him, precisely because he was pronouncing a eulogy of a close relative or perhaps even of his own father? Isidore spoke of the occasion and of his delivery in his letter to Manuel II. On his emotions, cf. Kalligas' observations, *Byzantine Monemvasia*, p. 172: "Isidore in his description carefully hides how much he was moved. . . ." On this eulogy and the occasion of the delivery, cf. *infra*, nn. 54 and 55.

24 *Arch. Segr. Vaticano, Arm. XXXI*, tom. 52, fol. 64^r (as quoted in *PaL* 2: 4 n. 5): *Orbitus D<omini> Cardinalis Ruteni: Anno a nativitate Domini MCCCCLXIII, die vero Mercuri XXVII mensis Aprilis, reverendissimus in Christo pater dominus Cardinalis Rutenus appellatus Ysidorus Rome diem suum extremum. Eius anima in pace requiescat.* Cf. *infra*, ch. 7, nn. 30 and 32.

25 Pierling, p. xxi, intimates that Isidore earlier was a disciple of the Neoplatonist philosopher, Georgios Gemistos Plethon, at Mistra. James Hankins goes further and makes the emphatic statement that Isidore "had almost certainly been a student of Pletho"; cf. his "Cosimo de' Medici and the 'Platonic Academy'," *JWarb* 53 (1990): pp. 156, 157; repr. and enlarged with appendices in *idem, Humanism and Platonism in the Italian Renaissance*, Storia e Letteratura. Raccolta di Studi e Testi 220, 2 (Rome, 2004), p. 208. Joseph Gill, more circumspect in his research and writings, states, "Isidore probably did [study under Plethon], for his writings at this time display a decided Platonic tendency and an antagonism to Aristotle [which he later displayed especially at the Council of Ferrara-Florence]." Cf. Gill, *Personalities of the Council of Florence*, p. 66. However, Gill, in the "Introduction" to *Isidorus Arch. Kioviensis et Totius Russiae. Sermones inter Concilium Florentinum Conscripti. . .* , eds. G. Hofmann and E. Candal, CFDS, Series A, vol. X, fasc. 1 (Rome, 1971): p. vii, modifies his earlier interpretation and asserts that *philosophiam sub Georgio Gemisto Plethone studuit*. If he was a student of the philosopher, then Isidore (who was a number of years senior to Bessarion, at least thirteen) emerges as a contemporary of Cardinal Bessarion, each being a student of Plethon. It is known that Bessarion studied under Plethon in 1431, and then perhaps Isidore might have studied with the master in the 1420s, although we have no concrete evidence to substantiate this claim. Thus the issue is quite plausible, although Isidore himself nowhere makes the assertion that he was a student of Plethon. It is significant, as we shall see later, that there was a very close relationship between the two cardinals, Isidore and Bessarion, especially at the Council of Ferrara-Florence and thereafter into the 1460s. Plethon does not associate himself with Isidore in any of his written works, perhaps for good reason since his writings are not intended to recognize associates or students, and any such claims of a strong bond between the two men, between teacher and student, are purely speculative. On the importance of Plethon to rhetorical literature, Platonism, and neo-paganism, cf. F. Masai, *Pléthon et le platonisme de Mistra* (Paris, 1956); C.M. Woodhouse, *George Gemistos Plethon: The Last of the Hellenes* (Oxford, 1986); and N. Siniossoglou, *Radical Platonism in Byzantium: Illumination and Utopia in Gemistos Plethon* (Cambridge, 2011), among others.

26 On these critical years, which would have resulted in the willing surrender of Constantinople to Bayezid I Yıldırım ["the Thunderbolt"], if the battle of Ankara and the rout of the Ottoman forces by the Mongols of Timur (Tamburlaine/Tamerlane) had not intervened, cf. now D. Khatzopoulos, *Le premier siège de Constantinople par les Ottomans, 1394–1402* (Montreal, 1995); and the modern Greek translation by the author, with additions: *Ἡ Πρώτη Πολιορκία τῆς Κωνσταντινουπόλεως ἀπὸ τοὺς Ὀθωμανοὺς (1304–1402)* (Athens, *sine anno*). Older literature includes *MP*, pp. 139 ff. and Appendix 9 for an evaluation of sources and dates; *LCB*, pp. 328–330; G. Roloff, "Die Schlacht bei Angora," *Historische Zeitschrift* 161 (1943): pp. 244–262; H.A. Gibbons, *The Foundation of the Ottoman Empire: A History of the Osmanlis up to the Death of Bayezid I (1330–1403)* (New York, 1916), pp. 250 ff.; H. Hookham, *Tamburlaine the Conqueror* (London, 1962), *passim*; and S.J. Shaw, *History of the Ottoman Empire and Modern Turkey*, 1: *Empire of the Gazis: The Rise and Decline of the Ottoman Empire (1280–1808)* (Cambridge, 1976), p. 307, with modern Turkish scholarship on the events.

27 That the plague was perhaps a more immediate concern in the decision to surrender the city to Bayezid has not been examined by modern scholarship. Cf., e.g., the brief chronicle entry 22 for 1402/6910 in *CBB* 1: 28 (p. 184): οἱ δὲ ἐν τῇ Πόλει λ<ο>ιμοκτονηθέντες, ὁ λαὸς ἔφυγεν. ἔλαβον δὲ τὰς κλεῖδας τῆς Πόλεως τινὲς τῶν ἀρχόντων καὶ ἐπορεύοντο ἐν τῷ Κοτυαείῳ πρὸς τὸν σουλτάνον – τοῦ παραδοθῆναι τὴν Πόλιν. While the spelling of the ms. states λιμοκτονηθέντες, we believe that this is a reference not so much to famine but to the plague, since both words sound identical when voiced. It is possible that λοιμοκτονηθέντες is after all the true reading referring to the plague. That the surrender of Constantinople had become imminent is a certain fact. The initial negotiations for its implementation may have begun as early as the summer of 1401. Cf. *RKOR* 3195 (p. 74). This surrender had been discussed in detail in *MP*, pp. 200 ff.; and in Khatzopoulos, *Ἡ Πρώτη Πολιορκία*, pp. 197–200. For additional contemporary testimonies, cf. *MP*, p. 207 and n. 14.

28 Khatzopoulos, *Ἡ Πρώτη Πολιορκία*, pp. 228–249.

29 Kalligas, *Byzantine Monemvasia*, p. 170: "It is certain that when Manuel arrived in Constantinople from the Peloponnese in June 1403, after his journey to the West, Isidore had either traveled with him or had preceded him there." While the evidence is far from "conclusive," as there are no documents to support either opinion expressed by her, we may ask a legitimate question: Did Isidore and his talents come to the attention of the emperor while the latter was in the Morea at this time or did Manuel decide to bring the young gifted Moreot (his own relative in some unspecified way?) to the imperial city to receive what was presumed to be a first-rate education? The emphatic statement of Kenneth M. Setton, *PaL*, pp. 3, 4 n. 5, that "Isidore first emerges in the light of history as a very young man in the year 1403" must also be seen as an opinion, for there are no surviving documents that speak of Isidore at this early date. Ziegler, *Die Union des Konzils von Florenz*, p. 58, first notices him in 1409. The earliest date for the appearance of Isidore in history is 1414 and not 1403 as scholars have assumed for a long time. This will be discussed *infra*, nn. 43–48.

30 G. Cammelli, *I dotti bizantini et le origini dell'umanismo*, 1: *Manuele Crisolora* (Florence, 1941): 128 ff.; I. Thomson, "Manuel Chrysoloras and the Early Italian Renaissance," *Greek, Roman and Byzantine Studies* 7 (1966): pp. 63–82, esp. 80; and *MP*, p. 231.

31 *MP* devotes an entire chapter to Manuel II as a scholar, ch. 7 (pp. 395–443), and defines his literary activity as "the cornerstone of his being" (p. 410). *MP* further observes (p. 409) that, given his literary and military talents, under "more favorable opportunities," he could have been "the East Roman Marcus Aurelius."

32 For the state of education in Constantinople in the decade of 1401–1410, with particular emphasis on Manuel II's efforts to educate his children, cf. M. Philippides, *Constantine XI Dragaš Palaeologus (1404–1453): The Last Emperor of Byzantium* (forthcoming), ch. 2, sec. III. On the low state of learning in Constantinople in the first half of the fifteenth century, cf. the notable observations of I. Ševčenko, "Intellectual

28 The rise of Isidore

Repercussions of the Council of Florence," *Church History* 24/4 (1955): p. 294 and *passim*.

33 It should be observed that at this time, in spite of the unfavorable circumstances brought on by the long blockade of Bayezid I, Constantinople managed to educate an impressive number of notable intellectuals, both Greek and Italian, who made the difficult voyage to the imperial city to receive training in the ancient Greek language and in classical Greek literature. Many of these scholars found their way to Italy before and after the fall in 1453 and contributed immensely to the Italian Renaissance. On this *generatio mirabilis*, cf. among others S.P. Lampros, *Ἀργυροπούλεια: Ἰωάννου Ἀργυροπούλου Λόγοι, Πραγματεῖαι, Ἐπιστολαί, Προσφωνήματα, Ἀπαντήσεις καὶ Ἐπιστολαὶ πρὸς Αὐτὸν καὶ τὸν Υἱὸν Ἰσαάκιον. Ἐπιστολαὶ καὶ Ἀποφάσεις περὶ Αὐτόν. Προτάσσεται Εἰσαγωγὴ περὶ Ἰωάννου Ἀργυροπούλου, τῆς Οἰκογενείας Αὐτοῦ καὶ τῶν Ἀργυροπούλων καθ' Ὅλου* (Athens, 1910); D.J. Geanakoplos, *Greek Scholars in Venice: Studies in the Dissemination of Greek Learning from Byzantium to the West* (Cambridge, 1962; repr. as *Byzantium and the Renaissance* [Hamden, 1972]); idem, *Interaction of the "Sibling" Byzantine and Western Cultures in the Middle Ages and Italian Renaissance (330–1600)* (New Haven and London, 1976); idem, "Italian Renaissance Thought and Learning and the Role of Byzantine Emigré Scholars in Florence, Rome, and Venice: A Reassessment," *Rivista di studi bizantini e slavi* 3 (1984): pp. 129–157; K.M. Setton, "The Byzantine Background to the Italian Renaissance," *Proceedings of the American Philosophical Society* 100 (1956): pp. 1–76; D.A. Zakythinos, "Τὸ Πρόβλημα τῆς Ἑλληνικῆς Συμβολῆς εἰς τὴν Ἀναγέννησιν," *Ἐπετηρὶς τῆς Φιλοσοφικῆς Σχολῆς τοῦ Πανεπιστημίου Ἀθηνῶν* 5 (1954–1955): pp. 126–138; and K.S. Staikos, *Χάρτα τῆς Ἑλληνικῆς Τυπογραφίας: Ἡ Ἐκδοτικὴ Δραστηριότητα τῶν Ἑλλήνων καὶ ἡ Συμβολή τους στὴν Πνευματικὴ Ἀναγέννηση τῆς Δύσης*, 1: *15ος Αἰώνας* (Athens, 1989). Most recently, cf. Maria Mavroudi, "Translations from Greek into Latin and Arabic During the Middle Ages: Searching for the Classical Tradition," *Speculum* 90/1 (2015): pp. 29–59.

34 The earliest letters of Isidore, published by Regel, *supra*, n. 3, are addressed to Guarino. The tone and the jesting material indicate that the two were close friends, probably since the days of their literary training in Constantinople.

35 Cammelli, pp. 131 ff.; *MP*, p. 231 n. 57; and M. Baxandall, "Guarino, Pisanello and Manuel Chrysoloras," *JWarb* 28 (1965): pp. 183–204.

36 An example of his exquisite calligraphy at an early stage in his career and life is provided by his transcription of Manuel II's *Funeral Speech/Ἐπιτάφιος* for Theodoros I, housed in the Bibliothèque National de France, Départment des Manuscrits, *Supplément grec 309*. His *codex* also bears a masterpiece of Greek portraiture; cf. Helen C. Evans, ed., *Byzantium: Faith and Power (1261–1557)* (New Haven and London, 2004), no. 1 (p. 26); and Philippides, "The Fall Constantinople 1453: Classical Comparison and the Circle of Cardinal Isidore," p. 371 n. 97. For Isidore's activities as a copyist of ancient texts, cf. C.G. Patrinelis, "Ἕλληνες Κωδικογράφοι τῶν Χρόνων τῆς Ἀναγεννήσεως," *Ἐπετηρὶς τοῦ Μεσαιωνικοῦ Ἀρχείου* 8–9 (1958/1959): pp. 63–124, esp. 87: "Ἰσίδωρος καρδινάλιος [δρᾶ 1409–1464]."
Isidore's interests in calligraphy go beyond the task of a copyist. As *Codex Vat. gr. 914*, fols. 1ʳ–3ʳ demonstrates, he had a profound curiosity in the art of ink making, providing not only a recipe for its production, but also expounding upon the process. For a substantial analysis of this text and a critical edition with commentary, cf. Ph. Nusia, "Ἀνέκδοτο Κείμενο περὶ Σκευασίας Μελανιοῦ, Κινναβάρεως, Βαρζίου, Καταστατοῦ, καὶ Κόλλησις Χαρτιοῦ (15ος αι.)," in N. Tsirones, Mp. Lengas, and A. Lazaridu, eds., *Βιβλιοαμφιάστης 3: Τὸ Βιβλίο στὸ Βυζάντιο. Βυζαντινὴ καὶ Μεταβυζαντινὴ Βιβλιοδεσία. Πρακτικὰ Διεθνοῦς Συνεδρίου. Ἀθήνα 13–16 Ὀκτωβρίου 2005* (Athens, 2008), pp. 43–62, esp. 55–62.

37 It is known that he had continued his studies upon his return to the Peloponnese and developed a skill in copying manuscripts, although he spent substantial time in Mistra and Monemvasia. Cf. A. Papadakis, "Isidore of Kiev," *ODB* 2: 1015–1016; and Kalligas, *Byzantine Monemvasia*, p. 177.

The rise of Isidore   29

38 On Isidore and the Vatican Library, cf. Mercati, ch. 3 (pp. 60–102).
39 *MP*, p. 263 n. 109, notes that the documentation for these trips is "scanty" at best, and the journeys were probably of a personal nature, even though a document describes Chrysoloras as an "ambasciatore dell'imperatore di Costantinopoli."
40 This trip is much better documented than the previous voyages of 1404 and 1405–1406; cf. *RKOR* 3318 (pp. 95, 96); Cammelli, pp. 144 ff.; and *MP*, p. 263.
41 In Constance, Chrysoloras fell ill and died on the 15th of April 1415; cf. *MP*, p. 322. His stay in the city coincides with the gathering of the Council of Constance and the trial of Jan Hus, the Czech professor, regent of Charles University, priest who preached at the Bethlehem Chapel in Prague, and religious reformer. The question must be raised: Did Chrysoloras go to Constance to confer with the papal leadership and perhaps seek to obtain agreement for military assistance? This is a topic that has not been explored. As we will note in the next chapter, religious reformers dominated this council among others, although some, if not the majority, of the attendees were strong supporters of the papacy.
42 Theodoros died in 1407, but the month and exact day of his death remain problematic; cf. *MP*, p. 272, n. 126, for the particulars on the uncertain and ambiguous evidence. The generally accepted date of Theodoros's death is generally the summer of 1407. Cf., e.g., A.G. Mompherratos, *Οἱ Παλαιολόγοι ἐν Πελοποννήσῳ* (Athens, 1913), p. 29: Τὸ θέρος 1407 ὁ Θεόδωρος Ι μετὰ μακρὰν ἀσθένειαν ἀπέθανεν ἐν Μιστρᾷ. Georgios Sphrantzes's authentic chronicle, the *Minus*, in *Georgios Sphrantzes, Memorii 1401–1477. In anexa Pseudo-Phrantzes: Macarie Melissenos Cronica, 1258–1481*, ed. and trans.V. Grecu, Scriptores Byzantini 5 (Bucharest, 1996); *The Fall of the Byzantine Empire: A Chronicle by George Sphrantzes 1401–1477*, trans. M. Philippides (Amherst, 1980); and *Georgii Sphrantze Chronicon*, ed. and trans. R. Maisano, CFHB 29 (Rome, 1990), is of no help. It treats this period under a general chronological heading: 3: ἀφ' οὗ δὴ ιβου ἔτους μέχρι καὶ τοῦ καου [1403–1413], and telescopes into this summary a number of events that differ chronologically, including the death of the despot of the Morea: καὶ τοῦ θανάτου τοῦ δεσπότου κὺρ Θεοδώρου τοῦ πορφυρογεννήτου εἰς τὸν Μυζιθρᾶν. *MP*, p. 272 n. 126, is more specific: Theodoros probably died in June.
The title of Manuel's speech, as it appears in the manuscripts of the period, reads (with minor variations): Τοῦ Εὐσεβεστάτου καὶ Φιλοχρήστου Βασιλέως Κυροῦ Μανουὴλ τοῦ Παλαιολόγου Λόγος Ἐπιτάφιος εἰς τὸν Αὐτάδελφον Αὐτοῦ Δεσπότην Πορφυρογέννητον Κῦρ Θεόδωρον τὸν Παλαιολόγον Ῥηθεὶς Ἐπιδημήσαντος εἰς Πελοπόννησον τοῦ Βασιλέως. G.T. Dennis, *The Letters of Manuel II Palaeologus*, CFHB 8 (Washington, DC, 1977), points out, pp. 159, 160 n. 1, that this long address has also survived in an epitome of a sort, revised by Manuel himself: *Codex Scorial gr. 14 (R-I-14)*, fols. 257–270.
43 The confusion dates back to the *quattrocento*, when Laonikos [Nikolaos] Khalkokondyles, *Laonici Chalcocandylae Atheniensis Historiarum Libri Decem*, ed. I. Bekker, CSHB, Book 1 (Bonn, 1843), pp. 202, 203, states that Manuel II during his voyage to the Morea in 1408 pronounced the speech "as if he were a tragedian at his [brother's] grave": Ἐμμανουῆλος ὁ Βυζαντίου [Constantinople's] βασιλεύς ... ἐπὶ τῷ ἀδελφῷ ἤδη τελευτηκότι [Theodoros I] λόγον ἐπικήδειον ἐξετραγῴδει δεξιῶν ἐπὶ τῷ τάφῳ αὐτοῦ. For a new edition and the first complete English translation of Khalkokondyles, cf. A. Kaldellis, ed. and trans., *The Histories*, Dumbarton Oaks Medieval Library, 2 vols. (Cambridge, MA and London, 2014). The same confusion also seems to appear in an unclear statement of Isidore himself, in his *Panegyric* to Manuel II and John VIII. Cf. *ΠκΠ* 3: 164: ὁ βασιλεὺς ἐκεῖνος [Manuel II] ... ἧκεν εἰς Πελοπόννησον ... τοῦ φίλου καὶ ἀδελφοῦ τῶν ὧδε ἀπάραντος καὶ πρὸς τὰ ἀμείνω πορείαν μεταστάντος ... ὃν καὶ πενθήσας ἀξίως κατεκόσμησεν λόγοις ἐπιταφίοις, γενναίοις πάνυ δεξιοῖς. For selections from the text, cf. *infra*, Appendix. Influenced by these misleading statements, modern scholars have been led astray as well; cf. *MP*, p. 525.
44 A summary of the chronological problems and the confusion associated with this document is supplied in *MP*, Appendix 22 (pp. 525–527). The chronology has now become

easier to understand because of the "new" evidence; cf. *infra*, nn. 51 and 52. Armed with this new information, it now appears that the older view of Lampros is closer to the truth than the later conclusions of Zakythinos (cf. *infra*, n. 50). S.P. Lampros, "Μία Ἐπιμνημόσυνος Τελετὴ ἐν Μυστρᾷ," *Σπαρτιατικὸν Ἡμερολόγιον* 11 (1910): pp. 33–42, has concluded that the terminus ante quem for the recital was 1419, when Theodoros II married Cleopa Malatesta, that is, Isidore in his letter would have mentioned her among the audience, as she would have attended the ceremony. In fact, the arguments offered by Zakythinos in favor of a date of 1409 have now been effectively invalidated.

45 Lampros edited and published the text in *ΠκΠ* 3: 132–221. His student, I.K. Bogiatzides, after the death of his mentor, continued the editorial work for this and the later volume. Exactly when Isidore composed the speech is unknown, but, because of its contents, it must have been after the naval battle near the Ekhinades (Curzolari) islands in the Ionian Sea, near Naupaktos (Lepanto), in 1427. On this event and its historical circumstances, cf. Philippides, *Constantine XI Dragaš Palaeologus*, ch. 4, sec. II, since Isidore himself recounts the consequences of this naval victory over Carlo Tocco and his son Turnus/Turno. Cf. Isidore's own statements, which assist us in providing a terminus ante quem for his speech, in *ΠκΠ* 3: esp. 196, 197. We should observe that his long speech clearly displays Isidore's superior classical education and mastery of ancient Attic. It contains substantial references to antiquity and is composed in an admirable ancient Greek style, even though Bogiatzides unjustly criticized its style. We wonder whether Bogiatzides, p. γ´ of the introduction: μετ᾽ οὐκ ὀλίγων αὐτοῦ σολοικισμῶν καὶ βαρβαρισμῶν, would have expressed this criticism if he had known that it had been composed by Isidore. Bogiatzides attributes the text to an anonymous writer, since the ms. does not contain the author's name in the incipit, added by a later hand that reads: *In Constantinopolitatum Imp. Et Constantinopolim ipsam encomion panegyricum; in quo praeter cetera, quod Imperator Constantinopoli a Turcis periclitante, ipse ad petenda ab Italis et Germanis auxilia profect. suscep.* The work was eventually attributed to Isidore by Mercati, pp. 2 ff. The authorship by Isidore and the approximate date of its composition 1429 are further confirmed by O.J. Schmitt, "Kaiserrede und Zeitgeschichte im späten Byzanz: ein Panegyrikos Isidors von Kiew aus dem Jahre 1429," *Jahrbuch der Österreichischen Byzantinistik* 48 (1998): pp. 211 and n. 11, and 241, 242. On p. 211, he states: "Was Länge und Inhalt anbetrifft, last sich nur eine zeitgenössische Rede mit Manuels II. Werk vergleichen der 1429 am Hofe Johannes' VIII. vorgetragene Panegyrikos Isidors, des späteren Metropoliten von Kiew." Cf. R. Estangüi Gómez, *Byzance face aux Ottomans. Exercice du pouvoir et contrôle du territoire sous les derniers Paléologues (Milieu XIVe–milieu XVe siècle)*, Byzantina Sorbonensia 28 (Paris, 2014): p. 451 n. 446. Bogiatzides, however, realized the exceptional importance of this work, e.g., p. γ´ of the introduction: πολυτιμοτάτου δὲ διὰ τὰς περιεχομένας ἱστορικὰς εἰδήσεις ἀγνώστους ἀλλαχόθεν. He recognized that it is more than a speech, for it provides us with precious historical information on the events of the period that are embedded in the rhetorical text. In addition to the battle of Ekhinades and the treaty that followed, which was sealed with the marriage of Constantine XI, the son of Manuel II, to the daughter of Tocco, it is the only Greek text that addresses in detail the long voyage of Manuel II to the west during the blockade of Constantinople by Bayezid I, thus providing us in a narrative form a detailed Greek view of the emperor's journey abroad. It is a pity that modern scholarship has largely overlooked the precious historical details furnished by Isidore in this *Encomium*.

46 The funeral address has been edited and published on a number of occasions: *PG* 156 (Paris, 1866): cols. 181–308; Lampros, *ΠκΠ* 3: 11–119; and definitively, Julian Chrystostomides, Προθεωρία εἰς τὸν τοῦ βασιλέως Μανουὴλ Παλαιολόγου ἐπιτάφιον εἰς τὸν ἀδελφὸν Θεόδωρον. *Manuel II Palaeologus: Funeral Oration on His Brother Theodore*, CFHB 26 (Thessalonike, 1985).

47 Manuel's letter to Chrysoloras, requesting improvements on the text, has survived. Cf. Dennis, *The Letters*, no. 56 (pp. 158–160). Also, e.g., the opening statements, p. 159: στέλλω σοι τὸν πρὸς τὸν ἀδελφὸν Ἐπιτάφιον, ὃς ἐμοὶ δεδημιούργηται δακρύοντι μᾶλλον ἢ γράφοντι . . . οὔκουν οὐδὲ τουτὶ τὸ βραχύτατον γράφειν ἀδακρυτὶ δύναμαι.

48 His brief reply is simply titled Προθεωρία. On this work and its text, cf. Chrysostomides, pp. 67–69.
49 For a Greek-English bilingual edition, cf. C.G. Patrinelis and D.Z. Sophianos, *Manuel Chrysoloras and His Discourse Addressed to the Emperor Manuel II Palaeologus/Μανουὴλ Χρυσολωρᾶ Λόγος πρὸς τὸν Αὐτοκράτορα Μανουὴλ Β΄ Παλαιολόγο* (Athens, 2001). The importance of this text had been indicated prior to the edition; cf. C.G. Patrinelis, "An Unknown Discourse of Chrysoloras Addressed to Manuel II Palaeologus," *Greek, Roman and Byzantine Studies* 13 (1972): pp. 497–502.
50 The suggestions of Chrysoloras survive in one ms., Meteora, *Metamorphosis 154*, in seventy-five folios, the first of which is missing; the ms. had already been identified by Nikos Bees in 1967, but was not published until 2001 (*supra*, n. 49). On its history and "dormant period," cf. Patrinelis and Sofianos, p. 38.
51 This is the sound conclusion reached by Patrinelis and Sofianos, and is based on internal evidence within the text, which employs future terms in regard to a potential audience; cf., e.g., p. 79: τίς δὲ καὶ τῶν ἀκουσομένων τούτου [*sc.* Ἐπιταφίου] and again πολλῶν τῶν ἀκουσομένων ... καὶ θαυμασομένων. At the same time, the new conclusion negates the arguments of D.A. Zakythinos, "Μανουὴλ Β΄ ὁ Παλαιολόγος καὶ ὁ Καρδινάλιος Ἰσίδωρος ἐν Πελοπονήσῳ," in *Mélanges offerts à Octave et Melpo Merlier, à l'occasion du 25ᵉ anniversaire de leur arrivée en Grèce*. Collection de l'Institut Français d'Athènes 94 (Athens, 1957): p. 6, who was under the impression that the speech was pronounced in the spring of 1409, which Zakythinos believes was on the second anniversary of the death of Theodoros. Cf. Estangüi Gómez, pp. 377, 378 nn. 79–82 and 385 n. 121.
52 Before the publication and the analysis of Meteora, *Metamorphosis 154*, scholars had assumed that the emperor sent his letter and speech to Chrysoloras late in 1409 or early in 1410. It was also assumed that the speech was composed in 1409 as the earliest evidence for Plethon's residence at Mistra. Moreover, scholars had further assumed that Isidore was already in the Morea in 1409, since he brought the Ἐπιτάφιος with him. Armed with the Meteora manuscript, Patrinelis and Sofianos quite reasonably conclude, p. 46: "the writing of Manuel's funeral oration and letter to Chrysoloras, the earliest evidence of Georgios Gemistos Plethon's presence and Isidore's presence at Mistra ... must be shifted to some years later." Cf. Estangüi Gómez, p. 451 f.
53 Dennis, *The Letters*, p. 168 n. 1, points out that the date can be extrapolated from a letter that Guarino wrote in January of 1418. Dennis reviews the evidence and concludes that Manuel composed his letter before October 1417 (cf. the following note for specifics).
54 On this letter, cf. Lampros, "Μία Ἐπιμνημόσυνος Τελετή," p. 40. The complete text of this letter appears in Dennis, *The Letters*, no. 60 (pp. 166–169). The request for a translation comes at the conclusion of the letter: φανέρου τε οἷς ἂν γνοίης καὶ πρὸς τὴν Λατίνων φωνήν, εἰ δὲ βούλει, τὴν ἰδίαν τοῦτο [Ἐπιτάφιον] μεταβάλλειν ἀξίου ... σύ ... τοῦτο ποίει, δείξεις ἂν κἂν τῷδε τὸν εὔνουν. The translation would have been a difficult task. Guarino never attempted to comply with the request, but he passed it on to Ambrogio Traversari, as Dennis, *ibid.*, p. 18 n. 3, indicates, deriving his evidence from a letter of Guarino, whose pertinent text he quotes: *Ipse etiam imperator humanissimam quondam ad me nisit epistulam et funebram pro eius fratre orationem quam ipse confecti; oratio est ... copiosa et miro contexta verborum et sententiarum ornatu ... ad fratrem Ambrosium nostrum mittam*.
55 His letter addressed to the emperor, τῷ βασιλεῖ κῦρ Μανουήλ, has been published as Letter 5 (pp. 65–69), in Regel.
56 In Regel's edition, this letter is published and numbered as the fifth (pp. 65–69), and is next to last. This position in relation to the other letters is of course misleading, for it implies that it was written at a later time.
57 *Ibid.*, p. 65.
58 *Ibid.*: ὡς ταύτῃ δή μοι μᾶλλον λυσιτελεῖν καὶ μὴ οὕτως ἀποκναίειν τὴν Ἀττικὴν ἀκοήν, πρὸς ἣν Πλάτωνος καὶ Δημοσθένους γλῶτταν καὶ τῶν κατ᾽ αὐτοὺς μόνον προσήκει φθέγγεσθαι.
59 *Ibid.*: ἡδέως τοιγαροῦν ἀκούοις, ὦ βασιλεῦ. πρότερον δὲ ἐρῶ σοι λόγον βραχὺν μέν, γλώττης δὲ ἀρίστης δεόμενον καὶ μείζονος ἢ κατὰ τὴν ἐμήν.

32 *The rise of Isidore*

60 *Ibid.*: ὁ δῆμος οὐχ Ἑλλήνων, ἀλλὰ βαρβάρων ἦν. ἡ δὲ τούτων ὠμότης καὶ τῶν Σκυθῶν ὑπερηκόντιζεν ... οὐδὲ τῶν ἀγροτάτων θηρίων διέφερον. Isidore also reports on a local practice that involved ritual mutilation, which seems to have surprised him greatly, as he refers to it as τὰ πρώην δεινά. On this detail in his report, cf. some scholarly observations: S.P. Lampros, "Τὸ Ἔθος τοῦ Μασχαλισμοῦ παρὰ τοῖς Μανιάταις τῶν Μέσων Αἰώνων," *NH* 2 (1905): pp. 181–186. Lampros points out that the testimony of Isidore must be read together with the observations, on the same custom, of Ioannes Argyropoulos's rhetorical comparison of Manuel II to previous emperors, as included in the ms. 817, Bibliothèque National de France, Départment des Manuscrits. In addition, cf. S. Kougeas, "Περὶ τῶν Μελιγκῶν τοῦ Ταϋγέτου ἐξ Ἀφορμῆς Ἀνεκδότου Βυζαντινῆς Ἐπιγραφῆς ἐκ Λακωνίας," *Πραγματίαι τῆς Ἀκαδημίας Ἀθηνῶν* 15 (1950): pp. 29, 30. This was an ancient custom reported by numerous authors in antiquity, which somehow had survived the passing of centuries only to be mentioned again in the *quattrocento*.

61 Regel, p. 66: ἐντεῦθεν δὴ καὶ μετέωρον τὴν ἀκοὴν εἶχον, ὥσπερ οἱ τὰ μεγάλα μυστήρια πάλαι μυούμενοι.

62 *Ibid.*: ἐπεὶ δὲ καὶ παρὰ τὴν τῶν Σπαρτιατῶν ἐγενόμεθα μητρόπολιν [Mistra], λόγος ἔρρει πολὺς καὶ τὸ βιβλίον ἅπαντες ἐζήτουν καὶ περὶ ἐκείνου πολὺν ἐποιοῦντο λόγον. θᾶττον γὰρ ἢ πτηνὸν τὸ πτερὸν τῆς φήμης διαδρομὸν πάντας ἀνέπεισεν ἐκεῖνο ζητεῖν.

63 *Ibid.*, pp. 66, 67.

64 In Lampros's edition, the text of the address occupies 107 printed pages (with an *apparatus criticus*), pp. 11–118.

65 This is the opinion of Zakythinos, "Μανουὴλ Β´," p. 48, who estimates that Theodoros, who had been born in 1400, as estimated by Lampros, was too young to be entrusted with this task. On Theodoros Gazes [Gaza], cf. Staikos, 1: 67–89.

66 Staikos, *ibid*. Demetrios had been an old associate of Theodoros I.

67 On this topic, cf. the penetrating remarks of *MP*, pp. 424, 425, on the emperor's own style and degree of difficulty in his Greek composition, as they apply not only to the emperor's style, but also to that of all Byzantine educated intellectuals of the *quattrocento*.

68 It was probably at this time that Isidore also wrote a letter (Letter 4 in Regel, p. 64) to his friend Khortasmenos, whom Kalligas, *Byzantine Monemvasia*, p. 173, identifies as Ioannes Ignatios Khortasmenos, the later metropolitan of Selybria; cf. H. Hunger, *Johannes Chortasmenos (ca. 1370–ca.1436/37)*, Wiener byzantinische Studien 7 (Vienna, 1967). In this correspondence, Isidore speaks of a letter he sent to the emperor concerning the ceremony at Mistra: καὶ περὶ τῆς ἐπιστολῆς δέ, ἣν ἀνήγκαμεν τῷ πάντ᾽ ἀρίστῳ καὶ θειοτάτῳ βασιλεῖ [Manuel II].

69 *Supra*, n. 36, for particulars. The ms. was acquired by the Bibliothèque nationale de France after the French Revolution of 1789, but it is unclear how it found its way to France. The text received the attention of art historians in the nineteenth century; cf. H. Bordier, *Description des peintures et autres ornaments contenus dans les manuscripts grecs de la Bibliothèque nationale* (Paris, 1883), pp. 281, 282.

70 *Supra*, nn. 62 and 63.

71 On the Byzantine imperial costume, cf. A. Hofmeister, "Von der Trabea Triumphalis des römischen Kaisers über das Byzant. Lorum zur Stolader abendländischen Herrescher," in P.E. Schramm, ed. *Herrschaftszeichen und Staatssymbolik: Beiträge zu ihrer Geschichte vom dritten bis zum sechzehnten Jahrhundert*, 1 (Stuttgart, 1955), pp. 25–50; yet, as I. Spatharakis, *The Portrait in Byzantine Illuminated Manuscripts* (Leiden, 1976), p. 265, has justly observed: "Although much has been written on imperial costume, a systematic examination of it is still required." On the portrayal of medieval Greek emperors in general, cf. in the classic but rare work of S.P. Lampros, *Λεύκωμα τῶν Βυζαντινῶν Αὐτοκρατόρων* (Athens, 1930), which reproduces various portraits in black and white within the limits of the available technology of the period. For a comparison of Manuel II and John VIII as travelers and as subjects in western art, cf. C. Marinesco, "Deux Empereurs byzantins en Occident: Manuel II et Jean Paléologue," *Comptes rendus de l'Academie*

des Inscriptions et Belles-Lettres, January–March, 1957 (Paris, 1958), pp. 23, 24; and *idem*, "Deux Empereurs byzantins, Manuel II et Jean VIII Paléologue, vus par des artistes occidentaux," *Le Flambeau* 40 (November–December, 1957): pp. 758–762. In addition, cf. the informative discussion of Manuel's portraits in *MP*, Appendix 24, pp. 531–551. On the *Funeral Speech*'s masterpiece of late Byzantine illumination, cf. Spatharakis, pp. 234–236, who further compares it with another manuscript, Musée du Louvre, Paris, Ivories A 53, containing the portraits of Manuel's family. This ms. contains the text of Pseudo-Dionysius the Areopagite and was brought to the Royal Abbey of Saint-Denys by Manuel Chrysoloras himself, as a personal gift of Manuel II. Cf. *MP*, pp. 263, 264. It bears the following dedication, cf. *ibid.*, p. 545, with a photograph of the actual text. The dedication reads as follows in Chrysoloras's own orthography and pronunciation; cf. *MP*, p. 545:

> τὸ παρὸν βϊβλϊον, ἀπεστάλη παρὰ τοῦ ὑψηλοτάτου βασϊλέως καὶ || αὐτοκράτορος ῥωμαίων κϋροῦ μανουὴλ τοῦ παλαιολόγου εἰς τὸ μο||ναστήριον τοῦ ἁγίου Δϊονϋσϊου τοῦ ἐν παρϋσϊῳ τῆς φραγγίας ἢ γαλατίας || ἀπὸ τῆς κωνσταντϊνουπόλεως δϊ' ἐμοῦ μανουὴλ τοῦ χρϋσολωρᾶ, πεμ||φθέντος πρέσβεως παρὰ τοῦ εἰρημένου βασϊλέως, ἔτη ἀπὸ κτίσεως || κόσμου, ἑξακϊσχϊλϊοστῷ ἐννεακοσϊοστῷ ἕξκαιδεκάτῳ. ἀπὸ σαρκώσεως δὲ || τοῦ κϋρίου χϊλϊοστῷ τετρακοσϊοστῷ ὀγδόῳ. – ὅς τϊς εἰρημένος βασιλεὺς ἦλθε πρότερον εἰς τὸ Παρϋσϊον πρὸ ἐτῶν τεσσάρων.

In addition, cf. H. Belting, *Das illuminierte Buch in der spät-byzantinischen Gesellschaft* (Heidelberg, 1970), pp. 75, 76.
72 Letter 5 in Regel, pp. 65–69; cf. *supra*, n. 56.
73 Letter 3, *ibid.*, p. 63.
74 *Ibid*. Isidore uses the phrase, "the chariot of Zeus," in his first letter to Guarino, which was probably written sometime after this letter. Cf. par. 3, line 4, *ibid.*, p. 60: καὶ τρόπον δή τινα τῷ πτηνῷ Διὸς ἅρματι.
75 Letter 3, *ibid.*, p. 63: στοῶν κάλλη . . . ναῶν ὡραιότης . . . οἰκιῶν καὶ ἀγρῶν κτήσεις, . . . ὠνίων πλῆθος καὶ ἀφθονία παντοίων βρωμάτων, ἃ πολλὰ μέν εἰσι παρ' ὑμῖν [in Constantinople], καλλίω δὲ μᾶλλον ἢ πολλά.
76 Letter 1, *ibid.*, p. 59. Cf. par. 1, lines 1 and 2.
77 *CBB* 1:246: ἐν ἔτει ͵ϛϡιη΄ [6918 *anno mundi*, that is 1409] ἐγέγονεν τὸ ἕβδομον θανατικόν. Perhaps this wave of the plague originated in Crete. Cf. T.E. Detorakis, "Ἡ Πανώλης ἐν Κρήτῃ. Συμβολὴ εἰς τὴν Ἱστορίαν τῶν Ἐπιδημιῶν τῆς Νήσου," *Ἐπιστημονικὴ Ἐπετηρὶς Φιλοσοφικῆς Σχολῆς Πανεπιστημίου Ἀθηνῶν* 21, ser. 2 (1970): pp. 118–136, esp. 122 f.
78 *CBB* 1: 247.
79 *Minus* 5.2: ἐν μηνὶ Αὐγούστῳ ἀπέθανε καὶ ἡ δέσποινα κυρὰ Ἄννα ἡ ἀπὸ Ῥωσσίας λοιμώδει νόσῳ.
80 *Ibid*. 5.1: ἐν τῷ χειμῶνι τοῦ αὐτοῦ δὴ ἔτους ᵃ1416/1417° θανατικοῦ γενομένου ἐν τῇ Μαύρῃ Θαλάσσῃ. Sphrantzes then lists a large number of his relatives who had succumbed to the wave of this plague.
81 As is clearly implied by the conjunction καί,, before the prepositional phrase εἰς τὴν Πόλιν; cf. *ibid.*: τοῦ δ' αὐτοῦ θανατικοῦ γενομένου περὶ τὸ ἔαρ καὶ τὸ θέρος καὶ εἰς τὴν Πόλιν.
82 *Ibid.*: περὶ τὸ ἔαρ καὶ τὸ θέρος.
83 According to several Muscovite chronicles, the betrothal had been arranged by 1410/1411. Cf. E. von Muralt, *Essai de chronographie byzantine, 1057–1453* (St. Petersburg, 1871; repr. 1966), n. 5. Gibbons, p. 232, is under the erroneous impression that Anna married John VIII in the last years of Bayezid's reign; for an explanation of this error, cf. *MP*, p. 153 n. 45. In addition, Runciman, "The Marriages of the Sons of the Emperor Manuel II," 1, p. 276. On Anna, cf. *PLP* 9: no. 21349 (p. 64) [s.v. Παλαιολογίνα, Ἄννα]. Doukas 20.3 emphasizes the fact that Lady Anna was still young, 14 years of age,

34 The rise of Isidore

when she died; she had married John VIII three years earlier but had not been crowned queen because of her youth:

> ὁ βασιλεὺς Μανουήλ... στείλας εἰς τὸν ῥῆγα Ῥωσίας ἠγάγετο νύμφην [sc. τῷ υἱῷ αὐτοῦ, that is John VIII] τὴν θυγατέρα αὐτοῦ. καὶ ἁρμόσας ταύτην, μετακαλεσάμενος τὸ ὄνομα αὐτῆς Ἄνναν, οὐκ ἠβουλήθη στέψαι τότε εἰς βασιλέα. ἦν γὰρ ἡ κόρη τὸ ἑνδέκατον ἄγουσα ἔτος. σεραιομένων δὲ τριῶν ἐτῶν καὶ λοιμικῆς νόσου καταλαβούσης τῇ Πόλει καὶ ϖολὺ ϖλῆθος λαοῦ διὰ τοῦ βομβῶνος τεθνηκότος, ἐτελεύτησε καὶ ἡ βασιλὶς Ἄννα, μέγα ϖένθος καταλιϖοῦσα τοῖς ϖολίταις.

84 *Ibid.*: τοῦ βομβῶνος.
85 Letter 1 in Regel, p. 59: ἄρτι τοῦ μετοϖώρου τὴν τοῦ θέρους ὥραν διαδεξαμένου νοσοῦντι νόσον μακρὰν καὶ βαρεῖαν, τὴν λοιμώδη. In addition, cf. *CBB* 2: 407.
86 Cf., e.g., Doukas 20.3: ϖολὺ ϖλῆθος λαοῦ διὰ τοῦ βομβῶνος τεθνηκότος.
87 Letter 1 in Regel, pp. 59, 60:

> ἀλλὰ καὶ τοῦ λοιϖοῦ, φημὶ δὲ λοιϖὸν τὸ μεμνῆσθαι σε ἡμῶν, ὥσϖερ εἰ οὐκ ἔγραφες, τῶν μὴ καλῶν ἐτίθουν, οὕτω σου γεγραφότος τῶν καλῶν τίθεμαι, καὶ τὸ μηδὲ τῆς ϖρὸς καθυφεῖναι ϖαλαιᾶς ἐκείνης φιλίας, μᾶλλον δὲ καὶ τῷ τοῦ χρόνου μήκει συμϖαρεκτείνεσθαι δεῖν οἶμαι ταύτην, καθάϖερ τῶν φ[υτῶν] ὁϖόσα τοῖς γεωργοῖς ἀρδείας τετυχηκότα τυγχάνει. ἀλλὰ σὺ μέν ἄϖαξ ἐϖιστέλλεις τοῦ ἔτους καίτοι, τί λέγω, ὅτε δύο ϖαρῳχηκότεν ἐτῶν μόλις ἥκει μοι γράμματα ϖαρὰ σοῦ, καὶ ταῦτά γε καλῶς εἰδότος ὅϖῃ τε γῆς εἰμι ϖολλῶν τε ὄντων τῶν ὡς ἡμᾶς αὐτόθεν ἀφικνουμένων.

88 *Ibid.*, p. 60. Cf. par. 4.
89 Patrinelis, "Ἕλληνες Κωδικογράφοι τῶν Χρόνων τῆς Ἀναγεννήσεως," pp. 87 ff. For an example of a late work, cf. B.L. Fonkich and F.B. Poljakov, "Ein unbekanntes Autograph des Metropoliten Isidoros von Kiev," *BZ* 82 (1981): pp. 96–101; and esp. *Codex Monac. gr. 157.*
90 *Supra*, n. 36.
91 For the career, the "humanism," and the (rather overrated) contribution of Plethon to Neoplatonist thought, to the revival of Platonic studies, and to the Italian Renaissance, cf. Woodhouse.
92 E.g., Ioannes Dokeianos was a noted copyist of ancient manuscripts and a scholar of some merit. Cf. the remarks in *ΠκΠ* 1: μδ´–μστ´; a partial list of the titles of books in his possession survives (*ΠκΠ* 1: 254) and indicates that his interests were similar to those of any other educated Greek of the Palaiologan period. For the archaic tendencies in his style, cf. the brief remarks in M. Philippides, "Herodian 2.4.1 and Pertinax," *CW* 77 (1984): pp. 295–297. On Ioannes Dokeianos as a scholar and humanist, cf. S.P. Lampros, "Αἱ Βιβλιοθῆκαι Ἰωάννου Μαρμαρᾶ καὶ Ἰωάννου Δοκειανοῦ καὶ Ἀνώνυμος Ἀναγραφὴ Βιβλίων," *NH* 1 (1904): pp. 295–312. In addition, cf. *PLP* 3: no. 5577 (p. 57); and Alice-Mary Talbot, "Dokeianos, John," *ODB* 1: 645.
93 In addition to Mistra, Kalavryta also seems to have enjoyed conditions favorable for a "revival of learning." Zakythinos has convincingly argued that this intellectual and artistic resurgence was only restricted to the elite, the privileged few, while the rest of the population of the Morea did not share in this high culture; cf. D.A. Zakythinos, *Le despotat grec de Morée (1262–1460)*, 2: *Vie et institutions* (Athens, 1953): p. 310. His views are accepted in J.V.A. Fine, Jr., *The Late Medieval Balkans: A Critical Survey from the Late Twelfth Century to the Ottoman Conquest* (Ann Arbor, 1987), p. 541.Years later, Cyriacus of Ancona encountered a rich library in Kalavryta, which contained a notable copy of Herodotus; cf. W. Miller, *Essays on the Latin Orient* (Cambridge, 1921), p. 149; and V. Laurent, "Le Vaticanus latinus 4789. IV. Alliances et filiations des Cantacuzènes au XVe siècle," *REB* 9 (1951): pp. 64–105, esp. p. 78. On the intellectuals in the Morea, cf. A.E. Vacalopoulos, *Origins of the Greek Nation: The Byzantine Period 1204–1461* (New Brunswick, 1970), ch. 13. For the "renaissance" of the Morea, cf. among others, S. Runciman, *The Last Byzantine Renaissance* (Cambridge, 1970); idem, *Byzantium and the Renaissance* (Tucson, 1970); I. Ševčenko, "The Palaeologan Renaissance," in W. Treadgold, ed.

Renaissances before the Renaissance: Cultural Revivals of Late Antiquity and the Middle Ages (Stanford, 1984), pp. 144–171; and I.P. Medvedev, *Византийский Гуманисм XIV–XV вв.* [= *Byzantine Humanism in the Fourteenth and Fifteenth Centuries*] (Leningrad, 1976). Vacalopoulos, ch. 13, further identifies this "renaissance" with national awareness; in his view the revival, which, he believes, amounts to a "national consciousness," came to an end with the Turkish conquest, when the last remaining scholars fled to the West. The contribution of scholarly refugees to the Italian Renaissance is fully discussed in Geanakoplos, *Greek Scholars in Venice; idem, Interaction of the "Sibling" Byzantine and Western; idem, Constantinople and the West: Essays on the Late Byzantine (Palaeologan) and Italian Renaissances and the Byzantine and Roman Churches* (Madison, 1989); the collection of essays by various authors in *Venezia e l'Oriente fra Tardo Medioevo e Rinascimento*, ed. A. Pertusi, Civiltà Europa e Civiltà Veneziana, Aspetti e Problemi 4 (Venice, 1966); and Staikos.

94 Letter 1 in Regel, pp. 60, 61.

95 *CC* 1: 74. The Bolognese Codex, *Bibl. Univ. lat. B 52*, busta 22, fols. 40^r–42^v, which has preserved this important letter of Isidore, reminds us in a note (printed in *CC* 1: 53) that the original text of Isidore was in Greek and that we only possess its Latin translation. The translator maintains that he attempted to retain the flavor and style of the Greek original text of the epistle, even though he was not an expert in the Greek language, as he admits:

> Habes iam, Alberte dilectissime grecam epistolam factam latinam, etsi satis inepte traductam. Malui enim <me> rudem ac indoctum iudicari abs te, quam pervicacem. Usus autem sum sermone facili et ilaro et, it ita dicam, puerili, ne tibi videar alius esse quam sum, tardo scilicet ac rudi ingenio. Potuissem enim hinc inde vocabula exquisite mendicari et expiscari, sed nolui et re minima rem maximam facere atque ostentare, quo me tenuis ac exiguissime supellectilis non est. Ipsam ergo penes te serva nec ulli cures edere, ne in tanta doctissimorum virorum copia temerarious ac presumptuosus fuisse videar, qui tantum mihi arrogem, ut grecam profiteri scientiam ausus sim, cuius vix prima rudimenta delibarim. Tuus Lianorus de Lianoriis etc.

For the full text of Isidore's letter, cf. *infra*, ch. 5, sec. 3.

96 The cardinal's information on the sultan's reliance on astrology should not be dismissed easily. Turkish sources confirm this superstitious trait in the sultan's character. H. Inalcik, "Istanbul: An Islamic City," in *idem, Essays in Ottoman History* (Istanbul, 1998), pp. 249–271, esp. 250, has the following comment on the sultan's reliance on the supernatural:

> Mehmed the Conqueror believed that the conquest would be the work of Allah, a miracle of His providence. The sufi Şeyh Aq-Semseddin, a follower of the famous mystic philosopher of light, "Umar" al-Suhrawardi, became murşid (spiritual guide) to the sultan and the army during the siege. The young sultan asked the murşid to go into religious retreat to know the divine decision of the exact date of the conquest. The conquest did not occur on that date that the murşid gave, rather the Christians recorded a naval success on that day. The letter written by the Şeyh to the sultan has been discovered in the palace archives.

It should be added that Mehmed II was not the only sultan who relied on the advice of astrologers. His father, Murad II, had employed diviners during his siege of Constantinople and was also under the influence of a holy man, whom Ioannes Kananos names "Mersaites," clearly a reference to the title murşid, but the imam's name was actually Seid-Bokhari (cf. *LCB*, p. 348), as is attested by the eyewitness account of the siege of 1422. Ioannes Kananos, *Georgius Phrantzes. Ioannes Cananus. Ioannes Anagnostes*, ed. I. Bekker, CSHB (Bonn, 1838), pp. 466, 467, relates:

> αὐτὸς δὲ ὁ μέγιστος καὶ πολὺς παρ' ἐκείνοις ὁ εὐγενὴς πατριάρχης, ὃν εἶχον προορατικὸν καὶ προφήτην, τοὔνομα Μηρσαΐτης [murşid] τῇ Περσικῇ διαλέκτῳ, ἀπέστειλεν ἀποκρισιαρίους πρὸς τὸν δεσπότην Τούρκων [Murad II] καὶ εἶπεν "ὅρα μὴ συνάψῃς πόλεμον ... ἕως ὅτε ἐγὼ νὰ φθάσω καὶ νὰ δηλώσω τὴν ὥραν τῆς συμπλοκῆς τοῦ πολέμου, ὡς ὁ μέγας ἡμῖν διδάσκει Ῥασοὺλ ὁ προφήτης." ... ὁ

δεσπότης Τούρκων [Murad II] δουλοπρεπῶς ὑπεδέξατο τοῦτον [murşid]. αὐτὸς δὲ σοβαρὸς καὶ μεγαλοϋπέροχος ἑωρᾶτο πᾶσιν ... καὶ πάντες οἱ Μουσουλμάνοι ἀληθῆ καὶ βέβαια κρατοῦσιν πάντα τὰ λαληθέντα ἐκ τούτου, καὶ πάντες τὴν κέλευσιν ἔμενον τὴν ἐκείνου, ἵνα προστάξῃ τοῦ πολέμου τὴν ὥραν.

For the most recent edition and English translation of Kananos, cf. A.M. Cuomo ed. and trans., *Ioannis Canani de Constantinopolitana Obsidione Relatio*, Byzantinische Archiv 30 (Boston and Berlin, 2016).

97 Letter 2 in Regel, pp. 61, 62, which, we will show, is earlier than Regel's Letter 1.
98 Letter 2, *ibid.*, p. 61: ὅσον εἰσηνέγκαμεν κρότον ἀναγνόντες σου τὴν ἐπιστολήν ... οὐδὲ λέγειν ῥαδίως ἂν ἔχοιμεν. τοσοῦτον ἤσθημεν, ὅ τε ἀναγινώσκων ἐγὼ οἵ τε ἀκροώμενοι πάντες ... ἡ δὲ μᾶλλον ἡμᾶς κατεῖχεν ἢ αἱ Σειρῆνες τοὺς παραπλέοντας. ἀλλὰ οὐδ᾽ Ὀδυσσεὺς ἄν, οἶμαι, ταύτην παρέδραμε.
99 *Ibid.*: Γουαρῖνος ὁ καλός, κοσμήσας μὲν τὴν πατρίδα καὶ πρὸ τῆς πατρίδος Ἰταλίαν πᾶσαν τῇ πατρίῳ φωνῇ, κοσμήσας δὲ καὶ τὴν Ἑλλάδα τῶν ἐκείνων Ἑλλήνων παιδείᾳ.
100 This assumption is still encountered. Cf., e.g., Kalligas, *Byzantine Monemvasia*, p. 171: "The letters ... are compiled in chronological order and from their contents it can be deduced that they were written between autumn 1409 and roughly 1417."
101 The first group of four letters was published by A.W. Ziegler, "Vier bisher nicht veröffentlichte griechische Briefe," *BZ* 44 (1951): pp. 570–577; the remaining four were published by *idem*, "Die restlichen vier unveröffentlichten Briefe Isidors von Kijev," *OCP* 18 (1952): pp. 135–142. Cf. T.V. Kushch, "Исидор Киевский как Эпистолограф [= Isidore of Kiev as an Epistolographer]," *Античная древномь и средние века 39* (=*К 60-летию д.и.н. профессор Валерия Павловича Степаненко*) (2009): pp. 375–382.
102 *Codex Vat. gr. 914* is discussed *in extenso* by Mercati, ch. 1.
103 Kalligas, *Byzantine Monemvasia*, p. 175.
104 Ziegler, "Vier bisher nicht veröffentlichte griechische Briefe," Letter 1 (p. 575): ἀλλὰ τοιαῦτα μὲν πέμπειν οὐκ οἶδα, ἃ δὲ οἶδα, τῶν ἀπὸ τῆς Πάτρας ἄνευ σοι πεμφθέντων.
105 *Ibid.*: ἀλλ᾽ ἐγγύτερον ἐλπὶς ἡμᾶς ἀφικνεῖσθαι παρ᾽ ὑμᾶς τοὺς Ἀχαιούς.
106 *Ibid.*, pp. 574, 575.
107 A quotation from Homer; cf., e.g., *Odyssey* 1.64: τέκνον ἐμόν, ποῖόν σε ἔπος φύγεν ἕρκος ὀδόντων. In addition, cf. *Odyssey* 3.230, 5.22, 19.492, 21.168, and 23.70; *Iliad* 4.350 and 14.83. This epic formula had been widely adopted and had become a favorite proverb among Byzantine intellectuals.
108 Ziegler, "Vier bisher nicht veröffentlichte griechische Briefe," Letter 1 (p. 575).
109 Kalligas, *Byzantine Monemvasia*, p. 174, suggests that this letter may have been written in 1414, but she was not aware of the "new" chronology, which has modified the *Funeral Speech* of Manuel II and has consequently "readjusted" the chronology that also involves Isidore. Thus her date for this letter is decidedly too early.
110 Ziegler, "Vier bisher nicht veröffentlichte griechische Briefe," Letter 2 (pp. 575, 576).
111 Kalligas, *Byzantine Monemvasia*, p. 176; there is nothing in the letter nor in the manuscript to indicate who was the intended recipient.
112 Ziegler, "Vier bisher nicht veröffentlichte griechische Briefe," Letter 2 (p. 575).
113 Perhaps the work that he had copied for Guarino, Xenophon's *Anabasis* (*supra*, text with n. 88), had something to do with the lively interest that he displays in *Perserei*. For Isidore's comparisons of the Ottoman sultan to the great king of ancient Persia, cf. Philippides, "The Fall of Constantinople 1453: Classical Comparisons and the Circle of Cardinal Isidore," esp. pp. 366–376.
114 Thus Ziegler, "Vier bisher nicht veröffentlichte griechische Briefe," letters 2, 3, and 4 (pp. 575–577) appear to be addressed to the despot. Cf. Kalligas, *Byzantine Monemvasia*, pp. 175–176. The remaining letters from the manuscript, letters 5, 6, 7, and 8 were published separately by Ziegler, "Die restlichen vier unveröffentlichen Briefe," pp. 135–142. They are in a pleasant style, full of classical allusions, but add nothing to our knowledge.

Letter 8 (p. 142) emphasizes the interest of Isidore in the occult, wherein he compares himself to an ancient soothsayer: οὐκ ἄρα ἦν ἐγὼ μάντις πονηρὸς οὐδέ τις φαῦλος εἰκαστής.
115 *PaL* 2: 18, presents a confused and confusing chronology on this point. It is implied that John VIII came to the Morea in 1426, while the actual date is of course 1427, as is stated correctly in *PaL* 2: 31. Similar is the confusion (or misprint?) in *LCB*, p. 364, wherein Nicol is under the impression that John VIII went to the Morea in 1426. The correct date, 1427, appears in D.M. Nicol, *The Immortal Emperor: The Life and Legend of Constantine Palaiologos, Last Emperor of the Romans* (Cambridge, 1992), p. 8. The actual chronology is well preserved in the *Minus* 14 and 15.1. In 15.1, Sphrantzes relates: καὶ τῷ αὐτῷ ἔτει μηνὶ Νοεμβρίῳ ἐξῆλθεν αὐτὸς δὴ ὁ βασιλεὺς ἀπὸ τῆς Πόλεως καὶ ἀπῆλθεν εἰς τὸν Μορέαν τῇ κϛῃ Δεκεμβρίου. This is one of the most unambiguous sequences in Sphrantzes. His chronology presents, for once, no problems whatsoever and there is no justification for any confusion. John VIII went to the Morea in the early winter of 1427. The date is further confirmed by an entry in a short chronicle, which speaks of the arrival in the Morea of Constantine, who had accompanied his brother, John VIII. Cf. *CBB* 1: 41.6 (p. 322): ἔτους ͵ϛϡλζ΄, μηνὶ δεκεβρίῳ, ὁ δεσπότης ὁ κῦρ Κωνσταντῖνος <ἦλθεν εἰς τὸν Μωρέαν>. S. Runciman, *Mistra: The Byzantine Capital of the Peloponnese* (London, 1980), p. 72, implies that the battle at Ekhinades took place soon after 1427. The standard date cited for this victory is 1427; cf. *PaL* 2: 18; and *LCB*, p. 364. If so, it took place before the arrival of John VIII, which occurred during the last days of December. Alternatively, the battle may have occurred in the late winter or the early spring of 1428.
116 E.g., N. Cheetham, *Mediaeval Greece* (New Haven and London, 1981), p. 205, who, however, telescopes numerous events into one paragraph and even fails to mention the victory at Ekhinades.
117 Presumably, he was Demetrios Laskaris Leontares (Leontarios, Leontaris); cf. *PaL* 2: 19 n. 60. On the noble status of this Leontaris, cf. M.C. Bartusis, "The Kavallarioi of Byzantium," *Speculum* 63 (1988): 343–350, esp. 350.
118 On this discourse, cf. *supra*, n. 45. The historical sections of this speech, with the first translation into a modern language, and with limited commentary, are given *infra*, Appendix.
119 Zakythinos, *Le despotat grec de Morée*, 1, p. 200; and Nicol, *The Immortal Emperor*, p. 8.
120 *Minus* 16.6.
121 The manuscript is contained in the *Codex Vat. gr. 1823*, fol. 126ʳ. It was first published by Mercati, pp. 151, 152. The text has been re-edited with divisions into paragraphs for easier reading and reference. Some textual errors have been corrected and the punctuation has been reworked.

2 Isidore and the Council of Basle

1 Prelude to Basle

The decade of the 1430s proved to be not only crucial but also decisive for the survival of the few territorial remnants of the once glorious Byzantine Empire. This was a period in which the Byzantine emperor John VIII involved himself in extensive diplomatic endeavors to forge an alliance with the papacy and western European states for the survival of his declining empire. But the West also sought to court Byzantine favor to weaken papal resolve to maintain supremacy over Christendom and its adherence to the doctrines of *Caesaropapism* and the "Petrine Doctrine." The former was the Byzantine belief that the emperor was the superintendent of the church[1] and the converse of this doctrine was the forged papal notion that the Byzantine emperor Constantine I the Great had relinquished ecclesiastical, if not also political, dominion to the highest Roman Church authority, namely the pope. The "Petrine Doctrine" was the notion that Roman preeminence over all Christendom was directly inherited from the Apostle Peter. Diplomacy, though complex leading up to the two councils,[2] was not the only approach, nor was it solely confined to the secular arena. On the contrary the multitude of religious questions, the rupture between the Roman and Avignonese churches referred to as the Great Schism, the creation of rival papacies, the question of the East-West schism ascribed to the scholar and statesman Patriarch Photios that dates back to the ninth century, the conciliar movement,[3] the rise of reformative religious factions, and especially the military needs of the imperial state, among other factors, steered John VIII to involve his government in two religious councils. The first to be addressed in this chapter, the Council of Basle (1431–1449),[4] a reforming body that had constituted itself as the representative of the universal church, called upon the Byzantine delegates to thrust themselves into the forefront of discussions concerning ecclesiastical issues then confronting and troubling the papacy and the western states. The second, to be addressed in Chapter 3, the Council of Ferrara-Florence (the main years of 1438–1439, although the inclusive dates are 1438–1445), achieved church union and subordinated Byzantine religious influences to papal partialities as the leading spokesman for dogmatic issues.[5] But for the empire the preeminent issue was to avoid failure in obtaining substantial military aid and personnel from the West, and ultimately to preclude the final collapse of their diminishing state into the out-reaching hands of its Ottoman foe.

Isidore was a leading figure at both councils. At least to 1430, his intellectual and ecclesiastical activities are centered at Monemvasia in the Morea with some digressions and stays at Mistra where most probably he came under the influence if not also the tutelage of Plethon.[6] As early as 1410, Isidore was called upon to compose a "blessing" for Cyril, the newly elevated metropolitan of Monemvasia who would recite the "blessing" before the main gate of the fortified city before entering it to assume his seat. Seventeen years later, Isidore accompanied Cyril to Constantinople[7] and perhaps this is reflective of the prominence that had been accorded to him for his literary and ecclesiastical skills, and noticeably his links to the Palaiologan family. A most notable achievement in his early career, however, was his role in preparing documentation for the metropolitan of Monemvasia. Isidore competently drafted two petitions that were addressed to the patriarch at Constantinople.[8] The first is particularly important because it reveals Isidore's familiarity (and his presumed knowledge, as well as the ease with which he could deal with sources) with the *Chronicle of Lacedaemonia and Monemvasia* and with a rendition of the *Chronicle of Monemvasia*.[9] He demonstrated his knowledge of the historical roots of Monemvasia, the role the Slavs played in the Peloponnese, and the nature and causes of the jurisdictional dispute between the metropolitans of Corinth and Monemvasia; his opinion was accepted by the emperor. Thus Isidore's earlier studies and literary achievements prepared him well for his subsequent role that brought him to Constantinople to address the needs of the imperial court and patriarchal hierarchy. In 1430 he entered the private imperial monastery of Saint Demetrios and three years later he became superior or abbot of the institution.

More concrete is the evidence for Isidore's later appointments:

Metropolitan of Kiev and of All Rus' (1437–1442);
Titular Metropolitan of Kiev and of All Rus' (1442–1458);
Cardinal-Priest (1439–1451);
Cardinal-Bishop of Sabina (1451–1463);
Titular Latin Patriarch of Constantinople (1452–1453, and again 1459–1463);
Latin Archbishop of Nicosia (1456–1458); and
Latin Archbishop of Kiev and of All Rus' (1458–1463).

A parallel must be drawn with the appointments of Bessarion, a close associate of Isidore:

Metropolitan of Nicaea (1437–1439);
Cardinal-Priest (1439–1449);
Cardinal-Bishop of Sabina (1449?);
Cardinal-Bishop of Tusculum (1449–1468);
Cardinal-Bishop of Sabina (1468–1472); and
Titular Latin Patriarch of Constantinople (1463–1472).

The listing of ecclesiastical offices held by Isidore remains argumentative among modern scholars and raises one main issue of immediate concern to us. Although papal literature and interpretative works in recent centuries award Isidore with the designation of "Titular Latin Patriarch of Constantinople" for the years "1452–1453," the validity of this address remains suspect.[10] The question must also be raised: Did Isidore attempt to promote himself for elevation to the office of "Titular Latin Patriarch of Constantinople"?; or probably more correctly: Did he seek to become the "Greek Patriarch of Constantinople"? We know that after the death of Patriarch Joseph while attending the Council of Ferrara-Florence, Isidore did seek the office of patriarch. Sylvestros Syropoulos[11] cites the words of the grand *protosynkellos* following an angry exchange with Isidore: Δέσποτα Ῥωσίας, οὐ γενήσῃ πατριάρχης ἐὰν δὲ γένῃ, κάθελε πρῶτον ἐμέ, "Despot of Rus': You will not become patriarch. If you do get appointed, depose me as your first act." Later, Syropoulos[12] states that Isidore "craved" the patriarchal appointment. In 1452 Sphrantzes did encourage the emperor, Constantine XI, to designate Isidore "Patriarch of Constantinople,"[13] but the emperor declined to do so because of strong anti-unionist opposition and because the appointment would have required the obedience of all Greeks, as Sphrantzes recounts.[14] Thus Isidore, in acts of self-promotion, may have directly contributed to the present scholarly confusion. If he could not obtain the Greek title, then he would have been content with the Latin. We are confronted with the issue of what is historical and what is perceived to be on the basis of questionable evidence. Nestor-Iskander, therefore, may not be far-fetched in making frequent references to a "patriarch" during the siege of 1453, whether he be a Greek or a Latin. These are not simple literary embellishments, but may acknowledge that Nestor-Iskander was aware of Isidore's attempts at self-promotion and even of his legitimate claim of a patriarchal title. Certainly, Isidore was the highest-ranking ecclesiastic within the city during the siege of 1453 and he may have used this fact to his advantage.[15]

2 At Basle

Early in 1433, the Council of Basle dispatched two legates, Antonio, the bishop of Suda, and Alberto de Crispis, to Constantinople to gain Byzantine favor and support for their respective positions. (The papacy also sent representatives.) John VIII was amenable to their overtures, viewing this as an excellent opportunity to obtain western military assistance for his beleaguered city.[16] The patriarchal official, a *megas ekklesiarches* (μέγας ἐκκλησιάρχης, grand ekklesiarkh of Santa Sophia)[17] and *dikaiophylax* (δικαιοφύλαξ, subaltern judge or judge general of Constantinople),[18] Sylvestros Syropoulos, reports the following on the Basle embassy:[19]

ἦλθον τοίνυν οὗτοι μετὰ γραμμάτων εἴς τε τὸν βασιλέα καὶ τὸν πατριάρχην, καὶ ἔδειξαν ὅπως ἡ ἐν Βασιλείᾳ σύνοδος ἔχει τὸ κράτος καὶ τὴν ἰσχὺν πλέον τοῦ πάππα καὶ κρεῖττον ἢ ἐκεῖνος πράξει αὕτη τὰ περὶ τῆς ἑνώσεως, καὶ οἱ πλείους καὶ κρείττονες τῶν ῥηγῶν τῇ συνόδῳ πρόσκεινταί τε καὶ πείθονται, καὶ πρὸ πάντων ὁ βασιλεὺς τῶν Ἀλαμανῶν ὁ Σιγισμοῦντος, κἀκεῖθεν γενήσεται μᾶλλον ἡ ὑπὲρ τῶν Γραικῶν ἀρκετὴ βοήθεια.

They came with the letters [from the Council of Basle] to the emperor and patriarch. They pointed out how the Council of Basle had more authority and power than the pope; how it could better than him [the pope] carry out union [of the churches]; how the majority of kings, the most powerful, adhered to the council and were submissive to it, as was indeed the emperor of the Germans, Sigismund; only from there sufficient aid would come to the Greeks.

The council was designated the *Seventeenth Ecumenical Council*, as was the later Council of Ferrara-Florence, understanding the latter to be an extension of the former. The primary literature for the period, however, numbers them as the *Eighth*. The Council of Basle was one of several reforming councils that convened in the fifteenth century to curb papal autocracy and limit the authority of the papal *curia*. At its inception, the council stated its purpose. Three objectives were defined at its first session held on 14 December 1431.[20] First, the council sought to eliminate heresies that had had a destructive impact upon the Western Church and continued to rend it apart. Next, and perhaps a most troublesome feature for the assembly, was the prevalence of wars between western Christian states and provinces. Its pervasiveness drained vital resources needed for the maintenance of peace and tranquility in the West. And finally, the council noted the numerous vices present within the church and sought to purify its institution.

Prior to the formal sitting of the Council of Basle and in the last year (1431) of the pontificate of Martin V, one of the chief proponents of a synod, discussions had been conducted setting forth the initiatives for the convocation of a church council that would include representatives from the Eastern and Western churches. Sylvestros Syropoulos furnishes us some personal insights on the Byzantine issues discussed in the preliminaries leading up to the synod. We should give particular attention to the dispositions and reluctance of Patriarch Joseph to participate in such a body, remaining unwavering in his views and maintaining them for the balance of that decade. It is unclear, however, whether or not these feelings were conveyed to Isidore, although we should assume that the latter was aware of the patriarch's positions on convening and participating in an ecclesiastical body. Isidore, as we shall observe below, although at variance in his thinking with Patriarch Joseph, was obedient to him. Sylvestros Syropoulos relates:[21]

ἀλλὰ καὶ ὁ πατριάρχης ἔκτοτε λίαν ἡγούμενος ἐπαχθὲς τὸ γενέσθαι τὴν σύνοδον ἐν τόπῳ καὶ ἐξουσίᾳ λατινικῇ καὶ λέγων πολλάκις ὡς εἰ ἐκεῖσε γένηται, οὐκ ἔσται καλὸν τὸ συμπέρασμα τῆς συνόδου, καὶ δεικνύων ἑαυτὸν μηδόλως βουλόμενον ἐκεῖσε παραγενέσθαι, ἐν μιᾷ τῶν ἡμερῶν καθήμενος ἐν τῷ κελλίῳ αὐτοῦ μετὰ καὶ ἐκκλησιαστικῶν ἀρχόντων, παρόντων καὶ δύο ἐκ τοῦ παλατίου ἀρχόντων, εἴρηκεν, ὅτι. λέγουσι γενέσθαι τὴν σύνοδον ἐν τῇ Ἰταλίᾳ καὶ ἀπελθεῖν τοὺς ἡμετέρους καὶ καρτερῆσαι ἐν τῇ συνόδῳ, καὶ ἔχειν τὰς ἐξόδους καὶ τῆς ὁδοῦ καὶ τῶν σιτηρεσίων παρ' ἐκείνων. ἐν γοῦν τῷ ἀπελθεῖν οὕτω καὶ ἐκδέχεσθαι καὶ τὴν ἡμερησίαν τροφὴν ἐξ ἐκείνων, ἤδη γίνονται δοῦλοι καὶ μισθωτοί, ἐκεῖνοι δὲ κύριοι. καὶ πᾶς δοῦλος τὸ θέλημα τοῦ κυρίου αὐτοῦ ὀφείλει ποιεῖν καὶ πᾶς μισθωτὸς τὴν ἐργασίαν τοῦ μισθοῦντος αὐτὸν ἐργάζεται καὶ πᾶς ὁ μισθῶν τινα τούτου χάριν τὸν μισθὸν παρέχει ἵνα ὁ μισθούμενος πληροῖ πᾶν ὅπερ ὁ μισθῶν αὐτὸν προστά[ξε]ι. εἰ δὲ μή γε, οὐ παρέχει αὐτῷ τὸν μισθόν. εἰ γοῦν ἐκεῖνοι κρατήσουσι τὸ σιτηρέσιον, τί ποιήσουσιν οἱ ἡμέτεροι; καὶ εἰ οὐ θελήσουσιν ὑποστρέψαι τοὺς ἡμετέρους δι' ἰδίων ἐξόδων τε καὶ πλευσίμων, τί ἄρα ἔξουσιν οὗτοι ποιῆσαι; κατὰ τί οὖν συμφέρει τούτους τοὺς ὀλίγους, τοὺς ξένους, τοὺς πένητας, ἀπελθεῖν εἰς τοὺς πολλούς, τοὺς πλουσίους, σοφούς, τοὺς ὑπερηφάνους, τοὺς ἐντοπίους, καὶ εἰς αὐτοὺς δουλωθῆναι; εἶτα καὶ περὶ πίστεως καὶ εὐσεβείας συζητεῖν καὶ διδάσκειν αὐτούς, οὐκ ἔνι τοῦτο καλόν, οὐκ ἔνι. ἐμοὶ δοκεῖ ὅτι οὐδόλως συμφέρει ἡμῖν τοῦτο. δύναται δὲ ὁ βασιλεὺς ποιῆσαι ἐνταῦθα τὴν σύνοδον, εἰ θελήσει, καὶ ἄνευ ἐξόδων, ἐπεὶ οἱ ἐλευσόμενοι ἐκ τῆς Ῥωμαϊκῆς Ἐκκλησίας ἐνταῦθα δι' ἰδίων ἐξόδων ἐλεύσονται. εἰ δὲ καὶ ἐξόδων δεηθῇ, δύναται ἐπέκεινα τῶν ἑκατὸν χιλιάδων συνάξαι ὑπέρπυρα. καὶ εὐθὺς μὲν ἀκουσθὲν τοῦτο δόξει ἀπίθανον. ἐγὼ δὲ δείξω πῶς ἔσται τοῦτο καὶ δυνατὸν καὶ εὔκολον.

Since then the patriarch found the matter of convening a synod in a Latin place and under Latin authority offensive, and he often stated that if the synod were held there, its conclusion would not be good. He indicated that he personally had no wish to attend. One day, as he was sitting in his cell together with church lords (and two palace lords were also present), he said: "They say that the synod will be held in Italy. Our side will travel and will attend the synod. They will pay our travel expenses and our stay. If our side indeed travels in this manner and accepts its daily food rations from them, our side will be reduced to the status of servants and hirelings. The other side will be the lords. Every servant must carry out his master's will. Every hireling works on the projects that his employer orders him to complete. Otherwise, he will receive no salary. If they withhold food, what will our side do? If they decide to have us return, at their own expense and with their own ships, how will they accomplish it? Why should a few poor foreigners visit so many rich, wise, and haughty [men] and be enslaved? So it does not seem a good thing to me to hold discussions and instruct them on piety. It does not seem to be to our advantage at all. The emperor has the authority to convene the synod here, should he wish to do so; and he can do so without incurring any expenses, as those from the Roman Church, who will come here, will do so at their own expense. For his own needs, he can avail himself with the collection of one hundred thousand *hyperpers*. If one hears this, one will likely consider it absurd. Yet I will show how it is both possible and an easy task."

Patriarch Joseph from the outset advocated the notion that the synod should be held in Constantinople. He believed that this was both a good and an honorable approach, and would be of great advantage to the Byzantines. He even enumerated the sums of moneys that could be raised among the eastern high clerics.[22] His proposals had widespread support among the Orthodox Greeks and especially the anti-unionists who viewed the formative ideas for a synod to convene in Basle with deep suspicion.

But John VIII was aware that both the conciliarists and the papacy claimed sole responsibility for addressing and resolving the issues confronting the fading Byzantine Empire. In 1431, he initially appointed a delegation of three to travel to Basle. The group reached Kallipolis and upon learning of the death of Pope Martin V returned to the imperial city. They believed that at that moment their mission had been rendered purposeless. John VIII was dismayed at their return and believed that their mission should not have been discontinued with the death of the pope. Among the initial group of appointees, several soon subsequently refused to participate further in the synod at Basle.[23]

The emperor, seeking to preserve an advantage in the disputes between the conciliarists and papists at Basle, and especially to obtain western military assistance, thus nominated another delegation of three to attend the assembly. The Byzantine delegation named on the 15th of October 1433 bore three letters, the first of which is found only in a Latin rendition, bearing the leaden seal (*molybdobullon*) of Patriarch Joseph.[24] The second letter, affixed with the imperial golden seal (*chrysobullon*) and extant both in a Greek and Latin version, bears the appointments of John VIII and was accompanied by a third letter addressed to the synod.[25] Each of the first two letters identified the membership of the delegation.[26] At the head of the group was Demetrios Palaiologos Metokhites, the grand domestic, who also held the honorific titles of *protovestiarios* (πρωτοβεστιάριος/πρωτοβεστιαρίτης, first lord of the imperial wardrobe) and *megas stratopedarkhes* (μέγας στρατοπεδάρχης, grand army commander), and had the more meaningful title of governor of Constantinople.[27] He is cited first in both letters, perhaps demonstrating that the emperor's relative was the lead delegate whose mission was secular in nature, that is, to secure western military aid. Isidore, hieromonk (ἱερομόναχος) and *kathegoumenos* (καθηγούμενος, abbot), is placed second in the letters, thus entrusting him with the task to elaborate the Byzantine position on theological issues then confronting the Western and Eastern churches and states. The third legate was a nobleman of his household, Ioannes Dishypatos (Disypatos, Dissipato),[28] who appears, at least according to the sources, to have played not a prominent but rather a lesser role at Basle.

Having instructed his delegates to Basle of his proposals and intentions to gain as many concessions as possible, John VIII was aware that the pope had the advantage in making good on his promises of aid, but was continuously prejudiced to the condition of church union, whereas the conciliarists were dependent upon the goodwill of their respective states, many of which were involved in petty struggles, within and externally, with numerous rivals. Thus, as it became apparent over the course of three years, from 1433 to 1436, John VIII and Patriarch Joseph (who, it was evident, preferred to support the absent Eugenius at the Basle assembly)[29] were aware that money and patronage were the pope's key assets and he was most likely to come to the aid of the beleaguered empire, although as events would demonstrate in 1453, the year of the fall of Constantinople, the papacy for numerous reasons failed to provide adequate funds, supplies, and manpower for the defense of the imperial city; perhaps the absence of concern had been related to their own diminished resources or to other needs of the church that took precedence.[30]

Upon its arrival, the Byzantine delegation almost immediately found itself in the enviable position of being intensely courted both by Pope Eugenius IV and the conciliarist assembly at Basle. The pope believed that "the Eastern Emperor and the leading prelates of the Greek Church were particularly anxious at the moment for healing the Schism [of 1054], since only if this were achieved could they hope for substantial help from the West against the Turks."[31] Advancing the notion of "the church union" of the Byzantine and Roman patriarchates, Eugenius forced the hand of the conciliarists, who were composed of a significant element identified with high churchmen, disgruntled duchies and nobles, western universities (in particular Paris and central European institutions, notably Charles University in Prague), and of more moderate heretical movements (conspicuously among the Hussites[32] in Bohemia). This disparate body sought to democratize the papacy and to weaken its monarchic and authoritative stance. Thus both factions labored to gain Byzantine allegiance and support for their respective positions. Each promised substantial military aid in the form of arms and manpower.[33] In addition, each proffered financial inducements as monetary contributions to satisfy the travel and lodging expenses of the Byzantine delegation. Later, these financial considerations were also renewed to attend a council at Ferrara, although the Basle assembly had considered as possible locations of the future council seven sites, including Constantinople, Avignon, Savoy, as well as Basle.

A question at this juncture must be raised. What was the role of Isidore at the Council of Basle? He has preserved no detailed account to elaborate what in fact he had been instructed by the emperor and patriarch to accomplish in his private and public negotiations with leading clergymen at this assembly, nor of his contributions in the preparation of documents. It is disconcerting for scholarship that no substantive memoir of his attendance at this meeting is extant. Obviously, he, as well as the other two delegates, had received imperial and patriarchal instructions and we can only surmise the Byzantine position from the outcome and from one significant document. And yet, a disquieting issue must be raised. The western delegates at Basle made a charge that the Greek delegation, thus including Isidore, was engaged in acts of duplicity and in bad faith by simultaneously involving themselves in private discussions on identical issues with both the pope and the council. The Byzantine delegation, without denying the charge, could only retreat to the position that they were following the instructions of imperial and patriarchal authorities.

One document is now attributed to Isidore and merits scrutiny in assessing his contributions. This is a lengthy discourse, dated July [24?] 1434,[34] and is an autograph that can definitely be attributed through the tools of paleography to the pen of Isidore. This short essay can be read with ease in translation, which is done *ad sensum* (as Manuel Chrysoloras would have termed it) and not *ad verbum* (which would be impossible because of the style). The discourse reads:

Πρὸς τὴν ἐν Βασιλείᾳ Σύνοδον

1 πρῶτον μέν, ὦ θεία καὶ ἱερὰ σύνοδος, τὴν παρὰ τοῦ θεοῦ βοήθειάν τε καὶ συμμαχίαν ἐπικαλοῦμαι τῶν ἐγκωμίων ὑμῶν ἁπτόμενος, καὶ ταῦτα τηλικούτου πράγματος, ὑπὲρ οὗ πᾶς τις ἄν, οἶμαι, κατόπιν λέγων πολλῷ τῆς ἀξίας τῶν ἡμετέρων φανεῖται λειπόμενος ἔργων ἀλλ' οὐδ' εἰ τῶν πάλαι καὶ τῶν νῦν περιῆσαν τὰ μέγιστα περὶ λόγους τὰ πρῶτα φερόντων εἰς ταὐτὸν συνελθόντες, ἀξίως ἂν καὶ ἁρμοζόντως τοῖς ὑμετέροις ἔλεγον πράγμασι. καὶ πλείω μὲν ἂν ἴσως ἔλεγον καὶ καλλίω, ἐφικέσθαι δὲ τοῖς πράγμασιν ἱκανῶς οὐδ' ἐκείνους ξύμπαντας οἶμαι ἄν. οὕτω τῶν ἡμετέρων ἐλάττους ἔργων καὶ πράξεων ξυμβαίνει πάντων τοὺς λόγους γενέσθαι. εἰ δὲ τοῦθ' οὕτως ἐπὶ τῶν πολλῶν, τί ἂν ἐπ' ἐμοὶ γένοιτο, καὶ ταῦτα περὶ λόγους ὀλίγην ἔχοντι τὴν ἰσχύν, ἄλλως τε οὐδ' ἔχοντι κατὰ σῶμα οὕτω τῆς μακρᾶς ἐκείνης ἀπαλλαγέντι καὶ πολυημέρου νόσου καθαρῶς, ἀλλ' ἔτι λείψανα φέροντι ταύτης; λόγος γὰρ τῶν φιλοσόφων καὶ ἀληθής γε τὰς ψυχὰς συμπάσχειν τοῖς σώμασι.

2 ἔπειθ' ἡμῶν δέομαι μετ' εὐμενείας ἀκοῦσαί μου τοὺς λόγους μηδὲν ὑπιδομένους μήθ' ὥς ἔχω περὶ αὐτοὺς ἀδυνάτως, μήτε πρὸς τὸ μέγιστον ὑμῶν ἀφορᾶν ἀξίωμα, εἰ λέγειν ὅλως ἐγχειρῶ πρὸς ὑμᾶς, πρὸς οὓς καὶ ἀντωπεῖν οὐκ ἔδει μ' ἄν. τί γὰρ τῶν καλῶν τῶν ἀπ' αἰῶνος ὑφ' ἁπάντων θαυμαζομένων οὐκ ἴδοι ἄν παρ' ὑμῖν; ἀρετὴν ἄρα, ἢ θεοῦ τε ἐστι καὶ τῶν μεγάλων ἀνδρῶν, ὅσοι πρὸς θεὸν τὴν ἔφεσιν ἀνατείνουσι καὶ δι' ἧς θεῷ οἰκειοῦνται καὶ ἧς ἄνευ οὐδὲν ἂν γένοιτο προσῆκον ἀνθρώπῳ κατὰ λόγον καὶ τὴν αὐτοῦ ζῆν ἐθέλοντι δημιουργίαν καὶ ἣν μόνην ἁπάντων εἴληχεν ἄνθρωπος ἀφομοιούμενος θεῷ δι' αὐτῆς, ἥπερ οὐρανοπολίτας τοὺς κεκτημένους ἐπιδείκνυσιν αὐτήν; ποῦ τοίνυν ἴδοι τις ἂν καὶ πλείους καὶ καθ' ἕνα καὶ μᾶλλον ξύμπαντας θάλλοντας ἐπὶ ταύτῃ καὶ ἐπανθοῦντας ὡς φοῖνιξ, κατὰ τὸ προφητικὸν ἐκεῖνο λόγιον ἢ ὑμᾶς αὐτούς, οἳ πᾶσαν τὴν οἰκουμένην ὥσπερ ἕτερος ἀποστολικὸς χορὸς ἀθροισθέντες ἀγῶνα παρ' ὑμῖν αὐτοῖς προὐθήκατε μέγιστον τοὺς μὲν κακῶς ἀπερρωγότας ἐπανορθῶσαι Χριστιανῶν καὶ εἰς τὴν προτέραν ἐπαναγαγεῖν εὐσέβειαν, οὓς δ' αὖ ἔχοντας μέν ὑγιῶς καὶ κατὰ τοὺς θείων τῶν πατέρων εὖ ὅρους καὶ ἀποστολικῶς ὁδεύοντας οὐκ οἶδ' ὅπως ὁ χρόνος δὲ διαίρεσιν ἐποιήσατο τοῦ ἑνὸς τῆς ἐκκλησίας ἱεροῦ σώματος καὶ τὴν τομὴν βαθεῖαν ὁ μακρὸς ἀπειργάσατο χρόνος καὶ διάστασιν οὐ μικράν τινα οὐδὲ φαύλην ἐνεποίησεν.

3 ἀλλ' ἐς τοσοῦτον ὁ τῆς κακίας ὥπλισεν ἀμφοτέρους κατ' ἀμφοτέρων ἄρχων καὶ δημιουργός, ὡς καὶ λόγοις κατ' ἀλλήλων ὁπλίζεσθαι καὶ ἀκροβολίζειν ἄμφω τὰ μέρη καὶ πρὸς ἄλληλα, καὶ ταύτην ἰάσασθαι τὴν διάστασιν κατὰ νοῦν ἔθεσθε, καὶ πρέσβεις ὡς ἐκείνους ἀπεστάλκατε πάντα τρόπον τὸ καλὸν ποθοῦντες καὶ σεβάσμιον εἰρήνης καὶ ὁμονοίας, ἣν ἡ τοῦ θεοῦ ἐκκλησία, σῶμα τὸ πρῶτον ἢ ἐτεθήλει τελοῦσα, χρόνους ὅτι πλείστους αὐτὴν ὁ πονηρὸς διέστησε, καὶ τούτους τῶν πατριαρχικῶν ὑπὲρ τούτου πολλάκις πρότερον πρεσβευσαμένων, κἂν ὁ καιρὸς ἐκεῖνος τὸ μέγα καὶ σεπτὸν ἰδεῖν οὐκ εἶχε τοῦ καλοῦ τούτου χρῆμα, ἀλλ' ὑμῶν γε, ὡς ἔοικεν, ἀπέκειτο τῇ ἄκρᾳ ἀρετῇ καὶ συνέσει, ἄπαντα λόγον νικώσῃ θελῆσαι τὴν ἕνωσιν καὶ θελήσαντας ἐπισπεῦσαι καὶ ἐπισπεύσαντας εἰς ταὐτὸ συνελθεῖν καὶ συνελθόντας παρ' ἀμφοῖν τῶν μερῶν πᾶν ὅ,τι κάλλιστόν τε ὑψηλότατον τελεσθῆναι, συναιρομένου θεοῦ, τοῦτο καὶ μόνον ὑμῶν εἰς τέλος προαγαγόντων. τίς ἆρ' ἱκανὸς ἐπαινέσαι κατ' ἀξίαν τὴν προθυμίαν, τὴν σπουδήν, τὴν ἐς ταὐτὸ πάντων ὑμῶν συνδρομήν, τὴν πρὸς ἀλλήλους μετὰ τῆς χάριτος τοῦ θείου πνεύματος ἕνωσίν τε καὶ κοινότητα καὶ τὴν ἐς ἀλλοδαπήν, πρὸς ἕκαστον, πάλιν χρόνιον προσεδρίαν οὖσαν ὡς οἰκείαν προσμένειν αὐτῇ τῶν οἰκείων ἑκάστου καὶ πατρίδος καὶ πόλεως τοσοῦτον ἀπεσχοινισμένου τὸν χρόνον; πρὸς τοῦτο τὸ μέγιστον ἔργον καὶ λαμπρότατον βουλευομένῳ μοι τὴν ὑμῶν ἱερὰν καὶ ἁγίαν ἕνωσιν τῇ θείου πνεύματος χάριτι ἀξιῶσαι καὶ παρακαλέσαι καὶ πεῖσαι καὶ ὅτι τάχιστ' αὐτὸ τελεσθῆναι καὶ μηδ' ἡντινοῦν ὑπὲρ τούτου θέσθαι τὸ παρ' ὑμᾶς ἀναβολήν, μετὰ μικρὸν καὶ δὴ τοῦτο ποιήσω κατὰ καιρὸν ἐκείνου μνησθεὶς τὸν προσήκοντα.

4 τανῦν δὲ τοῖς εἰρημένοις τὸν λόγον ἐπιθήσομεν. τῆς θείας ὑμῶν ἀπὸ περάτων ἕως περάτων ἀρετῆς διαδραμούσης οὐδὲν παρήκατε τῶν ὅσα Χριστιανοῖς δίκαια τυγχάνει καὶ ὅσια, ἀλλὰ πάντα θεσμόν, πάντα δίκαια, πάντα νόμιμα ὅσα τελεῖ τῇ θειοτάτῃ Λατίνων ἐκκλησίᾳ, ὅσα πόλεσι καὶ παντὶ δήμῳ καὶ γένει, τοῦτ' ἐπὶ νοῦν βαλλόμενοι, θείας δὲ ἄντικρυς τοῦτο προνοίας, ἐπείπερ καὶ θεοῦ ἔργον ἀληθῶς. τούτων τὰ μὲν ὥς ἄριστα διευθετήσατε, τὰ δὲ διευθετοῦντες ἄρτι τυγχάνετε, τὰ δὲ καὶ μέλλετε διευθετεῖν. τίς οὖν ἱκανὸς γένοιτ' ἂν ἀξίως ὑμῶν ἐπαινέσαι τὰ μεγάλα καὶ θειότατα ἔργα; τίς διάτορον καὶ λαμπρὸν καὶ διαπρύσιον τὴν φωνὴν ἀναλαβών, ἐπὶ τοσοῦτον ἠχήσει, ὥστε ἀπὸ τῶν ἄκρων ἕως τῆς οἰκουμένης ἐξυμνῆσαι μεθ' ὅτι πλείστης καὶ οἰκειοτάτης τῶν περάτων τῆς εὐφημίας, τοσαῦτα καὶ τηλικαῦτα ἔργα διαπραττόντων ὑμῶν ἀξιεπαινότατά τε καὶ ἀξιάγαστα, ὧν οὐδ' ὁ πᾶς αἰὼν τὴν μνήμην λήθης βυθὸς παραπέμψει, οἷα δὴ τἀνθρώπινα γίγνεσθαι πέφυκεν;

5 σοφίαν δέ, ἣ καὶ αὐτὴ τοῦ θεοῦ τε λέγεται καὶ ἔστι καὶ ἧς κατὰ χάριν μεταλαμβάνουσιν ἄνθρωποι, ἧς καὶ ἡ ἔφεσις φιλία ταύτης λέγεται, ἐπιπολῆς ἡψάμεθα ἄκροις, ὅ φασι, τοῖς δακτύλοις, οὐ μὲν οὖν ἀλλ' ἐς βάθος καὶ πόρρω σοφίας ἐθόντες καὶ τοῖς ἀδύτοις τῶν ἱερῶν μυστηρίων αὐτῆς ἐγκύψαντες ἠρύσασθε πᾶν ὅσον ἐφικτὸν ἀνθρωπίνῃ καὶ χωρητὸν φύσει. ταύτης δὴ τῆς εἴτε βούλει σοφίας ἢ φιλοσοφίας τίς εἴληφεν ἄρτι τὸ κράτος κατὰ πάντων ὅσον ἐν θεολογίαις ὑψηλόν τε καὶ θεῖον, ἧς οἱ

μεμυημένοι καὶ μόνον ἴσασι τὰ μυστήρια, καὶ ὅσον ἐν τοῖς ἱεροῖς καὶ θείοις κανόσιν, ὑπὲρ ὧν ὑμεῖς ἄρτι τοὺς ἀγῶνας ὑφίστασθε ὡς ἂν ἔχωσι τὸ κράτος ἀκλόνητον καὶ τὴν ἰσχύν, ἔτι τε τῶν τελεταρχικῶν χαρίτων καὶ δωρεῶν τοῦ θείου πνεύματος μυστηρίων τελειωτικὴν δύναμιν, ὧν ὑμεῖς καὶ μύσται καὶ μυσταγωγοὶ τυγχάνετε.

6 τίσι τῶν πάντων ἤ περ ὑμῖν οὕτως ἐξήσκηταί τε καὶ τετελείωται καὶ εἰς μεγίστην ἐπιμέλειαν ὑπὲρ ἁπάντων ἐσπούδασται, μᾶλλον δὲ ἀεὶ καὶ σπουδάζεται τῶν Χριστιανῶν; ἆρα καὶ τίς ἱκανὸς πρὸς ἀξίαν ὑμῶν ἐπαινέσαι τὸ ὕψος πάντων ἕνεκα τῶν εἰρημένων; πολλοῦ γε καὶ δεῖ. ἀλλ᾽ ἐπεὶ τὰ μὲν ἔργα διαπράττεσθ᾽ ὑμεῖς ὡς ἄριστά τε καὶ ὑψηλότατα, οἱ δὲ τούτων ἐλάττους καὶ κατόπιν τυγχάνουσιν ἔπαινοι, ἀνάγκη δὲ παρὰ τῶν λεγόντων ὁπωσοῦν ἀνακηρύττειν ταῦτα, καθόσον αὐτοῖς ἐφικτόν, προανακρουσάτω καὶ συναράσθω Δαυὶδ ὁ θεῖος ἡμῖν πρὸς τὸν ὑμῶν ἔπαινον. ἀκούσατε ταῦτα πάντα τὰ ἔθνη. ἐνωτίσασθε πάντες. οἱ κατοικοῦντες τὴν οἰκουμένην, ὅπως εὐφρανθῆτε εὐφροσύνην καὶ χαρὰν ἀγαλλιάσεως, ἐφ᾽ οἷς ἡ θεία καὶ ἱερὰ συνάθροισις αὕτη καὶ πράττει καὶ βούλεται τὸ τῆς εἰρήνης καὶ ὁμονοίας καλόν, ὅπερ ἐστὶ τῶν ἀρετῶν τὸ ἀκρότατον, καὶ ἐπείγεται καὶ ἐφίεται τοὺς Εὐρωπαίους ἐς ταὐτὸ συνελθεῖν τοῖς Ἀσιανοῖς καὶ γενέσθαι σῶμα καὶ μέλος ἓν τὴν ἐκκλησίαν τοῦ Χριστοῦ, ὃς τῷ ἰδίῳ αἵματι περιποιήσατο ταύτην, πολλοῖς τέρασι καὶ σημείοις ὡς θεὸς στηρίξας καὶ βεβαιώσας αὐτὴν καὶ εἰρήνην καὶ ἀγάπην τοῖς θείοις καὶ ἱεροῖς μαθηταῖς ἐπιτάξας καὶ ἀποστόλοις, ἐπὶ τῇ ὁμολογίᾳ τοῦ θείου πηξάμενος αὐτὴν τὴν πέτραν, καὶ τοῖς λοιποῖς σὺν αὐτῷ παραδοὺς ἱεροῖς ἀποστόλοις τὸ πνεῦμα τὸ ἅγιον αὐτοῖς ἐχορήγησεν, δι᾽ οὗ κύκλῳ τὴν οἰκουμένην ἐσαγήνευσαν πᾶσαν περιελθόντες, εἰρήνην ἕκαστος τῷ προσδεχομένῳ παρέχων παντί.

7 αὕτη χρόνου κατεῖχε τὴν ἐκκλησίαν Χριστοῦ χιλίους, οἶμαι, καὶ πρός. εἶτ᾽ οὐκ οἶδ᾽ ὅθεν, ἐνέπνευσε δ᾽ οὖν ὁ φθονερὸς καὶ ἀρχέκακος δαίμων κατὰ τῆς ἐκκλησίας Χριστοῦ καὶ στάσιν κεκίνηκε κατ᾽ αὐτῆς αἰτιῶν οὔ τοι καλῶν οὐδὲ μεγάλων οὐδὲ βλαπτόντων τὰ μέγιστα μέρος ἑκάτερον, ἀναρριπίζει τὸ σχίσμα, καί, τὸν καιρὸν εὑρὼν συμμαχοῦντα. ἑνόσει γὰρ τὰ ἡμέτερα τηνικαῦτα ὑπὸ τῶν ἐμφυλίων. διάστασιν καὶ ῥῆγμα κἀκ τούτων τραύματα ἑκατέρων ἐμποιεῖ ταῖς ψυχαῖς. καὶ ῥέων ὁ χρόνος, οὐδὲν τοῦ μεγάλου καὶ ἱεροῦ τῆς εἰρήνης ἐπιμνησθέντος χρήματος ἢ μνησθέντος μέν, ἀγενῶς δέ, μέχρι τοῦ νῦν μείζω πολλῷ καὶ περιφανεστέραν πεποίηκε τὴν διάστασιν, ὀλίγον ἐν τῷ μεταξὺ πάνυ χρόνον τῶν μερῶν συνελθόντων ἑκατέρων. εἶτα πάλιν χείρω τοῦ προτέρου τὰ μετὰ ταῦτα φανέντα τὴν οἰκουμένην ἐνέπλησε πᾶσαν ζοφερᾶς καὶ σκοτεινῆς τῆς ἀχλύος, τοσαύτην ἔριν κατ᾽ ἀλλήλων καὶ φιλονεικίαν πραγματευσάμενος, ὡς καὶ ἀλλήλους ἑτερόφρονας ἡγεῖσθαι καὶ μηδὲν πάγιον καὶ βέβαιον ἐν ἐκείνοις ἔχειν ἐν οἷς ἑκάτερος ἐρρίζωται δόγμασιν, ἀλλ᾽ ἕκαστον τὸ ἑαυτοῦ μόνον συνορᾶν ἐκείνου τε ὑπεραγωνίζεσθαι καὶ ἐπεκδικεῖν αὐτό, οὐδὲν ὑπὲρ καταστάσεως καὶ εἰρήνης καὶ ὁμονοίας τῆς τῶν ἐκκλησιῶν ἐπιβλέποντα καὶ μηδ᾽ ὑγιὲς

ἐννοεῖν τινα τὸ παρ' ἅπαν ὑπὲρ τοῦ μεγάλου τῆς μιᾶς ἐκκλησίας τοῦ Χριστοῦ σώματος.

8 ἄρτι δὲ τοῦ θείου καὶ ἱεροῦ ταῖς ψυχαῖς ἡμῶν ἐπιλάμψαντος πνεύματος, ὑμεῖς ἐκ πάντων μερῶν συνελθόντες πᾶν ὅ,τι κράτιστόν τε τῆς ἐκκλησίας καὶ προῦχον Χριστοῦ ὅσον ἐν ἀρετῇ, ὅσον ἐν σοφίᾳ καὶ γνώσει, ὅσον ἐν ἐπιστήμῃ τῆς ἱερᾶς θεολογίας καὶ ὅσον ἐν πείρᾳ τῶν τῆς ἐκκλησίας ἱερῶν κανόνων καὶ νόμων καὶ ὅσον ἐν τοῖς ὑψηλοῖς πᾶσι τῶν μαθημάτων καί, ἁπλῶς εἰπεῖν, πᾶν τὸ προῦχον ἐν πᾶσι καλοῖς, κατὰ νοῦν ἐθήκατε τὰ πάλαι διερρωγότα συνάψαι τμήματα καὶ εἰς εἰρήνην καὶ ὁμόνοιαν τὴν ἐκκλησίαν ἐπαναγαγεῖν καὶ μίαν ὥσπερ τὸ πρότερον ἀποκαταστῆσαι πρὸς τὸν αὐτοκράτορα Ῥωμαίων καὶ τὴν ἱερὰν τῶν Γραικῶν πρέσβεις πέμψαντες ἐκκλησίαν ἀνακαλεῖσθε, οὐκ ὀλίγον τὸν πόνον τῆς τοσαύτης τῶν σταλέντων ὑπομεινάντων ὁδοῦ, μακρᾶς πάνυ καὶ δυσχεροῦς τυγχανούσης, κἀκείνων πολλάκις ὑπὲρ τούτου πρεσβευσάντων, οὐκ οἶδ' ὅπως δὲ τῶν πρέσβεων ἐπανελθόντων παρ' ἐκείνων πρὸς οὓς ἐπρέσβευον ἀπράκτων.

9 καὶ μηδὲν οἴεσθαι μικρὸν καὶ ἀδρανὲς τὸ Γραικῶν εἶναι γένος. αὐτὸ μὲν γὰρ ἴσως καθ' ἑαυτό, χρόνους ἤδη συχνοὺς πολιορκηθέν, ὠλιγώθη τε καὶ ἐκακώθη, ἀλλ' οὐκ εἰς τέλος ἐξετρίβη. φυλάττει γὰρ ἐκ μέρους αὐτὸ Κύριος. Πελοπόννησός τε γὰρ ὅλη τῇ βασιλείᾳ Ῥωμαίων ὑπείκει καὶ Λῆμνος καὶ Ἴμβρος καὶ περὶ τὴν Κωνσταντίνου τὸ πλεῖστον τῆς Θρᾴκης μέρος. ἔτι δ' αὖ πλὴν τῶν ἀρχῶν καί τινων τῶν ἐν τέλει Κέρκυρα πᾶσα, Κεφαλληνία, Ζάκυνθος, Ἰθάκη, Λευκάς, Ἤπειρος πᾶσα, Ἰλλυρικόν, Ἀχαΐα, Φωκίς, Βοιωτία, Ἀττική, Ἑλλάς, Μακεδονία, Θρᾴκη. Μυσία ἡ ἄνω, Μυσία ἡ κάτω, Εὔβοια, Κυκλάδες νῆσοι, Κρήτη, Ῥόδος, Κύπρος, Χίος, Λέσβος, ταῦτα πάντα Γραικῶν οἴκησίς ἐστιν. καὶ πᾶσα δὲ ἡ περὶ τὴν Ἀσίαν ἀρχὴ πάντων βαρβάρων τὰ πλεῖστα Γραικοῖς ᾤκησται. εἰσὶ δ' αὖ καὶ Σύρων ἄθροισμα πλεῖστον. ἀλλὰ καὶ βασιλεῖαι παμπληθεῖς καὶ κατὰ γλῶτταν διάφοροι τῇ Γραικῶν ὑπείκουσι ἐκκλησίᾳ. ἥ τε γὰρ Ἰβήρων μεγίστη βασιλεία καὶ ἡ Λαζῶν καὶ πρὸς τούτοις ἡ Ζηκχῶν ἐπαρχία καὶ ἡ Ἀλανῶν ἥ τε Τζαρκασῶν καὶ ἡ τῶν Γότθων ἥ τε Μολδοβλαχία καὶ πρὸς τούτοις ἡ καλουμένη Βλαχία μεγάλη καὶ ἡ τῶν Τριβαλλῶν. οὐ μὴν καὶ ἡ τῶν Ἀλβανιτῶν ἀρχὴ καὶ περὶ τὰ ὑπερβόρεια ἡ τῶν Ῥῶς μεγίστη κατὰ τὸν Οὐγγράτην δημοκρατία καὶ ὁ τῆς μεγάλης Ῥωσίας μέγας καλούμενος ῥήξ ἕτεροί τε ῥῆγες ἐν ἐκείνῃ καὶ ἡ κάτω πᾶσα Ῥωσία τῶν ῥηγῶν ἄνω καί τινων περὶ ἐκείνους ἅπαντας τὸ ὑπήκοον ὑπείκει τῷ Κωνσταντινουπόλεως. τοσαῦτά εἰσι καὶ πλείω μᾶλλον τὰ προσοικειωθησόμενα ὑμῖν.

10 ἀλλ' ὑμῶν γε τῆς ἀρετῆς ἄρτι καθάπερ ἡλιακῶν ἐπιλαμπούσης ἀκτίνων, ἀντιβολῶ καὶ δέομαι τὴν σπουδὴν καὶ προθυμίαν ἣν τὸ πνεῦμα τὸ ἅγιον ὑμῖν χορηγεῖ ἐπιπιστεῦσαι προαγαγεῖν εἰς τέλος, φεισαμένους μηδενὸς τὸ παρ' ἅπαν ὅσα πρὸς τὴν θείαν τῆς ἐκκλησίας ἕνωσιν ἀφορᾷ, ἵνα μιᾶς ἀναφανείσης καθάπερ τὸ πρότερον καὶ εἰς ταὐτὸ συνελθούσης, ἡ μὲν ἐκκλησία Γραικῶν τῶν Λατίνων ἐκκλησία τυγχάνῃ, Γραικοὶ δ' αὖ ὡς πρὸς οἰκείαν τὴν Λατίνων μετὰ τῆς προσηκούσης

ἀγάπης προσέρχωνται, ἑκάτεροι τῶν παρ' ἑκατέρων ἀνθ' ὅτι πλείστης ἀπολαύοντες τῆς ἡδονῆς τῶν ἀγαθῶν, ὥσπερ ἦν τὸ πάλαι. ἀμοιβαὶ τοίνυν καὶ μισθοὶ καὶ ἀνταποδόσεις τοῖς περὶ τὸ μέγα καὶ θειότατον χρῆμα τῆς θείας ἐσπουδακόσιν ἑνώσεως πρὸς μὲν θεοῦ τιμαὶ καὶ στέφανοι τοῖς δοθεῖσι πάλαι πατράσιν ἁγίοις ἰσοστάσιοι, οἷς ἡ τῆς ἐκκλησίας ἔκκλησις Χριστοῦ ἐπιμέλειά τε καὶ σύστασις καὶ ὑπὲρ ἧς ἀγῶνας καὶ πόνους μυρίους ὑπέστησαν, φεισάμενοι ἑαυτῶν οὐδαμῶς, ἀλλὰ πάντα πόνον καὶ μόχθον τέρψιν ἡγούμενοι καὶ χαράν, πρὸ δὲ ἀνθρώπων ἀθάνατον ἕξετε τὴν εὔκλειαν, ὑπό γε τῶν ἔτ' ἐσομένων εἰς αἰῶνα τὸν ἅπαντα στήλην ἕκαστος ταῖς ἁπάντων ἐναποθέντες ψυχαῖς μείζω καὶ πολλῷ γε μείζω τοῦ παρὰ Ῥοδίοις κολοσσοῦ, ὃν ἐκεῖνοι τῷ Ἡλίῳ πάλαι ἀνέθεσαν, τῶν ἐκ τοῦ παντὸς αἰῶνος ἐς δεῦρο ἀνθρώπων δυνηθέντων μηδαμῶς ἴσον ἐκείνῳ ἀπεργάσασθαι. ἀλλὰ τί φημι ἀνδριάντα μέγαν καὶ χειροποίητον; οὐρανομήκη τὴν στήλην ἕξετε ἀπὸ ἀνίσχοντος φαινομένην μέχρις ἡλίου δύνοντος.

11 διὰ ταῦτα πάντα τοίνυν τὸν ἀγῶνα τουτονὶ μετὰ τῆς πολλῆς καὶ μεγάλης προθυμίας, ἧς ἄρτι κέκτησθε δέομαι τῆς ὑμῶν θείας καὶ ἱερᾶς ἀκρότητος ὅτι τάχιστα σπεύσαντας συμπερᾶναι, ἵνα τὰς εἰρημένας νῦν διὰ ταχέως ἀμοιβὰς καὶ πρὸς θεοῦ δέχησθε καὶ πρὸς ἀνθρώπων, εὐφραινόμενοι τὴν ἀληθῆ χαρὰν καὶ πρέπουσαν ἱεροῖς ἀνδράσιν ἀγαλλίασιν.

12 ἀλλὰ μὴν ὑπὲρ εἰρήνης πρότερον ἐπιμνησθείς, ὑπὲρ ἧς τὸν ἀγῶνα τουτονὶ τὸν μέγαν ἐς μέσον προὐθήκατε καὶ πάντα νοῦν καὶ διάνοιαν εἰς τὸ ταὐτὸ συναγηοχότες τὸ μέγιστον τοῦτο καὶ ἱερὸν τῆς εἰρήνης ἀνὰ τὴν οἰκουμένην σπεύδετε ξύμπασαν ἐπικυρῶσαι χρῆμα, μετὰ ταῦτα καὶ περὶ τῶν ἄλλων ἐρῶ οὐχ ὅσον καὶ σοφίας ὑμῖν μέτεστι καὶ γνώσεως καὶ ἱερᾶς θεολογίας ἔτι τε τῆς τῶν τε νόμων καὶ ἱερῶν κανόνων πείρας καὶ πάσης ἱεροτελεστικῆς τοῦ θείου πνεύματος δωρεᾶς, ἀλλ' ὅσον ὅ τε παρὼν ἀπαιτεῖ χρόνος καὶ τῶν ἡμετέρων λόγων ἰσχὺς ἀναλόγως ἂν εἴποι τούτῳ δὴ τῷ βραχεῖ καιρῷ τῆς ὑμῶν θείας καὶ ἱερᾶς συνάξεως.

13 εἰρήνη τὸ μέγα πρᾶγμα καὶ ὄνομα τὰς ἀγγελικὰς καὶ οὐρανίους συνέχει δυνάμεις, τῷ ἑνὶ καὶ πρώτῳ καὶ μεγάλῳ καὶ τριστηλίῳ τῆς θεότητος παρισταμένας φωτί, τὴν θείαν ἐκείνην καὶ ἄρρητον ἐντρυφώσας τρυφὴν τὴν ἀπὸ τῆς μακαριωτάτης τριάδος ἔλλαμψιν δηλαδή, καὶ διὰ τῆς εἰρήνης συνέχονταί τε καὶ συνδέδενται ἡνωμέναι τῷ τῆς ἀγάπης δεσμῷ, καὶ δὴ τὸν νοητὸν αὕτη συνέχει κόσμον ὡς μέγιστον ἐγγίζοντά τε καὶ πλησιάζοντα τῷ ὑπὲρ πάντα λόγον ἀκηράτῳ καὶ ἀπροσίτῳ φωτὶ τῆς θεότητος. αὕτη συνεκτικὸν καὶ ἑνοποιὸν τυγχάνει παντὸς ἀγαθοῦ. τοὐναντίον δ' αὖ ἔχθρα διάστασιν καὶ μερισμὸν καὶ ἔριν ποιοῦσα.

14 ἔχθρα δὲ καὶ ἔρις καὶ τῦφος οὐδὲ τὸν νοητὸν ἀφῆκε πάλαι κόσμον ἐν τῇ ἑαυτοῦ καταστάσει μένοντα πάντοτε λαμπρόν, ὡς ἐδημιουργήθη, ἀλλ' ὁ τῷ πρὶν μὲν φωτεινός, ὕστερον δὲ δι' ἐκείνης γεγονὼς συγκατέσπασεν ἑαυτῷ πολλὰς δυνάμεις οἰκείας ἑαυτῷ καὶ συνδημιουργοὺς τῆς κακίας, ἀρχηγὸς ἐκείνης καὶ παρ' ἑαυτῷ ἔχει κόσμον ὅτι κἀξ ἐναντίων συγκεκραμένων τῶν μερῶν ὅταν πλεονάζῃ

μηδεμία τῶν ἀπ' αὐτῶν ποιοτήτων εἰρήνη καὶ τάξις συνέχει τὸ πᾶν ἐν αἰθρίᾳ καὶ λαμπρᾷ τῇ κοσμικῇ καταστάσει ἰσονομίας ἐν πᾶσι τελούσης. ὅταν δὲ στάσις ἐν αὐτῷ γένηται μάχη τε, σύγχυσις τηνικαῦτα κατακρατήσει, ἀταξία καὶ λύσις γίνεται καὶ φθορὰ σχεδὸν τοῦ παντὸς καὶ τὸν ὡραιότατον καὶ κάλλιστον τουτονὶ κόσμον ἀμορφία συνέχει καὶ ζάλη καὶ σκοτομανία, οὐδ' ὁρᾶσθαι τὸ παρ' ἅπαν τυγχάνοντος ἀνεκτοῦ.

15 ἀλλὰ δὴ καταβῶμεν ἐπὶ τὸ μικρὸν μὲν τοῦ κόσμου μέρος, μέγιστον δὲ βασιλεῦον παντὸς τοῦ κόσμου καὶ ἄρχον ὡς ὁ θεὸς ἐκέλευσε, τὸν ἄνθρωπον. ὅταν μὲν γὰρ τὸ καθ' ἑαυτὸν οὗτος ὥς ἔχει φυλάττῃ καὶ τὴν τάξιν τηρῇ τῆς ψυχῆς καὶ κατάστασιν, εἰρήνην ἄγων σταθερὰν καὶ βεβαίαν, τηνικαῦτα μᾶλλον ἔοικεν ἀγγελικῷ χορῷ κατὰ ῥυθμὸν καὶ τάξιν βαίνοντι τὴν προσήκουσαν. ὅταν δ' ἐκπέσῃ τοῦ καθ' ἑαυτόν, ἔρις γίνεται καὶ μάχη. ἐπιθολοῦσα δὲ αὕτη τὸ ἡγεμονικὸν ἐκείνου καὶ ἐπισκοτοῦσα, ἀλαμπῆ καὶ ἀμαυρὰν τὴν ψυχὴν ἀπεργάζεται, προσεοικυῖαν φάσμασί τισι σκοτεινοῖς, ἀσύστατον ἑαυτὴν ἐν πᾶσι ἑτερρορεπῆ δεικνῦσα.

16 ἀλλ' ἴδωμεν ὅσον καὶ οἷον τὸ τῆς εἰρήνης χρῆμα. εἰρήνη τοιγαροῦν μετὰ λαμπροῦ τοῦ σχήματος βασιλείαν συνέχει, εἰρήνη δημοκρατίαν, ἀριστοκρατίαν καὶ πᾶσαν ἑτέραν ἀρχὴν συνέχει νόμιμον. εἰρήνη γὰρ τὰς πόλεις αὐξάνει, καλλωπίζει, ἐπίδοσιν μεγίστην ἐπάγει παντί, καὶ ἄρχοντι καὶ ἀρχομένῳ. αὕτη καὶ οἰκίας κατὰ μέρος συνιστᾷ καὶ χώρας ἀοικήτους οἰκουμένας ποιεῖ καὶ τὰς ἐρήμους ἐξημεροῖ καὶ πάντα τρόπον αὔξει, πᾶν ἐφ' ὅπερ ἂν ἐπιβλέψῃ καὶ προβαίνειν ἐπὶ τὸ βέλτιον οἰεῖ, καί, ἁπλῶς εἰπεῖν, πᾶν ὅ,τι κάλλιστόν τε καὶ ὑψηλότατον ἥδε κατεργάζεται, καὶ ταύτης ἄνευ οὐδὲν ἐν τῷ βίῳ χρηστόν. πᾶν δὲ τοὐναντίον πολέμους ἔχθρα κατεργάζεται, οἱ δὲ πόλεμοι φόνους καὶ φθορὰν ἀνθρώπων, κωμῶν, πόλεων, ἐπαρχιῶν. ἅπτεται καὶ μέχρι τῶν ἀλόγων συμπάσχει γὰρ τοῖς ἀνθρώποις καὶ ταῦτα.

17 τί τὴν μεγάλην καὶ εὐρυάγειαν καθεῖλε πόλιν τῶν Τρώων; οὐκ ἔρις καὶ μάχη; τῶν δὲ Βαβυλωνίων τὸ περιαδόμενον τί καὶ καθεῖλε λαμπρότατον καὶ ὀχυρώτατον καὶ μέγιστον τεῖχος; τὴν δὲ ἱερὰν τῶν Ἱεροσολύμων πόλιν οὐ αὕτη καθεῖλεν; οὐχ ἥδε τὸ τῶν Ἑβραίων γένος δοριάλωτον ἅπαν ἐς τῶν Ἀσσυρίων ἀπήγαγεν; οὐ τὴν μεγίστην Ἀσσυρίων καθεῖλε ἀρχήν; οὐ τὴν Περσῶν; οὐ τὴν Ἑλλήνων; οὐ τὴν Ῥωμαίων; πόσαι πόλεις ἐν Ἰταλίᾳ τὸ πάλαι κατηρειπωμέναι καὶ κατηθαλωμέναι ὑπ' αὐτῆς ἐς δεῦρο διετέλεσαν; ἄρτι Γαλατίαν, θάλλουσαν μὲν τὸ πρῶτον, νῦν δὲ συνεχομένην καὶ φθειρομένην συχνῶς ὑπὸ Βρεττανῶν οὐκ ἔχθρα καὶ μάχη κατ' ἀμφοτέρων ὁπλίζεται, κἀκείνους ὁπωσδήποτε ταύτῃ συμφθείρουσα; ἔνθα δ' ἂν ἐπικρατήσῃ, οὐ τὸν μέγιστον ἐμποιεῖ τούτοις ἀφανισμόν; ἄνωθεν δὲ καὶ ἐς δεῦρο τί καὶ βίβλοι γέμουσιν; οὐ τῶν ἐξηνδραποδισμένων γενῶν, ἔτι τε χωρῶν καὶ πόλεων τραγῳδίας καὶ ἱστορίας;

18 διὰ ταῦτα πάντα τοίνυν ἀναβάσεις ἐν τῇ καρδίᾳ ὑμῶν, ὦ θεία καὶ ἱερὰ θέμενοι σύνοδος, τῇ τοῦ θείου πνεύματος χάριτι εἰρήνην κατὰ νοῦν σχεδὸν ἔθεσθε πάσῃ τῇ οἰκουμένῃ βραβεῦσαι, καὶ πολὺν ποιεῖσθαι τὸν ἀγῶνα, παντὶ προμνηστεύοντες γένει τὸ ταύτης καλόν τε καὶ τίμιον,

μεμνημένοι, ὅτι ὁ Χριστὸς αὐτὸς οὐδὲ ἕτερον ἐπιφέρει ἑαυτῷ, οὐ τὸ παντοδύναμον, οὐ τὸ προνοητικόν, οὐδὲν τῶν τοιούτων, ἀλλὰ τὸ τῆς εἰρήνης καὶ τὸ τῆς ἀγάπης. ἐγώ εἰμι φάσκων ἡ εἰρήνη. ἐγώ εἰμι ἡ ἀγάπη. ταύτην τὴν θείαν καὶ ἱερὰν τῆς φωνῆς ἔννοιαν μιμούμενοι, πάντα τρόπον ὑπὲρ ταύτης σπουδάζετε, ὡς τοῦ εἰρηνοποιοῦ μαθηταὶ καὶ διδάσκαλοι τῆς εἰρήνης. ἀλλὰ ταῦτα μὲν οὕτως καὶ φιλεῖτε καὶ σπεύδετε κυροῦν ἐν παντὶ γένει.

19 κατὰ τὸ ἀνῆκον ἡμῖν, ὦ θεία καὶ ἱερὰ σύνοδος, τὸν πρέποντα ἔπαινον τῆς καλῆς καὶ θεαρέστου προθυμίας ὑμῶν, ἧς ἔχετε ὑπὲρ τῆς ἑνώσεως τῶν ἐκκλησιῶν τοῦ Χριστοῦ ἐχρῆν μὲν ἀρτίως εἰπεῖν. ἐπεὶ δὲ ὁ παρὼν οὑτοσὶ καιρὸς φαίνεται μὴ εἶναι ἱκανός, τοῦτο καὶ δὴ λέγω τὸ βραχύτατον. θεὸς ὁ ποιῶν ἀεὶ θαυμάσια καὶ νῦν ἐνέπνευσεν ὑμῶν ταῖς ψυχαῖς, ἵνα τὸ μέγα τῆς ἑνώσεως καὶ ἱερὸν τῆς εἰρήνης τελέσητε χρῆμα. ὑμῖν γάρ, ὡς ἔοικεν, ἡ μισθαποδοσία τοῦ μεγάλου τούτου καλοῦ καὶ ἐν τῷ νῦν αἰῶνι καὶ ἐν τῷ μέλλοντι ἀπόκειται, σὺν θεῷ τελεσθέντος καὶ εἰς ἔργον προβάντος. τὴν ἀνεκλάλητον οὖν ἐκείνην χαρὰν ἕξουσι καὶ εὐφροσύνην πάντες ὅσοι ἂν πρὸς τὸ τοιοῦτον ἔργον συνδράμωσι μετὰ χρηστῆς καὶ ἀληθοῦς προθυμίας.

[Address] to the Synod at Basle

1 Divine and sacred Synod: I will first call upon help and assistance from God, as I begin your praise; then I will address the importance of the subject, whose value, in my opinion, no prominent speaker from our times or from antiquity may seem to be equal to, or do appropriate justice to, our subject in this gathering. I do not believe that anyone from any time could exhaust the significance of the matter before you, even if he spoke at length, in suitable terms. It so happens that no speech can equal the importance of your deeds and actions in this matter. If this is the case with any speaker, what could I accomplish? I am not a strong public speaker and I am physically weak, as I have not quite recovered from that illness that lasted many days and I still endure its after-effects. In the true saying of the philosophers, the soul also suffers along with the body.

2 I beg you to listen to my words with good will and to overlook the fact that I am not equal to my task, in this consideration of such an important matter, with which you are concerned. I am attempting to address you, even though I should not appear before you. Who among you could fail to see the beauty of this matter, which has been admired over the centuries? Virtue comes from God; it is through virtue that great men, who are inclined to follow God, approach God. Without virtue man would not have an appropriate reason to live in God's creation. It is through virtue alone that man assimilates to God. Those who demonstrably possess it should be called citizens of the heavens. Where else could one encounter more individuals who flourish with virtue like the phoenix (according to that famous, wise saying of the prophets)? You yourselves from all over the

world have gathered here, like the chorus of the apostles, and have undertaken the greatest labor to correct those Christians who have badly broken away and to restore them to their former piety. In the past they held sound dogmas according to the rules set by the divine fathers and followed the way of the apostles. Yet somehow time created the division of the single sacred body of the Church. The subsequent long period transformed an original simple scratch into a formidable, wide chasm.

3 The master and creator of evil armed both sides, which then began to argue and fight with each other. Now you are proposing to eradicate this gulf and dispatched ambassadors to those who desire to find a satisfying resolution in every way, as they embrace peace and harmony, which, in early times and for a long time afterwards, characterized the flourishing body of the Church. Yet the wicked one brought about their long separation, even though many patriarchs attempted to find a resolution. In their times, however, the advantages of pursuing this goal were not realized. The task has fallen upon you, prominent as you are with the greatest virtue and intelligence, and you are determined to achieve union. Without hesitation you hastened to assemble a congregation to include both sides in order to achieve the most beautiful and highest objective. With God's help, this was your avowed goal. Who can adequately describe your good will, your persistence, and your efforts to bring about, in the Holy Spirit's grace, a common union that would include everyone, both at home and abroad? You took residence here in this city, and made it into your home; for many years during you were isolated from your own countries and cities. I also believe in this greatest and most shining goal of the holy and sacred union, with the Grace of the Holy Spirit, and I beg and implore you to bring about this conclusion as soon as possible. Do not postpone it, as our times demand it, as I will mention briefly.

4 Let me touch upon this subject. Your virtue has spread over all borders and you have overlooked nothing that Christians hold just and holy. Your activities are lawful to the most divine Church of the Latins, to cities, and to all communities and people. Your mind was set upon a goal that touches upon God's will. You are truly carrying out God's work. You have made excellent arrangements, which continue to the present day and will take us into the future. Who can adequately praise your great and most divine accomplishments? Who can raise a voice to such level of loudness to declare and to chant, in shining tones approaching all the limits of oratory, throughout the world, the praise of what you have achieved? Your work is worthy of praise and glory, to emerge out of the depths of forgetfulness, contrary to what happens in human affairs.

5 Wisdom is also said to come from God and human beings gracefully share in it, not by just touching upon it lightly; we touch upon it firmly, as we approach the heights of wisdom and enter the sanctuaries of sacred mysteries, at least as far as human nature can share in them. Only those who are initiated into these mysteries can grasp the power of this wisdom (or

philosophy). Only those who probe into theology, into the heights of the divine, and into sacred and divine laws, on whose behalf and preservation you have undertaken this mighty struggle to confirm the power of graceful ceremonies, can realize God's gifts and the powerful mysteries of the Holy Spirit, whose initiates and mystics you happen to be.

6 You have so struggled and have brought to realization, with the highest zeal, your apprehension to work on behalf of Christians. Can anyone summon a power strong enough to praise your highest achievements that I have enumerated? I do not believe so. You carry out your work in the best and most lofty way. Any praise would be inadequate, in spite of the fact that necessity demands that such praises be pronounced, as far as it can be done. Let divine David take up his lyre and sing your praises along with me: "All nations, hear my words: let the inhabitants of the world come together and experience enjoyment and joy of delight" in the actions of this divine and sacred assembly, which wishes to establish the pleasures of peace and harmony, up to the ultimate point of virtue, when you summoned the inhabitants of Europe and of Asia to join the common goal and become one body, as members of the Church of Christ, who founded and confirmed the Church with His own blood, and, as a God, supported and solidified it with many miracles commanding peace and love, which he passed on to His divine and sacred disciples and apostles. He fashioned this divine rock and passed it on, with the Holy Spirit, to the sacred apostles. They encircled and enchanted the entire world in their travels and each one preached peace to all.

7 Peace reigned over the Church of Christ for a thousand years and more, I believe. Then out of nowhere, the ancient spiteful demon of evil created a rebellion against the Church of Christ with minor ugly reasons, which were not extremely harmful to either side; yet they brought us the schism, as it was also suited to those times. Our conditions were not healthy because of civil wars back then. So there was a division and a break and the wounds of each side filled all souls. Time passed on and no one recalled the immense boon of sacred peace, which was rather despised all the way to our own times. The division became more pronounced and there were few meetings between the two sides. What had occurred seemed worse than it was, as time went on, and the world was filled with a marked fog of darkness. The demon promoted strife and made each side to think that it was different from the other. Nothing remained settled and confirmed and the uncertainty was rooted in belief. Each side only fought for the establishment of its views and neglected the great goal of defending the body of the single Church of Christ.

8 Recently the divine and the holy have illuminated our souls; you came together. You have considered all that is best and virtuous for the Church of Christ; you decided to join the pieces torn asunder through wisdom, through the science of sacred theology, and through the experience of the sacred canons and laws; in one word, you decided to bring back the

state of the ancient Church to peace and harmony through sacred canons and laws. So you dispatched ambassadors to the emperor of the Romans [Greeks, John VIII Palaiologos] and called upon the sacred Church of the Greeks, thinking nothing of the toils that your ambassadors faced on this long and difficult journey. They came often and announced their mission, but somehow they failed to accomplish their goal.

9 Do not think that the nation of the Greeks is small and unmoving. It has been under siege for many years during which it lost territories and came under stress. Yet it has not been totally worn out. The Lord protects it to a great extent. All of the Peloponnese is included in the empire of the Romans; so are Lemnos, Imbros, and the greatest part of Thrace in the vicinity of the city of Constantine [Constantinople]. In addition to other areas under tribute, there is all of Corfu, Kephalonia, Zacynthos, Leukas, all of Epeiros, Illyria, Achaea, Phocis, Boeotia, Attica, Hellas, Macedonia, Thrace, Upper and Lower Mysia, Euboea, the Cycladic islands, Crete, Rhodes, Cyprus, Chios, and Lesbos. All these areas are inhabited by Greeks. All territories in Asia under the barbarians [Turks] are mostly inhabited by Greeks. They are also [inhabited by] a great number of Syrians. There are many other kingdoms, which do not speak Greek, but are under the Greek Church. The great kingdom of Iberia [Georgia], the kingdom of the Lazians [Lazikans], the regions of Chechens, Alans, Circasians, and Goths, not to mention Moldowallachia, Great Wallachia, and the area of the Triballians [Serbs]. In addition, there is the land of the Albanians and to the extreme north the most extensive democracy of the Rus' (along the Ungrates) and the so-called king of Great Rus', along with other kings in the area, as well as lower Rus' with its upper and neighboring kings. All these are subjects of the emperors of Constantinople. These neighboring nations surpass in number your neighbors.

10 The rays of the sun illuminate your virtue. I respond and I beg that you zealously hasten, under the influence of the Holy Spirit, to reach our goal. Spare nothing that will bring about the union of the Church so it may recover its former status through harmony between the Church of the Greeks and the Church of the Latins. May the Greeks embrace with affection the Church of the Latins as if it were their own. Let both sides enjoy the pleasurable advantages, as it was in the past. Rewards, benefits, and advantages over the divine, and the most loveable to God union will come. Honor from God and victorious wreaths will equal what has been awarded to the ancient holy fathers, who established the Church of Christ with care and countless toil. They had spared nothing of themselves but derived only pleasure and joy from their labors. Those who are alive now and by future generations will award you for eternity and immortal glory. Each one of you will leave behind a monument that will be greater than the Colossus of Rhodes, which the Rhodians had dedicated to Helios. Human beings have not achieved as much to equal that monument. Why am I talking about a huge statue that was made by human hands? Your monument will reach the heavens and will be evident from the rising to the setting sun.

11 For all these reasons and for the struggle that you have undertaken with such great zeal, I beg your divine and sacred attitude that you have recently displayed and that you hasten to bring our goal to a conclusion, as soon as possible, so that you will receive shortly the divine rewards and so that you will experience, with delight, the true joy and bliss appropriate to holy men.

12 I will address the subject of peace, on whose behalf you propose to undertake this grand labor and on which you have focused your mind and intelligence, hastening to realize this greatest and sacred goal of establishing peace throughout the world. Then I will turn to a few other matters and I will touch upon wisdom, knowledge, sacred theology, laws, and sacred canons, ritual, and the contribution of the Holy Spirit; I will proceed, in full understanding of the demands of time and of my innate strength. My time is brief, but this much your divine and sacred assembly has allotted.

13 Peace is a grand subject. The name alone combines the angelic powers of Heaven's enlightenment and is further supported by the one and foremost Trinity of the divine (that is, the divine and inexpressible luxury emanating from the most blessed illumination of the Trinity). These are bound together and are connected through peace and by the bond of love. Peace supports the intelligible world, touches upon, and approaches the light of the divine with its purest and untouchable qualities. Furthermore, peace solidifies and unites all goodness. Its opposite, enmity, creates separation, division, and strife.

14 Enmity, strife, and conflict did not allow the world to remain forever in its ancient shining form but they broke it into numerous powers who were the con-creators of evil. They became the masters of evil, affecting the old order and its descendants. Then you see the state of the intelligible world containing an excessive amount of these mixed qualities, which create neither peace nor order which could bring about a calm constitution of equal laws for everyone. In the presence of these disturbances war comes about and confusion reigns with the attending disorder, dissolution, and total destruction for everything. This most beautiful and best world no longer exhibits is orderly shape; weakness and total darkness emerge, which cannot be tolerated under any circumstances.

15 Let us consider a small part, which, nevertheless, is the greatest, governing and reigning part of the world, as God has ordained: the human being. When man governs himself and observes the order and constitution of his soul by maintaining a steady and secure peace, then there is steadiness and order, following the appropriate pace of a chorus of angels. But when man loses control of himself, strife and war appear, which confuse man's leadership qualities and create darkness, the absence of light. His soul is also darkened. The soul then becomes a dark specter displaying inconsistency and indecisiveness.

16 Let us see in what way peace is superior. Peace produces shining empires. Peace produces democracy, aristocracy, and every other form of

lawful government. Peace augments, beautifies, and greatly promotes every city, every lord, and every subject. It also creates homes, and makes uninhabited regions civilized; it even tames deserts and promotes habitation everywhere. It improves all conditions and, in one word, it is responsible for beauty and for the most desirable conditions. Without peace there is nothing good in life. On the contrary, one encounters wars and enmity. Wars produce murders, destruction of human life, and the elimination of villages, cities, and provinces. It even affects animals, which also suffer along with human beings.

17 Did war not destroy Troy of the wide streets? Was there no strife? Was there no war? Who can forget the fate of Babylon, whose famous great walls were so strongly fortified? Did it not destroy the sacred city of Jerusalem? Did it not enslave and carry away the Jewish nation into Assyria? Did it not destroy the greatest empire of the Assyrians, the empires of the Persians, of the Greeks, and of the Romans? How many cities were ruined in Italy and remained in this state until our own times? Recently, it has affected Galatia [France], which flourished in the past but now is under stress and is often destroyed by the Britons. Were not enmity and war responsible? Did they not arm both sides? Do they not create the greatest destruction wherever they appear? Are not books full of such cases? Do histories not talk of enslaved nations and of the tragedies of countries and cities?

18 Consider such matters in your heart, divine and sacred assembly, and, with the grace of the Holy Spirit, make it your intention to award peace to the entire world. It is a noble struggle you are undertaking, if you take into account the beauty and honesty that come with peace. Remember that Christ offers nothing else. He does not offer absolute power and anticipation. Nothing of the sort. He only offers peace and love. He says: "I am peace. I am love." Follow the divine and sacred meaning of this word. Spend all your time on behalf of peace, especially since you are the disciples of the peacemaker and also are teachers of peace. Embrace it with devotion and establish it in every nation. For all these reasons and for the struggle that you have undertaken with such great zeal, I beg your divine and sacred attitude that you have recently displayed and that you hasten to bring our goal to a conclusion, as soon as possible, so that you will receive shortly the divine rewards and so that you will experience, with delight, the true joy and bliss appropriate to holy men.

19 Divine and sacred synod: I have praised, as I ought, your recent manifest and admirable zeal, which is also pleasing to God, on behalf of the union of the Churches of Christ. Since I do not have sufficient time, I will only state that God performs miracles and now has inspired your souls to conclude the great and sacred goal of achieving peace. There will be a reward for you, on account of this great boon, in the present and in the future, if God approves and brings the work to a proper conclusion. All who assist with good intentions and true zeal for the conclusion of this goal will experience inexpressible joy and delight.

In terms of style, the Address is a composition that displays the erudition of its author in Attic Greek. Isidore's Atticism has little that Demosthenes or Isocrates would have recognized; it is more typical of the style of the Byzantine Greeks of the *quattrocento*, who preferred the Attic style of the second sophistic. Libanios, Philostratos, or Aelius Aristides would have read Isidore's prose with ease and with a certain degree of admiration for his expression. For modern or classical Attic tastes, though, his style can be termed verbose, as the author uses too many words to express one thought. Isidore's essay is a typical oration of the learned Byzantines and their adherents who continued it in the sixteenth century, among them Markos Musuros, Janos Laskaris, and Demetrios Khalkokondyles, who represented Greek scholarship in Renaissance Italy. John W. Barker has aptly described this style of late Byzantine composition, which is also encountered in Manuel II's literary compositions:[35]

> Obscure and unusual tricks of Classical style are seized upon and used to absurd extremes. Logical syntax is distorted almost beyond recognition, and word order beyond all reason. Infinitives are used recklessly in place of participles; participles are exploited by the bushel as nouns. Key words are deliberately omitted ... vague and imprecise words are gleefully strewn about at every opportunity. Grammar and vocabulary become pawns in a learned game, in which one expert vies with the other to achieve a nirvana of esoteric enigma. Maintaining the Hellenistic tradition with remarkable fidelity on the one hand, and mirroring on the other the rhetoric typical of early Renaissance humanists. . . [they made] each work an exercise in empty and stylized patterns. In the process, content and substance are often lost or ignored and are almost always subordinate to demands of style and displays of elegance.

Isidore's essay was originally composed in Attic Greek, but was subsequently translated into Latin by the Sicilian humanist Giovanni Aurispa.[36] Whether Isidore lacked sufficient proficiency in Latin or was reluctant to furnish a Latin version himself remains an unanswered question. It is most probable that he delivered the address in Attic Greek, which few in the audience at Basle could understand, hence the need for a Latin translation. He had demonstrated a reluctance to employ foreign languages throughout much of his lifetime, favoring the use of his beloved Attic Greek. It is reasonable to assume, therefore, that he addressed the audience in Attic Greek, given his penchant for the dialect.

In terms of content, it is surprising that Isidore, a well-educated cleric, has very little to say about theological matters. While he does make reference to and cites the standard platitudes about God's will and the inspiration of the Holy Spirit, he does not address the real problems that the Council of Basle is facing, nor does he confront the synod's and Greek Church's difficulties with the papacy. Isidore's main theme is the survival of the Greek state against the onslaughts of the Islamic threat and, by extension, the unification of Christendom and its churches as a powerful force to counter the threat confronting the Byzantines. Thus Isidore in many ways expresses the current views of the imperial leadership at Constantinople and his observations and arguments would have been heartily approved by John VIII, who was determined to achieve union in order to become the recipient of military and financial aid from Catholic Europe and in this way resist the encroaching Ottoman expansion. The elaborations of Isidore expressed in the essay are the views of the emperor as we encounter them in the composition of Sylvestros Syropoulos about the councils of Basle and Ferrara-Florence. Isidore suppresses the concerns and problems of the Greek Church and those of Catholicism for the survival of the imperial state. If anything, this essay clearly demonstrates that Isidore is closer to the emperor in his perception of the issues than to those of the majority of the Greeks who wished to remain free of papal domination and various interferences. It is clear that unification and the anticipated rewards that would result through the unification of the churches are Isidore's main concerns. He is, at least initially at the councils, less a theologian and more a practitioner of *Realpolitik*, although as events would later demonstrate, Isidore did address questions of Christian dogma, both in the Greek and Latin contexts.

But in his Basle address, he begins with an introduction, which, through classical precedents, evokes a *captatio benevolentiae*. He praises his audience for their willingness to undertake church unification. While this theme remains alive throughout the speech, he takes the opportunity to provide his own interpretations based on history and not on theology. He harkens back to the "ancient" order of the church when, he believes, everything was in order for a period of a thousand years and suggests that in recent centuries, through the intervention of the devil, the schism occurred.[37] He then draws upon ancient precedents to illustrate the ills that division brings and makes the generalization that all evil has as its source the absence of peace. He takes time to point out the importance of the Greek "empire." Even though it has been diminished in size, he makes the curious argument that the subjects of the Turks are Greeks and proceeds to list the territories still controlled by Constantinople. While there is exaggeration here, as he seems to include the Ionian Islands that were then under Latin rule, and other territories that were not a part of the "empire," we may suggest that he manufactured a hyperbole to impress upon his audience the territorial extent of the "empire." Moreover, he utilizes the fact that many eastern territories still subject themselves to the ecclesiastical authority of the patriarch, even though they are politically independent from Constantinople.

Thus the essay includes a certain amount of exaggeration as well as simplification in advancing theological arguments. Whenever Isidore suggests theology, he borders on suggesting paganism. The terms that he uses for mystery religions and initiation rites are closer to those in usage in late antiquity and not in the Christian context of the late medieval period. He conveys the simple thought that it is the devil that has put everything into confusion and the Council of Basle should be praised in its efforts to restore the "ancient peace" to the church.

We should express one further thought. Though his communication is couched in philosophical and theological argumentation, he does not neglect to cite the western ecclesiastical and secular difficulties and issues then linked to his imperial state. By drawing this analogy, Isidore before the general congregation of the Council of Basle makes a strong plea and justification for church union. He calls upon the general congregation to arrive at the formation of *unum Ecclesiæ sanctum corpus*, "one holy body of the church"[38] that then was divided. His emphasis was upon the fragmented Christendom and the problems that had ensued over the course of centuries. He relates that this division arises because, in the Latin rendition, there are,[39]

> *non iura, non æquitates, non ritus, non consuetudines, non leges. Omnia enim quæ Christi Ecclesiæ conferunt, quæ civitatibus, quæ populis, quæ generi hominum, divina quadam providentia, divina industria tractatis.*
>
> No laws, no equalities, no religious customs, no usages, no agreements. Truly, all things brought together upon the church of Christ, which are being brought to the states, which are brought to the peoples and to human kind, have been handled by a certain divine providence and a divine energy.

For comparative purposes, it is very difficult to contrast the Greek text with the Latin translation of Aurispa, who also utilized an *ad sensum* approach. He exercised literary license and provided an improved text without distorting the essential ideas conveyed by Isidore.

The statements of Isidore reveal his strong belief in and an adherence to the notion of church reunion between East and West, and an admission of the willingness of the Byzantine "empire" to be a strong advocate for unification under one head, the pope. These statements clearly contravened the resolve of the council to weaken the claim of papal supremacy and to limit the powers of the Roman *curia*. He is also aware of conflicts in the West and cites the political divisions in Italy, the struggles between Venice and Genoa, the involvements of the papacy and other peninsular states in these struggles that could limit the quality and quantity of military aid and personnel for the defense of the empire, and the Hundred Years' War between England and France (which he designates, in his classical mode, as Britannia and Galatia/Gallia). Isidore has thus demonstrated a breath of knowledge concerning affairs in the West and was well aware how these might have a negative impact upon the primary imperial goal to salvage the few remnants of the once glorious Byzantine Empire with the arrival of western aid.

Perhaps a more significant attestation of Byzantine involvement in western ecclesiastical and political questions is a summary document that provides the potential Byzantine position on issues at the assembly. The text bears no signature to indicate either authorship or a collective group of contributors, nor does it state its immediate origin within the assembly. It is dated 1434 and bears the title[40] *Sequuntur Avisamenta. Dominorum deputatorum in facto pecuniarum reperiendarum pro adventu Græcorum ad hoc sacrum generale concilium Basileense, etc.,*

"Notices Follow. Of the lords selected to find money in the real world for the arrival of the Greeks to this holy general council of Basle." The text lists thirty-one items of conciliar and Byzantine concern, but also includes issues raised before the general assembly at Basle. The document is an excellent summary statement to deputations present at the council and defines their financial needs for attendance; it is also indicative of the complex doctrinal and other issues confronting the council. And most significantly, the text demonstrates the preeminent position to be accorded to the arriving Greeks.

A mutual agreement to achieve union of the Greek and Roman churches, a *concordat* commonly identified as *Sicut pia mater* (*As a Pious Mother*)[41] between the Greeks and the Basle assembly in a public session, was reached on the 7th of September 1434, whereby the former solemnly promised to abide by the provisions of the accord. The document addresses a number of significant issues, but throughout remains optimistic in tone. It expressly desires to end the religious and military assaults upon the Bohemians (or rather the Hussites) and to bring to a conclusion the centuries-long theological discord between the Byzantines and Rome. The agreement notes that the conciliarists sensed early on in their conclave that the Byzantines were desirous of church union and dispatched a delegation to Constantinople; the emperor and patriarch graciously received the Basle representatives. The emperor, it notes, "straightaway" appointed three ambassadors to participate in the conciliar council. Thereafter, in general congregation at Basle, the Byzantine delegates expressed a most fervent desire for church union and daily they revisited this desire for union. The document stresses, however, that the Byzantine delegation made clear that union could only be achieved in a universal synod, at which both eastern and western churchmen would participate in the deliberations and could come to common agreement. Accord was thus reached on several points. First, substantive attention was devoted to a forthcoming site, where the council would continue its deliberations and at that same time make provision for the maintenance of the delegates in the host city. Among the cities proposed were Constantinople, although the choice remained unresolved, granting to the Latin delegates the option to select one of their own urban centers. The text notes that John VIII and Patriarch Joseph placed limitations upon naming certain sites, because they were not mentioned in previous instructions. To preclude failure to arrive at agreement upon a future site, the document nominated a number of places: Bologna, Milan (or another Italian city), Calabria, Ancona, Buda (in Hungary), Vienna, and lastly Savoy.[42] But to avoid a stalemate over the issue of a future meeting place, the Byzantine delegation promised that the emperor, the patriarch, and the other members of their delegation would attend the forthcoming synod. On this note, *Sicut pia mater* affirmed Byzantine sincerity for achieving church union and the council in turn made provision for the transfer of a substantial sum of money, 8,000 ducats, to the Greeks for convening a congregation of eastern prelates in Constantinople in preparation for their attendance at the future synod.

Assurances were given of military assistance in the form of archers, although the initial draft of the document called for the dispatch of "two large galleys and two light galleys and 300 crossbowmen [to] be sent for the protection of the city [Constantinople]."[43] The large galleys would then transport the imperial and patriarchal delegation to the site of the future synod. This commitment of military assistance was to take place by August 1435. Although the costs of dispatching and the maintenance of crossbowmen in the imperial city were to be funded by the Basle assembly, the primary reason for their dispatch was to assist in the defense of Constantinople during the absence of the emperor against a possible Turkish assault or to suppress an internal revolt led by anti-unionists.

Lastly, we encounter in *Sicut pia mater* clarification for the meaning of some phrases, since there apparently was a lack of clarity among the Latin and Greek delegates. In providing elucidation, Isidore must have played a prominent role, since he was more proficient in understanding ecclesiastical terminology than his lay counterparts. The Latins brought up four phrases for further elaboration. First, they sought to determine the Greek understanding of *synodus universalis* ("universal synod"). The Byzantine position was that the pope and eastern patriarchs or their procurators should be present at the future synod. Lesser ranking prelates or their representatives should also participate. Perhaps most noteworthy was the stipulation that both the emperor and the Constantinopolitan patriarch be present and participate in the synod. Like the first seven ecumenical councils recognized by the Eastern churches, the emperor was to enjoy a preeminent place at the head of the gathering, even if a shared role, was to have a function in the discussions, and was to have a voice in the final decisions. Next, the phrase *libera et inviolata* ("free and inviolate") was explained by the Greeks to imply that there would be uninhibited discussion without obstacles or violence to any of the speakers. Third, the Latins sought the Greek understanding of *sine contentione* ("without contention"), which the Greek ambassadors explained meant the absence of quarrelsome discussions and ill-tempered contentiousness among the delegates or delegations. They maintained that the discussions should be necessary, peaceful, honest, and charitable. And lastly, the Latins sought a clarification of *Apostolica et canonica* ("Apostolic and canonical"), to which the Greeks replied that the synod should define what it understood this phrase to imply. The Byzantine delegation did stress that their emperor be accorded the same rights, honors, privileges, and dignities as the pope, thus equating the two heads of a synod.[44]

In the same document, the Greeks requested that Eugenius IV be informed of the provisions in *Sicut pia mater* and that his consent be given to its contents. The conciliarists were willing to seek his assent for the benefit of the faith and ecclesiastical unity. Doubtless, this instrument was revolutionary in its tone and contents, and may explain why hereafter the pope labored zealously to undermine the decisions of the Basle assembly and to gain an advantage as the sole head of the church at any future gathering.

John VIII signified his approval of the provisions of *Sicut pia mater*. He issued a formal document, dated 26 November 1435, of which only Latin renditions are extant.[45] Bearing no title, the contents of the text restress the role and participation of the pope in a future gathering and the importance of church union. John VIII lists his ambassadors to Basle and cites them by name, including Isidore. He then cites the Basle ambassadors to his own imperial city: John of Ragusa, who was of the order of public professors and a *magister* in sacred books; Henry (Heinrich) Menger, a knowledgeable doctor and a canon in Constance; and Symeon Fréron, a baccalaureate in sacred theology and a canon at Orléans. Sylvestros Syropoulos[46] also identifies the three legates, but identifies them respectively as "Brother John,[47] Henry Mancer,[48] and Brother Simon."[49] The legates were sufficiently funded to meet all their needs and were granted the power and authority to arrange all matters leading to the convocation of an ecumenical synod.[50] Their role in the imperial city and the contentious discussions that extended over a number of days will be discussed presently.

In the meantime at Basle, during the years 1435 and 1436, while Isidore conducted negotiations directly with the pope, the Byzantine delegation reaffirmed its commitment in general congregation and in the presence of the assembly's commissaries and expressed the fervent wishes of the emperor, patriarch, and the Eastern Church for union. They did, however, emphasize their view that union could only be achieved in a universal synod, recognizing that the provisions of *Sicut pia mater* had elapsed through no fault of the Byzantines or the conciliarists, but rather because of intervening negotiations. However, the provision of military aid did materialize and forces were dispatched in 1436. The reaffirmation of imperial and patriarchical sincerity is again noted in the proceedings of the twenty-fourth session held on the 14th of April 1436, and in the document addressing matters concerning the Greeks.[51] This document also makes an interesting provision. There must have been apprehension for the safety of John VIII and Patriarch Joseph to travel to a future site. What prompted this concern is not made clear, nor is evidence furnished as to who may have posed a threat to the Byzantine delegation and under what circumstances. The conciliarists were concerned about the security and freedom of the Greeks and thus guaranteed their status as delegates, free of any impediments or threats to their wellbeing. Also, their unrestricted travel, entry into and egress from cities, maintenance, and free expression in debates without hindrance from anyone were guaranteed. Hereafter, both groups for the remainder of the year labored to make preparations for reconvening the general assembly at Ferrara.

It became evident by 1437 that the papacy had gained the upper hand in discussions and had won the allegiance of Constantinople. Further, it was noticed that throughout 1435 and the following year, Isidore and his colleagues held private discussions with the pope and his representatives. But in the meantime, disputes among the delegations had arisen within the Council of Basle over a number of essential points. The *concordat*, *Sicut pia mater*, in essence had lapsed by 1437, but the promised military aid for the defense of Constantinople did materialize. According to the document, 300 archers were authorized. Part of the contingent was to be provided by the papacy, while the other part was to be furnished by the Basle assembly. Each group was to be transported on their respective ships. The papal vessels arrived before the others and gained the advantage to transport Patriarch Joseph and 700 delegates, while John VIII traveled on his own ship.

In the same year, Eugenius IV submitted a document to the Basle assembly titled: *Bulla Domini Nostri Papæ. De assensu præstito in materiis Græcorum,* "A Bull of Our Lord the Pope. Concerning the assent prescribed in Greek matters." The pope emphatically points out *ut Græci ad unitatem Romanæ atque catholicæ ecclesiæ reducerentur,* "so that the Greeks may be led back to the unity of the Roman and Catholic Church";[52] thus the discussions of the conciliarists were rendered fruitless. The pope's intent at this juncture may have been not only to weaken conciliarist resolve, but also to negate their numerous issues that had drawn disparate delegations to Basle and to reinforce his primacy as head of the church. For Eugenius, it appears to have been a foregone conclusion that the Byzantines were desirous of church unity and it was futile for the conciliarists to continue their efforts to woo the Greeks, although the conciliarists also affirmed their desire as stated in the documentation for the twenty-fourth session (14 April 1436) to achieve union of the two churches. The following year, the theme of concord between the papacy and the Constantinopolitan patriarchate and *imperium* was reaffirmed in *Alia Bulla Patens Domini. Nostri papæ in que inseruntur capitula concordata cum Græcis, etc.,* "Another Available Bull of the Lord, Our Pope, which includes an agreement with the Greeks."[53] Hence, Eugenius reserved for the papacy the sole responsibility for achieving union between the two churches and he undermined the efforts of the Basle assembly to win the Byzantines over to their cause. Hereafter, the documents produced in the next five years at Basle demonstrate the intense rivalry between the conciliarists and the papacy, each attempting to encourage the Byzantines to adopt their positions. For the Byzantine delegation, including Isidore, their primary mission remained to accept the notion of the union of churches and to secure western military aid for the salvation of their imperial state. In time, the Basle assembly relented, bowing to papal pressures, left its work unresolved, and accepted the proposal to reconvene at Ferrara on the 18th of January 1438 in order to begin the work of church union. But in spite of these initial achievements and of the negotiations with the conciliarists and papists, the notion of a church union remained *anathema* to many Greeks, particularly the monks and a significant proportion of the Constantinopolitan populace, who especially viewed the Roman papacy with disfavor and deep suspicion, questioning papal intentions toward the Greeks and the fear of Latinization of their church. Historical precedent and deep memories played significant roles in the formulation of the negative Byzantine outlook toward Rome, especially when viewing the consequences of the crusader conquest and sack of the imperial city in 1204 and the aftermath. Geanakoplos, however, sums up well the respective positions of the three groups as Basle:

> the Greeks were more familiar with the traditional papal prestige than with the new phenomenon of western conciliarism, and indeed conciliarism as a movement soon proved to be ephemeral . . . he [John VIII] . . . preferred

to negotiate with a single absolute authority rather than the factious fathers at Basel.[54]

But then the declining empire had only to look eastward and accept the further realization that the Ottoman Turks also rejected the notion of church union between Rome and Constantinople, being informed of the ensuing negotiations and viewing the remnants of the Byzantine Empire as within their sphere of influence and domination.[55] Thus, the Byzantines entered a phase in the second half of the 1430s and the decade of the 1440s wherein their substantial need for western military aid was compounded by renewed Ottoman pressures and territorial aggressions. Indeed, the international politics played a more decisive role than the religious postulations of the conciliarists and papists at Basle.

3 Byzantine issues resulting from Basle

The arrival of the Basle delegation, headed by John of Ragusa, is substantially recorded by Sylvestros Syropoulos.[56] His account, addressed from the perspective of the patriarchate, is one of the rare detailed texts to provide us with information on the difficulties of the negotiations with the Basle envoys. Nor was there unanimity within the Byzantine court and the patriarchate; rather, there were contested questions often testing the resolve of the emperor and of the patriarch, often reaching a breaking point in their relationship.

A few days after their arrival, John of Ragusa, Henry Menger, and Symon Fréron made a formal visit to the patriarch. Each side rendered to the other the customary honors. John of Ragusa first reiterated that the Basle synod had a great desire to enact church union and was prepared to assume all responsibility and expenses for transporting the emperor, patriarch, and other eastern Church Fathers to the proposed synod site. He concluded by saying that this delegation was dispatched to Constantinople to cooperate and to takes steps for all necessities. Henry Menger then spoke and noted that they had brought with them scribes, but the latter had fallen ill to an infectious disease en route to the imperial city. He lamented that their delegation was deprived of the skills of the scribes. Perhaps most notable are the words of the third envoy, Symon Fréron. He argued that church union would be a great benefit to Christianity, and especially that the western lords would greatly assist their eastern counterparts, assuming that he implied military assistance.[57]

Patriarch Joseph responded positively to their words, but with a caveat. He acknowledged that church union was highly desirable. Although he was willing to undertake and contribute toward the completion of "God's work," he then indicated that the projected journey would be difficult for him because of ill health and his advanced age. In terms of the promises and pledges of the Basle envoys, he contrasted himself as another (doubting) Thomas.[58] During the weeks of the Basle envoys' presence in Constantinople, time and again he reiterated his skepticism about a successful conclusion to the negotiations.

The meetings with the patriarch were complicated by two other circumstances. Accompanying the Basle envoys were the Byzantine delegation of John VIII and the papal representative Christoforo. The patriarch received Metokhites, Isidore, and Dishypatos, but they were not accorded the customary courtesies. Of this discourteous reception, rumors almost immediately circulated within the imperial court and the city that disparaged the accomplishments of the Byzantine legation to Basle and focused on the fact that there was disagreement among the three legates. Whether there was disbelief concerning their accomplishments, the issue of church union must have been disturbing to the Orthodox anti-unionist elements and fueled misstatements of what had transpired. And that the patriarch had not received the Byzantine legates with the customary courtesies appears to have become common knowledge among the urban populace. In a number of circles, the absence of rendering courtesy was viewed as a slight to the emperor and a negation of the envoy's achievements at Basle. Thus, Isidore came to be viewed within the patriarchal circle with suspicion, given the evidence provided by Sylvestros Syropoulos in his memoir.

Not to undermine his efforts at church union and the reception of military assistance from the West, the emperor commanded high churchmen, abbots, and confessors to assemble before the patriarch. John VIII as well attended this gathering and took his place as *katekhoumenos* (κατηχούμενος) to the right of the patriarch. To preclude further misstatements of what had transpired at Basle, the emperor directed the three Byzantine envoys to provide an account of what had taken place.[59] Metokhites, the leading spokesman for the envoys, related of the courtesies extended to them by the high clergy at the synod and of the amiable conversations that they had had. He stated that they were regularly informed of the proceedings, were permitted to address "both" factions at the synod, were allowed to voice the Byzantine concerns, and received satisfactory answers for these problems. Metokhites stressed that the three envoys were in agreement to accept only those things that they had requested. He denied that there were divisions among them. Rather, he stated, they found solutions to Byzantine concerns and under oath reached agreements that were delineated in the decree to be presented by the Basle legates. Isidore and Dishypatos confirmed what the leading envoy had stated. The emperor was pleased with their statements and then called upon the patriarch to speak. But when he began to speak, the emperor happened to laugh. The patriarch was saddened and viewed the incident as one to mock him, although John VIII denied this intent. Thereafter, Patriarch Joseph refused to continue to speak and no attempts at imperial conciliation were successful.[60] Clearly, this meeting had ended on an unfortunate note and would make difficult future relations between the two leaders. On a positive note, the Byzantine envoys to Basle spoke highly of John of Ragusa, who had made himself available to the Greeks and had been eager to provide for their comfort.[61]

A few days later, the patriarch assembled his immediate circle of high clergy and others. He announced that the emperor had conferred with the Latin envoys and had come to the decision to cooperate with them. John VIII indicated that he would compel Patriarch Joseph to cooperate with the Latin envoys and would require him to travel to the synod. The patriarch considered these demands unbearable. He could not bring himself to cooperate with the emperor. He made clear that he would resist if he found a proposal favoring union not to his liking. He found himself abandoned by the emperor and had only his immediate ecclesiastical circle to look to for support. The patriarch then sought their advice and asked for their assistance in this matter. His clerics urged him to remain brave and unyielding. They promised to defend their church. Having gained their collaboration, the patriarch felt encouraged to meet with the emperor on the following day.[62] Thus, the lines were drawn between emperor and patriarch. The discussions between the patriarch and his high clergy fueled the passions of the anti-unionists and there was no retreating on the issues.

The following day, a Friday, John VIII summoned Patriarch Joseph to meet with him at the Nea Ekklesia, a church within the complex of the great palace. This was to be a private meeting between the two men and the clergy accompanying the patriarch were to remain seated outside the structure. The two then summoned the *mesazontes*, the emperor's confidants, and the grand domestic, and there followed the high priests and the Byzantine legates to Basle, thus including Isidore.

After completion of their discussions, the patriarch was directed by the emperor to state what had been agreed upon between them. Noting that John of Ragusa and his colleagues had requested that the Byzantines announce what the Council of Basle had accomplished, that was done. In addition, the Latin delegation asked that the Basle decree that they had brought with them be presented to those present. The latter requested a reading of the document and with trepidation they were alarmed at the contents of its preamble. The synod, it reads, had agreed to exert efforts to correct the "ancient heresy of the Greeks," much as they were attempting to correct that of the Hussites.[63] This caused such consternation among the Greek high clergy that a succession of meetings ensued with the Basle delegates to resolve the contentious statements. To the Byzantine side in these negotiations, the *mesazontes*, the patriarch, and his immediate circle of high clerics, were added Demetrios Angelos Philommates (a γραμματικός, an imperial secretary),[64] Georgios Scholarios (the scholar and later a strong anti-unionist), and Brother Manuel (a translator).[65]

The Byzantine participants sought a correction to the preamble and requested that the author of this offensive statement be identified. Maintaining that they had never deviated from the apostolic, synodic, and patristic traditions, the Greek legates argued that this statement was creating a scandal among them and demanded a correction to the preamble. The Latin legates affirmed that this was not done on purpose and alleged that a secretary had included this condemnation of the Byzantines. Denying that the Latins had ever held the Byzantines to be heretical, the legates claimed that they were not doing so at present and that the inclusion of that statement had been an error. The Latins then asserted that the Byzantine envoys, thus also Isidore, to the Council of Basle had seen a draft of the decree and could have raised objections and asked for a correction to the preamble, but had failed to do so. The Greeks present at this gathering then concluded among themselves that John of Ragusa and his colleagues had been endowed with great powers by their synod and could recast the decree, affix a seal, and deliver it to the emperor and patriarch.

At a second meeting of both sides, restating that the offensive preamble was not done on purpose, they could not submit to the Byzantine demand for a correction. John of Ragusa and his colleagues held that they were not entrusted with the power or authority to make a correction. They would, however, in a letter confirm the correction to the preamble and promised that the Basle synod would approve this change. The Greeks remained firm and refused to accept the proposal of a letter. They insisted that the preamble had to be rewritten and emended then and there. They reiterated that publicly the Latins had branded them as heretics and on this note the second meeting abruptly adjourned.[66]

A third meeting was arranged. Again, the contentious issue arose and the Byzantines persisted in their demand for a correction. The Latins countered with the statement that they had suggested a method for correction, but that it was unacceptable to the Greeks. The Latins also countered with the argument that they did not have the power to make a bull in the imperial city. They did propose to write another preamble, making the correction that the Greeks demanded, and would rewrite the decree for their approval. However, they noted that the revised document would be sent to Basle with one of their members for approval and would be sealed with a bull. All sides were satisfied with this approach, although one Byzantine skeptic raised the question of whether or not the synod would accept and confirm the revised document.[67]

In the ensuing days, discussions continued regarding the participation of the patriarch and other Byzantine high churchmen at the proposed universal synod. The Greeks expressed concern citing the declining health of the patriarch, the advanced age and infirmities of leading ecclesiastics, and the difficulties of travel that would be imposed upon them. The future site of the synod and the nominated nine locations ruled out distant travel to the more remote among them, excluding Basle and Savoy.[68] There appeared no immediate compromise on a location and accord was not reached.

Two other difficulties arose regarding the Greek presence at the forthcoming synod. Sylvestros Syropoulos and the confessor Lord Matthaios raised these concerns. First, they observed that if the emperor, patriarch, and other high ecclesiastics were away from the imperial city at a time of war the defense of the city could not be carried out effectively. The emperor and his immediate party would be required to return hastily to their city and to abandon the synod, leaving the work of church union undone. The second issue concerned expenses of return passage. The patriarchal chronicler and the confessor raised a question: Should no agreement be reached on the convocation of a future synod, who would bear the costs of return passage for the Byzantine participants? Would the Council of Basle provide passage on their galleys and thus bear the costs? A confidant of the emperor, Loukas Notaras, stressed that they had addressed the first concern and elaborated that the emperor, a number of high lords about him including the military units accompanying them, and the churchmen would be required to return to Constantinople. Notaras clarified further that the ecclesiastics would play no role in a conflict and were generally and normally useless in the city's defense. Concerning the issue of payment for return passage, he maintained that this should be addressed at a later meeting.[69]

John of Ragusa and his colleagues addressed the second concern at a subsequent consultation. They pointed out that they were confident that church union would be achieved and they had not considered the cost of return passage. They did, however, stipulate that should church union fail to be achieved, the Byzantines would then be responsible for payment of their own return passage. A number of Byzantine legates at this meeting became upset over these hidden expenditures. Suspicious of Latin intents, the Greeks stipulated that a written statement be included in the Basle decree. John of Ragusa and his colleagues agreed to add this requirement to the document and the matter was settled.[70]

As discussions extended over a prolonged period and the issues were relatively minute in content, John VIII intervened and expressed his position on church union. He concluded that the schism had lasted for too long and, as he enumerated, "very close to five hundred years."[71] His mathematics was faulty. The Photian Schism occurred in the mid-ninth century and the formal inception of the schism in 1054. It is unclear from the sources which event he had in mind. The first would have been approaching 600 years and the second looming on 400 years. The emperor believed that if church union were accomplished, both the Greeks and Latins would benefit, improving both church structures in countless ways.[72]

Attention now turned to the presence of Christoforo, the papal representative, at these negotiations. He was instructed by the Latin delegation from Basle to gain the pope's approval on the arrangements that had thus far been agreed upon for a future synod and to obtain a statement from the pope that he would attend the future assembly. The Latins were displeased with Christoforo's responses, believing that he was evasive. They became angry and demanded that he submit in writing all that had been agreed upon. He was willing to do this, but even this seemed not to satisfy the Basle envoys and they displayed their contempt for Christoforo. The following day, however, Christoforo produced a written statement detailing, in acceptable form, that he had the power and authority to cooperate with the Basle envoys and that the pope would accede to the agreements that had been concluded.[73] Excluded, however, were guarantees of return passage for the Byzantine delegation should church union not be achieved. The Latin delegates maintained that they lacked the power to make this guarantee. John of Ragusa and Kantakouzenos then engaged in a lively exchange over the issue of what authority and power the Basle envoys were granted to make changes to the original decree. The Latins argued that it was impossible for them to make alterations to the decree, but after consulting among themselves they concluded that they could include a provision for safe-conduct for the emperor, patriarch, and Byzantine delegation to a future synod, although the issue of return passage appears to have been left unresolved. In addition, they would present to the delegates at the Council of Basle the new draft of the preamble and other changes to the original decree. Henry Menger was then designated to return to Basle with the documentation, obtain their approval with a seal, and dispatch the sealed documents.[74]

The only unresolved question was whether or not the patriarch would attend the forthcoming council. The Latin envoys visited and conferred with him. They urged him to attend and to give his consent to make the arranged travel. He hesitated again, arguing that his advanced age and poor health precluded him from making this difficult journey. Exasperated with his responses, the Latin legates demanded that he agree to make the journey, to which he replied: "If the pope travels to the synod, I will go too."[75] The legates stressed that "a pope" will come to the synod, the implication being whether he come from Rome or Avignon. Patriarch Joseph then insisted upon assurances that the pope in Rome would attend and the Basle envoys gave confirmation. On this vague note agreement was achieved.

There was one further stipulation. Since the populace of Constantinople was aware of the offensive preamble, the Byzantine negotiators insisted that the revised preamble be read to the public and that it would be announced that the Greeks would attend the universal synod. The following Sunday, a gathering of Constantinopolitans and others took place in the Holy Church of the Resurrection of Christ. The revised preamble was read. Loukas Notaras, perhaps speaking for the emperor, added a few statements. Thus the preamble and the Basle decree were completed in a revised form. The new document, along with imperial and patriarchal letters, was dispatched to the Basle synod. Likewise, Christoforo returned to Rome to announce to the pope what had transpired.

What was the role of Isidore during the course of these negotiations? Obviously, he was present. But the emperor and patriarch, and their immediate circle, played the primary roles. As a representative of John VIII, Isidore maintained his fidelity to the emperor throughout these discussions, although his submission to patriarchal authority must have come into question.

4 The Muscovite reaction

The question next arises: How do Russian sources and scholarship view the proceedings at Basle, in view of the fact that Isidore was soon to become the metropolitan of Kiev and of All Rus'? Although the Muscovites purportedly had sent Iona (Jonas), the bishop of Riazan and acting metropolitan of Kiev and of All Rus',[76] whom we shall discuss more extensively in the next chapter, as a part of a Rus' delegation to Basle, his late arrival precluded the Rus' from having any substantial influence upon its deliberations or a role in its decisions. The Muscovite delegation, if in attendance (and there is substantive justification for questioning their presence), must have had some concerns about Isidore's prominent position at the council and the part he played in the often undocumented private negotiations. Also, were the Muscovites so preoccupied with their own internal political, military, and religious affairs that their legate or legates, though perhaps aware of the substance of the discussions, could ignore the proceedings at Basle and the consequences that it might portend for Muscovy? It would seem that domestic issues outweighed the discussions at Basle, even though they must have been cumbersome for the Muscovites who remained isolated from and suspicious of Byzantine imperial and patriarchal relationships with western prelates at this assembly and what this signified for their own metropolitanate. In essence, the Rus' delegation at Basle, if in attendance, of its own volition remained unproductive in the process of resolving delicate questions and apparently estranged from the overall proceedings.

Contemporaneous fifteenth-century Rus' sources and those of the next century, especially the annals/chronicles,[77] are strangely reticent concerning the matters discussed at Basle. Questions for theological disputation, such as the "*filioque*" insertion in the Nicene Creed, the notion of the existence of a Purgatory, and the dispute over the use of leavened versus unleavened bread, among other matters, concerned the Muscovites little at the moment. Of express importance to them was the matter of ecclesiastical authority – the claim of the primacy of the pope at Rome over the Constantinopolitan patriarchate and its implications for the Rus'. Even modern Russian sources treat lightly the issues addressed by this assembly.[78] It is true that the Rus' metropolitanate was a branch of the Constantinopolitan patriarchate, and thus was subject to overall Byzantine jurisdiction and ecclesiastical confirmation of its metropolitans. But at the same time, the Muscovites were seeking a path to establish their ecclesiastical autonomy, an autocephalous church, independent or at the least semi-independent of both Constantinople and Rome.

By the onset of 1437, Isidore had completed his mission along with the other members of the Byzantine delegation to the Council of Basle. His return to Constantinople ushered him into a new phase in his rise in the ecclesiastical hierarchy. At the same time, he was to achieve new literary successes that brought him added prominence at the expense of his rivals. But the path to eminence was by no means free of torturous encounters and was fraught with many vines and thorns strewn along the unpaved road. His credentials as a pro-unionist were clearly established at Basle and, thereafter, he appears to have remained unwavering in this position. Whether in later years he had doubts about what had been achieved, he does not express these concerns either in his letters or other writings. How steadfast he remained in his support of church union is best understood in his role as a papal legate to numerous Orthodox areas and herein we have a better understanding of his determination to remain a loyal papal advocate for church union.

Notes

1 D.J. Geanakoplos, "The Council of Florence (1438–1439) and the Problem of Union Between the Greek and Latin Churches," *Church History* 24/4 (1955): pp. 325 and 337 n. 11.
2 The issues of *Caesaropapism*, at least the papal advocacy of jurisdictional primacy over the Eastern churches, and of church union between East and West in the century (if not in fact the four centuries) leading up to the Council of Ferrara-Florence is addressed by D.J. Geanakoplos, *Byzantine East and Latin West: Two Worlds of Christendom in the Middle Ages and Renaissance: Studies in Ecclesiastical and Cultural History* (Oxford, 1966), esp. pp. 84 ff. For the Basle Council and especially the complex secular diplomacy and the political issues prior to the assembly, cf. J.M. Buckley, "Diplomatic Background of Byzantine Support for the Papacy at Ferrara-Florence, 1438–1439," Unpublished Doctoral Dissertation, George Washington University, 1970, esp. chs. 13–30 (pp. 218–478). For an intelligent discussion of the Petrine primacy from an Orthodox perspective, cf. the essay of A. Papadakis, "The Byzantines and the Rise of the Papacy: Points for Reflection, 1204–1453," in M. Hinterberger and C. Schabel, eds. *Greeks, Latins, and Intellectual History 1204–1500*, Bibliotheca 11 (Leuven, Paris and Walpole, MA, 2011), esp. pp. 21–29 and 35–40.
3 The fundamental position of the conciliarists was their theoretical belief that in matters of ecclesiastical jurisdiction, the authority of a church council was superior to that of a pope. This notion dates its roots to the Council of Constance (1414–1418) and its stance to weaken the absolutist powers of the popes. The conciliarists further maintained that they had received their authority directly from God and their authority was superior to that of the papacy in matters of faith, schism, and reform. Cf. E. Jacob, *Essays in the Conciliar Epoch* (Manchester, 1953), *passim*; H. Herre, *Concilium Basiliense: Studien und Quellen zur Geschichte des Concils von Basel* (repr. Mendel, 1971), *passim*; idem, "Handschriften und Drucke Baser Konzilsakten," in *Deutsche Reichstagsakten unter Kaiser Sigmund*, Part 4/1: 1431–1432, 10/1 (Göttingen, 1957), pp. xcvi–ci; J. Helmrath, *Das Basler Konzil. Forschungsstand und Probleme* (Cologne and Vienna, 1987), *passim*; and J.W. Stieber, *Pope Eugenius IV, the Council of Basel, and the Secular and Ecclesiastical Authorities in the Empire: The Conflict over Supreme Authority and Power in the Church* (Leiden, 1978), *passim*.
4 For the documentation of the council, cf. the editions of S. Brant, *Decreta & acta Concilii basiliensis. . . , bound with Acta scitu dignissima docteq[ue] concinnata Constantiensis concilii celebratissimi. . .* (Basel, 1499); J.D. Mansi, *Sacrorum Conciliorum, Nova et Amplissima Collectio, in qua præter ea, quæ Phil. Labbeus et Gabr. Cossartius. . .* 30 (Venice, 1792), cols. 669–1221; *Monumenta conciliorum generalium seculi decimi quinti. Concilium Basiliense, scriptorum*, eds. F. Palacký, E. von Birk, K. Stehlin and K.W. Hieronimus, 1–4 (Vienna and Basil, 1857–1935); and E. Cecconi, ed., *Studi storici Concilio di Firenze. Con documenti inediti o nuovamente dati all luce sui manoscritti di Firenze e di Roma. Part 1: Antecedenti del Concilio* (Florence, 1869). Also, J. Haller, *Concilium Basiliense. Studien und Quellen zur Geschichte des Concils von Basel*, 1–4 (Basil, 1896–1905; repr. Nendeln, 1971).
5 For a succinct discussion of the doctrinal issues addressed at Basle and later at Ferrara-Florence, cf. the essay of D.J. Geanakoplos, "An Orthodox View of the Councils of Basel (1431–49) and of Florence (1438–39) as a Paradigm for the Study of Modern Ecumenical Councils," in *idem, Constantinople and the West*, pp. 260 ff. The article was initially published as "Die Konzile von Basel und Florentz (1431–49) als Paradigma für das Studium moderner ökumenischer Konzile aus orthodoxer Perspektive," *Theologische Zeitschrift* 38 (1982): pp. 330–359; and reprinted in its present form with corrections in the *Greek Orthodox Theological Review* 30 (1985): pp. 311–334. For the conflict between the notions of papal authority versus conciliar, cf. Zanaida V. Udal'tsova, "Борьба византийских партий на Флорентийском соборе и роль Виссариона Никкйского в заключении [= The Struggle of the Byzantine Delegation at the Council of Florence and the Role of Bessarion of Nicaea in the Conclusion of Union]," *BB* 3 (1949): pp. 107 and 113, 114.

6 There exists no direct evidence, unlike that which survives for Bessarion, that Isidore had studied with Plethon. Nowhere in his works does Plethon cite Isidore by name, although this is not unexpected, since his focus was on diverse subjects and weightier philosophical questions. Cf. *PG* 160: cols. 821–1020. Also, Woodhouse, pp. 37, 38, who further states on p. 141 that "possibly" Isidore was a student of Plethon. For an extended discussion of whether or not Isidore was a student of Plethon, cf. *supra*, ch. 1 n. 25.

7 The purpose of their visit was to resolve a jurisdictional dispute with the metropolitan of Corinth and to return the see of Maina/Mani/Mane to the governance of the metropolitan of Monemvasia. The emperor himself, John VIII, intervened in the matter and returned the see to Monemvasia.

8 For the texts of the petitions, cf. S.P. Lampros, "Δύο Ἀναφοραὶ Μητροπολίτου Μονεμβασίας πρὸς τὸν Πατριάρχην," *NH* 12 (1915): pp. 255–318; and Mercati, *Scritti d'Isidoro*, pp. 9–17. Related to Isidore's activities in Monemvasia, Laurent, "Isidore de Kiev," pp. 150–157, having carefully reviewed all evidence at hand, mainly primary sources, has concluded that Isidore was not Metropolitan of Monemvasia for that period, contrary to earlier scholarly interpretations and especially that of Zakythinos, "Μανουὴλ Β΄ ὁ Παλαιολόγος," pp. 45–69, esp. 64–69, who holds that Isidore was metropolitan of Monemvasia from 1412 to 1430. Given Isidore's extreme youth at the time, in 1412, he would have assumed the seat, if he had in fact done so, about the early age of 17 or perhaps in his early twenties. There is the possibility that he was in his early thirties, which would make him eligible for ordination to this position. Given his lack of significant accomplishments within the church thus far, let alone the question of ordination to the priesthood, it is quite improbable that Zakythinos's conclusion is true. Laurent stresses the silence of the Synodicon that lists no Isidore for the period in question. On this scholarly disputation, cf. *PaL* 2: 3, 4 and n. 5, where doubts are expressed about Zakythinos's position. Further, Ziegler, *Die Union des Konzils von Florenz*, pp. 58, 59, addresses the question of whether or not Isidore was metropolitan of Monemvasia. He concludes that in 1429 Isidore received the provisional appointment of metropolitan from the patriarch, although his tenure in this office was brief since he had moved on to Constantinople the following year. This is plausible, although again the Synodicon makes no reference to him.

9 For literature on the three renditions of *Chronicle of Monemvasia* and related texts, cf. Kalligas, *Byzantine Monemvasia: The Sources*, pp. 3 ff.

10 *PaL* 2: 4 n. 5. In a recent correspondence, Thierry Ganchou has brought to our attention that *Arch. Serg. Reg. Vat. 398*, fol. 56^r–56^v, nowhere states that Isidore was given the title of "Latin Patriarch of Constantinople," especially at the earlier date of 1452. This source only states: *vicario per nos in dictis locis ad temporalem et spiritualem jurisdictionem exercendam deputato*. On this quotation, cf. the citation of Nicolai Iorga, *NE* 2: 461, 462. Thus, as Ganchou stresses, Pope Nicholas V appointed Isidore successor to the late Giovanni Contareno (Contarini), who, however, according to Mercati, *Scritti d'Isidoro*, pp. 134, 135, Appendix 6: "Un atto patriarcale di Gregorio Mamma dell'a 1455," was designated in 1450 for the "patriarcha constantinopolitano" with authority only for the jurisdiction and revenues of patriarchal properties in Crete and Negroponte, then under Latin domination. Sylvestros Syropoulos, *Les "Mémoires" du Grand Ecclésiarque de l'Eglise de Constantinople Sylvestre Syropoulos sur le concile de Florence (1438–1439)*, ed. and trans. V. Laurent, CFDS 9 (Rome, 1971), IX.18 (p. 502) cites a papal statement at the conclusion of the Council of Ferrara-Florence negotiations (1439) and the claim that they had their own Latin Patriarch of Constantinople, Giovanni Contareno (Contarini). Syropoulos may have transposed dates, since Contareno was not, if true, given the title of Latin Patriarch of Constantinople until 1450. However, there remains the possibility that Syropoulos is correct in this citation, since his work was written in the early or mid-1440s, which then raises new questions that we are not prepared to clarify in this study. One point we should stress is that since 1261 and the termination of the Latin occupation of Constantinople the papacy appears to have continued the practice of

designating a Latin Patriarch of Constantinople, although the designees did not reside in the imperial city and little notice is given of them in the papal sources. Father Gill in his *CF* is generally critical of Syropoulos, going to the extreme to accuse him of emotionalism, if not exaggeration, in recounting the personages and events at Ferrara-Florence. For Gill's criticisms of Syropoulos, cf. *ibid.*, pp. xi–xvi and 233, 234. Michael Angold, on the other hand, in his *The Fall of Constantinople to the Ottomans: Context and Consequences* (Harlow, 2012), p. 76, comes to the defense of Syropoulos and asserts that "Sylvester Syropoulos wrote an account of the council of Ferrara Florence which ranks among the most accomplished historical works produced by a Byzantine." For a significant interpretation of the work of Syropoulos, cf. D. Geanakoplos, "A New Reading of the Acta, especially Syropoulos," in G. Alberigo, ed. *Christian Unity: The Council of Ferrara-Florence 1438/39–1989*, Bibliotheca Ephemeridum Theologicarum Lovaniensium 97 (Leuven, 1991), pp. 325–351. In addition, there is no suggestion within Mercati's study that either Contareno or later Isidore was ordained and formally given the title of "Titular Latin Patriarch of Constantinople." However, expanding upon this earlier reference, Father Georg Hofmann, "Quellen zu Isidor von Kiew als Kardinal und Patriarch," *OCP* 18 (1952): p. 152, states: "Der Kardinalbischof von Sabina, Isidor von Kiew, wurde am 24. Januar 1452 Nachfolger des lateinischen Patriarchen von Konstantinopel, und die Verwaltung der Patriarchatsgüter des lateinischen Patriarchen von Konstantinopel, Johann Contareno." The *Curriculum Vitae Isidori*, included in *Isidorus Arch. Kioviensis et Totius Russiae*, CFDS, Series A, vol. X, fasc. 1, pp. vii, viii, gives no notice that Isidore was designated "Titular Latin Patriarch of Constantinople." In point of fact, the *Curriculum* does not cite any Latin positions held by Isidore and cites only his Greek offices. The source for Hofmann's claim that Isidore was elevated to the titular Latin seat in Constantinople in 1452 remains suspect. On the other hand, if we carefully examine *Arch. Serg. Reg. Vat. 398*, fol. 56, that is addressed as *Calistus etc. Venerabili Fratri Philippo Archiepiscopo Cretensi, salutem etc.*, and is dated the seventh Ide of July, 1455, the first year of his pontificate (the pontificate of Nicholas came to a conclusion in the same year upon his death); G. Hofmann, "Papst Kalixt III, Entscheidet die Frage ob der lateinische Patriarch von Konstantinopel eine kirchlicher Ernennung in den lateinischen Bistuemern Kretas vornehmen darf," in *Miscellanea Giovanni Mercati, 3: Letteratura e Storia Bizantina*, Studi e Testi 123 [Vatican City, 1946], p. 218, revises the date to 24 January 1452, attributing the document to the pontificate of Nicholas V, and this is puzzling given the salutation of Calixtus III, Isidore was not awarded the title of "Titular Latin Patriarch of Constantinople" until the death of the exiled Orthodox Patriarch Gregory III Mammas in 1459. The pertinent sections of *Arch. Serg. Reg. Vat. 398* read:

> *Sane pro parte tua nobis nuper exhibita petitio continebat, quod, licet archiepiscopi vel primates in diocesibus suffraganeorum suorum foraneos officiales constituere nequeant iuxta canonicas sanctiones, tamen venerabilis frater noster Ysidorus, episcopus sabinensis ac perpetuus commendatarius ecclesie constantinopolitane, pretextu quarundam litterarum in forma brevis per felicis recordationis Nicolaum papam V predecessorem nostrum sibi concessarum quondam vicarium seu foraneum officialem in diocese tua cretensi provincie constantinopolitane preter consuetudinem inibi approbatam et contra santiones predictas constituere et deputare molitur in tuam iniuriam et contemptum. . . . Nos igitur, qui in iusticia cunctis fideliter debitores existimus, huiusmodi supplicationibus inclinati litteras predictas revocantes, cassantes et annullantes illasque ad statum debitum et rationabilem reducentes, quod episcopus sabinensis prefatus sive alius commendatarius vel administrator ratione eiusdem constantinopolitane ecclesie vel pro tempore existens constantinopolitanus patriarcha, perpetuis futuris temporibus nisi in casibus a iure permissis dumtaxat et non alias in tua et suffraganeorum tuorum diocesibus vicarium sive officialem huiusmodi constituere et deputare possit seu debeat.*

For a more thorough discussion of this papal bull and the award to Isidore, cf. Hofmann, "Papst Kalixt III," pp. 218, 219 n. 19; and cited *infra*, n. 24, esp. p. 348, wherein he stands partially corrected. Further, neither *Vat. Reg. 468* nor *Vat. Reg. 470* states that Isidore

74   *Isidore and the Council of Basle*

had earlier been named either "Titular Latin Patriarch of Constantinople" or "Latin Patriarch of Constantinople." We also encounter other differences in the primary sources to complicate this discussion. E.g., N. Iorga, ed., *NE* 2: 29, records that on the 28th of September 1452 a refugee in Rome, Roberto, deposited 200 florins *prototidem solutis rev^{mo} d. patriarchae Constantinopoli pro subventione expensarum suarum*. This does not imply that Isidore held the patriarchal title of the city, only that the patriarchal office received this sum for its maintenance.

11 X.10 (p. 486).
12 X.24 (p. 510).
13 36.12.
14 36.5–6.
15 On Nestor-Iskander's report that he had seen "the patriarch," whom he names as both Athanasios and Anastasios, cf. *supra*, ch. 1, n. 1.
16 Cecconi, p. 186 f.
17 Ruth Macrides, J.A. Munitiz, and D. Angelov, *Pseudo-Kodinos and the Constantinopolitan Court: Offices and Ceremonies*, Birmingham Byzantine and Ottoman Studies 15 (Farnham, 2013), p. 169. On this church office that was established in the fifteenth century, cf. J. Darrouzès, *Recherches sur les ΟΦΦΙΚΙΑ de l'Eglise byzantine* (Paris, 1970), pp. 59, 60, 101–103, and 285–288.
18 Macrides, *et al.*, pp. 281 and 309; and Darrouzès, pp. 109–111.
19 Sylvestros Syropoulos II.22 (p. 126).
20 *Decrees of the Ecumenical Councils*, 1: *Nicaea I to Lateran V*, ed. N.P. Tanner (Washington, DC, 1990), p. 456.
21 II.19 (120).
22 *Ibid*.
23 *Ibid.*, 20 (122). Complications resulted in the meantime and Sylvestros Syropoulos addresses these from an Orthodox perspective. Cf. his account of the difficulties, *ibid.*, II.21 and 22 (pp. 124 and 126).
24 *Orientalium Documenta Minora*, CFDS, series A, ed. G. Hofmann, 3, fasc. 3: (Rome, 1953), doc. 3 (6, 7). In the heading of the letter, it bears the date of 13 October 1433, but was signed two days later.
25 *Ibid.*, doc. 4 (8, 9). The accompanying letter, dated 28 November 1433, appears as document 5, *ibid.*, p. 9, but without accompanying text and only a brief notice. Cf. Cecconi, doc. XIV (pp. xxxvi, xxxvii); and doc. XV (p. xxxviii), dated 11 November 1433, for the imperial mandate to the delegation.
26 Sylvestros Syropoulos II.23 (pp. 126, 127). Cf. Cecconi, docs. XIV (pp. xxxvi, xxxvii) and XXX (pp. lxxxviii–xcii). For their difficult journey to Basle, cf. Gill, *Personalities of the Council of Florence*, p. 66.
27 Cf. V. Laurent, "Le dernier gouveneur byzantine de Constantinople: Démétrius Paléologue Métochitès," *REB* 15 (1957): pp. 197–206.
28 Little is known of him, although the family name was prominent during the Palaiologan era and the families were linked through marriage. For a citation of him in the agreement of 7 September 1434 between the council and the Greeks, cf. Cecconi, doc. XXXII (pp. xcvi–xcix); and Tanner, 1: 478–482.
29 Cf. Haller, 1: 361, and doc. LXXIX.
30 For the failed efforts and a contrast of events in 1438 and 1452–1453, cf., e.g., W.K. Hanak, "Pope Nicholas V and the Aborted Crusade of 1452–1453 to Rescue Constantinople from the Turks," *BS* 65 (2007): pp. 337–359. The prelude to Basle and the ongoing intense rivalry between the Basle reformers and the papacy is competently recounted by Sylvestros Syropoulos II.7–9 (p. 108–111), 13 (pp. 114, 115), and 19–32 (pp. 120–137). For the most courteous and engaging statements in the prefatory remarks of the Byzantine delegation, cf. Mansi, 30: cols. 680–685. Ziegler, "Isidore de Kiev," p. 402, attributes these remarks to Isidore, although this may not be accurate, since Demetrios Palaiologos Metokhites was the head of the delegation and the preparation

Isidore and the Council of Basle   75

of the document was most probably a joint effort of the three delegates. It is possible, however, because of Isidore's oratorical skills that he delivered the remarks, thus leading to the confusion of authorship. Further, Isidore set the tone for his ecclesiastical position, one that he unwaveringly maintained throughout his lifetime. For further analysis of the arrival and the immediate events, cf. Pierling, 1: 11 ff.; and *CF*, p. 50.

31 W.T. Waugh, "The Councils of Constance and Basle," in J.B. Bury, *et al.*, eds. *The Cambridge Medieval History* 3 (Cambridge, 1936), p. 35.

32 The Hussites, though condemned as a heretical body well over a decade earlier at the Council of Constance, had been invited to Basle on the 10th of October 1431, and were promised safe-conduct in session four on 20 June 1432 to participate in a liberal discussion of their theological views. Cf. Tanner, 1: 460, 461; but conspicuously absent in Cecconi 1. The Hussites, however, placed conditions for their participation, and after some delay, arrived on the 4th of January 1433. On the Hussites and their attendance at Basle, cf. J. Gill, *Constance et Bâle-Florence* (Paris, 1965), pp. 133, 135, 139, 140, 165, 167–170, 172–174, and 179. Also cf. Miladá Paulová, "L'Empire byzantine et les Tchèques avant la chute de Constantinople," *BS* 14 (1953): p. 160:

> Les catholiques eux-même reconnaissaient cette analogie entre les Grecs et les Hussites, donnant ainsi involontairement naissance en Bohême à l'idée d'établir une Union avec l'Eglise byzantine. Ce fut ainsi qu'Enée Sylvius reprocha aux Taborites d'avoir copié le calice des Grecs. Toutefois, au XVe siècle, des nouvelles parvinrent en Bohême des vastes actions politico-religieuses et enfin, de l'union de Florence meme.

She adds (p. 161): "Et au concile de Bâle, nous pouvons constater que ce sont déjà les Tchèques qui réclament la presence, bien que vainement, des Grecs." On the Czech presence and involvement in the proceedings of the Council of Basle, cf. *ibid.*, pp. 162 and 166–169.

33 The question of military aid and financial assistance for the Byzantine delegation's attendance at Basle and also Ferrara-Florence has been addressed by Sylvestros Syropoulos II.32 ff. and 196 ff. Cf. A. Black, "Popes and Councils," in C. Allmand, ed. *The New Cambridge History* 7 (Cambridge, 1998), pp. 70, 71; Geanakoplos, *Byzantine East and Latin West*, pp. 92, 93; *idem*, "Byzantium and the Crusades, 1354–1453," in K.M. Setton, ed. *A History of the Crusades* 3: *The Fourteenth and Fifteenth Centuries*, ed. H.W. Hazard (Madison, 1975), pp. 91, 92.

34 The Greek text was only recovered in the twentieth century by S.P. Lampros. Having extracted the essay from *Palatino gr. 226*, fols. 180^v–183^r, he published it in *ΠκΠ* 1: 3–14. His comments in the "Introduction," pp. ιζ´–ιη´, declare that he was unaware of the identity of the author, whom he cited as "Anonymous." Moreover, Lampros was under the impression that this speech was delivered during the Council of Ferrara-Florence and this notion led him to publish it under the title of Ἀνωνύμου ϖρὸς τὴν ἐν Φλωρεντίᾳ Σύνοδον. After his death, a committee undertook a revision of his materials and concluded that it was indeed a speech delivered at Basle. One of the collaborators involved in the process of reviewing Lampros's materials, I.K. Bogiatzides, his student and protégé, realized that various humanists had translated this text into Latin and thus it was delivered during the Synod of Basle. He arrived at this conclusion based upon an appended Latin note (*ΠκΠ* 1: νγ´) that reads: *Propositio facta per dominum legatum in concilio Basiliensi in publica congregatione ambaxiatoribus graecorum*. With this realization, Bogiatzides was able to make many corrections to Lampros's edition based upon the Latin translations and he republished a much-improved Greek text in an Appendix, pp. 324–335, to the same volume. However, Bogiatzides remained unaware of the true author of the Greek text and published the work under the title of Ἀνωνύμου ϖρὸς τὴν ἐν Βασιλείᾳ Σύνοδον. Next, Mercati, pp. 1–4, on the strength of the handwriting of the *Palatino gr. 226* and on the strength of another Latin note accompanying Aurispa's translation, *ibid.*, p. 2 n. 3: *Translatio, facta per Aurispam, orationis graecorum factae in Congregatione Basiliensis per alterum oratorum ipsorum graecorum, de graeco in latinum, per archiepiscopum Rucensem, tunc*

abatum Sancti Demetrii Ordinis Basilii, was able to demonstrate that the author was indeed Isidore, who at that moment was undeniably the abbot of Saint Demetrios Monastery in Constantinople and was a member of the Greek delegation. Although scholars have assigned no title to the Latin rendition, its incipit is: *Primum quidem, o sacrosancta synode*. Cf. Cecconi, doc. XXIX (pp. lxxx–lxxxvii), which may serve as a working title, since the first three words of the first paragraph are generally and normally employed to title a document. Further, Cecconi (p. lxxx) assigned authorship to Isidore, but only identified him as the abbot of Saint Demetrios Monastery and the "archbishop" of the Ruthenians (Rus'). Cf. also Mercati, pp. 1–4, who is critical of Bogiatzides for having overlooked the much earlier work of Cecconi.

35 *MP*, p. 424.
36 The attribution to a translator reads: *Translatio, facta per Aurispam, orationis græcorum factæ in Congregatione sacri Concilii Basiliensis per altum oratorum ipsorum græcorum, de græco in latinum, per archiepiscopum Rucensem, tunc abbatem Sancti Demetrii Ordinis sancti Basilii*. Cecconi, p. lxxx; as well as Gill, *Personalities of the Council of Florence*, p. 67, accept that the translation into Latin issues from the pen of Aurispa. Also, Aurispa was known to have traveled to Constantinople. It is unclear from the evidence at hand whether he and Isidore had met prior to the Council of Basle or had collaborated in the matter. For a comprehensive treatment of Aurispa's contributions, especially at the Council of Ferrara-Florence, cf. Lidia Caciolli, "Codici di Giovanni Aurispa e di Ambrogio Traversari negli anni del Concilio di Firenze," in P. Viti, ed. *Firenze e il Concilio del 1439. Convegno di Studi Firenze, 29 novembre–2 dicembre 1989*, Biblioteca Storica Toscana 29, 2 (Florence, 1994), pp. 559–647.
37 Isidore apparently is making reference to the ninth-century "Photian Schism" that led to the split in Christendom two centuries later, the division of 1054 that had not been healed by the early fifteenth century. On the Photian Schism, cf. the eloquent study of F. Dvornik, *The Photian Schism: History and Legend* (Cambridge, 1948). Cf. his Appendix III: "Unpublished Anonymous Greek Treatises on the Councils," pp. 452–457; "List of Manuscript's Quoted," pp. 459–461; "List of Sources," pp. 462–473; and "Bibliography," pp. 474–487.
38 Cecconi, p. lxxxi.
39 *Ibid.*, p. lxxxii.
40 Mansi, 30: cols. 871–873. Also, *Monumenta Conciliorum generalium sec. decimi quinti*, 2: 753–756.
41 The document is conspicuously absent in the collection of Mansi. However, the text is to be found in Cecconi, doc. XXXII (pp. xcvi–xcix) and for his elaboration upon it, cf. *ibid.*, pp. 58–92. On the document, cf. Gill, *Personalities of the Council of Florence*, pp. 36, 37 and 67, 68; and *CF*, pp. 54, 55.
42 The question of where to hold the synod was reviewed on the 7th of May 1437 (this date, the 7th, is not given by Cecconi, rather Tanner, 1: 510). Two sites were proffered: Basle and Avignon. The latter location must have been especially objectionable to Eugenius, for it was the seat of a rival pope. It is unlikely that either site was acceptable to the Greeks, for by now Isidore, in particular, had returned to Constantinople and it was unlikely that his two colleagues would find acceptable such choices, if only for the reason of difficulty of travel, but more so for association with a rival pope. For the session in question, the twenty-fifth, cf. Cecconi, doc. CXXI (pp. cccxxvii–cccxxxii).
43 For the full text of the document and its specific contents, translated into English, cf. *CF*, pp. 43, 44. The original Latin version appears in G. Hofmann, ed., *Epistolae pontificiae ad Concilium Florentinum spectantes*, Part 1: *Epistolae Pontificiae de Rebus ante Concilium Florentinum Gestis (1418–1438)* (Rome, 1940), doc. 26; and Cecconi, doc. VI (p. xviii), where the specific passage reads: *Item ut mittantur galee tenues due et balistarii trecenti ad custodiam civitatis, sintque capitanei galearum et balistariorum quos Imperator iusserit sibique fidem iureiurando firmet*. Also, Haller, 1: 339; and Tanner, 1: 478–482. It is more than coincidental that Isidore, as a papal legate, was familiar with the value of crossbowmen and personally retained 200 in 1452–1453 to aid in the defense of the imperial city. On this, cf. *SF*, p. 374.

44 The issue of seating at the head of the council reemerges at the outset of the Council of Ferrara and proved to be a thorny matter that almost precluded the council from reconvening later at Florence. On the latter, cf. *CF*, pp. 106, 107, and 142 ff.

45 Hofmann identifies two versions of the emperor's declaration: Florence, Biblioteca Mediceo-Laurenzia, *Codex Strozzi 33*, fol. 123ᵛ; and Biblioteca Vaticana, *Codex Palat. 597*, fol. 105ʳ. For the *Codex Strozzi 33*, cf. Hofmann, *Orientalium Documenta Minora*, doc. 13 (18, 19).

46 II.27 (130).

47 He is the renowned John Stojkovicǎ of Ragusa. Among his many accomplishments he had held the post of doctor of theology at the Sorbonne and was a companion of Cardinal Giuliano Cesarini during the struggles against the Hussites; he had been named delegate to the Council of Basle early in 1431; he had been designated envoy on numerous papal missions; and he was later, in 1442, consecrated cardinal by Pope Felix V. On Stojkovicǎ, cf. B. Duda, *Joannis Stoikoviç de Ragusio OP doctrina de cognoscibilitate Ecclesiae* (Rome, 1958); and J. Kubalik, "Jean de Raguse. Son importance pour l'ecclésiologie du XVᵉ siècle," *Revue des Sciences Religieuses* 157 (1967): pp. 150–167.

48 He may have been French. He is distinguished as a doctor of dogma.

49 He was a colleague of Henry Menger and was an envoy of the Council of Basle to the Vatican.

50 Sylvestros Syropoulos II.27 and 29 (pp. 130 and 132). Syropoulos (p. 27) relates that upon completing an agreement for the convening of an ecumenical synod and a location for its meeting, one of the three delegates would return to Basle to complete arrangements for the dispatch of galleys to transport John VIII and Patriarch Joseph to the new site. Also, the galleys would bring crossbowmen to guard Constantinople during the absence of the emperor. The other two envoys were to remain in the imperial city and would provide funds for the expenses of the council and would complete preparations awaiting the arrival of the galleys that were also bringing with them 8,000 florins. Aboard these vessels bound for Constantinople were the three envoys of John VIII, Metokhites, Isidore, and Dishypatos.

51 Cecconi, doc. LXXXIII (pp. ccxxi–ccxxiii).

52 Mansi, 30: col. 874.

53 *Ibid.*, cols. 910–913.

54 Geanakoplos, "Byzantium and the Crusades," p. 92; and *idem*, *Byzantine East and Latin West*, pp. 92–94. Cf. Waugh, pp. 35–38; and Black, pp. 70–73. Geanakoplos is correct in his interpretation. Early in 1435, John VIII had dispatched instructions to Ioannes Dishypatos to conduct primary negotiations with the papacy, thus circumventing the discussions with the fathers at Basle. As we have previously observed, the latter made charges of duplicity against the Byzantine delegation of negotiating with the pope and his representatives, while pretending at the same time to demonstrate their good faith in their discussions with the fathers at Basle. It is known that Isidore had played, in the meantime, a leading role in these private discussions with the pope and his envoys, the full contents of which are unknown to us with the exception of some details. On this topic, cf. *CF*, p. 59.

55 Although the issue of Greek informants, and perhaps even of Latin informers, in the process to acquire and supply information relative to ecclesiastical and secular negotiations, and of the transmission of valuable intelligence to the Ottoman Turks, has not been extensively studied, but simply alluded to, we may safely speculate that contemporaneous Byzantine writers were cognizant of informants both at Basle and later at Ferrara-Florence. To assuage Murad II, John VIII must have dispatched a delegation or, at the very least, a letter to calm the apprehensions of the sultan.

56 II.27–50 (130–158). For the variants texts, cf. *ibid.*, Recension B, II, pp. 580 ff., that repeats the essential information, but not the complete version found in the previous citation.

57 *Ibid.*, II.28 (132). Concerning the audience at the patriarchal palace, cf. Cecconi, pp. cl–clviii and cxcix.

58 Sylvestros Syropoulos II.29 (pp. 132 and 134).

59 *Ibid.*, II.31 (p. 134).
60 *Ibid.*, II.32 (pp. 136 and 138).
61 *Ibid.*
62 *Ibid.*, II.33 (p. 138).
63 *Ibid.*, II.34 (pp. 138 and 140).
64 Cf. *PLP* 12: no. 125; and Sylvestros Syropoulos II.3; and II.21.
65 Sylvestros Syropoulos II.36 (pp. 140 and 142). Questions have been raised regarding the offices held by Scholarios. More recently, see the essay of T. Ganchou, "Géôrgios Scholarios, 'Secrétaire' du Patriarche Unioniste Grègorios III Mammas? Le Mystère Résolu," *Le Patriarcat Œcuménique de Constantinople aux XIVe–XVIe siècles: Rupture et Continuité. Actes du colloque international Rome, 5–6–7 décembre 2005*, Dossiers Byzantins 7 (Paris, 2007), pp. 117–194.
66 Sylvestros Syropoulos II.37 and 38 (pp. 142 and 144).
67 *Ibid.*, II.39 (144). Cf. Cecconi, p. clxxi. At a later gathering (requested by the emperor) of Byzantine delegates appointed to negotiate with the Latins, John dismissed concerns about the contents of the preamble. The charge of heresy was a Latin issue to please their constituents and was not intended to demean the Greeks. Further, at a later meeting a new draft of the preamble was presented to the Byzantine delegation. Finally, the latter found the text acceptable and the matter was resolved. Cf. Sylvestros Syropoulos II.43 (p. 148), and 45 (p. 152).
68 Sylvestros Syropoulos II.40 (pp. 144 and 146).
69 *Ibid.*, II.41 (p. 146).
70 *Ibid.*, II.42 (pp. 146 and 148).
71 *Ibid.*, II.44 (pp. 148, 150, and 152).
72 *Ibid.*
73 *Ibid.*, II.46 and 47 (pp. 152 and 154).
74 *Ibid.*, II.48 (pp. 154 and 156).
75 *Ibid.*
76 *РИБ* 19 (1903): pp. 436, 437. A recently discovered account of Iona makes no reference of a journey to Basle. The claim of the Russian Historical Library must remain suspect. For the document in question, cf. "Новонайденная духовная граммота Митрополита Ионану [= A Newly Discovered Ecclesiastical Writing of Metropolitan Iona]," in A.I. Pliguzov, *et al.*, eds., *Рускии феодалъный архив XIV-первой трети XVI в.* [= *The Russian Feudal Archive, from the Fourteenth to the First Third of the Sixteenth Century*] 3 (Moscow, 1988), pp. 640–654. Further, the "Register of Incorporation" for the Council of Basle, based upon primary Latin sources, fails to cite by name the Greek and Slavic delegates present at the assembly. On this, cf. the unpublished doctoral dissertation of D.L. Bilderback, "The Membership of the Council of Basle," Seattle, The University of Washington, 1966, pp. 242–380, although caution should be addressed in the use of this study, since its main concern is to list the Occidental European delegates and not the Oriental. The lengthy list contains the names of a number of leading prelates who were numerically in the minority, while the majority of the attendees included doctors, masters, representatives of chapters, monks, and clerics of inferior orders.
77 The Russian series, ПСРЛ, shows no concern for the proceedings at Basle; it does not relate Iona's attendance at or participation in the discussions of the council. Reflective of the absence of citation is *ibid.*, *Московский Латописныый скодъ конца XV вѣка* [= *The Muscovite Annalistic Code at the End of the Fifteenth Century*], ПСРЛ 25 (Moscow-Leningrad, 1949).
78 Illustrative of this brief and general treatment are two works: F.I. Uspensky, *История Византийский имперій* [= *A History of the Byzantine Empire*] 3 (Moscow-Leningrad, 1948), p. 771 f.; and B. Ia. Ramm, *Папство и Русь в X–XV веках* [= *The Papacy and Rus' in the Tenth–Fifteenth Centuries*] (Moscow-Leningrad, 1959), p. 224 f.

3 The rise of Isidore and the Council of Ferrara-Florence

1 Metropolitan of Kiev and of All Rus'

Having achieved commendable successes at Basle, at least from the Byzantine viewpoint, Isidore returned to the imperial city. He had demonstrated his skills in ecclesiastical and secular diplomacy, and presumably resumed his position even if ever so briefly as abbot of Saint Demetrios monastery. His stay in the imperial city proved to be rather short-lived, for soon after his return he was nominated in early 1437 by the patriarch and the patriarchal synod and then confirmed by the emperor to the office of the metropolitan seat of Kiev and of All Rus'.[1] Though formally he was elected by the Synod of the Ecumenical Patriarch, he was, as we have previously noted, closely linked to the imperial Palaiologan family and thus received his appointment with the concurrence of both the patriarch and emperor. Isidore was a suitable candidate for the office. As was customary within patriarchal and imperial circles over the course of a number of centuries, and a practice that continues to the present, promising young men were extensively educated and highly trained for privileged ecclesiastical offices, after a strict selective process.[2] Thus Isidore (also cited as Sidor in medieval Slavic sources) was well prepared for the Kievan seat, because of his learning, training, and experience.

The scene in internal and external affairs for Muscovite Rus', however, was indeed complex during the decade of the 1430s.[3] The grand prince of Moscow was the youthful Vasilii II Vasil'evich (the "Blind," also cited as the "Dark," because he had his sight taken from him while held captive by a rival c. 1448); known for his lack of distinguishing qualities, he was unfaltering in enforcing his policies of state unification and the preservation of Orthodoxy; yet he was confronted with internal princely discords in addition to external threats. Family members, both of domestic and foreign origin, generated these discords. At the same time, Rus' church authorities exercised considerable influence upon the grand prince, some supporting his efforts and others favoring their own provincial princes. In seeking, then, to consolidate his political authority as the grand prince, Vasilii faced the opposition of independent-minded princes who pursued their own policies and were not in favor of a centralized princely authority at Moscow. Involved in these disputes were Vitovt, the grand duke of Lithuania, and his successor Svidrigailo. Vasilii's task was indeed formidable and made all the more difficult, since the Muscovite Rus' remained under the Mongol yoke, although the Mongol administrative control had been weakened; yet a *yarlik* (charter) as a symbolic act of subservience was still issued for an acceptable grand princely candidate by these Asiatic rulers. Thus at this juncture, the Mongols played no small part in resolving disputes among numerous Rus' princes and Muscovy's foreign rivals. They attempted to preserve as much of their hegemony and influence as was possible under these fluid conditions.

Upon the death of the Greek-born metropolitan Photios[4] in 1431 (the year 1433 is erroneously given in some scholarly works) the grand prince, acceding to the desires of the Muscovite Synod, supported Iona's provisional nomination as metropolitan, bearing the title of metropolitan-designate, and placed him in the position at least in an acting capacity until his confirmation and consecration by the Constantinopolitan patriarch. Iona was the bishop of Riazan and was favored by the Muscovite Synod. Hereafter, the chronicle evidence and secondary literature concerning Iona's confirmation becomes confusing. J.S. Luria provides an interesting if somewhat inaccurate observation of what then followed. He relates:[5]

> These chronicles [Muscovite and others], and historians after them, confirm that Iona traveled to Constantinople and received the conditional consent of the patriarch to take on the duties of the metropolitan see. Earlier chronicles, however, say nothing of Iona's trip and the patriarch's promise; documents on Iona's trip appear in the manuscript tradition considerably later, contradict each other, and in my opinion, show signs of later falsification. Iona's recently discovered testament[6] says not one word about the trip.

Although much of the statement remains accurate and is applicable to the late fifteenth- and sixteenth-century annals and contemporaneous works, there arises the question of whether or not Luria has confused two dates, namely 1431, the year of Iona's nomination as provisional metropolitan pending his confirmation by the patriarch, and 1437, the year when he traveled to Constantinople to seek confirmation and ordination for this office. Citing the *Московский Летописный свод Конца XV Века*, Luria appears to have misread the citation, which states:[7]

О поставлении на митрополью Русскую Иону владыку Рязанского. В лѣто <69>57 [1449]. Мѣсяца декабря 15...сними единомысленни на поставление на митрополию Ионы владыкы Рязаньского. А преже того, коли въ Царѣградѣ былъ о не — правлении митрополии, и онъ и от свѧтѣншего патриарха и от всего еже о нем свѧ —щеннаго собора благословенъ последи Сидора [Исидора] на митрополию.

Concerning the consecration upon the Rus' metropolitan [seat] of Iona, the bishop of Riazan. In the year <69>57 [1449, or rather correctly 1448]. In the month of December the 15th ... with their agreement[8] on the consecration to the metropolitan seat of Iona, the bishop of Riazan. But prior to this, inasmuch as there was in Tsargrad [Constantinople] a modification for the metropolitanate and [for] him, and from the most holy patriarch and all that concerned him, the sacred and blessed synod elevated Isidore to the metropolitan [seat].

The annalistic entry refers to the events of 1437 and makes no reference to 1431 when Iona was first designated for the seat. Further, there is no written evidence, either Muscovite or Byzantine, to establish that Iona went to Constantinople at this earlier date or thereabouts to be accepted provisionally or to be consecrated metropolitan of Rus'. It is very unlikely that he had made this journey that was probably prevented by Muscovite and Byzantine internal and external matters. The eastern Muscovite Orthodox high clergy had supported Iona's election. But almost simultaneously the grand duke of Lithuania, Svidrigailo, with the consent of the western Orthodox high clergy subject to his political jurisdiction, selected Gerasim to be the metropolitan of Kiev and of All Rus'.[9] Thus Gerasim from 1432 onward administered the western Orthodox dioceses from his seat at Smolensk. It is noteworthy that Lithuania at the moment occupied Kiev and much of the surrounding territory, but Gerasim did not attempt to reside at that center. Two years later, in 1434, Gerasim traveled to Constantinople, where his nomination was approved, having demonstrated his support for church union, and he was consecrated metropolitan.[10] The Constantinopolitan authorities, at the expense of denying the position to Iona, favored Gerasim's election and consecration. It is understandable, then, that for the period of 1432 to 1435 Iona had no legitimate claim to the metropolitan seat of Kiev and of All Rus', for another held the office. It was only after Gerasim was executed, burned at the stake in July 1435, having been charged with political heresy or specifically treason, that Iona and the Muscovites could now again attempt to legitimize his office as metropolitan and seek his consecration. It is plausible that after 1432 it was neither possible nor practical for the grand prince of Moscow to dispatch Iona to Constantinople for confirmation. Also, until the papal-conciliar issues were resolved at Basle, the office of the Rus' metropolitan centered at Moscow remained in an indeterminate state, with no clear resolution possible for its immediate need for a consecrated metropolitan.

Iona was at last dispatched to the imperial city to be confirmed and consecrated. The sources do not indicate the year, but most probably it was early 1437, or perhaps late in the previous year. The Byzantines appear to have been aware of his coming and were prepared to deal with this anti-unionist candidate. He presented his credentials for the office of metropolitan to the patriarch, and also sought the concurrence of the emperor.[11] Iona was denied confirmation and instead Isidore was designated for the position, having been selected by the patriarchal synod.[12] It was essential for the Byzantines to maintain their ecclesiastical jurisdiction over the Rus' seat in order to achieve the union of churches and to secure papal or conciliarist military aid for the defense of the imperial city. Isidore was a strong proponent of church union and had faithfully served the interests of the emperor and the Byzantine Church. His nomination for the Kievan seat was a foregone conclusion, for he had been nurtured for this position and had demonstrated his allegiance to the Constantinopolitan authorities.

The early sixteenth-century *Патриаршая или Никоновская Лѣтописъ*, the first of four texts that we shall examine, records Isidore's reception in Moscow in a most favorable light for the grand prince. The text reads:[13]

Прииде изо Царяграда на Москву Исидоръ митрополитъ. Тое же весны, въ вторникъ Свѣтлыя недѣли, по Велицѣ дни, прииде на Москву изо Царяграда отъ патриарха Иосифа на митрополью Исидоръ митрополитъ, Гречинъ, многимъ языкомъ сказатель и книженъ; и приятъ его князь велики Василей Васильевичь честнѣ, и молебная пѣвше въ святѣй соборнѣй церкви пречистыя Богородици, и сотвори нань пирование велие князь велики Василей Васильевичѣ, и дары свѣтлыми и многими одари его.

The Arrival from Tsargrad [Constantinople] to Moscow of Metropolitan Isidore. In the Spring[14] on the Tuesday of Bright Week, after the Great Day [Resurrection or Easter Sunday], Metropolitan Isidore, a Greek, came to Moscow for the metropolitanate from Tsargrad [Constantinople], from the Patriarch Joseph. [He was] a speaker of many languages and learned.[15] The upright grand prince Vasilii Vasil'evich received him and celebrated supplications in the holy cathedral church of the Most Pure Mother of God; and the grand prince Vasilii Vasil'evich held a great feast for him and bestowed upon him many holy gifts.

But after illustrating the cordial reception accorded to Isidore, the entry then provides a lengthy passage, demonstrating the differences of opinion that almost immediately had arisen between them. The passage relates:[16]

О Исидорѣ митрополитѣ. Того же лѣта Исидоръ митрополитъ всеа Русии начатъ глаголати великому князю Василью Васильевичю, сице глаголя, яко преосвященный киръ Иосифъ патриархъ и благочестивый киръ Калуянъ царь Мануиловичь Греческий Константинаграда совѣтоваша со всѣмъ священнымъ соборомъ и со князи и з бояры, еже быти осмому собору съ папою и со всѣми Римляны, мятежа ради и раскола Греческия церкви съ Римъскою, и землямъ и царствиамъ о любопрении и разтворении пречистаго тѣла и честныя крови Христовы, еже въ кисломъ хлѣбѣ и во опрѣсноцѣ, и о Святѣмъ Дусѣ, и тако быти подвизашеся прежней ходатай собору тому. Глагола ему князь велики: «при нашихъ прародителехъ и родителехъ соединения закона не бывало съ Римляны, и язъ не хощу, понеже не приахомъ мы отъ Грекъ въ соединении закона быти съ ними». Исидоръ же митрополитъ не послуша сего, но тщашеся вседушно, хотя ити на осмой соборъ къ папа Евгению и къ патриарху Иосиоу и киръ къ Калуяну царю Греческому въ Римскую страну. И рече ему князь велики Василей Васильевичь: «отче Исидоре, мы теб'в не повел'вваемъ ити на осмон соборъ въ латыньскую землю, ты же, насъ не слушаш, хощеши тамо ити; но се ти буди в'вдомо: егда оттуду възвратишися къ намъ, принеси къ намъ нашу христианскую в'вру Греческаго закона, якоже приаша прародители наши отъ Грекъ». Онъ же тако об'вщася сътворити и клятну на ся възложи ничтоже странна и чюжа не принести отъ Латынъ въ Рускую землю отъ осмаго ихъ собора, но православие истинное соблюсти Греческаго закона, мнася мудр'ве мудр'вишихъ, и учинися з безумными въ сограсии.

Concerning Metropolitan Isidore. In this year [6945/1437] Isidore, the metropolitan of All Rus' began to relate to the grand prince Vasilii Vasil'evich, how the most holy lord Patriarch Joseph and the devout lord, the emperor Kalojan [= "Good John," John VIII, the son of] Manuel, of the Greek City of Constantine [Constantinople], consulted with all the priestly council and with the princes and with the nobles, that being with the papists and with all Romans [Latins] at the Eighth Council, because of rebellion and schism of the Greek church from the Roman, and the lands and the empires concerning a disagreement of the mixing of the most pure body and precious blood of Christ, whether in sour [leavened] and in unleavened bread, and of the Holy Spirit, and thus the foregoing had driven that one [him] to attend this council. The grand prince said to him: "Among our forefathers and parents there was no law of union with the Romans, and I do not desire [it], because it was not brought to us from the Greeks to have a unification law with them." Metropolitan Isidore did not adhere to this, but hastened full of spirit, desiring to go to the Eighth Council, to Pope Eugenius and to Patriarch Joseph, and to the lord Kalojohn [John VIII], the Greek emperor, [and] to the Roman land. And the grand prince Vasilii Vasil'evich said to him: "Father Isidore, I will enjoin you not to go to the Eighth Council in the Latin land. You do not listen to us; you desire to go there. But it will be apparent to you: When you thereafter return to us, bring to us our Christian faith of the Greek law, as our forefathers brought [it] from the Greeks."[17] He thus vowed, taking an oath upon himself, to impose nothing strange nor foreign from the Latins upon the Rus' land from the Eighth Council, but to observe the true Greek Orthodox laws, countenancing the wisest of the wise, and repair from the senseless toward concord.

Unlike the *Patriarchal or Nikon Annal*, the late fifteenth-century *Muscovite Annalistic Code* provides an earlier variant text addressing Isidore's arrival in Moscow and his discussion with the grand prince. This passage relates:[18]

О Сидор'в митрополит'в, какъ прииде из Царяграда на Москву. В л'вто <69>45 [1437] прииде из Царяграда на Москву митрополит Сидоръ въ вторникъ св'втлыя нед'вли по велиц'в дни, и приать его князь велики честно. Онъ же сы подсерж'ваемъ бысть сатаною и по мал'вх временех своего пришествия начат дръзновенно тщатися к соборному путшествию, и пов'вдаша,

ıако быти нынѣ в Римьстѣи земли събранью осмаго собора, мятежа ради и
разскола еже Грѣчьстѣи церкви с Римскою о растворении сватаго тѣла и крове
божиıа сватѣмь жрътвенницѣ, еже в кисломъ хлѣбѣ растворение, даж и въ
пресноцех, и ‖ прочее о сватѣмъ дусѣ, и тако нарицашеся прежнии исхода-
таи збору тому. Благовѣрныи же великии кнази Василеи Васильевичь богомъ
вразумѣваемъ глаголаши ему, да не поидет на составление осмаго збора
латыньского, ниже съблазнитьса в ересех их, и възбраниаше ему о сих. К сему
же повелѣ и еще глаголати ему, ıако да останетсıа таковыıа мысли съвръшати,
и много глаголаши ему, и не послушаше сицевых, но ıако ненсто сıа дѣıаше.
И по сем ркоша ему: «вѣси ли, отче, заповѣдь сватыхъ правилъ сватыхъ
отецъ, ıако же о сих богоносции отци сватии, седмыи съборъ съвръшивше
и въ сватыхъ правилѣх Устав и божественыи законъ сватыхъ апостолъ весь
положивше, и сватую вѣру православна запечатлѣша проповѣдью отца и
сына и сватаго духа, чтуще сватую троицю, едино божество нераздѣлимо.
О осмом же соборѣ съставлıающих проклıатию предаша и анафема их нар-
екоша и с еретикы их отлучи единосложно, богу спротивнаıа дѣлающин. Он
же сих никако же послушати можаше. Благочестиıа же ревнитель и споспѣшник
истиннѣ благовѣрныи кнази великы Василеи Васильевичь сицеваıа рече к нему:
«о, Сидоре, дръзновенно дѣеши, в латыньскую земл идеши и составление
осмаго собора побѣдаеши, его же отрекошасıа сватии отци. Нынѣ же, аще и не
останешисıа мысли своеıа, но буди вѣдаıа, егда възвратишисıа оттуду к намъ,
‖ то принеси к нам изначальствѣнѣишее прежьнее благое съединение нынѣшнее
въснавшее в нас благочестие и Устав божественаго закона и правлениıа сватыıа
церкви. Он же зѣло тıажькскую о сих клıатву на сıа положи, рекуще, ıако ничто
же странна и чюжа не принести от латынъ в Русскую земл иесъ осмаго их
собора, но ıатьсıа, рече, крѣпцѣ стоıати о православии и по сватѣмъ правилом
побарати о благочестии. Лжесловеснѣ бо глаголаше сиıа, скрываıа мысль злую
в сердци своемь, хотıа съвратити люди божиıа с истиннаго пути сватыıа
вѣры и соединити к латыном, мнѣвъ себѣ единого мудрѣиша въ всѣх…».

Concerning Metropolitan Sidor [Isidore], how he arrived from Tsargrad [Constantinople] to Moscow. In the year <69>45 [1437], Metropolitan Sidor arrived in Moscow from Tsargrad on the Tuesday of Bright Week after the Great Day [Resurrection or Easter Sunday], and the grand prince received him with honor. He [Isidore] was satanically surrounded by those [followers][19] and in a short time after his arrival he began with audacity to exert himself for a journey to the council and disclosed how now there was in the Roman lands a gathering of the Eighth Council, because of the rebellion and the schism between the Greek Church and the Roman, concerning a mixing of God's holy body and blood in the holy gifts, whether in the separate sour [leavened] bread and that in the unleavened, and ‖ further concerning the Holy Spirit; and thus drawing upon the preceding he chose to depart for this assembly. The Orthodox grand prince Vasilii Vasil'evich with godly comprehension said to him: "Do not go for the forming Latin Eighth Council. Be not seduced by their heresy," and prohibited these to him. He enjoined to them and again said to him how such thoughts remained to lead astray and said much to him. He [Isidore] did not listen to such views, but acted as a madman. And following this [the grand prince] said to him: "Father, if you have influence, correct the sacred precepts of the holy fathers, as these are God-given to the holy fathers, accomplished at the Seventh Council and set forth in the holy precepts, and all was placed in the divine law of the holy apostles and inculcated in the teachings of the sacred Orthodox faith of the Father, the Son, and the Holy Spirit, being the Holy Trinity, one indivisible divinity." Concerning the composition of the Eighth Council, malediction betrayed it and reproached them as anathema, and declared the full body anathematized as heretics, working in opposition to God. He [Isidore] in no way would listen to these [words]. The Orthodox grand prince Vasilii Vasil'evich thus said to him, the pious zealot and veritable promoter: "O Sidor, speaking in confidence, you are going to the Latin land and communicating the gathering Eighth Council, that is disavowed by the holy fathers. For the present time, if you do not cease your thoughts, it will be known when you return to us from there, || bringing this to us as formerly the most immemorial favorable union currently celebrated by us the blessed and the decree of the divine law, and the administration of the sacred church." With difficulty, he took an oath upon himself, stating that he would bring nothing strange nor foreign from the Latins to the Rus' land, from the Eighth Council, but cling, he said, to stand firmly for Orthodoxy and to struggle for the sacred precepts concerning piety. Because he had spoken falsely, concealing evil thoughts in his heart, he sought to lead astray the people of God from the true path of the sacred faith and to unite with the Latins, being of the opinion that he also was the wisest of all.

The third text to be considered, *Софийская Вторая Лѣтописъ* [= *The Second* (Redaction) *of the Sofia Annal*],[20] which was compiled in the first half of the sixteenth century, after 1520 but before 1550, preserves both the moderate language of *The Patriarchal or Nikon Annal* and the harsher invectives found in *The Muscovite Annalistic Code*. The *Sofia Annal* relates about the arrival of Isidore:[21]

О осмомъ соборѣ. Въ лѣто 6946 [1438] въ лѣта же и во дни благочестиваго великаго князя Василіа Васильевича всеа Русн, пришедшу нѣкогда Сидору митрополиту на Руьскую землю, на второн недѣли по Велицѣ дни, и тако ему почтену бывшу отъ великаго князя, онъ же постригаемъ бысть сатонию, по малѣ времени своего пришествіа начатъ дрьзновено касатисм къ соборному путншествию; повѣдаше мко быти нынѣ въ Римстѣн земли собрани юсмаго собора, мятежа ради и раскола еже Греческой церкви съ Римскою, о растворении тѣла Господня и крови на святомъ жертвенницѣ, да еже въ кисломъ хлѣбѣ растворение даже и въ опрѣсноцѣхъ, и прочее о святомъ Дусѣ, и тако нарицашесм прежнии несходатаии собору тому. Благовѣрный же великии князь Василен Васильевичь, Богомъ вразумлмемъ, глаголаше ему, да не пондеть на составление осмаго собора латыньского, ниже съблазмитсм въ ересехъ ихъ, возбраняше ему о сихъ; къ сему же и еще глаголаше ему, яко да останетсѧ таковыѧ мысли свершати, и много глаголаше ему, и не послушаше сицевыхъ, но яко ненстовъ сѧ дѣѧше. По сихъ рекоша ему: «вѣси, отче, заповѣдь святыхъ правилъ святыхъ Отецъ, яко о сихъ богоносни Отци святии, седмый соборъ совершивше и во святыхъ правилѣхъ уставъ божественый законъ святыхъ Апостолъ весь положивше, и святу юврѣру православиа запечатлѣша проповѣди юОтца и Сына и святаго Духа, чтуще святу юТроицу, едино божество нераздѣлимо; о осмомъ же соборѣ съставляющ ихъ проклятi юпредаша.» Онъ же сихъ никакоже послушати можаше. Князь же велики по сихъ рече ему: «то идеши на осмый соборъ, емуже недостоить быти по правиломъ святыхъ Отецъ; да аще возвратишисѧ оттуду къ намъ, и то принеси къ намъ древнее благочестие, еже приѧхомъ отъ прародителѧ нашего Владимера, а нова и странна не приношаи къ намъ, понеже аще что принесеши къ намъ ново, то намъ неприѧтно будетъ.» Того же лѣта, мѣсѧца августа 15 день, поиде Сидоръ въ Римъ, на осмый соборъ, похорони въ княгни єУпраксею. Онъ же съ клѧтвою юобѣщасѧ, рекъ, не принести ему нова и странна, но крѣпцѣ стоѧти по православии и по святымъ правиломъ поборати; злу юже мысль скры во сердци своемъ, хотѧ люди Божiа совратити со истиннаго пути, мнѣвъ себе мудрѣнша паче всѣхъ.

Concerning the Eighth Council. In the year 6946 [1438, correctly 1437]. In that year and on the day of the pious grand prince Vasilii Vasil'evich, in the second week after the Great Day [Resurrection or Easter Sunday], Metropolitan Sidor arrived by carriage in the Rus' land. And thus the grand prince honored him. He [Isidore] was satanically tormented; after a short time he began with audacity to concern himself with a journey to the council. He disclosed how the Eighth Council was now gathering in the Roman lands because of the rebellion and schism between the Greek Church and the Roman, concerning a mixing of the Lord's body and blood in the holy gift that is indeed blended in the leavened bread and even in the unleavened bread, and concerning the Holy Spirit. And thus drawing upon the preceding he chose to go to this council. The Orthodox grand prince Vasilii Vasil'evich with godly comprehension said to him: "Do not go to the forming Latin Eighth Council, nor be seduced by their heresy," and prohibited these to him. | | He further added to this, how such thoughts would not stop to lead astray and said much to him: "Do not listen to such views, you act as a madman." And following this, the [grand prince] said to him: "Weigh, Father, the sacred precepts of the holy fathers, as these are God-given to the holy fathers, accomplished at the Seventh Council [Nicaea II, 787] and set forth in the holy precepts, all placed in the divine law of the holy apostles, and placed in the sacred Orthodox faith and confirmed in the teaching of the Father, the Son, and the Holy Spirit, being the Holy Trinity. Concerning the composition of the Eighth Council, malediction betrayed it." He [Isidore] in no way would listen to these. The grand prince following this said to him: "You are going to the Eighth Council. It is unworthy of the precepts of the holy fathers.

When you return from there to us, do bring to us the ancient piety | | that was received by Vladimir [I] from our ancestors, but do not bring to us the new and strange, because if you bring us the new, that will be disagreeable for us." In this year [1437] on the 15th day of the month of August, the funeral of Princess Eupraxia, Sidor went to Rome for the Eighth Council. He took an oath, himself stating, that he would not bring to him [the grand prince] the new and strange, but firmly stand for Orthodoxy and struggle for the sacred precepts.[22] He concealed evil thoughts in his heart, desiring to lead astray God's people from the true path, being of the view that he, more than others, was the wisest.

The fourth text, the *Книга Степенная Царского Родослвія* [= *The Book of Degrees of Tsarist Relationships*] of the 1560s, relates in the Fourteenth Degree[23] of Isidore's election to the metropolitan seat of Kiev and All Rus'. Preserving a harsh condemnation of Isidore and his ministry, the text reads:[24]

О несущемъ митрополите Исидоре, како лукавнова на православіе и како облечеся безуміе его, и о подвизе благочестивыхъ. И тогда преже пришествіа святаго Іоны предвари прити во Царьградъ отъ Рима зломудренный Исидоръ и некоимъ богопротивнымъ коварством дерзну восхитити поставленіе отъ патріарха на престоль Россійскіа митрополіа. Царь же и патріархъ вельми пожалиша, ако ускориша поставити Исидора, || блаженному же Іоне, ако неволею пропочествующе, глаголаху сице: «Но обаче, ими же судьбами весть Богъ, егда Исидору некое преложеніе будетъ, и тогда ты богоизбранный Христовъ святитель готовъ благословенъ воспріати богожелаемый тебе престолъ Россійскіа митрополіа»; еже и бысть последи Божимъ благоволеніемъ. И тако отпущенъ бысть и пріиде во свою епископью на Рязань. По мале же времени Исидору пришедшу на Москву, великій же князь Василій Васильевичь, неведый его развращеннаго ума и ако суща митрополита пріатъ его честне. Пребывшу же ему на Москве 4 месяц, и поиде въ Римъ на осьмый соборъ, идеже ждаху его 6 месяцъ, не соборующе, Римьскій папа Евгеній и Цареградскій патріархъ Іосиф и царь Иванъ Калуанъ. Тамо же царь глаголаше сице, ако «въ Руськой земли большее православіе и вышшее христіаньство, въ нихъ же есть || великій государь и царь, братъ мой, Василій Васильевичь, ему же мнози царіе и князи и з земльами своими служатъ». И того ради славнаго имени ждаху къ себе пришествіа Исидорова, ему же великій князь Василій много восбраняше, ако не достоитъ таковому собору быти, онъ же клятвами страшьными и тяжькими клятся, ако не побарати ему по Римлянехъ, ни хвалити Латиньскаго развращенія, ни закона, но крепко стояти о православіи.

Concerning the non-existent metropolitanate of Isidore, how [he was] cunning toward Orthodoxy and how he was invested with his madness, and concerning the exploitation of the devout. And when prior to the coming of the holy Iona, preceding the arrival to Tsargrad [Constantinople] from Rome[25] of the pernicious thinker Isidore and some ungodly [and] insidious [ones], they dared to aspire to place the patriarchal [nominee] upon the metropolitan seat of Moscow. The emperor [John VIII] and the patriarch [Joseph] conferred extensively on how to hasten the consecration of Isidore || [and] how to explain the constraint of the blessed Iona, stating thus: "Since both, for whom the will of God is their destiny, though Isidore somewhat will be a substitute, and then you the chosen of Christ the God, the prelate prepared for the elevation. God willing, you received the throne of Rus'"; – that the last was the beneficence of God. And in this way he [Iona] was dismissed and went to the episcopacy in Riazan. After a short time Isidore came to Moscow. The grand prince Vasilii Vasil'evich was unaware of his depraved intellect and how frankly he had obtained the extant metropolitan [seat]. He remained in Moscow four months, and went to Rome[26] for the Eighth Council, where he stayed for six months, not in council, [but meeting] with the Roman Pope Eugenius and the Constantinopolitan Patriarch Joseph and the Emperor John Kalojan. There the emperor thus stated how "in the Rus' land the majority is Orthodox and most are Christians. Among them there is || the grand prince and tsar [?], our brother Vasilii Vasil'evich, whom many emperors[27] and princes with their lands serve [him]." And for the sake of this honorable land, he [the grand prince] awaited the arrival of Isidore, to whom the grand prince Vasilii prohibited many [things], as it was not proper to attend such a council. He [Isidore], with dread and pain, took an oath that he would not struggle for the Roman, nor praise the Latin seduction, nor [their] law, but stand firmly for Orthodoxy.

Unlike the contemporaneous polemical literature that condemns the Latins in vitriolic terms, the passage in the *Patriarchal or Nikon Annal*, though forthright, does not damn Isidore for his views. Rather, the grand prince has made a clear statement of his objection to church union and his position on certain theological issues. Isidore, too, has made clear his intention to attend the council, over the objections of the grand prince. Thus the stage was set for a confrontation between the two men upon Isidore's return from Florence. *The Muscovite Annalistic Code*, however, reflects the acerbic language then in vogue and its tone is often harsh when addressing Isidore and his activities. *The Book of Degrees of the Tsarist Relationships* provides a brief statement of Isidore's arrival, often negative in tone, and does not preserve the theological disputation between the grand prince and the metropolitan. The book does raise a suspicion: Why did Isidore depart so quickly for the Council of Ferrara-Florence, but first go to Rome (if in fact this is true, although there is no evidence to support this contention since Pope Eugenius IV had earlier fled the city and the claim does not appear to have validity) where he remained for some months and for what purpose? This may be a misstatement, or it is implied that he went to the Roman land and not to the city itself. Further, did Isidore realize that a precarious situation was developing for him in Moscow and thus he sought to escape its immediate consequences, or did he have imperial and patriarchal instructions to set out as expeditiously as possible for the Eighth Council? Unfortunately, the surviving literature does not clearly answer nor shed light on these questions. The lesser Rus' annals are as well denigrating toward Isidore, although often their passages are brief and add little that is new.[28]

That Isidore had exacerbated the issues during his brief stay in Moscow and encountered resistance to his views and designs is apparent in the Rus' sources, if they are only partially accurate in reporting his arrival, reception, and departure. What remains unclear is the question: Did the Greeks, upon nominating him for the metropolitan seat, miscalculate Muscovite Rus' reaction? Certainly the question of Rus' aid for the relief of the imperial city was not a factor, since the Muscovites had their own internal problems and limited resources, and were in no position to send men and materials to aid in the defense of Constantinople. It is very doubtful that the Byzantines had contemplated such an outcome. Further, there is no evidence that the Byzantines sought military assistance in various forms from the Muscovites. And there is no evidence that the Muscovite Rus' had offered substantial military aid. Rather, the Greeks were determined to maintain the Muscovite metropolitanate as a subordinate unit of the patriarchate. Beyond this fact, we cannot make the assertion that Byzantine diplomacy had blundered with the appointment of Isidore. Iona was especially unacceptable to the emperor for the apparent reason that he did not support church union and had remained unwavering on this issue throughout the 1430s and 1440s. The Constantinopolitan officials as well were inflexible in supporting church union, for upon this rested their hope of obtaining western reinforcements and materials for the defense of their imperial city against the awaited Ottoman Turkish onslaught.

2 The Council of Ferrara-Florence

Isidore, traveling leisurely to Ferrara, appears to have made no attempt to attend the preliminary meetings leading up to the formal and public sessions at Ferrara. He departed Moscow either on the 15th of August or the 8th of September 1437.[29] Isidore enjoyed the role of a tourist for approximately the next twelve months, recording in detail the places that he had visited in Livonia, the Holy Roman Empire, and Italy, and the sights that he had encountered along the way.[30] He rarely devotes attention to prominent individuals encountered en route, nor does he address topics discussed. His early departure for the council provided him with an opportunity that he apparently relished to tour numerous cities and sites, and to raise funds during the course of the journey for the maintenance of his traveling staff, which numbered over 100,[31] and to receive suitable gifts for himself, thus becoming the basis for the travel account. He arrived in Ferrara on the 18th of August 1438.[32] His return journey to Moscow in 1440 carried him through Istria, Croatia, Hungary, Poland, and Lithuania, and also took nearly a year to complete.

The main sessions of the council at Ferrara had formally begun on the 8th of October, but its stay there was short-lived, ending on the 13th of December.

A variety of explanations are given for its relocation, among them the appearance of the plague the previous summer and its devastating consequences for the delegates and especially the Muscovite Rus' entourage that, upon its arrival, suffered heavy losses of humankind. The delegates then reassembled in Florence,[33] gathering there in January 1439. Only sixteen[34] general sessions are assigned to Ferrara, whereas ten, the sixteenth through the twenty-fifth, are ascribed to Florence for the dates of 26 February to 24 March 1439.[35] However, a number of minor sessions were held at Ferrara and Florence that addressed specific issues. Much of their work, nonetheless, focused on church union, although theological disputations occurred within the sessions. The most heated and extended debates centered on the issue of *filioque*, the procession of the Holy Spirit from both the Father and the Son. The Latin Church had incorporated the doctrine into their rendition of the Nicene Creed, whereas the Eastern churches, notably the Byzantine, claimed to retain the original version of the creed, thus excluding the *filioque* concept and maintaining that the Holy Spirit proceeded only from the Father.

Isidore's attendance in Florence merits particular attention. In his travel account, Isidore, most probably recorded by his assistant and companion Gregory, relates his observations in that city and his visit to Orsanmichele, though the site is not identified, where he viewed Latin images. He found one in particular to be worthy of comment:[36]

И ес въ градѣ томъ икона чюдотворна, образъ пречстыа Бжіа Мтре; и ес предъ иконою тою въ божнницѣ нецѣлѣвъшихъ людеи за 6000 доспѣты вощаны, въ образъ людеи техъ; аще кто застрѣленъ, или слѣпъ, или хромъ, или безъ рѫкъ, или великъ члкъ на конѣ прикѣхавъ, тако устроени, іако живи стоатъ, или старъ, или унъ, или жена, или дѣца, или опрочиа, || или какого потрщие на немъ было, или недугъ каковъ въ немъ быль, и како его простюло, или какова іазва, тако тои и стоитъ доспѣтъ.

> There is in that city a thaumaturgic image – a likeness of the Most Pure Mother of God. And before this image in its encasement there are 6,000 fully waxed human likenesses of those people who had been healed. If someone has been shot by an arrow, or is deaf, lame, without a hand, or a great man who arrived by horse, they are thus arranged as if they stand alive, whether aged, young, a woman, a maiden, a lad, || or however they were attired, or whatever infirmity they had, and how erect they were, or whatever the pestilence, thus it is fully developed in those standing.

The passage does not clearly establish that Isidore venerated the likeness of the Mother of God. Given that Muscovite clergy and perhaps others had accompanied him to the shrine, it is doubtful that Isidore made a public display. Rather, he may have said in the privacy of his person the appropriate religious responses. Also, no Muscovite or other sources relate this event; hence we have only this one source to draw upon.

The Byzantine delegation of 700, excluding John VIII and his immediate entourage that had sailed on his imperial vessel, arrived aboard papal vessels on the 16th of February, in time to participate in some of the early contentious debates.[37] But the proceedings began on an inauspicious note. Upon their arrival, the first stop being Venice, the Byzantine delegation suffered the experience of viewing its treasures that had been looted from Santa Sophia, other churches, and secular structures by the knights of the Fourth Crusade.[38] In spite of this unfortunate experience, the discussions proceeded and focused upon some preliminary dogmatic issues, as the differences between Roman and Byzantine interpretations, although these appear to have been limited to specific topics as the existence and functions of Purgatory, the use of leavened versus unleavened bread in the Eucharistic ceremony, and the role of the pope as the supreme head of the Catholic Church and his governance of and authority over all Christendom.[39] Upon the direction of the Byzantine emperor, the contentious question of *filioque*, the procession of the Holy Spirit from the Father or both from the Father and the Son, was not to be introduced by Byzantine theologians.[40] However, when the public sessions did convene at Ferrara and continued later at Florence, the addition of *filioque* to the Nicene Creed became a topic of substantive discussion between the Greek and Roman theologians, often contentious with and within each of the groups.[41]

Isidore, upon his arrival in August and months after the disputations had begun, deferred to Bessarion (a strong proponent of church union) and to Mark Eugenikos (the metropolitan of Ephesus and a staunch anti-unionist theologian) to continue the dogmatic debates, although he did participate in the discussions. His role as the metropolitan of Kiev and head of the Muscovite Rus' representatives lessened his position as orator, perhaps because he headed a non-Greek ecclesiastical delegation, but this did not preclude him from speaking on behalf of John VIII and the Greek delegation as he did on a number of occasions. During the ensuing deliberations with the Latin and Greek spokesmen, Isidore played a significant consultative role, often offering guidance to the emperor and being called upon by him to offer his advice on specific matters and to act as an imperial intermediary with the pope.[42] His role as the metropolitan of Kiev and of all Rus', thus, did not preclude him from furnishing valuable assistance and counsel to the emperor and he emerged as a strong advocate for the emperor's positions on a number of issues.

He was named one of six orators for the eastern churchmen at the public sessions in Ferrara and later in Florence, although Bessarion and Eugenikos were designated principal speakers, each reflecting divergent positions on dogmatic issues and in particular the questions of *filioque* and church union.[43] The silence of Isidore in the early sessions was noticeable and Ludovicus, the archbishop of Florence, questioned him. The archbishop may have intended to provoke and to urge the metropolitan of Kiev to speak and to state his positions on outstanding questions.[44] Isidore appears to have been comfortable with a limited speaking arrangement, for it left him unencumbered by theological concerns, which appear not to have been his main interest, and rather free to concentrate on matters of *Realpolitik* with the pope and his representatives, and to act often when called upon as an intermediary between the emperor and the pope. He did, on the other hand as we shall observe, concern himself with the prolonged discussions on *filioque* and other dogmatic questions. On the 1st of November at the sixth session, he set out to prepare a response to Andrew of Rhodes, thus siding with Bessarion on the question of authority to make alterations to the Nicene Creed. It is unclear whether Isidore delivered his prepared remarks or, rather and more likely, they were given to Bessarion, who incorporated them into his own text and then presented a rebuttal to the position of Andrew of Rhodes.[45]

Isidore articulated a number of written responses, but these contributions to the debates have received a modicum or little mention in modern sources that interpret especially the theological proceedings at Ferrara and at Florence. We should caution that the Occidental literature, both the primary and secondary sources, is heavily slanted to documenting and analyzing the Latin positions. Thus, we should indicate that reconstructing the dates when his written responses were delivered is problematic. Few are furnished and even those calendar notices are questionable. However, in reconstructing his written and oral contributions, we should first cite a short essay that he prepared in early October that places emphasis upon the themes of peace and charity among the disputants at the council;[46] a brief work of mid-October on the procedural customs to be adhered to by the Council of Ferrara;[47] and a third work, a draft of an address that is dated to late October and presents his views on opposing an addition to the Nicene Creed, namely the *filioque* phrase.[48]

In addition to the named texts and others,[49] two responses of Isidore during the disputations at Florence have been preserved both in Greek and Latin. In the first, delivered on the 24th of March, Isidore replies to Cardinal Andreas de Santacroce, who solicited his response, and Isidore rejoins:[50]

Quoniam autem rev. pater in hiis duabus congregationibus multa dixit et diversa, et adversis patribus et Orientalibus et Grecis Latinis, ac amplificando potius; nam vestra paternitas vere loquebatur in hiis congregationibus per VIII horas et plus, ex quibus omnibus partim errant auctoritates sanctorum, que pro nobis faciebant, partim sue Occcidentalis <ecclesie> communium, quoniam anima nostra accipit per sensus, presertim ea, que dicuntur per auditum; ea autem, que prolixe dicuntur, adducunt societatem ad aures, quia infesta est auribus societas verborum, quia sensus auditu leditur posse omnia transmittere ad animum, que prolixe dicuntur; propterea volumus, que per vestram paternitatem dicta sunt, in scriptis etiam ut detis nobis eas auctoritates allegatas in his libris, qui fuerunt Latinorum, ut partim nos possimus conferre cum auctoritatibus, que apud nos reperiuntur, partim, ut legamus in his libris, ut melius intelligamus; postea circa ista omnia diligenter considerabimus.

Because, on the other hand, the reverend father has said many things and in disagreement with these two assemblies, the Oriental and the Latin Greeks, he has enlarged capably. Your fathers speak faithfully in these assemblies during the eighth hour and beyond. All factions stray to support the sacred, which appears to us that your side, the Occidental <ecclesiastical> communion, is drawn to this association in relation to the aural, because the association is hostile to hearing the word, [and] because the sense of hearing, having been prejudiced, is able to convey all to the soul of which it is willing to speak. Therefore in the books that are implied through the adornments of the fathers, in the writings that indeed preclude us from supporting the allegations that are in these Latin books, so that in part we are able to attribute to the authors who are in the works we may discover, that in part we may gather from these books, [and] that we may somewhat understand. Thereafter, as such, we may carefully take up all.

The second preserved account of Isidore[51] is a rejoinder (no date is ascribed in the text, although it appears to have been delivered in the initial sessions at Florence) to a lecture by Rupecremata, after a sermon on the form of the Holy Eucharist by the fellow Dominican Iohannis de Torquemada:[52]

Si putarem aliquam contrarietatem inter ea, que dicta sunt per magistrum, facerem longum sermonem. Nam necesse est in contradictionibus aut confirmare aut confutare. Sed quoniam puto adiutorio dei esse concordes, per tria, que dicam, breviter me expedio. Et primo dico ex tempore; nam hoc missale, quo utimur, est traditum a Basilio et beato Grisostomo, utebamur ante tempus scismatis, nec aliqua facta est mutatio; tamen Occidentalis ecclesia numquam de hoc verbum fecit, ut cum fuerimus concordes et ad eundem finem tendentes, quemadmodum nostri considerantes, quod nostri videntes, quod ecclesia Romana semper permisit, ideo videtur, quod tempore sumus concordes, secundum rem dicimus idem et dico, quod credimus, quod id quod conficit ministerium, esse sermone domini et taliter per orationem sacerdotis dicimus sacrum effici hoc modo. Et quoniam credimus dominicam vocem esse effectricem divinorum munerum et semel a deo, cuius causa semper operatur illa vox semper replicatur a sacerdote et suscipit sacerdos, quod illa vox replicata aptetur, ut sit eadem vox cum voce domini et ut ita aptetur, invocatur spiritus sanctus et supplicat sacerdos, ut per virtutem spititus sancti concedatur gratia, ut vox repetita efficiatur ita effectiva, ut verbum dei fuit, et ita credimus consummativam fieri per illam orationem sacerdotis, et probo, quod dominice voces habent operationem ut semina, quia sine semine non potest effici fructus, ita in hac dominica voce; tamen, ubi cadit semen, eget aliis instrumentis, ut sacerdotis, altaris et orationum. Unde credimus per hoc esse vobiscum concordes. Quod autem addatur in diffinitione propter rationes vestras dixit pateritas vestra, quod est necesse propter discordiam, et dico, quod esset, si hec difficultas esset contraria, sed non est mota, ut fuerint disputations, et ideo, cum non fuerint controversie, quare debet deduci in dubium? De alia particula, in quibus considerantur IIII^{or} ad confectionem sacramenti, nos id[em] sentimus, quod vos, quod requiritur panis tritici et vinum de vite et sacerdos et quod per altare et principaliter per verba dominica. Et quoniam in omnibus his sumus concordes, vos dicitis, quod debet poni propter declarationem rudium. Rudes ita clare tenuerunt, et ita tenebunt, unde non est necessarium hoc poni in diffinitione; nam multe questiones sunt et de baptismate; si de omnibus vellemus providere, tempus non sufficeret. Cum autem hec dixerim ex me, supplico sanctissimum dominum nostrum et reverendos patres, ut non exigat[ur] alia diffinitio.

If we cleanse some of the contradictions in it [Rupecremata's address], which are spoken through the master, we will create a lengthy sermon. It is necessary for us in speaking against [these] contradictions either to confirm or to suppress [them]. But I will in a few words explain, seeing that with the help of God to clarify [what is] to be harmonious with the Trinity of which I speak. And first I [will] speak as the occasion demands. For this missal, which we use, is the tradition of [Saint] Basil and the blessed [Ioannes] Chrysostom that was used before the time of the schism. Some facts have not changed. Nevertheless, the Occidental clergy never makes [reference] to this word. Indeed, with most avoidance of harmony and to the achievement of this end, in what manner you consider ours to the extent that you view as of our country, and the assembly of Rome on each occasion concedes, therefore perceiving, the fact that agreements are temporary. We mention the following as the same and speak what we believe to the extent that it brings about [our] ministry, to be a discourse of the Lord and as such through the orations of the priests we devote the sacred producing this in the present. And since we trust the statements of the Dominican to be a product of divine presence and ever from God, whose cause at all times labors to review always that utterance on each occasion from the priest and upholds the priest, whereas that speech adapts to the review. In the same way as the assertion approves with the voice of God and thus so adapts, invoking the Holy Spirit and entreats the priest that he thankfully submit through the virtue of the Holy Spirit, that the statement repeats, making thus practical, [and] that has been the word of God. And in this fashion we rely upon the summation having been made through that priestly sermon and I approve because the Dominican has spoken as an author, which without an author would not confirm a fruitful authority as in this oration of the Dominican. However, where the seed falls, it is without other tools, indeed the priestly, the altar, and the sermon. How can we trust by this to be called to agreement? And moreover if we conceal through disavowal by reason of calculation, you speak of the dress of the fathers, as far as it is necessary to disagree, and to say, since it would be if this difficulty would be contradictory, but it is not a movement, how might they have been disputable? And therefore, may they not be debatable, wherefore it is due to lead to doubts? Of other parts in what manner we consider the fourth, the composition of the sacrament, we perceive it, like you, we require bread of wheat, wine of the vine, and a priest, and over an altar and principally by the word of the Lord. And because in all this we are in agreement, you say that with rudeness we have set aside the clarification. Thus they brusquely maintain clarity and in this fashion they hold fast, whence this assertion is not to be disputed. There are many questions for us and of baptism. If we convulse from all to look forward, there is insufficient time. On the other hand, I myself may have said these [statements]. I beseech our most sacred lords and reverend fathers, do not reflect upon all of the questions.

Also, between 17 April and 10 June 1439, Isidore prepared a brief response to the lengthy disputation of the Latin orator Giovanni da Montenaro, a provincial of Lombardy. Da Montenaro addressed the patristic literature enunciating the interpretations on the procession of the Holy Spirit from the Father and the Son (the *filioque*). The Latin texts that he cited were not made available to the Greek orators and this caused dismay among them. After da Montenaro had concluded his discourse, a long pause ensued and finally in exasperation Isidore raised a procedural issue, noting that the Greeks did not have copies of his documentation and were at a loss to respond to his theological argumentation concerning the procession of the Holy Spirit.[53] The Latins, however, during the *filioque* discussions, applying Aristotelian logic to the debates and even drawing upon the rational writings of Saint Thomas Aquinas, charged that the Greek orators displayed no specificity in their argumentation. Even John VIII was appalled at the "ignorance" of his orators, whether pro- or anti-church union, in their responses to the Latin speakers. Georgios Scholarios (who later after the fall of the imperial city in 1453 was appointed patriarch of Constantinople under the chosen name of Gennadios II), one of the most knowledgeable and learned Byzantine theologians at the council and a pro-unionist at the moment, was horrified at the lack of learning among the Greek delegates. Like the emperor, he impugned the "ignorance" of the Greek delegation.[54] Isidore did not dispute the emperor or Scholarios, and even appears to conclude that the Greek orators were ill prepared for these detailed expositions, whether because of a lack of knowledge or of preparation. Illustrative of his contributions to the debates, he presented during the month of April an eloquent discussion on the connotations of the Greek prepositions ἐκ (from) and διὰ (through) at Florence. Isidore argues that there was little differentiation in their meanings and prepositional usage, and employed this argumentation to support the Latin interpretation of *filioque*.[55]

To bring the impasse to a conclusion and to resolve the divisions within the Greek deputation, Isidore invited select bishops, those of Melenikos and Drama, along with other high Orthodox churchmen to a sumptuous dinner, as recounted by Sylvestros Syropoulos. While for weeks the papacy had denied sustenance and maintenance to the Greeks until they had relented and accepted the proposals of the pope and the Latin wing at the Council of Ferrara-Florence, the provision of a lavish meal was a welcome sight for those present. After they had dined, Isidore addressed the gathering and as a teacher he persuaded them to accept his arguments in favor of *filioque*. The guests accepted his position, but later upon their return to Byzantium a number of them recanted and damned Isidore for his actions.[56]

In the end, after months of wrangling amongst themselves and with the Latins, and in a climate of much distrust and misunderstanding, John VIII prevailed upon his Greek delegation to accept church union. Without a declaration of unity, he recognized that he could not hope for military aid from the West to relieve his beleaguered imperial city and protect the few remaining territorial remnants of the once glorious and extensive Byzantine Empire. The *Decree of Church Union*[57] was formally adopted on the 6th of July 1439, although the signatories, both Greek and Latin, applied their autographs the previous day. Isidore was a signatory to the *Decree*. His inscription reads:[58]

> *Isydorus archiepiscopus Ciebiensis ac totius Russie ac locum tenens apostolico sedis sanctissimi patriarche Anthioceni domini Dorothei*[59] *affirmans et diffiniens subscripsi.*
>
> Isidore, the Archbishop of Kiev and of All Rus', and also the region held by the apostolic seat of the most sacred Patriarch of Antioch, Lord Dorotheos, I sign affirming and forging anew.

Isidore's autograph in Greek, like the Latin in its context, reads:[60]

> Ἰσίδωρος μητροπολίτης Κυέβου καὶ πάσης Ῥωσίας καὶ τὸν τόπον ἐπέχων τοῦ ἀποστολικοῦ θρόνου τοῦ ἁγιωτάτου πατριάρχου Ἀντιοχείας κυροῦ Δωροθέου στέργων καὶ συναινῶν ὑπέγραψα.

Within several months after the signatories had adhered their autographs to the *Decree of Union*, Pope Eugenius IV embarked upon a letter writing campaign, promoting the role of Isidore at the church council and specifying his additional ecclesiastical jurisdictions within Muscovy and in particular in Eastern Europe. Thus, Isidore emerged thereafter as a major player in papal diplomacy in the Slavic lands and its implementer of church union for the following decades.

The first letter, of concern to us, was addressed from Florence by Eugenius IV to a general audience, and is dated the 15th of August 1439. The heading of the missive defines Isidore's papal appointments and the extent of his ecclesiastical jurisdictions over given territories. It reads:[61]

> *Eugenius etc. venerabili fratri Isidoro Kyew ac totius Russie Metropolite, in Lithuanie, Lyvonie et Russie provincias ac in civitatibus, diocesibus, terris et locis lechie, que tibi iure Metropolit[an]o subesse noscuntur, apostolice sedis legato, saltutem etc.*
>
> Eugenius, etc., concerning the Reverend Father Isidore, the Metropolitanate of Kiev and of All Rus', in Lithuania, Livonia, and Rus' provinces, and in the civilized centers, dioceses, lands, and select places, which we acknowledge to be subject to you and the jurisdiction of the Metropolitanate, the seat of the apostolic legate, greetings etc.

Aside from defining his ecclesiastical powers and the dominions subject to the rulers of these regions, the letter established Isidore as the apostolic rather than the papal legate for these jurisdictions, although we should not differentiate between the two distinctions, since the same high ecclesiastical office administers them. The letter is broadly addressed and does not solely concern the grand prince of Moscow. Further, if the pope intended the letter to influence the rulers of Poland and Lithuania, his overture was made all the more difficult by the fact that these rulers were anti-papal and pro-Basle in their outlook and preferences. Thus Isidore's task in these realms was not to be an easy one.

On the same day, the pope addressed a second letter,[62] a formal appointment of Isidore as his apostolic legate and the extent of his jurisdictions. The heading of the letter reads: *Eugenius etc. universis et singulis, ad quos presentes littere nostre pervenerint, salutem etc.*, "Eugenius, etc., the universal and the one [head], to whom[ever] our presentation of the letter reaches, greetings etc." The pope then addresses on the same day a third letter to the grand prince of Moscow. To the best of our knowledge, the text of the letter survives only in a Medieval Church Slavonic rendition that appears in the *Second Sofia Annal* (**Софнйскаѧ втораѧ лѣтопнсь**) and reads:[63]

Еугеній епнскупъ, рабъ рабомъ Божінмъ, превысокому кнѧзю Васнлью Васнльевнчу Московскому н всеѧ Русін велнкому царю спасеніе н апостольское благословеніе. Благодарнмъ Вседръжнтелѧ Бога, ѩко нынѣ, по многѣхъ трудѣхъ, Духа свѧтаго благодатн помощію, восточнаѧ церковь съ намн едина есть, еже ко спасенію юндетъ душъ многнхъ людій н къ твоей похвалѣ н славѣ пншетсѧ. Къ сему еднначеству многое положеніе н поспѣшеніе честнѣйшаго брата нашего Сндора мнтрополнта твоего всеѧ Русн, отъ апостольскаго престола посла, нже за свое благое крѣпчайше потруднлсѧ о соединенін; того раді потребно есть помогатн ему комуждо во всѣхъ дѣлѣхъ, наипаче в сіхъ дѣлѣхъ, еже предстояніе нмѣтъ къ достонінству едину н чіну церковному, врученну ему. А твое превысочайшее просімъ въ Господа нашего н съ болшімъ желаніемъ н со многімъ раченіемъ, сего мнт_ рополнта о оправданін н о добрѣ церковнѣмъ прежерѣченѣмъ, да прінмешн Бога ради н насъ дѣлѧ, занеже то съ желаніемъ н со многімъ раченіемъ къ тебѣ о немъ приказываемъ; по всѣхъ вещехъ, еже нматн вѣдатн отъ него о церковнѣй пошлннѣ предъстоѧніе, да будешн помощнікъ ему усердно со всею своею помощію, еже да будетъ хвала н слава отъ людей, а отъ насъ бладословеніе, а отъ Бога вѣчное дарованіе да нмашн. А дана во Флорентін, свѧщеньства нашего въ 9-е лѣто.

The Bishop Eugenius, the servant of the servants of God, to the most high prince of Moscow and of All Rus' Vasilii Vasil'evich, for the welfare of the grand tsar and the apostolic blessing. We give thanks to the Almighty God, for now after much labor, the Holy Spirit thankfully aiding, the Eastern Church is one with us. Thus it is written to be the salvation of the souls of many people and for your praise and glory. With this unification, much circumstance and diligence of our esteemed brother Sidor [Isidore], your Metropolitan of All Rus', who for our good labored with strength for union, is dispatched from the apostolic seat. For the sake of this, it is necessary for whomever to assist him in all deeds, particularly in those endeavors that have precedence toward the dignity of oneness and the church's ceremony I commit him. And in our Lord we beseech your Excellency, and with the greatest desire and with much zealousness, having previously stated concerning the justification and concerning the ecclesiastical benefit of his metropolitanate, for the sake of God accept [him] and our work, because this we enjoin you with the desire and with much assiduity concerning him. On all matters inquire of him concerning the present ecclesiastical custom. Thus you will fervently be the helpmate to him with all your assistance that will gain popular commendation and glory, and from us you will have the blessing and from God an eternal gift. Given in Florence in the ninth year of our holiness.

We are not informed in the Muscovite sources of the immediate reaction of the grand prince to this correspondence. Only later, after the arrival of Isidore, does the polemical literature reflect the harsh responses to his metropolitanate and the question of church union, among other issues.

Soon after, on the 28th of November 1439, Eugenius IV addressed a letter to John VIII, specifying the jurisdictions of Isidore. The communication reads:[64]

> *Eugenius Episcopus, servus servorum Dei, carissimo in Christi filio Ioanni Paleologo Romeorum imperatori, salute et apostolicam benedictionem.*
>
> *Cum esset profecturus ex Venetiis venerabilis frater Isidorus Ruthenorum archiepiscopus, ut [per] Hungariam et Germaniam rediret in patriam, casus accidit mortis clare memorie Alberti Romanorum, Hungarie et Boemie regis, quamobrem consultum est predicto ar[chiepiscop]o a dominio Venetorum ceterisque, qui illa noverunt itinera, fore tutius sese navigationis longitudini atque periculis exponere, quam illud terrestre iter ingredi, per q[uod] guerris implicitum et latrocinis obsessum maiora et certiora subiret pericula.*
>
> *Nos etiam audito de suspicione ipsa, que dicto archiepiscopo erat proposita, eiusdem fuimus se[nte]ntie.*
>
> *Veniet itaque domino et deo protegente Constantinopolim viis, que tibi sibique vibuntur cum tutiores tum etiam commodiores, in patriam accessurus.*
>
> *[Q]uare licet sciamus tuam celsitudinem optime intelligere magnam esse ipsius viri virtutem non dubitemusque te illum ex corde diligere, tamen, cum nos etiam eum [a]memus, quem novimus et in obtinenda unione multum fideliter et diligentissime laborasse, et speramus plurimum in ea conservanda profuturum, non potuimus [ab]stinere, quin has ad te daremus, predictum archiepiscopum singulari quodam modo comendantes. Nihil enim hoc tempore nobis acceptius facere poteris quam sip r[edictu]m archiepiscopum in hac sua profectione necessariis favoribus prosequeris.*
>
> *Datum Florentie, anno incarnationis dominice millesimo quadringentessimo [tricesi]mo nono, quarto kalendas decembris, pontificates nostri anno nono.*

Bishop Eugenius, the servant of the servants of God, beneficent in Christ, to the son [and] Roman Emperor John Palaiologos, greetings and apostolic benediction.

Upon departure from Venice, he would be the venerable father Isidore of the Ruthenian archdiocese, but is returning [through] Hungary and Germany to [his] native land [Muscovite Rus'], the occasion occurred, being distinct in the death and memory of the king Albertus of Rome, Hungary, and Bohemia, for which reason he is otherwise to advise the archbishop and the lord of Venice that he has altered the route. He himself will set forth to navigate the length and hazards [of these lands], as that land journey begins, through which the entwining warfare and brigandage are major hindrances and the contentions become a test.

I repeat, we ourselves also hear of the suspicion that the archbishop had set forth. We have been of the same opinion.

And so the lord came and furnished to God the Constantinopolitan influence, which to you may view at that time with the protectors as also accommodating, having come to the Father.

On which account we may understand your eminence to perceive the greatest good to be the manliness of men, not the uncertainty you prize through prudence. However, we are still mindful that many faithfully [accept] the new and in obtaining the union labored most diligently. And we hope for the majority to sow deeply in this, not abstain drunkenly. Rather, we offer this to you. The archbishop alone in a certain way will make publicly known what is commended. But indeed, we accept nothing at this time to bring about later, supposing that possibly the predictions of the archbishop follow necessarily favorably at his departure.

Given in Florence, in the year of the Incarnation of the Lord, the thousandth four hundredth thirty-ninth, the fourth Kalends of December, the ninth year of our pontificate.

For all his efforts in bringing about church union and resolving some dogmatic questions during the debates at Ferrara and Florence, and perhaps more so because Isidore was the confidant of and the intermediary to the pope for John VIII, in late 1439, on the 18th of December, the pope rewarded him with the nomination and elevation to the rank of cardinal. The formal ceremony of consecration took place at a later date. Also earlier, in mid-August of the same year, Isidore was nominated apostolic legate for Muscovite Rus' and the neighboring territories in Poland and Lithuania. His mission as metropolitan was to ensure church union in those Eastern Slavic areas. Clearly, Isidore had achieved considerable prominence within the papal circle and hereafter the popes were dependent upon his diplomatic skills, dispatching him to numerous areas in Eastern Europe and the Balkans to accomplish the union of churches.

3 The return to Muscovy and the aftermath of Florence

A substantial literature was produced soon after the return of Isidore to Moscow. Much of the Slavonic literature is polemical in tone and its content is disapproving of his participation in the Council of Ferrara-Florence, of his return to Moscow, of his pronouncements concerning church union, and even of his own acts that proved disturbing for the Muscovite Rus'.

Following the concluding events at Florence, Isidore set out to return to Moscow, taking a circuitous route that brought him to Buda, where he prepared a letter for the Muscovite Rus', Poles, Lithuanians, and Germans. The letter is a good summary statement of the key dogmatic issues of concern for the Muscovite Rus' that were resolved at Ferrara-Florence, although the Muscovites subsequently denied that they had been informed of these attainments. The original Greek text of the letter is lost and we rely upon a Slavonic rendition, *Vat. sl. 12*, fols. 536ᵛ–537ᵛ, in the Vatican archives that is assigned the date of the 5th of March 1440.[65] The text of the letter reads:

Исидоръ милостию Бжиею прѣсвцныи архиєпсп и всеа Русии, легатос і от ребра апельскаго седалища лѧтьцкаго и литовьскаго и немецькаго, всѣм і всѧкомȣ хрстовѣрнымъ с прибавлениемъ вѣры своеа вѣчьное спасние въ Гѣ.

Возрадȣнтеса і възвеселитеса вьси ннѣ, ѧко црквь восточнаа [и западнаа], коликое бремѧ разделени быша и едина ко единеи враждебны, а ннѣ истинным соеди—ениемъ соединишасѧ во изначалествениѣишее во свое соедние и въ миръ і въ единачество древнее, без всѧкого разделениа. Вси жъ хсоименитии, и какъ латыни, такъ и грекове, и ти иж[е] вьси подлежатъ стеи соборьнеи цркви костѧнтинопольстеи, еж[е] сȣть рȣсь, и сербн, и влахи, и инии вьси хрстиании роди, примете тое ж[е] и престое единачество с великою дховною радостию и чтию. И напред млю васъ въ Гѣ ншго Іс Ха, еже с наме млсть створивьшаго, чтобъ никакова розъдѣлениа въ васъ с латынею не было, зане ж[е] вси есте раби Гѣ ншего Іс Ха і во имѧ его крщнни. Вы же, латинстии роди, тѣх всѣхъ, иже въ гречестеи вѣре сȣть, истинно вѣрȣите, без всѧкого размышлениа, сȣт бо вси крщнии, крщние иже сто ес и неиспытно от римьскиа цркви, еже истинно и равно ес, ѧко ж[е] и тое цркви крщние. И даале бы межи васъ никакове злое размышление не было о тѣх дѣлех, но какъ латыни, такъ и прежъ реченнии грекове къ единеи цркви смотрение имѣли, еж[е] бо единым едина ес. И когда греки въ земѧи сȣть латыньстеи, или гдѣ ес въ ихъ земли латыньскаа цркви, чтобы есте вьси къ бжстнеи слȣжбе зъ дерьзновениемъ прибегали и тѣла Іс Хева смотрѣли и сокрȣшениемъ срдца чьсть воздавали, ѧко ж[е] і во своих црквах чинѧт. ǁ

На покаание приходѧт къ латинскимъ попомъ и тѣло Бжие от нихъ приемлютъ, а латыни тако ж[е] длъжни сȣть вь их црквь итти і бжственьныа слȣжбы слȣшати и с теплою вѣрою поклѧнѧтисѧ томȣ ж[е] Іс Хеву тѣлȣ, поне ж[е] истинно Іс Хево тѣло, так же ещно от греческаго попа въ кислом хлѣбе, какъ і от латыньскаго попа ещно въ преснои хлѣбе. И того ради обое достоино ес дръжати прѣсночное и кислое. А латыни тако ж[е] приходѧтъ ко греческим попомъ на покаание и причастие Бжие от нихъ приемлют, поне ж[е] обое то едино ес. Тако бо вьселеньскии зборъ кончалъ въ ѧвьленномъ послѣднии въ чтнеи большеи цркви слȣжиѣвше во градѣ Фролентин подъ лѣты воплощениа Гна 1439–го лѣта, мцѧ июлѧ въ 6 дн.

Isidore, by the grace of God consecrated archbishop of Kiev and of all Rus', the legate and from the apostolic seat of Latvia, Lithuania, and Germany, to all and to each believer in Christ, with an augmentation of their faith, everlasting salvation in the Lord.

Now all exalt and rejoice, as the Oriental [and the Occidental] Church[es] that were divided for some time and hostile to one another, but now are brought back to a true union, the most original in their unification, in peace and the most ancient harmony without any division. All peoples who bear upon themselves Christ's name, and thus the Latins and as well the Greeks, all of them indulged in the holy church council of Constantinople, who are Rus', Serbs, and Vlachs [Wallachians], and all of the other Christian nations, received this most sacred union with great spiritual joy and reverence. And I now beseech you in the Lord our Jesus Christ, who made grace for us in order that there would be no division among us with the Latins because all are servants of our Lord Jesus Christ and are baptized in His name. You, the Latin nations truly believe without any reflection those who are of the Greek faith, for all are baptized. With due attention of the Roman church, the baptized are holy and true, and alike all are baptized in the church. And further among you there should be no consideration of ill will concerning these affairs, but as the Latins, and so as previously stated the Greeks had looked to one church, for one is unity. And when the Greeks are in Latin lands, or when in their lands there are Latin churches, in order that all hasten to the divine liturgy with temerity and they view the body of Jesus Christ with humility and honor and render the heart as they performed in their churches.

For the sacrament of penance they will go to the Latin priests and will receive the Body of God from them, and the Latins in the same way are bound to go to their [Greek] churches and go to the divine liturgy, and with fervent faith worship this the Body of Jesus Christ, for truly it is the Body of Jesus Christ, as it is consecrated by a Greek priest in leavened bread, so also it is consecrated by a Latin priest in pressed bread. And it is necessary to retain both the flat [pressed] and the leavened. And the Latins should also come to the Greek priest for the sacrament of penance and receive Holy Communion from them, for both of these are one. For the Council of [Ferrara-]Florence concluded thus in a public session, a divine liturgy in a great church in the city of Florence in the year of the incarnation of the Lord 1439, in the month of July on the sixth day.

Of the numerous ecclesiastical issues addressed by the Council of Ferrara-Florence, Isidore considered in this communication only three, the sacraments of Baptism, Penance, and Holy Communion. While he had given assurances to the grand prince of Moscow that he would not introduce into Muscovy any of the Latin theological positions, he did not uphold his pledge. Now that he was a cardinal in the Roman Church, he felt obligated to preach their teachings, contrary to the ultra-Orthodox traditions of the Muscovites. Also, Isidore was a representative of both the Eastern and Western churches and may have felt a need to breach the divide between them, but at a modest level in addressing only three sacramental issues and apparently more so to the Latins than to the Greeks or Rus'. Concerning the Sacrament of Baptism, a divide persists to the present between the Roman Catholics and the Orthodox. Since medieval times, the Byzantine churchmen have maintained that the Latin practice of administering the Sacrament of Baptism was invalid, because the Romans had initially performed a single immersion unlike the Byzantines who performed three, and then later the Romans modified their practice to simply infusion, having abandoned immersion.[66] Although subsequent to the reception of this communication the Muscovite lay and ecclesiastical authorities assumed the posture of being unaware of the achievements at Ferrara-Florence, certainly this communication should have piqued their interest. But in denial, they seem to believe that their churchmen had not attended the sessions of the council, when in fact they had and the Muscovite authorities were well aware of what had transpired. Thus the Muscovite annals and other literary sources should be used with caution.

In the meantime, while en route to Moscow, to placate the Orthodox Christians of Poland and Rus' who harbored suspicions concerning his ministry, Isidore composed another letter, dated the 27th of July 1440. It is addressed to the elders of Chelm' (Cholm', Kholm'), among others, and reads:[67]

Благословенние Исидора, митрополита киевскаго и всеа Русн, легатоса и от ребра апостольскаго сѣдалища ляцкого и литовъского и немецкого, в Холмъ о Стѣмъ Дсѣ сыномъ нашого смиреннна, старостам холмъским и воеводам и кто коли ни ес, так же и заказником и всимъ православным.

Пишем вашен мьсти, иж бил нам челом попъ Вавила от стого Спаса от Столпа, а сказывает, что же ден обиды чынится ему велми много; да и сад ден церковный у него обирают, а чымъ то он у тое церкви жыветь и Бога молит, о всем хрестианстве. И благословляю вашу млс, чтобы есте о томъ онекане мѣли, како бы церков Божаа и тот попъ никим былн не обидны, и садов бы церковных у него не обирали, и ни чего церковного не брали, зань же ден и старыны тое б церкви и попомъ ее; ∥ ни от кого обид не чынило ся, и чтобы и ныне вашымъ опеканьем та богомоля стояла с покоем, а тотъ бы попъ от нее прочь к иной церкви не шол, жыл бы туто и молил Бога никим не обнижень, зан же кто обидит церков Божю, тот самому Божю закону противляется.

А нам сущимъ православным хрестианом ляхом и русі, достонт исполняти Божа церкви и их сщенъников, а не обидети, есмо бо ныне, дал Богъ, одна–на брата хрестиане, латынни и русь; и того ради прынмете от Вседержителя Бога блгдат и милост, а от нашог смиреньа блгсловене и молитву.

А писан лист в Холмѣ мсца июля въ 27 днъ, в лѣт 6948, индикта въ 2.

The blessed Isidore, metropolitan of Kiev and of all Rus', legate to the apostolic Lateran seats of Latvia, Lithuania, and Germany [not the Holy Roman Empire, but the area maintained by the Teutonic Knights], in Chelm', in the Holy Spirit, in the humility of our Son, to the elders and the voevodas [military leaders?][68] of Chelm', and whoever there is, so also to the administrators and all Orthodox.

We write to your graces, that for us Babylas, who was the leading priest for the saintly Salvatoros of Stolpa, states that an affront to him made him very much [resilient], so that he would reap for himself in the divine garden and that he would reside there in that church and pray to God for all of Christendom. And I bless your graces that you will be uplifting for their teaching, for it is the church of God and this priest is not contumelious to anyone and he will not reap in the garden of their [Orthodox] church and will not bring in anything of their [Roman] church, because these [teachings] were made by the ancient church and its priests, || nor will he himself make an affront to anyone. And so that your teachings will now continue to be prayed in peace, this priest will be apart from it and will not enter other churches. Thus he will reside there and pray to God that no one will be offended, because whoever gives offense to the church of God, that one himself will be in opposition to God's law.

And for us it is necessary that the Orthodox Christians in Liakhia [Poland] and Rus' fulfill God's church and their priests, and do not offend, for they are now one, one Christian brotherhood of Latins and Rus', that is favored by God. And for the sake of this you will receive from the Almighty God indulgences and graces, and from our humility blessings and prayers.

The leaf was written in Cholm' on the 27th in the month of July 1440, the second indiction.

Isidore, attired in a red hat symbolizing his office of cardinal and following a Latin Cross in procession, arrived at the main gate of the city of Moscow on the 19th of March 1441. He performed the customary religious service prior to entering the town.[69] The *Second Sofia Annal*[70] then relates in substantial detail the events that transpired on that and subsequent days. If Isidore had sought to placate the Muscovite Rus', his initial and subsequent actions demonstrate otherwise. To compound matters, he had brought back in chains the esteemed Rus' churchman, Simeon of Suzdal. A full explanation of Isidore's reasoning for this action is not clearly evident, although the cardinal had learned in the meantime that Simeon was disseminating anti-unionist propaganda in Novgorod. However, Simeon in his account, Исидоровъ соборъ и хожение его (*The Council of Isidore and His Journey*),[71] rather discreetly does not furnish an explanation why he had to be brought back in chains. There then followed the celebration of a liturgy in the Uspensky (Annunciation) Cathedral,[72] during which Isidore invoked the name of the pope in the appropriate prayers. The grand prince and the Rus' clergy were insulted by what they deemed to be the cardinal's brazen actions. The grand prince refused to receive benediction from Isidore. The liturgy was concluded with a reading of the *Decree of Union*. Shortly thereafter, Isidore was deposed as metropolitan and three days after his arrival he was placed under arrest and confined to the Chudov Monastery. In the meantime, the grand prince directed that the cardinal/metropolitan be judged by a synod composed of the leading archbishops and bishops in Muscovite Rus'. The main charge against Isidore was that he preached a волкохыщаго ересь (wolf-like heresy),[73] whose teachings were in opposition to the true Orthodoxy of the Muscovite Rus'. He was questioned by members of the Muscovite Synod, without any admissions on his part of heretical actions. Awaiting trial and under the threat of being burned at the stake or buried alive, Isidore escaped in September 1441 from the monastery. He must have had the assistance of others, perhaps even with the connivance of Muscovite authorities and the grand prince himself who were eager to be rid of him. On this point, the Muscovite annals allude to this possibility, but the matter is never fully clarified.[74] But what is clear in the *Second Sofia Annal* is that Isidore was accompanied by his loyal companion Gregory, with whom he proceeded to Rome and permanent exile from Muscovite Rus'.[75] Further, Gregory is identified as the "Black," hence the "Bulgarian Gregory," or "Black" could signify his monastic order.

Soon thereafter, Iona, the bishop of Riazan, most probably acting as the metropolitan designee following the deposition of Isidore, convened the Muscovite Synod to address the crucial issues for the Muscovite Rus'. The Synod composed a letter from the grand prince to the Byzantine emperor, expounding upon their theological views and explaining the deposition of Isidore. The text of the letter reads:[76]

Державнѣишiи и боговѣнчаннѣишiи высочаншiи царю Греческiи! братъ свѧтаго ти царства великiи кнѧзь Московскiи и всеѧ Русiи достоиное посылаю свѧтому ти царству. Вѣмы убо извѣстно отъ божественаго Писанiа, ѩко прежде Божiе ю благодатiю и многыми его неизреченными щедротами, истинное благочестiе, еже въ Господа нашего Iисуса Христа въ Троицѣ славимаго истиннаѧ православнаѧ христiанскаѧ вѣра непорочнаѧ, провозсiа и возрасте въ царьствующемъ преименитомъ градѣ, въ отечьствiи свѧтаго ти царства, отъ благочестиваго свѧтаго самодержьца всеѧ вселенныѧ великаго кнѧзѧ Константина. По многыхъ же паки временехъ и лѣтѣхъ прародитель нашъ, свѧтыи и равныи Апостоломъ, ѩко же есть намъ достоино сице глаголати о немъ, великiи кнѧзь Владимеръ Кiевьскыи и всеѧ Русiи, еще въ поганьствѣ сыи, осiанiемъ же пресвѧтаго и живоначалнаго Духа, начатъ посылати во всѧ страны и далнѧѧ градовы и мѣста искати и испытовати: каѧ есть вѣра блага и богопрiѧтна? посыланiе же о томъ и изысканiе на многѣ, до Рима убо и до инѣхъ многыхъ мѣстъ, еже видѣти Латынску ювѣру, истокмо же се, но и богомерзскаго Моамефа повелѣ видѣти вѣру и служенiе: и сихъ испытавъ, и видѣ всѧ ѩко не суть добра, ниже богопрiѧтна, но паче богоненавидима, Латынству убо никакоже внѧтъ, оканнаго же и богомерзскаго Моамефа злочестивую ересь всѧческы поплевавъ отвѣрже. Послѣди же посла въ царствующiи градъ видѣти Греческую вѣру; они же посланiи его видѣша истинную и православную вѣру христiаньскую Греческую ѩко свѣщу на свѣтилницѣ многосвѣтлѣ свѣтѧщу, и повѣдаша ему. Онъ же сiа убо слышавъ сладцѣ и со вниманiемъ, множае стрѣлы уѧзвенъ бысть богоразумiемъ, и възрадоваса духомъ и възвеселиса сердцемъ и все юсовѣстiю, и безпрестаннымъ раченiемъ вжелѣвъ, абiе приступаетъ къ бани божественаго крещенiа и очищаетсѧ прежнѧго злочестiа водою и духомъ, съкрушаетъ же и отечьскыѧ идолы, заповѣдаетъ же и въ всемъ своемъ отечьствiи, во многочеловѣчнѣи Рустѣи земли, да всѣ вкꙋпѣ свѧтое крещение въсприимꙋтъ, малии же и велиции, богатии и ꙋбозии, всѧкъ чинъ и възрастъ, отъ велможъ и до простыхъ, отъ старець и до сꙋщихъ; еже бысть Божие юблагодатию, въскорѣ вси ꙋбо крестишасѧ, и Христовымъ именованиемъ названи быша и благочестие ѕѣло процвѣте, тма же невѣрствиа, всеконечно отгнасѧ. Взимаетъ же себѣ онъ великии новыи Констѧнтинъ, а реку благочестивыи царь Рꙋскыа землѧ Владимеръ, на свое отечьство, на новопросвѣщенное православное христианьство, отъ свѧтыа великиа съборныа и апостольскыа церкве царствꙋющаго града Премꙋдроста Божиа, и отъ царьствꙋющаго въ тогдашнее времѧ свѧтаго царѧ, и отъ правѧщаго Божию церковь свѧтѣишаго патриарха и божественаго еже о нѣмъ свѧщенного събора, на Рꙋскую землю митрополита; по немъ же ꙋкрѣплѧеми и сдержими благочестиемъ сынове его и внꙋцы его и правнꙋцы его по роду также творѧхꙋ, отъ времене до времене вземлюще митрополитовъ на свое отечьство, на Рꙋськꙋю землю, отъ царьствꙋющаго града, овогда Грека, иногда же отъ своеа землѧ поставлѧемаго свѧтѣишимъ вселенскымъ патриархомъ нашего Рꙋсина, а не отъ Рима, ни отъ папы, ни отъ Латынъ. Се же все тако бысть и до времене господьства приснопамѧтнаго господина моего и отца моего, великаго кнѧзѧ Василиа Дмитреевича, и до преженочившаго приснопамѧтиво отца нашего, преосвѧщеннаго Фотиа митрополита Киевьскаго и всеа Рꙋси; и благодатию Божиею землѧ наша и сꙋщихъ окрестъ насъ братии нашеи великыхъ кнѧзеи державы, и помѣстихъ кнѧзеи и начальниковъ елико кто подъ собою имѣетъ, вси сꙋть въ благочестии и въ православнѣи вѣрѣ живꙋще христианстѣи, и въ свѧтую живоначальую единосꙋщнꙋю и нераздѣлимꙋю Троицю вѣрꙋюще во Отца и Сꙋна и свѧтаго Дꙋха: отъ предания и заповѣдания оного свѧтаго великаго прародителѧ нашего и до сего настоѧщаго времене, въ немъже и мы нынѣ Божие юблагодатию жительствꙋемъ донелѣ же Богъ благоволитъ. имѣмъ нынѣ четыреста и пѧтьдесѧтъ лѣтъ и пѧть лѣтъ, Богомъ наставлѧеми, благочестие имꙋще. По преставлении же сего преженочившаго отца нашего, прежереченнаго приснопамѧтнаго преосвѧщеннаго митрополита Фотиа, за нꙋжу нахождениа безбожныхъ Ягарѧнъ и межꙋꙋсобныхъ ради бранеи и христианскаго ради ꙋстроениа и дꙋховныа ползы, понꙋдихомъ ити къ намъ отца нашего Іону епископа Рѧзаньскаго, мꙋжа сꙋща дꙋховна, въ добродѣлномъ житии отъ младенства многа лѣта поживша; послахомъ же съ нимъ и посла нашего, честнѣишаго боꙗрина нашего Василиа, съ прошениемъ ко свѧтому вашему царствꙋ, и свѧтѣишему патриархꙋ и къ божественому свѧщенному събору съ грамотами нашими, и словомъ есмѧ къ вамъ наказали, дабы намъ того епископа Іону поставили на митрополию. Не вѣмы же ꙋбо за кое лѣто нашего еста прошениа не приали, ни грамотамъ нашемъ, ни послу нашемꙋ, ни нашимъ посланымъ съ нимъ словесемъ не внѧсте, того еста намъ Іону епископа на митрополи юне поставили; и тому есмы не вмалѣ подивилисѧ, что ради сие къ намъ таково бысть, и въ размышлении быхомъ, или за помедлѣние нашего къ вамъ посланиа, или свое высочанишее поставивше тако сътвористе: о комъ къ вамъ ни послахомъ, ни ꙋ васъ кого просихомъ, ни требовахомъ, того еста къ намъ послали, а реку сего Исидора. И Богу вѣдомо, аще не быхомъ того нашего изначалнаго православнаго христианство съблюдали и страха Божіа аще не быхомъ въ сердци имжли, то никакоже не хотѣхомъ его пріати отъннудъ; но за вашего посла моленіе и за свѧтѣйшаго патріарха благословеніе, а за оного съкрушеніе и многое покореніе и челобитіе, едва едва пріахомъ его. Егда же понуди насъ покореніе его многое и челобитіе, пріахомъ его ико отца и учителѧ, съ много ючести юн благимъ усердіемъ, по прежнему, ѧкоже и онѣхъ преднихъ свѧтѣйшихъ митрополитовъ нашихъ Рускыхъ; мнѧще, ѧко да и сей единъ отъ нихъ есть, не вѣдуще, еже напреди хощетъ отъ него кое дѣло быти. А надѣемсѧ, тое все повѣдалъ вамъ церьскій посолъ, ѧкоже приде къ намъ предиреченый сей Сидоръ и отъ перваго дне начатъ тщатисѧ къ съборному путешествію колико възбранѧхомъ ему, онъ же начатъ извѣты сицевы творити, глаголѧ: ико немощно ми есть да не понду; аще бо не понду, имамъ отъ свѧтѣйшаго патріарха вмѣсто благословеніа клѧтву пріати, понеже убо прежнін азъ есмь ходатай бываемому събору и нужу имамъ всѧчески поити, ѧко и рукописаніе свое дахъ на себе, еже понду. И ѧко не възмогохомъ увѣщати его и отъ путнаго шествіа възбранити, и много паки глаголахомъ ему о сихъ: аще же убо пондеши и паки аще имаши възвратитисѧ къ намъ, то принеси въ намъ древнее наше благочестіе и православну ювѣру, еже пріахомъ отъ прародителий нашего Владимера, еже держитъ великаа съборнаа апостольскаѧ церковъ Греческаа; а ино странно и ново и чюже отъ тоа съборныѧ церкве не приношай намъ, понеже аще и принесеши что ново, то непріатно будетъ намъ то. Онъ же съ клѧтво ювѣщасѧ, ѧко не принести ему нова и странна ничтоже; нынѣ же приде къ намъ, много странна и чюжда принесе въ наше православное христіаньство, чрезъ божественаа и свѧщеннаа правила свѧтыхъ Апостолъ и богоносныхъ Отецъ и чрезъ божественое законоположеніе, еже предано свѧтыми Апостолы и богоносными Отцы свѧтѣй съборнѣй апостольстѣй церкви Греческѣй, всему православному христіаньству, еже послѣже Божіе юблагодатію, ѧкоже и преже писахомъ, насъ свѣтъ богоразумія осиа и крещеніе въ покаанію оставленіе грѣховъ просвѣти насъ, и христіанское имѧ на насъ есть. Принесе же къ намъ отъ Римскаго папы писаніе, въ немъ же о свѧтомъ Дусѣ двѣ началѣ Латына утвердиша въ своей ихъ церкви исповѣдовати; и опрѣсночнаа мудрствующе, ѧко истинно есть, рекоша нищуще, въ безкваснѣмъ и кваснѣмъ хлѣбѣ тѣлу Христову сотворѧтисѧ достоитъ; еще же и о усопшихъ писма глаголетъ, еже намъ убо недоумѣнно ѧвлѧетсѧ сіе: пишетъ бо въ посланіи своемъ сице папа: иже во истиннѣй, рече, вѣрѣ исповѣдани Божимъ смотрѣніемъ конецъ пріаша и покаанія плоды не доспѣша принести о согрѣшеніихъ своихъ, о нихъже имъ духовніи отцы заповѣдаша, и таковіи очищеніемъ мукъ опнистѧтсѧ по смерти, и прочаа. Самъ же убо Исидоръ во своихъ ему когда грамотахъ, идѣже посылаѧ писаше, нарицаа себе легатоса отъ ребра апостольска сѣдалница Лѧтьскаго и Литовьскаго и Нѣмецкаго, и запечатлѣваше писаніа своа зелеными запечатлѣніи, и предъ собою повелѣваше распѧтіе латыньски извааннно носити, объ нозѣ единѣмъ гвоздемъ пригвозденѣ, по всему

Латынскые обычаи въсприимъ держаше; еще же и въ двѣ церкви, наша же убо православныя и Латынскіа, еже въ Лятьской земли и въ Литовьской и въ Нѣмецкой, отъ папы благословеніе приятъ, рече, учителемъ и настоятелемъ себе называше, злочестинѣ двоеженствуа; еще же и помяновеніе папино имене въ святѣй нашей съборнѣй и велицѣй церкви въ служеніи своемъ сътвори; къ сему же подда и поработи насъ подъ отлученную, многыхъ ради ересей, святыми и богоносными Отцы Римскую церковь и Римскаго папу еже добрѣ вѣсть святѣйшее ваше владычьство, яко прежде многыхъ лѣтъ не имѣетъ совокупленіа и приобщеніа Римскаа церкви и Римскіи папа и прочее все еже подъ нимъ Латиньство съ четырми святѣйшими патріархи; надо всѣми же сими сътвори его всему нашему православному христіанству отца и учителя, и всѣмъ церквамъ главу, пасти и рядити и пещися всѣми церквами, и на всѣхъ концѣхъ вселенныя имѣти его перваго, неистиннѣ и неправеднѣ называюще его въ писаніи ономъ намѣстника блаженному и верховному апостолу Петру. Не токмо же до сего сътвори, но и ина многая странна и чужа отъ православныя христіанскіа вѣры внесе въ наше православіе, ихъже и не писахомъ здѣ. Мы же убо сіа слышавше и видѣвше, подвигохомся прежде, потомъ же надежю възложивше на неизреченныя судбы Божіа и благодаривше человѣколюбіе его, созвахомъ боголюбивыя епископы отечьства нашего, елицы обрѣтошася въ тое время близъ насъ, Ростовскаго Ефрема, Суздальскаго Аврамія, Рязанскаго Ѵону, Коломенскаго Варлама, Сарайскаго Ѵова, Пермьскаго Герасима, такоже и архимандритовъ и игуменовъ и прочихъ священноиноковъ и иноковъ земля нашея немало, и повелѣхомъ имъ възрѣти въ таа божественая и священая правила святыхъ Апостолъ и богоносныхъ Отецъ, еже приахомъ отъ святыа великіа съборныя апостольскыя Божіа церкве Гречьскіа, вашего истиннаго православіа, и тое принесенное его отъ папы посланіе повелѣхомъ прочитати намнозѣ; и явися всѣмъ нашимъ боголюбивымъ епископомъ Руськымъ, и честнѣйшимъ архимандритомъ и пренодобнымъ игуменомъ, и прочимъ священноинокомъ и инокомъ, и всему нашему православному христіанству, яко чюже есть и странно отъ божественыхъ и священныхъ правилъ Исидорово все дѣло и прихоженіе. И того ради послахомъ къ святому царю, и къ святѣйшему ти владычьству, и ко всему божественому и священному събору пословъ нашихъ; а съ ними послахомъ и тое писаніе папино писано полатынѣ и по вашей Гречьской грамотѣ, еже принесе къ намъ Исидоръ за папиною печатію. И просимъ святѣйшее ти владычьство, да съ святымъ царемъ и со всѣмъ божественымъ и освященнымъ съборомъ възрѣвше въ святаа ваша и божественаа правила Гречьскаа и во оно папино посланіе, и разсудивше, и за нужю далечнаго и непроходнаго путюшествіа, и за нахоженіе на наше христіанство безбожныхъ Агарянъ и за неустроеніе и мятежи еже въ окрестныхъ насъ странахъ и господарей умноженіа, свободно намъ сътворите въ нашей земли поставленіе митрополита; еще же и за сію нужю, яко и духовная дѣла вся каждому православному христіаннину, и наша съкровенная, а господскаа потребнаа словеса и дѣла нужно намъ дѣлати съ митрополитомъ, толкованно младыми человѣкы, отъ нихъже лѣпо естъ что тяити, и тіи прежде инѣхъ увѣдаютъ. И того ради просимъ, послѣте къ намъ честнѣйшее ваше писаніе, іако да помощію Божіею и благодатію свя́таго Духа, и споспѣшеніемъ святаго ти царства, и благословеніемъ святѣйшаго патріарха, и еже о немъ божественаго и священнаго събора, но святымъ правиломъ, събравше въ отечьстви нашемъ въ Рустѣй земли боголюбивыи епископи отечьства нашего, по благодати святаго Духа избравше кого человѣка добра, мужа духовна, вѣрою православна, да поставитъ намъ митрополита на Русь; понеже и прежде сего за нужу поставленіе въ Руси митрополита бывало. А мы о всемъ хощемъ, Божіею благодатію, но изначальству нашего православнаго христіанства, посыланіе и совопрошеніе и любовь имѣти съ святымъ ти царствомъ, и святѣйшаго патріарха благословенія и молитвы требовати и желати хощемъ, донелѣ же Богъ благоизволитъ и земля наша доколѣ имет стои и а никакоже раздачно отъ васъ имать быти наше православное христіанство до вѣка. Просимъ же о семъ святое ти царство, да со извѣщеніемъ о всемъ и съ честнѣйшимъ нашимъ писаніемъ отпустите сихъ нашихъ пословъ неиздержно, да навыкше о здравіи и благопребываніи святаго царства, возвеселимся духовнѣ, всегда и нынѣ и присно и въ вѣки вѣкомъ, аминь.

To the mightiest and the most divinely ordained, the most supreme emperor of the Greeks! I dispatch to your holiness, to your holy kingdom, a worthy brother from the kingdom of the grand prince of Muscovy and of All Rus'.

It is therefore also known from divine scripture how from the beginning the benevolence of God, His pronounced bounteousness, and veritable devotion, that the true pure Orthodox Christian faith is extolled in our Lord Jesus Christ in the Trinity, conveyed and augmented to the preeminent imperial city, to the sacred fatherland, this empire, from the pious saintly autocrat of all of the universe, the great prince Constantine [I, the Great]. Once more over much time and years our forefather, the holy and the equal of the Apostles, for it is necessary for us to speak of this about him, the grand prince Vladimir of Kiev and of all Rus', who then was a pagan, was enlightened by the most holy and life-creating Spirit, began to dispatch to all lands and distant towns, to seek places to scrutinize: What is their faith and theology? It was timely to have emissaries for this, hence to Rome where they considered the Latin faith and to many other places. Not only this, but he even commanded to view the faith of the godless Mohammed and [their] divine service. And having investigated these and seeing how all were not suitable, not receiving God but rather were godless, therefore no one would accept Latinism [and] from the ungodly and impious Mohammed the irreligious heresy, for in every way they despised the repudiation. In the end he [Vladimir] dispatched to the imperial city to observe the Greek faith. They, the envoys, his men, saw the true Greek Orthodox Christian faith, how the candle shone triumphantly over the lamps, and they related this to him. He thus willingly and with attention listened, and many buttresses were stung by the divine knowledge, rejoiced through the spirit, and enlivened the heart and all of the conscience. And desiring through unceasing zealousness to advance quickly to the divine bath of Baptism and to cleanse past impiety through the water and the spirit, to shatter the idols of the ancestors, to order this in all of their homeland, in the numerousness of the Rus' land, indeed all bathe in holy Baptism, the small and the large, the rich and the poor, all ranks and ages from the great lords to the simple, and from the elders even to the weaning children, so that they would be the divine blessing. The sooner all were baptized and were known by the Christian name, and piety flourished much, a great multitude of the unfaithful without doubt were driven away. He, the new Constantine the Great, gathered about himself, but it is said [that] the most pious tsar of the Rus' land, Vladimir, [introduced] into his native land for the newly baptized Orthodox Christianity the divine wisdom of the holy great councils and the apostolic church of the imperial city, and from the imperium in the most recent times of the holy tsar and the most righteous law of God from his holiness the patriarch, and concerning it that the divine of the holy councils [decreed] a metropolitan for the Rus' land. For this to strengthen and to sustain his pious sons, grandsons, and great grandsons, and also the created generations, from time to time they would receive from the imperial city metropolitans for their fatherland, the Rus' land, at times a Greek, and sometimes the universal patriarch would consecrate from our land our most holy Rusin, but not from Rome, nor from the pope, nor from a Latin. It was this way to the rule of my ever-memorable lord and my father, the grand prince Vasilii Dimitrievich, and to the preceding our ever-memorable father the most reverend Photios, the metropolitan of Kiev and of All Rus'. And for our blessed divine land, those who were around us brought authority to our grand prince, and the princely landed gentry and as much as possible the heads who were under them all were pious and abided in the Orthodox Christian faith, and in the holy life-giving consubstantial and indivisible Trinity, believing in the Father, the Son, and the Holy Spirit. Through the devotion and the precepts of our holy great forefather, even to the present time, through which we now are God's benefactors to the utmost, the dwelling of divine favor. We now have had the divine teachings, its piety, for 455 years.[77]

After the death of our foremost reposing father, of the aforementioned ever-memorable metropolitan Photios, following whom there arrived the godless Hagarite, and the inter-disputants on account of quarrels and of the Christians because of organization and spiritual advantages, we were urged to go to our father Iona, the bishop of Riazan, a man who was spiritual and who for many years from youth was devoted to a virtuous life. We dispatched with him our most upright boyar Vasilii with a petition to your holy empire, to the most holy patriarch, and to the most divine Holy Synod with our credentials and we enjoined with these utterances to you that you place for us this Bishop Iona on the metropolitan seat. We did not at once marvel at this that because of this it was so for us, and we turned to reflection or after we lingered on a letter to you or that your eminence performed such an action. About which there was no response to you, nor among you there was no one to petition for our needs. You had sent him to us, that is to say Isidore. And indeed to God, if this our immemorial Orthodox Christianity had not been maintained and if we had not had the fear of God in our hearts, then we would desire that no one henceforth would accept him. But we pray for your reply and for the blessing of the most hallowed patriarch, and for the one forceful surprise, and the many appeasements and petitions. We simply received him. When he provoked us with many appeasements and petitions, we had received him as a father and teacher with much honor and favorable eagerness after the previous as him a great most blessed metropolitan of our Rus'. Surmising that he was the sole spokesman from them, he did not know beforehand of some act to be desired of him. But we anticipated that the emperor's envoy told all of this to you about the arrival of this aforementioned Sidor and from the first day he began to go on a journey to the council and of the many prohibitions to him. He began to accuse others of doing [this], stating: "Since he was powerless, he would not go. But if I do not go, we have instead from the most blessed patriarch to acknowledge a sacred oath, as therefore the previous I will go to the extant council and I have need in every way to go, as you placed a decree upon yourselves, thus I will go." And since we were unable to exhort him and prohibit a reasonable journey and again we said much to him concerning this: "But if you go and when you have returned to us, do then bring back to us our pious Orthodox faith that we accepted from our forefather Vladimir, that retained the great council of the Greek apostolic church. But do not bring us an otherwise strange, new, and foreign synodical church, for if you bring something that is new, it will not be in accord for us." He promised with an oath how he would bring nothing new and strange to him. He now returned to us; he brought many strange and foreign [practices and beliefs] to our Orthodox Christianity, to go along with the divine and consecrated precepts of the holy Apostle and divinely born Father and to go along with the heavenly law-giving that was delivered to the holy Apostles and the divinely born Fathers of the Greek holy apostolic church councils, all Orthodox Christians who hereafter [enjoyed] God's benevolence. As we previously wrote, for us the world of the knowledge of God shone, baptism toward repentance to abandon sins enlightened us, and the Christian name is upon us. He brought us a letter from the Roman pope in which concerning the Holy Spirit the Latins affirmed two causes to profess in their own church. And philosophizing the azymous [unleavened bread] that it is veritable, it speaks of the deficiency in making worthy in unleavened and leavened bread the body of Christ. Yet, concerning the latter nourishment they say how therefore for us this appears perplexing, for the pope writes of this in his letter[78] that indeed, he says, we contemplate the profession of a faith in God admitting the conclusion and the fruits of repentance will not ripen to bring over their transgressors, entrusting spiritual fathers among others of them, and such bitter wined torments are seized upon after death, and the following. Because Isidore himself at one time in his very own writings, that he had hastened to dispatch the missive, he nominated himself a legate to the Lateran apostolic seats of Latvia, Lithuania, and Germany, and sealed his letter with a green signet. He issued a command to carry before himself the object, the Latin crucifix, holding it impressively. So that to the two churches, therefore carried into the Orthodox and Latin that were in the Latvian, Lithuanian, and Germanic lands, he brought the papal blessing. He said that he was designated teacher and superior for the sacrilegious bigamists. Still, in his divine service in our sacred cathedral and great church he made mention of the named pope. He subjected and restrained us to this under [the threat of] excommunication, because of the many heresies, by means of the holy and God-bearing Roman paternal church and the Roman pope. Thus he brought the good news to your most sacred sovereignty, as many years prior there was neither unity nor association with the Roman church and the Roman pope, and all other Latins under him with the four most holy patriarchs. It is necessary for all that he do all of this for our Orthodox Christian fathers and teachers, and for all church superiors to nourish, to adorn, and to care for all of the churches, and for all ends of the world to have him first, the unbelievers and the iniquitous to denominate him in their writings the glorious superior and the supreme apostle Peter. They not only strive toward this, but even many other lands and foreigners, [taking] from our Orthodox Christian faith, add to our Orthodoxy that is not written here. We therefore heard this, observed, and drew the former to us. Then an expectation was placed upon an unspoken divine destiny and thanked His philanthropy. Our fatherly bishops beckoned the love of God. As much as possible at this time we discovered in our proximity Ephrem of Rostov, Avram of Suzdal, Iona of Riazan, Barlam of Kolomensk, Iova of Saray, Gerasim of Perm', so also the archimandrites, abbots, the faithful priesthood, and the countless monks of our land. We enjoined them to return to those divine and sacred precepts of the holy Apostle and the bearers of God that we received from the grand holy divine apostolic councils of the Greek Church, our true Orthodoxy. And that which he introduced in the papal letter, we perused the newness for a long time. All appeared to our God-loving Rus' bishops, upright archimandrites, reverend abbots, and other clergy and monks, and all of our Orthodox Christians how all of Isidore's activities and arrival were foreign and unfamiliar to our divine and holy principles.

And for the sake of this, we dispatch our envoys to the devout emperor and to you the most pious sovereign, and to the entire divine and sacred Synod. But with these envoys and this papal document written in Latin and according to your Greek decree, still Isidore brought to us with a papal seal. We beg your most holy sovereignty that the blessed emperor and the divine and consecrated Synod restore your sacred and divine Greek laws, deliberate on its papal writing, the future needs, the impractical journey, the influx upon our Christianity of the godless Hagarite, the disorder and sedition that encircles our land and the mastery of expansion. Establish for us in our land a consecrated autocephalous metropolitan. And again for this need as well as all spiritual needs of each Orthodox Christian and our approval, and the necessary seigniorial sanction and the efforts required of us to work with a metropolitan, the interpretations of the young people for whom it is appropriate to conceal, these among others we advise. For the sake of this we beseech that you send us your most honorable letter, how through the aid of God and the blessed Holy Spirit, through the aid of your sacred empire, the blessed most holy patriarch, and that concerning them the divine and sacred Synod. But through the holy principles we gathered in our native land, in the God-loving Rus' land, our paternal episcopate, through the benevolence of the Holy Spirit such good men were chosen, spiritual men, believing in Orthodoxy, do change for us the metropolitanate in Rus', because of the need prior to this there was in Rus' an ordained metropolitan. And we desire this, the benevolence of God. But from the inception of our Orthodox Christianity, you dispatched, debated, and we had admiration for your sacred empire and blessed most holy patriarch. We request prayers and desire the wish as long as God consents, our land has standing, and no way relinquishes from you to have retained our Orthodox Christianity for ages. We ask your sacred empire of this, that with the information concerning these and with our most upright letter give leave to these our envoys without charge, and that you accustom with the judiciousness and the prosperity of the sacred empire. We seek enlightenment now, always, ever, and for all times. Amen.

This letter is an excellent summary statement of the Muscovite Rus' adherence to a "true Orthodox Christianity." It is subtle in its approach, respectful in tone, and not intended to be provocative, either toward the Byzantine emperor or toward his patriarch. Rather, the text seeks to convey the notion that the Muscovite Rus' had preserved over the centuries the true Orthodox faith introduced by Vladimir I and had maintained an unwavering belief in its teachings and laws. They call upon the Greeks to recognize this, in the hope that the agreements reached with the Latins at the Council of Ferrara-Florence will in no way alter their historical and traditional Orthodox outlook. The Rus' letter even reflects upon Isidore's strong support of the *Decree of Church Union*, but restates their wish that he bring nothing new and foreign from the council. Most significant is the Muscovite Rus' request that Constantinople grant to them an autocephalous metropolitanate, yielding to them the privilege at greater ecclesiastical independence, although remaining within the sphere of Byzantine patriarchal authority. At the same time the Muscovites admit that prior metropolitans at times were Greeks and at times they were of Rus' stock. Also of significance is the Muscovite position of being consistently anti-Muslim. Their fear of Islamic inroads as the Byzantine was clearly justified if one examines the historical record of the Kievan and Muscovite Rus'. Puzzling, however, is their equating the Muslims with the Latins. The letter does subtlety advocate the candidacy of Iona for the metropolitan seat, but at the same time it stresses the un-Orthodoxy of Isidore, arguing that his actions and pro-Latin ceremonies upon his arrival were both alien and new to Muscovite religious principles. On this note, the letter concludes the Muscovite position on sundry questions. It remains historically unclear whether the Byzantines ever responded to the correspondence. No such document has survived. It is only certain that if there was no reply, then this was license for the Muscovite Synod to elevate Iona to an autocephalous metropolitan seat later in that decade.

Notes

1 Ramm, p. 228, citing *ЯИБ* 19: 436, 437, claims that Pope Eugenius IV was instrumental in convincing the Byzantines to nominate Isidore for the vacant seat at Moscow. The assertion may be plausible. But aside from this claim and the validity of its statement, we have no other Vatican, Greek, or Muscovite corroborating sources to support or to refute this contention, which may be part and parcel of Muscovite anti-Latin polemical literature that emerged soon after the fall of Constantinople in 1453 and was quite vociferous thereafter, even achieving the prominence of historical fact. For a study of this issue, cf. A.S. Pavlov, *Критические опыты по истории древнейщей греко-руски полемники пртив латиям* [= *Critical Essays on the History of Ancient Greco-Rus' Polemics Against the Latins*] (St. Petersburg, 1878), *passim*; A.N. Popov, *Историко-лутертурный обзор древне-русских полемических сочнений против латинян (XI–XV в.)* [= *A Historical-Literary Survey of Ancient Rus' Polemical Works Against the Latins (Eleventh–Fifteenth Centuries)*] (Moscow, 1875; repr. London, 1972), pp. 363, 364, and *passim*; and P. Sokolov, "Был-ли Мсковскій Митрополитъ Исилоръ палскмъ легатомъ для москвы [= Was the Muscovite Metropolitan Isidore a Papal Legate to Moscow]?" in *Чтения въ Историческомъ Обществе Нестщра-Лутопица* 20/2 (Kiev, 1908), pp. 23–38. Gill, *Personalities of the Council of Florence*, p. 46, makes the significant observation that in 1436 Bessarion was designated *hegoumenos*/abbot of the monastery of Saint Basil, granting him a position comparable to that of Isidore, and "shortly afterwards he [Bessarion] was elected to the See of Nicaea, at about the same time that Mark Eugenikos became Metropolitan of Ephesus, Isidore Metropolitan of Kiev and All Russia, and Dionysius Metropolitan of Sardis." Hereafter, there follows a close parallel in the careers of Isidore and Bessarion, each holding similar offices, if not also interchanging them. It is highly doubtful that the pope supported the elevations of Mark Eugenikos and Dionysios, for both were anti-union proponents, and it was highly improbable that they were in the pope's good graces. But illustrative of John VIII's desire to maintain balance between the pro-unionist and pro-Orthodox elements within his empire, these appointments clearly exemplify his political and theological point of view. There appears, however, confusion in the sources on when this nomination was extended, whether in late 1436 or later in early 1437. *Vat. gr.* 776, fol. 209^v, would have Isidore receiving the appointment in late 1436 and soon thereafter departing for Moscow. For this journey and his stopover in L'vov (L'viv), cf. P. Schreiner, "Ein byzantinischer Gelehrter zwischen Ost und West. Zur Biographie des Isidor von Kiew und seinem Besuch in Lviv (1436)," *Bollettino della Badia Greca di Grottaferrata* 3/3 (2006): pp. 215–228.

2 Cf. A-E. Tachiaos, "The Greek Metropolitans of Kievan Rus': An Evaluation of Their Spiritual and Cultural Activity," *Harvard Ukrainian Studies* 12–13 (1988–1989): p. 431 f.;

and for the substantive literature on the subject of training and preparation, *ibid.*, p. 430 n. 1. The article was reprinted in *idem, Greeks and Slavs*, pp. 349–364.
3 On these complex problems, cf. Vernadsky, *The Mongols and Russia*, pp. 294–297 and 299–302.
4 Photios was a Moreot born in Monemvasia, who maintained a correspondence in the 1420s with Isidore. For Isidore's correspondence, cf. *ГИМ No. 284*, fol. 335ʳ. A brief description of the text appears in B.L. Fonkich, "Греческие писцы эпохи возрождения [Greek Scribes in the Renaissance Epoch] [Part] 3," *BB* 42 (1981): p. 126. Photios's death in 1431 is confirmed by the *Никаноровская Льтопись (Nikanorov [Monastery] Annal)*, ПСРЛ 27 (Moscow-Leningrad, 1962), p. 102. Cf. *Сокрвщенный Льтописный Сводъ 1495 г.* [*The Abbreviated Annalistic Code of the Year 1495*], ПСРЛ 27: 209, under year 6939/1431. The *Патриаршая или Никоновская Льтопись* [*Patriarchal or Nikon Annal*], ПСРЛ 12 (St. Petersburg, 1901), p. 10, furnishes an elaborate tale of an angel visiting him prior to his death. We should further notice that Muscovite Rus' was emerging as a centralizing force among the Rus' provinces and its princes were the leading advocates for this trend. Photios was well aware of this movement and whether or not he conveyed this to John VIII and perhaps even to Isidore in their correspondence is unclear. On this, cf. A.-E.N. Tachiaos, "The Testament of Photius Monembasiotes, Metropolitan of Russia (1408–1431): Byzantine Ideology in XVth-Century Muscovy," *Cyrillomethodianum* 3 (1983): 89 f.; repr. in *idem, Greeks and Slavs*, p. 377 f.
5 J.S. Luria (Lur'e), "Fifteenth-Century Chronicles as a Source for the History of the Formation of the Muscovite State," in M.S. Flier and D. Rowland, eds. *Medieval Russian Culture*, California Slavic Studies 19/2 (Berkeley, Los Angeles, and London, 1994), pp. 52, 53.
6 Pliguzov, pp. 640–654.
7 ПСРЛ 25: 270. For two variant texts in the same source, cf. ПСРЛ 12: *Патриаршая или Никоновская Льтопись* [= *The Patriarchal or Nikon Annal*] (St. Petersburg, 1901), p. 74, one brief and the other expanding the passage, that do not appreciably alter the information. Also, cf. ПСРЛ 23: *Ермолиская Льтопись* [= *The Ermolin Annal*] (St. Petersburg, 1910), p. 154; *ibid.*, 27: 115; *ibid.*, 27: 347; *ibid.*, 28: *Льтописный Сводъ 1497 г.* [= *The Annalistic Code of the Year 1497*] (Moscow-Leningrad, 1963), p. 110; *ibid.*, 28: *Льтопись Сводъ 1518 г.* [= *The Annalistic Code of the Year 1518*], pp. 277, 278; *ibid.*, 30: *Владимирский Льтописецъ* [= *The Vladimir Annalist*] (Moscow, 1965), p. 134; and *ibid.*, 31: *Мазрискийслий Льтописецъ* [= *The Mazurin Annalist*] (Moscow, 1968), p. 106.
8 That is, Rus' synodal members.
9 ПРСЛ 12: 20. It is noteworthy that the *Muscovite Annalistic Code* makes no reference to the appointment of Gerasim, nor relates anything regarding him. Thus reference to him is totally excised from this work. Cf. ПСРЛ 25: 248 ff. This is also true of two later chronicles, the *Хроника Литовская* [*The Lithuanian Chronicle*] and *Хроника Быховциа* [*The Bykhov Chronicle*]. Cf. the appropriate sections in, respectively, ПРСЛ 32 (Moscow, 1975), pp. 80 f., and 152–155.
10 For the complex political issues of the early 1430s, cf. S.M. Soloviev, *История Россий с древнейших Времен* [*A History of Russia since Ancient Times*], 2 (vol. 4) (Moscow, 1960), pp. 577–582; Vernadsky, *The Mongols and Russia*, pp. 298, 299 and 308; and Ramm, pp. 222, 223.
11 ПСРЛ 22: 506. Paradoxically, few major Rus' annals mention Iona's journey to Constantinople to seek confirmation for this office.
12 *РИБ* 19: 436, 437. Sophia Senyk, "The Patriarchate of Constantinople and the Metropolitans of Rus', 1300–1600," in *Le patriarcat œcuménique de Constantinople aux XIVᵉ–XVIᵉ siècles: rupture et continuité. Actes du colloque international Rome, 5–6–7 décembre 2005*, Dossiers byzantins 7 (Paris, 2007), p. 99, makes the astute observation:

> [G]rand [P]rince Basil II of Moscow wrote to the patriarch [Joseph] announcing Iona's election, and indeed all documents referring to the election, take pains to point out that the patriarch had promised at the time of the election of Isidore as

metropolitan of Kiev, when already Moscow proposed Iona, that Iona would succeed Isidore should the latter die first.

This claim is limited to Muscovite sources, and there is no reference to a patriarchal promise in the Greek works. For the Muscovite references, cf. *РИБ* 6: 575–586; and *Руский Феодалный Архив*, ed. A.I. Pliguzov, et al., 1 (Moscow, 1986), pp. 88–91.

13 ПСРЛ 12: 23.
14 *Ibid.*, p. 23 nn. 1 and 2, wherein the notes demonstrate that the renditions of this annual furnish two dates for his arrival, 6945/1437 and 6946/1438. The former is the accepted year of arrival.
15 Sylvestros Syropoulos confirms Isidore's substantial knowledge and learning. Cf. his treatment of Isidore, *passim*, wherein Syropoulos is at times complimentary of Isidore. On the other hand, for a recent treatment of Isidore as a treacherous individual during the proceedings at Ferrara-Florence and thereafter upon his return to Moscow, cf. Maria Pia Pagani, "Il 'perfido' protagonista: Isidoro di Kiev al concilio di Firenze del 1439," in Gabriele de Rosa and Francesca Lomastro, eds., *L'età di Kiev e la sua eredità nell'incontro con l'Occidente. Atti del Convegne Vicenza, 11–13 aprile 2002* (Rome, 2003), esp. pp. 159–169. She notes no manuscript sources and relies upon printed works that support the Latin positions in the proceedings at Florence.
16 ПСРЛ 12: 23, 24.
17 O. Halecki, *From Florence to Brest (1439–1596)* (Rome, 1958), p. 42, maintains on the evidence of Muscovite sources that "the metropolitan received the desired permission to go to the council." The evidence, however, in this and subsequent Muscovite accounts does not indicate such precise language, unless the Rus' accounts are intended to be misleading. Cf. Pierling, 1: 16 ff.; and E.E. Golubinsky, *Исторія Русской Церкви* [= *A History of the Russian Church*], 1 (2nd ed., Moscow, 1901), pp. 414–440.
18 ПСРЛ 25:253. An almost identical rendition of this text appears in ПСРЛ 8:*Продолженье Льтниси но Воскрсенскому Списку* [= *A Continuation to the Annal according to the Voskresensk Transcript*] (St. Petersburg, 1859), pp. 100, 101. The *Muscovite Annalistic Code* indicates a borrowing from the Voskresensk Transcript, but with emendation.
19 Like him, those who were proponents of church union.
20 This annal was first published in ПСРЛ 6 (St. Petersburg, 1855; repr. Leningrad, 1925). The citations that follow are taken from the 1855 redaction, part 2. A recent rendition (Moscow, 2001) subscribes to modern textual editing with questionable orthographic substitutions and additions.
21 ПСРЛ 6: 151, 152.
22 Father John Meyendorff, an ordained Russian Orthodox priest and scholar, interprets this passage to read: "Isidore also accepted the task of assuring victory of Orthodoxy at the council, as he was convincing the Russian grand-prince to support the council." Cf. J. Meyendorff, "Was There an Encounter Between East and West at Florence?" in Alberigo, p. 162 n. 22.
23 ПСРЛ 21/2 (St. Petersburg, 1913): ch. 19, pp. 506, 507.
24 *Ibid*.
25 Correctly, this should read Basle, unless the scribe intended the term to imply the Roman lands.
26 The city of Rome is not implied here; rather, the scribe may be citing Rome to mean the Latin lands. Given his textual materials, the scribe should have been aware that the council was meeting in Ferrara and then continuing its deliberations at Florence.
27 Unless a gross exaggeration, this term should rather be understood to imply Caesars, or senior provincial princes, and certainly not emperors who would be subordinate to a grand prince.
28 Notably, cf. ПСРЛ 23: 149.
29 The dates for his departure from Constantinople and first arrival in Moscow are at variance in the sources. The question is further compounded by differing dates given in

the annals of his departure for and arrival at Ferrara. No clear resolution can be made of these incongruities and even his personal travel account raises questions of when he first arrived in Moscow, then soon departed for Ferrara-Florence, and later returned to Moscow.

30 A number of significant studies have appeared, preparing critical editions and analyses of his travel account. Among them, cf. N.A. Kazakova, "Первоначальная Редакция 'Хождения на Флорентийлий Собор' [= The First Redaction of 'The Journey to the Council of Florence']," *ТОДРЛ 25: Памятники Русской Литературы X-XVII вв.* [= *Monuments of Russian Literature Xth–XVIIth Centuries*] (Moscow, 1970), pp. 60–72; "Хождение Митрополита Исидора иа Флорентїискїи Соборъ [= The Journey of Metropolitan Isidor to the Council of Florence]," in J. Krajcar, ed. *Acta Slavica Concilii Florentini. Narrationes et Documenta*, CFDS 11, series A (Rome, 1976), columnar texts in Old Slavonic and Latin; *Библиотека Литературы Древней Руси* [= *A Literary Library of Ancient Rus'*], eds. D.S. Likhachev, et al., 6 (St. Petersburg, 1999), pp. 464–487, medieval and modern Russian texts on facing pages; "Reisebericht eines unbekannten Russen (1437–1440)," in G. Stökl, ed. *Europa im XV. Jahrhundert von byzantinern Gesehen* (Graz, Vienna, and Cologne, 1954), pp. 151–189. Most recently, cf. P. Bádenas de la Peña and A. L. Encinas Moral, "Anónimo ruso sobre et viaje de Isidoro de Kiev ad Consilio de Florencia," *Erythei* 35 (2014): pp. 251–299, with a Spanish translation and the Slavonic text. For a textual study of the several renditions of the travel account, cf. J. Krajcar, "Metropolitan Isidore's Journey to the Council of Florence. Some Remarks," *OCP* 38 (1972): pp. 367–387; O. Kresten, *Eine Sammlung von Konzilsakten aus dem Besitze des Kardinals Isidoros von Kiev.* Österreichische Akademie der Wissenschaften. Philosophisch-Historische Klasse Denkschriften, 123 (Vienna, 1976); and M. di Branco, "Da Ferrara a Firenze. Gli itinerari delle delegazioni conciliari (Gennaio-Febbraio 1439) e le visite di Eugenio IV e Giovanni VIII a Pistoia," *Rendiconti* 19 (2008), esp. pp. 740–742. For additional studies of the travel account, cf. T. Frommann, *Kritische Beiträge zur Geschichte der Florentiner Kircheneinigung* (Halle, 1872), pp. 112–121, and *passim*; and S. Kolditz, *Johannes VIII. Palaiologos und das Konzil von Ferara-Florenz (1438/39). Das byzantinische Kaisertum im Dialog mit dem Westen*, Monographen zur Geschichte des Mittelalters, Band 60, 1 (Stuttgart, 2013), p. 37 n. 183.

31 Simeon of Suzdal, *Acta Slavica Concilii Florentini. Narrationis et Documenta*, ed. J. Krajcar, CFDS, Series A, 9 (Rome, 1976), p. 55. The full account by Simeon of the travels of Isidore and the Muscovite delegation, and their participation in the discussions on various issues at Ferrara and Florence, appears both in Latin and Slavonic renditions in *ibid.*, pp. 51–76. The account from a Muscovite viewpoint relates further the roles of John VIII and Patriarch Joseph at the council, but adds little that is new or in opposition to the accounts of the Greeks and Latins. Simeon does provide some insights on the roles played by leading Rus' clerics at the council. For recensions of Simeon's account, cf. J. Krajcar, SJ, "Simeon of Suzdal's Account of the Council of Florence," *OCP* 39 (1973): pp. 103–130. But as Father Krajcar evaluates (pp. 103, 104) the value of the account, he stresses:

> One aspect only, I believe, has not been sufficiently examined, viz. how far is Simeon's Account credible and what spirit prompted and animated him in writing the pamphlet. Though an eyewitness, Simeon does not offer trustworthy evidence on the personalities of the Council and his presentation of theological discussions is a mere farce. He gives, however, an insight into the moods of the common people, servants and attendants, Russian and Greek alike. His writing is also of importance for learning the aftermath of the Council in Muscovy and for studying the beginnings of Muscovite ideology.

32 CFDS, series B, 5, fasc. 1; *AG*, p. lxxi. Cf. Pierling, p. 22; and G. Hofmann, "Die Konzilsarbeit in Ferrara," *OCP* 3 (1937): p. 408.

33 For the proceedings in Florence, cf. *idem*, "Die Konzilsarbeit in Florenz," *OCP* 4 (1938): pp. 157–188 and 372–422.
34 Isidore lists thirteen, perhaps only those in which he had participated or of which he had immediate knowledge. Simeon of Suzdal lists seventeen, p. 61.
35 Cf. Krajcar, "Metropolitan Isidore's Journey," pp. 274–275, who addresses the problem of the number of general (not minor) sessions at Ferrara and later Florence. The numbers are confused in the various sources.
36 CFDS 11: fol. 124^r–124^v (pp. 28, 29). For a variant English translation from the Latin rendition, the *Peregrinatio*, of the Хождение, cf. Annemarie Weyl Carr, "Labelling Images, Venerating Icons in Sylvester Syropoulos's World," in Fonti Kondyli, *et al.*, eds., *Sylvester Syropoulos on Politics and Culture in the Fifteenth-Century Mediterranean. Themes and Problems in the Memoirs, Section IV*, Birmingham Byzantine and Ottoman Studies 16 (Farnham, 2014), p. 86.
37 For an extensive discussion of the preliminaries leading to the departure of John VIII and Patriarch Joseph for the Council of Ferrara-Florence and their passage, cf. especially Sylvestros Syropoulos III.6 ff. and IV.1–10; and the briefer treatment in *CF*, pp. 88–91 and *passim*. Most recently, cf. Fondyli, and esp. the essays of Elizabeth A. Zachariadou, "The Ottomans, the Greek Orthodox Church and the Perils of the Papacy," pp. 23–32; R. Price, "Precedence and Papal Primacy," pp. 33–47; Vera Andriopoulou, "The Logistics of a Union: Diplomatic Communication through the Eyes of Sylvester Syropoulos," pp. 49–67; and Fotini Kondyli, "The Logistics of a Union: The Travelling Arrangements and the Journey to Venice," pp. 135–153.
38 Sylvestros Syropoulos IV.25 (p. 222).
39 For a succinct compilation of the theological issues addressed at the Council of Ferrara-Florence, cf. Angold, p. 21.
40 *CF*, pp. 114 ff.
41 On the difficulties of the extended *filioque* discussions, *AG*, pp. 400 ff., 426 ff., *passim*, and esp. the lucid argumentation of Georgios Scholarios, pp. 428–431. Cf. *CF*, ch. 5: "The Addition to the Creed;" and ch. 7: "Union: The Procession of the Holy Spirit." For a discussion of the procession of the Holy Spirit, cf. Waugh, 8: 39. On the role of Christian Humanism in these theological disputations, cf. G. Podskalsky, *Von Photios zu Bessarion. Der Vorrang humanistisch geprägter Theologie in Byzanz und deren bleibende Bedeutung.* Schriften zur Geistesgeschichte des östlichen Europa, Band 25 (Wiesbaden, 2003), *passim*.
42 Cf. Sylvestros Syropoulos VIII.9 (p. 398), VIII.21 (p. 408), and VIII.27 (p. 414).
43 Eugenikos, according to a source, departed Ferrara during the month of September 1438. His absence was brief. He did return and participated in later public sessions, but afterward often absented himself for sundry reasons. He was not a signatory to the accord inaugurating the union of churches and remained a firm anti-unionist during and following the council. Cf. *ПкП* 1:277.
44 This exchange took place on the 8th or 9th of October 1438, during a conciliar session. Cf. *Andreas de Santacroce, advocatus consistorialis, Acta Latina Concilii Florentini*, ed. G. Hofmann, CFDS, series B, 6 (Rome, 1955), p. 33. For a brief treatment of Isidore's theological views within the context of Byzantine religious thought of that period, cf. P. Schreiner, "I teologi bizantini del XIV secolo e i padre della Chiesa, con particolare riguardo all biblioteca di Isidoro di Kiev," in M. Cortesi, ed. *Padri Greci e Latini a Confronto (Secoli XIII–XV). Atti del Convegno di studi della Società Internazionale per lo Studio del Medioevo Latino (SISMEL). Certosa del Galluzzo Firenze, 19–20 ottobre 2001* (Florence, 2004), pp. 133–141.
45 On this point, cf. *CF*, pp. 152–156 and 153 n. 8.
46 *Codex Vat. gr. 1896*, fols. 214^r–216^v.
47 *Codex Vat. gr. 706*, fols. 166^r–169^v. A Latin summation appears in Isidore, *Sermones*, X/1: viii–ix; and the full Latin and Greek texts of Ποῖα ἐν τῇ Συνόδῳ ἐστὶ τὸ Βέλτιον Ποιητέα / *De Modo Procedendi in Concilio*, in *ibid.*, pp. 1–8.

48 *Codex Vat. gr. 1896*, fols. 181ʳ–184ʳ. For a Latin summation, cf. Isidore, *Sermones*, X/1: ix. For the full Latin and Greek texts of Λόγος Πρῶτος κατὰ τῆς ἐν τῷ Συμβόλῳ Προσθήκης/*Sermo prior contra Additionem as Symbolum*, in *ibid.*, pp. 9–16.

49 Among other texts (in manuscript and other formats) that have been published: Λόγος Συμβουλευτικὸς περὶ Ὁμονοίας τῷ Συμβόλῳ/Exhortatoria Oratio ad Concilium, on the procession of the Holy Spirit and a discussion of the prepositions, ex and per, *Codex Vat. gr. 706*, fols. 12ʳ–22ʳ, in addition, the Latin and Greek texts being in Isidore, *Sermones*, X/1: 54–80, with a Latin summation in *ibid.*, pp. x–xii; further, a second major work, *Codex Vat. gr. 1896*, fols. 139ʳ–156ᵛ, on the procession of the Holy Spirit, Isidore's Λόγος Δεύτερος κατὰ τῆς ἐν τῷ Συμβόλῳ Προσθήκης/Sermo Alter Contra Additionem ad Symbolum, the Latin and Greek texts being in Isidore, *Sermones*, X/1: 17–53, with a summary on *ibid.*, pp. ix, x; the results of the Council of Florence in *Codex Vat. gr. 1858*, fols. 44ʳ–50ʳ, the Latin summation is found in Isidore, *Sermones*, X/1: xii; and corrections to the former in *Codex Vat. gr. 1904*, fols. 112ʳ–113ʳ; and the apographa in *Codex Vat. gr. 1152*, fols. 173ᵛ–183ʳ. The last two texts are summarized in Isidore, *Sermones*, X/1: xii. Both the full Latin and Greek text (*Codex Vat. gr. 1858*, fols. 44ʳ–50ʳ) of Isidore's Πῶς δεῖ τὴν Ἕνωσιν ἐκτελεῖσθαι/Sermo de Unione Florentina Exsequenda, appears in Isidore, *Sermones*, X/1: 81–94.

50 *Andreas de Santacroce*, fol. 130ᵛ (6: 222). The Latin text is addressed in this study for its clarity rather than the Greek.

51 *Ibid.*, 148ʳ, 148ᵛ (251).

52 *Ibid.*, 146ᵛ–148ʳ (248–250). Cf. *CF*, pp. 274, 275 and 280, 281.

53 *Codex Vat. gr. 706*, fols. 121ᵛ, 122ʳ. Cf. *supra* the like response of Isidore to Cardinal Andreas de Santacroce. Apparently the failure to provide cited Latin texts was an ongoing issue between the Greeks and Latins. The Latin legates at Florence, like Ferrara, saw no need to furnish them to their Greek counterparts, either from a contemptuous position for their peers or because they were hardened in their argumentation, believing its rationalization to be superior to one based upon faith.

54 Georgios Scholarios, *Ouvres complètes de Gennade Scholarios*, eds. L. Petit, X.A. Sidéridès, and M. Jugie, 3 (Paris, 1931), p. 87, 88.

55 Cf. Sylvestros Syropoulos VIII.33 (p. 420) f. and VIII.35–36 (pp. 422 and 424). For a lengthy discussion of this complex question, cf. the Latin summation especially in Isidore, *Sermones*, X/1: pp. ix–x; *CF*, pp. 245 ff.; Geanakoplos, "A New Reading of the Acta," p. 336 and n. 42; and C.N. Tsirpanlis, *Mark Eugenicus and the Council of Florence: A Historical Re-evaluation of His Personality* (New York, 1979), pp. 89, 90, and *passim*.

Years earlier in a correspondence with his friend Manuel Chrysoloras, c. 1415, Isidore addressed the meaning of φίλος and its implications for the current argumentation. On this, cf. Podskalsky, pp. 35, 36; and Ziegler, "Die restlichen vier unveröffentlichen Briefe Isidores," pp. 135 and 138 ff.

56 Sylvestros Syropoulos IX.18 (p. 452). Aside from this small group of Greek clerics that had attended his dinner(s), following the signing of the *Decree of Church Union*, a large number of Greeks rejected the outcome. For a comprehensive treatment of this subject, cf. Marie-Hélène Blanchet, "L'èglise byzantine à la suite de l'Union de Florence (1439–1445). De la contestation à la scission," in *Byzantinische Forschungen 29* [= *VIIIᵉ Symposium Byzantinon. L'Eglise dans le monde byzantine de la IVᵉ croisade (1204) à la chute de Constantinople (1453)*] (Strasbourg, 7, 8 et 9 novembre 2002) (2007), pp. 79–123. Cf. idem, ed., *Théodore Agallianos. Dialogue avec un moine contre les Latins* (1442), Byzantina Sorbonensia 27 (Paris, 2013), esp. ch. 3: "L'Unione de Florence et ses répercussions."

57 The Latin text of the *Decree* along with the signatories appears in *Andreas de Santacroce*, fols. 153ᵛ–157ᵛ (6: 260–266); and *CF*, pp. 412–415, but without the autographs. For some analyses of the *Decree*, cf. G.R. Evans, "The Council of Florence and the Problem of Ecclesiastical Identity," in Alberigo, p. 178.

58 *Andreas de Santacroce*, fol. 156ᵛ (6: 265). *AG*, p. 465, however reads: *Isidorus metropolita Kioviensis totiusque Russiae, et locum tenens apostolicae sedis sanctissimi patriarchae Antiocheni*

domini Dorothei, contentus subscripsi. Isidore's endorsement appears soon after that of the emperor, given the fact that he was the procurator for the absent patriarch of Antioch.
59 Dorotheos, the Patriarch of Antioch, was unable to attend the proceedings at Ferrara and Florence, and in his absence Isidore was designated his replacement with all rights and privileges of the patriarch. To what extent he exercised the patriarchal privileges remains unclear from the extant texts. If anything, he appears to have maintained an air of decorum and with prudence did not display the trappings of that high office.
60 In *Epistolae Pontificiae ad Concilium Florentinum Spectantes*, ed. G. Hofmann, CFDS, Series A, part 2 (Rome, 1944), p. 77. The complete Greek version of the *Decree of Church Union* appears in *ibid.*, pp. 68–79, doc. 176. However, with slight revision, particularly the last phrase, *AG*, p. 465, reads: Ἰσίδωρος μητροπολίτης Κιαίβου καὶ πάσης Ῥωσίας, καὶ τοπορητὴς τῆς ἀποστολικῆς καθέδρας τοῦ ἁγιωτάτου πατριάρχου Ἀντιοχείας κυρίου Δωροθέου, ἀρκετὸς ὑπέγραφα. Cf. Hofmann, "Die Konzilsarbeit in Florence," pp. 413–417.
61 For the full text of the letter, cf. *Epistolae Pontificiae ad Concilium Florentinum Spectantes*, pp. 93–94, doc. 202. Cf. *Vat. Reg. 365*, fol. 190^r, 190^v. For Isidore's further role and activities in Poland and Lithuania, cf. Kolditz, 1: 352 f. and n. 280, and 378, 379.
62 *Epistolae Pontificiae ad Concilium Florentinum Spectantes*, pp. 94, 95, doc. 203. Cf. *Vat. Reg. 365*, fols. 190^v, 191^r.
63 ПРСЛ 6 (St. Petersburg, 1855): pp. 160, 161. A manuscript rendition of the papal letter is also to be found in the Mazurin Collection, *Codex No. 1530*, fols. 540^r–541^r, deposited in Moscow at the Центральный Государственный Архив Древних Актов (the State Central Archive for Ancient Acts). The letter is reproduced in *Acta Slavica Concilii Florentini. Narrationis et Documenta*, ed. J. Krajcar, SJ, CFDS 9 (Rome, 1976), pp. 138–139. Another rendition of the letter also appears in the Продолженіе Лѣтописи Воскресенскому Сриску [= Continuation of the Annal according to the Voskresensk Transcript] 8: pp. 108, 109. The latter has some orthographical and terminological alterations, but these do not amend the intent of the letter nor its thoughts. A reference to the letter but without the full Cyrillic text of the correspondence appears in *Epistolae Pontificiae ad Concilium Florentinum Spectantes*, pp. 95, 96, doc. 204. For additional renditions, cf. CFDS 9: p. 138.
64 *Epistolae Pontificiae ad Concilium Florentinum Spectantes*, pp. 143, 144, doc. 233. *Cf. Vat. gr. 133* for the Greek text of the letter. Additionally, two other papal letters in support of Isidore's ministry should be briefly noted in our study. An epistle, dated the 25th of March 1442, was addressed by Eugenius IV to Baron Doldio and to Casimir, the grand duke of Lithuania, commending the episcopacy of Cardinal Isidore to their regions. Cf. Hofmann, *Epistolae Pontificiae*, 3: pp. 66, 67, doc. 259. For the Greek text, cf. *Codex Vat. gr. 1018*. The second brief communication, dated the 11th of June 1445, is addressed by Eugenius IV relative to Isidore and the union of churches to a general noble audience. Cf. *ibid.*, 2: 104, 105, doc. 282. For the Greek text, cf. *Vat. gr. 133*.
65 For a printed version of the manuscript, cf. Krajcar, *Acta Slavica Concilii Florentini*, pp. 140–142. A rendition of the letter with significant orthographical and phraseological alterations appears in the *Second Sofia Annal*, ПСРЛ 6: pp. 159, 160. The Krajcar text is herein employed. It remains unclear from all extant sources whether the monk Gregory (identified as of Greek stock, but more often and perhaps correctly as the "Bulgarian"), who was also a longtime companion of Isidore, was instrumental in translating the original Greek letter into Church Slavonic. Further, J. Gill, SJ, "Isidore's Encyclical Letter from Buda," in A. G. Welkykyi, ed., *Analecta Ordinis S. Basilii Magni. Miscelanea in Honorem Cardinalis Isidore (1463–1963)*, 4/1–2 (Rome, 1963), pp. 1, 2, has erred. He has added a preamble to the text that is borrowed from the *Second Sofia Annal* and is not a part of the original letter. Further, his citation, claimed from the *Second Sofia Annal*, is questionable. The polemical addition in the *Second Sofia Annal* correctly reads:

Сіи же Сидоръ злочестивыи принмъ отъ папы велию честь; и тако идущу ему от Рима в путь свои на Руськую митрополию. принде въ градъ нарицаемыи Будинъ, мѣсяца марта въ 5 день. Оттѹду пославшѹ емѹ своа писаниа въ Латьскѹ юн въ Литовьскѹю землю и на всю Рѹсь православнаго хрестьианства.

This impious Sidor received from the pope a great honor. And so he set out from Rome on his journey to the Rus' metropolitanate. He arrived at the town named Buda on the fifth day of March. From here he sent his letter to the Latvian and to the Lithuanian lands and to all of the Rus' Orthodox Christendom.

66 Gill, "Isidore's Encyclical Letter," p. 5.
67 Krajcar, *Acta Slavica*, doc. V (pp. 144–145). Cf. *Vat. sl. 12*, fols. 18ᵛ, 19ʳ. For the complex issues addressed in this letter and subsequent correspondence, cf. Halecki, *From Florence to Brest*, pp. 56–69.
68 The term *voevoda* is more common in usage among the fifteenth-century Balkan Slavs. Its use herein may be evidence that Isidore's companion, Gregory, was instrumental in translating the original Greek text into Slavonic.
69 For a further description of Isidore's arrival, cf. Krajcar, "Simeon of Suzdal's Account of the Council of Florence," pp. 128–130.
70 ПСРЛ 6: 161, 162. Cf. M. Cherniavsky, "The Reception of the Council of Florence in Moscow," *Church History* 24/4 (1955): pp. 348–351; and a detailed account of succeeding events in *CF*, pp. 359 ff.
71 In *Acta Slavica Concilii Florentini*, CFDS 11: pp. 51–76 (text).
72 Simeon of Suzdal identifies the church as that of the Blessed Virgin. *Ibid.*, fol. 20ʳ (71).
73 ПСРЛ 6: 162.
74 *Ibid.*, p. 163 n. (unnumbered), gives the date of his flight as the 15th of September 1441, six months after his confinement. The note further states that he departed Moscow, went to Tver where he was briefly incarcerated, and then proceeded to Lithuania, from where he continued his journey to Rome.
75 *Ibid.*, p. 162. For the leading secondary literature on this topic: the charges, trial, and escape, cf. Cherniavsky, p. 357 n. 19.
76 ПСРЛ 6: 162–167. The editors of this annal questionably date the letter to 1438. This is highly improbable, since John VIII was in Italy attending the Council of Ferrara-Florence, as was Joseph, the sitting patriarch of Constantinople. Correctly, the letter should be assigned to the year 1441 or later, after Isidore had departed Muscovite Rus'. Further, *Акты Историческіе* 1 (St. Petersburg, 1841), pp. 71–75, notes that this letter was also sent to the patriarch of Constantinople, Metrophanes II (1440–1443). Cf. *infra*, n. 77.

There remain further chronological issues concerning correspondence between Moscow and Constantinople. V. Malinin, *Старецъ Елеазарова Монастыря Филоѳей и его Посланія. Историко-Литературное Изльдованіе* [= *The Elder of the Eleazarov Monastery, Filothei and His Correspondence. A Historical-Literary Inquiry*] (Kiev, 1901), pp. 444, 445, cites a letter sent by the grand prince of Moscow to the patriarch of Constantinople, Metrophanes II, in 1441. The contents of this correspondence appear to be very similar, even in language and tone, to that of the 1443 letter. Cf. *ibid.*, n. 1651; and *РИБ* 6: pp. 525–528. However, according to *ibid.*, 6: pp. 526–535, the letter was never sent because the emperor had accepted the union of churches. Cf. Vernadsky, 3: p. 312. The letter of 1443 may have been prompted because the patriarchate under the leadership of Metrophanes had acquired the reputation of being ineffectual in its dealings with its ecclesiastical subordinates and was noted for rarely responding to written requests. The Second Sofia Annal also raises editorial questions, mainly mislocated texts on the printed pages and the letter section in particular should be used with caution, as two columns are not parts of the letter. For other renditions of the letter in Muscovite archives, cf. ПСРЛ 6: 165–167, the unnumbered notes. However, of all the Muscovite annals, only the *Львовская Льтопись* (*L'vov Annal*) includes a briefer rendition of the letter. Cf. ПСРЛ 20/1 (St. Petersburg, 1910), pp. 251–254. For a substantially revised and emended text, that includes a significant section referencing the dogmatic issues leading up to the conversion of Kievan Rus', but is deleted from the cited letter, cf. *Сфійская Вторая*

Летопись, ПСРЛ 6 (Moscow, 2001), pp. 93–97. There appears to be no conclusion in this revision, for the letter leads into a vitriolic discussion of Isidore's metropolitanate and advances the claim of Iona to the metropolitan seat of Kiev and of All Rus'.

77 Assuming that their calculation is accurate, if we accept the year of 988 as the year of the baptism of Vladimir and his conversion of Kievan Rus' to Byzantine Christianity, then this letter would have been written and transmitted to Constantinople in 1443, and certainly not in 1438. Further, the contents of the letter do not support the earlier date. Halecki, *From Florence to Brest*, pp. 73–74, concurs with the year 1443.

78 The statement that the pope referenced dogmatic questions resolved at Ferrara-Florence in his letter to the grand prince of Moscow is puzzling. We have previously cited, *supra*, pp. 99, 100, the papal letter to the grand prince that Isidore bore with him on his return to Moscow and that letter does not include these dogmatic discussions. Unless the *Second Sofia Annal* is in error, does the annal imply that there was a second letter from the pope to the grand prince that Isidore brought with him or did the metropolitan append to the original papal letter to include this dogmatic information? Or does the reference to a letter rather imply that the Muscovite Synod was responding to the *Decree of Church Union* and other letters that Isidore had previously addressed to various lands? This uncertainty needs to be explored further in future research. Further, it is doubtful that Isidore would willingly cooperate and furnish to the Muscovite Synod copies of his letters to other rulers. Rather, it is more probable that Muscovite bishops in attendance at Ferrara-Florence furnished the grand prince and the Synod detailed accounts of the dogmatic agreements that had been reached at the church council. This then appears to be the basis for the reference to dogmatic issues in this letter.

4 The papal emissary

1 The first mission to Constantinople: a failure

The first mission that Isidore undertook on behalf of the pope brought him to Constantinople. He appears to have been there in 1450 but his stay was brief. Very early on in this mission, he came to the realization that nothing constructive could be accomplished on behalf of the union, given the political and religious climate in the imperial city. The scene favored the anti-unionists, who had gained an upper hand. As details of this trip are not reported extensively or in detail by our sources, most scholars have overlooked Isidore's mission and his efforts remain largely undocumented; nevertheless, the mission did occur and the evidence for it is cited below. That the cardinal traveled to the imperial city is beyond doubt and can be established through the information provided by Ioannes Argyropoulos, a Greek unionist who had firmly embraced the conclusions reached at the Council of Ferrara-Florence. At this time, in 1450, Argyropoulos had taken up residence in Constantinople where he was teaching under the auspices of the court at the imperial property known as the Xenon.[1] As a proponent of church union, Argyropoulos undoubtedly had contacts with Isidore, while the latter was in Constantinople. Thus, in one of the rhetorical compositions that Argyropoulos sent to the pope he mentions Isidore by title and thus establishes the cardinal's presence in the imperial capital.[2] This composition admits Argyropoulos's declaration of his strong adherence to church union. He further requests that the pope entertain his sons who were about to visit Rome. This *epistula* is loaded with classical references, as the author must have been aware of the pope's humanistic tendencies and his love of classical literature.[3] At the beginning of this *opusculum*, Argyropoulos includes the following statement:[4] πλείστην ὅτι χάριν οἶδα τῷ θεῷ μὲν πρῶτον, ὦ πάτερ πατέρων καὶ κύριε κυρίων τῶν ἐπὶ τῆς γῆς, εἶθ᾽ οὕτω καὶ τῷ αἰδεσιμωτάτῳ μοι κυρίῳ καρδιναλίῳ, "Father of fathers and lord of the lords on earth: I am in the greatest debt, first of all to God, and then to my lord, the most reverend cardinal."

As Lampros reasoned, the reference to the "cardinal" must be a reference to Isidore; in theory it could also designate Bessarion but, as is well known, Cardinal Bessarion was in Italy at this time and occupied the episcopal seat of

Bologna (1450–1455). Consequently, Isidore must be implied as the cited cardinal. There is additional evidence that places Isidore in Constantinople. Ubertino Pusculo provides us with a poetic narrative from the conclusion of the Council of Ferrara-Florence through the siege and fall of Constantinople in 1453. Pusculo is the only other source that has preserved some details, in fact the only details that we possess, with regard to this mission of Isidore.[5] Pusculo introduces Isidore in his poem and his information probably represents a general knowledge about the Greco-Rus' cardinal that must have been in circulation at that time. Pusculo had no contacts at the imperial court and was without influential protectors or patrons. He had come to Constantinople as a student to become proficient in ancient Greek.[6] Pusculo states:[7]

> *Romae erat insignis pater Isidorus, habebat / Praesul qui populos sacro sub jure Ruthenos / Olim Graeca secans jam dudum dogmata, postquam / Errorem novit, cupiens reparare salutem. / Sprevit opes (magnis opibus gaudebat) honesti / Captus amore pio, sua pulsus limina liquit / Patria pro vero vanos contempsit honores. / Quem pius Eugenius collegit. Talibus illum / Pro meritis dedit esse suum ad pia sacra ministrum, / Et jussit populis illum praesse Sabinis.*
>
> In Rome was the distinguished Father Isidore, who, as a prelate [metropolitan], used to have the Ruthenians under his ecclesiastical jurisdiction. Some time ago he had separated himself from the Greek dogmas, after he had educated himself about their error. He wished to restore sound dogmas. He despised wealth and delighted in major tasks. He fell in love with piety and moved away from his own country. Pope Eugenius [IV] took him into the college [of cardinals]. Because of his accomplishments he made him his minister and placed him in charge of the Sabines.

After this introduction, with its emphasis on Isidore's Catholic conversion, Pusculo continues and mentions a few items that must have been on the cardinal's agenda on this trip:

> *Hic patriae antiquum servans pietatis amorem, / Nam genus is magna Danaum ducebat ab urbe, / Sollicitus revocare suos erroribus, urbem / Threiciam ad magnam tendit: regemque senatumque /[8] Urbis adit: mandata ferat quae pandit: et ultro / Quae papae Eugenio jurarunt foedera, poscit / Observare pie; tabulis, quae scripsit in amplis, / Quique manu, aspiciant; ruptae nec crimina legis / dira clada luant. Deserta ad signa redire, / A quibus errarunt jam dudum, hortatur. At illum / Ut Danai in longum duxerunt arte Pelasga / . . . / . . . nullamque datur sperare salutem; / Urbem Romanam repetit legatus: / . . . / Grajorum exponit, pulsat qui nuncius aures / Pontificis cumulatque graves sub pectore curas.*
>
> He piously maintained his old affection for his homeland, which brought him back to the city of the Danaans [Greeks]. He was anxious to eradicate the errors of his compatriots and travelled to the great city in Thrace [Constantinople]. He came to the emperor and the senate of the city and reported on his mission. He demanded the pious enforcement of their pact

with Pope Eugenius. He showed them many tablets that had been written and asked them to avoid criminal charges and the consequent dire punishment. He urged them to abandon their ancient errors. Yet the Danaans [Greeks] put him off with their Pelasgian [ancient] tricks . . . and afforded him no hope for restoration. The legate returned to Rome. . . . The ambassador reported on the Greeks and talked to the pontiff who was aggrieved.

Thus in a few words we are informed that this was an official mission. Isidore came in the capacity of a papal legate but was unable to enforce the pope's demands and wishes that undoubtedly included the formal endorsement of church union and its ceremonial celebration in Santa Sophia. Having achieved nothing, Isidore returned to Rome. Perhaps it was then that he produced a written report about the state of ecclesiastical affairs in Greece, which still remains in manuscript form.[9]

2 The second mission to Constantinople: warlord and gift-bearer

In the spring of 1451, Emperor Constantine XI Dragaš Palaiologos, the successor and brother of John VIII, dispatched his ambassador, Andronikos Bryennios Leontaris, to the Vatican, seeking military aid and relief for his beleaguered city.[10] Additionally, the diplomatic activities of the emperor were widely known and soon after the fall of the imperial city Antonio Ivani da Sarzana in his *Expugnatio Constantinopolitana* (composed in the winter of 1453/1454) makes mention of them:[11] *Dragas, Graecorum imperator, interea ratus hostem novo tempore reversurum, ad summum Pontificem Imperatoremque Romanum atque regem Alphonsum et Venetos nonnullos alios principes oratores mittit, qui nuntient nisi ei auxilientur, sese Teucrorum conatibus nequaquam obsistere posse*, "Dragaš the emperor of the Greeks was under the impression that the enemy [Turks] would come back once more, and he sent numerous noble emissaries to the highest priest [Pope Nicholas V], to the Roman Emperor [Frederick III], to King Alfonso, and to the Venetians to announce that, unless he received help, he would find himself unable to resist the Turks."

The letter that Leontaris carried to the pope has not survived. It is usually stated that its contents can be reconstructed from the papal reply, but the pope's views may not have answered the requests of Constantine XI. In fact, the letter of Nicolas V assumes a didactic tone and even scolds the emperor for his inactivity in enforcing papal supremacy in Constantinople. It is quite probable that Constantine's concerns were passed over in silence in partiality to papal demands and the pope's letter was interpreted as an ultimatum.[12]

Yet we may reconstruct the general tone of Constantine's letter to the pope from the remarks of the leader of the anti-unionist faction in Constantinople, Georgios Scholarios,[13] who was destined to become the intractable enemy of Isidore. Scholarios, who at the time had access to the imperial court and was often consulted by the emperor and his confidants, addressed a communication to the emperor that is dated 12 March,[14] without citing a year, but from the contents of the composition and his references to current affairs we may be certain that the year was 1452.[15] In Scholarios's view, Leontaris unnecessarily complicated the ecclesiastical situation by not enforcing the emperor's message, which included a request that the Vatican send its delegation of scholars to discuss anew matters involving Orthodox and Catholic dogma through public disputations and discussions as the Greek hierarchy had planned:[16]

> ἡ καλὴ ϖρεσβεία τοῦ Βρυεννίου ἐνέϖλεξε τὰ ἐκκλησιαστικὰ ἡμῶν ταῦτα τῆς ϖίστεως, ὡς ἀκούομεν. ἀντὶ γὰρ συνόδου ἐνταῦθα γενησομένης διὰ ἀϖοκρισιαρίων τοῦ ϖάϖα σοφῶν, ὡς ἂν γένοιτο μετὰ λόγων ἐλευθερίων καὶ ἐξετάσεως τῶν διαφορῶν ἡμῶν φανερᾶς ζήτησις ἐκκλησιαστικὴ καὶ κανονική, ἅϖερ ἐζήτησαν οἱ ἡμέτεροι ἐκκλησιαστικοὶ αἰδεσιμώτατοι ϖατέρες γράψαντες, οὐχ ἑκόντες καὶ τοῦτο, ἀλλὰ ἠναγκασμένοι καὶ βεβιασμένοι τὰς συνειδήσεις . . . ἔρχεται ϖρέσβυς, ὡς ἀκούομεν.

The good embassy of Bryennios [Leontaris] has complicated our ecclesiastical affairs, as we hear. Instead of a canonical public synod that was to take place here with the scholarly emissaries of the pope, marked by unprejudiced arguments (as our ecclesiastical, most reverend father had requested in writing, surely not willingly but under force and compulsion that violated their conscience, it is quite clear), we hear that an emissary is on his way to us.

Indeed the pope's reply was not very encouraging, for Nicholas V had demanded, above all, the enforcement of the terms of the union of churches that had been concluded in the proceedings of the Council of Ferrara-Florence, which had never been pursued with any enthusiasm by the lay populace and lower clergy in Constantinople; in fact, any accommodation with the papacy had been steadily eroding and had even worsened following the disastrous crusade of Varna.[17] The defeat of the western armies at Varna had left the imperial capital of the Greeks more vulnerable than ever. Thus the pope's unsympathetic reply to the emperor's plight has been interpreted as an ultimatum:[18] no aid would be forthcoming unless the union had been formally accepted, enforced, and celebrated in its entirety. The pope followed up these demands by dispatching to Constantinople his legate Isidore.

In the spring of 1452, Pope Nicholas V directed Isidore, in the capacity of official legate of the Vatican to Constantinople (but with no ecclesiastical jurisdiction over the city, although he would be the highest-ranking churchman in the city)[19] with instructions to enforce the union that had been concluded at Florence. According to a contemporaneous Greek source, this mission was understood to have originated at the behest of the emperor, who desperately needed a military alliance with Catholic Europe against the Ottoman sultan, Mehmed II, who was preparing a major and final attack upon Constantinople. The emperor, in return for western military aid, had offered to enforce the terms of the union of the Greek and Latin churches, which had been accepted by a majority of the delegates present at Florence. Constantine demanded a military alliance and offered in return the formal enforcement of the union in his capital.[20] Isidore was of the conviction that his mission would achieve the desired results only if he came to the Greek capital in charge of forces to strengthen its defense against the expected Ottoman attack. Isidore's first stop was at Naples[21] before he moved on to the Aegean and the Levant. In every port of call he made numerous attempts to recruit a mercenary force that would give the appearance of an advanced group of a substantial western army that was assembling to relieve the imperial capital from the Turkish threat.[22] It was his assumption that only under such circumstances would the Greeks agree to the union and formally accept the papacy's terms. His journey took considerable time and Isidore reached Constantinople's harbor only in the fall of 1452. Apparently, he produced numerous detailed accounts of his adventures in a series of letters addressed to Bessarion. None of these letters appear to have survived and we are not even certain that they ever reached Bessarion. Isidore himself had his own doubts about their fate and he seems to imply that either his letters or their replies were lost due to the uncertain circumstances and the upheaval that ensued:[23]

> *Saepenumero anteactis temporibus ad vestram reverentiam scriptitavi, a qua nec responsionem quidem ullam accepi; quid in causa fuerit, ignoro. Illud coniectare licet: aut meae tibi redditae non sunt aut ad me tuae non sunt delatae baiulorum forte neglegentia, quod etiam bello et rerum asperitati tribuere possumus, aut – quod tertio loco relinquitur – tua nobis irata est atque adversatur reverentia.*
>
> On a number of occasions in the past I wrote numerous letters to your reverence, but I never received a reply. I know not the reasons for this but I may attribute it either to the possibility that my letters were not delivered or to the possibility that your letters never reached me, due to official negligence brought about by the cruel war. The third possibility is that Your Reverence may be angry and irritated with me.

Fortunately, in the same letter Isidore supplies a summary of these adventures to his friend, Bessarion, which he composed after the fall of Constantinople and his escape from the city, and after he had reached safe haven in Crete on the 6th of July 1453. At least, we may form a general impression of the circumstances that accompanied his voyage to the Levant, but one wishes that the details treated in the earlier letters had been preserved. The surviving letter is by far the earliest testimony to document the events of the siege, composed by an authoritative eyewitness, who was involved with the strategy formulated by the Greek imperial court. But even so, we lack the original Greek text written by Isidore; we possess only its translation into Latin, admittedly, as the translator states, a humanistic exercise, by a contemporary of Isidore. In this letter the cardinal alludes to his long voyage that brought him to Constantinople in 1452:[24]

> *Cum circa mensem Maii superioris anni* [1452] *Romam reliquissem, nullum penitus inde praesidium vel auxilium referens . . . omnia me adverse atque infeliciter*

succedere ceperunt. Omitto autem nunc singula. Tantisper sex menses in itinere cucurrerunt, cum vix et tandem sextum et vigessimum mensis Octobris diem ad infelicissimam urbem Constantinopolim pervenimus, hoste ac ferro clausam et undique circumseptam.

When I left Rome in May of the previous year [1452], bringing with me neither soldiers nor substantial aid ... I fell into adversity and bad luck. I will not speak of every individual instance for now. And so my voyage stretched into six months and I only managed to reach the most unfortunate city of Constantinople on the twenty-sixth day of October. The city was already under military blockade by the enemy and had been surrounded on all sides.

In addition to the cardinal's own testimony, Leonardo Giustiniani, the archbishop of Lesbos,[25] passed on his own brief statements. Leonardo became a close associate and admirer of Isidore, in the course of the siege. The argument can be made that Leonardo was attracted to Constantinople through the recruiting efforts of the cardinal once the latter reached the island of Chios. Leonardo states that much. Isidore, if one accepts Leonardo's testimony, recruited him by requesting his assistance in accomplishing his religious mission to Constantinople. Also, Isidore needed his help in theological matters and in persuading the Greeks to accept the union formally:[26] *cum igitur reverendissimus pater D<ominus> cardinalis Sabinensis [sc. Isidorus] pro natione Graecorum legatus, in eius famulatum me ex Chio voca<vi>sset, ego summa cum animi mei diligentia, ut fidem sanctae Romanae ecclesiae fortiter constanterque, uti debitum exigit, defensarem,* "and when the most reverend father, the lord cardinal of the Sabines [Isidore], who was sent to enforce the union with the Greeks, summoned me to join his retinue from Chios, I consented to go in order to defend, with all my mental strength, the faith of the Holy Roman Church, as it was my duty."

Early on, before the beginning of the siege, the Latin bishop fell under the spell of the Greek cardinal and the two of them worked closely together thereafter.[27] It is very likely that Leonardo accompanied Isidore to Constantinople on the last leg of the latter's voyage from Chios. Not a great deal is known about Leonardo's earlier career. He had been born in Chios at the beginning of the fifteenth century or a few years earlier and he must have been close to Isidore in age. Later in Italy, Leonardo joined the Dominicans as a student and moved on to Perugia around 1426. He most probably came to Lesbos in July 1444, to become the island's archbishop. By 1449 he returned to Italy where he made the acquaintance of numerous influential ecclesiastics and humanists, including Cardinal Domenico Capranica, Poggio Bracciolini, and Lauro Quirini. Leonardo[28] is placed squarely within the humanistic sphere by Cyriacus of Ancona who had met him, as he notes in a letter of 1444:[29] *Vidimus et inter praeclaros eo loco viros Leonardum, venerandum religione ac divinarum et humanarum litterarum peritissimum hominem, quocum multis cum nobilibus splendido in symposio fuimus,* "we saw Leonardo, one of the well-known men of that place, very reverend in his faith and a scholar of theology and the humanities, and spent time with him in the course of a dinner with many noblemen." Cyriacus mentions Leonardo

128 *The papal emissary*

once again in a letter of 27 August 1444, which was probably composed in Constantinople:[30] *Hodie ... reverendissimum patrem Leonardum, Lesbeum pontificem, ad hanc urbem adventatem hylaritate revisimus*, "today ... when we came to that city, we visited again, with elation, the reverend father Leonardo, the bishop of Lesbos." Leonardo was an ecclesiastic with strong humanistic tendencies, who shared similar interests with that father of archaeology and epigraphy, and was well known among the active lovers of antiquity in the *quattrocento*.

The difficulties (*adverse atque infeliciter*) that the cardinal is alluding to during his voyage may have been partly due to unsettled weather, unsuitable for sailing in the Aegean during the summer months. Monsoonal effects during the summer, even at present, frequently lead to a low-pressure trough over Turkey. The weather is then characterized by what is now known as the *meltemi* (identified with what was called in antiquity *etesian*/yearly) wind that flows from high-pressure ridges over the Balkans toward the trough. During the period of the *meltemi* winds, the trough may extend relatively far to the south of the Aegean, beyond even the island of Rhodes. The prevailing pattern is encountered during June to October, with its maximum strength in July and August. Normally, the wind picks up in the early afternoon to a force of 4–5 Beaufort, and then grows to 5–7 during daylight, which continues through the night. This pattern can easily be repeated over many days, sometimes occupying a whole week.[31] By contrast, another eyewitness, Ubertino Pusculo,[32] reports that Isidore's mission was assisted by fair winds that allowed him an easy passage. Obviously, Pusculo was unfamiliar with the actual circumstances of the cardinal's progress. The poet had not traveled with Isidore, whom he may not have personally met. He writes a few years after the events and perhaps recalls the impression that Isidore may have wished to create upon his arrival. Certainly, the Greek cardinal would have presented a stiff upper lip and must have projected an optimistic outlook:[33]

> *Tendere ad urbem*
> *Legatus propere rursus tu, Isidore, juberis,*
> *Rursus si qua via est, Danaos, quae ducat in unum*
> *Cum pastore pio, et reddat quae legibus aequis.*
> ...
> *Actus adit, portusque capit spirante secundo*
> *Austro Bosporeos.*

You, Isidore, were ordered to hasten back and assume control of the way by which the Danaans [Greeks] could return to the pious shepherd [pope] and to just laws.

...

He [Isidore] left and reached the port at the Bosphoros [Constantinople] supported by a favorable wind from the south.

If Pusculo is to be trusted, Isidore arrived shortly after daybreak and was received with pomp and ceremony:[34] *Jam roseis aurora diem detexerat alis, / Legatus puppim eggreditur. Cui regia turba / Ad portam primi occurunt, fidique Latini: / Sublatumque in equo ad regem comitantu,* "already the dawn was uncovering the day with her rosy wings, when the legate [Isidore] disembarked. At the gate a throng from the palace met him and the Latins [Italians] were the first to run and meet him. He mounted a horse and was escorted to the emperor [Constantine XI]."

Despite the welcoming reception, the cardinal may have looked upon his mission with considerable dismay. While Pope Nicholas V had clearly intended the enforcement and celebration of the union of the churches with their corollary, the formal return of the Greek Church to the Catholic fold as the objective of his legate's mission, he had failed to provide his legate with any military force to ensure the success of the mission. His cardinal, however, had realized that all progress in the religious situation demanded tangible proof that the West was making preparations to relieve the deplorable state of Constantinople's defending forces against the might of the Ottoman sultan. To enhance the possibility of success for his mission, he concluded that he had to recruit and bring to the Greek capital a military force, even if it was necessarily a small unit. So he took it upon himself to gather, along the way, a modest band of mercenaries, whose salaries he may have intended to pay with funds supplied by the Vatican for his mission. Archbishop Leonardo, the devoted friend and admirer of Isidore, makes clear that the cardinal's goal, as intended by the pope, was to bring about religious union, which, from the Vatican's point of view, need not have implied immediate military assistance. After the fall of the city, Henry of Soemmern, who was associated with the Vatican, reviewed the cardinal's mission and declared it a success:[35] *Cardinalis autem Ruthenus [sc. Isidorus], natione graecus, qui per papam anno iam elapso Constantinopolim missus fuit ad inducendum Graecos ut ipsi primatum Ecclesiae Romanae etiam quoad iurisdictionem <super> omnes ecclesias orbis recognoscerent – quod et fecit,* "the Ruthenian cardinal [Isidore], a Greek by origin, was sent to Constantinople by the pope over a year ago in order to persuade the Greeks about the primacy of the Church of Rome and to make them recognize its jurisdiction over all churches in the world. He accomplished his mission."

The difficulties that Isidore mentions in his letter to Bessarion may also have been related to his efforts to recruit soldiers for the defense of the Greek capital. It would not have been an easy task. Service in the Turkish army promised to be more lucrative, even for Christian renegades and mercenaries. The careful preparations of the sultan had been widely advertised. Many Christians viewed service under the imperial standard less attractive, a major financial risk, and perhaps even certain death. The Islamic banner, when all factors are considered, was certainly more appealing. The fact is that the huge Ottoman army included numerous renegades and Christians in its ranks, who had been attracted to the sultan's camp with the prospect of booty.[36] Isidore's friend, Leonardo, comments with disapproval and dismay on these "renegades" in the Ottoman camp. Yet, the cardinal knew that he had to bring a token force in order to impress the Greeks and to facilitate the union. Thus, on his way to the capital, Isidore stopped at several islands, endeavoring to enlist volunteers and mercenaries to join his retinue.

His final stop before arriving in Constantinople was the island of Chios. Apparently the cardinal remained on this island for some time, waiting for the merchant owners of his Genoese ship to complete their local business before transporting him to Constantinople. Moreover, they were anticipating the arrival of another ship so that both vessels would make their entry into the Black Sea and on to the Genoese possession of Caffa. In all likelihood, the two ships sought a greater measure of safety by forming a convoy to pass through the Turkish occupied straits of the Dardanelles.[37] While on Chios Isidore recruited Archbishop Leonardo, who was destined to compose one of the most influential accounts of the siege. Leonardo had a very high opinion of Isidore and eagerly accepted the invitation to accompany him to the beleaguered capital of the Greeks.[38] Doukas also notes that Isidore recruited the main body of his force at Chios, significantly augmenting his contingent from the west:[39] καὶ ἐλθόντος ἐν τῇ νήσῳ Χίῳ, μετὰ νηὸς μεγίστης τῶν Γενουιτῶν, ἐποίησεν ἡμέρας ἱκανάς ... ὁ καδδηνάλιος οὖν ἔχων μεθ' αὐτοῦ τῶν Ἰταλῶν ἄχρι πεντήκοντα ἐρόγευσε καὶ ἑτέρους πλείστους ἐκ τῆς Χίου Λατίνους, "he came to the island of Chios aboard a very large Genoese vessel and remained there for a number of days ... the cardinal already had about fifty Italians in his retinue and he hired many other Latins on Chios." The total number of men in Isidore's contingent is not specified by Doukas. Nicolò Barbaro,[40] who has left us his precious diary of the siege,[41] however, specifies the size of the ship that brought Isidore to Constantinople:[42] *hor da poi pasadi ver quanti zorni, l'azonse una nave che vignia da Zenova, de Zenovexi, de portada de cantara trenta sie millia con el gardenal del Rosìa, che manda el papa per dover far la union,* "after a few days had passed, a ship of thirty-six cantars came from Genoa. Aboard were Genoese [individuals] and the cardinal of Rus', whom the Pope had dispatched to conclude the union." He specifies the exact number of Isidore's recruits:[43] *e dusse con si homeni 200 fra scopetieri e balestrieri per secorso de questa zitade de Costantinopoli,* "and he came with two hundred men, gunners and crossbowmen, to help the city of Constantinople."

The crossbowmen, in particular, were a precious commodity especially in the defense of cities and this contingent must have added a much-needed force for the defense of the walls.[44] Combining the statements of Doukas and the note in Barbaro one may then conclude that the main body of Isidore's mercenaries, about 150 men, was recruited from Chios. These troops were not members of elite units and expert warriors, but rather a motley force of questionable martial skills. We do not know what was their exact specialty in warfare. Barbaro, however, adds the observations that the cardinal's force included *scopetieri* and *balestrieri*, gunners and crossbowmen, who were always welcome for the defense of walled cities. With this modest force the cardinal and his convoy sailed to Constantinople and with the *meltemi* winds spent they finally entered the Golden Horn on the 26th of October.[45]

At long last the Constantinopolitans were presented with tangible evidence that the West had not abandoned them. The cardinal's small contingent implied future aid, provided that church union was finally accomplished. To the fanatical anti-unionists, however, this token band of Latin mercenaries led by a Greek cardinal in the service of the pope may have looked more like a police force, ready to apply pressure and demand the conclusion of the union through a force of arms. In the past, when the Greek emperor John VIII had traveled to Italy to attend the Council of Ferrara-Florence, care had been taken to recruit and transport to Constantinople Cretan crossbowmen,[46] ostensibly to enlarge the defending force, but in reality to help the emperor's regent maintain control over the population in the event there were ensuing riots protesting the union of the churches. It is possible that the previous "assistance" by a force of crossbowmen was now recalled, when the cardinal and his mercenaries entered the city.[47]

The days (or rather weeks) that the cardinal spent on Chios, whether detained by *meltemi* winds, in addition to the wishes of the owner to await the arrival of another ship to form a convoy to Constantinople, were profitably spent. Isidore recruited mercenaries, summoned other associates, and probably formed new or reinforced old contacts with the island's magnates. We should recall that on his escape route after the sack, noting that the island also played a major role during the conflict, it was on Chios that he secured firm passage to Venetian Crete, thus removing himself from the Ottoman danger.[48] Once we grasp that the cardinal put this stopover to good use, perhaps another possible link can be made. It is possible that at this stage in his voyage he became aware of a band of Italian *condottieri*, who were evidently acting like corsairs in the area and were, in fact, under a cloud of suspicion in Italy. Perhaps they had been operating in the Aegean to distance themselves from Italy and from Genoa, where numerous inquiries concerning the band's leader had arisen. Their leader, and in command of his own ship, was Giovanni Guglielmo Longo Giustiniani, apparently a young man if Leonardo is to be believed, who was destined to become the nucleus for the defense of Constantinople during the siege of 1453. He was officially appointed commander-in-chief and was placed in charge of all land operations in the defense of the city. He became Constantine's πρωτοστράτωρ or, as Leonardo correctly translates the term into Latin, imperial *dux militiae*.[49] It was his departure, after he was twice wounded, from the fortifications about the Pempton Gate that brought about the fall of the imperial city on the 29th of May.[50] While Isidore was lingering on Chios, we are told by one Greek source[51] that Giustiniani and his band were also in the vicinity of Chios. We do know that Giovanni Guglielmo Longo had already attached himself to the *albergo* of the Giustiniani of Chios,[52] whose coat of arms he had assumed for himself.[53]

Among the few documents that seem to refer to Giustiniani, there is a letter written by Nicholas Soderini, Florence's envoy in Genoa, which mentions the secret departure of Giustiniani with 700 men.[54] Giustiniani may have been seeking to remove himself from the jurisdiction of Italy, for charges against him were being prepared. He may have endeavored to anticipate formal charges of piracy and may have absconded to the Levant before he had to face formal summons.[55] Eventually, Giustiniani came to Constantinople, offered his valuable, as it turned out, services to the Greek emperor, who was delighted with the recruitment

132 The papal emissary

of the Genoese *condottiere* and his experienced band; they went on to form the nucleus of the defense. What remains unclear is what attracted Giustiniani to Constantinople. His eventual reward remains a mystery and promises, if any, made by the emperor are not divulged in the extant sources, but contradictory rumors were then in circulation.[56] In fact, we are not aware of any negotiations that may have occurred prior to Giustiniani's arrival. If any dialogues had occurred, they were well concealed by the imperial administration.

One fact does stand out. Giustiniani and Isidore were contemporaries and at the same site and within the vicinity on the island of Chios. Isidore was on Chios in the fall of 1452 while Giustiniani was operating in the nearby waters. Is it possible that the two individuals had encountered each other and that the cardinal enticed the *condottiere* to communicate with the administration in Constantinople to offer his services? Thus, was Isidore in some way responsible for attracting Giustiniani's valiant band to the imperial capital? Alternatively, could he be the catalyst responsible for bringing the existence of Giustiniani's band to the notice of the imperial administration late in the fall or early winter of 1452? Did he set in motion the wheels that eventually brought Giustiniani to the city and to his destiny? It is quite possible that the cardinal was a principal in this matter and that he played some unspecified role. Or is it an accident that the *condottiere* followed the cardinal to the city? The *condottiere* and his band finally arrived on the 26th of January 1453,[57] and were received with relief and joy. Perhaps the Greek cardinal was instrumental in their coming.

The arrival of such an important contingent could not have come as a surprise to the imperial administration. In the least, such events do not occur without due preparation and are seldom unexpected. It is unfortunate that Sphrantzes writes nothing of this important matter. The enlistment of Giustiniani and his band of mercenaries/pirates was a Constantinopolitan coup, perhaps the last notable achievement of the imperial chancery.[58] And one must wonder whether Isidore played a significant role in the negotiations during his voyage that brought him from Italy to Constantinople, by way of Chios, one of the bases of Giovanni Giustiniani. The appointment of Giustiniani as commander-in-chief proved to be a wise choice.

Isidore may have also carried a personal gift for the emperor, whose good will he desperately needed if his ecclesiastical mission were to succeed. There were reports in circulation that the cardinal presented the Greek emperor with a sword. This gift, if the story does not amount to a folktale and a fabrication, has attracted the attention of numerous scholars in the recent past, who have gone so far as to identify the cardinal's gift with a surviving sword that is found in the *Armeria Regia* in Turin. Upon its purchase in the Levant, along with numerous other old weapons from Ottoman Turkey, there was an attempt to provide this artifact with a glorious pedigree by identifying it as the sword presented by Isidore to Constantine.[59] The blade of the Turin sword/scimitar displays a poetic inscription composed of two lines in fifteen-syllable meter, a popular poetic form of Modern Greek folk poetry: Σὺ βασιλεῦ ἀήττητε, Λόγε Θεοῦ παντάναξ, / τῷ ἡγεμόνι καὶ πιστῷ αὐθέντῃ Κωνσταντίνῳ, "You invincible King, all-mighty Word of God, [and] ruler of all / to the lord and faithful master Constantine."

The inscription appearing in this usage does not make sense. The grammar is confusing with an absent main verb. In fact, the inscription on the Turin blade seems to have been added to the sword by someone who was aware of the more complete version of the dedication that was supposedly on the original gift by the cardinal and so it represents the "stitching together" of two lines from a more perfect distich that was supposedly engraved on the very sword that Isidore allegedly presented to Constantine XI. In other words, the inscription on the blade in the *Armeria Regia* of Turin is a forgery, probably dating to the nineteenth century and not earlier. The forger did not make an effort, for whatever reason, to copy the entire poem (whose complete text is known from elsewhere)[60] and only linked together two lines from it, to the detriment of grammar and perhaps meter, as the two separate fifteen-syllable lines have been joined into one thirty-syllable line.[61] We may speculate that the poem proved too long for the Turin blade and, accordingly, the forger shortened the text to a manageable size, having no qualms about the preservation of good grammar. Aside from this flaw, an unintelligible inscription, the Turin sword belongs to the classification of the Oriental scimitar, a well-known type that was carried by Janissaries in the sixteenth and seventeenth centuries. The configuration of the sword appears similar to the type of hunting sword that John VIII had brought with him to Florence in 1438/39, when Pisanello beautifully sketched it.[62] Both swords are of an Oriental design, but "Constantine's sword" lacks the cruciform hand guard (with tips turned upward and downward) and its blade is slightly wider than John's sword. Both swords are good specimens of the Oriental scimitar in the late Middle Ages and the early Renaissance. Perhaps the Turin sword, without the inscription, even dates to the fifteenth century, but there is no proof that Constantine ever handled it.[63]

Ultimately, a major suspicion about the authenticity of the alleged sword and the account that Isidore presented it to the emperor is the paucity, indeed absence, of any citation about this blade in the surviving sources from that tumultuous period. The first modern scholar to make reference to the cardinal's "gift" was A. G. Paspates, who states that Isidore presented a sword to the emperor either before or after the celebration of the union of the churches in Constantinople:[64] ὁ Ἰσίδωρος ἐλθὼν ἐν Κωνσταντινουπόλει ὡς ἱεράρχης καὶ πολέμαρχος προσέφερε τῷ Παλαιολόγῳ ξίφος εὑρεθὲν μετὰ τὴν ἅλωσιν καὶ μέχρι τοῦδε ἐν Βυζαντίῳ σωζόμενον, " Isidore came to Constantinople as a clergyman and as a warlord and presented Palaiologos with a sword, which was found after the sack and is still preserved in Byzantium [Constantinople]." Paspates then continues and quotes the following four- (and not two-) line poem that was supposedly etched on the blade of this sword. Paspates's version has preserved the integrity of the fifteen-syllable meter:[65]

Σὺ βασιλεῦ ἀήττητε, Λόγε Θεοῦ παντάναξ,
Νίκης βραβεῖα δώρησε κατὰ τῶν πολεμίων,

Τῷ ἡγεμόνι καὶ πιστῷ αὐθέντῃ Κωνσταντίνῳ
Ὥσπερ ποτὲ τῷ βασιλεῖ μεγάλῳ Κωνσταντίνῳ.

You invincible King, all-mighty Word of God, [and] ruler of all:
Grant victorious trophies against our enemies
To the lord and faithful master Constantine,
As you once did to Emperor Constantine the Great.

Thus the confused grammar of the inscription on the Turin blade finds its resolution. The forger only concerned himself to record the first and third lines of this poem, omitting, for whatever reason, line 2 which contains the main verb and line 4 which appeals to a historical precedent. Nevertheless, the inscriber must have been aware of the full poem as quoted by Paspates. The Greek scholar does not supply a source for his assertion, nor does he state whether he personally knew the whereabouts of the "genuine" sword or why he thought it to be the authentic item. Paspates was a meticulous scholar. That he failed to cite a document in a footnote suggests that there was no such document. Perhaps he had examined a sword and may have become convinced of its authenticity but proved unwilling to report further details in an effort to safeguard the sword's ownership or whereabouts. Another Greek scholar investigated this matter and discovered that there were several swords in existence in the nineteenth century with pedigrees claiming the honor of being the genuine article. He concluded that all were forgeries, beyond any doubt.[66]

The nineteenth-century Greek-speaking world witnessed a desire to recover relics associated with the last centuries of Byzantium. There is little doubt that this trend was related to the rebirth of the Greek nation and its accompanying nationalism after it secured freedom from the Ottoman Empire. As for the supposed sword of Constantine XI, the Greek community of Constantinople even purchased one of these swords and presented it to Constantine, the crown prince of Greece, on 1 December 1886, being under the impression that it was the true sword of Constantine XI, in spite of the existence of the Turin blade and of other scimitars claiming the same pedigree throughout the Aegean islands. Of course, for the Greek community this gift bore the stamp of authenticity.[67] It is painfully obvious that such authentic relics are no longer recoverable and the alleged sword of the last emperor belongs to the realm of mythology, and does not even qualify to be a legend. There were other swords in antiquity and in the Middle Ages that also attracted a similar lore.[68] The indisputable fact remains that no authentic source from the fifteenth century ever mentions the sword of the last emperor, which, in fact, becomes important long after the events of the fall of the imperial city had been concluded, when Constantine XI himself had been transformed into the "vanished emperor" who would return to lay claim to his lost empire. This legend states that Constantine was not dead, but sleeping, and that upon reawakening an angel would present to him the sword that he carried in the last battle. It was under these emotional circumstances in millennial prophecies that Constantine's sword assumed a supernatural significance and became an essential part of the story.[69]

3 Disputations

The arrival of Isidore and his contingent made it clear that at long last the union of the churches would be enforced and celebrated. The pope, however, remained dissatisfied with Constantinople's lack of a unionist or of any, for that matter, religious policy. That the Constantinopolitan court had ceased operating a "department of religion" must have been painfully aware to all those involved. Even in matters that pertained to Orthodoxy, state supervision appears to have come to an end. It is a well-known fact that the lack of initiative in Byzantine religious affairs even puzzled, in the last decades, the Orthodox Muscovite Rus', who had shown remarkable restraint when they officially asked the Greeks on more than one occasion for guidance on ecclesiastical matters and waited in vain for a reply from the patriarch to address the issues; the answers the Rus' had requested never came.[70] The fact remains that no effective religious administration had functioned in Constantinople since the last days of John VIII. This can further be seen in the simple matter of the coronation of Constantine XI, who was never formally crowned emperor.[71] Constantine personally embraced the religious harmony restored at Ferrara-Florence and had individually espoused Catholicism,[72] while he had taken no steps to conclude the union in his capital and had further allowed complete freedom to the anti-unionists to thunder their anathemas in public without restraint.[73]

Nevertheless, there were problems between the Vatican and Constantinople, problems that went beyond the sphere of theology and dogma. There were actual administrative issues within the Greek Church that the pope wished to resolve before he committed himself to supplying military and financial aid[74] for the beleaguered capital of Constantine. One of the thorny questions concerned the exiled unionist patriarch of Constantinople and the fact that there was no patriarch at the moment sitting in the imperial city. At the conclusion of his letter, the pope urged the emperor, among other things, to reinstate the unionist patriarch to his throne, who had abandoned his charge earlier, when he had realized that nothing could be accomplished in the face of stubborn anti-union opposition and a lack of support from the court. Thus in August of 1451, Patriarch Gregory III Mamas[75] abandoned his see and sought sanctuary with the pope in Rome.[76] Further, in his letter to the emperor the pope demanded the restoration of the patriarch with full authority:[77]

πρᾶττε ὅπως ὁ Κωσταντινουπόλεως πατριάρχης [Γρηγόριος] εἰς τὸν ἑαυτοῦ ἐπανήξει θρόνον, καὶ ἐπανήκοντι αἰδῶ καὶ τιμὴν καὶ ὑπακοὴν πάντας ἀπονέμειν διατάξαις, ὅσην δεῖ κατὰ λόγον ἀρχιερατικοῦ ἀξιώματος, ὥστε μηκέτι τὸν ἐν ἀξίᾳ ὄντα τοιαύτῃ καθάπερ τινὰ τῶν εὐτελῶν ἱερέων διάγειν τὸν βίον, ἀλλ᾽ ὡς δεῖ τὸν ἀληθῆ Κωνσταντινουπόλεως πατριάρχην.

See to it that the Patriarch of Constantinople [Gregory] returns to his throne as you issue orders that all should obey him with the appropriate respect and honor that is reasonably demanded by his high ecclesiastical post, and so that he no longer lives as if he were some humble priest, but as is his due as the true Patriarch of Constantinople.

This demand must have been well known to all, for the letter's contents appear to have been divulged. Thus Doukas was also aware of these two demands but, remarkably, he suggests that it was the emperor who initiated these questions and asked for the help of the Vatican to put an end to the Greek troubles. It was the emperor, according to Doukas, who asked the pope to send his representative to put an end to the religious schism and enforce the terms of the Council of Ferrara-Florence:[78]

ὁ βασιλεὺς ἦν στείλας ἐν Ῥώμῃ προλαβών, αἰτῶν βοήθειαν καὶ ὅπως συντεθῶσι τῇ ὁμονοίᾳ καὶ ἑνώσει τῇ γεγονυίᾳ ἐν Φλωρεντίᾳ καὶ λάβῃ τὸ μνημόσυνον ὁ πάπας ἐν τῇ Μεγάλῃ Ἐκκλησίᾳ. καὶ ὁ πατριάρχης Γρηγόριος ἐπανελεύσεται ἐν τῷ θρόνῳ αὐτοῦ. καὶ μετακαλεῖτο τινας ἀφικέσθαι τῶν τοῦ πάπα, ὅπως εἰρηνεύσῃ τὴν ἄσπονδον ἔχθραν τοῦ σχίσματος.

In the meantime the emperor [Constantine XI] had taken care to send [a message] to Rome, asking for help and for an alliance in accordance with the agreement and the union that had been achieved in Florence so that the pope's name be commemorated in the Great Church [Santa Sophia]; in this way Patriarch Gregory will return to his throne. So he invited some of the pope's men to come and make peace by eliminating the endless enmity created by the schism.

The problem has become rather complicated, as we are uncertain concerning the status of the patriarchal office after the departure of Gregory. If we comprehend the surviving contemporary Greek literature, we have to conclude that the post remained vacant after the departure of Gregory until the fall of Constantinople, although some scholars adhere to the notion that an Athanasios II occupied the seat in 1450,[79] but the literature on the subject is unconvincing. It was only after the fall that a Greek patriarch with expanded powers was appointed in Constantinople under the Osmanli administration as the head to the Greek minority within the Ottoman state.[80] No Orthodox patriarch appears to be in charge immediately before or during the siege. This view is underscored by the papal demand that Gregory had to be restored to his previous position with full authority. And yet there have survived rumors, with modern scholarly debate on this issue. These rumors purport that others somehow had occupied the seat. The main culprit in this "invention" of a successor to Gregory in Constantinople is, to a large extent, Nestor-Iskander,[81] who composed the Slavonic eyewitness siege of the fall.[82] He had been present in the Ottoman camp but at some point early on before the onset of the siege, he managed to escape, entered the city, and joined the defenders.[83] It is in this Slavonic narrative that curious comments are encountered relative to an existing patriarch. Nestor-Iskander relates that during the siege there was a council attended by the emperor, his nobility, the senate, and the patriarch.[84] Elsewhere[85] he relates that the patriarch was in charge at Santa Sophia during prayers. He even portrays the patriarch in Santa Sophia receiving the conquering sultan;[86] at this point Nestor-Iskander even identifies the patriarch as Anastasios. It is to Patriarch Anastasios, we are told, that the sultan entrusted the head of the slain emperor Constantine XI to be encased and preserved in gold and silver.[87] To complicate matters further the patriarch's name also appears as "Athanasios."[88] Was there really an Anastasios/Athanasios in charge of the Patriarchate after the departure of Gregory III? It is also possible that Nestor-Iskander erred and assumed that a high cleric was the patriarch. It has been speculated that Nestor-Iskander may have mistakenly believed that Isidore himself was the patriarch of Constantinople, given the fine robes that he wore because of his high rank.[89] The fact remains, understandably, that all our reliable Greek sources do not mention a patriarch and that Sphrantzes, with connections to the court and the emperor, seems certain that there was no patriarch, as he had advised Constantine XI to appoint Isidore to the position of Greek patriarch of Constantinople, and that would have complemented his existing (papal) title of Latin Patriarch of Constantinople. It, therefore, would have made him the highest cleric in the Greek Church.[90]

Thus Sphrantzes is explicit about the solution that he proposed to the problem of the vacant patriarchal throne, but, of course, he failed to address the papal demand that Gregory be restored and failed to recognize Isidore's title as Latin Patriarch of Constantinople:[91]

εὑρεθέντος καὶ γὰρ τοῦ καρδηναλίου Ῥωσσίας εἰς τὴν Πόλιν, μέσος ἐγὼ παρ' αὐτοῦ γέγονα εἰς τὸν ἀοίδιμον καὶ μακαρίτην αὐθέντην μου τὸν βασιλέα, ἵνα γένηται πατριάρχης. καὶ τὰ καὶ τὰ γένωνται παρ' αὐτοῦ καὶ τοῦ τότε πάπα, ἢ κἂν ἐκ δευτέρου νὰ μνημονευθῇ ὁ πάπας.

The cardinal of Rus' happened to be in the City and I argued, as his intermediary, to my late lord, the emperor, that he should be appointed patriarch in the hope that various advantages would come from him and then the pope, or at least that the name of the pope should be commemorated.

Thus Sphrantzes does not even allude to the possibility of Gregory's restoration that had been explicitly demanded by the pope. It is possible that one of the reasons that directed the emperor to reject his friend's advice was that the situation would be complicated even further if he appointed Isidore to the post as the titular head of the Greek Church while Gregory was still alive. Also, it would have created additional problems within the papacy, for two individuals loyal to the pope would then hold the same office, and this conflict could have postponed or at least protracted the anticipated aid from the West.[92] Nevertheless, the fact remains that Gregory was never reinstated in the imperial capital,

138 *The papal emissary*

even when Constantine yielded to other papal demands and even formally celebrated the union.

Sphrantzes, who had advocated the appointment of Isidore to the vacant patriarchal throne of the Greek capital, has preserved a picture of the deplorable situation that plagued the court in those turbulent days and takes the opportunity to explain why, in his own view, his suggestion was eventually rejected: Constantine was concerned about an actual civil war breaking out if Isidore were to ascend to the patriarchal throne:[93]

> καὶ πολλῶν λόγων καὶ βουλῆς καὶ μελέτης γενομένης ἔδοξε τῷ ἀοιδίμῳ βασιλεῖ ὅτι τὸ ἓν νὰ λείψῃ παντελῶς, διότι πατριάρχου γενομένου ἔνι χρεία πάντες, ἢ νὰ πείθωνται αὐτῷ, ἢ ἔχθρα νὰ γένηται καὶ πόλεμος μέσον αὐτοῦ καὶ τῶν μὴ πειθωμένων αὐτῶν. καὶ εἰς τοιοῦτον καιρόν, ὁποῦ μᾶς ἐπεμβαίνει ἔξωθεν πόλεμος, νὰ ἔχωμεν καὶ ἔσωθεν πόλεμον, πόσον κακόν.

After many deliberations and consultations, the late emperor decided to abandon the first alternative [*sc.* the appointment of Isidore to the patriarchal post], since the appointed patriarch required the obedience of all; otherwise riots and war would ensue between him and those who were unwilling to obey. Especially at this time, when we were facing war from without, what a misfortune to have a war within!

Perhaps the decision to remove Isidore from consideration for the ecclesiastical seat and to abandon the whole matter altogether amounted to yet another concession of Constantine to the anti-unionist mob. Sphrantzes states that Constantine rejected the elevation of Isidore in order to avoid strife within the capital. Isidore himself never hints, in his surviving letters, that he was ever under consideration for the post, as part of his mission was to reconfirm Gregory. Isidore never states anything about another possible patriarch in Constantinople and only announces to the pope in his first letter[94] to him (dated 15 July 1453)[95] that he had succeeded in commemorating the name of Gregory: *commemorabatur . . . reverendissimus patriarcha Gregorius, qui non solum tempore quo fuit in Constantinopoli in nulla altera ecclesia, verum et<iam> in suo monasterio nequaquam commemorabatur, verum . . . tota urbs eum commemorabatur,* "the most reverend Patriarch Gregory . . . was commemorated; during his residence in Constantinople he was never commemorated in any church, not even in his own monastery, but . . . the whole city commemorated him."

Soon after the arrival of Isidore in the imperial city,[96] Constantine, under pressure from the pope's legate who insisted on completing his mission,[97] ordered the leaders of the anti-unionists to assemble and to begin discussions for the acceptance of the union of churches at an early date in November.[98] In all likelihood, the emperor was displeased with this turn of events, for he knew that the majority of his clerics and his subjects was opposed to the union and to the terms that the cardinal had come to enforce. Doukas is explicit on this point:[99] ἦλθον εἰς τοὺς ἑνώσεως λόγους, καὶ εὑρὼν [*sc.* Ἰσίδωρος] τὸν βασιλέα εἰς τοῦτο κατανεύσαντα καὶ μερικοὺς τῶν τῆς ἐκκλησίας, "then the matter of union arose and he [*sc.* Isidore] discovered that the emperor and some members of the clergy were willing to accept the union." To emphasize his point, Doukas explains that at this time very few clergymen favored church union and that the emperor himself only pretended to be a supporter for union:[100] τὸ πλεῖστον οὖν μέρος τοῦ ἱερατικοῦ καὶ μοναχικοῦ τάγματος, ἡγούμενοι, ἀρχιμανδρῖται, μονάζουσαι, – τί λέγω, τὸ πλεῖστον!, . . . οὐδεὶς ἐξ ἁπάντων. καὶ αὐτὸς ὁ βασιλεὺς πεπλασμένως κατένευσεν, "the majority of the hierarchy and monastic orders, abbots, archimandrites, nuns (why do I say 'the majority'? What I mean to say is the absolute majority!) . . . there was not a single individual among this group in agreement. The emperor himself only pretended to agree." Doukas seems to be reporting rumors that must have been circulating in the city at the time. The impression that Constantine's support of the union was merely a pretense must have persisted in Constantinople,[101] as it even reached the cardinal's circle, and Leonardo voiced similar concerns. Leonardo was convinced that even when the union was concluded and celebrated, the Greeks had been totally insincere, as he succinctly described, in a memorable phrase, the Greek view of the union as fiction and not fact (*non . . . facta . . . sed ficta*).[102]

The kind reception that the emperor accorded to the legate did not conform to the sentiments and the absence of a warm welcome that he received from the anti-unionists who were clearly alarmed at his arrival. Their reaction is best gauged by the remarks of their leader, the obstinate Georgios Scholarios. On the day of the cardinal's arrival in Constantinople, Scholarios published a manifesto that lamented the future. This polemical tract was pinned to the door of his cell and in all likelihood it attracted great numbers of anti-unionists, who must have gathered before his cell while a literate person read aloud the contents. The very title of this *opusculum* demonstrates that it was directed against the cardinal, even though no mention of Isidore by name is made within the body of the work:[103] τοῦτο προσηλώθη τῇ θύρᾳ τοῦ δωματίου ἀπὸ τῆς α^{ης} Νοεμβρίου μετὰ τὸ ἐλθεῖν τὸν καρδινάλιον, "this [work] was nailed on the door of his cell[104] since November 1st, after the cardinal's arrival." It concludes by making his intentions plain: Scholarios would never yield and would never accept church union, for in his view such actions amounted to a separation from God.[105]

As leader of the anti-unionist circles, Georgios Scholarios wrote of the meeting that had been arranged, and perhaps even enforced by imperial command. He also makes clear in the preamble to the speech that this was their first, presumably public, meeting. Earlier, the "cardinal had arranged everything in private."[106] The anti-unionist faction again proved uncooperative and maintained its militant refusal to entertain any possibility of accommodation:[107] ἐλθόντος τοῦ λεγάτου ['Ισιδώρου] ἐν Κωνσταντινουπόλει καὶ ὄντος, καὶ ἀνάγκην ἐπάξαντος τῷ βασιλεῖ περὶ τῆς ἑνώσεως, συναχθέντες οἱ ὑπογεγραμμένοι ὁρισμῷ βασιλικῷ πολλάκις ἐν τῷ τοῦ Ξυλαλᾶ λεγομένῳ παλατίῳ, ταύτην τὴν ἀπόκρισιν δεδώκασι τῷ βασιλεῖ, "then the legate [sc. Isidore] came to the city; while he was there, he compelled the emperor to do something about the union; and so the following people frequently convened on a number of occasions, by imperial decree, in the so-called Palace of Xylalas,[108] and gave an answer to the emperor with their signatures appended to it." Isidore does not allude to these proceedings and does not mention the names of the individuals who maintained their anti-union stance. Thus in the letter he wrote to the pope from Crete Isidore only identifies Scholarios, but not his eight associates:[109] *Attamen Scholarius ille at alii octo monachorum sociorum suorum una cum eo unione praefate abalienaverunt se*, "nevertheless Scholarios and eight monks, his associates, kept away from the aforementioned union." The list[110] of the outspoken enemies of Catholicism cited by Scholarios includes Silvestros Syropoulos (the Greek historian of the Council of Ferrara-Florence),[111] Neophytos,[112] and Agallianos. The latter has left us an account of the anti-unionist view of the proceedings that had been initiated by Isidore. Agallianos does not have kind words for the cardinal and for Isidore's seven individuals, whom Agallianos believed to be the cardinals' close associates:[113]

> τὸ ἐν Ῥωσίας Ἰσιδώρῳ πονηρὸν πνεῦμα, καὶ ἕτερα ἑπτὰ τῆς πονηρίας πνεύματα λαβόμενον, ἐπεστράτευσε καθ᾽ ἡμῶν καὶ σφοδρὰν τὴν ἔφοδον ἐργασάμενον, κλύδωνά τε ἐξήγειρε μάλα δεινόν, πρὸς ὃν οὐκ ἴσχυσαν ἀντισχεῖν οἱ πολλοί, ἀλλὰ τὴν ἐξ ἡμῶν ὑγιᾶ διδασκαλίαν παρὰ φαῦλον θέμενοι ἢ ἀγνοίᾳ κλαπέντες ἢ φόβῳ κατασεισθέντες ἢ βίᾳ παρασυρέντες, ἅπαντες ἐγένοντο τοῦ καιροῦ πλὴν ἐμῶν, λέγω, ... ἀλλὰ διὰ τοῦτο ἦλθεν ἡ ὀργὴ τοῦ Θεοῦ ἐπὶ τοὺς υἱοὺς τῆς ἀπειθείας.
>
> The wicked spirit within Isidore of Rus' allied itself with seven other wicked spirits, and marched against us. They prepared and launched a mighty attack against us. It amounted to a great sea storm, which the majority proved unable to resist. And so they managed to pervert, steal through ignorance, shake through fear, and bring down through violence, our correct interpretation and lead all astray at that time, all, except us, I mean. ... But God's wrath fell upon these sons of disobedience.

On the other hand, under pressure from the court, the nobility supported Constantine's *Realpolitik* and sought a compromise to this problem. Contrary to the prevailing notion in modern scholarship, the leader of the nobility, the grand duke Loukas Notaras, labored on behalf of church union and parted company with his old friend Scholarios.[114] The exact time frame for their disagreement may be pinpointed to a letter[115] that Scholarios sent to the grand duke, in which he outlines his reasons why he would never support the union. By then the cardinal had arrived and the court had taken a reasonable course of action that would lead to church union. Scholarios must have depended on Notaras's support of his cause and he was probably surprised by the reply. In fact, the disagreement must have disturbed Scholarios, for he refers to it in his letter to the anti-unionist clerics that were about to hold discussions with the cardinal in

November. Scholarios had retained copies of his correspondence and was able to quote the grand duke's rebuke of his actions verbatim:[116]

ἔνι καὶ παρ' ἐμοὶ τὸ ἴσον τοῦ γράμματος ἐκείνου, καὶ ὁ μέγας δοὺξ ἀντεμήνυσέ μοι οὐκ οἶδ' ὅπως μάτην κοπιᾷς, πάτερ, ὅτι τὸ μνημόσυνον τοῦ πάπα περιέστη νὰ δοθῇ, καὶ ἀδύνατον ἄλλως γίνεσθαι. σωζομένου γοῦν ὅτι νὰ μηδὲν ἐμποδίσῃς, διότι οὐδὲν ἀνύσεις, ἂν χρῄζῃς νὰ ἔλθῃς νὰ συντύχῃς νὰ τὸ ποιήσωμεν.

I do have a copy of my letter [to Notaras]. The grand duke replied in the following manner: "You are laboring in vain, Father, as the pope's name will be commemorated. It has been decided. It cannot be otherwise. Make sure that you do not create any obstacles, for you will accomplish nothing; but do come, if you can, and contribute to its fulfillment."

Notaras seems to have been a key element in the campaign of the anti-unionists who clearly wished to gain his support. Scholarios was not the sole person who paid attention to him. There were others and there is evidence that Scholarios's right-hand man and associate, Theodoros Agallianos, also carried on a campaign to attract the attention of the grand duke. Agallianos composed a treatise in which he "reworked" the Greek unionist's thesis that he had written in support of the Latin dogma.[117] Although there is no internal evidence in Agallianos's speech to indicate the date of the composition, we would not be in error to conjecture that it was written at this time, during the period of debates. In this address Agallianos takes the opportunity to praise the grand duke's patriotism and personal qualities, and then continues, in flattering terms, to seek his patronage for the anti-unionists:[118]

τῶν μὲν εἰς τὸν ἐνδοξότατον μέγαν δοῦκαν [*sc.* Λουκᾶν Νοταρᾶν] ἐγκωμίαν χάριν ὁμολογῶ σὺν πᾶσι τοῖς ἄλλοις αὐτῷ κοινῇ τε γὰρ ἅπαντες ὀφείλομεν τὰς χάριτας τῷ τοιούτῳ ἀνδρί, προθύμῳ τε ὄντι περὶ τὰ κοινὰ καὶ ἐπωφελῆ, καὶ ἰδίᾳ ἕκαστος διὰ τὴν πρὸς ἕκαστον εὔνοιαν αὐτοῦ, κοινὸν πρυτανεῖον ἑαυτὸν ἀγαθοῦ καὶ πάσης χρείας καὶ βοηθείας ἑκάστῳ παρασχομένῳ.

I also along with all others, sing the praises of the grand duke [Loukas Notaras]. In common do we all owe a debt to such a man who is well disposed to our commonwealth and to good works. In private, each of us owes a debt due to his kindness that has been directed at each, as he has offered himself to be the treasury of goodness, providing all help and aid.

It is also interesting to observe that along with Agallianos, Scholarios, in all likelihood at this time, also composed a work, in which he specifically attacked Ioannes Argyropoulos and his Catholic views. This work survives and is titled: *Τοῦ Αὐτοῦ [Γενναδίου τοῦ Σχολαρίου] περὶ τῶν Ἀγγέλων πρὸς τὴν τοῦ Ἀργυροπούλου Γνώμην Ἀντιφερόμενον, By the Same [Gennadios Scholarios] Concerning the Angels, Opposing the Opinion of Argyropoulos.*[119] Thus both of the chief proponents of the anti-unionist camp composed works that were personally directed against Ioannes Argyropoulos. It is clear from our sources that Argyropoulos had been the recipient of imperial munificence for a substantial period of time. The court had financially supported his teaching school – the Academy in Constantinople – during the reigns of two emperors.[120] Furthermore, he had served as an imperial judge for some time, κριτὴς τοῦ δημοσίου τῆς Κωνσταντινουπόλεως, "public judge of Constantinople," and as an ἄρχων τῶν ἐκκλησιῶν, "lord of Churches."[121] In addition, he had been a devout Catholic, who knew Latin well and had received an advanced degree, a doctorate, from the University of Padua,[122] where had been granted the title of provost/*rector*,[123] and had become well versed in the scholastic methods of argumentation. While Agallianos was a close ally of Scholarios, Argyropoulos was the right hand to Isidore and probably the chief proponent of union who also could argue well and in accordance with the rules of scholastic logic for which the Latin West had become famous. He knew how to win arguments employing logic in the western fashion, a method that was unfamiliar to the Greeks. Thus, it would not be unreasonable to suppose that Argyropoulos, who had also attracted the attention of the grand duke Notaras,[124] was the chief advocate for the union camp, especially in disputations. Perhaps it was the influence of Argyropoulos and his arguments, in addition to *Realpolitik*, that convinced the grand duke to suggest to Scholarios that "he was laboring in vain"[125] in his opposition to the union.

The arrival of Isidore created considerable confusion within the anti-unionist camp. Apparently, the anti-unionists were delighted with the court's inactivity thus far. It soon became apparent, however, that the cardinal was going to press the matter of church union and his opponents charged that he was enforcing his will in haste and perhaps with the help of the Venetians and the Genoese in Constantinople.[126] Thus his arrival created further polarization within a city that was already perilously divided, and whose independent existence was more in question. But it was a matter of accepting union, which, it was hoped, would bring aid for political and military survival, or the converse of rejecting union, which would produce the urban center's inability to resist the overwhelming numerical superiority of the enemy.[127] The Greek cardinal brought reinforcements and then insisted upon the complete satisfaction of the pope and of Catholic Europe. The emperor had to agree to these demands, for he was well aware of the dangers that his capital was about to face. Literally, it was a matter of survival. Consequently, the anti-unionists began to feel some pressure. The inevitable rumors must have linked the name of Isidore with the patriarchal throne, especially since Sphrantzes and his friends in court favored Isidore's appointment to the post. Scholarios retired or perhaps he was urged to do so and then was encouraged to confine himself to a monastery. Clearly, by then he had become a *persona non grata* at court. From his cell at the Pantokrator Monastery[128] before he had taken monastic vows and then from the Kharsianites Monastery as a monk, the indignant Scholarios directed a thunderous campaign with a torrent of proclamations inciting the mob against the court.

Scholarios refused to participate in this gathering sponsored by the court but he kept a watchful eye over its proceedings.[129] He issued a written report[130] to enumerate what he thought were the best ways to defend the faith; the anti-unionists who had participated, among them Syropoulos and Agallianos, undoubtedly studied his report. This report has survived and perhaps we may form an impression of what was being discussed by the issues that interested Scholarios; otherwise, no "minutes" or *acta* have survived. Scholarios's report bears the following explanatory note instead of a proper title:

τοῦτο ἐστάλη τοῖς ἐκκλησιαστικοῖς, τῷ μεγάλῳ ἐκκλησιάρχῃ τῷ Σιλβέστρῳ καὶ τῷ μεγάλῳ χαρτοφύλακι τῷ Ἀγαλλιανῷ, τῇ ἡμέρᾳ ᾗ ἐμηνύθησαν οἱ ἐκκλησιαστικοὶ εἰς τοῦ Ξυλαλᾶ τὸ ϖαλάτιον. καὶ ἦν αὕτη ἡ ϖρώτη φορὰ μετὰ τὸ συσκευασθῆναι ϖάντα ἰδίως διὰ τοῦ καρδιναλίου καὶ τῶν τριῶν ἀρχιερέων τοῦ ἐνιαυτοῦ τούτου. τῇ ιε´ Νοεμβρίου.

This [report/composition/letter] was sent to the officials of the church, the grand *ekklesiarkhes* Silvestros [Syropoulos] and the grand archivist [Theodoros] Agallianos, on the day that these church officials were summoned to the Xylalas palace. This was the first occasion after the cardinal [Isidore] especially and the three high clergymen of this year had made all arrangements. On the 15th of November.

In this composition Scholarios submits all the arguments he could muster to demonstrate that the Council of Ferrara-Florence had been in error and he further points out the "innovations" that the Catholic Church had adopted and had thus departed from the ancient faith. In the process he alludes to the plight of Constantinople but he sees greater perils in church union and the secular survival of his city is of secondary importance to him. He again refers to his previous declarations that were of no actual value to the defense for the upcoming siege:[131] ϖερὶ δὲ τοῦ συμφέροντος τῇ Πόλει λέγω, ὅτι ἡ σωτηρία τῆς Πόλεως ἐκεῖνά ἐστιν ἃ ἐλάλησα ἐν τῷ μοναστηρίῳ τοῦ Παντοκράτορος, εἰ ἐγίνοντο καὶ ἔτι εἰ γενήσονται, καὶ οὐδὲν ἕτερον, "in regard to what is good for the city [Constantinople] I say that salvation for the City consists in what I said at the Monastery of the Pantokrator, if they have come about or will come about. I say nothing else." He continues to insist that he has provided a detailed report and has demonstrated that the emperor and the court were in error in yielding to the cardinal's demands:[132]

ἔτι ἐμήνυσα τῷ μεγάλῳ δουκί, μᾶλλον δὲ ἔγραψα ἐν ϖλάτει, ὡς οἶδεν ὁ τιμιώτατος μέγας ἐκκλησιάρχης καὶ ὁ τιμιώτατος δικαιοφύλαξ, νὰ ἀναφέρῃ τῷ βασιλεῖ, ὅτι ἃ βούλονται ϖοιεῖν ἔχουσιν ἅϖαν κακὸν ἐκ θεοῦ καὶ ἀνθρώϖων οἰκείων καὶ ἐξωτερικῶν καὶ ἐχθρῶν καὶ ἐκ συμμάχων, καὶ οὔτε ἕνωσις ἔσται ταῦτα, οὔτε μὴ ἕνωσις οὔτε ἔσται ϖλέον ἡ ἐκκλησία τῆς

> Κωνσταντινουπόλεως ἐν λόγῳ τοῖς ὀρθοδόξοις ἀπὸ τοῦ νῦν, ἐὰν ταῦτα συμπερανθῶσιν οὕτως ὡς βούλεσθε. ἐζήτησα ἐλθόντος τοῦ καρδιναλίου εὐθύς, ἀλλ' οὐκ ἠθελήσατε, τοῦτο πάλιν λέγω καὶ συμβουλεύω, νὰ ἔλθω εἰς τὸ παλάτιον, καὶ ἂς ἔνε αἱ τρεῖς τάξεις τῶν πολιτῶν, ἡ σύγκλητος, ἡ ἐκκλησία, καὶ ἡ πολιτεία, ἂς ἔλθῃ καὶ ὁ καρδινάλιος καὶ μετὰ Βενετίκων καὶ Γενουιτῶν ὅσους βούληται, καὶ νὰ δείξω πῶς τοῦτο ὃ κατεπείγει ὁ καρδινάλιος ἔνι εἰς ὅλα τὰ μέρη ἀσύμφορον.
>
> I even sent a message, or rather I wrote *in extenso*, to the grand duke [Loukas Notaras], as the most honorable grand *ekklesiarkhes* [Syropoulos] and the most honorable *dikaiophylax*[133] know, to report to the emperor [Constantine XI] that what they wish to accomplish will invite every evil from God, from men, from friends, and from external enemies. Consequently, neither union nor non-union will result. The Church of Constantinople will no longer exist for the Orthodox from this point on, if you enact your wishes. The moment the cardinal [Isidore] arrived, I made a request that you did not accept. Again I say and advise: allow me to come to the palace. Let there be present the three civil classes (the senate, the church, and the state); let the cardinal come with as many Venetians and Genoese as he wishes. I will demonstrate that what the cardinal is in a hurry to accomplish will bring no advantage to anyone.

That is the prime argument of his report and is directed against Isidore's actions, whose presence in Constantinople Scholarios clearly resented and he associated Isidore with the Italians.

The only arrangement the anti-unionists were willing to accept, in the final analysis, was their own position, which required the abandonment of the decisions concluded at the Council of Ferrara-Florence. Three times they had pressed their agenda that included the demand to re-argue the conclusions of Ferrara-Florence and endlessly tried to gain more favorable terms for themselves, that is, for the Church of Constantinople. They implied that they had not been at liberty to express their true positions at Ferrara-Florence and they now wished to do so by applying surgical procedures to the decisions that had been taken and had been accepted in Italy.[134] In addition, they demanded that western help to defend Constantinople should be divorced from the papal demand that church union be accepted and enforced.

We do not know from the surviving Greek sources who were the Greek supporters and associates of Isidore during these tense and acrimonious disputations. The accounts that survive all derive from the circle of Scholarios and the fanatical faction. Isidore's own thoughts have not survived, but evidently he dispatched frequent reports to the Vatican on the state of the ecclesiastical problems at this point in time.[135] Leonardo, however, supplies a few hints when he complains about the ecclesiastical entanglements in Constantinople:[136]

> *Intellexi plane, praeter Argyropilum, artium magistrum, Theophilumque Palaeologo hieromonacosque quosdam paucos et alios laicos, quod ambitio Graecos quasi omnes*

captivasset, ut nemo esset qui zelo fidei vel salutis suae motus primus videretur fieri by velle suae quasi opinionis et pertinaciae contemptor.

I realized clearly that besides [Ioannes] Argyropoulos[137] (the liberal studies professor and Catholic priest), Theophilos Palaiologos,[138] and a certain few hieromonks, as well as some lay persons, almost all Greeks had fallen victim to vanity. Consequently, there was no one who appeared motivated by religious enthusiasm or by the salvation of his soul to disregard opinion and obstinacy.

Leonardo further expresses his own resignation, as he found it personally impossible to reason with and come to terms with the Greeks:[139] *captabam perinde et mores et naturam Graecorum argumentisque sanctorum theologum dictis agebam intelligere quod eorum esset studium, quod propositum, quae rationes, quis finis eos a vera intelligentia debitaque oboedientia vel revocabant vel retrahebant,* "I tried to get a grasp of the customs and the character of the Greeks and tried to understand what they really wanted through the arguments and statements of their saintly theologians, as well as what they intended to do, especially their reasons that would keep them from an actual understanding and prevent them from the customary obedience."

Leonardo assigns personal motives for the Greek rejection of Catholic dogma, even though he believed that the Greeks saw the validity of the Catholic position. Thus the thorny matter of the procession of the Holy Spirit, the notorious *filioque*, was discussed and even though the Latin view was well presented, most likely with scholastic logic, whose art the Greeks had not mastered, Leonardo attributed the Greek rejection of the Catholic position to the obstinate character of Scholarios and his partisans:[140]

ex una parte ad fatendum articulum Sancti Spiritus urgebat eos conscientia, ex altera, ne meliorem Latini quam Graeci de veritate fidei intelligentiam habere credentur, elationis tumor eos adducebat. Verum, quoniam nec ratio nec auctoritas nec variae Scholarii, Isidori Neophytique opiniones adversus Romanae Ecclesiae fidem stare poterant.

On the one hand their own conscience was leading them to accept the article of [the procession] of the Holy Spirit but, on the other hand, inflated pride compelled them to believe that the Latins could not have a better understanding of the true faith than the Greeks. Neither their reasoning nor their authority, not even the various opinions of Scholarios, of Isidore [the hieromonk], and of Neophytos, could hold their own against the faith of the Roman Church.

After the decision was reached at the imperial court to accept, then to celebrate publicly, and to enforce the union,[141] even without anti-unionist approval,[142] the poisoned atmosphere in Constantinople became extremely polarized and public opinion became unfriendly, if not downright hostile to the imperial court. The imperial administration appears to have lost control over its own subjects, the vast majority of whom increasingly turned toward Scholarios for guidance and advice. Scholarios's most famous and most powerful manifesto appeared on 27 November, twelve days after the gathering at Xylalas, but before the formal celebration of the union.[143] We are left with the impression of a vast organization that Scholarios had assembled and was at his disposal, as in its very title the manifesto declares:[144] "the present [document] was distributed throughout the entire city in numerous copies, six months before the capture [of Constantinople] that took place on May 29." He addresses this document to the noble citizens of Constantinople and to all clergymen and lay members, τοῖς εὐγενεστάτοις πολίταις τῆς Κωνσταντινουπόλεως ἅπασιν ἱερωμένοις καὶ κοσμικοῖς, "to the most noble citizens of Constantinople; to all the members of the clergy and the lay." In this intractable text Scholarios sought to justify his actions and he stubbornly insisted that he had remained loyal to his emperor and to his homeland, at least in his Orthodox way:[145]

> εἰ μὴ ποθῶ τὴν εἰρήνην τῶν ἐκκλησιῶν καὶ τὴν ὁμόνοιαν τῶν χριστιανῶν ἁπάντων, ἀλλὰ τὴν ἀληθινὴν καὶ πνευματικὴν καὶ ἐκκλησιαστικὴν δικαίαν καὶ σωτήριον, μὴ εἰρηνευθείη μοι ἡ ζωή. εἰ μὴ πληροφορεῖ με τὸ συνειδὸς ὅτι ὀρθόν ἐστι καὶ ἀδέκαστον πρός τε τὸν βασιλέα καὶ τὴν πατρίδα καὶ ὑμᾶς πάντας καὶ ἰδίως ἕκαστον ἐν ἀγάπῃ εἰλικρινεῖ, μὴ συγχωρῆσαί μοι τὰς ἁμαρτίας ὁ Κύριος.
>
> If I do not desire peace between the Churches and harmony among all Christians (a true spiritual harmony of ecclesiastical justice and salvation), may I never find peace in my lifetime. If my motives are not righteousness and justice for my emperor, for our homeland, and for all of you (as I have sincere affection for each one of you), may the Lord never forgive my sins!

Doukas also relates Scholarios's retirement and his campaign against church union that he continued from within his monastic cell. He relates that after the Xylalas deliberations had concluded the anti-unionists (whom Doukas styles "schismatics") flocked to the cell[146] of Scholarios and begged for instructions:[147] τότε τὸ σχισματικὸν μέρος ἐλθὸν ἐν τῇ μονῇ τοῦ Παντοκράτορος ἐν τῇ κέλλῃ τοῦ Γενναδίου, τοῦ ποτε Γεωργίου Σχολαρίου, ἔλεγον αὐτῷ. "καὶ ἡμεῖς τί ποιήσωμεν;" "at that time the schismatic party came to the Monastery of the Pantokrator, to the cell of Gennadios (who was formerly known as Georgios Scholarios) and kept asking him: 'And what are we to do?'" According to Doukas, Scholarios then decided to publish a written declaration, stating his own convictions, cast in the form of advice: αὐτὸς δὲ [ὁ Σχολάριος] ἐγκλεισθεὶς καὶ χάρτην λαβὼν καὶ γράψας τὴν γνώμην αὐτοῦ, διὰ γραφῆς ἐδήλου τὴν συμβουλήν, "but he [Scholarios] locked himself in [his cell], took paper, and wrote his opinion. In the written piece he revealed his advice." It is not certain that Doukas has the same declaration in mind that has been preserved and was published on the 27th of November "throughout the entire city." But given the position in Doukas's narrative, between the Xylalas meeting and the formal celebration of the union, perhaps we can assume that Doukas is speaking of the manifesto, whose numerous copies were widely distributed. The problem, however, is that the declaration that Doukas attributes to Scholarios is much shorter than the one that has been preserved independently in Scholarios's *opus*. It is possible that Doukas provided a summary of the actual composition that was attributed to him by the Greeks after the fall (while he was conducting his interviews with survivors of the sack, as he happens to mention in this same section).[148] The passage of time, the events of the siege, and the period of captivity had undoubtedly affected and colored the memory of those informants, who probably furnished Doukas with the gist of the original detailed composition and not with an accurate verbatim quote. Doukas himself supplies the qualifier οὕτως, "in such a way," to indicate that he is not reproducing the exact text of the declaration. Alternatively, it is possible that Scholarios produced two different versions: one intended for the educated nobility and one for the general public who did not feel comfortable with his ancient Greek phrasing. It is quite plausible that if this is actually the case, then the shorter composition, with easier grammar and less archaic vocabulary, cited by Doukas, was intended for the general and ill-educated public.

Doukas's shorter version of Scholarios's declaration preserves the original spirit of the irascible monk that we encounter in the longer version within Scholarios's transmitted *opus*:[149]

> τὰ γραφέντα οὖν ἐδήλουν οὕτως. ἄθλιοι Ῥωμαῖοι, εἰς τί ἐπλανήθητε καὶ ἀπεμακρύνατε ἐκ τῆς ἐλπίδος τοῦ θεοῦ καὶ ἠλπίσατε εἰς τὴν δύναμιν τῶν Φράγγων καὶ σὺν τῇ Πόλει, ἐν ᾗ μέλλει φθαρῆναι, ἐχάσατε καὶ τὴν εὐσέβειάν σας; ἵλεως μοι, Κύριε. μαρτύρομαι ἐνώπιόν Σου, ὅτι ἀθῷός εἰμι τοῦ τοιούτου πταίσματος. γινώσκετε, ἄθλιοι πολῖται, τί ποιεῖτε; καὶ σὺν τῷ αἰχμαλωτισμῷ, ὃς μέλλει γενέσθαι εἰς ὑμᾶς, ἐχάσατε καὶ τὸ πατροπαράδοτον σέβας καὶ ὡμολογήσατε τὴν ἀσέβειαν. οὐαὶ ὑμῖν ἐν τῷ κρίνεσθαι.

> His written composition ran in such a way: "Wretched Romans [Greeks]: to what purpose have you gone astray and have distanced yourselves from God's hope and you place all hope on the might of the Franks [Europeans] and together with the city [Constantinople] that is about to be destroyed. Have you also lost your piety? Lord, have mercy on me! I am a witness before you. I am innocent of such fault. Do you know, wretched citizens, what you are doing? Together with your captivity, which is about to fall upon you, you have lost your ancestral piety and you have embraced impiety! Woe to you on the [day of] judgment."

It is curious to note that the original declaration, the *apologia* of Scholarios, does not in any way address the Constantinopolitans. It is couched in the first-person singular and lays out his motivation, designed to demonstrate his true faith. It makes no reference to future woes. In Doukas's version, Scholarios is playing the part of Pythia and predicts the torrent of woes that are about to fall upon the city and its citizens. Clearly, Doukas's version has been recast, perhaps unconsciously, in the minds of survivors to emphasize the disaster and the actions of Scholarios in the days preceding the fall, as recalled by survivors, not unlike the warnings of a modern Cassandra. Doukas concludes by saying that the original composition of Scholarios was longer than the text that he quotes and further adds that Scholarios withdrew himself from sight. This must have been an effective dramatic gesture on his part, as crowds gathered before his quarters and a literate person read his composition aloud:[150] ταῦτα καὶ ἕτερα πλείω γράψας καὶ εἰς τὴν θύραν τοῦ κελλίου αὐτοῦ προσηλώσας, ἐκλείσθη ἔνδον καὶ ὁ χάρτης ἀνεγιγνώσκετο, "after he wrote these [words] and many more besides, he nailed [the composition] to the door of his cell. Then he shut himself in and his paper was read again and again." Doukas further emphasizes that even in the course of the siege Scholarios maintained his opposition to the court:[151] ὁ δὲ Γεννάδιος οὐ διέλιπε καθ' ἑκάστην διδάσκων καὶ γράφων κατὰ τῶν ἑνωτικῶν, καὶ πλέκων συλλογισμοὺς καὶ ἀντιφάσεις, "not a day passed that did not see Gennadios [Scholarios] preaching and writing against the unionists, as he continued weaving syllogisms and contradictions."

After the union had been formally celebrated in the capital, Scholarios maintained his intransigent position and composed a letter to his former patron and partner in sedition, Despot Demetrios in the Morea, the younger brother of Constantine XI. He listed a number of reasons that prompted him to publish his manifesto of the 27th of November. Scholarios mentions, with unmistakable pride, the resources that he and his acolytes made use of, especially the labor of copying and distributing multiple copies of the declaration. Scholarios's motives, actions, and general attitude illustrate that the monk was treading upon the ground of treason, even though he would have undoubtedly preferred to see himself as a true champion of Orthodoxy and as a victim of the court's oppression in order to conclude the union for reasons of *Realpolitik*. One may even infer, from Scholarios's thunderous statements, the existence of a fifth column within the walls of Constantinople, operating without opposition from the court, which tread lightly with the anti-unionists. Scholarios and his accomplices took this opportunity to condemn the emperor's efforts to elicit military aid from the West for his capital and his harassed subjects:[152]

> σιωπῆσαι δὲ παντελῶς οὐδ' ἐν μέσοις τοῖς πειρασμοῖς ἔκρινα, καὶ διὰ τοῦτο συγγράφω τῇ πόλει πάσῃ συμβουλήν τινα σύντομον ἐν σχήματι διαμαρτυρίας καὶ ἀπολογίας ὑπὲρ τῆς σιωπῆς τὰς τῶν εὐσεβεστέρων γνώμας συνέχουσαν, καὶ ἡ τοῦ νοεμβρίου μηνὸς εἰκοστὴ καὶ ἑβδόμη τοῖς τε βασιλείοις αὐτοῖς καὶ ταῖς ἀγοραῖς καὶ ταῖς ἐν τῇ πόλει μοναῖς ἁπάσαις τὸ γράμμα ἐκεῖνο διέσπειρον τοσαῦτις ἐκγεγραμμένον σχεδόν, ὅσαι δὴ καὶ τοῦ μηνὸς αἱ ἡμέραι. καὶ τὸ σχῆμα τοῦ γράμματος, ἀπολογία γὰρ ὑπὲρ τῆς δῆθεν σιγῆς ἦν, καίτοι ποῦ τὸν πρόσθεν χρόνον ἐσίγων; ἐβόων μὲν οὖν τὴν ἀδικίαν τῆς πίστεως.

> I decided not to remain completely silent in the midst of temptations and for this reason I composed a short piece of advice for the city. It was in the form of a protest-apology over the silence, which was maintained

by the most pious individuals. On November 27 I distributed this letter in the palace itself, in the market places, and in all the monasteries of the city. The number of copies equaled the days of that month, numbering as many as the days of that month. I chose the genre of an apology to explain my supposed silence. But really, was there a time that I was silent? I had been loudly protesting the injustices suffered by our faith.

This chaotic religious situation had its ramifications in politics as well. The fact is that the last Greek emperor of Constantinople was never formally crowned in the required religious ceremony. That the patriarchal throne was vacant complicated this matter also, as the patriarch was required to officiate at this important ceremony of a formal coronation.[153] It is possible that the decision of the anti-unionists to oppose union to the bitter end had repercussions in this area as well. The consequence with the court's decision to accept the formal church union in the face of immense opposition generated by Scholarios and his associates meant, in practical terms, that no coronation could take place. And this matter of crowning the active emperor had to be passed over in silence for the time being. Perhaps it was the court's conclusion that, if the expected attack by the sultan were to fail, then this vital matter could be revisited in contented future days.

The anti-union faction took pleasure in informing Constantine of the reality of his ambiguous situation, of being an emperor without crown. And furthermore, they included the postponed coronation ceremony in their argumentation as a weapon in their arsenal by attempting to compel Constantine to renounce the union. Thus Ioannes Eugenikos, the brother of Markos, and a confirmed anti-unionist himself, directed a letter to Constantine after his accession. Although he respectfully addressed him as τὸν βασιλέα Κωνσταντῖνον Παλαιολόγον, "Emperor Constantine Palaiologos," he seized the opportunity to remind him that he was not actually an emperor, as there had been no coronation ceremony which would indisputably render Constantine as the official defender of the Greek Church:[154]

τῆς ποίας οὖν ἐκκλησίας ἐκδικητής ἐστι καὶ ὑπέρμαχος ἡ ἐκ θεοῦ βασιλεία σου, καὶ πῶς ἔχει νῦν αὕτη ἡ ἐκκλησία τοῦ Χριστοῦ καὶ ποῦ ταύτης θρέμματα καὶ τίς ὁ ποταπὸς ὁ ταύτης δοκῶν ποιμὴν καὶ προστάτης καὶ τίς ὁ στέψων σε πατριάρχης ὁτεδήποτε καὶ τῷ θείῳ μύρῳ χρίσων βασιλικῶς, καὶ τὴν σὴν εὐεργεσίαν καὶ ὁμολογίαν δεξόμενος;

Which Church will you, as God-approved emperor, protect and defend? What is the present condition of the Church of Christ? Where is its flock? Who is this wretch who currently pretends to be its pastor and patron? Who will be the patriarch to crown you? When on earth will he anoint you with the divine oil in the imperial manner and will thus become your dependent and confessor?

In addition, the other fervent follower of Scholarios, Theodoros Agallianos, emphasized, as late as 1452, the fact that Constantine had not been crowned, even though he refers to him as "reigning":[155] γέγραπται ταῦτα . . . *βασιλεύοντος τοῦ ὑστάτου τῶν Παλαιολόγων Κωνσταντίνου τρίτῳ ἔτει τῆς ἀρχῆς αὐτοῦ, ἔτι ἀστεφοῦς ὄντος διὰ τὸ τὴν ἐκκλησίαν μὴ ἔχειν προστάτην,* "I wrote these [words] . . . in the reign of the very last of the Palaiologoi, Constantine, in the third year of his reign, while he still remained without a crown because the Church lacked a defender."

The contemporaries of Constantine were sharply divided on this issue. The majority seems to have accepted the legitimacy of his position. He was *de facto* and *de iure* emperor, even if the required ceremony in the Great Church had been denied to him. The major writers of the period, Dokeianos, Kritoboulos, Sphrantzes, Khalkokondyles, and most compilers of the short chronicles, were sufficiently realistic to accept this state of affairs. Argyropoulos wrote a formal address to the new emperor in which he describes him as θειότατον βασιλέα, "the most divine emperor," and has no reservation in observing that Constantine had actually ascended the throne:[156] χαίρω μέν, ὦ θειότατε βασιλεῦ, ὁρῶν σε ἐπὶ τοῦ βασιλείου θρόνου καθήμενον, "I rejoice, most divine emperor, when I perceive that you, an individual excelling in everything, have ascended the throne." Similarly, Michael Apostoles,[157] also a unionist, accepted Constantine as θειότατον βασιλέα "most divine emperor." Others, however, failed to do so; and they were not all anti-unionists, but saw legitimacy in the view that the reigning emperor had not been crowned. Thus Doukas could never bring himself to accept the fact that the last Greek emperor had never been formally crowned and he considered John VIII as the last to have properly reigned in medieval Greece, but then Doukas contradicts himself by calling Constantine "the emperor."[158]

4 Isidore and the declaration of church union

The decision to celebrate the church union formally in Santa Sophia was made by the imperial court and was ratified by those in attendance at the meeting that took place in the palace. Doukas relates this, but the language of his text indicates that it was not a unanimous decision. Some of the court officials and clerics in attendance who had agreed to participate only "appeared" to ratify the decision. Doukas also begins the passage by stating that the emperor himself pretended to agree to the union:[159]

> καὶ αὐτὸς ὁ βασιλεὺς πεπλασμένως κατένευσεν. πλὴν ἐλθόντες οἱ φαινόμενοι κατὰ τὸ δοκοῦν τῆς ἑνώσεως ἐν τῇ Μεγάλῃ Ἐκκλησίᾳ, ἱερεῖς τε καὶ διάκονοι τῶν τοῦ κλήρου καὶ ὁ βασιλεὺς σὺν τῇ συγκλήτῳ, ἐβουλεύοντο κοινῇ ὁμονοίᾳ λειτουργῆσαι Θεῷ καὶ ἀποδόσαι τὰς εὐχὰς ἀδόλῳ γνώμῃ.

> Even the emperor himself pretended to give his assent. Finally, those who appeared to agree went to the Great Church [Santa Sophia]: priests and deacons from the clergy, the emperor, and the senate, and they expressed the wish in common agreement to have a divine liturgy performed and to express the prayers with a clear conscience.

The qualifiers that Doukas employs to suggest his doubts about the sincerity of the participants are obvious and include the participle φαινόμενοι/"appeared," and the adverb πεπλασμένως/"only pretended." But these qualifiers seem to be balanced, if not contradicted, by κοινῇ ὁμονοίᾳ/"in common agreement," by ἐβουλεύοντο/"expressed the wish," and by ἀδόλῳ γνώμῃ/"in clear conscience." The problems involved in the celebration of the union are apparent and Doukas himself, a unionist, must have felt conflicted. It would not be an exaggeration to conclude that similar feelings prevailed in Constantinople's atmosphere. Independently of Doukas, Leonardo shared his hesitation about the emperor's sincerity,[160] and further on expresses his famous conclusion that the union amounted to nothing more than a theatrical show:[161] *non ergo unio facta, sed unio ficta*, "indeed union was not a fact but a fiction." He returns to this topic again and simply states that the heart of the Greeks was not in it, as they failed to enforce it:[162] *celebrarant unionem Graeci voce, sed opera negabant*, "the Greeks celebrated the union in word but denied it in action."

It was perhaps the official position of the court to accept union in order to conform to the pope's demands and to hope, in accordance with the "carrot on the stick" principle, for the promised military aid against the sultan. But at the same time, the imperial representatives took care to express hesitation and their regret in order to pacify, in vain and unsuccessfully as it turned out, the anti-unionists, whose assistance in the defense of the city would be essential. At best, the anti-unionists would cooperate; in an unhappier case, they might protest by adhering to the "passive resistance" policy advocated by their leader, Scholarios; and at worst, they might form a "fifth column" within the city under siege and even actively labor on behalf of the sultan. Thus the imperial court was confronted with a terrible dilemma: a declaration of church union might bring substantial aid to the beleaguered city (that in the end failed to materialize),[163] but implied at the same time a further alienation of the anti-unionists, who by far were the majority within the city; on the other hand, placating the majority and rejecting union would alienate the pope and Catholic Europe and no aid would ever come. The ambiguity adopted by the court, to celebrate the union but allow a free hand to the anti-unionists to protest endlessly, may have been due to an official decision.

In this decidedly mournful atmosphere the celebration of church union finally took place in Santa Sophia, the most sacred of cathedrals in Greek Christendom, on the 12th of December 1452. Barbaro, who undoubtedly attended the festivities, devotes a few sentences to the event, even though he cites the wrong date, rendering it as one day later:[164]

> *Adi 13 dezembrio fo fatto la union in la giexia de Santa Sofia, con grandenissima solenitade de chierixie, en etiam ve jera el reverendo gardenal de Rosia, che jera mandà per el papa, etiam ve jera el serenissimo imperador con tuta la sua baronia, e tutto el populo de Costantinopoli; e in quell zorno ve fo de gran pianti in questa zitade, e questa union sì se intende, che i sia unidi come nui Franchi, e non aver più sisme in la giexia.*

On December 13, the union was concluded in the Church of Saint Sophia with great solemnity by the clerics. Present were [Isidore] the reverend cardinal of Rus' (dispatched by the pope), the most serene emperor with his barons, and the entire population of Constantinople. On that day there were great lamentations in this city. This union meant to unite them, as we Franks [Latins] are, and to have no more schisms in the Church.

Leonardo also devotes one sentence to the celebration, but he is clearly disappointed and has grave reservations about the sincerity of the participants:[165] *Actum est industria probitate praefati domini cardinalis [sc. Isidori], ut sacra unio, assentiente imperatore senatuque – si non ficta fuit – firmaretur celebrareturque secundo Idus Decembris, Spirid<i>onis episcopus sancti die*, "the lord cardinal's [Isidore's] energy and goodness saw to it that the sacred union was confirmed and celebrated with the consent of the emperor and the senate (provided that it had been genuine) on the second day of the Ides of December, on the feast day of Saint Spirid<i>on, the bishop."

Only one source, Pusculo, has furnished a long account of the ceremony, which is the main subject of his third book.[166] Pusculo has taken the opportunity to provide what emerges as the last description on record of Santa Sophia within a Christian setting[167] and the last occasion at which a Greek emperor of Constantinople and a Greek cardinal, the official emissary of western Europe's religious leader, collectively celebrated the liturgy and mass. The days of a Christian Santa Sophia were numbered, for it was destined to be converted into a mosque and eventually to be transformed into a Turkish-Islamic museum in more modern times.[168] Pusculo adds:[169]

> *Templum erat antiquum, media constructus in urbe, / Relligione ingens regum monumenta priorum / Excelsus servans, variisque insigne columnis. / Convexum coeli forma testudine fulget / Auratis desuper, pictisque coloris lapillis / Coelesti. Ingentes subeunt immane columnae / Rubrae, opus extructum, viridesque, et candida signant / Marmora: porphyreaeque tabulae, fulvaeque relucent / Parietibis latis. Distincta coloribus arte / Strata oculos stringunt pavimenta infratibus. Aere / Tres valvae insignes bullis, pulchro aurichalco / Ingentes duplices latae sonuere volutae / Cardinibus latum ante ipsam porrigitur aedum, / Vestibulum, foribus totidem, et simili ornamento / Insigne. Hic solio se rex componitur alto / Ad portam temple mediam, stratoque resedit / Quem circum Graji proceres funduntur. Ad illum / Ut venit, destras jungunt, mutuisque salutant / Vocibus a summo Nicolao principe dicta / Pace: salutato et legatus rege recumbit / Sede humili, parva, fuerat forte parata.*

There was an ancient church [Santa Sophia] erected in the middle of the city. This dignified monument of former emperors was universally revered and was marked by columns of various colors. Curved like a tortoise, its high dome shone above with golden and multi-colored mosaics. Enormous tall columns of red and green stone supported the structure; bright marble shone; and purple and yellow slabs illuminated the wide walls. The stone pavement, cleverly marked in color, greeted the eyes of visitors. Three huge double doors dressed in bronze, marked by relief-work, thundered as they were opened wide and turned inward on their hinges to reveal a large interior vestibule, with the same number of doors decorated in a similar and amazing fashion. To the central gate of the church the emperor was conveyed on his high throne. He was sitting on a coverlet and was surrounded by throngs of Greek nobles. After he arrived, they shook hands and greeted each other with the peace extended by the pope, Lord Nicholas. With the salutations over, the legate [*sc.* Isidore] sat on a small, low seat, which had been prepared for him.

Pusculo furnishes the only existing description of the proceedings and the circumstances for the declaration of church union that had taken place. Isidore rose and addressed the emperor. In his speech, which takes up fifty lines of Pusculo's work, Isidore states that he had been moved by patriotism to return to Constantinople, in spite of his advanced age (c. 67):[170] *vasti discrimina nunquam intrassem ponti, nec tantos ferre labores / Auderem senior: non tunc tua limina adirem. / Sed me communis patriae sors aspera movit / Rursus adire lares patrios*, "I would never have faced the dangers of the sea. I am an old man and should not have taken upon my shoulders such hard work. I would not have come to your city, but our common threat to our homeland forced me to retrace my steps to my sacred fatherland." He alludes to his arrival as pastor and warlord.[171] He reminds the flock and the emperor of the Ferrara-Florence Council and of the allegiance given to Pope Eugenius IV,[172] and announces that Pope Nicholas V was prepared to send aid, a point on which the unionist court was extremely sensitive, for they hoped that the forthcoming aid would be substantial and would justify their unpopular position to unite with the Catholic Church:[173] *Nec me pastorem contemnant. / Barbara contra arma quibus clause excidium exspextare queruntur, / Auxilia excipient. Aderunt terraque marique, / Armatae classes, magnusque exercitus armis*, "let them have no contempt, for, because I am a shepherd, as they complain that they are hedged in by the barbarian's [Turkish] army waiting for destruction. Help will come. It will come here by land and over the sea: armed armadas and a greatly outfitted army." Isidore concluded that if no help had arrived thus far, it was because God in anger had turned away from Constantinople.

We should be reminded that Pusculo provides this speech in a poetic form, although he does ascribe it to Isidore. Thus, in details, it may not be accurate. Pusculo was not a reporter, but rather a poet who perhaps in shorthand noted the main points of the cardinal's address. He was probably, but not with certainty, present at the ceremony, for it was a most important event in the city prior to the onset of the Ottoman siege. Having witnessed the ceremony, he had visual knowledge of the proceedings. We may, therefore, assume that indeed the cardinal spoke, whom Pusculo may have witnessed on this occasion, as he has the cardinal alluding to his own advanced age. Isidore must have delivered the address in some form, most probably extemporaneously rather than from a prepared text that would have been unlike him, and it is reasonable to assume that he raised points similar, if not identical, to those that Pusculo ascribes to him.

Pusculo also "recorded" the response of the emperor, Constantine XI:[174]

> *Talia dicta dabat legatus. Corde premebat / Rex curas, fixosque oculos tellure tenebat. / Tunc sic pauca refert: Mihi non est copia soli / Pontifici adjungi summon, nec cogere dignum / Est populum: placido fiant haec corde necesse est. / Sed tu si qua potes primum scrutare per artes / Tentamenta animos monachum primosque sacrati / Ordinis explora: placeat si foedere tali / Hacque via ulcisci Teucros; et morte levari; / Ex conare tamen populum allectare periclo / Attonitum. Interea cunctum explorare senatum / Quid sit opu facto, hunc et maturare jubebo.*

Such were the words of the legate [Isidore]. The emperor appeared concerned and kept his eyes fixed on the ground. Then he said a few words: "It is not solely up to me to join the pope and there is no dignity to compel my people. They must do so willingly. It is up to you to use all your cunning to convert the monks and the high clerics. I would be delighted to find any way to avenge myself upon the Turks and to wipe them out. Try to convert my people, who have been numbed by the impending danger. Meanwhile, let us ask the senate to find out what needs to be done and I will issue orders to implement it."

Barbaro notes, exercising a journalistic tone in his report, that the celebration was more an occasion for lamentation for the general populace and was distinctly marked by the absence of joy.[175] It is important to stress that, aside from Pusculo, no other surviving sources describe this celebration in detail. To the Greek anti-unionists, these proceedings were the work of the devil. The less said about them the better. The Latin Leonardo, on the other hand, did not believe that the Greeks were sincere and he did not bother to record the celebration of the union with a detailed description of the ceremony. Thus the realization of the ancient goal of church union was not amply recorded either by the Greeks or by the Latins. Among the other eyewitnesses, Barbaro, who was a sailor and a physician, was not overly interested in theology. Accordingly, he devoted a few sentences to the union without recording any details. And so it was left to the scholarly humanist Pusculo to record the event in classical hexameters. Pusculo may not have been blessed with Vergil's talents, but he was an eyewitness to the event and he gave poetic embellishment to Isidore's speech and to Constantine's response. Pusculo composed and circulated his poem at the moment when numerous survivors, including Isidore, were still alive in Italy. He would have incurred a charge of invention and of an imagination running wild had he departed from the historical essentials of the situation. As there were never any complaints voiced concerning the historical accuracy of his description, we may conclude that the substance of his poetical account must reflect substantial reality. The very least that can be said is that both the cardinal and the emperor spoke during the ceremony. It is interesting to note further that even at this late date Constantine persisted in his refusal to apply pressure upon the anti-unionists and publicly stated his position during the ceremony of church union. He evidently believed that it was the responsibility of the pope's representatives to convert the Greeks. To the chagrin and embarrassment of Leonardo, Constantine expected the pope's legate to do his part and convert the Greeks through argumentation and persuasion but without support or material aid from the court. But Isidore's powers of persuasion were limited, perhaps a limitation that he himself recognized, thus explaining in part his utter failure to convert the Greeks to Latinism.

This point has never been emphasized in scholarship, but it appears to have been a conscious decision by the emperor to keep himself and his court distant from the religious debate. Constantine relied upon Isidore to address the matter of "conversion" and the court simply refused to chastise or to enforce by decree Latin proselytization. Consequently, Leonardo arrived at the distinct impression that the emperor had been very weak and even cowardly in his dealings with the anti-unionists, whose leaders and their activities he had failed to check, but had allowed them a free hand to circulate their propaganda throughout the city:[176]

> *Ergo dixi: Paterisne, o imperator! Ut haec ambitio scindat Ecclesiam, ut hujus rei gratia divina ira magis magisque merito accendatur? Cur non e medio pertinaces illi tolluntur? Acquiescere imperator visus, metropolitasque Scholarium, Isidorum, Neophytum complicesque, judices constituit, verbo quidem, non facto. Nam pusillanimitatem imperator excussisset, hanc fidei illusionem vindicasset. Qui enim homnibus, Deo spreto, complacet, utique confundetur. Coercendi quidem illi errant, qui si fuissent, morbum pestiferum non propagassent. Sed ignoro, utrumne imperator, aut judices damnandi quibus correctionis virga, quamquam minae intercessissent, aberat.*
>
> Therefore I said: "Emperor: will you bear it? This aspiration [of the anti-unionists] will produce a schism in the Church and the wrath of God will rightly burn more ferociously than ever. Why are these offensive individuals still among us?" The emperor appeared to agree quietly and appointed metropolitans as judges over Scholarios, Isidore, and Neophytos, and their associates, but he had done so in word and not in deed. Indeed, if the emperor had forsaken his cowardice [towards them], he would have punished the deceitful appearance of their faith. He who pleases men and scorns God will be totally confounded. Those who deserved punishment wandered free. Had they been corrected, they would not have spread their pestilential sickness around. But I know not, whether we should condemn the judges or the emperor, as neither possessed the stick to correct and could only avail themselves of empty threats.

If we accept the evidence furnished by Pusculo, of the emperor's speech in Santa Sophia, and we assume that the poet reported an accurate record of this address, then we may conclude that Leonardo has mistaken imperial policy for personal cowardice. The emperor desired that the cardinal and his followers convert his people to their cause through persuasive argument. It was the imperial position that Isidore and his entourage would be responsible for persuading and converting the populace and the anti-unionists, and that the imperial court would not impose its will and would not apply pressure or enforce by decree or other means what the populace should embrace willingly. Thus the imperial court was also complicit in allowing the chaos to continue within the city. Leonardo is correct in his assessment of the existing situation, but for the wrong reason. It was not so much the cowardice attributed to the emperor, but a consequence of policy and of the emperor's conviction that the papal legate should teach, preach, and convert. The responsibility for these actions fell upon the shoulders of Isidore and his entourage. Imperial policy, however, failed. The papal contingent was unsuccessful in its efforts and the anti-union activities multiplied unceasingly. The imperial court simply did not proceed through force to impose church union.

Sphrantzes simply states[177] that the celebration of church union took place on the 12th of December. Doukas concentrates on the reaction of the anti-unionists and portrays the general climate of despair that subsequently reigned throughout the imperial city:[178]

> ἐν τῇ συμφωνίᾳ οὖν αὐτῇ ἔστερξαν τοῦ γενέσθαι λειτουργίαν κοινὴν ἐν τῇ μεγάλῃ ἐκκλησίᾳ, τελεσθεῖσα παρ' Ἰταλῶν καὶ Γραικῶν, καὶ μνημονεύσαντες τὸν πάπαν Νικόλαον ἐν τοῖς διπτύχοις καὶ τὸν ἐξόριστον πατριάρχην Γρηγόριον. τὰ τῆς ἱερᾶς μυσταγωγίας ἐπληρώθη ἐν μηνὶ Δεκεμβρίῳ ιβ΄... ἦσαν δὲ καὶ πολλοὶ οἳ οὐκ ἔλαβον προσφορὰν ἀντιδώρου ὡς βδελυκτὴν θυσίαν τελεσθεῖσαν ἐν τῇ ἑνωτικῇ λειτουργίᾳ. ὁ δὲ καδδηνάλιος ἀνιχνεύων πᾶσαν καρδίαν καὶ πάντα σκοπὸν τῶν Γραικῶν, οὐκ ἐλάνθανον γὰρ τὰ μαγγανεύματα καὶ αἱ ἀπάται τῶν Γραικῶν ... ἀλλ' ὡς αὐτοῦ τοῦ γένους ὢν σὺν ὀλίγῃ ὁρμῇ ἔσπευδε βοηθῆσαι τῇ πόλει, καὶ ἤρκει πρὸς ἀπολογίαν τῷ πάπᾳ ὅσον γέγονε, τὸ δὲ πλέον ἀνετίθετο τῷ θεῷ τῷ τὰ πάντα οἰκονομῶντι πρὸς τὸ συμφέρον.

> With this agreement, they decided to celebrate a common liturgy in the Great Church [Santa Sophia]. Both Italians and Greeks participated in it and they commemorated in the diptychs Pope Nicholas and the exiled Patriarch Gregory. The divine liturgy was celebrated on the 12th of December ... there were many who refused to accept the offering of bread, because it was in their opinion an abominable sacrifice performed in a unionist liturgy. The cardinal looked into the hearts and the designs of all Greeks, whose machinations and intrigues had not deceived him.... He was their compatriot and showed no hesitation in helping the city. He only reported to the pope what had occurred and put his trust for everything else in God who administers all in an advantageous manner.

The efforts of Isidore on behalf of conversion were acknowledged by Pusculo, who states that the Greek cardinal did his utmost to persuade and to convert the fanatical anti-unionists, in accordance with the emperor's directive issued on the 12th of December during the celebration of the union. But it was all in vain and his arguments fell upon deaf ears:[179]

> *Isidorus ... Verba dari monachos primos, altaeque Sophiae / Presbyteros, templique duces, quo plurima in urbe / Pulchra celebrantur, nunc hos, nunc instruit illos; / Hortatur, suadet, capiti se adjungere summo / Christicolum: soli pereant ne sponte relicti. / Praeterea et cives primos, ambique coactos / In simul affatur. Semotum singula quemquam / Admonet interdum. Frusta tolerare labores / Nocte dieque valet. Grajorum nescius artis / Perfidiae ac magnae, Grajus licet, arte Pelasga / Tractatur. Jam mensis abit namque unus, et alter: / Tantum verba habet, se mullum deflectere civem, / Aut monachum potuit, nec regis flectere mentem.*
>
> Isidore ... with his crafty arguments sometimes instructed the foremost monks and presbyters of the renowned Santa Sophia and sometimes the leaders of that church, where most of the beautiful rites in the city were celebrated. He urged them and tried to persuade them to unite with the highest lord of the Christians [the pope] and not perish willingly left by themselves. In addition, he employed similar arguments in his talks with the foremost citizens in various gatherings. He pressed his admonitions on those who were wavering. He performed labors with all of his strength day and night, but in vain. He was not familiar with the great tricks of sedition of the Greeks, the Pelasgian art, even though he was a Greek himself. Already a month went by and then another. He only spoke and proved unable to bring to his side neither monk nor citizen. He could not change the emperor's mind.

Clearly, Isidore had his hands full, but his arguments failed to prevail in the heated debates that went on for at least two months and proved unable to compel the emperor to use force in this matter.

In addition to his mediating duties between the imperial court and the Italians, not to mention his efforts to strengthen the neglected fortifications, Isidore had the thankless task, imposed upon him by the emperor, of "converting" Constantinople's populace to accept the union. His appeals fell upon deaf ears, as we have seen. His chief associates in this "mission impossible" must have included Argyropoulos and Argyropoulos's faithful student Michael Apostoles, as is attested by Leonardo[180] and Pusculo.[181] This nucleus of pro-unionists faced an impossible task and the atmosphere within the city was poisoned, turning from worse to worst after the celebration of church union. Even though in the folklore of the Greeks after the sack of Constantinople Santa Sophia played such an important role in the stories, legends, and myths, the sad fact remains that this major edifice had been "contaminated" by the Latin and papist presence. The result was that the beloved structure was avoided by the Orthodox and never again functioned properly as an ecclesiastical monument. Since that fateful day of the "celebration," it was viewed as an abode of demons and a pagan temple:[182]

> καὶ ἡ Μεγάλη Ἐκκλησία ὡς καταφύγιον δαιμόνων βωμὸς Ἑλληνικὸς αὐτοῖς ἐλογίζετο. ποῦ κηροί; ποῦ ἔλαιον ἐν ταῖς λυχναψίαις; τὰ πάντα σκοτεινὰ καὶ οὐδεὶς ὁ κωλύων. ἔρημον τὸ ἅγιον τέμενος ἐφαίνετο, προσημαῖνον τὴν ἐρημίαν, ἣν ὑποστῆναι μέλλει μετ᾽ ὀλίγον διὰ τὰς παραβάσεις καὶ ἀνομίας τῶν κατοικούντων.

And the Great Church [Santa Sophia] was considered by them [Constantinopolitans] to be a refuge of demons and a Hellenic [pagan] temple [after the celebration of the union]. Where were the candles? Where was the oil for the lamps? Everything was in darkness and there was no one to prevent it. Deserted seemed the holy church to be and it pointed to its future abandonment that it was going to suffer a short time afterwards, on account of the transgressions and lawlessness of the inhabitants.

It is significant that in the next sentence Doukas points an accusatory finger at Georgios Scholarios, the obdurate enemy of the emperor; the stubborn monk probably encouraged the pro-Turkish elements within the city and was responsible, directly or indirectly, for the formation of a fifth column working for Mehmed's victory:[183] ὁ δὲ Γεννάδιος ἔγκλειστος ἐδίδασκε καὶ ἀρὰς ὑπετίθει τοῖς τὴν εἰρήνην ἀσπαζομένοις, "but Gennadios [Scholarios] preached from within his monastic cell and heaped curses upon those who had embraced [religious] peace." Doukas adds a bitter comment with regard to the folly of the Greeks and their former contemptuous attitude towards the Great Church, which they believed had been contaminated by the Latins and the Catholic ritual at the celebration of union:[184]

> ὦ δύστηνοι Ῥωμαῖοι, ὦ ἄθλιοι, τὸν ναόν, ὃν ἐκαλεῖτε χθὲς πρὸ τοῦ χθὲς σπήλαιον καὶ βωμὸν αἱρετικῶν καὶ ἄνθρωπος οὐκ εἰσήρχετο ἐξ ὑμῶν ἐντός, ἵνα μὴ μιανθῇ διὰ τὸ ἱερουργῆσαι ἔνδον τοὺς τὴν ἕνωσιν τῆς ἐκκλησίας ἀσπαζομένους, νῦν ἕνεκα τῆς ἐπελθούσης ὀργῆς ὡς σωτήριον λύτρον ἐνδύεσθε; ἀλλ᾽ οὐδὲ τῆς δικαίας ὀργῆς ἐπελθούσης ἐκίνησεν ἂν τὰ σπλάγχνα ὑμῶν πρὸς εἰρήνην. καὶ γὰρ ἐν τοσαύτῃ περιστάσει εἰ ἄγγελος κατήρχετο ἀπ᾽ οὐρανοῦ ἐρωτῶν ὑμᾶς. εἰ δέχεσθε τὴν ἕνωσιν καὶ τὴν εἰρηνικὴν κατάστασιν τῆς ἐκκλησίας, διώξω τοὺς ἐχθροὺς ἐκ τῆς πόλεως, οὐκ ἂν συντίθεσθε. εἰ δὲ καὶ συνετίθεσθε, ψεῦδος ἂν ἦν τὸ συντιθέμενον. ἴσασιν οἱ εἰπόντες πρὸ ὀλίγων ἡμερῶν. κρεῖττον ἐμπεσεῖν εἰς χεῖρας Τούρκων ἢ Φράγγων.

O unfortunate Romans [Greeks]! O wretched men! You now flocked to that church, seeking a sanctuary of salvation, on account of the impending, the righteous wrath, and the very church that yesterday and the day before you used to call a cave of heretics. Not a single individual among you would dare enter to avoid contacting the pollution that the ones who embraced church union had brought about with their holy rites. Even righteous wrath failed to move your hearts to the path of peace. In this predicament that you found yourselves, if an angel had descended from heaven and asked you: "Will you accept church union and a road to peace, if I drive the enemy out of the city?", you would have rejected him. Even if you had agreed, your consent would have been false. They knew it well, those who a few days earlier had said: "It is much better to fall into the hands of the Turks than into the hands of the Franks [Western Catholics or Latins]."

The climate of chaos that Doukas asserts followed the acceptance of church union is further emphasized when he portrays the "treasonous" behavior of the court's grand duke, Loukas Notaras. Doukas held the strong conviction that Notaras had acted against union and that in fact he was the right hand of Scholarios, and that the two individuals cooperated closely to the detriment of Constantinople's defense. Doukas was not alone in holding a pessimistic opinion about the grand duke. With time Notaras's image became shrouded in controversy and he was never absolved of damaging activities. In fact, history has been unkind to the grand duke and numerous treasonable charges are attributed to him, focusing upon his controversial role in those difficult days.[185] Contrary to the prevailing notion in modern scholarship, Notaras himself labored in support of church union and parted company with his old friend Scholarios.[186]

Pusculo adds an interesting *coda* to his report on the festivities and on Isidore's activities in the capital. His report has not been taken into account by scholarship, but it is important at this point. He seems to suggest that the court's diplomatic machinery went to work without informing the cardinal and produced one last attempt to come to terms with the sultan's Porte.[187] It is quite probable that Constantine and his courtiers tried to open a channel to the Porte after the union had been celebrated, which very act would have suggested to the Porte that western help, if not an actual crusade, would soon be on its way to relieve the Greeks, but the court neglected, intentionally or unintentionally, to inform Isidore and the Latin leadership in Constantinople of this last minute mission. Had the court's secret attempt at rapprochement with the Porte become known, it would have made the imperial court appear duplicitous. But in the end, as Pusculo recounts, the court's initiative eventually was "leaked."

A few days later, he states, a faction of the court, headed by Loukas Notaras and Kantakouzenos, urged Constantine to make contact with the Porte and to point out to Mehmed that the Greeks had formally effected a reconciliation with the pope and that the West was prepared and willing to dispatch aid and reinforcements to the beleaguered city. The diplomatic goal of this mission would be to initiate a dialogue with the sultan and to coerce him to discontinue his energetic preparations for the conquest of the imperial city, to cease his mobilization of his armies, and to return to diplomacy and to the negotiating table:[188] *Primus Lucas dira odia cordi / Condita depromens obstat. Se adjungit eidem / Cantacusinus. Eat secretus nuntius ambo / Unanimes tractant Machmetto, pacis habendae*, "the first to stand in the way (hiding his deep and dark hatred) was Loukas [Notaras]. Kantakouzenos allied himself with him. Both individuals were of one mind and urged that a secret messenger be dispatched to negotiate peace with Mehmed." The emperor agreed to this plan and dispatched to the Porte a Greek merchant who personally knew Mehmed:[189] *Rex probat hoc gaudens, omnis collectus in unum / Concilium et numerus partum. Mercator in hostis / Basilicus camp Grajius vivebat . . . / . . . Machmetto notissimus. Huic dato ultro / Pacis onus. Scripto secretus nuntius affert / Quae facienda velint*, "the emperor approved of this [plan]. All fathers [senators] were summoned to a council. In the camp of the enemy lived a Greek merchant, Basilikos . . . who was well known to Mehmed. They [the Greeks] entrusted this man with the burden to [establish] peace. The secret messenger took with him written instructions of what they wished to be accomplished."

Leonardo as well may have been suspicious of the court's activities, for he too points out that an atmosphere of intrigue prevailed, laboring against the mission of the cardinal:[190] *Adversus enim legatum [sc. Isidorum] multi invidia clanculo torquebantur*, "against the legate [*sc.* Isidore], many secretly wove a web of hatred." It is also frustrating that we do not have other details about this embassy, which is overlooked by all sources, with the exception of Pusculo. Who, for instance, was in charge of this mission? Pusculo states that it was someone named *Basilicus*/Basilikos who remains totally unknown to us. We cannot even be certain of his name. Was "Basilikos" a real name? While the feminine form of this name/adjective, *Basilike*, survives (but not in the masculine form as a name and is occasionally met even nowadays), was *Basilikos* an actual name in the fifteenth century or a pseudonym, intended to disguise his real name and to protect him? Or perhaps is it to be understood as *basilicus/basilikos*, as an adjective, meaning "of the imperial court" (that is, βασιλικὸς τῶν ἀνακτόρων, "an imperial representative" or even "the emperor's man")? Did Pusculo intend to use it as an adjective coupled with the receding noun, *basilicus mercator*, "an imperial merchant?"

Pusculo adds the interesting statement that Isidore was kept in the dark about this attempt to establish contact with the Porte.[191] This account is not duplicated in any other source; yet, a peace mission at this time may not be totally out of the realm of possibility. In fact, it is precisely the fact that after the declaration of church union on the 12th of December, the imperial administration may have decided to use the celebration as its diplomatic pawn in further negotiations with the sultan and to force him to abandon his plans to lay siege to the city. Traditionally, the Porte had consistently felt uneasy towards any understanding between Orthodox Constantinople and Catholic Europe that might result in a crusade against the Ottoman Turks.[192] After all, Mehmed II had always feared such religious harmony among the Christians, not unlike the apprehensions of his predecessor, Murad II,[193] a fact that was known to the Greeks.

If Pusculo's account is accurate, one reason may have been isolated for the bad press that Loukas Notaras received in the works of numerous authors soon after his execution. We have noted that Notaras, for political and realistic reasons, supported the emperor's efforts to ratify church union and that on this subject he honestly disagreed with his anti-unionist friend Scholarios.[194] Yet in contemporary literature, Loukas Notaras emerges as a rabid anti-unionist. The famous portrait of the grand duke painted by the pen of Doukas, a Greek with pro-Catholic sentiments, supposedly views Notaras as having declared that he would rather see the turban in the middle of the city than the pope's miter. This is one of the memorable passages of late medieval Greek literature. Indeed, Doukas's portrayal of the grand duke is highly untrue and unjust, for Notaras was unlikely to have uttered such words.[195] Doukas may have been influenced by charges that had surfaced among the Greek refugees in Italy following the fall of the imperial city, claiming that Notaras had been a traitor of some sort, but lacking in specifics. If, on the other hand, Notaras had supported a policy of opening a dialogue between the Greek court and the Porte, and had argued in favor of new negotiations to diffuse the delicate situation at this late date, using as his bait the celebration of church union (for whose sanction he had worked as Constantine's loyal minister), his position may have been misinterpreted as a courtier's fawning attempt to please two masters. The grand duke would thus come under suspicion in the eyes of the unionists and anti-unionists alike. His deliberately ambiguous position would have cast him in the role of a villain, a part that he eventually assumed in various narratives addressing the aftermath of the sack of the city, when all parties involved were eagerly seeking scapegoats for the disaster. By then Loukas Notaras was dead. He had been beheaded upon the decree of the sultan and could not defend his reputation. A minor humanist in Italy, Ioannes Moskhos, composed a belated and perfunctory defense, which most probably had been commissioned by the grand duke's surviving daughter, Anna Notaras, then resident in Italy, to produce a heroic literary portrait of the last grand duke in order to counteract the endless gossip, the unflattering rumors, and the numerous charges with regard to her father's alleged treacherous behavior. The circulating confused and confusing picture of the last grand duke beguiled Doukas (and others) to present exaggerated and inaccurate portrayals of him, whose efforts on behalf of peace seem to have earned him the enduring hatred of Pusculo and the dislike of Latin residents in the imperial city, in spite of Notaras's extensive financial dealings with Italian states, merchants, and bankers. Furthermore, his support for church union and his devotion to Constantine cost him the friendship of the anti-unionists and, in many ways, both the grand duke and the emperor found themselves isolated, in an unenviable camp. Pusculo and Doukas wrongly placed Notaras at the head of the anti-unionists.[196]

The reputation of Notaras suffered considerably in the days following the siege and the sack. Leonardo was of the opinion that Notaras and Scholarios desired to present themselves as the only true supporters of church union, hoping thereby to gain favor with the pope. Thus Leonardo believed that Notaras was not against the union and that he simply desired to claim credit for its belated celebration in the capital:[197] *intendebat ex una parte Scholarius, ex altera, Chirluca* [Κὺρ Λουκᾶς] . . . *ut hi essent qui soli rem intellexisse viderentur, quique*

162 *The papal emissary*

primi laudarentur tantae unionis auctores, "on one side Scholarios, on the other Lord Loukas, were working hard to create the impression that they were the only ones who understood this matter and to be praised as the prime architects of such important union." It was at that moment that Leonardo probably formed a low opinion and even conceived contempt for Notaras, whose motives he considered to be insincere and mercenary. The fact remains that the grand duke attempted to initiate a dialogue with every element involved in the situation – the unionists, the anti-unionists, the Porte, and the Latin ecclesiastics in Constantinople, and this effort probably rendered him as an unsympathetic figure to all concerned. Loukas Notaras managed to please no one. His last offer of peace failed. Consequently, the reputation of the last grand duke suffered unfavorable treatment in contemporary literature.

We are better informed about an important gathering that took place in Constantinople immediately following the celebration of church union. The meeting took place in Santa Sophia on the same day as the declaration of union. Once the celebration had been completed and the papal demands had been formally accepted, the emperor applied pressure on the Venetians residents in the imperial city. He made those demands that he believed could be met by the Venetians once he and his court had met the conditions of the pope's ultimatum. Most of these developments were public knowledge and were noted by the residents of the imperial capital, including Barbaro. It is important to notice that the emperor was assisted in this effort by Isidore, who must have been working closely with the imperial court at the diplomatic level, concerning the Constantinopolitan Venetians and the mission to convert the Greeks to Catholicism. His efforts seems to have been dictated by the court, which was unwilling to inflict church union by force of arms. At this time the emperor was able to make demands that were also seconded by the papal legate. The emperor was painfully aware that he had no imperial fleet at his disposal and the defense of the harbor and the Golden Horn weighed heavily upon him. These were of crucial importance to him if Constantinople were to survive the upcoming siege. The Greek emperor must have reckoned that the sultan would launch his attack from both land and sea. Emirs and sultans of old, such as Bayezid I and Murad II, had failed to take Constantinople, precisely because they had no fleet to maintain a true blockade and had been unable to throw a tight cordon around the Greek capital. Mehmed took steps to remedy this situation.[198] Accordingly, Constantine must have had the protection of the Golden Horn in mind when he decided to press the resident Venetians, who, he hoped, would undertake the defense of the harbor.[199] In his view, the Italian permanent residents within his city had to do their part and commit themselves to the defense without further delay. In the sacred precinct of Santa Sophia, the imperial administration formally requested that the Venetian authorities detain all ships for the defense of the harbor:[200] *e li vera l'imperador, el gardenal de Rosìa, el vescovo de Metelin, e tuti i baroni del imperador, e tuti mercadanti de la nation, e la più parte del populo de questa zitade, e tuti digando per una voxe*, "present there [in Santa Sophia] were the emperor, the cardinal of Rus' [Isidore], the [arch]bishop of Mytilene [Leonardo], all the barons of the emperor, all merchants of the nation, and most of the people of the city. They all spoke with one voice." The public forum suggests that the emperor wished to demonstrate to his subjects that church union would immediately produce tangible results. He linked the union to the survival of the city and wished to demonstrate that there was an advantage to it in spite of the fulminations of the anti-union party.

The Venetians, however, were not prepared to yield to Constantine's demands and the debate continued for some time. At long last, Constantine indicated his displeasure with the attitude of the Venetians:[201] *e in questo raxonamento l'imperador si andò a disnar con tuti li suo baroni, e cusì fexe ognomo, e in questo zorno non fo fatta altra pratica, salvo raxonamento asai,* "during this debate the emperor went to dinner with all his barons; so did everyone else and on that day nothing else was achieved, except a great deal of debate." Important decisions were made the next day in a private forum, without the public present. In this way, no one would appear to lose face in front of the emperor's subjects or before the Venetian residents. According to Barbaro, on 14 December[202] Isidore, Leonardo, and a group of Greek noblemen held a meeting with the *bailo* of Venice, Girolamo Minotto,[203] and with his captain general, Gabriel Trevixan. Over dinner Isidore repeated the demand of the emperor. The *bailo* agreed with Isidore and urged the captain general to remain in Constantinople. Trevixan did not wish to make any commitments and threatened to depart on the very same night. At this point, Minotto took matters in his own hands, consulted with the Venetian merchants and decided, on his own authority, to detain the galleys in Constantinople's harbor.[204] In yet another council, Minotto's action received formal approval by a positive vote of those present. The Venetian ships were detained and were eventually deployed within the Golden Horn, even though fears were expressed that some captains would disregard the order and would depart. Accordingly, measures were taken to prevent all captains from leaving without proper authorization.[205]

Within the city itself, unionists and anti-unionists continued to dispute with each other. The church union did not become a serious deterrent for Mehmed. The proceedings of the 12th of December did not impede his military preparations. Only the anti-unionists were encouraged to intensify their campaign against their emperor's religious policies. The urban population remained hopelessly divided. Constantine refused to apply force against them. The leadership of the anti-unionists interpreted his inaction and refusal to limit their activities as a personal weakness and in the end there was no respite in their agitation.

Notes

1 There is a well-known depiction of Argyropoulos teaching from his cathedra that is included in the *Oxford Bodleian* 87 ms., fol. 35ʳ (cf. H.O. Coxe, *Recensionem codicum graecorum comtinens*, Catalogi codicum manuscriptorum bibliothecae Bodleiana, pars 1 (Oxford, 1853), p. 152. This picture is accompanied by the following caption identifying various pupils of Argyropoulos: ὁ Ἀργυρόπουλος καὶ διδάσκει Ἀντώνιον Πυρόπουλον ἰατρὸν καὶ Μανουὴλ Πυρόπουλον καὶ Πανάρετον Ἰωάννην ἰατρὸν καὶ Ἄγγελον

Δημήτριον καὶ Ἀγάλλωνα τὸν τοῦ Μόσχου καὶ Βρανὰν τὸν τοῦ πρωτομάστορος ἰατρὸν ἐν τῷ τοῦ κράλου ξενῶνι. For these pupils (who, notably, seem to be physicians), cf. Lampros, Ἀργυροπούλεια. Ἰωάννου Ἀργυροπούλου, p. κδ ´. In addition, cf. Staikos, 1: 15ος Αἰώνας, pp. 173–196, esp. 174–176, who also provides a reproduction of the Oxford depiction of the Xenon, no. 33 (p. 181); and Geanakoplos, *Greek Scholars in Venice*, pp. 75–79; and *idem*, "The Italian Renaissance and Byzantium: The Career of the Greek Humanist-Professor John Argyropoulos in Florence and Rome (1415–1487)," *Conspectus of History* 1 (1974): pp. 13–28. J. Harris, *Greek Emigres in the West 1400–1520* (Camberley, Surrey, 1995), does not discuss the teaching activities of Argyropoulos in Constantinople. For further details on this notable scholar, cf. *infra*, nn. 119–121.

2 Lampros, Ἀργυροπούλεια, pp. λβ ´– λε ´, was the first scholar to realize the historical importance of this work that firmly places Isidore in the imperial capital at this time and he fixes the date of the composition to 1450, prior to Argyropoulos's departure for Rome. The composition is addressed to Pope Nicholas V: Ἰωάννου τοῦ Ἀργυροπούλου τοῦ κριτοῦ τοῦ δημοσίου τῆς Κωνσταντινουπόλεως εἰς τὸν μακαριώτατον Πάπαν κὺρ Νικόλαον. It was first edited and published by Lampros, Ἀργυροπούλεια, pp. 129–141, but it has never been translated into a modern language. Moreover, no Renaissance translation into Latin exists.

3 Thus Argyropoulos quotes Homer and goes on to name Scylla, Charybdis, Eos, Herakles (p. 129), Odysseus, Zeus, the ancient Athenians (p. 130), Hesiod, Julius Caesar (with his own translation of the famous Latin dictum *alea iacta est* into Greek as ἐρρίφθω κύβος, "the die is cast"), Solon, Croesus, Sardis (p. 131), Cyrus, Kambyses, Mandane, Sibylla (p. 132), the Titans (p. 133), and Aristotle (p. 136 and p. 137), among other numerous biblical references to reinforce his confession that he is a true Catholic.

4 Ἀργυροπούλεια, p. 129.

5 Lampros points out the importance of Pusculo in this regard, but his observations on the mission of Isidore and on the significance of Pusculo's information have not been taken into account by modern scholarship in general. Cf. Lampros, Ἀργυροπούλεια, pp. λγ´–λζ´.

6 Pusculo's poem titled *Constantinopolis libri IV*, was edited by Bregantini on the basis of a single manuscript in Venice's Marciana and transcribed by G.M. Gervasi; another four manuscripts of this work exist but there is no modern edition of the entire work with an *apparatus criticus*. Bregantini's text was reprinted in A.S. Ellissen, ed., *Analekten der mittel- und neugriechischen Literatur*, 3 (Leipzig, 1857), Appendix, 12–83. On Pusculo, cf. *SF*, pp. 31, 32; and *infra*, n. 32.

7 Pusculo II.205–214 (p. 31).

8 Ellissen, p. 132, prints: *regemque, senatumque*.

9 The ms. in question, *Codex Vat. gr. 1858*, fols. 44^r–50^r, is briefly discussed by Mercati, p. 37 n. 5. This text has never been transcribed, edited, or published. It is written in the difficult cursive style of Isidore and still awaits a modern editor and publication. The contents of this manuscript have been briefly discussed in *CF*, pp. 389–391. Very likely Isidore in the composition advised Pope Nicholas of the formal papal "ultimatum" to Constantine XI, which included strong, perhaps even undiplomatic, language. On this ultimatum, cf. the following note.

10 Leontaris, seeking aid, was also dispatched as an imperial representative to other Italian powers: Venice, Ferrara, Rome, and Naples. He was well received in Rome and made a very favorable impression, as the pope himself states in his letter to Constantine XI. Cf. the opening statements in the translation of the Latin into Greek by the humanist Theodoros Gazes [Theodore Gaza], ΠκΠ 4: 49–63: Ἀνδρόνικον Βρυέννιον Λεοντάριν, ἄνδρα τῶν εὖ γεγονότων, ὃν πρεσβευτὴν πέπομφας ὥς ἡμᾶς ἡδέως εἴδομεν, καὶ τὰ σοῦ γράμματα ἀναγνόντες ἥδιον δὴ λέγοντος αὐτοῦ ἀκηκόαμεν. Leontaris's mission is discussed in *PaL* 2: 108; and *CF*, pp. 377–380. For the surviving documents on this embassy, cf. *NE* 4: 27 (p. 46); Constantine's letter of introduction, dated the 10th of March 1451; and *NE* 3: 254 f. For the desperate efforts of Constantine XI to awaken

the West to the Turkish threat, cf. R. Guilland, "Les Appels de Constantin XI Paléologue à Rome et à Venise pour sauveur Constantinople (1452–1453)," *BS* 14 (1953): pp. 226–244, esp. 231 ff.; and *idem*, "Αἱ πρὸς τὴν Δύσιν Ἐκκλήσεις Κωνσταντίνου ΙΑ ΄ τοῦ Δράγαση πρὸς Σωτηρίαν τῆς Κωνσταντινουπόλεως," *Ἐπετηρὶς Ἑταρείας Βυζαντινῶν Σπουδῶν* (1952): pp. 60–74. Also, cf. C. Marinesco [Marinescu], "Notes sur quelques ambassadeurs byzantins en Occident à la veille de la chute de Constantinople sous les Turcs," *Annuaire de l'Institut de philologie et d'histoire orientales et slaves* 10 (1950): pp. 426, 427. *PaL* 2: 108, lists all Venetian archival material pertaining to this matter. For a review of previous scholarship and a synthesis of the material, cf. now Hanak, "Pope Nicholas V," pp. 337–359, who also provides an English translation of the letter from the Latin (its Greek version is the work of Theodoros Gazes) that Nicholas V sent to the emperor (pp. 354–359). Kritoboulos, *Critobuli Imbriotae Historiae*, ed. D.R. Reinsch, CFHB 22 (Berlin and New York, 1983), describes the complicated situation with a few statements, 1.19: πρεσβείας ἔπεμπον πανταχοῦ, καὶ παρὰ τὸν μέγαν ἀρχιερέα τῆς Ῥώμης [Pope Nicholas V], ᾧ καὶ μᾶλλον εἶχον θαρρεῖν . . . δεόμενοι συμμαχίας τε καὶ ἐπικουρίας τὴν ταχίστην τυχεῖν. For other editions of the text, cf. Κριτόβουλος: Βίος τοῦ Μωάμεθ Β ΄, ed. P.A. Déthier *MHH* 21.1 (*sine loco* [Galata/Pera?], *sine anno* [1872?/1875?]; "*De rebus gestis Muhammetis II*," in C. Müller, ed., *Fragmenta Historicorum Graecorum*, vol. 5 (Paris, 1870; Paris, 1883); *Critobul din Imbros din domnia lui Mahomed al II-lea anii 1451–1467*, ed. V. Grecu, Scriptores Byzantini 4 (Bucharest, 1963); and C.T. Riggs, *Kritovoulos. A History of Mehmed the Conqueror* (Princeton, 1954; repr. 1970). Constantine's initial letter to the pope has not survived. The contents of the pope's letter were well known to the populace in Constantinople and they were probably familiar with Greek renditions such as the one by Gazes (ἐκ τῆς Λατίνης μεθερμηνευθεῖσα φωνῆς ὑπὸ Θεοδώρου τοῦ Γαζῆ, as the translator himself states in the title of the work). Doukas knew of the papal demands, especially the requirement to restore the exiled Gregory III Mamas to the patriarchal throne (cf. *infra*, text with nn. 75, 76, and 77). It was perhaps through this Greek translation that Ubertino Pusculo (cf. *infra*, nn. 32 and 33), alludes to the condition in his poem; cf. Pusculo IV.1020 ff. (not included in the selections printed in *CC* 1): *Heu nimium de te* [Constantine XI] *vates Nicolaus* [Pope Nicholas V] *hoc ipsum / Antistes cecinit summus; dum saepe vocaret / Te, sibi praedixit tempus patriaeque tibique / Hoc fore; cum lacrymans: Vereor ne numen Achivis* [Greeks], */ Dixit, opem neget*. Leontaris was active in the defense of Constantinople in 1453; cf. Languschi-Dolfin (independent from his source, Leonardo), Giacomo Languschi (Dolfin, Zorzi), *Excidio e presa di Constantinopoli nell' anno 1453*, in "Die Eroberung Constantinopels im Jahre 1453 auf einer venetianischen Chronik," ed. G.M. Thomas, *Sitzungs berichte der köngl. bayer. Akademie der Wissenschaften*, philos.-hist. Klasse 2 (Munich, 1866), p. 17: *A la porta carsea* [Χαρσία] *Leondario Brion cum Fabricio Cornero Candioto; TIePN*; and Pusculo (*CC* 1: 208): *Charsaeam servans Lontarius gente Briena / gaudet de socio clara de gente Fabruci, Cornaria. / Hic Venetus Cretem generosus habebat. / Fide, armis ambo tutantur sorte suprema*. For the Latin version of the pope's letter, cf. Hofmann, *Epistolae Pontificiae ad Concilium Florentinum Spectantes*, no. 304 (pp. 131–134; the Greek rendition: pp. 135–138). For other editions, cf. Hanak, "Pope Nicholas V," p. 337 n. 1, as well as his word of caution: "questions persist whether either the Latin or the Greek renditions, or both, are authoritative versions."

11 *TIePN*, p. 150.
12 E.g., S.P. Lampros, *Ἱστορία τῆς Ἑλλάδος ἀπὸ τῶν Ἀρχαιοτάτων Χρόνων μέχρι τῆς Ἁλώσεως τῆς Κωνσταντινουπόλεως (1453)* 6 (Athens, 1908; repr. Athens, 1998), p. 911: τῆς ἀπαντήσεως τοῦ πάπα, ἣν δυνάμεθα νὰ ὀνομάσωμεν τελεσίγραφον; Lampros repeats the same characterization for the pope's letter, ultimatum/τελεσίγραφον in the *Ἀργυροπούλεια*, p. λς΄; and *CF*, p. 378: "this reply is firm almost to the point of being an ultimatum." The Latin text is cast in a much harsher tone than the Greek translation by Gazes. For an English rendition of the Latin text, cf. Hanak, "Pope Nicholas V," pp. 354–359.

13 The most recent biography of Scholarios-Gennadios II is by T.N. Zeses, *Γεννάδιος Β΄ Σχολάριος: Βίος-Συγγράμματα-Διδασκαλία, Ἀνάλεκτα Βλατάδων* 30 (Thessalonike, 1980). This is a curious and extremely superficial work, whose avowed aim is to claim sainthood for Scholarios-Gennadios and to diminish the contribution of Bessarion to scholarship. It is amazing that after the passage of five centuries the old controversies and animosities between "Greek" and "Latin" should appear again! It also contains inaccuracies and often pure propaganda; cf., e.g., the comments of C. Livanos, *Greek Tradition and Latin Influence in the Work of George Scholarios* (Piscataway, NJ, 2006), p. 19: "[Zeses' study] has been criticized for the argument that many of the writings wherein Scholarios praises Latin authors were, in fact, papist forgeries." A true scholarly book-length biography of Scholarios in English, or in any other language, remains to be written. Much better, although a great deal shorter, than Zeses's hagiographical work, is J. Gill, "George Scholarius," *Unitas* 12 (1960; Eng. ed.), pp. 99–112; and cf. *idem, Personalities of the Council of Florence,* pp. 79–95. Indirectly, one may follow Scholarios's career through his association with Plethon; cf. Woodhouse, *passim.* On Scholarios, cf. *PLP* 11: no. 27304 (pp. 156–158). In addition, cf. now the thoughtful study of folkloric elements involving Gennadios II by M.G. Serges, *Γεώργιος Σχολάριος-Γεννάδιος Β΄ ὁ Πρῶτος μετά την Ἅλωσῃ Οἰκουμενικός Πατριάρχης: Ἐθνοϊστορική Μελέτη, Μελέτες για τη Βυζαντινή και Μεταβυζαντινή Ιστορία* 3 (Athens, *sine anno*). The importance of Scholarios as an intellectual figure and religious leader is never doubted, but his personality remains obscure and is still clouded in uncertainty, despite numerous scholarly publications on aspects of his work. Cf. the evaluation that was produced by J. Meyendorff, *Byzantine Theology: Historical Trends and Doctrinal Themes* (New York, 1979), p. 112: "[Scholarios is] an intellectual enigma."

14 Scholarios referred to this report in one of his works in which he demanded that all his writings be sent to Rome to demonstrate the errors of the Latins; cf. *ΠκΠ* 2: 129: ἔτι ὁ λόγος, ὃν ἔγραψα τῷ αὐτοκράτορι ἐν τῇ β΄ τοῦ μαρτίου.

15 The work has been published in *ΠκΠ* 2: 89–105, under the title: πρὸς τὸν βασιλέα Ἀπολογητικὸς [presumably, λόγος]. ἐπέμφθη αὐτῷ τῇ 12ῃ τοῦ Μαρτίου. It is perhaps notable that the manuscript belonged to Ioannes Dokeianos, one of the minor humanists of the Morea who had connections with George Gemistos Plethon, whose classical and neoclassical attitudes Scholarios abhorred. On this minor humanist, cf. P. Topping, "Greek MS 1 (The Works of Joannes Dokeianos) of the University of Pennsylvania Library," *The Library Chronicle* 29 (1963): pp. 1–15; and Philippides, "Herodian 2.4.1," pp. 295–297.

16 *ΠκΠ* 2: 89, 90. Scholarios emphasized this point once more in his *apologia* that was published on 27 November (cf. *infra,* n. 104), wherein he claims that he was opposed to Bryennios's embassy (*ΠκΠ* 2: 134): καὶ ὕστερον μετὰ τὴν πρεσβείαν τοῦ κῦρ Βρυεννίου, ἧς οὐκ ἐκοινώνησα (our emphasis).

17 Most recently on this topic, cf. C. Imber, *The Crusade of Varna, 1443–45,* Crusader Texts in Translation 14 (Aldershot, 2006).

18 *Supra,* n. 12.

19 It is unclear from our sources whether Isidore was sent to Constantinople at the emperor's invitation, in spite of Doukas's statement that it was so; cf. the following note. That the emperor issued such an invitation seems highly unlikely, given the prevailing and strong anti-unionist sentiment in the beleaguered capital and the total failure of Isidore's first mission. It appears more reasonable to accept the notion that Isidore was directed to Constantinople through the initiative of the Vatican. On this ambiguous point, cf. Hanak, "Pope Nicholas V," p. 347: "the invitation to send a papal legate remains unresolved in our sources." Pusculo cites the fact that Isidore came as a papal legate to Constantinople, III.487–490: *Tendere ad urbem / Legatus propere rursus tu, Isidore, juberis, Rursus qua si via est, Danaos* [Greeks] *quae ducat in unum, / Cum pastore pio, et reddat quae legibus aequis.*

20 Doukas 36.1: ὁ δὲ βασιλεὺς [Constantine XI Dragaš Palaeologus] ἦν στείλας ἐν Ῥώμῃ προλαβών, αἰτῶν βοήθειαν καὶ ὅπως συντεθῶσιν τῇ ὁμονοίᾳ καὶ ἑνώσει τῇ γεγονυίᾳ

ἐν Φλωρεντίᾳ. The mission of Isidore was well-known to the Greeks and even the laconic Khalkokondyles refers to it, as an after-thought, when he relates the actual siege [8.17 (pp. 190, 191); *PG* 159: cols. 388–389], by using two future participles of purpose in his construction. Thus Khalkokondyles indicates the objective of Isidore's mission, whom he identifies as "the cardinal of Sarmatia" (the ancient geographical term that Khalkokondyles employs consistently to signify medieval Rus'): καὶ καρδινάλιος Ἰσίδωρος Σαρματίας [= Ῥωσσίας] . . . ϖαρεγένετο . . . ὥς ξύνοδόν τε ϖοιησόμενος καὶ διαλλάξων τοὺς Ἕλληνας τῷ Ῥωμαίων ἀρχιερεῖ [pope]. Curiously, Georgios Sphrantzes, a member of the imperial administration and apparently a close advisor to the emperor, does not speak of the cardinal's mission but only complains that the pope failed to send any aid (overlooking the cardinal's contingent of mercenaries and Isidore's personal financial contribution for the upkeep of a section of the sea walls at their juncture in the northwest of the city with the land walls), and suggests by a genitive absolute construction that the cardinal "happened to be present" in the city, without a word about the cardinal's official mission. He relates, *Minus* 36.5: ἡ ἐκκλησία τῆς Ῥώμης καὶ τί ϖερὶ τούτου [that is, aid to Constantinople] ἐφρόντισεν . . . εὑρεθέντος καὶ γὰρ τοῦ καρδηναλίου Ῥωσσίας εἰς τὴν Πόλιν. Sphrantzes's sixteenth-century elaborator, Makarios Melissourgos-Melissenos, in the derivative *Maius*, slightly alters the wording and makes the complaint less indignant; he retains, however, the genitive absolute but omits καὶ after the participle. He notes in *Maius* IV.2.3 (p. 470): καὶ ἡ ἐκκλησία τῆς Ῥώμης, ϖερὶ τούτου ἐφρόντισεν. εὑρεθέντος γὰρ τοῦ καρδηναλίου τῆς Ῥωσσίας εἰς τὴν ϖόλιν. Sphrantzes's bitterness overwhelms him and eventually he states in heavy irony that the Greeks in the months following their submission to the pope received as much aid from the Vatican as had been sent to them by the sultan of Cairo. Further, *Minus* 36.6: διέβησαν ἰδοὺ μῆνες ἓξ καὶ τοσοῦτον λόγον ἐϖοιήσαντο ὑϖὲρ βοηθείας, ὅσον ὁ σουλτάνος τοῦ Κάρεως. The elaborator of the *Maius*, beyond his usual simplifying paraphrase, simply adds a gloss to "Cairo," to make it clear that Egypt is meant (IV.24.3): τοῦ Κάρεως, ἤτοι τῆς Αἰγύϖτου.
21 Mercati, p. 129 n. 3; and *CF*, p. 383.
22 Doukas, a Greek Catholic and supporter of the union, found great fault with the recalcitrant Greek anti-unionists and thought highly of Isidore, whom he described as an honorable, well-educated, and thoughtful individual, especially during the Council of Ferrara-Florence, 36.1: ἔστειλε δ᾽ ὁ ϖάϖας [Nicholas V] τὸν καδδηνάλιον Πολωνίας [*sic*], τόν ϖοτε ἀρχιεϖίσκοϖον Ῥωσίας Ἰσίδωρον, ἄνδρα συνετὸν καὶ σώφρονα καὶ ϖεϖαιδευμένον ἐν δόγμασιν ὀρθοῖς, Ῥωμαῖον τὸν γένος καὶ αὐτὸν ἕνα τῆς ἐν Φλωρεντίᾳ συνόδου ὑϖάρχοντα ϖατέρα τίμιον.
23 For details on this important *epistula*, cf. the following note. The text is quoted from *CC* 1: 64.
24 *Codex Bibl. Univ. lat. B 52*, busta 22, n. 1, fols. 40ʳ–42ᵛ. There can be no doubt that the original letter was composed in Greek, as the manuscript clearly states that this is a Latin translation from the original Greek by the humanist Lianoro dei Lianori: *Habes iam, Alberte dilectissime, grecam epistolam factam latinam*. This Latin version was first edited and published by G. Hofmann, "Ein Brief des Kardinals Isidor von Kiew an Kardinal Bessarion," *OCP* 14 (1948): pp. 405–414; selections (with Italian translation) were reprinted in *CC* 1: 64–80; for the extract in our text, cf. *CC* 1: 66–68. Hofmann, however, neglected to print Lianori's note; for the complete text of the note, cf. *CC* 1: 63:

> *Habes iam, Alberte dilectissime, grecam epistolam factam latinam. etsi satis inepte traductam. Malui enim <me> rudem ac indoctum iudicari abs te, quam pervicacem. Usus autem sum sermone facili et ilaro et, ut ita dicam, puerili, ne tibi videar alius esse quam sum, tardo scilicet ac rudi ingenio. Potuissem enim hinc inde vocabula exquisita mendicari et expiscari, sed nolui ex re minima rem maximam facere atque ostentare, quod me tenuis ac exiguissime supellectilis non est. Ipsam ergo penes te serva nec ulli curis edere, ne in tanta doctissimorum virorum copia temerarius ac presumptuosus fuisse videar, qui tantum mihi arrogem, ut grecam profiteri scientiam ausus sim, uius vix prima rudimenta delibarim. Tuus Lianorus de Lianoris.*

On this note, cf. Hofmann, "Quellen zu Isidor von Kiew als Kardinal und Patriarch," *OCP* 18 (1952): pp. 143–157, esp. 144 n. 2. On the numerous letters that Isidore wrote in Crete immediately after his arrival from Constantinople and for other contemporaneous literature associated with the cardinal, cf. *SF*, ch. 1: "Scholarship and the Siege of 1453." For the entire Latin text of this significant letter addressed to Bessarion and its English translation, cf. *infra*, ch. 5. The other letters that issued from the pen of Isidore while he was in Crete must have also been composed in Greek but in their case too only Latin renditions survive. Such is clearly the circumstance with the letter dated *pridie Nonas Julii MCCCCLIII: Epistola composita per ser Pasium de Bertipalia notarium ad instantiam reverendissimi domini domini Isidori cardinalis Sabiniensis* (*CC* 1: 60).

25 Biographies of Leonardo were written long ago and contain numerous inaccuracies; the oldest examples include M. Iustiniani, "Vita Leonardi," in *Caroli Pogii de nobilitate liber disceptatorius et Leonardi Chiensis de vera nobilitate contra Poggium tractatus apologeticus* (Abelini, 1657), cols. 43–48; and J. Quétif and J. Echard, *Scriptores Ordinis Praedicatorum*, 1 (Paris, 1729), cols. 816–818. In more recent times, the few facts known about the archbishop have been summarized by R.-J. Loenertz, "La Société des Frères Pérègrinants. Etude sur l'Orient Dominicain," 1, Inst. Hist. FF. Praed., Diss. hist. 7 (Rome, 1937). How the Genoese Leonardo became the bishop of Mytilene is explained in a document examined and summarized by Iorga, *NE* 3: 241:

> Le 8 juillet [1449], le gouvernment génois, anon-çantau cardinal de Fermo, grand-pénitentiaire, l'arrivée à Rome de l'archevêque de Mitylène, le prie de faire défendre par le pape l'union entre un fils de Dorin Gatilusio avec un fill de Palamède, sa cousine, union que sollicite l'archevêque susdit.

Further documentation can be found in *NE* 2: 432, 433:

> 21 juillet 1449. Le pape accede la demande faite par Léonard, archevêque de Mitylène, – don't l'église, bien que métropolitaine, n'avait pas de suffragants, "ex quo nonull: Greci eandem Eclesiam Mitilinenensem deridere ac eam ludibrio habere soleant," – de lui soumettre les evêques de Chio et des deux Phocées. Mais cette concess dion na saurait ètre préjudiciable asuc autres métropolitains soumis à l'Eglise romaine. – Le meme jour, l'Eglise de Mitylene n'ayant Presque pas de revenue ("aut asseris, nullius vel modici valoris [fructus]"), le pape accordè à Léonard, sa vie durand, l'administration et les revenues de l'Eglise d'Adria, vacante après la mort de l'evêque Lombard. – De plus, il confirme des despositions testamentaires de Léonard.

NE then quotes a section from a document, in which Leonardo is addressed by his formal title (*quod ordinis fratrum predicatorum professor existis*), which the archbishop himself cites, along with his other distinctions, in the opening of his report on the fall: *Epistula reverendissimi in Christo patris et domini Leonardi Ordinis Praedicatorum, archiepiscopi Mitileni, sacrarum litterarum professoris*. Leonardo's later life is not well documented. It was believed that he returned to the island of Lesbos, was captured by the Turks in the sack of Mytilene in 1462, was subsequently ransomed, and then wrote an account of this siege and sack entitled *De Lesbo a Turcis capta*. This work betrays, however, the hand of a different author. It is written in a less sophisticated style and prose and employs a different Latin idiom that betrays more parallels with the genre of the late medieval ecclesiastical sermon than with the humanistic precepts of composition employed by Leonardo in his account of the siege and the sack of 1453. In fact, the *De Lesbo* was composed by Archbishop Benedetto, the successor of Leonardo to the see of Mytilene. Benedetto was nominated to this post by Pope Pius II on 3 December 1459, after the death of Leonardo. The Latin text of this work was edited and published by C. Hopf under the erroneous title: *Leonardi Chiensis de Lesbo a Turcis capta epistola Pio papae II missa ex. cod. ms. Ticinensis* (Regimonti, 1866), who then reprinted it in his *Chroniques Gréco-Romanes Inédites ou peu connues publiées avec notes et tables généalogiques* (Paris, 1873; repr. Brussels, 1966), doc. 21, pp. 359–366. No English translation of this work exists. Leonardo returned to Italy in 1458 to contribute personally to a campaign to gain military aid against his old enemy, Mehmed II, who was now making preparations to attack Lesbos. Leonardo died in Italy in late February or early March 1459.

Leonardo's authentic work on the fall of Constantinople achieved fame through its translated versions. Thus one of the most influential renditions into Italian was first published by Francesco Sansovino in his immensely popular *Historia universale dell'origine et imperio de Turchi: nella quale si contengono la origine, l'usanze, i costumi, cose religiosi come mondani de Turchi: oltre ciò vi sono tutte le guerre cher di tempo sono state fatted a quella natione cominciando da Othomano primo Re di questa dente fino al moderno Selim con le vite ditu tutti i principi da casa Othomana* (Venice, 1564, 1568, 1571, etc.), pp. 304 ff. The Latin text of Leonardo was published by P. Lonicer in his *Chronicorum Turcicorum* 1 (Frankfurt am Main, 1584), pp. 315–336; his version was reprinted by L.T. Belgrano, "Prima serie di documenti riguardanti la colonia di Pera," *Atti della Società Ligure di Storia Patria* 13 (1877–1884), pp. 233–257; and as an appendix in Sreznevskii's edition of Nestor-Iskander, *Повѣсть о Царьградѣ*; and in *PG* 159: cols. 923–941, with the cautionary note in *CC* 1: 121; and by J.P. Déthier, *Anonymous Moscovita*, in *MHH* 21.1 (*sine loco, sine anno*), pp. 1047–1122. *CC* 1: 124–171, offers only selections with Italian translation and with improved Latin text but with serious omissions and incomplete *apparatus criticus*. Unfortunately, the important *Codex Mediol. Trivult. lat. N 641*, fols. 11^r–21^r, with its valuable marginalia and scholia, is not taken into account. Since this text provides a major eyewitness account of the siege and fall, a modern editor and a new edition with an *apparatus criticus* and the marginalia of the Florentine *codex* have become imperative. The most important complete printed version is the Lonicer edition and it is based only on one manuscript: *Codex Vat. 4137*, as is stated at the beginning of *PG* 159: cols. 923, 924, a version of the letter: *Abraham Bzovius in Annalium Baroni continuatione ad annum 1453, cui Historiam Leonardi Chiensis inseruit praefatam, num. 6, pag. 84 ad 90, ubi num. 7, descriptam hanc narrationem ex ms. Codice Vaticano 4137, inquit*. For other manuscripts of this work, cf. *SF*, ch. 1, I.4. In addition, on Leonardo, cf. now J. Schiel, *Mongolensturm und Fall Konstantinopels: Dominikanische Erzählungen im diachronen Vergleich, Europa im Mittelalter* 191 (Berlin, 2011), esp. pp. 162–180.

26 *PG* 159: col. 923; and *CC* 1: 124–126. The latter furnishes a variant text: *cum igitur reverendissimus pater, dominus cardinalis Sabinensis, pro unione Graecorum legatus, in eius famulatum me ex Chio vocasset, egi summa cum animi diligentia ut . . . defensarem*. Cf. *SF*, p. 15.

27 Leonardo, *PG* 159: col. 925 [*CC* 1: 125–127]. Barbaro notes that they appeared together on several occasions; cf., e.g., Barbaro 4 [*CC* 1: 11]: *e lì ve iera l'imperador, el gardenal de Rosìa, el vescovo de Metelin* [Leonardo]. For the editions of Barbaro's account, cf. E. Cornet, ed., *Giornale dell' assedio di Costantinopoli 1453 di Nicolò Barbaro P.V. correddato di note e documenti* (Vienna, 1856). This edition still remains the only complete printed form of the Diary. It has been translated into English by J.R. [Melville] Jones, *Nicolò Barbaro: Diary of the Siege of Constantinople* (Jericho, 1969); selections with improved text in *CC* 1: 8–38. There exists a Modern Greek translation by V.A. Lappa, *Η Πόλις Εάλω: Το Χρονικό της Πολιορκίας και της Άλωσης της Πόλης* (Athens, 1991), pp. 93–213. There also exists in Latin a partial translation of the journal, which some scholars have mistakenly assumed to be a fifteenth-century rendition of the original text composed in the spoken Venetian idiom of the period. This Latin ἐφημερὶς or journal is in actuality a later translation of Barbaro's text into Latin that was published under the title, *Nicolai Barbari Patricii Veneti Ephemerides de Constantinopoli anno 1453 obsessa atque expugnata*, in *PG* 158: cols. 1067–1078; for the original text and an English translation of the ἐφημερίς, cf. *SF*, Appendix 1.

28 For sources on his life, cf. *supra*, n. 25. Why Leonardo returned to Italy in 1449 is explained in a document summarized in *NE* 3: 241:

Le juillet [1449], le gouvernment génois, annonçant au cardinal de Fermo, grand pénitentiaire, l'arrivée à Rome de l'archevêque de Mytilène, le prie de faire defender par le pape l'union entre un fils de Dorin Gattilusio avec un fille de Palamède, sa cousine, union que sollicite l'archevêque susdit.

For further documentation of this visit, cf. *NE* 2: 432, 433. On Leonardo and his literary connections, cf. M. Philippides, "The Fall of Constantinople 1453: Bishop Leonardo Giustiniani and His Italian Followers," *Viator: Medieval and Renaissance Studies* 29 (1998): pp. 189–227.

29 E.W. Bodnar, SJ, and C. Foss, *Cyriac of Ancona: Later Travels*, The I Tatti Renaissance Library 10 (Cambridge, MA, 2003), letter 6 (pp. 15–27).

30 *Ibid.*, Letter 15, pp. 84–86. Bodnar and Foss, however, are in error when they identify a Leonardo mentioned elsewhere in Cyriacus's Diary with our Leonardo. Thus in Diary 3 (pp. 168–170) Cyriacus notes that he sent a copy of an inscription to *Leonardo Iustiniano, Veneto patricio nobili et amplissimo hieromnemonum ordine*; this Leonardo is identified by Bodnar in the Index (p. 448) with our Leonardo. This identification is in error, for our Leonardo was a Genoese. The Giustiniani family of Venice was well known, with connections in Constantinople and the Levant, and certain members of it even fought in the defense of Constantinople in 1453; in the Venetian dialect of the *quattrocento* their name is usually written as "Zustignan" but they are to be distinguished from the Genoese Giustiniani "*albergo*" of Chios, to which our Leonardo belonged. That our Leonardo was a Genoese is also made clear in his own narrative; see, e.g., *PG* 159: col. 929 [not in *CC* 1]: *O Genuenses... sed sileo, ne de meis*. The confusion here arises from the fact that Cyriacus's latinized form "Iustinianus" applies both to the Genoese Giustiniani and to the Venetian Zustignan. This confusion is absent in *Vita Viri Clarissimi et Famosissimi Kyriaci Anconitani by Francesco Salamonti*, eds. C. Mitchell and E.W. Bodnar, SJ, *Transactions of the American Philosophical Society* 86.4 (Philadelphia 1996), in which the Venetian Leonardo is identified correctly and the date of his death (1446) is also cited (27, 28; p. 147 n. 33).

31 For the evidence on the "etesian winds" in ancient literature, from the heliacal rising of Sirius (July 28) to September 28, in agreement with the latitude of Athens and close to the latitude of Constantinople, that is, the parameters of the Aegean, and for the equation of *meltemi* with "etesian", cf. W.M. Murray, "Do Modern Winds Equal Ancient Winds?" *Mediterranean Historical Review* 2 (1987): pp. 139–167; and W.T. Loomis, "Pausanias, Byzantion and the Formation of the Delian League: A Chronological Note," *Historia: Zeitschrift für Alte Geschichte* 39/4 (1990): pp. 487–492.

32 He was the "classical" poet of the siege; he had traveled to Constantinople to perfect his knowledge of ancient Greek and remained in the city throughout the siege. After his captivity he found his way back to Italy, via Rhodes, and composed a valuable poem describing the situation before and during the siege and sack. Thus Pusculo was a participant who had seen, met, and even conversed with many Italian and Greek defenders, whose activities, operations and positions on the wall he meticulously noted in his work. It is unfortunate that this primary document by an eyewitness still awaits a modern editor. The two existing editions are based on inferior manuscripts and on the Déthier edition of *MHH* 21.1, which is extremely rare. On Pusculo, cf. the following note.

33 Pusculo 3.487–490 (p. 51). The valuable testimony of Pusculo for the period from October through December, 1452, has been totally neglected by modern scholarship, which has been inclined to focus, albeit sporadically, on Pusculo's Book IV (the narration of the "more sensational" events and operations of the siege). No modern scholar has extensively utilized Pusculo's important observations on the celebration of the union in Constantinople and even Pertusi only includes a few lines from Book III in the selections he printed in *CC* 1. Isidore himself hints at the difficulties that he had encountered during his long voyage, when he mentions that *omnia me adverse atque infeliciter succedere ceperunt* (*CC* 1: 66). For the first edition of Pusculo's text, cf. *supra*, n. 6. More recently, Pertusi, *CC* 1: 124–171, has published a slim selection from Book IV with Italian translation. The *CC* 1 selection/text is quite an improvement over Bregantini's earlier edition and one eagerly awaits a complete and modern edition of this important eyewitness source. On Pusculo, cf. *SF*, I.A.7 and *supra*, n. 6.

34 Pusculo 3.500–503.
35 Henry of Soemmern [*CC* 2: 92]. *CC* 2 does not include the entire text of this fascinating letter. For a new edition of the complete Latin text with English translation, which recounts the adventures of Isidore during the early hours of the sack, his escape from Constantinople, and his arrival in Venetian Crete, cf. Philippides, *Mehmed II the Conqueror and the Fall of the Franco-Byzantine Levant to the Ottoman Turks*, pp. 121–133.
36 Leonardo 927 [*CC* 1: 128–130]; words within brackets represent the variant readings in *CC* 1 edition:

> *Excitatus itaque in furorem Deus, misit Mahometh [Mehemet] regem potentissimum Teucrorum [Theucrorum]; adolescentem quidem audacem, ambitiosum, temulentum, Christianorum capitalem hostem; qui Nonis Aprilis ante Constantinopolis [Constantinopoleos] prospectum, cum tercentis et ultra millibus [milibus] pugnatorum in gyro terrae castra papilionesque confixit. Milites majore numero equestres, quanquam [quamquam] omnes pedites magis expugnabant. Inter quos pedites ad regis custodiam deputati audaces, qui ab elementis Christiani [christiani] aut Christianorum [christianorum] filii, retrorsum conversi, dicti Genizari [genizari] ut [uti] apud Macedonem Myrmidones, quasi quindecim millia [milia].*

Beyond the Janissary regiments, the archbishop goes on to name a number of Christians who had been attracted to the Ottoman camp by the prospect of booty, *CC* 1: 130: *Sed quis, oro, circumvallavit urbem? Qui, nisi perfidi christiani, instruxere Theurcos? Testis sum quod Graeci, quod Latini, quod germani, Pannones, Boëtes, ex omnibus christianorum regionibus, Theucris commixti opera eorum fidemque didicerunt.*

37 Doukas 36.1: καὶ ἐλθόντος [*sc.* Ἰσιδώρου] μετὰ νηὸς μεγίστης τῶν Γενουιτῶν ἐποίησεν ἡμέρας ἱκανάς, ἕως οὗ οἱ ἔμποροι τῆς νηὸς πραγματεύσωνται καὶ δώσωσι τὰ χρειώδη καὶ λάβωσι τὰ ζητούμενα, ἀναμένοντες καὶ ἑτέραν ναῦν, ἥτις ἔμελλε συμπλέειν ἄχρι Καφᾶ.
38 Leonardo, *PG* 159: col. 925 [*CC* 1: 125–127]. It is evident throughout his narrative that Leonardo was a close associate and friend of Isidore. Barbaro notes that they appeared together on several occasions; cf., e.g., Barbaro 4 [*CC* 1: 11]: *e lì ve iera l'imperador, el gardenal de Rosìa, el vescovo de Metelin* [Leonardo].
39 Doukas 36.1.
40 On Barbaro and his role in the defense of Constantinople's harbor, cf. *SF*, ch. I, no. II.A.1.
41 For the editions and translations of this work, cf. *supra*, n. 27.
42 Barbaro 3 [*CC* 1: 10].
43 *Ibid.*
44 That crossbowmen were urgently needed and were much appreciated by the urban defense can be seen in the narrative of Leonardo, who goes out of his way to cite the services of Theodoros Karystenos, who, in spite of his advanced age, was an expert crossbowman and offered valuable service in the defense (Leonardo, *PG* 934 [*CC* 1: 148]: *Theodoros Caristino, senex sed robustus Graecus, in arcu doctissimus*), until he was killed during the final assault of 29 May as Isidore states in a letter to Bessarion (*CC* 1: 70): *ille Theodorus Carystenus irrumpentibus in rubem hostibus . . . summa fortitudini gloria occubuit.* Karystenos's superhuman efforts in the defense may have even impressed the Rus' eyewitness, Nestor-Iskander, who makes note of him (N-I 41 [pp. 56, 57]): Въсточный же Флабураръ Мустафа вскорѣ найде на Грекы со многою силою ... Феодоръ же тисячникъ совокупився съ Зустунѣмъ, "Mustafa, the standard-bearer of the east, came upon the Greeks with a large force soon thereafter. . . . Hurrying to his aid, Chiliarch Theodoros joined [forces with] Justinian."
45 Isidore's letter to Bessarion (the 6th of July 1453): *tandem sextum et vigessimum mensis Octobris diem ad infelicissimam urbem Constantinopolim pervenimus.* Barbaro also notes the arrival of Isidore but he fails to assign a specific date to the event; he states only that Isidore's ship arrived *hor da poi passadi ver quanti zorni.* The next date that he records in his narrative is *dì 10 novembrio*, so he has not contradicted the cardinal's text, but

he simply is not specific. Barbaro is in error, however, when he states that the cardinal came with one ship [*CC* 1: 10: *l'azonse una nave che vigna da Zenova, de Zenovexi . . . con el gardenal de Rosìa*]. Doukas 36.1 (cf. *supra*, n. 37 for the text), is unambiguous: two ships. Hanak, "Pope Nicholas V," p. 349 n. 54, suggests that the date of the cardinal's arrival is in doubt, pointing out that Doukas 36.1 suggests that he arrived in November (a date that is accepted by Vacapoulos, *Origins of the Greek Nation*, p. 191). Yet, one simply should give more weight to the cardinal's own words; surely, he knew the date of his arrival. That he arrived in November was a date that was debated before the cardinal's own testimony with the publication of his letter, when it became precisely known; and decades ago Lampros had deduced, from the various compositions of Scholarios, that Isidore had arrived before 1 November. Cf. *ΠκΠ* 2: ια΄, n. 4: γίνεται δῆλον, ὅτι, παρὰ τὰ συνήθως λεγόμενα, ὅτι ὁ Ἰσίδωρος ἔφθασεν εἰς τὴν Κωνσταντινούπολιν τὸν Νοέμβριον, ἀληθῶς κατέπλευσεν ὀλίγον πρὸ τῆς 1 Νοεμβρίου.

46 Syropoulos III.12: μετὰ δὲ τῶν κατέργων τούτων ἦλθε καὶ ὁ ... κῦρ Κωνσταντῖνος ... καὶ οἱ τζαγράτορες ἐκ τῆς Κρήτης. Recension B, 608: ἔφερον δὲ καὶ τοὺς τζαγράτορας ἐκ τῆς Κρήτης διὰ φυλακὴν τῆς Πόλεως κατὰ τὴν ἐν δεκρέτῳ συμφωνίαν. For details on that situation, cf. M. Philippides, *Constantine XI Dragaš Palaeologus (1404–1453): The Last Emperor of Byzantium*, forthcoming, ch. 4, sec. I.

47 There can be little doubt that the fanatical anti-union mob in Constantinople viewed the arrival of Isidore and his armed contingent with alarm, suspicion, and fear; cf. *CF*, pp. 383, 384.

48 Henry of Soemmern X [Philippides, *Mehmed the Conqueror*, pp. 128, 129]: *unde timens plurimum . . . ingressus quamdam parvulam navem devenit Chium, inde Cretam*.

49 Languschi-Dolfin 21 (fol. 317), identifies Giustiniani as *capitanio general in la terra*, "captain general of the territory." Other writers employ more generic terms. The Latin account of Giacomo Tetaldi twice designates *Giustiniani capitaneus constitutus*, "appointed captain." Cf. *Informations envoyées, tant par Francisco de Franc, à très reverend pere en Dieu monseigneur le cardinal d'Avignon, que par Jehan Blanchin & Jacques Edaldy marchant Florentin, de la prise de Constantinople par l'empereur Turc le xxix. jour de May MCCCCLIII, á laquelle ledit Jacques estoit personnellement*, eds. E. Martène and U. Durand, in *Thesaurus novus anecdotorum*, 1: *Tomus primus complectens regum ac principum, aliorumque virorum illustrium epistolas et diplomata benè multa* (Paris, 1717), cols. 1819–1826; *Veterum scriptorum et monumentorum historicorum, dogmaticorum, moralium amplissima collectio*, eds. E. Martène and U. Durand, 5 (Paris, 1729), pp. 785–800; J.R. Melville-Jones, *The Siege of Constantinople 1453: Seven Contemporary Accounts* (Amsterdam, 1972), pp. 1–10; and the new edition of the Latin Tetaldi, with English translation and commentary, in Philippides, *Mehmed the Conqueror*, pp. 133–219. In the short account of the siege by two Greek refugees, Thomas Eparkhos and Joseph Diplovatatzes, who found their way to Germany after the fall, and whose account still survives in a colorful German translation of the period, Giustiniani is simply identified as der Genuessen Haubtman, "the chief of the Genoese" (*NE* 2: 514–518). On Diplovatatzes and his family after the fall of Constantinople, who were associated with Bessarion's circle, and even traveled as far as England, cf. Harris, ch. 1; it is further pointed out, p. 22, that the same Thomas Eparkhos and George (not Joseph) Diplovatatzes had come to England in 1455. Diplovatatzes was endeavoring to raise a sum of money to ransom his wife and his children in Constantinople. On their account of the fall, cf. *SF*, ch. 1, no. I.8.

50 The only exhaustive study of Giustiniani's career, as far as it can be recovered, since we possess few unambiguous documents, is provided by M. Philippides, "Giovanni Guglielmo Longo Giustiniani, the Genoese *Condottiere* of Constantinople in 1453," *Byzantine Studies/Etudes Byzantines*, n.s., 3 (1998): pp. 13–54. Also cf. *SF*, ch. 6, sec. 2.

51 Kritoboulos, 25.1: τις ἀνὴρ Ἰταλὸς Ἰουστῖνος [Giustiniani] ὄνομα ... διέτριβε περί τε Χίον καὶ Ῥόδον καὶ ταύτῃ θάλασσαν λοχῶν. Leonardo uses similar phraseology,

implying that Giustiniani was a corsair: *mare decursitans* (*CC* 1: 132). During the siege Porte officials, perhaps the sultan himself, viewed Giustiniani as a "pirate" and a "corsair." In the course of the siege the sultan officially viewed the Christian ships in the harbor of Constantinople (including Giustiniani's) as pirate vessels; cf. Leonardo, *PG* 159: cols. 931 and 932 [not in the selections of *CC* 1]: *piratarum erant, quos imperator conduxerat, contra eas agere velle, quae inimicorum suorum essent*. Leonardo's report is also echoed in Languschi-Dolfin's vernacular version (Languschi-Dolfin 14 [fol. 315]), whose author renders Leonardo's piratarum-pirates as de corsari, "corsairs." In addition, one translator of Leonardo's Latin text into Greek, Pseudo-Sphrantzes, *Maius* 3.6.2, presents the same passage in a paraphrase and retains the reference to "pirates": αὗται αἱ νῆες οὐκ εἰσὶν ἐμπορικαί, ἀλλὰ πειραταί. The same reference to "pirates" is retained in the later anonymous chronicle *Codex Barberinus 111*, 18: τὰ ὁποῖα καράβια εἴχανε μέσα ἀνδρειωμένους κουρσάρους. In a work that was composed soon after the siege, before November 1453, Niccolò Tignosi (known also as da Foligno) knew of "corsairs" in the service of the emperor of Constantinople and seems to refer indirectly to Giustiniani and his company (*TIePN*, p. 104): *quoniam Bizantium praeter quosdam piratas Italosque mercatores nullos habere potuit defensores*. Giacomo Tetaldi, another eyewitness and defender of Constantinople in 1453, in his Latin version has no qualms about Giustiniani's status; Tetaldi concludes that he was a mercenary and records, in his Latin version (Philippides, *Mehmed the Conqueror*, XVII [pp. 184, 185]): *Erat hoc in loco intra civitatem constitutus capitaneus quidam nomen erat Ioannes, vir nobilis, natione Ianuensis, qui eo tempore imperatori Constantinopolitano deservivit sub tributo*. A similar paraphrase is found elsewhere (V, pp. 154, 155): *stipendiarius erat imperatoris Constantinopolitani*.

52 There were about 120 families that made up the *albergo* of the Giustiniani, which had been constituted in 1364; cf. P.P. Argenti, ed., *Hieronimo Giustiniani's History of Chios* (Cambridge 1943), 387: "J Giustiniani abitanti a Scio . . . erano di numero a tempi di loro dominio da cento vinti famiglie"; also cf. *PaL* 2: 112 n. 10. K. Hopf, *Les Giustiniani dynastes de Chios étude historique, traduite de l'Allemane par Etienne A. Vlasto* (Paris, 1888), p. 64:

> En géneral les Maonensi récurent en excellent termes avec les Ottomans jusqu'à la catastrophe de 1453, ou le héros Giovanni Guglielmo Longo (plu connu sous le nom de Jean Giustiniani) vint troubler cetter bonne harmonie, en prenant part à la défençe de Constantinople.

53 *Ibid.*, p. 174:

> Les armoires des Giustiniani de Chios étaient de gueules à la fortresse d'argent, surmontée de trois tours de même, maçoncées de sable, au chef d'or chargé de l'aigle de l'empire couronnée, à une tête regardant à dextre, qui leur avait été concédée par Sigismond. Cet écusson est ancore parfaitement visible aujourd'hui sur des marbles, dur de polais et de tours de Chiòs prequ'en ruines, comme aussi sur l'ancien palais de la Maona, à Gênes, dan la contrada de Giustiniani.

This was a more modern form of the ancient version, *ibid.*, p. 174 n. 1: "Les armoires primitives des Giustiniani étaient une fortresse d'argent surmontée de trois même, maçoncées de sable, sur champ de gueules."

54 *NE* 2: 477, 478:

> Jean Giustiniano ne partit pas avant le 25 juillet d'Albenga. Il prit, dans les eaux de la Sicile, un vaisseau de Biscaïe et un autre de Catalogne. Bien qu'il en eût encore deux, en secret, il était parti avec un seul vaisseau, portant 700 hommes d'équipage. Les Génois mêmes le craignaient, "perchè è conosciuto il più pericoloso et di maggiore animo huomo che si truovi in acqua salsa."

55 A letter of 15 December 1452 reports that a Giovanni Giustiniani and his ship captured a "Saracen" vessel transporting merchandise from Alexandria, and that the Genoese

authorities were about to appoint a commission to inquire about the circumstances surrounding this incident. Cf. *NE* 3: 277:

> le gouvernement de Gênes nomme une commision pour juger les réclamations présentées par quelques Génois contre Jean Giustiniano Longo, qui avait arrêté un grippo sarrasin et poursuivi un vaisseau genevois qui portait d'Alexandrie à Chio des marchandises appartenant à des Sarrasins.

56 Cf. the analysis and investigation in Philippides, "Giovanni Guglielmo Longo Giustiniani"; and in *SF*, ch. 6, sec. 2. Our sources apply various reasons for the decision of Giustiniani to come to Constantinople's aid, but none have ever been substantiated and no other documentation survives. Barbaro, who as a Venetian had no affection for the Genoese and was occasionally unfair in recording the actions of Giustiniani, states that the warlord came to help Constantinople *e per benefitio de la christianitade, e per honor del mundo* (Barbaro 13 [*CC* 1: 12]). Barbaro's statements are occasionally echoed in modern scholarship as well; cf., e.g., *CF*, p. 383: "The seven hundred men under Giustiniani Longo, the Genoese, were a personal contribution of a great soul to a nation in its agony." Kritoboulos I.25.1 states that Giustiniani came to Constantinople on his own initiative and adds that the emperor had promised, as Giustiniani's eventual reward, the island of Lemnos: ἦκεν αὐτόκλητος σὺν ταῖς ὁλκάσι βοηθήσων . . . εἰσὶ δὲ οἳ καὶ μετάκλητον αὐτὸν γενέσθαι φασὶ παρ' αὐτοῦ ὑπεσχημένου [*sc.* Κωνσταντίνου] μετὰ τὸν πόλεμον μισθὸν τῆς βοηθείας τὴν Λῆμνον αὐτῷ. Doukas agrees on the reward and further adds that the cession of Lemnos was confirmed by an imperial *chrysobull* (38): διὰ χρυσοβούλλου γράμματος τὴν νῆσον Λῆμνον. Another contemporary, who personally knew many of the participants on both sides of the siege, was the Greco-Venetian Nikolaos Sekoundinos. He was one of the first westerners to visit Constantinople in an official capacity following its conquest in the summer of 1453, when the Venetians were attempting to come to an understanding with Mehmed II and to ransom Venetian defenders and citizens captured during the sack. Sekoundinos earlier had served as the Latin-Greek translator during the Council of Ferrara-Florence, and, diplomatically skilled, he had access to the various courts in Italy and the Levant. Sekoundinos is probably the closest to the truth when he states that Giustiniani was promised a reward, without citing any specifics: *Januensis quidam Joannes Longus, vir profecto magni pretii, cum ducentis circiter nautis – nam onerariae navis praefectus, . . . stipendio imperatoris conductus.* Regardless of the promised reward, Giustiniani, if indeed he was the gentleman who was under investigation by the authorities of Genoa for piratical activities, may have elected to remove himself, at least for the time being, and may have chosen Constantinople as the proper environment in which to redeem himself and also to avoid being involved in court proceedings.

57 Barbaro 13 [*CC* 1: 12]: *In questo zorno, pur di 26 zener, vene in Constantinopoli Zuan Zustignan Zenovexe . . . perché l'intendeva la nezesitade che havea Constantinopoli, e per benefitio de la christianitade, e per honor del mundo.*

58 *SF*, ch.VII, sec. II.

59 V. Langlois, "Notice sur le sabre de Constantine XIV, dernier empereur de Constantinople, conservé à l'Armeria Reale de Turin," *Revue archéologique* 14 (1857): pp. 292–294; and more extensively, in *idem*, "Mémoire sur le sabre de Constantine XIV Dracosès, dernier empereur grec de Constantinople," *Revue del'Orient et de l'Algerie et des Colonies* (Paris, 1858), pp. 153–165. In addition, cf. X.A. Siderides, "Κωνσταντίνου Παλαιολόγου Θάνατος, Τάφος, καὶ Σπάθη," Ἡ Μελέτη 2 (1908): pp. 143–146; and Nicol, *The Immortal Emperor*, pp. 90, 91. In addition, cf. the discussion in Philippides, *Byzantine Imperial Cinders: Constantine XI Dragaš Palaeologus (1404–1453)*, ch. 8, sec. I.

60 Cf. *infra*, n. 63.

61 That this sword is a forgery was concluded by Siderides, pp. 143–145, after a detailed investigation.

62 Discussion of the Pisanello drawings of John VIII and his accoutrements on the occasion of his visit to Florence in connection with the Council of Ferrara-Florence in 1438–1439, as well as his impress upon various Italian artists, cf. Philippides, *Constantine XI Dragaš Palaeologus (1404–1453)*, ch. 4, sec. 4; L. Syson and D. Gordon, *Pisanello: Painter to the Renaissance Court* (London, 2001), pp. 29–34; and C.C. Bambach, in Helen C. Evans, nos. 318A and 318B (pp. 527–532), and nos. 319 and 319.1 (pp. 532, 533).

63 A drawing of the Turin sword/scimitar appears in G.A. Soteriou, "Τὸ Λεγόμενον Ξίφος τοῦ Κωνσταντίνου Παλαιολόγου," *Κιβωτὸς* 17/18 (1953): p. 240.

64 A.G. Paspates, *Πολιορκία καὶ Ἅλωσις τῆς Κωνσταντινουπόλεως ὑπὸ τῶν Ὀθωμανῶν ἐν Ἔτει 1453* (Athens, 1890; repr. Athens, 1986), p. 94.

65 *Ibid.*, p. 94. Nicol, *The Immortal Emperor*, p. 91 n. 47, also quotes the text from Paspates, but several errors have been committed: in line 2 Nicol has δώρησον (instead of the correct form δώρησε) and the form πιστῷ (line 3) lacks the required circumflex (present in Paspates's version).

66 Siderides, p. 146: Πόθεν ἔλαβεν ὁ Πασπάτης τὴν εἴδησιν ταύτην δὲν γνωρίζομεν, οὐδ' ἐμάθομεν ποῦ εὑρίσκετο [*sc.* τὸ ξίφος] ἐν ἔτει 1890, ὅτε οὗτος ἔγραφε, οὔτε νῦν [*sc.* 1908] ποῦ εὑρίσκεται, ἐὰν ἔτι σώζηται.

67 *Ibid.*, p. 145:

Ἑπομένως ἐπιτρέπεται, νομίζομεν, ἡ παραδοχὴ ταύτης μὲν ὡς γνησίας ἴσως, ἀπομιμήσεως δὲ τῶν ἄλλων, τῆς τε . . . τοῦ Τουρίνου . . . καὶ τῆς τῷ Διαδόχῳ . . . δωρηθείσης, προερχομένης ἔκ τινος νήσου τοῦ Αἰγαίου πελάγους, ἔνθα καὶ ἄλλαι τρεῖς ἢ τέσσαρες ὅμοιαι ὑπῆρχον πρό τινων δεκάδων ἐτῶν.

68 On the motif of the sword, so potent in medieval legends, cf., among others, J. de Vries, *Heroic Song and Heroic Legend* (Oxford, 1963), p. 133. For the mythical swords, wooden or otherwise, of Constantine XI, and for the folklore associated with such relics, cf. the analysis by S.D. Emellos, "Ὁ Κωνσταντῖνος Παλαιολόγος καὶ τὸ Ξύλινο Σπαθί του," in *Θρυλούμενα γιὰ τὴν Ἅλωση καὶ τὴν Ἐθνικὴ Ἀποκατάσταση* (Athens, 1991), pp. 50–59; and the brief remarks of Nicol, *The Immortal Emperor*, pp. 93, 94, who is unaware of Emellos's investigations.

69 On the legend of the "sleeping emperor," cf. Philippides, *Constantine XI Dragaš Palaeologus (1404–1453)*, "Introduction" and ch. 9; and *SF*, ch. 4.

70 In 1451 the Grand Prince Vasilii II had written to Constantine XI a respectful letter asking to receive the blessing of the patriarch, once a patriarch had been appointed (*РИБ* 9 [1880]: cols. 525–536). For further details, cf. J. Meyendorff, "Was There Ever a 'Third Rome'? Remarks on the Byzantine legacy in Russia," in J.J. Yiannias, ed. *The Byzantine Tradition After the Fall of Constantinople* (Charlottesville and London, 1991), pp. 45–60, esp. 48 ff. This was a consequence of the Muscovite realization of the unmitigated decline of the medieval Greek state under the late Palaiologoi. The Muscovites increasingly turned toward the patriarchate rather than the court, as the patriarchate's position, in their view, had been on the rise in the previous fourteenth century. And even the grand princes of Moscow had attempted to exercise some degree of independence from Constantinople. Vasilii II in particular, like his father, challenged the traditional position of the Greek emperor of being in charge of the entire οἰκουμένη, a world inhabited by all Christians. Thus his father ca. 1395 had taken the unprecedented action of deleting from the liturgy the name of the Greek emperor. He wrote a letter explaining his thesis that underscored the declining position of the Greek imperial administration. The patriarch of Constantinople replied in stern terms and strove to put such attempts to rest. On this incident, cf. E. Miklosich and J. Müller, *Acta et diplomata graeca medii aevi sacra et profana* 2 (Vienna, 1860): no. 447 (pp. 188–192), for the patriarch's reply (on whose basis the letter of the grand prince can be reconstructed); a partial translation and discussion of the patriarch's argument appears in *MP*, pp. 105–111; D. Stacton, *The World on the Last Day: The Sack of Constantinople by the Turks, May 29, 1453. Its Causes and Consequences* (London, 1965), pp.

176 The papal emissary

113, 114; W.V. Medlin, *Moscow and East Rome, A Political Study of the Relations of Church and State in Muscovite Russia*, Etudes d'histoire économique, politique et social 1 (Geneva, 1952), pp. 69–71; P. Charanis, "Coronation and Its Constitutional Significance in the Later Roman Empire," *Byz* 15 (1940/1941): pp. 64, 65; A.A. Vasiliev, "Was Old Russia a Vassal State of Byzantium?" *Speculum* 7 (1932): pp. 358, 359; and G. Ostrogorsky, "The Byzantine Empire and the Hierarchical World-Order," *Slavonic and East European Review* 35 (1956): pp. 1–14, esp. 9; a partial translation of the letter can be found in E. Barker, trans., *Social and Political Thought in Byzantium from Justinian I to the Last Palaeologus. Passages from Byzantine Writers and Documents* (Oxford, 1957), pp. 194–196.

71 Above all, upon his arrival in Constantinople from the despotate of the Morea, Constantine may have realized that a patriarch who had given his allegiance to the pope could not crown him, as the majority of anti-unionists in the capital would reject him. Thus the last Greek emperor did not receive either his crown or the sanction of an Orthodox patriarch in the most revered place of the Greek Middle Ages, the Church of Santa Sophia. Opponents of church union were quick to remind Constantine of the absence of the coronation ceremony and appear to have used a possible future ceremony as bait, in their efforts to force Constantine to renounce the union. He was *de facto* and *de iure* emperor, but the required religious ceremony in the church was postponed and was never performed. There is a growing interest in this matter among scholars who have often reviewed this anomalous situation: I.K. Bogiatzides, "Τὸ Ζήτημα τῆς Στέψεως Κωνσταντίνου Παλαιολόγου," *Λαογραφία* 2 (1923): pp. 449–456, remains the definitive work on this topic. Bogiatzides, p. 454, examines the historical precedents of such emperors as Manuel I Komnenos, who was invested with the purple by his father and was acclaimed by the troops; only later was he crowned in an official ceremony in Constantinople; Nicol, *The Immortal Emperor*, pp. 37, 38, repeats the same information as Bogiatzides. In addition, cf. Aikaterine Christophilopoulou, "Ἐκλογή, Ἀναγόρευσις καὶ Στέψις τοῦ Βυζαντινοῦ Αὐτοκράτορος," *Πραγματεῖαι τῆς Ἀκαδημίας Ἀθηνῶν* 22 (1956): pp. 199–201; in addition, cf. *eadem*, "Περὶ τὸ Πρόβλημα τῆς Ἀναδείξεως τοῦ Βυζαντινοῦ Αὐτοκράτορος," *Ἐπιστημονικὴ Ἐπετηρὶς τῆς Φιλοσοφικῆς Σχολῆς τοῦ Πανεπιστημίου Ἀθηνῶν* 13 (1962/1963): pp. 393–399. The more recent article by Margaret G. Carroll (Klopf), "Constantine XI Palaeologus: Some Problems of Image," in Ann Moffatt, ed. *Maistor: Classical, Byzantine and Renaissance Studies for Robert Browning* (Canberra, 1984), pp. 329–343, adds nothing new to this topic and simply speculates, p. 337, that Constantine may have postponed his coronation in Constantinople until he found a consort. Also cf. M. Kordoses, "The Question of Constantine Palaiologos' Coronation," in R. Beaton and Charlotte Roueché, eds. *The Making of Byzantine History: Studies Dedicated to Donald M. Nicol* (London, 1993), pp. 137–141. Also cf. Philippides, *Constantine XI Dragaš Palaeologus (1404–1453)*, ch. 8, sec. 5, for a fresh look into this matter and a review of all available evidence.

72 Leonardo, who had no affection for the anti-unionists, does not question Constantine's Catholicism. Cf. *PG* 159: col. 936 [not included in *CC* 1]: *At quid dicam arguamne principem, quem semper praecipuo honore veneratus sum: cujus fidem erga Romanam Ecclesiam intellexi.* Yet elsewhere in his narrative, Leonardo doubts Constantine's sincerity; cf. *infra*, n. 102.

73 *Ibid.*, col. 935 (not included in *CC* 1): *Severitas a principe aberat; nec compescebantur verbere aut gladio, qui neglexissent obedientiam. Idcirco quispiam suis efferebatur voluptatibus, blandimentisque ... demulcebant iratum imperatoris animum; delusus improbe a suis, bonus ille dissimulare malebat injurias.* In *ibid.*, col. 930 (not included in *CC* 1), Leonardo is even more specific: *Sed ignoro, utrumne imperator, aut judices damnandi quibus correctionis virga, quanquam minae intercessissent, aberat.*

74 The pope eventually did prepare a small fleet of five galleys and sent it for the relief of Constantinople. It never arrived in the capital. By the time the city fell, the papal fleet had only reached the island of Chios. It had only managed to set sail from Italy on 10 April 1453. Cf. Maria-Matilda Alexandrescu-Dersca Bulgari, "L'action diplomatique et

militaire de Venis pour la defense de Constantinople (1453)," *Revue romaine d'histoire* 13 (1974): pp. 247–267; F. Thiriet, *Régestes des deliberations du Sénat de Venise concernant la Romanie* 3 (Paris, 1961), p. 184 n. 2917; in addition, cf. Hanak, "Pope Nicholas V," esp. pp. 350–352.

75 There has been a needless controversy over his name and *PaL* 2: 4 n. 4, asks if he is improperly called Mamas. The controversy arose as a result of the deliberate insertions by Makarios Melissourgos-Melissenos, the sixteenth-century compiler of the *Maius* and elaborator of Georgios Sphrantzes's authentic *Minus*, to glorify his supposed ancestors in the fifteenth century. Makarios's family name was Melissourgos, one of humble origins, but he and his brothers wished to be associated with the illustrious family of Melissenos and they went so far as to produce a coat of arms for themselves to reflect the name Melissenos and not their own Melissourgos. Throughout the *Maius*, the compiler made additions at every opportunity to associate his "ancestors" with the prominent family of the Melissenoi and thus claim prestige and glory to himself and his relatives. While Sphrantzes in his authentic chronicle addresses Gregory only by his name (e.g., *Minus* 26.9: ὁ κὺρ Γρηγόριος ϖατριάρχης ἐγεγόνει), the equivalent passage in the elaborated *Maius* has been altered to include the surname "Melissenos" (*Maius* 2.19 [p. 342]: κὺρ Γρηγόριος ὁ Μελισσηνὸς ϖατριάρχης ἐγένετο). The compiler/forger, therefore, for his own purposes added "Melissenos" to the patriarch's name and made him a member of his own invented family. The controversy raises the question concerning Gregory's supposed surname: Was he a Mamas or a Melissenos? Clearly, the Melissenos reference is a later addition by the forger who exhibited questionable motives. It is the Melissenos reference that is questionable and not Sphrantzes's authentic Mamas. Consequently, every mention of "Melissenos" in the *Maius* (without a correspondence in the authentic *Minus*) is necessarily suspect. For the forgeries in the *Maius* that derive from the desire of the forger to connect himself with the illustrious medieval family of the Melissenoi, cf. I.K. Khasiotis, *Μακάριος, Θεόδωρος καὶ Νικηφόρος οἱ Μελισσηνοὶ (Μελισσουργοὶ) (16ος–17ος Αἰ.)* (Thessalonike, 1966), pp. 18–22; for a modern recreation of their (invented) coat of arms (employing their invented Melissenos connection), without tincture, cf. ibid, p. 182.

76 *Minus* 31.12: τὸν δ᾽αὐτοῦ ἔτους [1451] Αὔγουστον, διέβη ἀϖὸ τῆς Πόλεως ὡς φυγὰς καὶ ὁ ϖατριάρχης κὺρ Γρηγόριος. The modifier ὡς φυγὰς suggests that the patriarch departed in secret and took with him few possessions, if Sphrantzes actually intends the phrase to mean "as a refugee"; alternatively, Sphrantzes may mean "as an exile." In addition, the conjunction καὶ suggests that he had joined other unionists in this flight. The sixteenth-century elaborator of Sphrantzes (*Maius* 3.1) does not revise this statement. For some chronological (very likely unnecessarily imagined and invented) problems involving the date that Gregory III assumed the patriarchate of Constantinople, cf. *CF*, pp. 365, 366 n. 2.

77 *ПкП* 3: 61, 62; for another English translation, cf. Hanak, "Pope Nicholas V," p. 358 no. 13.

78 Doukas 37. For an allusion to the contents of the papal letters in Latin poetry by Pusculo, cf. *supra*, n. 10.

79 Cf. *supra*, ch. 1 n. 1.

80 For the patriarch as the head of the Orthodox millet, cf., among others, S. Runciman, "Rum Milleti: The Orthodox Community under the Ottoman Sultans," in Yiannias, *The Byzantine Tradition After the Fall of Constantinople*, pp. 1–17; idem, *The Great Church in Captivity: A Study of the Patriarchate of Constantinople from the Eve of the Turkish Conquest to the Greek War of Independence* (Cambridge, 1968); and, in general, K. Karpat, *An Inquiry into the Social Foundations of Nationalism in the Ottoman State: From Estates to Classes, from Millets to Nations* (Princeton, 1973).

81 For the early scholarship on this topic, cf. the bibliography cited in B. Unbegaun, "Les relations vieux-russes de la prise de Constantinople," *Revue des études slaves* 9 (1929):

pp. 13–38 [repr. *idem, Selected Papers on Russian and Slavonic Philology* (Oxford, 1969), pp. 1–26]; N.A. Smirnov, "Историческое Значение Русской 'Повести' Нестора Искендера о Взятий Турками Коистантинополя 1453," *BB* 7 (1953): pp. 50–71.

82 The first English translation appeared only recently, with a new edition of the Slavonic text: N-I. Other translations, partial translations, and renditions in various languages of this narrative include: M. Alexandropoulos, *Ή Πολιορκία καί Άλωση τῆς Πόλης. Τό Ρωσικό Χρονικό τοῦ Νέστορα Ίσκεντέρη* (Athens, 1978) (in Greek); Déthier, *Anonymous Moscovita,* in *MHH*, 21.1: 1047–1122 (in French); M. Braun and M. Schneider, *Bericht über die Eroberung Konstantinopels nach der Nikon-Chronik übersezt und erläutert* (Leipzig, 1943) (in German); and selections in Italian by Emanuela Folco in *CC* 1: 267–299. For a discussion of the manuscript tradition and stemma, cf. N-I, pp. 7–10; and *supra*, ch. 1, n. 1.

83 Until recently it had been assumed that Nestor-Iskander spent the weeks of the siege in the Ottoman camp. It has now been demonstrated that this view is erroneous, as Nestor-Iskander was present within Constantinople. In addition, cf. *SF*, ch. IV, sec. 4. This observation was first presented at the Twelfth Byzantine Studies Conference (Bryn Mawr, 1986): W.K. Hanak, "Who Was Nestor-Iskander?" in *Abstracts of Papers, 12th Annual Byzantine Studies Conference* (Bryn Mawr, 1986), p. 15; M. Philippides, "The Historical Value of Nestor-Iskander's Povest' o Tsar'grade," *ibid.*, pp. 13–15; and was further developed in N-I, "Introduction."

84 N-I 8 (pp. 28, 29): Днемъ же минувшимъ пакы царь съ патріархомъ и съ святители събравъ весь священническій чинъ, также и весь сигклитъ [σύγκλητος] цесарьскый и множество народа, "The days passed by: again the emperor, the patriarch with the presbyters (all gathered according to priestly rank), and all members of the emperor's council, as well as a multitude of the people."

85 *Ibid.*, 67 (pp. 79–81): Цесарь же съ патріархомъ и вси вонин поидоша въ велнкую церковь, "the emperor, the patriarch, and all soldiers went to the Great Church [Santa Sophia?]." Similar events are portrayed in another Rus' testimony related to Nestor-Iskander's text, and again the patriarch is designated Anastasios (as in Nestor-Iskander's text, cf. next note), the Книга Степенная Царского Родо-словия in ПСРЛ 21/1: 150, 151: Во градѣ же царь и царица и патріархь Анастасіе, "in the city the emperor, the empress, and Patriarch Anastasius."

86 N-I 81 (pp. 90, 91): Патріархь же и весь клирикъ ... Тобѣ глаголю, Анастасіе... , "the patriarch and all clergy.... 'I say to you, Anastasius...'"

87 *Ibid.*, 82 (pp. 92, 93): Патріархь же вземъ положи ю въ ковчезець сребранъ и позлащенъ и скры ю въ великой церкви подъ престоломъ, "the patriarch took it [Constantine's head], placing it in a silver chest; it was guilded and was then concealed under the altar of the Great Church [Santa Sofia]."

88 *CF*, p. 376 n. 3. There was an impression among scholars that a "synod" of anti-unionists took place in 1450, whose acta formally deposed Gregory and placed an Athanasios (Nestor-Iskander's "Anastasios"?) on the patriarchal seat. The two names are variants, perhaps deriving from the manuscript tradition of Nestor-Iskander, but Hanak, "Nicholas V," p. 349, labels "Anastasios" a pseudonym. Yet this synod, it has been shown, never occurred and therefore references to it are spurious; cf. C. Papaioannou, "Τὰ Πρακτικὰ τῆς Οὔτω Λεγομένης Ὑστάτης ἐν Ἁγίᾳ Σοφίᾳ Συνόδου καὶ ἡ Ἱστορικὴ Ἀξία Αὐτῶν," *Ἐκκλησιαστικὴ Ἀλήθεια* 15 (1895–1896): pp. 237, 238, 259, 260, etc. In addition, cf. Gennadios [Metropolitan of Heliopolis], pp. 117–123. Also cf. Unbegaun, "Les relations vieux-russes de la prise de Constantinople," pp. 27–30.

89 N-I, pp. 116, 117 n. 33.

90 Isidore had been granted the title of Latin Patriarch of Constantinople, succeeding Giovanni Contarini on 24 January 1452; it is notable that the pope did not give him a full appointment but most probably a titular nomination and limited his jurisdiction to Crete, Negroponte (Khalkis in Euboea), and a few Venetian possessions, in order to avoid further trouble with unionists and anti-unionists in Constantinople. Cf. *Archiv. Segr. Vat. 398*, fol. 50; and Hanak, "Pope Nicholas V," p. 348. Isidore himself seems to have

made no use of this title while in Constantinople, being aware that he was not conferred by the papacy with ecclesiastical jurisdiction over the city. On this question, cf. *supra*, ch. 2 n. 8.

91 *Minus* 36.5. The *Maius* 4.3 (p. 472) simply provides a paraphrase of the same text, rendered into the spoken idiom of the sixteenth century.

92 Gill is of the opinion that Constantine was correct in rejecting his friend's advice; cf. *CF*, p. 387 n. 2: "a suggestion that the monarch prudently did not accept." It should also be mentioned that nowhere in the numerous polemical literature that Scholarios produced in the last year of Constantinople's independent existence does he mention a patriarch. Would he have avoided to note this and even to provide the name of such an individual if the latter actually existed as the head of his beloved Orthodox Church?

93 *Minus* 36.6. The *Maius* 4.3 (p. 472) presents a slightly amplified version in his contemporary idiom:

καὶ πολλῶν συζητήσεων λόγων καὶ βουλῆς γενομένων ἔδοξε τῷ ἀοιδίμῳ βασιλεῖ τῷ αὐθέντῃ μου τὸ ἓν τῶν δύο μὴ γένοιτο παντελῶς, ὅτι τῷ γενομένῳ πατριάρχῃ ἀνάγκη ἦν οἱ πάντες πείθεσθαι αὐτῷ ἢ ἔρις καὶ ἔχθρα γενήσεται ἀναμεταξὺ αὐτοῦ καὶ αὐτῶν τῶν μὴ πειθομένων αὐτῷ. καὶ ἐν ἐκείνῳ τοῦ καιροῦ διαμέσῳ εἰ καὶ συμβῇ μάχη ἔξωθεν παρὰ ἐχθρῶν, καὶ ἔχειν ἡμᾶς καὶ ἔσωθεν, πόσον ἔσεται κακόν.

94 *CC* 1: 92–100.

95 *Ibid*., 100: *Datum Candiae, die XV Juliii LIII*^{e}.

96 Doukas 36.2: καὶ ὁ βασιλεὺς δεξιῶς ἀποδεξάμενος καὶ τιμήσας, ὡς ἔπρεπεν.

97 That official action on the part of the emperor was taken because of the cardinal's efforts is clearly stated by Leonardo, *PG* 159: col. 925 (not in *CC* 1): *actum est industria et probitate praefati Dominis cardinalis*.

98 *CF*, p. 384, states that it was 15 November, but cites no source for this date. Perhaps we can assume that this date is ultimately derived from a letter that Scholarios (who did not participate in the proceedings that took place at Xylalas) sent to Syropoulos and to Agallianos, dated in its title τῇ ιε΄ τοῦ Νοεμβρίου (*ΠκΠ* 2: 122).

99 Doukas 36.2.

100 *Ibid*.

101 Such rumors were also prevalent in Rome among the Latin high clergy, many of whom had maintained age-old doubts about the sincerity of the Greeks for church union.

102 *CC* 1: 128: *non ergo unio facta, sed unio ficta ad fatale urbem trahebat excidium*. Earlier the archbishop also questioned the emperor's and the nobility's sincerity, *PG* 159: col. 925 (not in *CC* 1): *ut sancta unio, assentiente imperatore senatuque (si non ficta fuit), firmaretur*. Elsewhere in the narration, Leonardo states that he believed the emperor to be a true Catholic; cf. *supra*, n. 72.

103 *ΠκΠ* 2: 120.

104 At the time Scholarios had left the Pantokrator, where he had taken refuge as a member of the lay clergy, and had taken up residence in the monastery of Kharsianites in preparation for taking monastic vows; cf. *ΠκΠ* 2: ια΄, ιβ΄. He wrote a composition, an *apologia pro vita sua* (*ΠκΠ* 2: 107–119; *Oeuvres complètes de Gennade Scholarios*, 4: 463–473), which he directed to the emperor on the occasion of taking up residence at the Kharsianites. Also, he appended to the work the following prooemium, *ΠκΠ* 2: 107 [*Oeuvres complètes de Gennade Scholarios*, 4: 473]: ἐγράφη ὅτε ἀνεχώρησε τοῦ παλατίου καὶ τῆς μονῆς τοῦ Παντοκράτορος, ἐν ᾗ πρότερον ᾤκει κοσμικός, καὶ ἀπῆλθε εἰς τὸ τοῦ Χαρσιανίτου κοινόβιον καὶ ἡτοιμάζετο πρὸς τὸ μοναχικὸν σχῆμα.

105 *Ibid*., 120–121:

οὐκ ἀρνήσομαί σε, φίλη ὀρθοδοξία. οὐ ψεύσομαί σε, πατροπαράδοτον σέβας, ἕως τὸ ἐμὸν πνεῦμα ἐν τῷδε μένῃ τῷ σώματι. μηδέν με πειράζετε πλέον, ἄνθρωποι, ὅτι ἐγὼ τοιαύτης τῆς ἑνώσεως οὐ κοινωνήσω ποτέ, ὅτι οὔτε μετὰ τῶν Λατίνων ἑνωθήσεσθε οὕτως καὶ τὰ τοῦ θεοῦ χωρισθήσεσθε καὶ ἀδοξία ἀΐδιον ὑποστήσεσθε.

106 *Ibid.*, 122: καὶ ἦν αὕτη ἡ πρώτη φορὰ μετὰ τὸ συσκευασθῆναι πάντα ἰδίως διὰ τοῦ καρδιναλίου [*sc.* Ἰσιδώρου].
107 *Oeuvres complètes de Gennade Scholarios* 3: 188–195, esp. pp. 188–189.
108 No trace of this building has survived nor has any other structure been identified as the palace; still pertinent are the comments of Lampros in *ΠκΠ* 2: ιβ′: "Τοῦ παλατίου τούτου οὐδεμία γίνεται μνεία παρὰ τῷ C. *du Fresne du Cange* (*Constantinopolis christiana, seu description Urbis – Constantinopolitanae*... [Paris, 1680]), τῷ [J.] Labarte: (*Le palais de Constantinople et ses abords* [Paris, 1861]) καὶ τῷ Πασπάτῃ (A. G. Paspates, *Βυζαντιναὶ Μελέται Τοπογραφικαὶ καὶ Ἱστορικαί*. Βιβλιοθήκη Ἱστορικῶν Μελετῶν 208 [Constantinople, 1877; repr. Athens, 1986]). Cf. *ΠκΠ* 2: ιβ′: Θεοδόσιον Ξυλαλὰν εὑρίσκομεν μνημονευόμενον ἐν τῷ κώδικι τῆς Ἀτεστίας (Estense) βιβλιοθήκης Μοδένης ὑπ' ἀριθ. 203. Ἴδε *Stadi italiani di filologia classica*. Τόμ. Δ v, σ. 506."
109 *CC* 1: 92. Isidore must have been thinking, without mentioning names, of some of the individuals that are included in the list of signatures furnished by Scholarios, for, in the latter's view, they were champions of Orthodoxy and he was proud to cite them; cf. the following note.
110 The document cited in *Oeuvres complètes de Gennade Scholarios*, 3: 193, lists the following names, which the prooemium admits are derived from a copy and not from the original document: εἶχε τὸ πρωτότυπον καὶ ὑπογραφὰς ταύτας. ὁ Νικομηδείας Μακάριος – ὁ Τορνόβου Ἰγνάτιος – ὁ Μολδοβλαχίας Δαμιανός – ὁ Πέργης καὶ Ἀτταλίας Θεόγνωστος – ὁ ταπεινὸς μητροπολίτης Δάρκου Ἀκάκιος – ὁ μέγας χαρτοφύλαξ καὶ ἀρχιδιάκονος ὁ Βαλσαμῶν – ὁ μέγας ἐκκλησιάρχης καὶ διάκονος Σίλβεστρος ὁ Συρόπουλος – ὁ ἡγούμενος τοῦ Στουδίου Θεόδοτος ἱερομόναχος – ὁ Ἰωσὴφ ἱερομόναχος καὶ πνευματικὸς πατήρ – ὁ Παντοκρατορινὸς ἡγούμενος Γερόντιος ἱερομόναχος – ὁ ἡγούμενος τῆς Περιβλέπτου Κύριλλος ἱερομόναχος – ὁ ἐλάχιστος ἐν ἱερομονάχοις καὶ πνευματικοῖς Νεόφυτος – Γερμανὸς ἱερομόναχος ὁ τοῦ ἁγίου Βασιλείου – ὁ ἱερομνήμων διάκονος Θεόδωρος ὁ Ἀγαλλιανός.
111 Laurent, *Les "Mémoires" du Grand Ecclésiarque de l'église Constantinople de Sylvestre Syropoulos*. There is an inaccurate translation and paraphrase of Syropoulos's *Memoirs* into Latin: R. Creyghton, *Vera Historia Unionis Non Vera* (Hagae-Comitis, 1660). No complete English translation of this important, albeit extremely partisan, work exists. The Syropoulos Project for graduate students at the Centre for Byzantine, Ottoman and Modern Greek Studies, IAA, University of Birmingham, has undertaken, in 2008, a partial translation into English of Section IV of the *Memoirs*.
112 Neophytos must have been a very active associate of Scholarios on behalf of the anti-unionist faction, as he also came to the attention of Leonardo, who cites him with contempt; evidently, he along with Scholarios and their other associates may have tried to put a stop to the gathering that the court had been planning; cf. Leonardo, *CC* 1: 126: *nec ratio nec auctoritas nec variae Scholarii, Isidori* [the anti-unionist ecclesiastic and not the cardinal, of course] *Neophytique opiniones adversus Romanae Ecclesiae fidem stare poterant*. Surely, he is the same individual who signed the document as "Neophytos, the most insignificant among hieromonks and spiritual [fathers]" (cf. the Greek text of his signature, *supra*, n. 110, no. 12). Neophytos must have exercised substantial influence at court. A Neophytos "the hieromonk" of the Kharsianites Monastery is mentioned by Sphrantzes and he may be the same person. It is known that the Neophytos of Sphrantzes had access to the court and also had connections with the imperial grand duke, Loukas Notaras; cf. *Minus* 33.5: καὶ ἐμηνύθη ὁ μέγας δοὺξ [*sc.* Loukas Notaras] διὰ τοῦ συντέκνου αὐτοῦ καὶ ἐμοῦ, ἱερομονάχου καὶ πνευματικοῦ τοῦ εἰς τὴν Χαρσιανίτου. The *Maius* (3.213 [p. 368]) simply affixes glosses: the forger inserts πατρὸς before Νεοφύτου and adds μονῇ after Χαρσιανίτου. It becomes evident that the two residences of Scholarios, first the Pantokrator and then the Kharsianites, were two extremely active anti-union centers and, by extension, anti-western and anti-administration. Neophytos and his anti-union activities were further known to Doukas, who cites him by name and

underscores his association with the court and his influence with the nobility (37.6: ἦν γὰρ αὐτὸς ὁ Νεόφυτος παρρησίαν ἔχων καὶ πνευματικεύων ἐν ἀνακτόροις καὶ μεγιστάνων οἴκοις) and further reported that he made every possible effort to restrain the Orthodox flock from taking communion from Latin and unionist priests after the celebration of the union in the imperial city.
113 For the entire speech of Theodoros Agallianos and for other surviving works by him, cf. C.G. Patrinelis, Ὁ Θεόδωρος Ἀγαλλιανὸς Ταυτιζόμενος πρὸς τὸν Θεοφάνην Μηδείας καὶ οἱ Ἀνέκδοτοι Λόγοι του. Μία Νέα Ἱστορικὴ Πηγὴ τοῦ Πατριαρχείου Κωνσταντινουπόλεως κατὰ τοὺς Πρώτους μετὰ τὴν Ἅλωσιν Χρόνους (Athens, 1966), pp. 91–129, esp. 97.
114 *CF*, p. 385 n. 178.
115 Scholarios refers to this letter in his advice to the clerics who were about to meet the cardinal; cf. *ΠκΠ* 2: 122–128.
116 *ΠκΠ* 2: 127.
117 It is titled: Τοῦ Τιμιωτάτου Δικαιοφύλακος τῆς Μεγάλης Ἐκκλησίας Κυρίου Θεοδώρου τοῦ Ἀγαλλιανοῦ Ἀνασκευὴ τοῦ ὑπὲρ τῆς Δόξης Λατίνων Βιβλίου Ἰωάννου τοῦ Ἀργυροπούλου.The treatise has been published: Lampros, *Ἀργυροπούλεια* pp. 234–303. On Ioannes Argyropoulos, who labored on behalf of Isidore, cf. *infra*, nn. 119–124. On Agallianos and his stance in these debates, cf. *supra*, n. 113, and *infra*, n. 133.
118 Lampros, *Ἀργυροπούλεια*, pp. 236–237. Agallianos continues with his fawning address to Notaras:

> τὰ δὲ κατ᾽ αὐτοῦ ταῦτα ἐγκώμια ἀντὶ πολλῶν καὶ μεγάλων τῶν προσηκόντων αὐτῷ βραχέα καὶ αὐτὸς εἶναι ὁμολογῶ, καὶ ἀνθρώπου πεφεισμένως ἄγαν καὶ ἄκροις ὡς εἰπεῖν δακτύλοις τούτων ἀψαμένου, τῷ βραχυτάτῳ τὸν ἐνεστηκότα ξυγχωρεῖσθαι χρόνον καὶ τῷ μήπω τὸν καιρὸν ἥκειν τῶν ἐγκωμίων τῶν τελεωτέρων ἴσως. τοῖς γὰρ ἀγαθοῖς ἅπας ἀνεῖται καιρὸς εἰς ἔπαινον.

119 This work in its entirety has been published by Lampros, *Ἀργυροπούλεια*, pp. ρ´– ρκε´. No English translation of this work exists.
120 For the teaching career of Argyropoulos, the best study remains that by Lampros in his long, detailed, and well-documented "Introduction" to the *Ἀργυροπούλεια*, pp. ε´– ριθ´. For the teaching activities of Argyropoulos at his Academy, cf. *ibid.*, pp. κζ´–λα´. Argyropoulos had been granted a building in which to conduct his teachings: the Kral's (King's) Xenon in Constantinople since the reign of JohnVIII. He was certainly involved in teaching activities with the καθολικὸν Μουσεῖον of the Kral's Xenon from 1440–1450. No trace of this famous building survives. It most probably was demolished after the fall of the imperial city. It is believed that the kral who established this edifice was Stepan II Uroš (1282–1320) and that the Xenon was associated with the Prodromos Monastery. On the nature of the lectures at the Xenon, cf. Argyropoulos's own comments and observations (*Ἀργυροπούλεια*, pp. 73, 74) and the impressions of Argyropoulos's famous pupil, Michael Apostoles (*ibid.*, pp. 228, 229). For the medical side of the educational process at the Xenon (as Argyropoulos was also a physician), cf. O. Lampsides, "George Chrysococcis, le médecin, son oeuvre," *BZ* 38 (1938): pp. 312–322; and *idem*, "Γεώργιος ὁ Χρυσοκόκκης ὁ Ἰατρός," *Ἀρχεῖον Πόντου* 24 (1961): pp. 38–41. On Argyropoulos, cf. Staikos, pp. 173–196; *supra*, sec. 1; and *supra*, n. 1.
121 He uses this title for himself in a report he sent to Pope Nicholas V in 1451; cf. *Ἀργυροπούλεια*, p. 129: Ἰωάννου τοῦ Ἀργυροπούλου τοῦ Κριτοῦ τοῦ Δημοσίου τῆς Κωνσταντινουπόλεως εἰς τὸν Μακαριώτατον Πάπαν Κὺρ Νικόλαον. Argyropoulos uses his title "lord of churches" in a letter to George Trapezountios, "of Trebizond," as the name is often but erroneously cited;Trapezountios was from Crete: τοῦ ἄρχοντος τῶν ἐκκλησιῶν.We are not certain what this title implies; nor what "churches" means. Is it a title that provides some sort of perhaps spiritual guidance over all churches in Constantinople or does it concern some other jurisdiction, perhaps Latin churches? On Argyropoulos, cf. *supra*, n. 1.

182 *The papal emissary*

122 The document granting him his doctorate has survived (*Archivio antico dell'Università di Padova. Acta Collegii Artistarum* no. 309 fols. CVIII⁶ and CIX), which is quoted in its entirety by Lampros, *Ἀργυροπούλεια*, p. ιθ´, n. 3.
123 He was granted this honor on 13 October 1444. Cf. ibid, p. ιζ´, where (p. ιη´) it is also pointed out that "provost"/*rector* in those times differed from the modern Academic position and only indicated an exceptional student.
124 It was Loukas Notaras who urged him to compose a treatise on the *filioque* issue with special reference to the Council of Ferrara-Florence. Argyropoulos, who signs himself as "teacher," completed this treatise. For the text, cf. *Ἀργυροπούλεια*, pp. 107–128. He included Notaras's imperial title in the address of his composition: τῷ Λαμπροτάτῳ καὶ Περιφανεστάτῳ Μεγάλῳ Δουκὶ Ἰωάννης διδάσκαλος ὁ Ἀργυρόπουλος. In the prooemium Argyropoulos takes time to sing the grand duke's praises *in extenso* and suggests that Notaras's intellect was worthy of Plato's Academy and the peripatetics, p. 108: νῦν δὲ φιλοσοφεῖς ἀκριβῶς, ὥσπερ τις ἐν Ἀκαδημίᾳ τραφεὶς ἢ πλοκὰς εἰδὼς λόγων, οὓς αὐτὸς ἔπλεξεν ὁ περίπατος. No English translation of this work exists.
125 *Supra*, n. 116, for the text.
126 Cf. Scholarios's comment, *ΠκΠ* 2: 126: καὶ μετὰ Βενετίκων καὶ Γενουιτῶν ... τοῦτο ὃ κατεπείγει ὁ καρδινάλιος.
127 Doukas 37.10, succinctly, if inaccurately, expressed it, since he unjustly attributed this comment to the grand duke: "either the papal miter or the Turkish turban (φακιόλιον ... Τούρκων ἢ καλύπτραν Λατινικήν)." For the extended passage, cf. *infra*, n. 195.
128 The famous Pantokrator Monastery was pillaged during the sack. After the fall the building became popularly known as the Zeyrek Camii when it was renamed after a scholar/holy man, Zeyrek Mehmed, who lived in the neighborhood of the mosque until his death, which occurred twenty years after the sack or early in the sixteenth century. On the conversion of the Greek churches into mosques after the fall, cf. the valuable work, with meticulous notes by the translator into English, entitled *The Garden of the Mosques: Hafız Hüseyin Al-Ayvansarayî's Guide to the Muslim Monuments of Ottoman Istanbul*, trans. and annotated by H. Crane (Leiden, Boston, and Cologne, 2000), and the comments on the Zeyrek Camii (p. 207). Paspates, who had read the learned Ottoman monograph, agrees with this testimony; cf. Paspates, *Βυζαντιναὶ Μελέται Τοπογραφικαὶ καὶ Ἱστορικαί*, p. 322:

> Ἡ ἐκκλησία αὕτη παρὰ τὴν συνήθειαν τῶν Ὀθωμανῶν, μετεβλήθη εὐθὺς μετὰ τὴν ἅλωσιν, εἰς ἀποθήκην τῶν μηχανῶν καὶ ἐφοδίων τοῦ αὐτοκρατορικοῦ ναυστάθμου. Ἀκολούθως κατὰ διαταγὴν τοῦ Σελὴμ τοῦ Δευτέρου ἀνηγέρθη μιναρές, καὶ μετεβλήθη εἰς τέμενος [mescidi]. Ὁ Σουλτὰν Σελὴμ διεδέχθη τὸν πατέρα αὐτοῦ Σουλεϊμὰν τῷ 1566ῳ, καὶ ἀπεβίωσε τῷ 1574ῳ. Ὅθεν ἐν τῇ ὀκταετίᾳ ταύτῃ μετεβλήθη εἰς τέμενος ἡ ἐκκλησία αὕτη, οὖσα ἀπὸ τοὺς χρόνους τῆς ἁλώσεως μέχρι τῆς ἐποχῆς ταύτης, ἀποθήκη τοῦ ναυστάθμου.

In addition, cf. J. Freely and A.S. Çakmak, *Byzantine Monuments of Istanbul* (Cambridge, 2004), pp. 211–220. Doukas 36.3: ἐν τῇ μονῇ τοῦ παντοκράτορος ἐν τῇ κέλλῃ τοῦ Γενναδίου, τοῦ ποτε Γεωργίου Σχολαρίου, is in error when he states that after the meetings in the Xylalas palace Scholarios was still in residence at the Pantokrator. He had already changed his residence to the Kharsianites Monastery. For Scholarios's residence in the monasteries, cf. *supra*, n. 104. Doukas was simply misled by his erroneous impression that the Pantokrator was the only nucleus of the anti-unionist resistance.
129 It is usually assumed that Scholarios had become a *persona non grata* at court and that he may have been prohibited from attending court functions. It is perhaps for this very reason that he publicly assumed his intransigent position and refused to attend this gathering of clerics (*ΠκΠ* 2: 122: ἐγὼ ἤθελον ἐλθεῖν, ὥσπερ καὶ ἀεὶ ποιῶ, ἀλλὰ οὐδὲν οἶδα καλῶς τί ἐστι τὸ βουλόμενον τῆς συνάξεως ταύτης). In order to soften the fact that he had been barred from court, he pretended to stay away from it by choice. This position,

we believe, is strengthened by the report he wrote. In its conclusion (to be quoted shortly in context) he writes: συμβουλεύω, νὰ ἔλθω εἰς τὸ ϖαλάτιον. He appears to be requesting an invitation and an opportunity to debate Isidore; cf. *infra*, text with n. 132.
130 *ΠκΠ* 2: 122–128. It is clear that by this time he had taken monastic vows and assumed the monastic name Gennadios, while he associates himself with the adjective "humble" that normally signifies a monk (p. 127): καὶ τί νὰ λαλῇ ϖλέον ὁ ταϖεινὸς Γεννάδιος.
131 *Ibid.*, p. 125.
132 *Ibid.*, pp. 125, 126.
133 In *ΠκΠ* 2: 122 Scholarios assigns the title τῷ μεγάλῳ χαρτοφύλακι to Agallianos; yet in the same composition (*ΠκΠ* 2: 125) he refers to him as δικαιοφύλαξ. In one of his own works, which was probably composed at this time since it concerns a composition that Ioannes Argyropoulos had drawn up to support the Latin dogma, Agallianos himself appears to have assumed the title of δικαιοφύλαξ for himself; cf. Lampros, *Ἀργυροϖούλεια*, p. 234: Τοῦ Τιμιωτάτου Δικαιοφύλακος τῆς Μεγάλης Ἐκκλησίας Κυρίου Θεοδώρου τοῦ Ἀγαλλιανοῦ Ἀνασκευὴ τοῦ ὑϖὲρ τῆς Δόξης Λατίνων Βιβλίου Ἰωάννου τοῦ Ἀργυροϖούλου. Also in the spring of 1452, Agallianos endorsed a note as ὁ δικαιοφύλαξ διάκονος Θεόδωρος Ἀγαλλιανός. For the text of this note, cf. Sophronios Eustratiades (Metropolitan of Leontopolis), " Ἐκ τοῦ Κώδικος τοῦ Νικολάου Καρατζᾶ," *Ἐκκλησιαστικὸς Φάρος* 6 (1910): pp. 200–206. Unfortunately, the *codex* that contained this note has vanished; on its fate, cf. Patrinelis, *Ὁ Θεόδωρος Ἀγαλλιανός*, p. 59 n. 240. On the roster of the anti-unionists who attended the gathering at the Xylalas palace the title μέγας χαρτοφύλαξ is assigned to Balsamon while Agallianos is identified by the title ὁ ἱερομνήμων διάκονος Θεόδωρος ὁ Ἀγαλλιανός; for the entire list of names with their titles, cf. *supra*, n. 110.
134 The position of the anti-unionists is still embraced in the polemical work of Zeses, *Γεννάδιος Β΄ Σχολάριος*, pp. 192–194, who ultimately advocates sainthood for Scholarios, whose polarizing stance he fails to recognize.
135 So Isidore states in the letter that he wrote to the pope after the fall of Constantinople and after he had reached safe haven in Crete (*CC* 1: 92–100). In his letter of 15 July to the pope he alludes to his earlier letters and reports (*CC* 1: 92): *postquam ego ab urbe Romana egressus sum, nonnullas literas Beatitudini Vestrae exposui*.
136 *CC* 1: 126.
137 On Ioannes Argyropoulos, who escaped from the sack and went to Italy to seek a professorial position, cf. *supra*, sec. 1; and the reconstruction of his life by Lampros, *Ἀργυροϖούλεια*, pp. ε΄–ρκε΄.
138 Elsewhere in his narrative (*PG* 159: col. 934 [*CC* 1: 148]), Leonardo emphasizes the Catholicism of Theophilos Palaiologos and his interest in literary scholarship: *Theodorus Caristino . . . Theophilusque Graecus, nobilis Palaeologo, litteris eruditus, e ambo catholici*. Theophilos is assigned a heroic death at the side of Constantine XI, whom, unlike numerous others, he refused to abandon in the final assault of the Turks on 29 May. For additional testimonies on this individual and his role during the siege, cf. *SF*, Appendix IV, no. 158 (652); and *PLP* 9: no. 21446 (p. 90).
139 *CC* 1: 126.
140 *Ibid.*
141 It should perhaps be emphasized that the decision to enforce and to celebrate the union was formally made (or was made public) after the gathering in the palace; cf. *Minus* 36.6: καὶ ϖολλῶν λόγων καὶ βουλῆς γενομένης. The *Maius* (4.2.3, p. 472) simplifies Sphrantzes's language but retains the same genitive absolute construction: καὶ ϖολλῶν συζητήσεων λόγων καὶ βουλῆς γενομένων. Doukas is in agreement and states that priests, deacons, the emperor, and the senate reached a common accommodation to enforce the union, 36.2: ἱερεῖς τε καὶ διάκονοι τῶν τοῦ κλήρου καὶ ὁ βασιλεὺς σὺν τῇ συγκλήτῳ, ἐβούλοντο κοινῇ ὁμονοίᾳ.
142 It seems that after the gathering at the Xylalas palace the emperor abandoned all hope for any reconciliation between the unionist and the anti-unionist factions. Sphrantzes

184 The papal emissary

reports the emperor's decision and one detects tones of resignation on the part of Constantine; cf. *Minus* 36.6: τοῦ δὲ μνημοσύνου, ἃς γένηται διὰ τὴν ἐλπίδα τῆς βοηθείας ἡμῶν εἰς ἀνάγκην. καὶ ὅσοι ποιήσουν τοῦτο εἰς τὴν Ἁγίαν Σοφίαν, οἱ ἄλλοι θέλωσιν εἴσθεν ἀναίτιοι καὶ εἰρηνικοὶ (slight elaboration in the *Maius* 4.2.3: τὸ δὲ μνημονεύεσθαι τὸν πάπαν γεννηθήτω ἕνεκεν ἐλπίδος βοηθείας ἐν τῇ ἀνάγκῃ ἡμῶν καὶ ὅσοι τοῦτο ποιήσωσι ἐν τῇ ἁγίᾳ Σοφίᾳ, οἱ ἄλλοι ἔσονται ἀναίτιοι καὶ εἰρηνικοί).

143 Scholarios, *Oeuvres complètes* 3: pp. 171–174 [= *ΠκΠ* 2: 131–135].
144 *ΠκΠ* 2: 131: [Γενναδίου τοῦ Σχολαρίου] ταύτῃ τῇ ἡμέρᾳ διεδόθη τὸ παρὸν εἰς ὅλην τὴν πόλιν εἰς ἴσα πολλὰ μεταγραφέν, πρὸ ἓξ μηνῶν τῆς ἁλώσεως, ἐν κθῃ τοῦ Μαΐου γενομένης. In the opening sentence the specific date of 27 November is mentioned: τῇ κζ´ Νοεμβρίου τελευταῖον Γεννάδιος [his monastic name, as he had already taken monastic vows] ὁ ἁμαρτωλὸς τοῦ θεοῦ δοῦλος καὶ ἐλάχιστος.
145 Scholarios, *Oeuvres completes* 3: p. 172.
146 It is not clear to us, from the evidence in our sources, exactly where Scholarios was residing at this moment in time. We have seen that he had earlier left the Pantokrator (*supra*, n. 104) and had taken up residence in the Kharsianites. Doukas clearly states that, after the meeting at Xylalas, Scholarios occupied a cell at the Pantokrator. Had Scholarios returned to the Pantokrator after he took monastic vows or has Doukas erred?
147 Doukas 36.3.
148 *Ibid.*, 37.3: ἔτυχον ἐγὼ [Doukas] μετὰ ταῦτα [the sack] μιᾷ τῶν εὐγενίδων αἰχμαλωτευθείσῃ καὶ διηγήσατό μοι.
149 *Ibid.*, 36.3.
150 *Ibid.*
151 *Ibid.*, 37.8.
152 Scholarios, *Oeuvres complètes* 3: 177.
153 On Constantine as "emperor without crown," cf. Philippides, *Constantine XI Dragaš Palaeologus (1404–1453)*, ch. 7, sec. 4.
154 The Greek text of the letter of Ioannes Eugenikos can be found in *ΠκΠ* 1: 123–134, esp. 125; for an analysis, cf. Bogiatzides, pp. 451–453. There exists no translation of this work in any modern language.
155 *CBB* 2: 7 (p. 636). A longer extract, in English translation, of the same chronicle can be found in Nicol, *The Immortal Emperor*, p. 58. The fact that Constantine had not been crowned was not entirely forgotten, in spite of the hagiographical lore that accumulated around his name. Thus an entry in a short chronicle reports the fact that he was still a despot at the time of his death; cf. *CBB* 1: 69.39 (p. 535): καὶ πάλιν ἐσέβησαν αὐτοὶ οἱ τῆς Ἄγαρ καὶ ἐπῆραν αὐτὴν ἐκ τῶν χειρῶν τοῦ Κωνσταντίνου δεσπότου, ἀστέπτου ὄντος, ὁ σουλτὰν Μεϊμέτης, ἐν ἔτει ´ςϡξα´, μαΐῳ κθ´ (our emphasis).
156 For this προσφώνημα, cf. *ΠκΠ* 4: 67–82 (wrongly attributed to Michael Apostoles); in addition, cf. Nicol, *The Immortal Emperor*, p. 39 nn. 6 and 7. Argyropoulos also composed a formal essay on kingship, which he presented to Constantine at this time. For its Greek text, cf. Lampros, *Ἀργυροπούλεια*, pp. 8–47; in addition, cf. Vacalopoulos, *Origins of the Greek Nation*, pp. 180, 181.
157 For Apostoles's composition, cf. *ΠκΠ* 4: 83–87.
158 Discussion of his contradictory position can be found in Bogiatzides, p. 449.
159 Doukas 36.2. It is interesting to note that the so-called Short Chronicles, the βραχέα χρονικά, make no reference to Isidore's arrival and mission, and in silence pass over the conclusion of the union and its celebration.
160 *PG* 159: col. 925 [*CC* 1: 128]: *sacra unio, assentientore imperatore senatuque (si non ficta fuit)*.
161 *Ibid.*
162 *Ibid.*
163 As Leonardo notes melancholically in his account, in the final analysis no substantial help ever came. *PG* 159: col. 929 [not in *CC* 1]: *Nam neque ex Genua, neque ex Venetiis, quibus pace eorum dicam mitti debuit, auxilium mittebatur. Necque aliunde spes erat, nisi ex Deo.*
164 Barbaro 4, 5 [*CC* 1: 11].

165 Leonardo, *PG* 159: col. 925 [*CC* 1: 125–127].
166 Pusculo III.481–646 (pp. 51–55); unfortunately, this important section was not included in the selected passages of the improved text in *CC* 1.
167 *Ibid.*, III.596–625 (p. 52). There are a few grammatical problems with the text, but we should recall that his text is based on that of a single manuscript and we are still awaiting a modern, collated, and reliable scholarly edition of Pusculo's poem with an *apparatus criticus*.
168 There exists a substantial literature with different emphases, historical, liturgical and theological, ceremonial, archaeological, architectural, and so forth, on this most famous structure of the medieval era. Cf. among others, C.A. Mango, *Hagia Sophia: A Vision for Empires* (Istanbul, 1997); R.J. Mainstone, *Hagia Sophia: Architecture, Structure and Liturgy of Justinian's Great Church* (New York, 1988); and R.L. Van Nice, *Saint Sophia in Istanbul: An Architectural Survey*, 2 vols. (Washington, DC, 1965 and 1986). For the centuries beyond the Byzantine period and for the fate of the building, cf. Natalia B. Teteriatnikov[a], *Mosaics of Hagia Sophia, Istanbul: The Fossati Restoration and the Work of the Byzantine Institute* (Washington, DC, 1998); R. Mark and A.S. Çakmak, eds., *Hagia Sophia from the Age of Justinian to the Present* (Cambridge, 1992); and R.S. Nelson, *Hagia Sophia, 1850–1950: Holy Wisdom Modern Monument* (Chicago and London, 2004). Still unsurpassed and rewarding remains the monumental work by a well-known astronomer who helped to demolish Percival Lowell's fantasies and ghosts of canals on Mars, E.M. Antoniadi, Ἔκφρασις τῆς Ἁγίας Σοφίας, 3 vols. (Athens, 1907–1909; repr. in 4 vols., Athens, 1983). For the role of this church in the days before and after the siege, cf. M. Philippides, "Tears of the Great Church: The Lamentation of Santa Sophia," *Greek, Roman and Byzantine Studies* 52 (2012): pp. 715–738, which further investigates the folk poems that arose as lamentations in response to the "celebration" of the union within the famous building.
169 Pusculo III.529–587 (pp. 52, 53).
170 *Ibid.*, III.531–534 (p. 52).
171 *Infra*, n. 172.
172 Pusculo III.570–572 (p. 53): *si firma volent decreta piorum / Sancta partum, Eugenio quae sunt promissa, fidemque / Quam scripsere albis cupient servare libellis*.
173 *Ibid.*, III.580–582 (p. 53): *Deus ipse benignus / Iratusque suas, hominum et simul obstruet aures, / Cum frustra auxilium implorent, nemoque juvabit*.
174 *Ibid.*, III.589–600 (pp. 53, 54).
175 *CC* 1: 11. *Supra*, n. 164.
176 Leonardo, *PG* 159: col. 930 (not included in *CC* 1).
177 *Minus* 36.6: καὶ γενομένου τῇ ιβῃ Δεκεμβρίου μηνός. The elaborator of the *Maius* 4.3 (p. 472) omits the participle γενομένου.
178 Doukas 36.5.
179 Pusculo III.634–646 (p. 54). Not in *CC* 1.
180 *CC* 1: 126:

> *Intellexi plane, praeter Argyropilum atrium magistrum, Theophilumque Palaeologo hieromonachosque quosdam paucos et alios laicos, quod ambitio ita Graecos quasi omnes capti[vi]vasset, ut nemo esset qui zelo fidei vel salutis suae motus orimus videretur fieri velle suae quasi opinionis et pertinaciae contemporat.*

181 Pusculo mentions the two scholars in company of each other and the verb he uses for Apostoles, in relation to Argyropoulos, suggests that they were closely associated, 3.661–667 (p. 55): *Carus Musis, et Palladis arte / insignis, plures docuit, dictisque retorsit / esse pios papaeque fidem servare, deoque / Argyropulus ea tunc tempestate Joannes. / Hunc sequitur tanto dignus doctore Michael Byzantinus: erat cognomen Apostolus illi*.
182 Doukas 37.5.
183 *Ibid*.
184 *Ibid*. 39.19.

186 *The papal emissary*

185 The situation offered fertile ground for all sorts of tales and alleged acts of treason to emerge; on this point cf. M. Philippides, "Rumors of Treason: Intelligence Activities and Clandestine Operations in the Siege of 1453," in M. Arslan and T. Kaçar, eds., *Byzantion'dan Constantinopolis'e Istanbul Kuşatmaları* (Istanbul, 2017), pp. 403–445.
186 *CF*, pp. 178 and 385.
187 The only detailed investigation and discussion of this effort is provided in Philippides, *Constantine XI Dragaš Palaeologus (1404–1453)*, ch. 8, sec. 1.
188 Pusculo III.617–621 (p. 54). Pusculo does not furnish the Christian name of Kantakouzenos. Was he Demetrios Palaiologos Kantakouzenos? On him, cf. Philippides, *Constantine XI Dragaš Palaeologus (1404–1453)*, ch. 7, n. 103; and *PLP* 5: no. 10962 (p. 92).
189 Pusculo III.628–632 (p. 54). There is one individual by that last name, John Basilikos, a merchant whose career extends beyond 1453; cf. K.-P. Matschke, "Leonard von Chios, Gennadios Scholarios, und die 'Collegae' Thomas Pyropulos und Johannes Basilikos vor, während und nach der Eroberung von Konstantinopel durch die Türken," *Βυζαντινά* 21 (2000): pp. 227–236. Could it be that John Basilikos and Pusculo's Basilicus are the same person?
190 Leonardo. *PG* 159: col. 930 [not in *CC* 1].
191 *Ibid*. III.633 (p. 54): *Isidorus nescius ipsi*....
192 *CF*, p. 88.
193 Cf. *supra*, ch. 3, sec. 2.
194 *CF*, p. 385; and *supra*, text with n. 115.
195 Doukas 36.10:

> ὁ δὲ Γεννάδιος ... ἔχων ἐκ τῆς συγκλήτου τὸν πρῶτον μεσάζοντα τὸν μεγαδούκαν [Λουκᾶν Νοταρᾶν] συνεργὸν καὶ συνίστορα, τὸν καὶ τοσοῦτον εἰπεῖν τολμήσαντα κατὰ τῶν Λατίνων, ὅτε εἶδον οἱ Ῥωμαῖοι τὸν ἀναρίθμητον στρατὸν τῶν Τούρκων, μᾶλλον δὲ κατὰ τῆς πόλεως, "κρειττότερόν ἐστι εἰδέναι ἐν μέσῃ τῇ πόλει φακιόλιον βασιλεῦον Τούρκων ἢ καλύπτραν Λατινικήν."

196 Pusculo III.732–739 (p. 56):

> *Abfuit a tali crudelis munere Lucas / Notarus. Ex primis multos quoque traxit inertes / Civibus in fraudem, et monachos hortatus iniquos / Perstare: ut contra teneant discordia summum / Dogmata pontificem. Gaudet contraria regi / Impius, ac tanto vestigial figere coetu, / Adversamque sequi indotus laetatur, et amens / Hisce viam. Sequitur major, numerosaque turba.*

This very negative picture of the grand duke, painted by Pusculo, Doukas, di Montaldo, and to a lesser extent by Leonardo (and his followers – Languschi-Dolfin, Pseudo-Sphrantzes, and the anonymous author of *Codex Barberinus Graecus 111*) has been uncritically accepted by some modern scholars, who also transform the grand duke into a villain. The most hostile modern portrait of Loukas Notaras has been that of the Marxist historian I. Kordatos in his popular (although highly speculative, rhetorical, misleading, and historically inaccurate) book, *Τὰ Τελευταῖα Χρόνια τῆς Βυζαντινῆς Αὐτοκρατορίας* (Athens, 1931), ch. 4.

197 Leonardo, *PG* 159: col. 930 (not included in *CC* 1).
198 The preparations of Mehmed II to create the first notable Ottoman armada were widely publicized. Kritoboulos 1.19.21 relates:

> πρὸ πάντων δὲ τοῦ ναυτικοῦ ἐπεμέλετο τριήρεις τὰς μὲν ἐκ νέου ναυπηγούμενος, τὰς δέ ... ἀνορθῶν ... ἔτι δὲ πλοῖα μακρὰ κατεσκεύαζε, τὰ δὲ καὶ κατάφρακτα, καὶ ταχείας ναῦς, τριακοντόρους τε καὶ πεντηκοντόρους ... πρὸς δὲ τούτοις ναυτικὸν συνέλεγεν ἐκ πάσης τῆς αὐτοῦ παραλίας Ἀσιανῆς τε καὶ Εὐρωπαίας.

199 Barbaro dates this event to the 13th of December and states that it took place on the same day as the celebration of the church union, but the Venetian physician had already erred with regard to this date. As we know, the union was celebrated a day earlier, on the 12th of December. Thus the date of the council must also fall on the 12th. Cf. the misstatement of Barbaro 5 [*CC* 1: 11]: *Adì 13 pur dezembrio fo praticado de retignir le galìe*

grosse de marcavo per conservation de Costantinopoli, e questa pratica fo fatta in la giexia de Santa Sofia.

200 *Ibid.*
201 *Ibid.* [*CC* 1: 11, 12].
202 Or was it the 13th of December? Cf. *supra*, n. 199.
203 Girolamo Minotto and his family were personally committed to the defense of Constantinople, a fact that was known to the sultan. During the siege, this family fought valiantly and its members were systematically executed upon an order of the sultan after the sack of the city. News of the fate of the Minotti was slow in reaching Venice and for a long time there was uncertainty as to their whereabouts. Marco Barbaro, *il genealogista*, enters the following note, dated 18 July 18 1453, to the journal of his relative, Nicolò:

> *Dopo presa la città, il Turco fece far cride, che chi avesse case in Costantinopoli gli dicesse, che egli le faria consegnare, et olti grechi et latini andarono a dirli dove erano le sue case, fra quali fu il nostro Bailo, e il Consolo Taragonense, et in vece delle case, il Turco feceli tagliar la testa, a esso Consolo, et a doi altri de' suoi, et al Bailo nostro et suo fiol, et a doi altri nostri nobeli.*

Girolamo Minotto had two sons who participated in the defense. Paolo was killed in battle; Zorzi and his father, Girolamo, were executed soon afterward, as Lomellino, the *podestà* of Pera notes, *CC* 1: 46: *Decapitari fecit* [Mehmed] *suis* [?] *diebus bailum Venetorum cum eius filio et aliis septem Venetis; et similiter consulem Catalanorum cum aliis quinque vel sex Catalanis*. News of their supposed captivity reached Venice in the guise of rumors and attempts were made to ransom Zorzi, who, it was believed as late as the beginning of August, was still alive and a prisoner of the sultan. On the other hand, no one could discover what had become of the wife of Girolamo Minotto during the sack. She appears to have simply vanished. Cf. *A.S.V. Senato Mar. R. 4*, fol. 202: *Cum omnibus notus sit miserabilis casus nobilis viri, ser Jeronimi Minotto, qui erat Baiulus Constantinopolis, qui sic ut habentur ductus est captivus in Turchia cum uxore et uno filio et perdidit omnem facultatem suam*. On the fate of the Minotti, cf. *PaL* 2: 133, 134 n. 87; and *CC* 1: 369, 370 n. 182. The most accurate information on the fate of the Minotti was brought to Venice by Catarino Contarini, another defender and also a prisoner of the Turks prior to being ransomed, who finally reached Venice by the 16th of August 1453. On him, cf. Stefano Magno, *NE* 3: 300:

> *Adì 16 agosto* [1453], *el venne con un grippo Cattarin Contarini da Constantinopoli, il quale se haveva scosso; per lo quale fu inteso della morte dada al bailo et suo fiolo et recuperation de i altri nostri Venetiani, et hebbe notitia del muodo del perder della cittade.*

The heroism of Girolamo in the defense of Constantinople has been noted by historians. Cf., e.g., C. Maltezou, *Ὁ Θεσμὸς τοῦ ἐν Κωνσταντινουπόλει Βενετοῦ Βαΐλου (1268–1453), Βιβλιοθήκη Σοφίας Ν. Σαριπόλου* 6 (Athens, 1970), pp. 51, 52:

> Οὐδεὶς ὅμως ἔδειξεν τὸ θάρρος τοῦ Gerolamo Minotto... [ὁ Minotto] ἐ[ν]όμιζεν ὅτι ἡ Βενετία θὰ ἐνίσχυε παντοιοτρόπως τὸν ἀγῶνα του... ἄνευ δὲ ἀναμονῆς ἀπαντήσεως,... ἀπηγόρευσε τὸν ἀπόπλουν τῶν βενετικῶν πλοίων καὶ ἐτάχθη εἰς τὴν ὑπηρεσίαν τοῦ αὐτοκράτορος... Θὰ ἠδύνατο νὰ ἀναμείνη τὴν ἐντολὴν τῆς μητροπόλεως, θὰ ἠδύνατο νὰ βοηθήση τοὺς ἀποίκους νὰ διαφύγουν τοῦ κλοιοῦ τῶν Τούρκων, θὰ ἠδύνατο τέλος ὁ ἴδιος νὰ λιποψυχήση. Ὅμως δὲν ἔπραξεν τοῦτο... Ὁ βάιλος προσέφερε τὴν βοήθειάν του, ὅτε ἡ χώρα του ἠρνήθη νὰ προσφέρη τὴν ἰδικήν της, ὁ βάιλος διὰ τῆς αὐτοθυσίας του ἔδειξεν εἰς τὴν Δύσιν, ὅτι ὤφειλε αὕτη νὰ εἶχε πράξει.

204 Barbaro 5 (not included in *CC* 1):

> *poi parla misser lo bailo digando: misser lo capetanio, io ve so confortar, perima per l'amor de Dio, e poi per honor de la cristianitade, e per honor de la signoria nostra de Veniexia, che vui dobiè romagnir qua in Costantinopoli a obedientia de l'imperador, e questo perchè la nostra signoria de Veniexia si l'avrà forte a bene de la romagnuda vostra.*

205 *Ibid.* 6 (not included in *CC* 1):

> *Come miser o bailo con i marcadanti intexe la opinion de miser lo capetanio, che el iera al tuo disposto de partirse in la dia hora, miser lo bailo con i marcadanti andò in terra, e lì fexe conseio de retegnir le galìe a defension de Costantinopoli, prima per l'amor de Dio, e può per honor de la cristianitade, in nel qual conseio fo reignude le galìe.*

Yet the Venetian authorities in Constantinople did not feel that this decree would prove a powerful deterrent to those wishing to leave. They eventually included a heavy financial penalty for anyone caught attempting to depart without authorization. Cf. Barbaro 7, 8 (not included in *CC* 1):

> *Abiando fato el conseio, che le galìe dovesse romagnir in Costantinopoli, non resta che i capetanii ad ogni modo voiana partirse, e pagar la pena de ducati 3000 per zascaduno, e però i marcadanti per prevalerse lor con sue mercadantie, convene far uno protesto, e protestar i capetanij che non se partisse.*

5 Defender, humanist, and survivor

1 Imperial councilor and legate

Isidore provides a summary of his experiences in Constantinople before the commencement of the siege in the first paragraph of his report to Pope Nicholas, which he composed soon after the fall of the city and his successful escape from the carnage. The opening paragraph of his *epistula*[1] reads as follows:

> *Postquam ego ab urbe Romana egressus sum, nonullas litteras Beatudini vestrae exposui et postissime de unione Graecorum cum ecclesia catholica facta et conclusa cum Deo esse, quae tamen iuxta tempus conveniens et condecibile facta est, nam valde delata et tardata est. Facta enim die XII mensis <Dece>mbris proxime elapsi tandem illa perfecta et conclusa, et tota urbs Constantinopolitana cum ecclesia catholica unita est et ubique commemorabatur Beatitudo vestra, postea reverendissimus patriarcha Gregorius, qui non solum tempore quo fuit in Constantinopoli in nulla altera ecclesia, verum et<iam> in suo monasterio nequaquam commemorabatur, verum, facta unione, tota urbs eum commemorabatur, ut fertur. Fuerunt enim omnes usque ad minorem una cum imperatore uniti et, gratia Dei, catholici usque ad horam et tempus nefandum ipsius desolationis et captivitatis urbis miserrimae Constantinopolitanae. Attamen Scholarius ille et alii octo monachorum sociorum suorum una cum eo unione praefata abalienaverunt se. Haec quidem omnia bene se ad certum tempus habebant.*

After I departed from the city of Rome, I drafted a few letters for Your Beatitude with regard to the union of the Greeks with the Catholic Church, which was accomplished and concluded with [the help of] God. You will find that it was done and concluded in a timely fashion, even though it had been delayed and postponed for such a long time. It was accomplished on the twelfth day of December of the last year. It was perfectly concluded and the entire city of Constantinople was united with the Catholic Church. Everywhere Your name was first commemorated and was followed by [the commemoration of the name of] the most reverend Patriarch Gregory (which had not ever been done in any church in Constantinople, including his own monastery) but, with the conclusion of the union, he was commemorated by the entire city, as it was said. All, to the last citizen, were united with the emperor and with the Catholics (thanks be to God!) until the horrible time and the hour of the destruction and captivity of the most miserable city of Constantinople. Yet, Scholarios and another eight monks, his associates, refused to participate in the union.[2] Such matters were accomplished in a satisfactory manner, up to a certain time.

His arrival had been controversial. While the Italian inhabitants were very respectful to him,[3] the Greek population must have felt nervousness and must have been suspicious of the true nature of the mission of Isidore, especially since he was accompanied by an armed contingent ostensibly to help in the upcoming siege. The populace may have viewed Isidore's mercenaries as his armed "gang" to enforce church union and to strengthen papal designs, demands, and will.

Girolamo Minotto, convinced the Venetians to stay and defend the harbor, but many of them did so unwillingly and problems continued throughout the siege.[4] We can state with confidence that Isidore played a key role in convincing the Venetians to remain and to defend the inner harbor of the Golden Horn. Apparently, the debate of 13 December achieved nothing; on the following day the cardinal and his friend Leonardo of Chios pressed their arguments again. In that debate, it should be noted, the emperor was not present, but evidently had entrusted his advisor to argue the case on behalf of the city. Again, the details are provided by Barbaro, who notes the importance of the cardinal in the course of the debate:[5]

> *In questo zorno, zoè di 14 dezembrio da può manzar, vene in galia da misser lo capetanio el reverendo gardenal de Rosia* [Isidore] *con el vescovo de Metelin* [Leonardo of Chios], *etiam ne vene misser lo bailo* [Girolamo Minotto] *con molti baroni del imperador e tutti nostri marcadanti . . . el gardinal se fo el primo che parla e dise; . . . non n'averemo dubito in questo inverno, che fuste de Turchi ne vegna a danizar el porto nostro, e a combater per altra via, e questo medemo si dise el vescovo de Metelin.*
>
> On that day, that is, December 14, after lunch, the reverend lord cardinal of Rus' [Isidore] with the bishop of Mytilene [Leonardo of Chios] came to the galley of the lord captain. The *bailo* [Girolamo Minotto] and many barons of the emperor, along with all our merchants also came . . . the cardinal was the first to speak and said: ". . . we have no doubt that the *fuste* [light ships] of the Turks will come and cause damage to our harbor. They will fight in every way." Similar arguments were voiced by the bishop of Mytilene.

Isidore was quite influential among this group. It was not just his prestige as a papal legate; the fact that he had contacts at the court must also have been factor. In addition, the primary reason that his arguments carried weight among the Venetians of Constantinople must have been the fact that Isidore had been granted Venetian citizenship and he was formally a citizen of Venice as well. For quite some time in the past decade he had been close to the Venetian Senate and he had been granted citizenship by the Grand Council on a vote of 637 to 19, with eight abstaining ballots, on 15 June 1443.[6]

The "barons" of the emperor further supported the arguments of the two churchmen, but it is doubtful that their words carried the same weight as the case presented by the churchmen and especially by the Venetian legate of the pope. It is perhaps significant that the counter-arguments of the Venetians were directed to the two churchmen, while, in their reply, the imperial courtiers seem to have been ignored and reference to them comes as an afterthought.[7] The Venetians added a threat when they simply stated that their galleys could depart on that very same night, with or without leave. This threat was taken seriously and the *bailo* called a council in the Venetian Church of San Marco of Constantinople, at which he applied pressure to retain the galleys and it was finally decided, by a vote of 21 in favor (with a single vote in opposition) to retain the galleys in Constantinople for the defense of the harbor. Thus the combination of efforts from the cardinal, the archbishop, and the *bailo*, won the day. The Venetian contingent proved invaluable in the defense of Constantinople and suffered enormous losses, both financial[8] and personal, during the sack and in the wave of executions that followed. Yet the decision enforced by the arguments of Isidore and by the steadfast nature of the *bailo* was not acceptable to all Venetians. In an effort to protect their cargo, some Venetian merchants, assisted by boat captains, drew up a document of formal protest,[9] signed by thirty-one individuals,[10] who however remained, in spite of their protest, to defend the city gallantly.

Having assisted in recruiting the local Venetians to protect the harbor and to guard the land and sea walls of Constantinople, Isidore turned his attention to a series of measures to renovate the walls and the defensive structures of the city.[11] It was indeed a major effort that occupied the administration until the beginning of the siege. The ancient fortifications had suffered a great deal of neglect over the centuries and they were in need of major repair, although efforts had been initiated during the reign of John VIII and of his successor Constantine XI to do something about the deplorable state of the major lines of defense. In the nineteenth century the surviving sections of the walls were surveyed and a number of inscriptions recording the repairs of 1453 were identified.[12] Some of the inscriptions mention the name of John VIII; a few include the name of his successor.

The reinforcement of the defenses was heavily handicapped by the inability of the court to pay for repairs.[13] In the days of Constantine XI[14] the imperial treasury was simply bankrupt and the emperor had to resort to desperate, albeit ineffective, measures to enrich his depleted finances. A typical attempt that proved fruitless is instructive. Constantine sought to impose a tariff on Venetian merchandise in Constantinople, mainly on wine and on imported hides. This desperate attempt to produce some funds for the court's depleted treasury met with incredible resistance from the emperor's Venetian allies and fellow residents[15] and from the official envoy from Venice, Nicolò da Canale, who later was destined to play a major role in the Levant.[16] Da Canale even threatened to abandon Constantinople unless the proposed taxes were rescinded.[17] In October of 1450 Constantine explained his actions to the doge and pointed out that his treasury was empty.[18] The Latin translation of the emperor's letter (dated the 23rd of October 1450) to the doge has survived.[19] Constantine explained his imposition of the tax as *pro utilitate urbis*, "for the welfare of the city."[20] This measure was finally rescinded and no funds entered the treasury.

Nothing seemed to alleviate the financial situation and no resources could be found.[21] By 1453 the situation had become desperate. In the period before the commencement of the siege and during the siege itself, the problems were so compounded that the emperor was left with no other choice but to "borrow" from churches and from dedicatory offerings. Eyewitnesses, who were moved by the emperor's pathetic actions, justified this emergency measure by appealing to precedents in antiquity and in accordance with the prevailing humanistic principles of the period. Leonardo describes these desperate measures to raise hard cash and cites similar emergency measures that had been taken long ago.[22]

What exacerbated this nightmare was also the fact that some of the prominent individuals in Constantinople, who were reputed to be extremely wealthy, also proved unwilling to contribute to the defense.[23] A typical example is afforded by Loukas Notaras,[24] the court's grand duke and the effective prime minister of the emperor, who was reputed to be immensely wealthy and who had heavily invested his fortune in Italian institutions. His investments had assured his daughters and one surviving son of a comfortable life in Italy after the fall of the imperial city. Notaras, however, was accused of having failed to contribute to the defense of Constantinople. By the 1470s charges of treason had mounted up[25] and Notaras's surviving daughter sought the services of a minor humanist in a futile attempt to rehabilitate her late father's reputation.[26] While the specific citation of Notaras may or may not be fair, it is simply a reflection of the general situation, in which individuals of means and of the upper classes simply failed to contribute to the common good for various reasons. We do not know how Notaras justified his position to deny his funds for the defense.[27] It is possible that the bulk of his fortune had been invested and transported to Italy with other members of his family, who had departed in the days before the siege. After the fall he was justly or unjustly accused of hoarding his wealth in order to donate it to the sultan, in a pathetic attempt to win his favor. This attempt, if it occurred at all, ultimately failed, as Notaras was a prominent victim in Mehmed's wave of executions following the sack.[28] In general terms, the emperor's inability to secure funds from his citizens for the defense of Constantinople was also noted by Barbaro's relative, Marco Barbaro, who supplied notes to the text of the journal and it must have been a well-known item in circulation among the population during the siege.[29]

It must have been a welcome relief to the emperor to find an individual willing to contribute to the defense fund. Isidore seems to be the only volunteer whose name is actually recorded as a contributor. The cardinal must have noted the dilapidated conditions of the fortifications during his previous trip and when he arrived with his contingent in 1452 he may have made provisions to transfer funds to assist in this endeavor. It is notable that he makes no mention of his contribution and never takes any credit for restoring a section of the fortifications.[30] We owe this information to the narrative of his friend and associate Leonardo, who states this fact a number of times in his narrative and suggests that the cardinal's funds were a personal contribution from his own money and not from the Roman Church. Thus Leonardo relates:[31] *Hieronymus Italianus, Leonardus de Langasco, Genuenses, cum multis sociis Chsyloportam et turres, quas Anemadas vocant impensis cardinalis reparatas, spectabant,* "Hieronymus the Italian, Leonardo de Langasco, and the Genoese with many allies defended Xyloporta ['Wooden Gate'] and the Anemades[32] Towers, which had been repaired with funds from the cardinal." Xyloporta[33] and the Anemades Towers are located to the north of the fortifications and west of the Golden Horn, an area that also received the attention of the Venetians before the commencement of the siege, for it seems to have been a weak sector, probably because of the absence of a moat and the reality that there was a single line of fortifications defending mainly the sector around the palace of Blakhernai. In addition to this problem, Greek laborers refused to assist in the repairs that were immediately needed during the siege unless they were to be paid at once in hard currency.[34]

The exceptional example of Isidore being willing to contribute to the defense from his personal funds is contrasted by Leonardo with the unwillingness of the locals to help in strengthening their own city against the enemy:[35]

> *Sed, o Graecorum impietatem, o patriae proditores, o avaros! quos cum saepenumero lacrymis perfusus inops imperator rogasset ut pro militibus conducendis pecuniam mutuarent, jurabant se inopes, exhaustos penuria temporum, quos posthac ditissimos hostis invenit. A paucis nihilominus quaedam ultronea oblatio est. Cardinalis Hercle omne studium adhibuit in ferenda ope, in firmandis turribus et muro.*
>
> Oh the impiety of the Greeks! What traitors to their fatherland! Avaricious individuals! How often did your emperor beg you, with tears in his eyes, to lend him money to hire mercenaries, and you swore that you were destitute, impoverished in these times of poverty! Yet the enemy discovered that you were so rich. Yet there were some voluntary contributions by a few individuals. By Hercules, there was the cardinal who spared no effort to render assistance in strengthening the walls and towers.

Exactly how Isidore made his contribution available for the repair of these towers is not known. Nevertheless it was a noteworthy expense, as another friend of Isidore tells us that the cardinal expended all he had on the repairs and had even resorted to selling his own vestments for the purpose.[36] One hopes that Isidore's contribution was spent appropriately, as there were again many rumors after the fall that the contractors, who had been entrusted with the renovations on the walls, had taken advantage of their position and had appropriated most of the funds for themselves to the detriment of the repairs that they had been hired to complete. An inscription on the walls has preserved the name of a contractor: Manuel Iagaris, who had been placed in charge of repairs during the months preceding the siege.[37] After the sack Iagaris was accused in the literature of the period of enriching himself at the expense of the repairs and of the general welfare. Iagaris was a member of the court and a few years earlier had been a member of the delegation that offered the crown to Constantine XI at Mistra.[38] Leonardo accuses Manuel Iagaris and his associate, the rabid anti-unionist hieromonk Neophytos from Rhodes, of blatant misconduct in the repairs of the fortifications. The archbishop includes a sardonic observation: their profits fell ultimately into the hands of the Turks and they failed to enjoy their ill-gotten gains.[39] We can only hope that the funds contributed by Isidore were put to good use and did not go into the coffers of the scheming contractors. During the siege the sector that was reinforced was not one of the primary targets of the Ottoman army, but it did come under attack late in the siege and was valiantly defended by Girolamo Minotto and his Venetians. This sector was never breached.[40]

Isidore was also assigned another area to defend during the siege.[41] Again our information is derived from his friend and close associate, Leonardo, who informs us that the cardinal defended the area about the Monastery of Saint Demetrios.[42] Isidore had been the abbot of that monastery before his appointment as metropolitan of Kiev and the Rus' Church. His familiarity with the monastery and its neighborhood must have been one of the deciding factors. Another contributing factor to his appointment to this command could have been that the area was defended by Loukas Notaras,[43] who may have come under suspicion by the court, because of his contacts within the Ottoman camp. So it was whispered in the city during the siege.[44] Further, Notaras had openly quarreled with the valiant *condotierre*, Giovanni Guglielmo Longo Giustiniani, Constantine XI's commander in chief at the critical sector on the western fortifications (the sector including the Gate of Saint Romanos and the Pempton) on the eve of the general assault. The issue between the two men was the question of the transfer of cannon from the relative safety of the sea walls commanded by Loukas Notaras to the dangerous sector of the land fortifications under the command of Giustiniani.[45] Could it be that in addition to the defense of the Saint Demetrios sector, Isidore was also meant to maintain a watchful eye over Notaras and over other monks and priests assigned to the defense of the sea walls[46] who were under the influence of anti-unionists and were not exactly pleased with the task assigned to them by the unionist administration? The sector of Saint Demetrios, as we have noted, was not a major target of the Ottoman army nor navy and Isidore was eventually able to leave his position on the day of the sack and to proceed to the neighborhood of Santa Sophia apparently without encountering any difficulty. He was eventually wounded, not at his sector, but in the immediate neighborhood of Santa Sophia.

2 Warrior and reporter

The exact activities of Isidore during the period of the siege are not known. He has not reported on these duties and in his surviving writings he appears self-effacing, as he also fails to mention his monetary contributions to the defense and his reinforcement of the walls. Leonardo provides a few passing notes. He states, for instance, that Isidore attended all meetings of the high command[47] and, consequently, must have been well informed concerning strategy and operations that were planned at the headquarters of the emperor and his officers, including the presence of Giustiniani, who was in charge of the most critical sector in the Mesoteikhion. Furthermore, Isidore was either accompanied by Leonardo to those meetings or Leonardo was kept informed by Isidore with regard to the daily decisions. Leonardo must have implicitly trusted his fellow churchman. If it were otherwise, he would not have known some important information that he has passed on to us. This information is not duplicated in other sources, whose writers were in Constantinople but had no direct contacts within the court. Thus, some of Leonardo's information comes from intimate knowledge of what was decided at these strategic sessions of the command, which Isidore must have discussed with him, while Barbaro, Ubertino Pusculo, Giacomo Tetaldi, and Benvenuto of Ancona, who were present in Constantinople, but were not members of the high command, fail to replicate. Isidore, therefore, must have been one of the sources, if not the main source, for Leonardo's account of the siege, who then went on to produce what has become the *regina narrationum* of the siege among historians.[48]

Undoubtedly, it was through Isidore that Leonardo[49] learned that Mehmed's grand vizier, Halil Çandarlı, whose friendly attitude towards the Greeks and their defense against the Ottoman army was generally known, was also informing the Constantinopolitan high command of the sultan's plans for offensive operations,[50] a fact that outside the court was not widely known throughout the city, but was suspected at the Porte. Eventually, Halil paid with his life for his treacherous activities. Apparently Loukas Notaras informed on Halil, whose correspondence he may have hoarded, in his attempt to gain favor with the sultan, as reported by Leonardo.[51] Leonardo further mentions that the sultan's vizier communicated with the Constantinopolitan court on this occasion, but the implication is that he had done so throughout the siege:[52] *Frequentes enim epistolae ad imperatorem ex Calilbascia portabantur,*[53] "frequently letters from Halil Pasha kept arriving." Leonardo either knew of this information by attending the court's strategy sessions himself as a "friend" of Isidore or the cardinal had communicated this information to him.

It is unknown whether Isidore personally took up arms and fought on the walls. He and Leonardo never mention their own activities on the walls. Nevertheless, Isidore was aware of the historical importance of the siege[54] and made detailed notes of the operations throughout the siege, as he relates in his letter to his friend, Cardinal Bessarion:[55] *Scripsi quoque pariter super omnia, mores ipsius Turci et curam eius ac vigilantiam ad totum orbem terrarum su<a>e dicioni subigendum et Christi nomen de terra delendum radicitus,* "I took notes about everything: the customs of the Turk himself and his care and vigilance to subjugate the entire world and to eradicate the name of Christ from the earth." Whether these notes survived or not remains unknown, for Isidore experienced numerous adventures before he reached safety one month after the sack. There is a statement in his letter to Bessarion that suggests that he had nothing to consult and that he remained confused and dazed,[56] even one month after the fall, when he was still unable to gather his thoughts and concentrate on what had really taken place. He suggests, nevertheless, that his information in this letter is not complete and that he intended to make available the details in person when he saw his friend. There are also indications that he withheld information on purpose. He was presumably unwilling to put certain events and incidents in writing; again he suggests that he will convey this information orally, and in person.[57]

During the siege Isidore and Leonardo must have observed operations together and must have discussed their significance in comparison to what they knew of antiquity. This may explain why similar comparisons appear in their narratives. They both compare Mehmed II to Alexander the Great and it is in Isidore's letter that we encounter the first attempt to connect Mehmed II with Alexander the Great. This comparison is also repeated in other letters of Isidore.[58] Leonardo was an ecclesiastic with strong humanistic tendencies and he was well known among the active lovers of antiquity during the *quattrocento*.[59] Leonardo was indeed aware of the comparison between Mehmed and Alexander, but chose not to utilize it frequently in his account. He only contrasts the sultan to the Macedonian king once, in connection with the sultan's crucial council, in the course of which Mehmed was persuaded by his advisors to launch the final assault on 29 May and to abandon all thoughts of a planned withdrawal. Once the young sultan makes his decision to launch the assault, he compares himself, in Leonardo's narrative, to Alexander the Great. Languschi-Dolfin follows suit and inserts the actual name of "the Macedonian." Significantly, Makarios Melissourgos-Melissenos omits reference to Alexander, while the text of the early seventeenth-century follower of Leonardo, the anonymous author of the *Codex Barberinus 111*, furnishes a more faithful paraphrase of Leonardo (and more accurately, via Sansovino's Italian translation of Leonardo's Latin account).

Leonardo also makes an indirect reference to Alexander the Great without declaring his name. He compares Mehmed's Janissaries to Alexander's bodyguard, presumably the *hypaspistai*, and amusingly, albeit erroneously, refers to them as the *Myrmidones*.[60] He then expresses the opinion that the "Myrmidones" can be equated with the famous Ottoman regiments, known in Turkish as *yeni çeri* or "new army," hence the Janissaries. On another occasion Leonardo portrays the sultan comparing himself to Alexander.[61] Is it more than coincidental that Cardinal Isidore uses a similar phrase:[62] *regem Alexandrum admirandum Macedonem cum minori potential subiuga<vi>sse totum orbem*, in his correspondence? This common phrase and shared sentiment may reflect an echo of actual conversations between the cardinal and his friend during the siege, while they were comparing notes on the operations and their significance.

Another comparison that the two churchmen share, which probably derives from their conversations during the siege, invokes the name of the Great King of Persia, Xerxes. The earliest writer to draw a comparison between the sultan and the great king is Isidore in his correspondence from Crete. He does so in one of his letters to Bessarion. This report is the initial reference and consequently a historically significant account of the siege operations. Isidore likens the floating bridge that the sultan constructed, denying absolute command of Constantinople's harbor to the Venetian defenders and threatening the sea walls of the city, to the bridge across the Hellespont that Xerxes had assembled in order to transfer his army to the European continent.[63] Isidore returns to the same topic in his letter of 8 July to Pope Nicholas V, and states that Mehmed's bridge did survive the siege and still remains standing in place at the time of his composition.[64] Leonardo also makes a similar comparison, in the same context.[65] He additionally furnishes a detailed description, including the measurements of the sultan's pontoon structure.[66] What is also of significance here is that another eyewitness of the siege, the classically minded Pusculo, also touches on Xerxes. Is it possible that the comparison initiated by Isidore and Leonardo had become a commonplace within Constantinople during the period of the siege and was even picked up by Pusculo? The mention of Xerxes in Leonardo clearly echoes Isidore and various other items that the two clerics discussed between themselves during the siege. Pusculo's references to Xerxes[67] implies that during the siege the association of Mehmed to Xerxes may have circulated among the defenders, Greeks and Italians alike. The reference to Xerxes is specific, as it applies to Mehmed's stratagem of a floating bridge, which in the final analysis was not comparable, in scale and size, to the bridge that the Great King had built across the Hellespont in the fifth century or to the channel that he cut across the peninsula of Mount Athos. The sudden fame of the Great King seems then to be a late phenomenon in Byzantine literature and we wonder about the origins of this perspective, which may ultimately find roots in "popular" prophecies and folk beliefs.[68]

Among the corpus of Isidore's letters, there are four epistles that bear a direct connection to the fall of Constantinople, to his adventures, and to the events that he had witnessed. Of the four letters the most significant is the earliest, which was written soon after Isidore had reached the safe haven of Candia, on 6 July. The original letter was composed in Greek, as it had been directed to Bessarion. The original Greek text has disappeared. We know that the surviving Latin text was rendered by a humanist in Italy as his exercise in translation from the Greek, a fact that the translator himself declares in a note.[69] On the same day another letter translated from Greek into Latin was dispatched from Candia. This letter was translated into Italian by the notary Pasio di Bertipaglia of Candia.[70] It is unknown whether Pasio translated a version of this text that was articulated by Isidore or whether he accomplished his translation from a written Greek version of this letter that had been presented to him by Isidore.[71] Soon afterwards, Isidore finished his formal report to Pope Nicholas V. It was accomplished as stated in the heading on the 8th of July,[72] but in its conclusion the 15th of July is cited.[73] Perhaps it took some days for a translation into Latin to be completed. We do not know the name of the translator, but Isidore could have availed himself of numerous bilingual humanists who were resident on Candia. The *incipit* of the letter suggests that it was given (in written form or dictated in Greek?) at the home of a notary who applied his seal.[74] It should further be noted that before Isidore composed these letters he took no respite from his adventures.[75] He seems to have provided oral accounts of his adventures and of the fall of Constantinople to various individuals on Candia whenever the situation demanded. It is also probable that he even produced a public oral recitation on the fall of the city. Thus a letter precedes Isidore's account of the 6th of July by one day[76] and was composed by a resident of Candia, Fra Girolamo of Florence, who was vicar of the Minorites in Crete. Another important associate of Isidore in Crete was the Venetian humanist Lauro Quirini, who obtained information from the cardinal, as he states,[77] and then utilized this evidence in his long letter of the 15th of July[78] to the pope.[79] Thus the remainder of the letters that Isidore composed at this time belong to his campaign of propaganda intended to ring the alarm bells among European leaders. He seems to have hoped for their intervention against the sultan.[80] He final composition is a letter to the duke of Burgundy, at a later date (the 22nd of February 1455), that adds no new information.[81]

We have selected two letters, to Bessarion and to the pope,[82] to quote presently, as they represent some of the earliest accounts, which have not been consistently quoted or utilized in modern scholarship. Yet, they represent the observations of a primary eyewitness. Together with the text of Leonardo, whose importance has always been valued and has been utilized, they become some of the more valuable early impressions of an individual who had participated in the siege, had been familiar with the headquarters of the defense, and had suffered during the sack of the city.

3 Two letters of Isidore

1 Isidore's letter to Cardinal Bessarion

Epistola rev<erendissi>mi d<omini> cardinalis Ruteni scripta ad rev<erendissi>mum d<ominum> Bessarionem episcopum Tusculanum cardinalem Nic<a>enum Bonnoni<a>e legatum. Capta Constantinopoli, idem cardinalis Rutenus e manibus Turcorum in Cretam insulam profugit. De gr<a>eco in latinum conversa.

Rev<erendissi>me in Christo pater et domine, salutem in omnibus plurimam.

1 *Saepenumero anteactis temporibus ad vestram reverentiam scriptitavi, a qua nec responsionem quidem ullam accepi; quid in causa fuerit, ignoro. Illud coniectare licet: aut meae tibi redditae non sunt aut ad me tuae non sunt delatae baiulorum forte negligentia, quod etiam bello et rerum asperitati tribuere possumus, aut, quod tertio loco relinquitur, tua nobis irata est atque adversatur reverentia, quemadmodum et Deus ipse, qui se quasi gravem, infestum praebuisse videtur illi miserrim<a>e atque infelicissim<a>e urbi et civitati, qu<a>e quondam erat et ab impiis quoque et atrocissimis infidelibus appellabatur Constantinopolis, nunc vero pessimo fato Turcopolis, cuius ego memor rivos profundo iuges atque incessabiles lacrimarum. Manus*

pr<a>eterea me dius fidius calamitates eius exarans vix moveri potest, mens mea tanquam hominis extra se positi ac paene insensati desidet continue, si quidem deambulans, iacens, stans, sedens, dormiens, vigilans, fontes lacrimarum emitto.

2 *Et per immortalem Deum, cuius oculis patent et manifesta sunt omnia, saepius ac saepius illum execratus sum ac maledixi crudelem ex Turcis, qui me sagitta fixit atque in sinistra capitis parte vulneravit ante ianuam cuiusdam monasterii, non tam acriter tamen ut eadem hora mihi vitam eripuerit, propterea quia eques eram et attonitus et spiculum ipsum magna in parte vires amiserat; sed me Deus, opinor, servare voluit, ut reliquas omnes tales ac tantas infortunatissim<a>e illius urbis adversitates conspiciam.*

3 *Repetamus enim ab <a>eterno cum plurimarum civitatum et parvarum et maximarum casus et ruin<a>e in diversis mundi partibus olim fuisse legantur, nulla unquam fuit, quae Constantinopolitan<a>e possit expugnationi ac direptioni comparari. Non Troi<a>e populatio, non Thebarum eversio, non Hierosolymorum trina destructio, non Antiochi<a>e, non Rom<a>e, non Alexandri<a>e, non cuiusvis alterius sive maioris sive minoris civitatis. Sed haec in praesentiarum recensere longum esset nec tempus plura patitur; postquam vero ad vos duce Domino venire constitui, pr<a>esens multa explicabo, qu<a>e litterarum ac epistol<a>e modum superant. Nunc paucula tantum perstringam, ut compendiose rei summam teneatis. Sic autem res se habet.*

4 *Cum circam mensem Maii superioris anni Romam reliquissem, nullum penitus inde pr<a>esidium vel auxilium referens, quam melius potui me ad iter paravi et profecto de urbe ipsa exiens, primo, ut aiunt, calcari et passu, omnia mihi adverse atque infeliciter succedere ceperunt. Omitto autem nunc singula. Tantisper sex menses in itinere cucurrerunt, cum vix et tandem sextum et vigesimum mensis Octobris diem ad infelicissimam urbem Constantinopolim pervenimus, hoste ac ferro clausam et undique circumseptam.*

5 *Quid igitur dixerim fecerimque ac mente volverim, non facile verbis aut scriptis complecti possem. Duorum mensium spatio classis coacta est atque adunata Christianorum ac perfecte et inviolate unita, quemadmodum et alias bis scripsi ad vestram reverentiam et quidem abunde satis et late. Cum autem res Christianorum splendide ac secunde procedere videbantur, quamvis et Turcorum quoque solertia pugnandi contra civitatem non cessaret [et] ardens studium et inexplicabile desiderium. Scripsi quoque pariter super omnia, mores ipsius Turci et curam eius ac vigilantiam ad totum orbem terrarum su<a>e dicioni subigendum et Christi nomen de terra delendum radicitus. Id enim mente sua exagitans commentatur et manum fortem pr<a>eparat ac exercitum et classem innumeram, peditum simul et equitum circiter trecentorum milium iudicatam, triremes, biremes and uniremes viginti et ducentas et navem unam onerariam sive rotundam; fabros omnes, telorum omne genus, instrumenta qu<a>eque mechanica et fabrilia congregat et exaggerat, qu<a>e ad capiendas et expugnandas urbes apta iudicantur, tormenta qu<a>evis, bombardas, catapultas et plurimas et maximas, ut eorum moles, monstra et portenta iudicares, quibus tandem Constantinopoli potitus est.*

6 *Inter cetera vero infinita tormenta, catapultas sive bombardas, tres erant, quarum prima quatuordecim talentorum lapidem proiciebat, altera duodecim, tertia*

decem. Cum autem reliquas omnes minores densiatas et fortitudo murorum substinerent, vires illarum trium et verbera crebro et assidue concutientium m<o>enia tollerare non poterant. Ad secundum enim ictum maxima pars deiecta est atque decussa murorum cum ipsis turribus. Tunc autem intelleximus perfectum esse atque impletum vetus oraculum, quod diu nostris annalibus servatum est, dicens: Vae tibi, civitas septicollis, cum te adolescens obsederit, quia tua m<o>enia fortissima demolita fuerint.

7 Subvertit itaque muros circa portam Sancti Romani et pr<a>eterea eam partem qu<a>e inter portas Fontis et Auream nuncupatas et antiquam Ventur<a>e portam erant et alteram qu<a>e Caligariorum appellabatur, apud quam dum accerrime pugnaretur fortissimus ille Theodorus Carystenus, irrumpentibus in urbem hostibus se opponens generose ac summa fortitudinis gloria occubuit. Totius enim circuitus pars illa debilior erat. Alia etiam plurima et maxima et terribilia breviter attingam.

8 Primum quidem cum validissimis catenis portus esset accinctus et clausus a parte montis Galat<a>e usque ad portam Pulchram triremes Venetorum quinque cum duodecim aliis onerariis sive rotundis navibus et quidem maximis portui et catenis mire Turcorum introitum prohibebant. Turci vero cum se illic frustra consistere animadvertent, in Dipplocioniam stationem se cum eorum navibus transtulerunt, ubi et classem instruxerunt. Paucis vero post diebus viam montanam trium milium passuum et ultra sterni iussit Turcus ad transiendas ab una parte montis Galat<a>e in alteram biremes et soliremes nonaginta duas, quas cum in portu eo modo traiecisset, portu potitus est et eius totaliter factus est dominus. Aliud iterum mirabilius est machinatus, quod et Xerxes quondam fecisse memoratur: pontem siquidem construxit et fabricavit maximum a mari Sanct<a>e Galatin<a>e usque ad m<o>enia Cynegi, quod duplo maius est spatium quam illius Hellespontiaci olim pontis a Xerxe fabricati, per quem non modo pedites verum etiam equites multi simul traducebantur.

9 Alium et tertium modum aggressus contra urbem versus portam Caligariorum a longe cuniculos quinque et subterraneos dolos effodit, per quos in urbem aditus pateret. Cumque ad murorum usque ac turri<u>m fundamenta applicuissent atque ipsa iam excidere conarentur, nostri pariter intus ex amussim de directri correspondentes cuniculos effoderunt. Sicque hostes ea parte fugati sunt atque depulsi et de melioribus multi sunt interempti cessavitque illius partis oppugnatio.

10 Machinamenta vero, moles, tormenta, catapultas et instrumenta, qu<a>e nunc falconia nominantur, quis enarraverit? Scalas <si>quidem amplius trecentas compegit, aggeres quoque ac terr<a>e tumulos instar collium ante muros congessit, castella pra<e>terea vastissimorum lignorum erexit, turres urbis exteriores ex<s>uperantia. Aliam insuper machinam excogitavit inauditam quidem et nostris temporibus numquam visam; forma enim quadranguli et solidissima, intus vacuam, domui cuipiam similem, et arte interna hominum inclusorum et rotarum cuilibet angulo suppositarum funibusque illigatis et aliis instrumentis volubilibus mobilem atque mire conducibilem, super quam scal<a>e imposit<a>e deferebantur, qu<a>e res opus effingebat Archimedis et Heronis, quod de per se et a casu moveri videbatur. Scal<a>e autem summitates murorum ac turrium <a>equantes tot<a>e erant tabulis circumquaque vallat<a>e, ne offendi possent ascensores ab his, qui m<o>enibus insidebant. Dicerem autem alia plura sed, ne fastidiosus sim, multa nunc omitto.

11 Inter haec quinquaginta et tres dies Turcus consumpsit Constantinopolim obsidens nec quicquam perfecit. Sed cum omnis cognitionis illud difficillimum est, quod futurum est, nobis oculos mentis occ<a>ecavit, illi vero ita aperuit, ut Martem potentissimum ac diem et horam eius accuratissime observaverit; habet enim diligentissimos astrologos Persas, quorum consiliis ac iudicio fretus summa qu<a>eque ac maxima sese consecuturum sperat. Vigessimo itaque nono die mensis Maii proxime peracti aurora illuscente, solis etiam radiis nostros oppugnantibus, mari ac terra urbem invadentes Turci ad eam partem maxime semiruptam circa Sanctum Romanum assiluerunt, ubi multi erant fortes viri Latini et Gr<a>eci absque tamen rege ac imperatore ipsorum, qui iam ab hostibus vulneratus ac trucidatus fuerat eiusque caput Turco postea dono datum est, qui eo viso plurimum ex<s>ultavit atque illi petulanti ludibrio improperavit et continuo in Andri<a>nopolim triumphandum misit.

12 Erat autem cum imperatore illo ductor quidam nomine Ioannes Iustinianus, quem multi incusant primam fuisse causam tant<a>e captivitatis et excidii: sed omittamus. Facilis autem erat in ea parte ad m<o>enia ascensus, quia, ut dictum est, quasi tota erat bombardis illisa ac prope decussa, propter quod et facile hostes in urbem irruperant, nemine illic invento, qui hostium impetum reprimeret aut eam partem defenderet.

13 Monstri autem simile erat civitatem ipsam totam pugnantem muris intus et extra oppugnatam. Illi quidem, qui in coenobiis erant, cum intellexerunt captam esse atque amissam totam urbem, enses et arma omnes abiciebant et servilem ac miserabilem diem aspiciebant pr<a>eter heroicos et fortes illos viros, qui et cominus ferientes et vulnerati moriebantur. Declarare autem tibi illius miserrimae urbis calamitates neque possum nec me conantem lacrim<a>e sinunt. O inexplicabilem ac funestum et execrabilem diem! O vocem crudelissimam atque deterrimam, quam ter in exercitu truculentissimus Turcus proclamavit miserandam civitatem illam pr<a>edam ac populationem et direptionem liberam Turcorum fore, cum primum capta esset, ut eos promptiores atque constantiores ad obsidionem redderet.

14 Vi<a>e quidem omnes strat<a>e ac angiporti sanguine et cruore fluentes cadaveribus c<a>esorum ac interfectorum erant plen<a>e. Trahebantur de domibus nobiles atque ingenu<a>e mulieres, reste ad collum ligat<a>e, serva simul et domina et nudis pedibus, quam plurim<a>e, filii quoque ac sorores eorum rapti atque a patribus divisi et matribus hinc et inde abducebantur. Videres autem Turcorum mancipia et servos vilissimos rapere atque distrahere delicatas illas atque pr<a>eclarissimas virgines s<a>eculares pariter et monachas (o sol et terra!), non tanquam boves aut pecudes vel aliquod aliud mansuetum atque domesticum animal, sed veluti gregem inmanium silvestrium et atrocium ferarum indomitarum in mediis gladiis percussoribus ac spiculatoribus et gladiatoribus circumstipatas ex urbe abstrahi.

15 Quid autem opus est omne vituperium, quicquid de templorum profanatione et spurcissimis inquinamentis sacrarum rerum fecerint, dicere? Quamprimum in templo quod Sanct<a>e Sophi<a>e appellabatur (nunc autem Turcicum masgidium), statuas omnes, iconas et imagines Christi, sanctorum ac sanctarum deiecerunt et confregerunt, omne vituperium in eas exercentes. Tabu<la>e quoque suggesti et aris atque altaribus insilientes furibundi ac ex<s>ultantes fidem nostram et sacrificia

Christiana deludebant et Mahometto laudes et hymnos decantabant. Sacrarii quoque postibus confractis sacra omnia et reliquias sanctas corripientes veluti vilissima et abiecta proiciebant. Quid autem in calycibus et consecratis vasis et pannis effecerint, silentio pr<a>etereatur. Mandelia quoque aurea et tabulas Christi et sanctorum imagines habentia, partim canibus, partim equis pro pr<a>es<a>epibus proponebant. Evangelia vero et ecclesiasticos libros pedibus conculcabant. <A>edificia item marmorea lucidissima atque splendidissima contrita sunt atque confracta omnia et idem in omnibus aliis templis factum est, ut nec sepulc<h>ris quidem marmoreis ullis pepercerint; quando omnia concusserint atque attriverint, pavimenta etiam ecclesiarum destructa et contusa et demum ea cuique summa voluptas et libido era<n>t in sacra maximum s<a>evire ac deformia et turpissima qu<a>eque reddere. Quis autem enumerare posset bona, res et supellectilia, quae primarum aedium ac domorum foribus concisis discerpebantur? Et sic una eademque lux et dies in <a>eternum memoranda et deflenda civitatem opulentissimam, magnificentissimam, illustrissimam, divinam penitus, evacuatam et deletam funditus vidit. Nihil enim reliquum fuit, quod non in manus impias Turcorum cum captivis pervenerit.

16 Non multos post dies Turcus omnes primores civitatis redemit simulans velle eos urbem inhabitare et in spem vit<a>e illos adducebat. Post tres dies decrevit ac iussit primo quidem duobus filiis Notar<a>e (alter enim gloriose dimicans interierat) capita in conspectu patris amputari, ipsi deinde patri, postea magni domestici filios tres pulcherrimos et optimos occidit et insuper patrem eorum. Dehinc illustrem dominum Nicholaum Gredetam <Goudelem?> et plurimos alios pr<a>eclarissimos viro interemit. Fecit autem et alia plurima et horrenda, dum etiam illic essem, quae longum esset enarrare.

17 Quomodo autem impias manus effugerim, brevi cognosces cum Italiam pervenero; perdisces enim tunc omnia. Cum autem in Italiam Turcus omnino transire deliberat cum fortissima manu exercituque maximo, trecentas enim triremes et parvas et magnas implevisse dinoscitur et naves onerarias maximas amplius quam viginti, pedestrem etiam exercitum et equestrem numero infinitum, et h<a>ec tu quidem vera puta, ego futura non dubito. Alexandri siquidem vitam quotidie audit arabice, gr<a>ece et latine.

18 Eapropter confestim ex Creta naviculam dimittens per fratrem Iohannem litteras dedi ad sanctissimum dominum nostrum papam et ad sacrum collegium cardinalium, item et ad regem Aragonum et ad maximas quasque Italiae civitates, quemadmodum et ad vestram Bononiam, hortans, excitans ac provocans eos, ut oculos ac mentem dirigant ad horum infidelium destructionem. Unde et vestra reverentia pariter dignetur occurrere ad hoc salutiferum, pium ac necessarium, opus, quam diutissime salvam et incolumem exopto.

Tu<a>e in omnibus reverenti<a>e
Isidorus cardinalis

In Creta, die sexta Iulii anno Domini M°CCCC°LIII°.
Finis. Τέλος. Ἀμήν.

Isidore to Bessarion

A Letter Written by the Most Reverend Ruthenian Cardinal
  To the Most Reverend Lord Bessarion, the Nicene Bishop of Tuscany and Legate to Bologna.

The Same Ruthenian Cardinal Escaped from the Hands of the Turks
  After the Capture of Constantinople and Fled to the island of Crete.
  It has been translated into Latin from the Greek.

1 On a number of occasions in the past I wrote numerous letters to Your Reverence, but I never received a reply. I know not the reasons for this but I may attribute it either to the possibility that my letters were not delivered or to the possibility that your letters never reached me, due to official negligence brought about by the cruel war. The third possibility is that Your Reverence may be angry and irritated with me, as is God Himself who seems to have shown His heavy and hostile side to that most wretched and hapless city and state, which was once called, even by savages and infidels, Constantinople but now, with the worst of luck, is known as Turkople. Its memory makes me groan deeply and makes me shed tears to no end. By god, its trials have paralyzed my arms. I seem to have lost my mind, as if I were an individual beside himself, forever unaware of his senses. I give forth fountains of tears when I walk, when I lie down, when I stand, when I sit, when I sleep, or when I am awake.

2 In the name of the immortal God, whose unsleeping eyes see everything, again and again do I curse and consign to hell that cruel Turk who pierced the left side of my head with an arrow in front of that legendary monastery [Santa Sophia]. It was not a serious wound that would claim my life, because I was on horseback and stunned, and the bolt was spent and had lost its force for the most part. Indeed, it is my opinion, God wished to save me so that I could witness all the remaining trials and disgrace of that most unhappy city.

3 We read in books that since the beginning of the world so many cities, both great and insignificant, in all parts of the world fell into ruin and yet the fate of none of them can be compared with the sack and rape of Constantinople, not the destruction of Troy, not the destruction of Thebes, not the three demolitions of Jerusalem, not that of Antioch, of Rome, of Alexandria, or of whatever other great or small city may come to mind. It is too much of a task to speak in detail and it would make too long a tale. Later I will give a detailed account in person but not in this letter, as I have decided to come to you, God willing. For now I will speak of a very few matters only, so that you may form a summary impression of what has occurred. Here is what happened.

4 When I left Rome in May of the previous year, bringing with me neither soldiers nor substantial aid, I had prepared myself to face a better journey; but as soon as I left the city [Rome], at my very first steps, as they say, I fell into waves of adversity and bad luck. I will not speak of every individual instance for now. And so my voyage stretched into six months and I only managed to reach the most unfortunate city of Constantinople on the twenty-sixth day of October. The city was already under military blockade by the enemy and had been surrounded on all sides.

5 I cannot easily express in words or in writing what I subsequently said, did, or thought. In the course of two months the Christian fleet was united and was deployed in perfect agreement, as I mentioned in my two other letters that I wrote to your Reverence, with all the appropriate details. The cause of the Christians seemed to advance in a splendid and perfect manner, even though the enthusiastic Turks, with their unattainable prize in mind, had not discontinued their clever attacks against the city, I took notes about everything: the customs of the Turk himself, his care and vigilance to subjugate the entire world, and his zeal to eradicate the name of Christ from the earth. He planned it in his mind and he reckoned the strength of the forces required: an infantry and a cavalry of about three hundred thousand, and an enormous fleet of biremes and triremes, of two hundred twenty-one cargo (or round) ships. In addition, he amassed and assembled engineers and every kind of weapon and engines and materiel appropriate for sieges and attacks upon cities: many heavy siege engines of all sorts, bombards, and catapults. You would think that he had amassed a mountain, the size of a monster, or an apparition; they were of help to him, in the final analysis, in his attempt to seize Constantinople.

6 Among the countless artillery pieces, there were three catapults (or bombards). The first ejected a stone [missile] weighing fourteen talents, the second a stone [missile] of twelve talents, and the third a stone [missile] of ten. While the strength of the walls resisted the force of heavy bombardment from all other lesser pieces, the fortifications could not withstand the might of those three combined, and their frequent and persistent strikes. At the second impact a large section of the walls, together with the towers, collapsed and was demolished. It was then that we realized that the ancient oracle preserved in our accounts had been fulfilled. It declared: "Woe to you, City of the Seven Hills, when a young man lays siege to you, your mighty fortifications will be destroyed."

7 He mined the walls in the area of the Saint Romanos Gate and in the section that extends between the Pege and the Golden Gates and the area between the ancient Ventura and the Kaligaria Gates. The heroic Theodoros Karystenos, who bravely opposed the enemies at the moment of their very entry and perished fighting most gloriously, superbly defended the latter. That entire sector had been weakened. I will briefly touch upon other important and terrible matters.

8 The harbor had been barred and enclosed by very strong chains stretching from the area of the Galatas Mount across [the harbor] to the Beautiful Gate. Entry into the harbor was effectively denied to the Turks by the chains and by five Venetian triremes and fifteen other merchantmen (or round, very large vessels). When the Turks realized that their efforts here would be in vain, they transferred themselves with their ships to a station in Diplokionion, where they deployed their fleet. A few days later the Turk [Mehmed II] ordered the construction of a three-mile level road through the mountains, to transfer, from the one side of Mount Galatas to the other, ninety-two biremes and uniremes, which he launched, in this manner, into the harbor, whose total control he thus assumed. Then he devised another admirable stratagem, which Xerxes, history tells us, was also supposed to have done in antiquity. He produced and built a very large bridge, from the shore of Santa Galatina to the walls of Kynegos (which is twice the distance over which Xerxes built a bridge across the Hellespont long ago). Over this bridge not only foot soldiers but also many horsemen could cross en mass.

9 Then he [Mehmed II] tried a third approach to take the city, against the Kaligaria Gate. From far away he dug five underground tunnels to gain entrance into the city. When they had approached the foundations of the walls and towers and demolition was imminent, our side from within dug five counter-mines in direct opposition. So the enemy was repelled and was forced to flee from that area, losing some of their better men. Attacks in that sector ceased.

10 Who can give an account of his engines, earthworks, catapults, artillery pieces, and cannon called "falcons" nowadays? He had more than three hundred ladders put together. He constructed earthworks that resembled mountains before the walls, in addition to castles made of such enormous wooden beams that they surpassed in height the outer towers of the city. Moreover, he produced an unprecedented engine that had not been seen until our day: in rectangular shape and extremely thick but hollow in the interior so that it resembled a house possessing an internal mechanism so it could move on wheels which rendered it mobile through superimposed ropes and other movable parts so that the entire structure could be directed; on top of it there were ladders. It seemed to have been devised by Archimedes or Hero, as it appeared to move on its own power at will. The ladders were as tall as our walls and towers and were protected by timber planks all around so that the attackers who were to mount the walls could not be harmed. I could mention countless other details but I have no wish to bore you and I will restrict myself to a few facts.

11 After fifty-three days of siege had passed, the Turks had achieved nothing. Yet any prediction about the future is always perilous; our mind's eye is blind to it. Thus somehow his eye was [blind] and he [Mehmed II] appointed the most suitable day to launch the most strenuous attack, as he consulted expert astrologers from Persia. He relied on their advice and judgment to achieve his greatest goal. On the twenty-ninth of May, a

little after the break of dawn, while the sun's rays were blinding our side, the Turks moved and attacked the city by land and by sea, concentrating their main assault on the semi-demolished sector around Saint Romanos, where many Greeks and Latins [Italians] had been posted together with their commander and emperor, who was wounded and killed by the enemy at that time. Afterwards his head was brought as a present to the Turk [Mehmed II], who looked at it and became elated. Without delay he dispatched it to Adrianople to be a part of his triumph.

12 Together with that heroic emperor was a warlord by the name of Giovanni [Guglielmo Longo] Giustiniani, whom many hold to be the primary cause of that enormous destruction and resulting captivity; but let me omit this matter. In any case, overrunning the walls was not a difficult undertaking in that sector because, as I stated earlier, the whole sector had been under incessant bombardment; that is why the enemy easily broke into the city, as no one had been left to repel the enemy attack or defend that sector.

13 It was like a nightmare: the fighting was both within and without the city itself. Those who were in monasteries took up sword and arms when they realized that the city had been lost and that they were facing the miserable day of enslavement. Like heroes of legend they fought mightily in hand-to-hand combat and fell down with wounds. I find myself unable to give an account of the misfortunes of that most unfortunate city. Tears come to my eyes and stop me dead. Oh, that indescribable funeral and cursed day! Oh, that most cruel and most foul proclamation with which that most savage Turk [Mehmed II] gave leave to the Turks to plunder, pillage, and denude that most miserable city for three days after its fall, in order to turn them into more willing warriors to carry out the siege.

14 All paved streets and narrow roadways were flowing with blood and were filled with the corpses of the slain and dead. Noble and free women were dragged from their homes and were bound from the neck. So many maids and mistresses were bound together and were barefoot. Sons were raped with their sisters. They were separated from their fathers and mothers and were taken away. We saw the lowest servants and slaves of the Turks snatching and leading away those graceful most noble virgins, both members of the lay and nuns (oh sun and earth!), as if they were cows, sheep, or any kind of domesticated animal. They were taken away from the city like a huge herd of wild undomesticated animals, with blows from swords, bolds, or knives.

15 Need I talk about the crimes of every kind, the acts of sacrilege against churches, and the foulest defilement of the sacred? As soon as they reached the Church that used to be called Santa Sophia (but now, of course, a Turkish *mescidi*), they tore down and shattered all statues, icons, and images of Christ, of male and female saints, and treated them to every kind of sacrilege. In fury they jumped and heaped themselves on altars and tables making sport of our faith and of the Christian sacraments and went on to chant praises and hymns to Muhammad. They broke down the doors

to the reliquaries and they threw out sacred relics as if they were the vilest and worthless of objects. I will pass over in silence their acts with regard to chalices, consecrated vessels, and vestments. With some of the golden clothes and covers that bore images of Christ and saints they clothed their dogs, with others their horses in their stables. They stomped on Gospels and ecclesiastical books. They destroyed shining splendid buildings of marble. They demolished everything and accorded the same treatment in all other churches. Not a single marble grave was spared. After they had demolished and leveled everything, they turned to the destruction and demolition of church pavements. What they really wanted at the deepest level was to act like savages and destroy everything in the most shameful manner. Who can give an account of the property, the possessions, the furniture, which were being snatched away through the shattered doors of buildings and homes? Together that dawn and day must be remembered, as they witnessed the most magnificent, most glorious city that was totally devoted to the Lord, become deserted and annihilated. There is nothing left, which did not fall, together with the captives, into the hands of the Turks.

16 A few days later the Turk [Mehmed II] ransomed the foremost citizens. He pretended that he wanted them to settle in the city and he created the hope that they would keep their lives. Three days later he issued a decree and commanded first that the two sons of [Loukas] Notaras (the third son had perished fighting heroically) be decapitated before their father's eyes and secondly that the father be decapitated. Next he executed the three handsome and very good sons of the grand domestic and then their father. Next he took the life of the illustrious lord Nikolaos Gredeta [Goudeles] and the lives of many others, of well-known men. He committed many other horrendous deeds while I was still there. It would take too long to enumerate them.

17 How I escaped from the infidels' hands you will find out as soon as I reach Italy; then I will tell you everything. In any case, the Turk [Mehmed II] is planning the invasion of Italy with a strong force and the greatest army. It is known that he is outfitting three hundred triremes, both large and small, as well as very large transports, more than twenty, in addition to countless infantry and cavalry. I am speaking the truth. I have no doubt about the future. Daily he reads the Life of Alexander [the Great] in Arabic, Greek, and Latin.

18 I sent a small boat from Crete and letters with Brother John to our most saintly pope and to the sacred college of cardinals. I also wrote to the king of Aragon and especially to the Italian cities, and to your own city, Bologna, urging, awakening, and, pressing on all of them to open their eyes and direct their attention to the destruction wrought by these infidels. I pray piously that Your Reverence enjoys good health and remains in a good state.

I remain servant to Your Reverence,
Cardinal Isidore

Crete, the 6th of July 1453 A.D.
The end. Amen.

2 Isidore's letter to Pope Nicholas V

Beatissime et suavissime pater,
  post debitam salutationem sanctorum et venerabilium pedum vestrae Beatitudinis humiliter me ipsum eidem commendo.

1 *Postquam ego ab urbe Romana egressus sum, nonnullas litteras Beatudini vestrae exposui et postissime de unione Graecorum cum ecclesia catholica facta et conclusa cum Deo esse, quae tamen iuxta tempus convenies et condecibile facta est, nam valde delata et tardata est. Facta enim die XII mensis <Dece>mbris proxime elapsi tandem illa perfecta et conclusa, et tota urbs Constantinopolitana cum ecclesia catholica unita est et ubique commemorabatur Beatitudo vestra, postea reverendissimus patriarcha Gregorius, qui non solum tempore quo fuit in Constantinopoli in nulla altera ecclesia, verum et<iam> in suo monasterio nequaquam commemorabatur, verum, facta unione, tota urbs eum commemorabatur, ut fertur. Fuerunt enim omnes usque ad minorem una cum imperatore uniti et, gratia Dei, catholici usque ad horam et tempus nefandum ipsius desolationis et captivitatis urbis miserrimae Constantinopolitanae. Attamen Scholarius ille et alii octo monachorum sociorum suorum una cum eo unione praefata abalienaverunt se. Haec quidem omnia bene se ad certum tempus habebant.*

2 *Postquam vero Mahometa hic iuvenis, Turcorum dominus, magnus amira nuncupatus, qui illius primi impiae conditoris legis malitia et nequitia est successor (ni enim ipso sit prior!), quanto etiam crudelius et magis tyrannicus est et maiorem habet potentiam et multitudinem exercitus abundabili malitia contra Christianos diabolum in eo ipso suscipiens fremuit et fremit, impetit et insilit, volens totaliter eos de orbe terrarum delere atque excerpere; qui contra omnes insultat atque insurgit. Tantum enim habet odium et abhominationem in eos, ut cum oculis Christianos perspexit, proprios oculos abluit et abstergit, quasi visione sua foedatus sit.*

3 *Talis enim existens, primo Constantinopolim obsedit, peroppidum quidem prope litus aedificavit. Postea conventiones et iuramenta quae habuit absque occasione destruxit et omnia cicumvicinia oppida et castra urbis Constantinopolitanae circuivit et omnes quos invenit Christianos cecidit et trucidavit. Postea omnes turres et castros expugnavit, cum mense Augusti nuper elapsi dimisit Constantinopolim et ad suas proprias regiones transmigravit. Et in mense sexto exercitum pedestrium et equestrium ultra numerum trecentorum milium et triremes magnas et parvas ducentas et viginti praeparavit, bombardas et alia industriosa tela instruxit et multa instrumenta confecit, quod difficile est ea numerare. Bombardas plurimas, quam mille, construxit, quarum tres fuerunt aliis maiores: prima enim proiciebat lapidem cuius mensura circularis erat XI palmorum, pondus cantariorum XIV; secunda autem mensura circularis decem palmarum et pondus cantariorum duodecim; tertia autem circularis mensura palmarum novem et pondus cantariorum decem. Reliquae autem fuerunt minores: una minor, alterae sclopeta innumerabilia erant. Sed omnes aliae bombardae*

nullam intulerunt laesionem, nisi solum illae tres quae lapides magnos prope iam septingentos proiecerunt et maximum detrimentum egerunt; per eas enim illa miserrima urbs per dies quinquaginta <et> unum terribiliter impugnabatur, cuius pro maiori parte muros in superficiem terrae ruptavit et devastavit. Aliae autem bombardae nullam egerunt laesionem, ut supra allegatum est, licet ac magnae ac validae etiam illae essent.

4 *Insuper alia magis nova et miraculosa mala egit, quae audientes mirari magnopere movent. Tempus enim provisum est portus Constantinopolitanus catena obserari et observari, cum ille portus reducitur in sinum et restringitur in angustum in civitatem Peram; quod factum est. Nam Venetorum triremes quinque et naves magnas duodecim numero cum salario instituimus pro securitate et custodia ipsius catenae. Quod cum amira nequam ille vidisset, statuit iter super colles et iuga fieri per tria miliaria et ultra; iussit quoque suis triremibus stantibus foris ligna sustinere et simul ea colligare per quae biremes LXXII numero deduceret, quas adeo per colles et iuga currentes perduxit ac si super mare ducerentur vento frequenti, habentes remos externos, vexilla et tentoria, ut de suo more est super mare portare; quas ad portum tandem deduxit. Deinde pontem super mare, qui usque ad hodiernum diem manet, construxit; habet enim distantiam de terra firma in Constantinopoli per miliare unum et tertium.*

5 *Construxit etiam <scalas> CCC et ultra, quarum aliquae erant observatae subtus fundamento quodam quadrangulo, quae quodam ingenio et industria intus movebantur et procedebant usque <ad> muros; scalae vero habebant desuper hamos ut, cum super muros adiacerent, hami illi ab inferiori parte habentes succursum, per aliquem non posse deici et deponi. Similiter erant velatae tabulis et indutae de sursum usque deorsum et circum circa, ne ascendentes queant a scallis depelli, sed valeant absque laesione et vulneratione ascendere. In aliis vero terram elevavit et castra lignea infixit. Alibi autem caveas faciebat sub terra, alias nonnullas mechanicas industrias exercebat: falcones et testudines nuncupabantur.*

6 *Verumtamen instabamus usque ad quinquagesimum quartum diem. In quanquagesimo vero <quinto> die, bello iam per universam noctem peracto et finito, exercitu exhausto et per ipsam muri devastationem mane ingresso, urbs Constantinopolitana, quae quondam felix et imperatrix omnium fuit urbium (nunc autem misera et infelicissima), capta est, die 29 Maii. Cuius captivitas omnes ab initio saeculi captivitates superat et excedit: Hierosolymorum ab Nabugodonosor<e> rege pauca equidem et parva fuit respectu tantae et tam magnae; ipsius quidem pecuniae ablatae sunt, populus autem non fuit pedibus et manibus colligatus, sed simul congregatus ad Babyloniam transductus est; et sacra eorum no abrepta, non conculcata, sed Assyriorum rex ea in aedibus suis cum reverentia observabat. Similiter et comparatio nulla in aliam civitatem potest fieri, quae huic potest adaequari.*

7 *Quapropter deprecor, exoro atque adhortor vestram Beatitudinem ut cito fiat aliqua providentia superinde, exinde omnem modum et industriam Beatitudo vestra teneat ad propugnandum et occurendum et conterendum huiusmodi novi Mahometi malignum propositum; quod equidem fiet, Domino disponente, si vestra Beatitudo curabit et festinabit in Italiam pacem fieri; quae cum Domino fiet, ut etiam alio consequatur bona quae Deus et vestra Beatitudo exoptat. Ego autem veniam cito ad vos,*

Deo dante, animam et corpus exponere pro fide Christiana et statu Christianorum; tunc etiam narrabo, exponens modos destructionis infidelium.

Vestrae Beatitudini humilis servus
Isidorus cardinalis se totum recommendat.

Datum Candiae, die XV Iulii LIIIo.

Most Blessed and Most Sweet Father:
My humble greetings with the due salutation
Before Your Beatitude's saintly and most venerable feet.

1 After I departed from the city of Rome, I drafted a few letters for Your Beatitude in regard to union of the Greeks with the Catholic Church, which was accomplished and concluded with [the help of] God. You will find that it was done and concluded in a timely fashion, even though it had been delayed and postponed for such a long time. It was accomplished on the twelfth day of December of the last year. It was perfectly concluded and the entire city of Constantinople was united with the Catholic Church. Everywhere Your name was first commemorated and was followed by [the commemoration of the name of] the most reverend Patriarch Gregory (which had not ever been done in any church in Constantinople, including his own monastery) but, with the conclusion of the union, he was commemorated by the entire city, as it was said. All, to the last citizen, were united with emperor and Catholics (thanks be to God!) until the horrible time and hour of the destruction and captivity of the most miserable city of Constantinople. Yet, Scholarios and another eight monks, his associates, refused to participate in the union. Such matters were accomplished in a satisfactory manner, up to a certain time.

2 Afterwards, the young Mehmed, the lord of the Turks, who is styled as "grand emir," who has succeeded (unless, of course, he surpasses) that founder [Mohammed] of the impious legislations [Islam] in malice and criminality, noted for his cruelty and tyrannical ways, possessing great power and an enormous army, he became possessed by the devil to move against the Christians and he groaned (and is still groaning), became restless, and launched his attack. He considers an abomination to look upon a Christian and he subsequently washes and cleanses his eyes to rid himself of the pollution.

3 Such was his attitude when he laid siege to Constantinople and first he erected a fortress by the sea [Rumeli Hisar]. He then violated all agreements and oaths that he had occasionally taken and surrounded all the neighboring towns and castles that belonged to Constantinople, putting to death and slaughtering all Christians he encountered. He then took by siege all towers and castles. In August of the past year he left Constantinople and moved back to his own territories. Six months later he prepared an

infantry and cavalry that numbered beyond three hundred thousand individuals, two hundred and twenty large and small triremes, bombards and other effective war engines, as well as other weapons of war, which would be too difficult to enumerate. He cast very many bombards, as many as one thousand. Among them, three were the largest. The first ejected a stone [missile] that measured eleven palms in circumference and weighed fourteen cantars; the second ejected a stone of ten palms that weighed twelve cantars; and the third ejected a stone of nine palms in circumference that weighed ten cantars. There were other smaller pieces. One was smaller and there were countless firearms. All the other cannons did no harm, but those three bombards that fired almost seventy large stones caused a great deal of damage. Under their bombardment that most unfortunate city endured fifty-one days of horrific warfare. A great section of its walls was devastated, was demolished, and was leveled. Nevertheless, the other bombards did no harm, as I have already indicated, but those [three] were the largest and most powerful pieces.

4 He performed other, quite unprecedented and even miraculous, evils, which would greatly astound the listener. Care had been exercised to guard and bar the harbor of Constantinople with a chain, as that port resembles a bay and it is enclosed, like a strait, across by the city of Pera. This was done. In addition, five Venetian triremes and twelve, in number, large ships under contract undertook to guard and secure the chain itself. When the emir realized that he could not do anything here, he decided to build a road that stretched over the hills and ranges to a distance beyond three miles. He also issued orders to transport wooden beams and to assemble seventy-two triremes to be transported overland over the hills and ranges (as if they were sailing over the sea, propelled by the wind, with oars extended over the sides, and with their standards and tents), resembling their normal way of traveling. Then he placed a bridge, which survives to the present day, over the sea. From the shores [of Pera] to the [shore of] Constantinople it covers a distance of one mile and one third.

5 He constructed three hundred ladders or more and some of them were protected by a square structure below. By a clever device and a great deal of effort they could be moved and positioned against the walls. The ladders had hooks attached on top so that, when they were placed against the walls, the hooks utilized their lower support and they could not be thrown off or be dislodged. Similarly they were covered with planks, from top to bottom and all around, so that those who were climbing could not be thrown off but were able to launch a mighty attack unharmed, under protection. In other areas he raised mounds of earth and deployed wooden castles. Still elsewhere he dug subterranean mines and used many other siege engines that we call "falcons" and "tortoises."

6 Nevertheless we resisted for fifty-four days. On the fifty-fifth day, after an all night attack, with our forces exhausted and the walls destroyed, early in the morning he gained entry, and the city of Constantinople that used

to be the happiest city, indeed the queen of cities (but now is miserable and most unfortunate) was taken on May 29. Its fate cannot be compared to the fate of other cities. It goes beyond comparison. When King Nebuchadnezzar took Jerusalem, it was not as rich and was small, with less extensive territory. To be sure, it was pillaged of its treasures, but its inhabitants' hands and feet were not bound. They were gathered and taken to Babylon. Their sacred vessels were not snatched or trampled, but the king of Assyria kept them in his temples with respect. Similarly, the fate of no other city can provide a comparison. Nothing equals this sack.

7 Therefore, I beg, plead, and urge Your Beatitude to make future plans quickly, with all the zeal that Your Beatitude possesses, to press on, to ward off, and to wipe out this new kind of evil that is presented by Mehmed. This will come about, with the Lord's permission, if Your Beatitude sees to it and hastens to arrange peace in Italy. If peace is established, with the Lord's help, then all the things that the Lord and Your Beatitude wish for will follow. With God's permission, I will swiftly come to you and offer my body and soul for the Christian faith and for Christendom. I will give an account of my plan that will lead to the destruction of the infidels.

The humble servant of Your Beatitude
Cardinal Isidore
With his total devotion to You.

Crete, the 15th of July 1453

4 The escape of Isidore

Isidore does not repeat the fictional details that Leonardo includes in his account, *dramatis causa*. Leonardo apparently embellished his account with episodes that are fictional in nature and he seems to believe that they should have taken place. Thus Leonardo mentions a dignified meeting of the emperor and his allies at which he delivered a noble speech on the eve of the final assault. It is very unlikely that such an address was delivered. Moreover, it is occasionally reported in secondary literature that there was a last mass, a liturgy, in Santa Sophia; this is another unlikely event.[83] The final assault of the sultan began during darkness in the early hours of 29 May[84] and the fighting at the walls ended a few hours later, at the break of dawn. The western fortifications had been overrun and the slaughter within the city had begun. We do not know how Isidore managed the situation at his sector. The main attack was directed at the western land fortifications and minor engagements appear to have taken occurred about the sea walls, precluding the dispatch of reinforcements to the critical sector of the land walls. Isidore himself and Leonardo provide no information on the fighting at the sea walls.[85]

When Isidore realized that the city had fallen, he abandoned his sector and moved to the southeast, towards the area of the Augoustaion and Santa Sophia,[86] which seems to have attracted most of the population in search of sanctuary and was under the influence of popular prophecies.[87] He could not have encountered armed conflicts along this route, even if he confronted throngs of the enemy entering the city, who were intent upon looting houses and seeking hidden treasures, before they turned their attention to human booty. We also know that he was on horseback, which was a definite advantage in avoiding the enemy, as pointed out by other eyewitnesses.[88] According to his own account, when he reached the church of Santa Sophia, the enemy had already penetrated deep into the imperial city and the slaughter had begun. Outside the doors of the church,[89] he was wounded on the left side of face by a spent arrow or perhaps a bolt; he seems to have suffered a slight injury. He was able to elude his pursuers, precisely because he was mounted on his horse.[90] It is interesting to note in passing that he relates nothing about his wound in his report to Pope Nicholas V. In the letter that was translated into Latin by Pasio di Bertipaglia, Isidore only states that he was able to escape through a "miracle of God" and again he fails to mention his wound. He does point out, however, with a degree of pride that he is the most truthful eyewitness to the disaster.[91] It should be emphasized that among the corpus of literature from the pen of Isidore that has survived, this is the only personal detail to be found. He never writes about himself, except in connection with the fall, in which we discover that he was wounded and that he was subsequently in a psychological state of depression. He further adds the all too human note of cursing the man who wounded him:

Et per immortalem Deum, cuius oculis patent et manifesta sunt omnia, saepius ac saepius illum execratus sum ac maledixi crudelem ex Turcis, qui me sagitta fixit atque in sinistra capitis parte vulneravit ante ianuam cuiusdam monasterii, non tam acriter tamen ut eadem hora mihi vitam eripuerit, propterea quia eques eram et attonitus et spiculum ipsum magna in parte vires amiserat; sed me Deus, opinor, servare voluit, ut reliquas omnes tales ac tantas infortunatissim<a>e illius urbis adversitates conspiciam.

In the name of the immortal God, whose unsleeping eyes see everything, again and again do I curse and consign to hell that cruel Turk who pierced the left side of my head with an arrow in front of that legendary monastery [Santa Sophia]. It was not a serious wound that would claim my life, because I was on horseback and stunned, and the bolt was spent and had lost its force for the most part. Indeed, it is my opinion, God wished to save me so that I could witness all the remaining trials and disgrace of that most unhappy city.

Henry of Soemmern also addresses this incident, supplying a few details and stating that Isidore had been wounded and that his face from that moment on was wrapped in bandages:[92]

Cardinalis autem Ruthenus, natione graecus, qui per papam anno iam elapso Constantinopolim missus fuit ... evasit. Per hunc Mahometum capta quidem Urbe, prope ecclesiam S. Sophiae accessit, putans illic esse armatos aliquot qui Turcis resisterent. Cum autem nullos inveniret resistere paratos et omnes fugerent, bonus pater voluit Turcis obviam procedure et pro Christi fide sanguinem fundere. Under per aliquod servitorum suorum coactus, fugit in ecclesiam, ubi captus est a Turcis . . . obvolutus . . . erat in facie pannis eo quod in facie sagittal vulneratus fuerat.

The cardinal of the Ruthenia, a Greek by birth, whom the pope sent last year to Constantinople, . . . has escaped. When Mehmed captured the city, he approached the Church of Santa Sophia. He believed that he would find there a number of armed men to resist the Turks. When he could locate no one prepared to offer resistance (for all were in flight), the good father expressed the wish to advance against the Turks and to pour out blood for his faith in Christ. Some of his own servants checked him and fled into the Church, where the Turks captured him . . . his head was covered with bandages because he had been wounded by an arrow on the face.

Thus a few details about the incident can be recovered. We discover that Isidore was not alone; rather, he had his retinue about him, who had assisted in bandaging his facial wound, and had conducted him indoors. In time, the enemy discovered that prisoners were valuable, perhaps more than booty, and the slaughter stopped in favor of anticipated ransom and monetary gain. What is also of interest is that Henry knew of the wound of Isidore even though nothing had been stated in the letter that the cardinal had sent to the pope. Isidore was exceptionally visible during his stay in Candia and the effects of his wound still must have been visible. The couriers who brought Isidore's letters to the *curia* in Rome somehow conveyed the fact, perhaps orally, that he had been wounded.[93]

Once again Isidore's luck held out and his captors did not identify him. He relates absolutely nothing about the circumstances of his captivity, the time he spent as a prisoner, or his escape to Pera. The letter translated by Pasio di Bertipaglia only mentions the miraculous circumstances that saved Isidore, without providing specific particulars.[94] Some general circumstances are cited by "a friend of Isidore," in his letter from Crete, dated the 15th of July:[95]

Captus itaque fuit et tanquam incognitus duobus diebus mansit in Thurcorum magno exercitu. Verum adiumento fuit reverendissimo domino cardinali quod quidam monachus senex interfectus fuit, cuius caput imperatori Thurcorum pro capite reverendissimi cardinalis allatum fuerat. Fama igitur dominum cardinalem obiise habebatur.

And so he was captured and unrecognized remained with the great army of the Turks for two days. What was of advantage to the most reverend lord cardinal was that some elderly monk had been killed, whose head had been brought to the emperor [sultan] of the Turks as the head of the most reverend cardinal. There was a rumor going around that the lord cardinal had perished.

From his phraseology, Henry of Soemmern seems to be quoting this friend of Isidore in his account, even though he adjusts the number of days that Isidore spent as a prisoner:[96] *captus est a Turcis et tanquam incognitus mansit tribus diebus in magno exercitu Teucrorum. Et erat ei praesidio quod famabatur et ab imperatore Turcorum credebatur occisus*, "he was captured by the Turks and unrecognized remained with the great army of the Turks for three days. What saved him was the rumor that he had been put to death by the emperor [sultan] of the Turks." Aeneas Sylvius Picolomini, who as Pope Pius II personally knew the cardinal and who must have conversed with him about the siege and fall, states in an *opusculum*:[97] *Isidorus cardinalis in eo tumultu captus, cum veste mutate non fuisse cognitus*, "Cardinal Isidore who was captured in that upheaval, was not identified, as he had changed his vestments."

Other eyewitnesses present during the sack had no news of the cardinal's fate and some simply admitted the fact. Thus Benvenuto, the consul of Ancona, states:[98] *item quod de reverendissimo domino cardinali nichil scit det<er>minate, nisi quod stabat super murum ad custodiam*, "item: nothing definite was known about the most reverend lord cardinal, except that he was guarding the top of the walls." Leonardo knew nothing about Isidore's fate and escape, and does not speak of it in his account.[99] The fact that Isidore was not identified while in custody greatly assisted in his escape.[100] There is no question that a price had been placed upon his head and, as noted by the Greek historian Khalkokondyles, he would have been executed on the spot if he had been identified:[101] ἐνταῦθα ἑάλω καὶ Ἰσίδωρος καρδινάλις Σαβοίων . . . καὶ εἰ μὲν οὖν αὐτὸν ἔγνω ὁ βασιλεὺς [Mehmed], ὡς εἴη καρδινάλιος Ἰσίδωρος ἀνεῖλέ τε αὐτόν, καὶ οὐκ ἀνίει διαφυγεῖν. νῦν δ᾽ οἰόμενος αὐτὸν τεθνάναι, οὐκ ἐποιεῖτο λόγον οὐδένα, "at this point Isidore, the cardinal of the Sabines, was captured . . . if the king [Mehmed] had recognized him, that he was Cardinal Isidore, he would have executed him and would not have allowed him to escape; but he was under the impression that he had perished and he paid no further attention."

According to the earliest testimonies that we have Isidore survived because the sultan was under the impression that the cardinal had perished in the early hours of the sack, during the indiscriminate slaughter. Early on, we are told, the sultan was presented with someone's head and he understood that the grizzly trophy was the decapitated head of Isidore, at which point he decided to pay no further attention and focused on the wave of executions of others who had been securely identified. Perhaps the head belonged to an unfortunate elderly monk who had no connection with Isidore. The tale of "the cardinal's escape" received a great deal of elaboration with time and eventually we encounter this fuller version:[102]

> [In] *nobilissimae Urbis excidio Isidorus cardinalis, pontificius ea tempestate ad Constantinum legatus, a Barbaris ad necem quaesitus, quo se praesentissimae cladi eriperet, fervente tumultu mutatis propere cum jacentis cadaver vestibus, ac fugientum turbae immistus urbe excessit incolumis. Verum, qui ementito cultu mortem effugerat, haud pari fortuna servitutem evasit: siquidem ab insequentibus victoribus captus, et quis esset ob rasum mentum vestemque peregrinam non agnitus nihilominus in servitutem abductus est. Interea cadaver, quod purpuratum Ecclesiae senatorem ex injecta Isidori veste mentiebatur . . . elati gaudio repererunt, et ejudem praecisum*

> caput roseo contectum pileo hastae infigunt: ac clamante praecone, Illud esse cardinalis Rutheni, per captae civitatis multa cum irrisione circumferunt.
>
> [During] the sack of the most noble city, Cardinal Isidore, the pontifical legate to Constantine [XI], who had been in that upheaval, was sought by the barbarians to be executed. He very cleverly escaped destruction, when he hastened to change his clothes with those of a stretched out corpse. He then joined the crowd fleeing the city without injury. But, while his deception saved him from death, his good fortune did not last long for him to evade capture. He was taken by his victorious pursuers and was enslaved but he was not recognized, as his chin was shaven and he wore strange apparel. Meanwhile, they found the corpse that was dressed in the purple robes of the Church that Isidore had discarded.... In joy and delight they cut the head off (bearing the red hat [sc. of the cardinal]) and fixed it on a lance. A public crier went ahead and proclaimed "this is the head of the Ruthenian cardinal," and they paraded it with good humor through many areas of the captured city.

This elaboration of the tale, with added details, relates that the cardinal escaped unhurt and took care, in an Odyssean stratagem, to change his clothes and wear the garments of a slain man. It is doubtful that Isidore effected this deception by himself, if this account contains any truth. He had been wounded and had been bandaged by members of his retinue; perhaps they as well would have exchanged his clothes for him. Moreover, the reference to the "shaven chin" is also puzzling. Had Isidore actually shaved his beard off in the manner of Latin clerics? His friend Bessarion was famous for his *barba graeca*, which may have also assisted in the propaganda of Latin clerics against him.[103] If Isidore had a shaven chin at this time, it was probably one of his actions before the last battle and assault. He probably realized the futility of the defense at that point and had decided to disguise himself before the commencement of the final assault. It would have been a simple matter to masquerade himself in this manner, since no one would immediately recognize him if they recalled his bearded face from earlier days. The beard was a sign of distinguishing Greek clerics from Catholic clergymen in those days and was further a personal declaration of unionist or non-unionist sympathies, evoking approval or disapproval in different cultures.[104] Henry of Soemmern clearly implies that the sultan became convinced that Isidore had been killed when he was presented with the bearded head of a monk of the order of Saint Basil. It is also interesting to note that this presentation also included the most prominent decapitated victims of the sultan: his kinsman Orhan and the Greek emperor, Constantine XI:[105]

> apportata sunt in conspectus eius in tribus lanceis per tres Turcos tria capita, quorum unum erat imperatoris Constantini, aliud cuiusdam militis Turci qui contra Turcos cum Christianis urbem defenderat et tertium erat cuiusdam senis barbati monachi de ordine Sancti Basilii, quod eidem dicebatur esse caput cardinalis Rutheni, licet in veritate non fuerat.

Three Turks brought him [*sc.* the sultan] three heads affixed to three lances. One of the three was the head of Emperor Constantine; the second belonged to a Turkish soldier [Orhan a distant relative of the sultan, in the care of the Greek emperor] who had defended the city on the side of the Christians; the third was the head of elderly bearded monk of the order of Saint Basil, which was said to be the head of Ruthenian cardinal. Of course, in reality, it was not.

We may perhaps conclude that Isidore, before the sack, had the appearance of a monk of the Saint Basil order, with a bearded face, and that he had probably taken on the appearance of a cleric in a Latin manner by shaving his beard before the final assault.

Moreover, in time we encounter a conflation of other unrelated incidents that had accumulated in the story of the cardinal's escape, such as the Cardinal's hat affixed on a lance and paraded through the devastated city for ridicule. The tale, unrelated to Isidore's adventures, first appears in the narrative of Leonardo, who states, in his detailed description of the excesses and sacrileges committed by the Ottoman army during the sack, the following incident:[106] *Crucifixum posthac per castra praeviis tympanis delundendo transportant: sputis, blasphemiis, opprobriis iterum processionaliter crucifigunt, pileum theucrale, quod* zarchula *vocant, capiti superponentes deridendo "Hic est Deus Christianorum,"* "they took around the crucifix through the camp to the accompaniment of the drum in a procession of blasphemies, foul language, and offenses. They placed upon it the Turkish hat, which they call *zarcula*, and in laughter they declared: 'This is the God of the Christians.'" This incident is undoubtedly the origin of the tale of the cardinal's hat paraded on a lance.

It is possible that Isidore was roughly mistreated while he was being transported to the Ottoman camp outside the western walls. It is likely that the Turks had difficulty bringing their human booty from inside the walls, as numerous gates were still sealed and others were congested with corpses and debris. Since there had been no breach of the fortifications, the prisoners had to be lifted up to the top of the walls and then lowered to the ground level of the Ottoman camp outside the walls. One description of the cumbersome operation survives:[107] γεμισθέντων τῶν πυλῶν τῆς τε Χαρσοῦς καὶ τοῦ Ἁγίου Ῥωμανοῦ μέχρις ἀψίδων αὐτῶν. ὡς καὶ τοὺς αἰχμαλώτους, γυναῖκάς τε καὶ παῖδας, μὴ δυναμένους ἐξελθεῖν, ἀλλ᾽ἐκ τῶν τειχῶν σχοινίοις χαλνῶντες αὐτούς, "the Gates of Kharsia [Edirne Kapı] and of Saint Romanos [Top Kapı] were congested [with dead bodies], all the way up to the arches. Later, the captives, women and children, could not be brought out but had to be lowered by rope from the walls."

Isidore's stay at the camp of the Turks must have filled him with anxiety. He undoubtedly felt discomfort and trepidation lest someone identify him and his identity became known. The fact that he was never recognized by any other prisoner, who could have tried to gain some advantage to ameliorate his own personal circumstances[108] with his captors by assisting them in identifying such a prominent person in the defense of Constantinople, qualified as a "divine miracle."[109] Most of Isidore's acquaintances in the city, both Greek and Venetian, were marked for death and the sultan exerted a great deal of effort to single them out among his prisoners. The sultan had his own informants within the city, possibly a fifth column that had been operating, whose members included fanatical anti-unionists who, without hesitation but with eagerness, would have stepped forward to assist the sultan in the selection of victims for the executioner and would have had no qualms identifying the pope's emissary. Isidore must have employed some kind of disguise to avoid detection and managed to be ransomed by some individuals who conveyed him to the relative, if uncertain, safety of the Genoese suburb of Pera.[110] Had he actually shaved his beard to avoid detection the night of the general assault before he had been seen by the multitudes in his "new" appearance? We do not know the identity of the individuals who ransomed the cardinal and spirited him away from the Ottoman camp. We only know that they were able to pay a modest price for his ransom. According to the earliest report by Henry of Soemmern, Isidore was ransomed for 100 ducats[111] three days after his capture:[112] *incognitus mansit tribus diebus in magno exercitu Teucrorum. . . . Tandem cardinalis ipse redemptus est pro C ducatis et vectus est in Peram mansitque absconditus*, "he remained in the extensive Turkish camp for three days. . . . Finally the cardinal was ransomed for one hundred ducats and was conveyed to Pera. He remained hidden." By the time Aeneas Sylvius Piccolomini composed his *Tractatulus*, the amount of the ransom had been drastically reduced and he even marvels at it:[113] *Isidorus cardinalis . . . tricentis asperis sese redemit, id est genus pecuniae admodum levis*, "Cardinal Isidore . . . was ransomed for three hundred aspers (so cheap was the price!)."

The safety that was offered in Pera was not absolute.[114] In theory the Genoese suburb of Constantinople had remained neutral during the siege and had traded in goods and provisions with both the Turks and the residents of the city. Nevertheless, numerous volunteers from Pera had assisted the defenders against the sultan's regiments in the final assault and some of those Genoese volunteers, including prominent individuals, had been captured in the sack.[115] Moreover, Giustiniani and his valiant regiment of *condottieri* from Genoa had provided the nucleus for the defense. The position of Pera was precarious at best and after the fall of Constantinople,[116] Pera's *podestà*, Angelo Giovanni Lomellino, hastened to surrender to the sultan, who granted the Genoese colony an *aman-name*, whose text has survived.[117] Because of the dangerous position of Pera, the safety of Isidore's haven must have been temporary and in spite of his difficult circumstances the cardinal must have realized that in time the sultan's agents would pick him up and he would be identified. The sultan's agents were probably combing through the suburb to identify concealed individuals throughout the month of June. This is implied in Henry of Soemmern's phrase that even within Pera, where he stayed for eight days, Isidore was forced to keep moving from hiding place to hiding place to avoid detection,[118] which was no doubt a difficult and complicated task, for he had been under considerable stress, fearful, and in pain from his wound.

We may further speculate that Isidore could not have arranged a departure from Pera without assistance. He had to have received considerable help, including the necessary financial means. Otherwise his escape from a city that was surrounded by the Ottomans and had formally surrendered to the sultan would have been impossible. The cardinal's patrons must have included some of the more prominent citizens in the suburb and may have included the head of the community, the *podestà* Lomellino, who was encountering his own personal problems within his family, in addition to the uncertain future of his public charge. Perhaps that is the reason that Isidore never contributed to the "bad press" that the Genoese of Pera encountered after the fall because of their ambivalent status of claiming neutrality during the siege, but at the same contributing to the war effort of the Constantinopolitans. Following the sack, they were accused of duplicitous behavior, even by some of their own citizens, even Leonardo. Thus the archbishop complains first about the "neutral" status of Pera, which proved, in his opinion, the greatest contributor to its own destruction. He believes that they should have openly sided with Constantinople and the Venetians.[119] Such accusations also surfaced during the siege and these difficulties occasionally disintegrated to mutual accusations of disloyalty. Leonardo reports one such occasion.[120] In one serious instance, the Genoese of Pera were accused of having informed the Porte of the defenders' plan to eliminate the Turkish boats that had been brought into the harbor. Leonardo was evidently suspicious of the actions of his countrymen, for he refuses to elaborate further on the incident and simply states: "I must be silent."[121] Barbaro, at the very beginning of his narrative, had restrained his natural Venetian bias against the Genoese and had even welcomed the arrival of the Genoese *condottiere* and his regiment in Constantinople. He initially expresses admiration for him. However, after his fateful retreat from the western walls, Barbaro exhibits characteristic language to describe his disapproval and even accuses the wounded warlord of intentionally creating panic within the city as he was marching to his ship and states with contempt:[122] "he was lying through his teeth!" Isidore, by contrast, never stated anything negative about the Genoese of Pera and he all the more so praised them for their contribution to the defense of Constantinople. He expresses his sorrow for the fate of Pera a number of times in his correspondence and he seems to be one of the few contemporary authors to defend the reputation of the Genoese of Pera.[123] We may assume that the critical factors in Isidore's mind for such expressions must have included the assistance that he had received from the Perenses while he was hiding in their colony and the substantial material help that he had received while he was among them, and then enabling and engineering his successful escape from the dangers within their neighborhood. He probably believed that he owed them a personal debt. Thus in his letter to the duke of Burgundy, Isidore emphatically praises the Genoese of Pera and provides the strongest defense against the charges that had surfaced against the Genoese:[124]

> *Nam cum pauci essemus, diu rem bellicam, quoad valuimus, gessimus, nec deerant nobis Ianuenses, qui omni conatu Urbem ipsam tutati sunt, et quamquam simulatu cum Teucro viverent hocque fieret statuto consilio, tamen noctu clam ad nos eos quos valebant ac poterant viros et sic subsidia mittebant frequentique senatu imperatorio*

aderant aliisque cum nationibus reipublicae tutandae consultabant. Etsi aliquis est qui ipsis improperet eorum culpa et defectu eam Urbem in deditione devenisse Teucrorum, salvae eorum pace, non consentaneum audietur, quia, cum in eo demmet ut nos periculo et discrimen laborarent, non debebant sui discrimini esse patratores.

We may have been few, but we successfully fought back, as long as we had strength. Indeed we were aided by the Genoese, who exerted every effort to defend our City. While they pretended, with an official decree, to live with the Turk, nevertheless every night they secretly sent to aid us their best and most capable warriors, attended the imperial senate, and even send dispatches to other nations to help our commonwealth. If one improperly suggests and even charges that the city fell to the Turks because of their lack of effort and absence, or because of the existing peace between them, one will not find me in agreement. We faced the same dangers and we labored on behalf of the same cause. They should not now defend themselves against such dangerous accusations.

With the Porte maintaining a close eye on the Genoese suburb, with the wave of unending executions in Constantinople, and with the current efforts of the sultan to capture all prominent citizens and defenders who had evaded capture and identification during the sack,[125] Isidore[126] must have felt uneasy and since his safety could not be maintained forever, he decided to make his move and to depart the suburb. Somehow his anxiety seems to be conveyed in the letter of Henry of Soemmern:[127] *postquam percepit Turcos accepisse Peram, iudicavit non esse tutum ibi remanere, et, ... non posset per loca christianorum fugere,* "after he heard that Pera would surrender to the Turks, he concluded that it would not be safe for him to stay any longer and ... he could not flee through Christian territory." Henry, our only source on this phase of Isidore's escape, then states that the cardinal boarded a Turkish galley that transported him to Asia Minor. It must have taken quite a bit of acting on the part of Isidore, not to mention bribing, to escape in this manner from the sacked city. According to Henry:[128] *intravit galeas Turcorum, in quibus mansit tribus diebus incognitus; obvolutus enim erat in facie pannis eo quod in facie sagitta vulneratus fuerat,* "he boarded a Turkish galley and stayed on board three days. He was not recognized, as his head was covered with bandages because he had been wounded by an arrow in the face." What must have been of use was also the new appearance of his face, without the beard. Beardless and covered with bandages he escaped detection.

Isidore reached Prousa (Bursa); while there he managed to attach himself to the company of a Turk. Together, they traveled to the old city of Phokaia, where a resident Genoese recognized him (one can only wonder whether this was possible because of the bandages, unless they had been removed and his beard had been growing) and he again came under suspicion. He then took a small boat that conveyed him to Genoese Chios and he could at last relax, since he had evaded all territory under the control of the Turks:[129]

Intravit Prusas in galeis Teucrorum, quibus in partibus finxit se esse quemdam pauperem captum redemptum quaerentem filios suos redimere captos Constantinopoli.

Et sic paulatim quodam Turco semper associatus est usque ad quemdam locum dictum Focis. Deinde, pertraseunte ipso cardinali, quidam Ianuenses eum agnoverunt et eum inadventer manifestare coeperunt. Unde timens plurimum, quia patria illa Turcorum erat, ingressus quamdam parvulam navaem devenit Chium.

The galleys of the Turks brought him to Prousa [Bursa]. He pretended to be an impoverished man who had been captured and then was ransomed, [and was] seeking to ransom his sons who were captured in Constantinople. Gradually, he tightly attached himself to a Turk, with whom he reached a place called Phokaia. Then, as the cardinal was traveling, a certain Genoese recognized him and inadvertently revealed his identity. He became anxious, because this region belonged to the Turks, and boarded a very small boat, which brought him to Chios.

From there he could arrange the longer leg of his journey to Venetian Crete, in greater safety and without anxiety. He had finally succeeded in escaping Constantinople, never to return.

In conclusion, the following is a tentative chronology of the crucial events that Isidore encountered on the day of the sack and that took place in the following weeks (Julian calendar):

> 29 May: Isidore was wounded in the square by Santa Sophia; assisted by his retinue he sought safety within the church. Isidore was captured and was then taken to the Turkish camp, successfully avoiding identification.
> 29–31 May: Isidore remained a prisoner in the Ottoman camp.[130]
> 1 June: Isidore was ransomed for a relatively small sum of money and was conveyed to Pera.[131]
> 1–8 June: Period of hiding and moving from house to house to avoid detection and identification by the sultan's agents.[132]
> 9–12 June: Isidore boarded a Turkish galley that conveyed him to Prousa/Bursa.[133]
> 12– June: An unspecified period during which Isidore traveled from Prousa/Bursa to Phokaia/Foca, to Chios, and then to Candia in Crete.[134]
> 5–8 July: Arrival in Candia, Crete.[135]

Notes

1 The Latin letter (dated: *Datum Candiae, die XV Julii LIII*) has been published, with Italian translation, in *CC* 1: 92–101. The text and the first English translation can be found in sec. 3 of this chapter. One should compare this opening paragraph to the letter that Isidore sent to his friend Cardinal Bessarion in Bologna. Because of its historical importance, the entire Latin text of this letter (dated: *In Creta, die sexta Iulii anno Domini M°C-CCC°LIII°*) and its first English translation is also cited in sec. 3 of this chapter. Selections from the letter to Bessarion, with Italian translation, appear in *CC* 1: 64–81. Leonardo further informs us that his original intent in accompanying Isidore to Constantinople was the reinforcement of church union, *PG* 159: col. 925: *Cum igitur reverendissimus pater, dominus cardinalis Sabinensis* [Isidorus]*, pro unione Graecorum legatus, in eius famulatum me ex Chio vocasset, egi summa cum animi mei diligentia ut fidem sanctae Romanae Ecclesiae fortiter constanterque, ut debitum exigit, defensarem.* Barbaro, on the other hand, in addition to the

mission of bringing about the union also emphasizes the military aspect of Isidore's journey to the beleaguered city, p. 10 (*CC* 1: 3):

> Hor da poi pasadi ver quanti zorni, l'azonse una nave che vigna da Zenova, da Zenovexi, de portada de cantara sie millia con el gardinal de Rosia [Isidore], che manda el papa per dover far la union, e dusse con sì homeni 200 fra scopetieri e balestrieri per secorso de questa zitade de Constantinopoli.

Filippo da Rimini (cf. *SF*, pp. 37, 38), the Venetian administrator of Corfu, also stresses the mission of the cardinal, which was intended to instill hope among the desperate population, pp. 156–157: *Eo tamen per Nicolaum pontificem summum legatus missus Isidorus cardinalis, qui bono faceret animo Thraces spem ingerens magnarum rerum.* Henry of Soemmern, who speaks of the cardinal's adventures during the sack and of his escape from the carnage, also writes of his original mission (Philippides, *Mehmed II the Conqueror*, pp. 128, 129 [*CC* 2: 86]):

> Cardinalis autem Ruthenus, natione Graecus, qui per papam anno iam elapso Constantinopolim missus fuit ad inducendum Graecos ut ipsi primatum ecclesiae Romanae etiam quoad iurisdictionem <super> omnes ecclesias orbis recognoscetur (quod et fecit, qui infra octo dies Romae expectatur), evasit.

Tignosi da Foligno, stresses the efforts that Isidore exerted on behalf of church union, *TIePN*, p. 114: *a cardinali similiter agebatur, quem illic Romana Ecclesia coegerat assistere ut, si posset, illorum animos retineret ne in haeresim iterum labarentur lapsosque retrahere, conaretur.* His role in promoting and achieving the union is also emphasized in a letter dated 15 July 1453, composed by a "friend"/*familiaris* of Isidore (who, as *CC* 1: 112 suspects, may be none other than Francesco Griffolini); cf. *CC* 1: 114: *Facta enim sancta unione, pro qua reverendissimus dominus cardinalis Ruthenus ex urbe recesserat.*

2 Cf. the information supplied by Leonardo, who also provides some names, which include the court priest Isidore, Scholarios, and Neophytos, whose recalcitrant attitude created immense problems for Cardinal Isidore. Cf. *PG* 159: col. 925:

> Verum quoniam nec ratio, nec auctoritas, nec variae Scholarii, Isidori Neophytique opiniones adversos Romanae Ecclesiae fidem stare poterant, actum est et industria et probitate praefati domini cardinalis, ut sancta unio, assentiente imperatore senatuque (si non ficta fuit!) firmaretur, celebraturque secundo Idus Decembris, Spiridionis [sic] episcopi sancti die.

Again he repeats the names of the same individuals, who formed the nucleus of the resistance, and accuses the emperor of failing to support strongly Isidore's efforts against the oppositions' "pestilential" activities. Cf. *PG* 159: col. 930 (not in *CC* 1):

> Acquiescere imperator visus, metropolitasque Scholarium, Isidorum Neophytumque complicesque, judices constituit, verbo quidem, non facto. Nam si pusillanimitatem imperator excussisset hanc fidei illusionem vindicasset.... Coercendi quidem illi errant, qui si fuissent, morbum pestiferum non propagassent. Sed ignoro, utrum imperator, aut judices damnandi quibus correctionis virga, quamquam minae intecessissent, aberat.

On Leonardo and his important composition that has inspired numerous imitators and followers, cf. M. Philippides, "The Fall of Constantinople: Bishop Leonard and the Greek Accounts," *Greek, Roman and Byzantine Studies* 22 (1981): pp. 287–300; *idem*, "The Fall of Constantinople 1453: Bishop Leonardo Giustiniani and his Italian Followers," pp. 189–227 (which cites previous scholarship); *idem*, "The Fall of Constantinople 1453: Classical Comparisons and the Circle of Cardinal Isidore," pp. 349–383; and J. Schiel, *Mongolesturm und Fall Konstantinopels: Dominikanische Erzählungen im diachronen Vergleich*, Europa im Mittelalter 19 (Berlin, 2011), esp. pp. 153–180. Leonardo's followers and imitators include Languschi-Dolfin, *Aeneas Sylvius Piccolomini* (Pope Pius II), "Riccherio," Makarios Melissourgos-Melissenos (Pseudo-Sphrantzes), the anonymous *Codex Barberinus 111*, and Francesco Sansovino; for information on the numerous imitators, cf. *SF*, pp. 19–26. For the sake of brevity in the footnotes of this chapter, we will quote only

Defender, humanist, and survivor 223

the duplications provided by Languschi-Dolfin, as this source appears to be the earliest imitator. Other followers will be ignored, with the understanding that they duplicate Leonardo's statements; they will only be cited if additional information is offered. For a plethora of correspondences between the imitators and Leonardo, cf. the analyses supplied by the scholarly literature cited earlier in this note.

3 Cf. the adjective applied to Isidore, "*reverendissimus*," which is also reflected in Barbaro's Venetian dialect; cf. e.g., 4 (*CC* 1: 11): *el reverendo gardenal de Rosia*; 5: (not in *CC* 1): *santissimo padre*; and 7 (not in *CC* 1): *Reverendissimo magnifico monsignor lo gardenal*.
4 On the heroic role of Girolamo Minotto and the other members of his family, many of whom, including the *bailo* himself, fell victim to the sultan's wave of executions after the fall, cf. *SF*, Appendix IV, nos. 132, 133, and 134 (p. 649). For a narrative of his role during the siege, cf. Maltezou, esp. pp. 50–52. In addition, cf. *supra*, ch. 4, n. 203.
5 Barbaro 5 (not in *CC* 1).
6 Details and documentation in *PaL* 2: 3, 4 n. 5.
7 Barbaro 5 (not in *CC* 1): *Dito che ave ognomo, respoxe messer lo capetanio: vui santissimo padre, e vui bon signor, e vui tuti che siete al prexente che me aldite.*
8 The earliest figures are provided by Barbaro 59 (not in *CC* 1): *Fu fatto presoni 60^m, e Turchi trovarono richezze infinite. Fustimà el danno de Cristiani ducati CC^m, de sudditi ducati C^m.* The Florentine merchant Giacomo Tetaldi, who was in Constantinople, fought on the walls, and swam to the safety of the Venetian ships during the sack, provides some of the earliest figures in his account, in Caput XXII entitled *De praeda Turcorum ex Constantinopoli et damno aliarum civitatum*. He estimates the following losses for the Venetians: *damnum vero quod perpessi sunt Veneti in hoc excidio fuit fere quadraginta millium ducatorum*. Then Tetaldi continues, stating that the same amount was lost by Genoa, while Florence lost 20,000 ducats. According to Tetaldi, the loss of the Venetians in war materiel amounted to the following sums:

> *Haec autem sunt armamenta seu casa bellica, quae Veneti praedicatae civitatis Constantinopolitanae pro defensione mutuaverunt et perdiderunt: octoginta fundibulae magna, 7000 brigandi, 4000 colubri, 4000 quadrigae cum balistis, 7000 fossoria, 7000 igniferas patellas, 12000 uncos, 2000 secures, 7000 malei, 40000 situlae, 7000 vasa vinalia pro potibus, 7000 bogas, 4000, ligones, et alia instrumenta plusquam 40000.*

Tetaldi then suggests that the Venetian losses in life were also high: *Item 6000 equestres et 16000 pedestres et 400 galaeae solutae pro integro anno*. A shorter summary is provided in his French account (ch. 21). For Tetaldi and his accounts, cf. Philippides, *Mehmed II the Conqueror*, pp. 21–26; Latin text (with English translation): pp. 134–217; French text: Appendix I (pp. 341–346). In addition, Barbaro also provides lists of names of numerous individuals who fell during the siege and of some who were taken prisoner and were later ransomed, 59 (not in *CC* 1): *Questi si sono i zentilomeni i qual fo morti in la bataia da turchi*; 60 (not in *CC* 1): *Questi si sono i nobeli, che scampò con le galie, e cun le nave in questo zorno*; 61 (not in *CC* 1): *Questi sono i nobeli che romaxe prexoni in tera in man de turchi*; 62 (not in *CC* 1): *i nobeli che se trova a questa prexa*; and 63 (not in *CC* 1): *Questi si son nobeli morti, da poi la prexa de la zitade de Constantinopoli*. For archival material on defenders and on fictional defenders, cf. *SF*, Appendix IV: "Some Defenders and Non-Combatants," pp. 625–661.
9 Barbaro 7, 8 (not in *CC* 1):

> *Abiando fato el conseio, che le galie dovesse romagnir in Constantinopoli, non rest ache i capetanii ad ogni modo voiano partirse, e pagar la pena de ducati 3000 per zascaduno, e però i marcadanti per prevalerse lor con le sue mercadantie, cunvene far uno protesto, e protestar è qui soto scritto.*

10 Barbaro 9, 10 (not in *CC* 1): *Questi tuti quanti soto scriti si sotoscrise al protesto sora scrito che el capetanio dovese romagnir in Constantinopoli*. The individual signatures include the following formula: io (followed by name and by patronymic) *ve protesto con quella aficazione* (or more commonly: *ve protesto in tuto e per tuto de sora è scrito*).

11 For a modern survey of the walls, towers, and gates, cf. our efforts in *SF*, ch. 5, pp. 297–359. For earlier descriptions, cf. Van Millingen, *Byzantine Constantinople*; Paspates, *Βυζαντιναὶ Μελέται*; the rather superficial account by G. Baker, *The Walls of Constantinople* (London, 1910; repr.: New York, 1975); B.C.P. Tsangadas, *The Fortifications and Defense of Constantinople*, East European Monographs 71 (Boulder and New York, 1980); and R. Janin, *Constantinople byzantine: Développement urbain et répertoir topographique*, Archives de l'Orient Chrétien 4A (2nd ed., Paris, 1964). Especially pertinent to the events of 1453 is *idem*, *La Géographie ecclésiastique de l'empire byzantin*. Additional topographical material can be found in the various travelers' reports collected in Majeska. Further details of topographical interest are also provided in accounts by western travelers; cf. J.P.A. Van der Vin, *Travellers to Greece and Constantinople: Ancient Monuments and Old Traditions in Medieval Travellers' Tales*, 2 vols. (Leiden, 1980). On medieval Greek fortifications in general, cf. C. Foss and D. Winfield, *Byzantine Fortifications: An Introduction* (Muckleneuk, Pretoria, 1985), esp. part 2, chap. 1, and pp. 56–59.

12 A pioneer in this field was the New England educated physician Paspates, *Βυζαντιναὶ Μελέται*, pp. 44 ff., who personally toured and meticulously examined the circuit of the walls and went on to record, publish, and discuss forty-one inscriptions (pp. 34–64) that he had detected and had identified *in situ*. In addition, cf. on the epigraphical evidence, S.D. Byzantios, *Ἡ Κωνσταντινούπολις, ἢ Περιγραφὴ Τοπογραφικὴ Ἀρχαιολογικὴ καὶ Ἱστορικὴ τῆς Περιωνύμου Ταύτης Μεγαλοπόλεως*, 1 (Athens, 1851), pp. 106 ff.; A. Mordtmann, *Esquisse Topografique de Constantinople* (Lille, 1892), pp. 11 ff.; and Van Millingen, *Byzantine Constantinople*, pp. 40 ff. For a modern survey of the western walls and the evidence that survives from the repairs that were carried out by John VIII, cf. *SF*, ch. 5. For the repairs that had been carried in the decade of 1430–1440, cf. M. Philippides, "Venice, Genoa, and John VIII Palaeologus' Renovation of the Fortifications of Constantinople," *Greek, Roman and Byzantine Studies* 56 (2016): pp. 377–397.

13 For an examination of the financial situation of Constantinople, cf. Philippides, *Constantine XI Dragaš Palaeologus (1404–1453)*, ch. 6, sec. I.

14 For earlier attempts to repair the fortifications by John VIII, cf. an anonymous *encomium*, which is especially informative about repairs at the moat, *ΠκΠ* 3: 292–308: ἐνταῦθα γὰρ αἱ διώρυχες περὶ τὸ τεῖχος καὶ οἱ τάφροι πάλαι μὲν εἰς βάθος ὠρύγησαν παρὰ τῶν τηνικαῦτα . . . χρόνου δὲ προϊόντος ἐν ὥραις χειμεριναῖς τῇ τῶν ὑδάτων ἐπιρροῇ κατὰ μικρὸν τὴν ὕλην ἐπισπωμένων ἐπληρώθησαν ταύτης ἄχρι τῶν ἄνω. The historical significance, unusual in a rhetorical showpiece of this genre, embedded in this anonymous Ἐγκώμιον εἰς τὸν Αὐτοκράτορα [Ἰωάννην τὸν Παλαιολόγον] (*ΠκΠ* 3: 292–308) was noted by Bogiatzides, who supervised the publication of *ΠκΠ*, vols. 3 and 4, after the death of S.P. Lampros, the original editor; cf. *ΠκΠ* 3: δ΄–ι΄ of the introduction. The passage quoted in our text can be found in *ΠκΠ* 3: 296. This anonymous source does not state exactly when John initiated this renovation program but presents a rather vague chronology; cf. *ΠκΠ* 3: 296: ἐπαναζεύξαντος τοίνυν τοῦ θειοτάτου βασιλέως μετά γε τῆς νίκης καὶ τῶν τροπαίων ἐκ τῆς τοῦ Πέλοπος. In addition, the panegyric of Isidore (whose true authorship was not known to Lampros), in *ΠκΠ* 3: 132–199, also provides a description of the moat, p. 136: τάφρος ὀρώρυκται πρὸ τούτου, ὡς μὲν εὐρεῖα, ὡς δὲ βαθεῖα, ὡς δὲ μήκιστος καὶ διὰ πάσης ὑποτρέχουσα τῆς ἠπειρωτικῆς ἐκείνης πλευρᾶς, τῶν χειλέων αὐτῆς ἀμφοῖν λίθοις μεγάλοις λογάδην τιτάνῳ προσερηρεισμένοις, συνηρμοσμένων καὶ συνδεδεμένων ἰσχυρῶς, ταῖν θαλάτταιν ἀμφοῖν προσαποδίδωσι. John also paid attention to the land fortifications and completed repairs on a tower near the Basilike Gate by the harbor (*ibid.*, p. 296):

> πύργος ἦν ἀτελὴς πρὸς τῇ λεγομένῃ Βασιλικῇ πύλῃ, ἐκ προγόνων μὲν ἀρχόμενος ἀνοικοδομεῖσθαι . . . διαβαίνων ἐγγύς που περὶ τὸ τεῖχος τοῦ ἄστεως καὶ θεασάμενος ἐπυνθάνετο τοὺς περὶ αὐτὸν εἰ δεῖ πέρας λαβεῖν τὴν οἰκοδομήν. καὶ τούτων, ὥσπερ εἰκός, κατανευσάντων, εὐθὺς ἐκέλευσεν ἐπιμελείας τυγχάνειν,

καὶ τοὺς προστησαμένους τοῦ ἔργου διαταξάμενος καὶ παραινέσας ὅπως ὀφείλει γίνεσθαι, ἀπηλλάγη. καὶ νῦν ἕστηκε παντόθεν σχεδὸν καθορώμενος.

He also erected two towers in the neighborhood of Blankas (*ibid.*, p. 297):

ἀλλὰ μὴν καὶ ἑτέρους δύο ἐν χώρῳ λεγομένῳ τοῦ Βλάγκα ἐκ βάθρων ἀνήγειρε, μεγέθει μεγίστους καὶ κάλλει διαπρεπεῖς καὶ μηδαμῶς ὄντας δευτέρους τῶν μάλιστα διαφερόντων. καὶ περιεστᾶσι κύκλῳ τοῦ ἄστεως οἱονεί τινα κόσμον παρέχουσι τῇ βασιλίδι τῶν πόλεων. ὁ μὲν ἔλαχε τὴν θέσιν πρὸς βορρᾶν ἵστασθαι, ἐπὶ πολὺ τὸν ἀέρα διαιρούμενος καὶ κατατέμνων, οἱ δὲ πρὸς μεσημβρίαν, οὐ πολὺ διεστηκότες ἀλλήλων.

John then completed repairs on the port of Kontoskalion (*ibid.*, p. 298).

15 D.M. Nicol, *Byzantium and Venice: A Study in Diplomatic and Cultural Relations* (Cambridge, 1988), pp. 390–392.
16 Nicolò da Canale would eventually become responsible for the fall of Negroponte/ Khalkis to the Turks; cf. Philippides, *Mehmed II the Conqueror*, pp. 30–33, p. 221 (with n. 18), and p. 247 (with nn. 260, 363, 365, and 367).
17 *NE* 8: 67, 68; for the documents of the period 2–17 August 1450, cf. *RdD* 3: 2830 and 2831.
18 Nicol, *Byzantium and Venice*, p. 391.
19 *NE* 3: 257, 258.
20 *Ibid.*:

> datum quod dabant pro sclavis capit<aneo> et portiaticum sclavorum, portiaticum aliarum rerum, exitum vini Venetorum, ut sit liber, scribaniam vegetum Jud<a>eorum Venetorum, medium <hy>perperum, quod exigebat co<m>merciarius noster ex qualibet vegete Jud<a>eorum, et quod de cetero Jud<a>ei Veneti non dent factionem aliquam in tempore ecessitates, ut ceteri Jud<a>ei; pro pellis et saumis et cariaticum, cum esset difficile nobis respondere, peti<v>it nos dilectus gener imperii mei, magnus dux Luchas Diermineftis [= Διερμηνευτὴς/Dragoman] Notara, ut transeat hoc in suo proprio salario et quod non petatur, donec veniat orator noster.

21 The situation is reflected in the coinage of the last Palaiologoi. Surviving coins that had been issued in the reign of Constantine XI are rare nowadays. There had been only one known coin dated to the regime of Constantine XI, a silver quarter-hyperperon, which had surfaced in 1974. A few other illegible copper coins may date back to Constantine's reign also. Finally, a hoard of low quality silver coins surfaced, which includes among them ninety coins of Constantine XI: 35 stavrata, 5 half-stavrata, and 50 one-eighth-stavrata. For an exhaustive study of the hoard in question, cf. S. Bendall, "The Coinage of Constantine XI," *Revue Numismatique* (VIe série) 33 (1991): pp. 134–142, with plates XIII–XVII.
22 *CC* 1: 146 provides an abbreviated extract of this passage; the complete passage, as quoted in our text, can be found in *PG* 159: col. 934:

> Quid autem imperator perplexus agat, ignorat. Consulit barones: suadent non molestari cives angustia temporis, sed recurrendum ad sacra. Auferri igitur et conflari iussit ex sacris templis sancta Dei vasa, sicuti Romanos pro necessitate temporis fecisse legimus, exque eis pecuniam insigniri darique militibus, fossoribus constructoribusque, qui rem suam, non publicam, attendentes, nisi ex denario convenissent, ad opus ire recusabant.

We encounter the usual echoes in Leonardo's followers: Languschi-Dolfin fol. 317 (pp. 18, 19):

> Al incontro lo Imperator non sa quello se debbe fare et consegliasse, lo confortano i baroni attento la angustia de tempi non molestar li citadini, ma ricorrer a li beni de le chiesie, unde fece i uasi d argento, croce, chalici, turriboli, e fece batter moneta per pagar soldati, et offosori, et

constructori, li qual tamen attendendo a le cose priuate, et non ale publiche, ricusauano lauorar se non erano pagati.

Not surprisingly, the same passage is encountered in the Greek text of the derivative *Maius* 3.5.7 (p. 401). Melissourgos-Melissenos followed Leonardo, but altered the classical precedents into a biblical reference:

> ἐπειδὴ καὶ χρημάτων ἐσπάνιζον τὰ βασίλεια διὰ τὸν μισθὸν τῶν στρατιωτῶν, προσέταξεν ὁ βασιλεὺς λαβεῖν τὰ τῶν ἐκκλησιῶν σκεύη ἅγια καὶ ἀφιερωμένα τῷ Θεῷ καὶ χρήματα ἐποιήσαμεν. Καὶ μή τις ἐγκαλέσειεν ἡμᾶς ὡς ἱεροσύλους ἕνεκεν τοῦ καιροῦ ἀνάγκης, καὶ ὡς ὁ Δαβὶδ πεπονθὼς πεινάσας τοὺς ἄρτους τῆς προθέσεως ἔφαγεν.

Another Greek paraphrase of the same passage, more faithful to its ultimate source, is provided in the *Codex Barberinus 111*, 7.13:

> Διατὶ ὁ βασιλεὺ εἶχε μεγάλην σύχυσιν καὶ δὲν ἤξερε πλέο τὸ τί νὰ κάμῃ καί, ἐπειδὴ δὲν τοῦ ἐδίδανε φλωρία οἱ πλούσιοι, δὲν εἶχε τί νὰ κάμῃ καὶ ἐπῆρε ἀπὸ τὶς ἐκκλησίες καὶ ἀπὸ τὰ μοναστήρια τὰ ἀσημικά τους καὶ τὰ ἔκαμνε μονέδα, ὡς καθὼς τὸ ἐκάμασι παλαιὰ οἱ Ρωμάνοι ἐς τὴν Ρώμα, καὶ ἐπλήρωνε τοὺς δουλευτάδες ὁποὺ ἐδουλεύαν εἰς τὰ τειχία.

The entire Greek text can be found in G.T. Zoras, ed., *Χρονικὸν περὶ τῶν Τούρκων Σουλτάνων* (κατὰ τὸν Βαρβ. Ἑλληνικὸν Κώδικα 111) (Athens, 1958); for an English translation of this early seventeenth-century *Codex Barberinus 111*, cf. M. Philippides, *Byzantium, Europe, and the Early Ottoman Sultans 1373–1513: An Anonymous Greek Chronicle of the Seventeenth Century* (Codex Barberinus Graecus 111), Late Byzantine and Ottoman Studies 4 (New Rochelle, 1990).

23 Cf., e.g., the comments of the *Codex Barberinus 111*, 7.12:

> Ὦ Ρωμαῖοι φιλάργυροι. Δημηγέρτες, τραδιτόροι, ὁποὺ ἐτραδίρετε τὴν πατρίδα σας, ὁποὺ ὁ βασιλέας σας ἤτονε πτωχὸς καὶ σᾶς ἐπαρακάλειε μετὰ δάκρυα 'ς τὰ μάτια νὰ τοῦ δανείσετε φλωρία διὰ νὰ δώσῃ καὶ νὰ μαζώξῃ πολεμιστάδες ἀνθρώπους νὰ βοηθήσωσι καὶ νὰ πολεμήσουνε, καὶ ἐσεῖς ἀρνίεστε μεθ' ὅρκους πῶς δὲν ἔχετε καὶ εἶστε πτωχοί! Ἀμμὴ ὑστέρου, ὅπου σᾶς ἐπῆρε ὁ Τοῦρκος, εὑρέθητε πλούσοι καὶ σᾶς τὸ πῆρε ὁ Τοῦρκος καὶ ἔκοψε καὶ τὸ κεφάλι σας ... Ὦ Ρωμαῖοι ἀκριβοί, μίζεροι, καὶ κακότυχοι, ὁποὺ ἐφάνη εἰς τὸ φῶς τόσον βίος, ὁποὺ σᾶς ἐζήτα ὁ βασιλέας σας δανεικὰ καὶ δὲν τὰ δώσετε νὰ βοηθήσῃ τὴν χώρα σας, μόνε τὸ ἀρνιέστε καὶ ἐλέγετε ὅτι: "δὲν ἔχομε καὶ εἴμεσταν πτωχοί," καὶ τώρα τὰ ἐπῆρανε οἱ Τοῦρκοι.

Identical sentiments are expressed in the narrative of Languschi-Dolfin (which might be the immediate source of the *Codex Barberinus 111* and which also depends, to a large extent, on the Latin text of Leonardo); cf. Languschi-Dolfin fol. 317 (p. 18):

> Et fu grande impieta de quelli baroni greci auari direptori de la patria. De li quali piu uolte el pouero Imperator cum lachrime domandaua, prestasseno denari per condur prouisionati. Et quelli iurauano esser poueri disfatti, che dapoi presi el Signor Turcho quelli trouo richissimi.

Also, cf. Languschi-Dolfin fol. 321 (p. 31): *et tutti li absconditti perueniano in man de Turci, o Greci miseri et miserabili che fingeui esser poueri. Ecco che sono uenuti in luce li uostri tesori, li quali teneui, et negaui uoler dar per subsidio de la citade.* Makarios Melissourgos-Melissenos follows but changes the ancient examples to biblical references, 3.5.7 (quoted *supra*, n. 26). For a stemma of the various degrees of correspondence among these followers of Leonardo, cf. Philippides, "The Fall of Constantinople 1453: Bishop Leonardo Giustiniani and His Italian Followers," p. 210; and, for further details, cf. the stemma in *SF*, Fig. 1 (p. 92).

24 On Loukas Notaras, his family, and his business connections, cf., among others, K.P. Matschke, "The Notaras Family and Its Italian Connections," *DOP* 9 [= *Symposium on*

Byzantium and the Italians, 13th–15th Centuries] (1995): pp. 59–72; idem, "Personengeschichte, Familiengeschichte, Socialgeschichte: Die Notaras im späten Byzanz," in L. Balleto, ed. *Oriente e Occidente tra Medioevo et Età Moderna. Studi in onore di Geno Pistarino*, 2 (Geneva, 1997), pp. 718–812; T. Ganchou, "Le rachat des Notaras après la chute de Constantinople ou les relations 'étrangères' de l'élite byzantine au XVe siècle," in *Migrations et Diasporas Méditerrannéenes (X^e–XVIe siècles)*.Actes du colloque des Conques (Octobre 1990), eds. M. Balard and A. Ducellier, Série Byzantina Sorbonensia 19 (Paris, 2002), pp. 149–229; A. Ducellier and T. Ganchou, *Les élites urbaines au Moyen Age* (Paris, 1997), pp. 39–54; C. Maltezou, Ἄννα Παλαιολογίνα Νοταρᾶ: Μιὰ Τραγικὴ Μορφὴ ἀνάμεσα στὸν Βυζαντινὸ καὶ τὸν Νέο Ἑλληνικὸ Κόσμο, Βιβλιοθήκη τοῦ Ἑλληνικοῦ Ἰνστιτούτου Βυζαντινῶν καὶ Μεταβυζαντινῶν Σπουδῶν Βενετίας 23 (Venice, 2004); and *SF*, Appendix II.

25 Cf., e.g., Adamo di Montaldo (on this secondary source, cf. *SF*, p. 46), who goes so far as to suggest that Notaras opened the gates to the Ottoman army, 22 (p. 37): *Quod patefacto ut ingerunt hostio per civem, quem Magnum Ducem cognominabant, copiarum introitus numero ingenti patuit.*

26 On the minor humanist, Ioannes Moskhos, a former student of George Plethon, cf. S. Mergiali-Falangas," Ἔνας Ἰταλὸς Οὑμανιστὴς καὶ Ἔνας Πελοποννήσιος Δάσκαλος: Σχέσεις Μάρκου Ἀντωνίου Ἀντιμάχου καὶ Ἰωάννου Μόσχου," *Modern Greek Studies Yearbook* 10/11 (1994–1995): pp. 579–584); Elizabeth A. Zachariadou, "Τὰ Λόγια καὶ ὁ Θάνατος τοῦ Λουκᾶ Νοταρᾶ," in *Ροδωνιά: Τιμὴ στὸν Μ. Ι. Μανούσσακα* (Rethymno, 1996), pp. 135–146; and *SF*, p. 45 n. 128.

27 Moskhos, in the piece that he wrote (which was commissioned by Notaras's surviving daughter in Italy), suggests, in a weak sophistic argument, that the grand duke proposed that all wealthy individuals contribute to a fund, an ἔρανος, and compete with one another in the amount of contribution; of course, nothing came of it, if the suggestion was ever made. Cf. M. Philippides, "An Ancient Business Success and a Medieval Failure: Lessons in Ethics from Old Business Approaches and Practices," in G. Prastacos, *et al.*, eds. *Leadership and Management in a Changing World* (Heidelberg, 2012), pp. 351–365, esp. 355–358.

28 Leonardo, *PG* 159: col. 943 [*CC* 1: 166]:

> *Vocatis igitur ad se [sc. Mehmed II] Chirluca ceterisque baronibus consularibus et reprehensis quod non suasissent imperatori vel pacem petendam vel dandam suae dicioni urbem, Chirluca . . . culpam retorquere curavit. . . . At Chirluca militiae poenam non evasit, qui protinus perditis primum in bello duobus liberis maioribus, alio impubere luxui regali reservato, coramque oculis tertio filio caeso cum ceteris baronibus decollatur.*

This information is echoed by Leonardo's followers as usual, cf. e.g., Languschi-Dolfin fol. 322 (pp. 31–32):

> *Et chiamato a se [sc. Mehmed II] chir Luca Notara mega duca et altri baroni greci, represe quelli che non persuadesse a lo Imperator, o inclinarsi a domandarli pace, o hauerli data libera la citade. Alhora Chirluca che cerchaua mettersi in gratia del Signor, et in disgratia Uenetiani et Genoesi de Pera, li qual fono quelli che dauano consilio, armi et militi et li qual uoltaua ogni copla, et per star in sua gratia lo imperator faceua resistentia, uogliando quello misero che sempre cerchaua gloria cum mendacio et scisma hauer mazor gratia. Callibasa . . . quello accuso esser amico de Greci lo qual cum frequente lettere a lo Imperator confirmo el suo animo a star forte et constante, et le sue lettere saluate in fede de questo apresento al turcho. . . . Ma Chirluca non scapolo la pena de la malitia sua, che nel suo conspetto fece occider do grandi sui fioli, laltro impubere zouenetto reservo a sua luxuria et lui in ultimo cum sui baroni fu decapitato.*

These rumors persisted as late as the 1470s and appear in Adamo di Montaldo's composition, p. 339:

> *Lucas, Magnus Dux cognomento honoris dictus, quem proditionis infamia reum fecit, vigesies centenis aureorum milibus extrusus est. Cumque noluisset natum regi libidinose eum rectius scelerate machinanti dare, dum benigne prius ac comiter habitus fuisset, in regis indignationem*

devenit. Quam quidem ob rem mox clamitantem e complexibus parentis arripi puerum jussit, cumque invitum violasset, eundem cum patre ac altero fratre morte multandum dedit, objecta de proditione civitatis culpa, quam perperam tradisse patrem asserebat.

Marco Barbaro, the kinsman of Nicolò, seems to have heard such rumors also, but he does not include the name of Notaras and only speaks of a courtier in his addition to his kinsman's journal, p. 66 (*CC* 1: 38):

Et dicesi che uno gran baron greco [Notaras?], *per farsi grato a esso Turco, gli mandò doi sue figlie con uno piato per una in mano, pieni de dinari, onde il Turco facea grande onore a ditto barone, et monstrava averlo molto grato. Vedendo li favori che avea costui, altri nobili grechi, ciascuno tolse quella quantità de denari che puotè, et per gratificarsi gli la portò a donare; lui accettò li presenti, et li portatori di essi metteva in grado onorato; ma chessato che fu tali presenti, el fece tagliare la testa a quanti lo avea presentato, dicendo che erano stati gran cani a non avere voluto prestarli al suo signore et avere lasciato perdere la città.*

It should be stressed that in his brief statement on the execution of Notaras, Isidore avoids all of these rumors and simply states facts (Hofmann, "Ein Brief," pp. 405–414 [omitted by *CC* 1]: *Post tres dies* [since the sack] *decrevit* [sc. Mehmed] *ac iussit primo quidem duobus filiis Notarae – alter enim gloriose dimicans interierat – capita in conspectu patris amputari, ipsi deinde patri, postea magni domestici filios tres pulcherrimos et optimos occidit insuper patrem eorum* [for an English translation, cf. *SF*, p. 600]).

29 Barbaro 66 [not included in the selections printed in *CC* 1]:

L'imperator essendo poverissimo, dimandò imprestido a suoi baroni di denari, loro si escusarono non ne avere, et poi Turchi trovarono assai denari, et a tal di quelli gentilhomeni fu trovato ducati 30ᵐ, e fu consigliato l'imperator non mettere angarie in queli tumulti, ma torre le argenterie de le chiese, et cosi si fece.

30 Even in his personal letter to his friend Bessarion, Isidore downplays his role; cf., e.g., his statement in paragraph 4 (for the entire letter, with translation, cf. *infra*, sec. 3): *Cum circam mensem Maii superioris anni Romam reliquissem, nullum penitus inde pr<A>esidium vel auxilium referens.*

31 *PG* 159: col. 935 [*CC* 1: 150]. Languschi-Dolfin repeats the information of Leonardo in the vernacular, fol. 318: *Hieronymo Italiano, Leonardo da Languasto Genoexe cum molti compagni la porta chsilo et le torre Anemade le qual el cardinal a sue spese hauea reparato diffensaua.*

32 On the proper name of these towers (Anemades and not Aveniades, as the name appears in very early editions) which were part of the Πενταπύργιον (that is, "the Fortress of the Five Towers"; cf. Paspates, Βυζαντιναὶ Μελέται, pp. 25–32), and on the scholarly controversy that resulted in an inability among scholars to identify them because the Renaissance editions contained an incorrect entry for their name, cf. *SF*, p. 355, n. 271. By the sixteenth century, the mistake had been detected by Leunclavius, who had received assistance from a learned Greek official of the Patriarchate, Theodosios Zygomalas, who cited the correct names for the towers. For Leunclavius's text, cf. *SF*, p. 355 n. 277.

33 On this sector, cf. our observations in *SF*, pp. 353–357.

34 Barbaro 50 (not in *CC* 1) relates an incident to illustrate this point, which took place at a critical moment, 28 May, as the siege was reaching its climax and the general Ottoman assault was about to commence:

Nui cristiani in questo zorno [May 28] *fessemo cara sette de manteleti, da meter a le merladure da laq banda da tera; fati questi manteleti, fo reduti a la piazza, e miser lo bailo* [Girolamo Minotto] *fexe comandamento ai griexi che portasse e questi prestamente a le mure, e mai griexi non i volse portar se prima i non fosse pagadi, e stete in contrasto quaxi sera per muodo, che nui venitiani convegnissemo pagar de borsa a chi i porta, e griexi nula si volse pagar; e quando che i manteleti fo zonti a le mura, el iera la note, e queli non podessemo conzare ai merli per la bataia, e si stessemo senza, e questo fexe l'avaritia lor griexi.*

35 *PG* 159: col. 934 [*CC* 1: 146]. He is imitated, as usual, by Languschi-Dolfin fol. 317 (pp. 18, 19):

> *Et fu grande impieta de quelli baroni greci auari direptori de la patria. De li qual piu uolte el pouero Imperator cum lachrime domandaua, prestasseno denari per condur prouisionati. Et quelli iurauano esser poueri disfatti, che dapoi presi el Signor Turcho quelli trouo richissimi. Tamen da alcuni li fo sponte prestato danari. Et lo cardinal Sabino de Rusia ogni studio pose in darli adiutorio in riparar torre et murri.*

36 *CC* 1: 114: *Facta enim sancta unione, pro qua reverendissimus dominus cardinalis Ruthenus* [Isidore] *ex Urbe* [Rome] *recesserat et vendita sua facultate tota usque ad vestimenta pro Urbis Constantinopolitanae.* Pertusi (*CC* 1: 111) supposes that the author is none other than Francesco Griffolini d'Arezzo.

37 No. 17 (p. 45) in Paspates' enumeration (*supra*, n. 15): Μανουὴλ τοῦ Ἰάγαρι. This family name is variously recorded in our sources: Giagaris, Jagaris, Iagaris, Iagros. On Manuel, cf. *PLP* 4, no. 7810 (p. 78). For the possible Russian origins of this name, cf. R.A. Klosterman, "Jagaris oder Gagarin? Zur Deutung eines griechishen und russischen Familiennames," *OCP* 204 (1977): pp. 221–237; in addition, cf. T. Ganchou, "Sur quelques erreurs relatives aux dernier défenseurs grecs de Constantinople en 1453," *Θησαυρίσματα: Περιοδικὸν τοῦ Ἑλληνικοῦ Ἰνστιτούτου Βυζαντινῶν καὶ Μεταβυζαντινῶν Σπουδῶν τῆς Βενετίας* 25 (1995): pp. 61–82, esp. 65 and 66, with accompanying notes. It is further likely that the same individual served as Constantine's emissary to Serbia in 1451; cf. I.A. Papadrianos, "Manojlo Paleolog, Vizantijski poslanik u Serbij 1451," *Zbornik Radova Vizantolo·kog Instituta* 7 (= *Mélanges G. Ostrogorsky 2*) (1954): pp. 311–315. Also cf. Papadopoulos, no. 184 (p. 94). Another member of the same family, Andronikos Iagaris, was an imperial envoy and, apparently, a μεσάζων of Constantine XI.

38 *Minus* 29.1: Ἀλέξιος Φιλανθρωπηνὸς ὁ Λάσκαρις . . . καὶ Μανουὴλ ὁ Παλαιολόγος ὁ Ἴαγρος . . . βασιλέα πεποιήκασι . . . τὸν δεσπότην κὺρ Κωνσταντῖνον.

39 *PG* 159: cols. 936, 937 [not in *CC* 1]):

> *At quid dicam? arguamne principem . . . an potius eos qui ex officio muros refidere debuissent? O quorum animae forte damnantur, Manuelis Giagari dudum inopis, et Neophyti hieromonaci Rhodii, si audeo dicere, praedonum, non conservatorum reipublicae, quibus veluti reipublicae tutoribus, aut ex aviis intestatisque bona relicta, muris ascribi debebant, privatis potius commodis impedebant. Primus viginti prope millium florenorum servus proditionis monachus, quos posthac reconditos urna septuaginta millium gazam reliquunt Teucris. Idcirco urbs praedonum incuria in tanta tempestate periit.*

Identical statements are repeated in Languschi-Dolfin fol. 318 (p. 22):

> *Ma per questo non e, da improperar lo Imperator, perche quello sempre haue bona fede in la romana chiesa, ma era uinto da pusillanimita, ma alcuni Greci, Manuel Jagari, et Neophyto Jeronaco Rodiani, ladri corsari non curauano conseruar el publico, hauendo gran richeze de auo quelle tegniua a suo priuati commodi. El primo hauea 70 millia ascosti in Zara lassati a Gazan Turcho. Et per poca cura de questi tali in tanti affani lassono perir la citade.*

Similar is the information supplied by Marco Barbaro in a note that he added to his kinsman's journal, p. 66 (not in *CC* 2):

> *L'imperator essendo poverissimo, dimandò imprestido a suoi baroni di denari, loro si escusarono non ne avere, et poi Turchi trovarono assai denari, et a tal di quelli gentilhomeni fu travto ducati 30^m, e fu consiglito l'imperatore non mettere angarie in queli tumulti. Ma torre le argenterie de le chiese, et così si fece.*

40 The major assault against this sector took place on 12 May, according to Barbaro 39 (*CC* 1: 23); for Barbaro's text, English translation, and discussion of the attacks, cf. *SF*, pp. 355–357.

41 Benvenuto, the Anconitan consul in Constantinople, whose fragmentary account was only recovered recently, twice stresses the importance of the military contribution of Isidore; cf. *TIePN*, p. 4: *Item quod de reverendissimo domino cardinali nichil scit det<er>minate, nisi quod stabat super murum ad custodiam*. Benvenuto fails to mention exactly which sector Isidore guarded. He returns again to Isidore's military contribution, *TIePN*, p. 5: *Item quod erant tantum homines ad custodiendum m<o>enias cum reverendissimo domino cardinali 7000*. For Benvenuto and his account, editions, and translations, cf. *SF*, p. 31, where it is pointed out that the ms. includes the following information in regard to the date of composition: "Venice, the 31st of July 1453."

42 *PG* 59: col. 935 [*CC* 1: 150]: *Cardinalis, a consilio nunquam absens, Sancti Demetrii regionem ad mare defensabat*. Languschi-Dolfin follows the prototype closely, fol. 317 (p. 20): *Lo cardinal mai se absentaua, ma diffensaua la porta de Dimitrij uerso el mar*. The exact location of the monastery remains unknown. Nevertheless, the general area can be identified through the comments of Stephen of Novgorod who visited Constantinople in earlier years and has left us an account of his tour. He places the area in the neighborhood of Kontoskalion; cf. his account in Majeska, p. 39 (English translation: p. 38): От Подрумия поити мимо Каньдоскали ... А оттоле идохом к святому Димитрию. Majeska (*ibid.*, p. 267) points out that "Stephen of Novgorod is the only known source suggesting an approximate location of the 'Imperial Monastery of St. Demetrius.'" Stephen also suggests that this monastery was the burial place of an emperor (*ibid.*, pp. 38, 39): ту лежит тѣло святаго царя Ласкарсафа (тако бо бѣ имя ему), и цѣловахом грѣшии тѣло его, "where the body of the holy Emperor Laskariasfa (such was his name) lies, and we sinners kissed his body." Stephen then adds another clue for the location of the monastery, near the Giudecca and the Jewish Gate of Constantinople: Тои есть монастырь царев, стоит при мори. И ту есть близ монастыря того живет жидов много при мори възлѣ городную стѣну, и врата на море зовутся «Жидовская», "this is an imperial monastery, standing near the sea. Many Jews live near the monastery, along the city wall above the sea, and so the gates are called 'Jewish.'"

43 Leonardo, *PG* 159: col. 950: *Chirluca curam portus totiusque maritimae regionis invigilabat ad deferendum praesidium* (followed by Languschi-Dolfin, fol. 317 (p. 20): *Cir Luca Notara hauea la cura deffensar el porto e la marina*). Barbaro duplicates the same information and specifies some further details, p. 19 (not in *CC* 1):

> *El mega duca, el qual sono el prinzipal homo de Costantinopoli da l'imperador in fuora, si avea in varda la marina de la banda del porto, et avea cavalli zento de rescossa, i qual jera d'agnora in sua compagna per dover dar socorso con quegli, dove jera de bisogno a la tera.*

In an original passage, without a dependency on Leonardo, Languschi-Dolfin also specifies that Notaras defended the Basilike Gate, fol. 317 (p. 17): *A porta basilica Luca Notara*, with whom Ubertino Pusculo agrees, 4.192–196 (p. 65) [*CC* 1: 208]: *Ac tu / Basileam, Luca, portam tibi, Notare, custos / commissam servas. Alias quae litora circum / aequoris aspiciunt portas diversa virorum / corpora legunt vicina et moenia servant*. Further, it is interesting to note that Neophytos the Rhodian and Manuel Iagaris (cf. *infra*, n. 41) also had commanding positions over monks and churchmen who were "manning" the sea walls in the sector near Notaras and Isidore. Cf. the Latin ephemeris of Barbaro (entire text and English translation in *SF*, pp. 578–596), p. 580 (April 6): *Legimus insuper quod magnus Dux* [Notaras], *primum secundum imperatorem locum tenens portui praefuit, ubi 100 ei equi parati stabant; quod muri maritime custodia monachis duce Manuele Giagaro ... ac Neophyto Rhodiensis comissa fuit*.

44 For the emotionally charged atmosphere and the rumors in circulation, involving "spies" and collaborators during the siege, cf. Philippides, "Rumors of Treason."

45 Leonardo, *PG* 159: col. 936 (*CC* 1: 152):

> *Interea capitaneus generalis Johannes Justinianus, totius fortunae observator, ut praesensit <ex> proclamatione Theucrum praesto daturum certamen, agebat confestim murorum, quos machina*

contriverat, reparationem; petivitque sibi a Chirluca, magno duce consulari, communes urbis bombardas quas contra hostes affigeret. Quas cum superbe denegasset: 'Quis me, capitaneus inquit, o proditor, tenet ut gladio non occumbas meo?' Qua ignominia indignatus, tum quod Latinus exprobasset eum, remissius post rei bellicae providentiam gessit. . . . At capitaneus Johannes, Mauricii Catanei praefecti, Johannis de Carreto, Pauli Bocchiardi, Johannis de Fornariis, Thomae de Salvaticis, L<e>odixii Gatilusii, Johannis Illyrici aliorumque ascitorum Graecorum consultu, acies munimentaque refecit. Cujus providentiam Teucrus commendans: 'Quam vellem, inquit, penes me praefectum illum Joannem honorandum!' Magnis hercle donis aureoque multo corrumpere illum studuit: cujus inflectere animum nunquam potuit.

Leonardo's information is replicated in the vernacular by Languschi-Dolfin fol. 318 (p. 21):

Infra questo tempo Joanne Zustignan capitanio general in la terra, che uedeua tutto el pericolo de la cita, come sentite la proclamatione facta per lo exercito del Turco, che uoleua dar la battaglia general alla citade, cum solicitudine riparo gran parte di muri ruinati. Insuper domando a Cir Luca Notara gran consegliero alcune bombarde da rebatter li inimici da la sua statione, et quelli cum superbia denego uoler dar. Al qual irato Joanne Zustignan disse o traditor, et che me tien che adesso non te scanna cum questo pugnal, da la qual uergogna disdegnato mega duca che uno Latino l hauesse improprato se portaua piu rimesso ale prouision de la cita, et Greci secretamente mal tolleraua che Italiani hauesse de difensar la citade.

Discussion of this important incident, which may have influenced Giustiniani's decision to retreat from his sector after he was wounded, in Philippides, "Giovanni Guglielmo Longo Giustiniani," pp. 13–54; and *SF*, p. 546.

46 Barbaro 19 (not in *CC* 1).
47 *PG* 159: col. 935 (*CC* 1: 150): *Cardinalis, a consilio nunquam absens.* . . .
48 Cf., e.g., the comments of Schiel, pp. 166, 167 and n. 61. It should be recalled, nevertheless, that, in spite of the evident primacy of this important source, we still lack an authoritative edition of Leonardo's complete text, which must include an essential *apparatus criticus*. For available manuscripts, some of which still need to be consulted, and the early editions from the fifteenth and the sixteenth centuries, cf. *SF*, pp. 18, 19, which have now been supplemented by Schiel, p. 166 n. 60, with citations of additional editions from the sixteenth century.
49 *PG* 159: col. 937 (*CC* 1: 154): *Calilbasia* [Halil Pasha] *enim, regis vetustior consularis baro, gravitate, consilio rerumque bellarum experientia pollens, Christianis favens, regi* [sultan] *semper dissuaserat ne urbem Constantinopolim molestaret.* The same information is encountered in Languschi-Dolfin's imitation of Leonardo fol. 319: *Alhora Calibassa piu uecchio graue de conseio, et perito de experientia de cose bellice sempre dessuadeua el Signor Turco non molestasse Constantinopoli.*
50 Thus Leonardo unambiguously states that as soon as the decision was made at the Porte to launch the final assault, Halil informed the Greek high command of the sultan's intention and gave advice concerning the course of action that the defense should undertake; cf. *PG* 159: col. 938 (*CC* 1: 156): *ut Calilbascia* [Halil Pasha], *senior consularis . . . consilium intellexit definitumque esse certamen, clam internuntiis admodum fidissimis uti amicus imperatori cuncta denunciat.* [Not in *CC* 1]: *hortaturque ut non expavescat . . . nec terreriminis eorum qui magis timuissent: nec indoctiore multitudine commoveri: custodies sint vigiles et pugnam perseverantes exspectent.* As usual, the information is repeated by Languschi-Dolfin fol. 319:

Come Calibassa uecchio conseijer intese chel conseijo . . . diffinir el zorno che se douea dar la bataglia, alhora per fidati nuncij come amico de Christiani tutta la deliberation del Signor tutto fa notto al imperator, confortando quello no se impaurica . . . ne per tal minaze impaurisse contra multituidine inexperta et facia far bone guardia.

51 *PG* 159: cols. 942–943 (a small extract, without the important details, in *CC* 1): *Chirluca . . . Calilbasciam vetustiorem, loco et prudential primum Teucri baronem, amicum admodum Graecis, quod crebris litteris ad imperatorem missis ejus animum a pacis consiliis detraxisset,*

232 *Defender, humanist, and survivor*

utque fortis staret persuasisset, accusavit; epistolas servatas in fide regi praesentavit. Cf. Languschi-Dolfin fol. 322, with identical information. If indeed this incident is true, it implies that Notaras had been hoarding intelligence information that Halil had been supplying to the defense and therefore Notaras's actions come into question. As the grand duke and prime minister of the emperor, he should have destroyed this evidence and should not have saved it to take advantage for his own purposes. It is no surprise that Leonardo adds, with a measure of delight, the following comment, *PG* 159: col. 943: *At Chirluca militia poenam non evasit: . . . decollatur.*

52 *PG* 159: col. 938 (not in *CC* 1) and duplicated by Languschi-Dolfin fol. 319: *Da qual bassa spesse lettere al imperator uegniuano portate.* For a further study of treasonable acts, spying, for agents, provocateurs, etc., cf. Philippides, "Rumors of Treason," *passim.*

53 The use of the imperfect tense implies that many letters came on different occasions, a fact that is also emphasized later in the bishop's narrative.

54 This becomes evident in his various comparisons with other cities, which had suffered a similar fate in antiquity. He touches upon this subject in all the literature that he produced after the fall; cf., e.g., his comments to Bessarion, 3:

> *Repetamus enim ab <A>eterno cum plurimarum civitatum et parvarum et maximarum casus et ruin<A>e in diversis mundi partibus olim fuisse legantur, nulla unquam fuit, quae Constantinopolitan<A>e possit expugnationi ac direptioni comparari. Non Troi<A>e populatio, non Thebarum eversio, non Hierosolymorum trina destructio, non Antiochi<A>e, non Rom<A>e, non Alexandri<A>e, non cuiusvis alterius sive maioris sive minoris civitatis.*

Similar comments with different comparisons of biblical origin can be found in his report to Pope Nicholas V, 6:

> *Cuius captivitas omnes ab initio saeculi captivitates superat et excedit: Hierosolymorum ab Nabugodonosor<e> rege pauca equidem et parva fuit respectu tantae et tam magnae; ipsius quidem pecuniae ablatae sunt, populus autem non fuit pedibus et manibus colligatus, sed simul congregatus ad Babyloniam transductus est; et sacra eorum no abrepta, non conculcata, sed Assyriorum rex ea in aedibus suis cum reverentia observabat. Similiter et comparatio nulla in aliam civitatem potest fieri, quae huic potest adaequari.*

55 The complete text and English translation will be quoted in presently.

56 Ibid.: *Quid igitur dixerim fecerimque ac mente volverim, non facile verbis aut scriptis complecti possem.*

57 This was his practice when he provides a short account of an incident, the withdrawal of Giustiniani from the critical sector of the assault, which precipitated the disaster, as the Turks overran the undermanned sector, the Mesoteikhion, and entered the fortifications, without ever achieving a breach of the walls; on this event, cf. *SF*, pp. 525–546. Isidore seems to suggests that the incident was also controversial in his own mind but he implies that he intended to speak about it with Bessarion in private, 11: *Erat autem cum imperatore illo ductor quidam nomine Ioannes Iustinianus, quem multi incusant primam fuisse causam tant<A>e captivitatis et excidii: sed omittamus.*

58 Dated the 7th of July 1453 (*dat<A>e VII Iulii MCCCCLIII* from Candia) and addressed to "the exalted lord priors of the palace and of the community of Florence," in which he adds further that the sultan's cruelty surpasses the cruelty of Thyestes. Echoes from this letter appear in the text of another letter (dated the 26th of July [1453]: *die 26 Julii*), which the cardinal addressed to the "Glorious Doge of Venice, Francesco Foscari" (*inclito duci Venetiarum Isidorus miseratione divina sacrosancta Romanae ecclesiae episcopus Sabinus cardinalis Rutinensis appelatus*). Cf. Hofmann, "Quellen zur Isidor als Kardinal und Patriarch," pp. 143–157: *(Magnificis dominis prioribus palatii et communitatis Florentinorum): Nam numquam Nero crudelissimus, numquam Thyestes, qui proprios filios edendos patri trad<d>idit . . . regem Alexandrum admirandum Macedonem cum minore potentia subiuga<viss>e totum orbem, et hunc, qui iam imperiale regnum Constantinopolis obtinuit et habet innumerabilem exercitum non posse totum orbem submittere.* The learned cardinal was perhaps confused with his

Defender, humanist, and survivor 233

reference to Thyestes. Thyestes in classical mythology had been the victim; he was served a dinner of his own children by his brother Atreus. These are the earliest citations and comparisons on record between the sultan and the Macedonian king, but eventually there was wide circulation of this comparison among humanists. The nucleus of this account appears to originate with Cardinal Isidore and his fellow humanists in Crete. This comparison found appeal in the humanistic circles of the West and was then taken up by others in their narratives. The comparison propagated by Isidore and Leonardo during the siege was further elaborated by the cardinal and by his literary circle on Crete. It was then dispatched in early reports to the West and was further expounded upon before it found wide appeal and distribution among humanists in Italy. On this topic, cf. the details in Philippides, "The Fall of Constantinople 1453: Classical Comparisons and the Circle of Cardinal Isidore," *passim*.

59 Leonardo is placed squarely within the humanistic sphere by Cyriacus of Ancona, arguably the first epigraphist for Greek archaeology, who had met him, as he notes in a letter of 1444 (Bodnar and Foss, letter 6 [15–27]): *Vidimus et inter praeclaros eo loco viros Leonardum, venerandum religione ac divinarum et humanarum litterarum peritissimum hominem, quocum multis cum nobilibus splendido in symposio fuimus*. Cyriacus mentions Leonardo once again in a letter of the 27th of August 1444, which was probably written in Constantinople (Bodnar and Foss, Letter 15 [84–86]): *hodie . . . reverendissimum patrem Leonardum, Lesbeum pontificem, ad hanc urbem adventatem hylaritate revisimus.*

60 Perhaps that is a copyist's error for *Macedones*? It should be remarked in passing that the Turkish expression "Janissary" proved difficult to couch in Latin or in the ancient Greek language. The most successful equivalent seems to have been coined by Laonikos Khalkokondyles, who consistently refers to this corps as οἱ νεήλυδες. Other authors and especially accounts composed in the various Italian vernaculars of the period seem to have had trouble with it and very often produce phonetic approximations to the Turkish word. Cf., e.g., Giacomo Rizzardo's usage in his account of the siege and fall of Venetian Negroponte/Khalkis to Mehmed II: *Vedendo il Signore che Turchi, e giannizzeri, e azappi con altre sue genti li face van di queste truffe di trafurar Franchi*; or Fra Castellana's usage in his account of the same siege: *qualche xiiij milia Tanengarii, cioè Cristiani rinnegati*. For new editions with English translation and historical commentary on these Italian texts, cf. Philippides, *Mehmed II the Conqueror*, chs. 6 and 7 respectively. Khalkokondyles's effort towards Hellenization produced the accurate translation of νεήλυδες but was never widely adopted in Modern Greek, since in the vernacular the term γενίτσαρος-ιανίτζαρος was preferred and became a loan word; in fact, it was already used in the fifteenth century by Greeks to designate the foreign mercenaries of the Byzantine emperor. On this point, cf. Elizabeth A. Zachariadou, "Les 'janissaires' de l'empereur byzantin," in *Studia Turcologica Memoriae Alexii Bombaci Dicata*, Instituto Universitario Orientale, Seminario di Studi Asiatici 19 (Naples 1982), pp. 591–597 [= *idem, Romania and the Turks (c. 1300–c. 1500)* (London 1985), Study 11]. On this peculiar Ottoman institution, see A.E. Vacalopoulos, *The Greek Nation, 1453–1669: The Cultural and Economic Background of Modern Greek Society* (New Brunswick 1976), pp. 73 ff.; S. Vryonis, "Seljuk Gulams and Ottoman Devshirmes," *Der Islam* 41 (1965): pp. 224–252; *idem*, "Isidore Glabas and the Turkish Devshirme," *Speculum* 31 (1956): pp. 433–443 [repr. in *idem, Byzantium: Its Internal History and Relations with the Muslim World*, Collected Studies (London 1971), Studies 12 and 13, respectively]; B. Papoulia, *Ursprung und Wesen der "Knabenlese" im osmanischen Reich* (Munich 1964), and its review by S. Vryonis in Byzantium, Study 14.

61 *PG* 159: col. 937 (not in *CC* 1): *An Macedonis potentia mea maior fuit, cui orbis minore cum exercuit paruit?* Languschi-Dolfin follows Leonardo closely, fol. 319: *utrum la mia potentia sia magior de quella d Alexandro macedonico, al qual cum minor exercito del mio tutto el mondo obedite*. For the plethora of comparisons among humanists in Italy, who compare Mehmed to Alexander, Isidore and Leonardo initiated the comparison, cf. Philippides, "The Fall of Constantinople 1453: Classical Comparisons and the Circle of Cardinal Isidore," esp. pp. 356–372. The Italian circle includes such humanists as Lauro Quirini,

da Rimini. Tetaldi, Aeneas Sylvius Piccolomini (Pope Pius II), Tignosi da Foligno, and numerous others.
62 Hofmann, "Quellen zur Isidor als Kardinal und Patriarch," pp. 143–157: *Magnificis dominis prioribus palatii et communitatis Florentinorum: Nam numquam Nero crudelissimus, numquam Tiestis* [Thyestes], *qui proprios filios edendos patri trad<d>idit.* After 1453, within the shelter of the Vatican, he borrowed from the library at least one work on Alexander; cf. Mercati, *Scritti d'Isidoro*, p. 82: *In secunda vice portavit libros sequentes prefatus Re<verendissi>mus dominus cardinalis Ruthenus xxv mai anno predicto. . . . Item unum librum in papiro forme mediocris, vocatus De gestis Alexandri Magni.*
63 *CC* 1: 72:

> *Aliud iterum mirabilius est machinatus, quod et Xerxes quondam fecisse memoratur: pontem siquidem construxit et fabricavit maximum a mari Sanct<A>e Galatin<A>e usque ad m<o>enia Cynegi, quod duplo maius est spatium quam illius Hellespontiaci olim pontis a Xerxe fabricati, per quem non modo pedites verum etiam equites multi simul traducebantur.*

64 *Ibid.*, p. 96: *Deinde pontem super mare, qui usque ad hodiernum diem manet, construxit: habet enim distantiam de terra firma in Constantinopoli per miliare unum et tertium.*
65 The bridge was admired by several eyewitnesses, who, independent of Leonardo and Isidore, also make reference to it, but without any learned allusions to Xerxes. Bishop Samuel's impressions were recorded in a contemporary German translation (*NE* 4: 86):

> vnd liessen sy in das Tayl des Mers czwischen den vorgenanten Stetten [Pera and Constantinople], vnd mochten da ein Pruck von aynem Tayl zu dem andern, darinnen leyten sy grosse Vas; vnd darauf leytten sy Püchsen vnd Füesslewt ein grosse Menig. vnd auff die selben Vass mochten sy aber ayn Pruck vnd mochten ein zwifächtige Wer auf das Wasser.

Similarly, the two refugees Eparkhos and Diplovatatzes also speak of this operation and of its impact upon the defenders, and their impressions have been preserved in a contemporary German translation; cf. *NE* 2: 516:

> Item: als er pei Petra auf daz Wasser ist kumen in ir Lantwer, do hat er alle Fesser genumen, die er mocht zu Wege pringen, und haben die an ein ander gepunden, und haben dar auf gepruck, und auf dem Wasser gestritten sam auf dem Land, und haben do gehabt mit ein 1000 Leittern, die wurffen sie an die Mauren; auch ward ein Loch geschossen, ein gross Loch, in die Statmaur, sam Sant Sebolds Kirchhof; dez haben sich die Genuessen unterwunden, sie wollens wol hervaren mit iren Schissen, – die dann hetten vil Schif; es was auch geboten in des Turcken Here vor finfzehen Tagen daz ein itlicher solt ein Leittern tragen, auf dem Wasser und auf dem Land.

The Florentine Tetaldi also notes this bridge, Caput VIII (Philippides, *Mehmed II the Conqueror*, pp. 166–168): *Similiter et pontem mira ingeniositate fabricati fecit de vasis, afferibus, trabibus et plancis, mille habentem passus in longitudine et septem in latitudine, ut sui ad nostros pertingere possint super mare ex transverso ambulantes et civitatis muris appropriquantes.* Leonardo is followed by Languschi-Dolfin closely, fol. 315:

> *Non contento perho de queso inzegno, el Turcho per altro modo cercho spauentarne. Et fece construir uno ponte longo 30 stadij sono miglia . . . dal mare fino alla ripa de la terra, fatta la zatra fermata sopra le botte ligate per diuider el porto, per lo qual ponte exercito poteua correr apresso el muro de la cita, apresso la giesia, imitando la potentia di Xerse el quale de Natolia in Grecia tradusse lo suo exercito per lo stretto de Hellesponto.*

66 *PG* 159: col. 931 [*CC* 1: 138; the text within <> is omitted by *CC* 1]:

> *Proinde hoc ingenio non contentus Theucrus aliud quoque, quo nos terreret magis, construxit, pontem videlicet longitudinis stadiorum circiter triginta, ex ripa urbi opposita maris qui sinum scinderet, vasis vinariis colligatis, subconstructis confixisque lignis, quo exercitus decurreret ad*

murum prope urbis iuxta fanum, <*imitatus Xerxis potentiam, qui ex Asia in Thraciam Bosphoro exercitum traduxit*>.

As usual his text is imitated in the vernacular by Languschi-Dolfin fol. 315 (cited in the previous note).

67 Pusculo 4.536–544 (71, 72) [omitted in the selections offered in *CC* 1]:

> *atque una consternere Pontum / Ponte superstructo; et cuneos transmittere siccis / Ipsi urbi pedibus tumidum super aequor et undas. / Xerxem fama canit quondam stravisse frementem / Hellespontiacum pontum, et junxisse rejunctam / Ponte Asiam Europa, siccis atque agmina plantis / Innumera ex Asia Europae immisisse.*

68 Echoes of the comparison of Mehmed to Xerxes are also encountered in Greek secondary literature on the siege of 1453, suggesting that the Great King of Persia had been a subject of conversation among the Greeks and that the comparison between the two potentates may actually date back to the days of the siege. We may be encountering a distant reverberation of actual conversations and observations voiced by participants in the defense and perpetuated by survivors of the sack. Thus Kritoboulos alludes to Xerxes in connection with another Ottoman stratagem that made a deep impression on the defenders, the transfer of light craft of the Turkish fleet overland and their launch into the harbor of the Golden Horn. The strategic intention of the sultan was to by-pass the chain-boom that had denied entry of the Ottoman fleet into the Golden Horn, and thus force the defense to thin out its scanty forces, as the walls of the harbor now had to be defended. Indeed, it was a very successful tactic when combined with the sultan's pontoon bridge. The combination of transferred boats and a floating bridge presented a major threat to Greek defenses. The Byzantines and their allies were forced to redeploy sparse military resources. Kritoboulos remarks that this tactic of the sultan, the transfer of some boats over the hills of Pera, surpassed the achievements of Xerxes, 1.42.6: ἐγὼ νομίζω καὶ τῆς Ξέρξου τοῦ Ἄθω διορυγῆς μεῖζον εἶναι τοῦτο πολλῷ καὶ παραδοξότερον καὶ ἰδεῖν καὶ ἀκοῦσαι. Kritoboulos's comparison is independent from that drawn by the two ecclesiastics. Doukas is in complete agreement with these sentiments and he also mentions Xerxes, compares Mehmed II to Alexander the Great, and calls the sultan the "modern Macedonian," 38.8:

> ὁ Ξέρξης τὴν θάλασσαν ἐγεφύρωσεν καὶ ὡς ξηρὰν ὁ τοσοῦτος στρατὸς ἐπάνω ταύτης διῆλθεν. οὗτος δὲ ὁ νέος Μακεδὼν ... ὕστατος τὴν γῆν ἐθαλάσσωσεν καὶ ὡς κατὰ κυμάτων τὰ πλοῖα ὑπὲρ τῶν κορυφῶν ἐπέζευξεν. ἀλλ' ὑπὲρ τὸν Ξέρξην οὗτος. καὶ γὰρ ἐκεῖνος διαβὰς τὸν Ἑλλήσποντον, παρὰ τῶν Ἀθηναίων αἰσχύνην ἐνδυθεὶς ὑπέστρεψεν, οὗτος δὲ τὴν ξηρὰν ὡς ὑγρὰν διαβὰς τοὺς Ῥωμαίους ἠφάνισεν καὶ τὰς χρυσᾶς ὄντως Ἀθήνας τὰς κοσμούσας τὸν κόσμον, τὴν βασιλίδα τῶν πόλεων εἷλεν.

69 The text of the note from *Codex Bibl. Univ. lat. B 52*, busta 2, n. 1, fols. 40ʳ–42ᵛ, is quoted in *CC* 1: 53:

> *Habes iam, Alberte dilectissime, grecam epistolam factam Latinam, etsi satis inepte traductam. Malui enim* <*me*> *rudem ac indoctum iudicari abs te, quam pervicacem. Usus autem sum sermone facili et ilaro et, ut dicam, puerile, ne tibi videar alius esse quam sum, tardo scilicet ac rudi ingenio. Potuissem enim hinc inde vocabula exquisita mendicari et exspicari, sed nolui ex re minima rem maximam facere atque ostentare, quod mee tenuis ac exiguissime supellectilis non est. Ipsam ergo penes te servas nec ulli cures edere, ne in tanta doctissimorum virorum copia temerarius ac presumptuosus fuisse videar, qui tantum mihi arrogem, ut grecam profiteri scientiam ausus sim, cuius vix prima rudimenta delbarim. Tuus Lianoru de Lianoriis etc.*

70 As is made clear in the *incipit*: *Epistola composite per ser Pasium de Bertipalia notarium ad instantiam reverendissimi domini, domini Isidori cardinalis Sabinensis.* We follow the punctuation of L. Silvano, "Per l'epistolario di Isidoro di Kiev: La lettera a papa Niccolò V de 6 luglio 1453," *Medioevo Greco* 13 (2013): pp. 241–258.

236 *Defender, humanist, and survivor*

71 It is only recently that the complete text of this letter composed by Isidore and translated by Pasio saw its *editio princeps*; previously we had only selections published in *CC* 1: 58–64. Finally, we have a reliable text of the entire letter from the *Codex Marc. 496*, fols. 330ʳ–331ʳ: cf. Silvano, pp. 241–258 (Latin text with Italian translation, pp. 246–251), who thoroughly discusses the manuscript in question and produces a commentary on the contents of the text.

72 *CC* 1: 90: *Datum Cretae in domibus residentiae nostrae sub sigillo nostro quo utimur anno a nativitate Domini M.CCCC. Quinquagesimo tertio, die octava Iulii potificatus sanctissimi in Christo patris et domini nostri domini Nycolay divina providential papae quinti anno septimo.* On this letter, cf. *SF*, p. 29.

73 *CC* 1: 100: *Datum Candiae, die XV Julii LIIIº.*

74 *Supra*, n. 73: *in domibus residentiae nostrae sub sigillo nostro.*

75 Henry of Soemmern was under the impression that Isidore's health had suffered during the period of his adventure; cf. Philippides, *Mehmed II the Conqueror*, pp. 128, 129 (*CC* 2: 92):

>   *devenit [Isidorus] . . . inde Cretam, in qua stabat, mediocriter valens, VIIIa Iulii novissime praeterii.* Isidore himself in the opening paragraph of his letter to Bessarion indicates that he had been in a state of clinical depression: *mens mea tanquam hominis extra se positi ac paene insensati desidet continue, si quidem deambulans, iacens, stans, sedens, dormiens, vigilans, fontes lacrimarum emitto.*

76 *CC* 2: 38: *Ex <Candia> die quinta Julii in loco Sancti Francisci Candiae MCCCC<LIII>.* On Fra Girolamo, cf. *SF*, p. 36.

77 Quirini knew the affection with which Pope Nicholas V regarded manuscripts and classical scholarship, and chose to include the mention of the cardinal together with the irreparable loss of literature in the sack; cf. *TIePN*, p. 74: *Ultra centum et viginti miia librorum volumina, ut a reverendissimo cardinali Rutheno [Isidoro] accepi, devastata.* Nevertheless, after his early liberation, Bishop Leonardo was able to buy books within the devastated city; cf. the information in *SF*, pp. 16, 17 and n. 61.

78 On the same day Isidore completed his letter to the pope. Could it be that both letters, Isidore's and Quirini's, were simultaneously sent to the pope, were dispatched on the same boat from Crete, and were carried by the same courier?

79 *TIePN*, p. 90: *Data Candidae Idibus Iulii 1453*. On Quirini and his account, cf. *SF*, p. 36.

80 To be discussed in the next chapter.

81 Cf. *SF*, pp. 29, 30.

82 Of course, the letter translated by Pasio is of equal importance; however, we chose not to include it, as this letter adds nothing of import to the letters by Isidore and can be consulted in Italian translation by Silvano (*supra*, n. 73).

83 For discussion of the two fictional episodes, the emperor's speech and the liturgy in Santa Sophia, cf. Philippides, "Tears of the Great Church: The Lamentation of Santa Sophia," p. 721 and n. 18.

84 Barbaro states that the sultan inspected his troops, prior to the general assault at the third hour before daylight, p. 51 (*CC* 1: 30):

>   *In questo zorno de vinti nuove de mazo del mile e quarto zento e cinquanta tre a ore tre avanti zorne, Macome bei, fio che fu de Morato turco, vene personalmente a le mure de questa zitade de Costantinopoli, per dar la bataia zeneral.*

Leonardo does not state the precise time, but he seems to allude to the early hours when the battle commenced, *PG* 159: col. 940 (*CC* 1: 158): *Tenebrosa nox in lucem trahitur nostris vicentibus; at dum astra cedunt, dum Phoebi praecurrit Lucifer ortum . . . consurgit exercitus.* Pusculo places the withdrawal of Giustiniani at the rise of the morning star (3.973–975, *CC* 1: 212): *Lucifer aurorae venientis pallidus ortum / ducebat, portans casumque diemque . . . Joannes abiit.* He further states that the Janissaries entered soon thereafter (3.986, 987, *CC* 1: 212): *Iam digitis fulgens roseis Aurora rubentem / aethera reddebat noctisque fugaverat umbram.*

85 The only event is recounted by Doukas 39.23, who suggests that in the vicinity of the Kynegion the Turks entered the Aya kapı and proceeded to plunder the church of Santa Theodosia (present day mosque of Gül Camii); on this incident and the identification of this church as Gül Camii, cf. *SF*, pp. 265 ff. It is coincidental that 29 May was the feast day of Santa Theodosia and Isidore relates this information to Pasio di Bertipaglia who further notes the superstitious nature of Isidore, who must have believed this day to be "unlucky" (Silvano, p. 248 [*CC* 1: 60]): *O diem infelicem, si fas est infelicem dici diem qua natalitia Sanctae* [Silvano: *beatae*] *Theodosiae virginis et martiris colerentur.*

86 Isidore does not mention the church by name. He only calls it *cuiusdam monasterii*, but this is not unusual. In the vernacular of the time, Santa Sophia was known as ἡ μεγάλη ἐκκλησία or, more commonly as τὸ μέγα μοναστήρι; cf. Philippides, "Tears of the Great Church: The Lamentation of Santa Sophia," which also provides an analysis of a popular poem then in circulation. In this well-known example of popular literature, Santa Sophia is referred to as "the grand monastery." Henry of Soemmern in his letter makes clear that it was Santa Sophia; cf. *CC* 2: 92: *prope ecclesiam S. Sophiae accessit.*

87 For a discussion of those prophecies as reported by numerous writers of the period, cf. *SF*, ch. 4, sec. II, and esp. pp. 227–231.

88 Thus the Anconitan consul, Benvenuto, who was present during the siege and sack, points out the particular advantage of having access to a horse, for it provided a quick means to escape from the enemy. Benvenuto stresses, as his account breaks off, that most of the officers in charge of sectors died because they had lost their mounts; *TIePN*, p. 5: *omnes provisores . . . interfecti errant . . . quia manserunt pedestres in platea.* On Benvenuto, cf. *supra*, n. 44. Isidore himself claims that his horse was of great advantage in his survival; cf. his letter to Bessarion, 2: *eques eram. . . .*

89 Letter to Bessarion, 2: *ante ianuam cuiusdam monasterii.*

90 *Ibid.*

91 Silvano, p. 250 (*CC* 1: 64): *Ego denique dolens Isidorus . . . qui huius crudelissimi excidii* [of Constantinople] *verissimus testis sum et impiorum manus nutu divino mirabiliter evasi.* He also emphasizes his status as an eyewitness in his propagandistic letter to "all Christians" of July 8; cf. *CC* 1: 84: *quod omnes actus et opera praefata propriis oculis vidi, et ego ipse cum viris Constantinopolitanis omnibus una passus sum.*

92 Philippides, *Mehmed II the Conqueror*, pp. 128, 129 (*CC* 2: 92–94).

93 Of course this is speculation. Henry could have discovered information about Isidore's wound from another letter that has not survived. Henry includes some of the epistolography of Isidore in his sources and he does mention that he tried "to piece together" what had happened in Constantinople, naming some of his sources, which seem to include Fra Girolamo the Minorite who was in Crete (cf. *SF*, p. 36). But in his surviving letter Fra Girolamo says nothing about Isidore. Henry mentions the following sources that he utilized (Philippides, *Mehmed II the Conqueror*, pp. 128, 129 [not in *CC* 2]):

> *Hanc totam seriem rei gestae college fideliter ex diversis epistoli scriptis ad diversos de ista material. Quarum una scripta est domin<i>o Venetorum per dominum Iacobum Lauredanum, generalem capitaneum eorum super mare; alia per ducem Venetorum scripta est domino papae tribusque aliis cardinalibus; <alia domini cardinalis> Ruthenis, qui de hac re unam papam, alia domino cardinali Firmano; tertia<m>que patens erat omnibus Christifidelibus. Et ex duabus aliis scriptis domino Firmano (quorum unam scripsit ipse agens, familiaris et domesticus dicti cardinalis Rutheni, aliam vicarius ordinis minorum provinciae Candiae). Quarum omnium copias habeo, ex copiis domini Firmani.*

94 *Supra*, n. 93. These "miraculous" circumstances may have become proverbial with time, as they are also cited by Leonardo Benvoglienti, in a letter of 22 November 1453; cf. *CC* 2: 110: *el Turcho cerchò con grande instantia questo Cardinale per farlo morire essendo in Costantinopoli; da a questo chi'o comprando, per divina dipensatione et miracolo è stato preservato.*

95 *CC* 1: 116. The friend may have been Francesco Griffolini d'Arezzo (*CC* 1: 112). In the immediate hours following the fall of the imperial city, it is unclear how and when

238 *Defender, humanist, and survivor*

Isidore disposed of his regal ecclesiastical robes. He, himself, provides no specific information on this. Obviously, he had to disguise himself as a Greek commoner to avoid detection, knowing well that Mehmed II was seeking his head. Numerous accounts, as the one cited of exchanging robes with an elderly monk, provide some questionable information. A version, without providing a source for this account, appears in Ch. Mijatovich, *Constantine Palaeologus. The Last Emperor of the Greeks, 1448–1453. The Conquest of Constantinople by the Turks* (London, 1892), p. 225, who writes:

> Cardinal Isidore with the aid of faithful servants, laid aside his purple robes, and put on the clothes of a common soldier. The body of a Latin volunteer was then dressed up in the robes of the Cardinal, and left lying in the street. The Turks came upon it, cut off the head of the supposed Cardinal, and carried it on a pike in triumph through the streets. Meanwhile, Isidore had fallen into the hands of other Turks; but he seemed so miserable and so useless as a slave that his Turkish master soon set him at liberty for a small sum of money.

96 Philippides, *Mehmed II the Conqueror*, p. 128 (*CC* 2: 92–94).
97 *Pii Secundi Pontificis Maximi de Captione Urbis Constantinopolis Tractatulus*, pp. 116, 117; text and English translation in Philippides, *Mehmed II the Conqueror*, pp. 94–119.
98 *TiePN*, p. 4.
99 Leonardo finished and sent his report to the pope by the 16th of August, as he states (*PG* 159: col. 944; *CC* 2: 170): *Data Chii, XVI die Augusti, 1453*). He never mentions the adventures of Isidore in his *epistula*, and the probabilities are that he was unaware of the adventures of his friend. By the time Leonardo completed and sent his report Isidore had passed through Chios on his way to Crete. Is it possible that the two friends missed each other during Isidore's brief stay on the island of Chios, where Leonardo had also fled?
100 The sultan was energetically engaged in identifying those prominent citizens, members of the court, and defenders whom he had marked for execution. Cf., e.g., Doukas, who states that the sultan had compiled written lists of his marked prisoners and paid the sum of 1,000 aspers per man to acquire them from their captors, 40.5: μαθὼν [Mehmed] . . . τὰ ὀνόματα τῶν εὐγενῶν τῶν ἐν παλατίῳ διαπρεψάντων ὀφφικιαλίων, πάντων τὰ ὀνόματα κατέγραψεν. καὶ ἐν τοῖς πλοίοις καὶ ἐν ταῖς σκηναῖς συναθροίσας οὖν πάντας ἐξηγόρασεν, ἀνὰ χιλίων ἄσπρων δοὺς τοῖς Τούρκοις.
101 Vol. 2: 8. 24 (pp. 198, 199 [= *PG* 159: col. 393]). For a Latin translation of this passage, cf. the next note.
102 Isidorus S. R. E. Cardinalis, *Notitia* (*Purpura Docta, Monachii 1714*, parte III, p. 105), *PG* 159: cols. 947, 948. The same note translates into Latin Khalkokondyles's comments (for the Greek passage, cf. *supra*, text with n. 102), *PG* 159: col. 952:

> *De Isidoro cardinal agens Laonicus Chalcondylas haec habet: In hac rerum turba miserabili (loquitr de urbis Constantinopolitanae direptione) captus est cardinalis isidorus Sarmatarum antistes, qui ductus in Galatium urbem renditus est, sedconscensa navi profugit in Peloponnesum. Si rex Turcarum virum hunc novisset, videlicet quod cardinalis esset, certe eum intefecisset; cum eum inter coeteros occisum putaret, nullam eius rationem habebat.*

103 In fact, Bessarion's beard may have contributed to his loss of the papal throne during the conclave of 1455, which was also attended by Isidore. On the circumstances of this conclave, cf. A. Kyrou, *Βησσαρίων ὁ Ἕλλην*, 2 (Athens, 1947), pp. 31–33. This event will be discussed in ch. 7, text with n. 27.
104 For the custom of the Latin Church to present its clerics with a clean shaven face, cf. *Corpus Christianorum, Continuatio Mediaevalis LXII, Apologiae duae: Gozechni epistola ad Walcherum; Burchardi, ut videtur, Abbatis Believallis Apologia de Barbis*, ed. R.B.C. Huygens (with an introduction on the history of the beard in the Middle ages by G. Constable) (Turnholt, 1985). The situation was similar to what we encounter in the Late Antiquity; cf., e.g., the disapproval that Emperor Julian ("the Apostate") had to face because he had

chosen to wear "the philosopher's beard," which prompted him to compose the satirical piece, *The Hater of the Beard, Μισοπώγων*.
105 Henry of Soemmern 5 (p. 124); *CC* 1: 86.
106 *PG* 159: col. 942 (*CC* 1: 166). Leonardo is followed by his imitator, Languschi-Dolfin fol. 322: *Dapoi tolseno Christo crucifix, et cum timpani et tamburli cum sputi e blasfemie derisorie posta sopra la capo el xarcula ditto sessa turchesca cridando deceuano: questo e dio de Christiani.* The incident was also known to Pope Pius II, as he reports it in his *Tractatulus* (*supra*, n. 97), with similar phraseology, pp. 112, 113:

> *Simulacrum crucifixi quem colimus, et verum Deum esse fatemur, tubis et tympanis praeeuntibus raptum ex urbe, histes ad tentoria deferent, sputo lutoque foedant, et ad nostrae religionem irrisionem iterum cruci affigunt. Exinde pileo quem sarculam vocant, capiti eius imposito, corona undique facta, his est, inquunt Christianorum Deus.*

"Zarchula/xarcula/sarcula," or, more properly in Turkish, *zerkulah*, indicates the distinctive white headdress of the Janissary regiments. It had clearly impressed the contemporary Italians who had seen it and is even mentioned by Barbaro 27 (*CC* 1: 17), who identifies the Janissaries as "the sultan's slaves," when he comments on the costumes of the various Ottoman regiments:

> *per niun modo non se podeva veder tera, che zà la iera cuverta da lor Turchi, massimante de janissarii qual sono o soldadi del Turcho, che sono i più valtentomeni che abia il Turco, etiam ne iera assaissimi schiavi del signor, i qual se cognose ai capeli bianchi, e i Turchi natural porta i capeli rossi, i qual se chiama axapi* [*azab*].

Giacomo Rizzardo, in his account of the fall of Khalkis/Negroponte to Mehmed II, also refers to the *zerkulah* (for this account, with English translation, cf. Philippides, *Mehmed II the Conqueror*, pp. 220–247), pp. 244–245: *Mandò per loro, e fece loro levar il zargolla di testa e mise loro capelli ungareschi in testa.*

107 The sixteenth-century anonymous Ἔκθεσις Χρονικὴ (for a modern edition, English translation, and commentary, cf. M. Philippides, *Emperors, Patriarchs and Sultans of Constantinople: An Anonymous Greek Chronicle of the Sixteenth Century* [Brookline, 1990], 32 [p. 48]).
108 Doukas reports a story in which a prisoner offers in return for his freedom to identify Loukas Notaras and Orhan, a distant relative of the sultan, who had fought with the Greeks against the Ottoman army, 40.4: Τότε εἷς τῶν αἰχμαλώτων τῶν Ῥωμαίων καταπραγματευσάμενος τὴν αὐτοῦ ἐλευθερίαν εἴρηκε . . . "εἰ ἐλευθερώσεις με σήμερον, ἔχω σοι δοῦναι τὸν Ὀρχὰν καὶ τὸν μέγα δοῦκα [Loukas Notaras] ὁμοῦ." Numerous incidents of this type undoubtedly took place throughout the Ottoman camp.
109 In Isidore's own words in the letter dictated to Pasio (Silvano, p. 250 [*CC* 1: 64]): *Ego . . . denique dolens Isidorus . . . nutu divino mirabiliter evasi.* Also for the "miracle," cf. the opinion of Benvoglienti quoted *supra*, n. 94. Even in his propagandistic literature (cf. next chapter), Isidore insists upon this "divine miracle" that had saved him and he even suggests a biblical comparison, when he likens himself and his circumstances to Jonah and the whale. Cf. his letter addressed to all Christians (*universis et singulis Christi fidelibus*), which was given at his quarters in Crete (*in domibus residentiae nostrae*) on the 8th of July (*die octava Iulii*) (*CC* 1: 84): *de manibus impiorum me Deus eripuit, ut Jonam ab utero ceti*.
110 Thus the mention of Isidore as a prisoner in a Venetian folk poem of the period is entirely fictional and Isidore only appears *dramatis causa* in the list of the sultan's prominent prisoners. The poem, an *anonimo Veneto*, belongs to the popular genre of the lamentations over the fate of Constantinople and is entitled *Questo è lamento de Costantinopoli* (*CC* 2: 296–315). Cf. ll. 279–280 (*CC* 2: 306): *Io vidi el cardinal / De Rosìa legato e in pregione*. This printing involves an emendation that can be accepted; cf. *CC* 2: 475 n. 37: *Ho correto la lezione "Loria" (che non ha alcun senso) . . . in "Rosìa"*.

111 The insignificant amount of ransom (whether ducats or aspers) becomes evident when it is compared with the exorbitant amounts that were demanded and were extorted for Venetian prisoners. Cf., e.g., the information supplied by Barbaro 61 (not in *CC* 1):

> *Tuti questi nobeli da Veniexia, i qual fo prexoni in man del turco, tuti tornò a Veniexia, i qual tuti se ave taia, chi ducati doamilia, chi ducati mile, e chi ducati otozento, in men de uno ano tuti so tornado a Veniexia.*

112 Henry of Soemmern 9; Philippides, *Mehmed II the Conqueror*, pp. 128, 129.
113 *Tractatulus*, ch. XII; Philippides, *Mehmed II the Conqueror*, pp. 116, 117. Perhaps it should be noted that the grammar of Aeneas Sylvius's phraseology also allows the possible interpretation that Isidore "ransomed himself" but this version is unlikely. His money, if he had any on him, must have been taken from him after he was captured and it is unlikely that he would have found himself able to navigate through the captured city to get to Pera across the Golden Horn. Others must have ransomed him and escorted him to Pera.
114 Isidore himself described the danger that faced Pera in his letter of the 22nd of February 1455 (*data Romae die XXII Februarii MCCCCL° quinto*) to the duke of Burgundy (*a tergo: Illustri<ssi>mo principi excellentissimo domino Philippo Burgundiae duci*) (*CC* 1: 108): *Nam capta Constantinopoli eamet hora et Pera in potestatem pervenit Teucrorum, destructis moenibus et rem ipsorum penitu deletam ac labefactam.* Isidore emphasizes again his witness status and clearly alludes to the immediate period after he had been ransomed and conveyed to Pera (ibid.): *Ego, qui praesens eram, possum verum de omnibus perhibere testimonium.* The early letter of Isidore through the pen of Bertipaglia also makes mention of the dismantling of its walls and the problems Pera was facing. Thus Isidore supplies our earliest testimony deriving from an eyewitness about the condition of the suburb. Cf. Silvano, p. 248; *CC* 1: 62: *Quoniam etiam christianissima et latina civitas Perae, quae a Januensibus possidebatur, ab eisdem hostibus [Turcis] capta et dilacerata, in qua etiam omnes similes horrendas crudelitates exercuerunt et deiectis turribus, moeniis et lapideis magnificis parietibus eam ut rus constituerunt.* Similar information is repeated in his letter to the pope, in which he ties the fate of the two cities together and also mentions details that are encountered as part of the conditions that are included in the sultan's *aman-name* to Pera (*CC* 1: 84):

> *Urbs igitur Constantinopolitana extincta est nec ullum sensum illa nunc habet; hac eadem etiam hora et civitas Pera nuncupata extincta est, quam demum Thurci occupant nunc et gubernant, cuius muros usque ad terram diripuerunt, quaae servituti adeo tradita est, quod non sinunt in exaltation sacratissimi corporis et sanguinis Christi tintinnabulum aut ullam campanam sonari aut pulsar; ymmo crucem quae supra magnam turrim fuit una cum ipsa turri in ruinam miserunt; cuius denique civitatis totam rempublicam perdiderunt et destruxerunt, gabellas et nonnullas alias impositiones et gravamina omnibus a maiore usque ad minorem ponere instituerunt.*

Among Greek authors, Doukas was also aware of the precarious position of Pera, 39.31: Ταῦτα ὁ Ζάγανος ἐκώλυσε τοὺς Φράγγους τοῦ Γαλατᾶ [Pera] μὴ ἀναχωρῆσαι. πλὴν ὅσοι ἐδυνήθησαν φυγεῖν, ἔφυγον. τότε συμβουλευθέντες οἱ λοιποί, ἔλαβον τὰς κλεῖς τοῦ κάστρου σὺν τῷ ποδεστάτῳ αὐτῶν [Angelo Giovanni Lomellino] καὶ ἀπῆλθον προσκυνήσοντες τῷ τυράννῳ [Mehmed].
115 One of those individuals was the nephew of the *podestà* of Pera, who had been taken prisoner and whose fate remained unknown in the early days after the fall. Eventually, by 30 August, it was discovered that Lomellino's nephew had turned renegade and converted to Islam during his captivity, and eventually became an official at the sultan's Porte; on this event, cf. *SF*, pp. 13, 14. Cf. the confused and emotionally stressed letter that the *podestà* wrote on the 23rd of June (*CC* 1: 42–51). On Lomellino's account, cf. *SF*, pp. 13, 14.
116 Angelo Giovanni Lomellino, the *podestà*, was well aware of the danger and he points out in a memorable phrase in his letter (*CC* 1: 44): *nam semper cognovi. Amisso Constantinopoli, amisso isto loco* [Pera].

117 The *aman-name* of Mehmed, signed by his chief Porte official Zaganos, has survived in its original Greek version (the diplomatic language of the Porte) and in a translation in the Italian vernacular. For the Greek and Italian texts, cf. Philippides, *Mehmed II the Conqueror*, Appendix II (pp. 347–350).
118 Henry of Soemmern 9 (Philippides, *Mehmed II the Conqueror*, pp. 128, 129 [*CC* 1: 94]): *et vectus est in Peram mansitque absconditus VIII diebus fugiendo de domo in domum occulte*.
119 *PG* 159: col. 929 (*CC* 1: 134–136):

> Sic simulata illa pax urbi profuit. Ego, iudicio meo, ni fallor, arbitror apertam guerram Perensibus a primo salubriorem quam fictam pacem: <et> quidem Theucrus neque castrum, quod demolitions eorum causa fuit, condidisset, neque guerram posthac tam terribiliem intuilisset. O Genuenses iam quodammodo cicurati! Sileo, ne de meis loquar, quos externi cum veritate diiudicant.

A short paraphrase is offered by Languschi-Dolfin (fol. 315), in which the personal complaints of Leonardo are not included.

120 *PG* 159: col. 932 (*CC* 1: 140–142): *At posthac inter Venetos et Genuenses Galatae oborta dissensio est, quod alter alterum fugae suspicionem improbrasset*. The information is repeated in Languschi-Dolfin (fol. 316): *Dapoi naque gran discension, fra Ueneti, et Genoexi de Pera, che l uno al altro imputaua che uoleuano fuzi*.
121 *PG* 159: col. 933 (*CC* 1: 144): *Etenim res haec detecta relataque Theucris egit, ut, dum nostri percutere voluere, ipsi prius percussi sint. Sed quid dicam, beatissime Pater? Accusarene quempiam licet? Silendum mihi est*.
122 Thus upon the arrival of Giustiniani, Barbaro states (13; *CC* 1: 12): *vene in Constantinopoli Zuan Zustignan Zenovexe . . . perché l'intendeva la nezesitade che havea Constantinopoli, e per benefitio de la christianitade, e per honor del mundo*. His retreat and withdrawal from the last battle is depicted in different colors, 55 (*CC* 1: 33):

> Vedando questo, Zuan Zustignan, zenovexe da Zenova, se delibera de abandoner la sua posta e corse a la sua nave . . . e scampando questo che iera capetanio, vignando el ditto per la tera criando: "Turchi son intradi dentro la tera"; e menteva per la gola, che ancora i non iera intradi dentro . . . tuti si se comenza a meter in fuga, e subito tuti abandona le sue poste.

In the course of his narrative Barbaro loses all patience with the Genoese and proceeds to describe them in extremely negative terms, cf., e.g., 30 (*CC* 1: 20): *i maledetti Zenovexi de Pera rebeli de la fede cristiana*.

123 *Supra*, n. 115.
124 *CC* 1: 108.
125 Isidore was not the only "wanted" person. Other prominent defenders were also sought; cf. e.g., the testimony of Angelo Giovanni Lomellino, who emphatically states that the sultan was searching for the Bocchiardi brothers and Maurizio Cataneo, who, like Isidore, had gone into hiding in Pera. Cf. *CC* 1: 46–48: *Inquisivit* [*sc.* Mehmed] *Mauritium Cattaneum et Paulum Boccardum, quise occultaverunt; dimisit in loco isto sclavum pro custodia loci*. Cataneo and the Bocchiardi brothers eluded the sultan's agents and, like Isidore, managed to escape to Italy. Again, here the efforts of the *podestà* must have been effective. Both Cataneo and the surviving Bocchiardi brothers appear in a legal document of the 9th of February 1461: R. Predelli, *I Libri Commemoriali*, 10 (libro xv) (Venice, 1876–1924), no. 73 (pp. 142–143) [*1461, ind. IX, Febbraio*]:

> Istrumento di malleveria prestata ai tre giudici delegati nominati nel. n. 72 – i detti giudici delegati e mediatori promettono che Venezia pagherà ai due reclamanti 4500 ducati d'oro, metà in cupo ad un anno, a titolo di dono grazioso. Tutti gli interessati dichiarano di approvare e accettare da Troilo ed Antonio Buciardi (o Buzzardi) veneziani, a favore di Maurizio Cattaneo e Nicolò Pizzamiglio, per 4300 ducati che verrebero rimborasti dai Buzzardi alla Signoria, se i due genovesi non potessero ottenere dal governatore e dal consiglio degli anziani di Genova l'approvazione del documento n. 72. Fatto testimoni ed atti come nel n. 72.

For documents regarding the Bocchiardi brothers and Cataneo, cf. *SF*, Appendix IV, nos. 15–17 (p. 635), and no. 29 (pp. 636, 637), respectively. Unlike Isidore we do not know how these individuals escaped from the vicinity of Constantinople.

126 Isidore must have been well informed about the executions that were taking place, as he had received information about them. Thus, he mentions the execution of the grand duke, Loukas Notaras, without submitting any of the rumors that eventually accumulated on this controversial figure (cf., e.g., *SF*, Appendix II [pp. 597–618], and on the execution of Goudeles, cf. his letter to Bessarion 16 [not in *CC* 1]).
127 Henry of Soemmern 9 (pp. 128, 129); and *CC* 2: 94.
128 *Ibid.*
129 *Ibid.*, 9 (*CC* 2: 94).
130 Letter by the "friend/*familiaris*" of Isidore (*CC* 1: 116): *captus . . . incognitus duobus diebus mansit in Thurcorum magno exercitu.*
131 Henry of Soemmern 9 (*CC* 2: 94): *incognitus mansit tribus diebus in magno exercitu Teucrorum . . . redemptus est pro C ducatis* [Aeneas Sylvius Piccolomini, *Tractatulus* 12: *tricentis asperis*] *et vectus est in Peram.*
132 *Ibid.*, 9 (*CC* 2: 94): *vectus est in Peram mansitque absconditus VIII diebus fugiendo de domo in domum occulte.*
133 *Ibid.*: *intravit galeas Turcorum, in quibus mansit tribus diebus incognitus . . . intravit Prusas.*
134 *Ibid.*: *intravit Prusas . . . usque ad quemdam locum dictum Focis. Deinde . . . ingressus quamdam parvulam navem devenit Chyum, inde Cretam.*
135 The specific date of Isidore's arrival cannot be established with any accuracy. Henry of Soemmern simply states that he was recovering in Crete on the 8th of July (*CC* 2: 94): *inde Cretа, in qua stabat, mediocriter valens, VIII[a] Julii novissime praeteriti.* The earliest letter of Isidore is the one that he dictated to di Bertipaglia, which bears the dictation date of the 6th of July. On the same day, as it is stated, Isidore composed his letter to Bessarion. His letter to all Christians is dated the 8th of July (the original text in Greek has not survived); so "the 8th of July" could be the date Isidore composed the text or it could reflect the date that his Greek text was translated into Latin. His Latin report to the Pope Nicholas V bears the date of the 15th of July. The latest he could have arrived in Crete would then be the 5th of July, that is, the day previous to when he dictated his letter to di Bertipaglia.

6 Cretan interlude

1 Early propagandist

Numerous ships, individually and in assembled flotillas, escaped from the carnage during the sack of Constantinople. The largest contingent of vessels comprised a sizeable Venetian flotilla that made its way through the Aegean to the island of Euboea and its port of Negroponte/Khalkis. From there dispatches were sent to Venice to announce the fall of the imperial city. Their arrival triggered major concern in Negroponte. Another smaller Genoese contingent of seven craft probably conveyed Leonardo and the mortally wounded Giustiniani to Chios. Yet other boats, loaded with refugees, slowly made their way to Candia in Venetian Crete. The Cretan ships that were present during the siege and had defended the Golden Horn, under their commanders Antonios Philomates, Sgouros,[1] and Hyalinas, also joined the exodus along with the Venetian galleys. During the siege the Cretan crews had been stationed in the harbor to assist the Venetian fleet in charge of the sea walls and the harbor. Perhaps some crewmen had disembarked and had valiantly defended three towers, although our testimony with the regard to this is late and may prove to be unreliable as it originates with the elaborated text by Pseudo-Sphrantzes.[2] The three Cretan ships that escaped with the Venetian flotilla reached Crete one month later, as recorded by a scribe at the monastery of Ankarathos.[3] Other smaller contingents must have also made their way to the Greek and Venetian possessions, thus raising further alarm throughout the Aegean islands.[4]

At noon on the 29th of May, the Venetian flotilla set sail and made its escape. The galley of Alvise Diedo was the lead ship and was followed by the galley of Girolamo (Jeruolemo) Morozini (Morexini). A third galley proceeded under the command of Dolfin Dolfin, but could only move with difficulty, for she had lost 140 of her crew. She was followed by the galley of Gabriel Trevisano (Trivixan/Trevixan), even though the Turks had captured him and another had to command the vessel. Then came the three ships from Crete under Venier, Philomates, and Hyalinas. A fourth galley from Crete under Grioni became the single casualty.[5] She was seized by the Turks, but Barbaro[6] fails to provide specific information on the incident. To this list of departing vessels we should

244 *Cretan interlude*

add that of Sgouros and his ship. He too arrived in Crete a month later with the other Cretan captains and their vessels.

In addition to the Venetian and Cretan vessels, there were seven Genoese ships. Their captains also moved through the Dardanelles to the Aegean. All of these craft were destined to be bearers of ill tidings to the western world. Yet even before these ships brought confirmation of the fall of Constantinople, rumors of doom had already spread throughout the Greek islands. Thus as early as the 11th of June the Paduan Paolo Dotti in Candia dictated a letter, in which he outlined his suspicion that the Greek capital had been taken.[7] His premonition was confirmed exactly one month after the sack, when the three Cretan ships with the numerous refugees on board finally reached Candia. Their account of unbelievable grief spread throughout the town. On the evening of the same day, Friday, the 29th of June, a scribe at the Monastery of Ankarathos recorded his personal reaction to the event:[8]

ἔτε <ι> αυνγ´, ἰουνίου κθ´, ἡμέρα ϛ⁀ᵗ, ἦλθαν ἀπὸ τὴν Κωνσταντινούπολιν καράβια τρία Κρητικά, τοῦ Σγούρου, τοῦ Ὑαλινᾶ, καὶ τοῦ Φιλομάτου. λέγοντες ὅτι εἰς τὴν κθ´ τοῦ Μαΐου μηνός, τῆς ἁγίας Θεοδοσίας ἡμέρα τρίτη, ὥρα γ´ τῆς ἡμέρας, ἐσέβησαν οἱ ἀγαρηνοὶ ἐς τὴν Κωνσταντινούπολιν, τὸ φωσάτον τοῦ Τούρκου τζαλαμπῆ Μεεμέτ, καὶ εἶπον ὅτι ἐπέκτειναν τὸν βασιλέα τὸν κὺρ Κωνσταντίνον τὸν Δράγασιν καὶ Παλαιολόγον. καὶ ἐγένετο οὖν μεγάλη θλῖψις καὶ πολλὶς κλαυθμὸς εἰς τὴν Κρήτην διὰ τὸ θληβερὸν μήνυμα ὅπερ ἦλθε, ὅτι χεῖρον τούτου οὐ γέγονεν οὔτε γενήσεται. καὶ Κ<ύριος> ὁ Θ<εὸς> ἐλεῆσαι ἡμᾶς, καὶ λυτρώσεται ἡμᾶς τῆς φοβερᾶς αὐτοῦ ἀπειλῆς.

In the y<ear> 1453, on the 29th of June, a Tuesday, three Cretan ships arrived from Constantinople: they belonged to Sgouros, to Hyalenas, and to Philomates. They said that on the 29th of the month of May (the day of Santa Theodosia), a Tuesday, the descendants of Hagar [Turks], the army of the Turkish çelebi [prince] Mehmed, entered Constantinople. They also said that they killed the emperor, Constantine Dragaš, also called Palaiologos. There ensued much grief and a great deal of mourning on Crete, on account of this grievous piece of news. Nothing worse than this has happened nor will happen. May the L<ord> our G<od> have pity on us and deliver us from His terrible threat.

For many refugees the haven in Crete did not signal the end of their difficulties. In fact, two of those captains who had reached Candia continued to feel the impact of the fall of Constantinople in the next decade. Antonios Hyalinas lost almost his entire fortune in the sack and was subsequently beset by debtors. Such was his plight that the Venetian Senate attempted to alleviate his condition with an official decree, in view of his services during the siege. In 1456, Antonios Philomates and his brother Markos were still in such financial struggles that the *Signoria* also came to their rescue by generously allowing them to purchase grain from Apulia and to transport it to Crete for sale.[9]

More famous than either of the unfortunate captains was another refugee, Cardinal Isidore, who also found his way to Crete at this time. He as well made his way to Candia. Henry of Soemmern reports Isidore's adventures in a brief dated the 11th of September 1453.[10] The fall of the imperial city was felt deeply by the inhabitants of Candia. It is quite possible that Isidore provided an account of his impressions of the disaster to an assembly of local magistrates. He may have even given a public recitation of the events of the siege and of his adventures.[11] He went on then to compose a series of long letters intended to communicate the sad news to western Christendom. Meanwhile, the local population went into heavy mourning. A formal lamentation on the sack, composed by a Jewish resident of Candia, Michael ben Shabettai Kohen Balbo, survives.[12] His sentiments match the universal grief that is detected throughout Europe immediately after the sack. As far away as London, the event is noted in chronicles:[13] "Also in this yer, which was the yer of Ower Lord god MCCC-CLiij was the cite of Constantyn the noble lost by the Cristen men, and wonne by the Prynce of the Turkes named Mahumet."

Candia clearly became a focal point and gathering place for the surviving refugees. Numerous survivors with their families and noblemen, accompanied by their entire household of service members, flocked to this immigrant center. The arrival of such a large group must have taxed the resources of Candia, whose authorities encountered the immense problems of feeding and housing the refugees. Many had to be divided among the religious institutions. Certain individuals, however, received more attention, because of their noble station, but we know less about the treatment of the countless souls who were of the lower social orders. Because of his important position and appointments, including that of papal legate, Isidore was fortunate to receive exceptional treatment upon his arrival and he was provided with a residence during his stay. It was at this dwelling that Isidore took advantage of his favorable reputation among the Italian humanists present in Candia and he began to issue a flood of letters that are of historical importance. In addition, these letters served as propaganda, for the efforts of Isidore were directed toward the Italian powers that, as he clearly hoped, would result in a reaction, the launching of an old-fashioned crusade to liberate Constantinople. Consequently, he composed a number of letters that were then dispatched to Italy:

Letter I, *Epistola composita per Pasium de Bertipalia notarium ad instantiam reverendissimi domini Isidori cardinalis Sabiniensis,* "a letter put together by Pasio di Bertipaglia, a notary, at the instigation of the most reverend Lord Isidore, the cardinal of Sabina," is dated the 6th of July 1453, from Crete: *Ex Candida insulae Cretae pridie Nonas Julii MCCCLIII.* It was obviously composed in Greek by the cardinal and was then translated into Latin by Pasio di Bertipaglia.[14]

Letter II is historically significant,[15] for it contains a detailed description of the siege and is devoid of propaganda. This dispatch, addressed to Bessarion, contains pertinent material concerning the land operations of the defenders: *Epistola reverendissimi patris domini Isidori cardinalis Ruteni scripta ad reverendissimum dominum Bisarionem episcopum Tusculanum ac cardinalem Nicenum Bononiaeque legatum,* "A Letter Written by the Most Reverend Ruthenian Cardinal to the Most Reverend Lord Bessarion, the Nicene Bishop of Tuscany and Legate to Bologna." It bears the same date as the previous letter: *in Creta, die sexta Iulii.* This meaningful letter was unsurprisingly composed in Greek, but the original with the Greek text has vanished and we only possess its Latin translation by Lianoro de Lianori.[16]

Letter III is the only *epistula* of Isidore that scholars were aware of for a substantial period of time. It belongs more to the genre of propaganda than to history, for it includes generalities intended to awaken Christendom to take up arms against the Turks. It is exceptionally uninformative with regard to the events of the siege. It is addressed to *universis et singulis Christi fidelibus,* "to the universal and the individual faithful of Christ," and is dated the 8th of July, *die octava Iulii.* In its traditional printed form, this letter is an abstract and not a verbatim citation of the manuscript text made by Antonino, the archbishop of Florence, who, in his *Chronicon,* part III, ch. 13, states: *Haec in substantia sunt in litteris praedictis, etsi aliqualiter verba immutata,* "in substance these matters are to be found in the aforementioned letter, even though I have somewhat changed the phraseology." Antonino's version is encountered in most printed editions that are not directly taken from manuscripts but from his abstract. Moreover, the text of this abstract was printed from a particularly unreliable manuscript.[17] This was probably the best-known letter by Isidore[18] and it survives in eight manuscripts of the fifteenth century and one of the seventeenth.

Letter IV to Pope Nicholas V is Isidore's official report in his capacity as papal legate to Constantinople. It contains a description of the siege in abbreviated form. It is not as extensive as his Letter II to his friend Cardinal Bessarion. Nevertheless, it includes important details that could be of use to a historian interested in the siege. Like all his letters from this crucial period, it appears to have been composed in Greek and then translated by an Italian humanist into Latin. It bears the date of the 8th of July: *die octava Iulii,* as stated in the heading, but at the conclusion of the letter the 15th of July is cited: *Datum Cretae, die XV Julii.*[19]

Letter V (dated: the 26th of July, *die 26 Julii*) is addressed to Francesco Foscari, the Doge of Venice, and adds nothing of importance to a discussion of the operations during the siege. It has more value as a work of propaganda and has more in common with **Letter III**.[20]

Letter VI, without a date cited anywhere in the manuscript, but probably written on the 6th of July[21] to Cardinal Domenico Capranica. This letter records generalities and cites the impact of the fall on the Aegean region.[22]

Letter VII is addressed to the city and the authorities of Florence, *Magnificis dominis prioribus palatii et communitatis Florentinorum,* and is dated the 7th of July: *Datae VII Iulii.* It enumerates some atrocities committed during the sack and reports the alleged designs of Mehmed II for world domination. It further highlights the panic detected throughout the islands of the Aegean after the fall.[23]

Letter VIII is addressed to the city of Bologna (*ad communitatem Bonnoniae*), the see of Cardinal Bessarion, and is dated the 7th of July. Like **Letter VII**, it considers the Turkish threat to Europe and provides no new information on the siege.[24]

These letters and the views expressed therein by Isidore influenced the manner in which the West assessed, in its attempt to comprehend the incomprehensible, the monumental disaster that befell Constantinople and the new reality that was emerging in the Levant. The western humanists attempted to interpret this transformation in humanistic terms through a classical filter. Humanists pointed out that the monumental struggle that had been played out in antiquity and had often been described by ancient writers in an obsessive fashion was now undergoing a process of revival, rising out of the ashes of the conflict between the Occident and the Orient. It no longer took the form of "Greek against Persian" or "Roman against Parthian." Its fifteenth-century reincarnation generalized Christian against Muslim and western Latin Christendom in opposition to the Islamic Ottoman Empire. It amounted to a great deal more than a struggle between competing religions. Indeed it was understood as a struggle for survival, a war between conflicting ideologies competing to eliminate established ways of life through aggressive military encounters. In the *quattrocento* the Turkish military machine engulfed, annexed, and absorbed all remnants of the old and tired empire of the Byzantine Greeks, which had survived for over 1,100 years and had promulgated the fiction that Constantinople and her Caesars had been the only direct heirs and only legitimate successors to the Roman Empire. While the Byzantine Empire existed, it was a buffer zone, although at times very thin, and was a demarcation line between Latin West and Islamic East. Finally, the fifteenth century witnessed the elimination of this buffer zone and Latin Europe came to face a depressing reality: sooner or later there was to be direct conflict with the Ottoman Turks. Thus far the struggle had been played out in the Aegean Sea region and the southern Balkans. When the Turks launched raids deep into Hungary, Serbia, Transylvania, Bulgaria, and Albania, the Italians began to take serious notice of this threat, which translated into real concern and panic among the northern Italian cities that had maintained ties with the Orthodox Christian states in the east and awaited an inevitable confrontation and an all-out war.

European humanists struggled to grasp the fall of Constantinople in a scholarly context. While the image of the Turk as a savage barbarian continued to be employed in the contemporaneous literature, a few intellectuals attempted to bring the Turks into the context of their humanistic sphere. And in time the Turk was rehabilitated in some circles and was even welcomed into a world familiar to humanists, as a long-lost relative. The Turks had already been perceived as descendants of the ancient Trojans. And this notion gained widespread popularity after 1453. The mythical assimilation of the Turk into a descendant of the ancient Trojans had been created in the late fourteenth century when the West employed a Latinized term to designate a Turk, who thus became known as not only *Turcus* but also as *Teucrus*. And *Teucri* was the term the celebrated Vergil used in antiquity for the Trojans in his *Aeneid*. The Italians were not unique in this scholarly transformation and assimilation of a newcomer into a familiar ancient group, a term designated by humanists as ἔθνος. In the Middle Ages the Byzantine Greeks themselves had employed classical terms, which no longer made sense, to indicate contemporary ethnic groups. Thus in medieval Greek literature, among the educated Byzantine Greeks, the Turks were often styled as "Persians," the Albanians as "Illyrians," the Slavs as "Thracians," "Sarmatians," and "Triballians," the Mongols as "Scythians," and the Hungarians as "Pannonians." While the term *Teucrus* gained momentum in the West, it should be emphasized that not all humanists accepted this equation. Francesco Filelfo and Nikolaos Sekoundinos, the latter a brilliant simultaneous Greco-Italian translator of Latin into Greek and Greek into Latin during the Council of Ferrara-Florence, continued, for instance, to employ the more accurate phonetic approximation of *Turci*. The assimilation of Turk into Trojan became more common after the fall of Constantinople, and it was in the very fall of Byzantium that some humanists found another correlation. It was then said that the Ottoman Turks avenged the sack of Troy that had taken place in antiquity and that Mehmed II, the Turkish sultan, rectified the murder of Priam and his family by the Achaean Greeks of the Bronze Age, when he plundered the capital of Byzantium.

2 Two major themes in Isidore's letters from Candia

In the early literature on the fall, the conqueror of Constantinople, Sultan Mehmed II Fatih, is frequently compared to the ancient Great King of Persia, Xerxes, who had invaded Greece in 481–480 BC, but, unlike the Ottoman sultan, had met with disastrous consequences. This particular comparison between the ancient Great King and the contemporary Ottoman sultan found appeal, as we shall presently see, in the early accounts on the fall of Constantinople. These accounts were composed by authors who interacted with each other and who also enjoyed a considerable familiarity with classical Greek literature. Thus these individuals created an early circle of eyewitnesses and humanists who exhibited a strong interest in the fall of the Byzantine capital. They attempted to become familiar with a contemporary disaster through the eyes of classical antecedents. In addition, they were perhaps reminded of the fact that Xerxes had sacked Athens before he was met with a naval defeat at Salamis. These humanists were perhaps anticipative that Mehmed like Xerxes would lose the war, in spite of the fall of Constantinople, which then would be recovered by the Christian West in the near future. They envisioned and placed their hope in Christian crusader armies, as the Athenians had recovered Athens after the Persian sack in 480 BC.

The earliest witness to produce a comparison between the Ottoman sultan and the Persian Great King is Cardinal Isidore in his correspondence from Crete. He did so in his letter to Bessarion. Specifically, Isidore compares the floating bridge that the sultan had constructed in the course of the siege to deny absolute command of Constantinople's harbor to the Venetian defenders and further to threaten the sea walls of the city to the bridge that Xerxes had built across the Hellespont in order to transfer his army into Europe.[25] Cardinal Isidore returns to the same theme in his letter of the 8th of July to Pope Nicholas V. He further adds the observation that Mehmed's bridge still remained intact after the fall.[26] Isidore was not unfamiliar with this comparison, as he had already indicated in his youthful literary preferences an acute interest in ancient Persia and the *Perserei*. He had been steeped in classical Greek literature and his educational background was based on Attic Greek. In this comparison between the sultan and the Great King, Isidore is closely followed in the statements of Leonardo, who also produced a similar thought in the same context concerning Mehmed's famous bridge.[27] Leonardo also furnishes a detailed description of the bridge, providing its specific dimensions and measurements.[28] And his numerous literary imitators closely emulated this prototype and ensured the continuation of this comparison in humanistic literatures. Thus Leonardo is paraphrased by Languschi-Dolfin,[29] Sansovino,[30] and the *Codex Barberinus 111* (but without the reference to Xerxes).[31] Melissourgos-Melissenos also suppresses classical allusions and only provides a simple description of the bridge.[32] It should be observed, nevertheless, that in the previous paragraph of his text, Melissourgos-Melissenos does include some allusions to antiquity, when he describes Mehmed's transfer of his boats overland and over the hills of Pera, and their launch into the Golden Horn. Perhaps the reference to Xerxes in the sources that he had consulted encouraged him to allude as well to Cleopatra, Augustus, and Niketas the Patrician.

Pusculo[33] also arrived at the same observation.[34] As we have previously noted, Pusculo had traveled to Constantinople in order to perfect his Greek and was then caught up in the storm of the monumental events of 1453. He was a participant in the defense, and had seen, met, and even conversed with many Italian and Greek defenders, whose activities, operations, and positions on the walls he meticulously records in his work. During the sack Pusculo, like Isidore, was captured by the Turks, as he himself records in a biographical couplet at the end of his work. Pusculo appears to have spent a year in captivity before he found his way to the island of Rhodes that was then protected by the Order of the Knights of Saint John. From Rhodes Pusculo returned to Italy. There he sought employment in the service of the influential cardinal of Santa Croce and the bishop of Fermo, Angelo Capranica, who was a close friend of Bessarion.[35] Capranica also had an interest in the events of the siege, as we can gather from a paragraph in a letter that was written by Henry of Soemmern with regard to the adventures of Isidore during the siege of Constantinople and of his difficulties. Henry informs us of Capranica's interests at the end of his letter.[36] Pusculo's poem, however, is of the utmost value for the historian. It is unfortunate that this primary source document still awaits a modern editor. Pusculo's work was printed in the eighteenth century,[37] but that inferior edition used only the manuscript housed in Venice's Marciana Library; the same text, without improvements, was reprinted in the nineteenth century.[38] The reference to Xerxes in Leonardo echoes Isidore and items that the two clerics discussed during the siege. Echoes of the comparison of the siege of 1453 suggest that the Great King of Persia had been a subject of conversation among the Greeks and that the comparison between the two potentates may actually date back to the days of the siege.

In the late Palaiologan era, even John VIII, who had embarked upon an ambitious program to strengthen the fortifications of Constantinople, in happier days was compared to Xerxes.[39] Part of John's project included repairs to the moat along most of the length of the land fortifications, which had been long overdue. Upon completion of work on the moat he received praise from his contemporaries, who compared his achievement to other projects from antiquity. For these efforts, John VIII was compared to Xerxes. Exactly when the emperor instituted these renovations is unclear in the sources and the precise chronology itself remains elusive. An anonymous author of an *encomium* cites a number of restorations that were undertaken and completed. This author stresses the particular attention that was devoted to the moat that had been long neglected.[40] The anonymous author does not state exactly when John VIII initiated this renovation program. He presents a rather vague chronology of events.[41] In addition, a Greek panegyric composed by Isidore[42] himself also provides a description of the moat.[43]

At an early age Isidore emerged as a copyist of ancient manuscripts. Thus certain manuscripts of ancient works reproduced by his hand survive and illustrate his interests. An example of his impressive calligraphy can be seen in an exquisite *codex* that contains Manuel II's *Funeral Oration* on his brother Theodoros I, the despot of the Morea/Peloponnese.[44] Notable among Isidore's intellectual interests[45] are his preferences for astrology[46] and the occult, as evidenced by the *Astrologika* and Pseudo-Ptolemy,[47] for medicine,[48] and for rhetoric.[49]

There was an oracle in wide circulation among Greek intellectuals in the decade prior to the siege. The forewarning itself purports to date to Xerxes's invasion of Greece in 480 BC and is attributed to the Delphic Pythia, but unlike traditional Delphic oracles, its text[50] is not written in meter but in archaic prose. The last of its predictions refers to Constantine Palaiologos, who in his capacity as despot of the Morea/Peloponnese in 1443 fortified the Isthmus of Corinth, known as the Hexamilion. When Constantine fortified the Isthmus, his achievement was hailed as a Herculean labor and numerous notables anticipated that the Turks would never be able to penetrate the Peloponnese. Constantine's project created quite a sensation that was echoed in contemporaneous literature. He was congratulated by Bessarion, who sent him a warm letter, in which he advised the despot to govern the Peloponnese efficiently and urged him to achieve some autonomy for the peninsula.[51] Bessarion heartily approved of the fortification program.⁵² The oracle most probably was composed prior to 1446,⁵³ before the Turks overran the fortifications and the troops of Constantine were routed, contrary to the oracle's optimistic predictions.

Constantine's fortification of the Hexamilion made its mark at the popular level, since it helped to lay a foundation for a mythic aura about the person of the despot. This predisposition of Constantine to attract folklore to himself eventually accelerated after his death and mysterious "disappearance" on 29 May. He became a very potent mythic figure in the folklore of the Greeks throughout the period of the Turkish domination.⁵⁴ His myth fueled the hopes of the enslaved Greeks during the following dark centuries, when the last emperor of Greek Constantinople was transformed into a figure bearing a symbolism equivalent to that of King Arthur, whose return and eventual reconstitution of the lost "empire" were eagerly awaited. Even before his death, Constantine had attracted his share of millennial lore and became the subject of oracular literature. Although he is not actually named in the versions of the Pythian prophecy (which, after all, may have even existed before he repaired the fortifications, but it was eventually attached to him), it is evident that the renovation of the Hexamilion metamorphosed him into a Messianic figure, who was imagined to deliver the Peloponnese from its relentless enemy.

A number of important personalities took interest in this popular oracle, as the manuscript tradition of the oracle's text testifies.⁵⁵ Significantly, one version that has survived was written by the hand of Ioannes Dokeianos,⁵⁶ a second by the hand of Cyriacus of Ancona, and a third notable version (with extensive commentary) by the hand of Isidore.⁵⁷ The part of this oracle that refers to Constantine concludes with a prediction to the effect that a Fury ("a bronze-legged Erinys") will destroy the might of the enemy and the Isthmus will be fortified.⁵⁸ Isidore provides his own exegesis of these enigmatic lines:⁵⁹

> τουτέστιν ἐλεύσεται αὐτοῖς ἡ δύναμις ἡ ἀνταποδοτικὴ τῶν κακῶν, ἡ ἰσχυροὺς πόδας καὶ πολλοὺς ἔχουσα καὶ χεῖρας ὁμοίως, καὶ καταβαλεῖ τῶν Τούρκων τὴν δύναμιν, ὅταν δέξηται ὁ ἀγὼν στέφανον, ἤγουν ὅταν τιμῶνται καὶ στεφανῶνται οἱ στρατιῶται ἐν τῷ πολέμῳ καὶ διὰ τὴν τιμὴν καὶ τὸν στέφανον χέωσι οἱ στρατιῶται τὰ αἵματα αὐτῶν εὐκόλως τηνικαῦτα στήσεται τὸ ἐν Ἐξαμιλίῳ τεῖχος ἰσχυρὸν καὶ ἀρραγές. τὸ γὰρ παλαιὸν οἱ Ἕλληνες τοὺς ἀγωνιζομένους ἐν τῷ Ἰσθμῷ διὰ πίτυος ἐστεφάνουν ὥσπερ οἱ Ἀργεῖοι διὰ σελίνου καὶ Ὀλυμπίασι δι' ἐλαίας καὶ οἱ Δελφοὶ διὰ μηλέας κλάδοις.

They will become strong again to retaliate with a strength possessing many feet and arms and will destroy the might of the Turks, when the contest receives its crown, that is, when the soldiers are honored and crowned in war and easily pour out their blood for the sake of honor and the crown [of victory]. At that time the Hexamilion wall will be strong and impregnable. In antiquity the Hellenes crowned the athletes at the Isthmian games with pine, as the Argives used celery; at Olympia olive branches were used; and at Delphi apple branches.

More pertinent for our purposes is the introduction that Isidore supplies in his exegesis of this "Delphic oracle," as he makes explicit mention of Xerxes:

ἐν τῇ πόλει τοίνυν Δελφῶν Ἀπόλλωνι νεὼς ἀνεῖτο, ἐν ᾧ καὶ τοῖς Ἕλλησιν ἀνὰ τέτταρα ἐτελεῖτο τὰ ἔτη μεγάλη καὶ λαμπρὰ καὶ ἐξ αὐτῶν ἐφοίτων καὶ ἀπαρχαιὰ ἀνετίθεντο καὶ δεκάται τῷ Πυθίῳ. ἐν ἐκείνῳ καὶ χαλκοῦς ἦν τρίπους καὶ κόρη τις ὑποκαθημένη τοῦ νεὼ τοῖς ἀδύτοις καὶ κάτοχος τελοῦσα τῷ δαίμονι τοῖς ἐρωτῶσι τὰ μαντεύματα προὔλεγε, τὰ μὲν ἑξαμέτρῳ τόνῳ, τὰ δ' οὑτωσὶ καταλογάδην. ἀλλ' ὁπότε δὴ Ξέρξης, Ξέρξης ἐκεῖνος, ἐστράτευσε κατὰ τῆς Ἑλλάδος, ἐν τοῖς Ἰσθμοῦ ὅσοι δὴ Πελοποννησίων ἀθροισθέντες, ὧν Λακεδαιμόνιοι τὸ κεφάλαιον, τὸ πρῶτον τειχίζουσι τὸν Ἰσθμὸν τῷ φόβῳ τοῦ βαρβάρου προληφθέντες (οὔτε γὰρ τὸ πρῶτον οὔτ' ἄχρι τοῦ νῦν στρατὸν ἐκίνησέ τις καὶ κατὰ γῆν τοσοῦτον καὶ κατὰ θάλασσαν). πέμπειν τοίνυν ἐκεῖνοι πευσόμενοι τοῦ Ἀπόλλωνος, εἴπερ ὁ κατὰ τὸν Ἰσθμὸν περίβολος. θεοπρόπους οἶμαι ἐκάλουν τοὺς ἀφικνομένους ἐπὶ τῇ πεύσει, ἅτε δὴ πρέποντας ἐπὶ τῇ πεύσει τῷ θεῷ. ἐρωτῶσιν οὖν τηνικαῦτα, τὰ δ' αὐτοῖς ἡ Πυθία χρεῖ.

There was a temple dedicated to Apollo in the city of Delphi, where the Hellenes celebrated an important, illustrious, and well-known festival every four years. All cities offered public sacrifices and sent representative priests to attend and to offer first fruits and tithes to the Pythian god. They had a bronze tripod there and there was a maiden who had access to the innermost chambers of the temple. She was possessed by the god and gave oracles to those who asked. Some were in the form of a hexameter, others in plain speech. And when Xerxes (that famous Xerxes) invaded Hellas, those Peloponnesians who had gathered at the Isthmus (the Spartans being the most important), were the first to fortify the Isthmus, for they were in fear of the barbarian (no one, up to the present time, has mobilized so many land forces and such a great fleet). They sent for Apollo's advice with regard to the defensive perimeter at the Isthmus. I believe that those who went to inquire of the god's opinion were termed "god-questioners." They asked and Pythia answered.

It can thus be demonstrated that Isidore had already developed an intellectual interest in Xerxes, whose deeds and name he had come upon while researching sources to interpret the oracle,[60] in addition to his familiarity with the Great King and Persia from the days when he was a young scholar immersed in classical studies. It is not that surprising then that the achievements of Xerxes sprang to his mind during the siege. He had already familiarized himself with this figure and was probably acquainted with the notion that John VIII's repairs of the moat had also earned that emperor a comparison with the ancient Great King.[61]

Isidore also contributed, and most likely initiated, in the contemporary literature dealing with the fall of Constantinople another theme, which is subsequently picked up in numerous accounts. Mehmed II Fatih becomes a comparable figure to Alexander the Great, the best-known ancient figure in the medieval Levant.[62] The comparison would have been inevitable, as the magnitude of the disaster deeply affected the terrified Christian population of the Balkans and the Aegean region.[63] Isidore himself, on 8 July, dispatched a letter to all Christians, in which he indicated the fright that Mehmed was already initiating new activities and supposed preparations to continue his conquests immediately after his sack of Constantinople.[64]

Besides Isidore, the earliest comparison on record is that of the 11th of June, *Candiae, XI Junii* <1453>, between the sultan and the ancient Macedonian king and is provided by the Paduan lawyer Paolo Dotti (*Missiva domini Pauli de Dotis, juris utriusque interpretis, olim ordinarii Paduae, relegati in Candiam, narrans de expugnatione civitatis illustris Constantinopolitanae*), who was a resident of Crete at that time. Dotti was a friend of Lauro Quirini[65] and composed a short account of the fall of Constantinople, which he wrote before Isidore initiated the torrent of his own letters to the west. Dotti characterizes the sultan as "a new Alexander":[66] *Omnes istinc Christianorum partes de huiusmodi afflictione timent, quia huic pagano terribili pro Alexandro altero nuncupato coniuncta est voluntas pessima et potestas maxima*, "every Christian region has been so afflicted with fear. This terrible infidel (nicknamed a new Alexander) possesses a most frightening will and the greatest might."

The earliest mention that Isidore makes of a correlation between Alexander and the Ottoman sultan was in his letter of the 6th of July (*in Creta, die sexta Iulii anno Domini M°CCCC°LIII°*) to Bessarion (*ad reverendissimum dominum Bisarionem episcopum Tusculanum ac cardinalem Nicenum Bononiaeque legatum*), which we have previously examined in connection with the siege.[67] It is in this letter that we encounter his first attempt to link Alexander the Great and Mehmed II, who, Isidore claims, was making hasty preparations to launch the invasion for his next target, Italy. This correspondence is an initial expression of his propaganda:[68] *et haec tu quidem vera puta, ego futura non dubito, Alexandri siquidem vitam quotidie audit arabice, graece et latine*, "and take this as the truth. I do not doubt what will happen: daily he hears the life of Alexander in Arabic, Greek, and Latin." Isidore pursues this comparison in his letter dated the 7th of July (*Dat<a>e VII Iulii MCCCCLIII*) that was addressed: *Magnificis dominis prioribus palatii et communitatis Florentinorum*, "the exalted lord priors of the palace and of the community of Florence," in which he further adds a humanistic note that the sultan's cruelty surpasses that of Thyestes.[69] Verbal echoes from this letter appear in the text of another communication (dated the 26th of July [1453]: *die 26 Julii*), which the cardinal addressed to the "Glorious Doge of Venice, Francesco Foscari" (*inclito duci Venetiarum Isidorus miseratione divina sacrosancta Romanae ecclesiae episcopus Sabinus cardinalis Rutinensis appelatus*).[70] These are his earliest citations and comparisons on record. The nucleus of them seems to originate with Isidore and his fellow humanists on Crete. This comparison finds further appeal in the humanistic circles of the West and was then taken up by others in their narratives. With time, the comparison that originated with this literary circle in Crete was further elaborated and was widely imitated in the West.

A famous member of the cardinal's circle on Crete was Lauro Quirini, who had conversed with Isidore about the operations of the siege. Quirini also found a place in his narrative (finished on the Ides of July, that is, the 15th of July: *data Candidae, Idibus Iulii 1453*) to assert that Mehmed thought of himself as "the modern Alexander": *hic ex diversis signis et iudiciis in tantam superbiam exultatus est, ut non dubitet dicere regem Alexandrum Macedoniae admirandum cum minori potentia subiuga<vi>sse totum orbem*, "he [*sc.* Mehmed II] is so arrogant and from many indications so proud that he does not hesitate to say that the famous king, Alexander of Macedon, had conquered the whole world with a smaller army [than his own]." Quirini further adds that the sultan was an avid reader of Arian's history of the Macedonian king,[71] echoing the statements of Isidore that the sultan was familiar with multi-lingual texts on the life of Alexander: *quam ob rem sese principem orbis terrarum gentiumque omnium, id est alterum Alexander, et esse et dici vult. Unde et Arianum, qui res gestas Alexandri diligintissime scripsit, quotidie ferme legere consuevit*, "he thinks of himself as the prince of the entire world and of all nations and that he is another Alexander. He wishes to be so styled. Consequently, he daily, as a rule, reads avidly Arian, who wrote a detailed account of the deeds of Alexander."

Quirini's narrative, which is based on the information the author received from Isidore and from other unnamed refugee sources, constitutes the earliest and longest account of the siege by a humanist who was not an eyewitness, but had obtained oral information from survivors. His narrative also furnishes very early observations and details on Ottoman strategy and tactics, especially with regard to the Turkish final assault of 28–29 May. Moreover, it was perhaps in conversations with Isidore that the name of Nero was invoked, for both Isidore and Quirini cite the Roman emperor in their accounts of the siege. Isidore refers to Nero as an example of cruelty in his letter to the doge and to the community of Florence. Nero also appears in the narrative of Lauro Quirini, again as an example of cruelty:[72] *etenim, quis Nero tam saevus, ut hoc horribile flagellum ad Christianum exstirpandum*, "who was as cruel as Nero, such a horrible scourge intended to eliminate Christians." Quirini returns to Alexander once more in his account but he does not make a comparison to the sultan. In this instance, he urges the pope to take up the struggle against the Turks and he is attempting to inspire him with examples from antiquity, citing such well-known figures who were familiar to the humanists as Scipio, Julius Caesar, Aemilius Paulus, and Pompey the Great, in addition to Alexander.[73] Once more, the pope was a humanist with unquestionable interests in antiquity and Isidore also took advantage of the pope's intellectual proclivities to cast the disaster of Constantinople in terms that humanists, in general, would appreciate and thus rekindle the embers for a western crusade to recover the Byzantine capital.

Leonardo also was an ecclesiastic with strong humanistic tendencies and was well known among the active lovers of antiquity during the *quattrocento*.[74] He was familiar with the comparison between Mehmed and Alexander, probably through his association with Isidore during the siege, but chose not to make frequent use of the association in his narrative. He compares the sultan to the

Macedonian king once, in connection with the sultan's crucial council, during the course of which Mehmed was persuaded by his advisors to launch the final assault and to abandon all thought of a projected withdrawal. In Leonardo's narrative, the young sultan makes his decision to launch the attack and compares himself to Alexander the Great.[75] Languschi-Dolfin follows his prototype, but also inserts after the name the description "the Macedonian."[76] Significantly, Makarios Melissourgos-Melissenos makes no reference to Alexander,[77] while the text of the early seventeenth-century follower of Leonardo, the anonymous author of the *Codex Barberinus 111*, presents a more faithful paraphrase of Leonardo's text (or perhaps it derives from Sansovino's Italian translation of Leonardo's Latin account).[78]

Leonardo also explains the origins of the Janissaries,[79] which he attributes to the peculiar Ottoman institution of the "*devşirme*," or παιδομάζωμα, the "child tribute" collected from Christian subjects in the Balkans and Asia Minor to form the dreaded corps of the sultan:[80] *inter quos pedites ad regis custodiam deputati audaces, qui ab elementis christiani aut christianorum filii retrorsum conversi, dicti genizari, uti apud Macedonem Myrmidones, quasi quindecim milia,* "among his infantry are the most fearsome who have been selected to be the king's [sultan's] bodyguard. They were Christians when they were little or have Christian origins, but they were converted [to Islam] and are called Janissaries, as were the Myrmidones with the Macedonian. They are as many as fifteen thousand." Languschi-Dolfin closely emulates Leonardo.[81]

Nikolaos Sekoundinos also produces a description of the character of the sultan in one of his speeches that he pronounced in early 1454. During the previous summer of 1453, Sekoundinos had visited the Porte on behalf of the *Serenissima* and probably had an opportunity to observe Mehmed II, with whose officials he had been negotiating for the release of the remaining Venetian prisoners that had been captured during the sack.[82] Sekoundinos was one of the earliest western visitors to come to Constantinople after the fall. In his work, he states that the sultan was an avid reader of ancient history and was especially interested in Sparta, Rome, and Carthage. But of particular interest to the sultan, according to Sekoundinos, were Alexander the Great and Julius Caesar, whose examples he wished to emulate:[83]

> *Tenet praeterea duos medicos, quorum alter latine, later graece est eruditus. Hic familiarissime utitur eorumque ductu veteris historiae cognitionem habere voluit, neque visus est Lacedaemoniorum, Atheniensium, Romanorum, Carthaginiensium aliorumque regum et principum rebus festis accommoda<vi>sse animum, Alexandrum Macedonem et Gaium Caesarem praecipue sibi imitandos delegit, quorum res gestas in linguam suam traduci effecit; in quibus legendis vel audiendis mirum delectatur in modum. Aemulationem enim gloriosa quadam illis se parem conatur ostendere, gloriaeque at laudis studio inflammari videtur atque ardere.*
>
> He has in his service two physicians, one of them is versed in Latin and the other in Greek. He has become extremely familiar with ancient history and desires such knowledge. He seems to have accommodated his

disposition to the deeds of the leaders of the Lacedaemonians, the Athenians, the Romans, and the Carthaginians. He especially chooses to imitate the Macedonian Alexander and Julius Caesar, whose histories he has taken care to translate into his language. He finds great pleasure in reading or hearing their histories. He attempts to demonstrate that he is their competitor, equal to them, and burns with desire to match their glory and praises.

Sekoundinos's passage exercised considerable influence on subsequent literature and helped to formulate the standard western literary portrait of the Ottoman sultan. An echo from his text appears to be present in an account that was added to an original business-like report on the siege operations that had been composed soon after the sack by the Florentine Giacomo Tetaldi,[84] in which Augustus is added to the list of Caesar and Alexander, as the sultan is again portrayed as an avid reader of ancient history:

Narrantibus his qui cum principe Turcorum aliquando conversati sunt . . . invenitur et eius statum optime noverant constat illum fuisse tunc temporis viginti trium circiter annorum. Ferunt quoque ipsum plus quam dici vel cogitari possit, delectari in humani sanguinis effusione. Propter quod invenitur anhelo quotidie stragem sitiens, ambition indefesse studens, damnantiones ardenter affectans, nella continue desiderans, discordias infatigabiliter fovens, triumphos modibus omnis amans, principatum totius orbis affectuosissime diligens, immo plusquam Alexander Magnus, Iulius, vel Augustus, vel alii quique potentes imperatores huius mundi. Aestimat denique maiorem et ampliorem virtutem et potentiam se habere quam omnes qui fuerunt ante ipsum; quapropter coram se recitari facit annales historias temporum antiquorum, quatenus ex is posset latius de singulis informari, ut tandem pervenire posset ad Venetos et Romanos et notitiam de duce Mediolanensi ac eius potentia haberet.

Those who have, at some point, conversed with the prince of the Turks and know his circumstances very well are in agreement that he is about twenty-three years old. They also say that more than can be expressed or thought of, he delights in shedding human blood. And so it is concluded that he eagerly thirsts for slaughter daily, that he is full of ambition, that he enthusiastically applies punishment, that he constantly desires war, that he loves triumphs of all sort, and that he thrives to create a world empire that will surpass those of Alexander the Great, of Julius [Caesar], of Augustus, or of any other powerful emperors throughout the world. He thinks that his power and strength surpass all of those who have preceded him. Accordingly, he has historical annals from antiquity recited in his presence, for he wishes to be informed in detail about individual events, with the objective of extending his power to Venice and Rome and also to be noticed by the duke of Milan.

Later in 1453 Nicolò Tignosi da Foligno composed an account titled *Expugnatio Constantinopolitana*. This work is in fact an appendix to a letter that he addressed to a friend and furnishes extensive observations on the personality of Mehmed II, and he comments on the international situation following the fall.[85] His information derives from an otherwise unknown eyewitness from Perugia, probably a merchant, who managed to conceal himself during the sack and subsequently escaped, as he reports.[86] The inevitable comparison of Mehmed II to Alexander, which first appeared in the compositions of Isidore, also appears in Tignosi's account. However, this author has included, for added effect, the figure of the Roman emperor Caligula:[87] *Quasi novus Caligula terrorem respicientibus incutit moribusque dicitur antiquorum studere <in> historiis et illorum facinora cum admiratur, se Alexandrum Macedonem superaturum aestimat, et Caesarem Octaviumque imitaturus firmissime credit se posse toto orbe potiri*, "like a new Caligula, he has infused terror in all witnesses and is said to have studied ancient histories and to have admired the crimes of the ancients. He estimates that he has surpassed Alexander the Macedonian and that he is about to emulate Caesar Octavius [Augustus]. His firm belief is that he will assume control of the whole world."

Languschi-Dolfin makes a similar comparison in a section of his work that is independent of the Latin[88] narrative of Leonardo, by which he has occasioned a notable debate among scholars. Languschi-Dolfin states[89] that Mehmed II adopted Alexander the Great as his idol. Moreover, he suggests that a companion of Cyriacus of Ancona[90] and another Italian read daily to the sultan the works of Diogenes Laertius, Herodotus, Livy, Quintus Curtius, the papal chronicles, and the chronicles of the emperors, of the kings of France, and of the Lombards. In another section, independent from Leonardo's narrative, Languschi-Dolfin again makes mention of Alexander and Caesar in comparison to Mehmed, and at this juncture Hannibal is also added to the distinguished company.[91]

Thus, based on Isidore's early propaganda, a tale took form, which states that Mehmed II Fatih enthusiastically devoured ancient texts, whose heroes and protagonists, both good and bad, he strove to emulate. This legend enjoyed a wide circulation among humanists. Because of the classical precedents established by Isidore,[92] it was unquestionably accepted and disseminated throughout Italy. Aeneas Silvius Piccolomini also mentions it in his letter[93] (dated the 18th of July) to the famous philosopher, Cardinal Nicholas of Cusa: *et quamvis est natura barbarus abhorretque literas, gesta tamen maiorum cupide audit, ac Iulium Caesarem, et Alexandrum Magnum omnibus anteponit, quorum illustria facta superare posse confidit atque contendit; nec se minus aptum ad subingendum orbem dicit*, "although he is a barbarian by nature and hates literature, nevertheless he avidly listens to the deeds of the ancients and prefers, above all, those of Julius Caesar and of Alexander the Great, whose illustrious deeds he challenges and is convinced that he will surpass. He says that he is an equal to them and that he will conquer the world."

Influence from the propaganda of Isidore can be detected as late as the 1470s. One of the last *quattrocento* humanists to produce an account on the fall of Constantinople was Adamo di Montaldo.[94] His text in several sections reveals echoes of this earlier propaganda. Thus Montaldo discusses the supposed interests of the sultan in literature and these familiar themes reappear:[95]

> *Literarum curam continuam gerit. Habet enim Arabem, quotidianum sibi familiarem, quondam peritum philosophia virum.... Praeterea duorum physicorum, alterius graece, alterius latine peritorum, domesticam sibi conversationem effecit. Horum trium virorum opera historiarum veterum novam quidem habet cognitionem perplacuit. Lacedaemonios et Carthaginenses, resque celebriter ab iis gestas exigui pendens, Gaji Caesaris atque Alexandri Magni morem,... complectitur....Amborum gesta in asiaticam linguam converti.*
>
> He shows interest in literature, as he daily keeps close to himself an Arab well versed in philosophy.... Moreover, he converses with two physicians: one is an expert in Greek and the other in Latin. He delights to gain the knowledge of the three men on ancient history. He embraces the accomplishments and the glorious deeds of the Spartans and the Carthaginians, and the character of Julius Caesar and that of Alexander the Great.... He has translated their histories into his Asiatic language.

Adamo di Monaldo returns to similar thoughts with a humanistic emphasis at the conclusion of his narrative.[96] He was clearly influenced by the humanistic *topos* that had been formalized by the time he wrote his composition.

It may be concluded that Isidore reinforced, if he did not actually originate, a *topos* that would have been a welcome observation to humanists of the early Renaissance, enforcing their view of the value of the classics in their attempt to understand the circumstances of their world through the filter of antiquity. Alexander the Great himself, a keen student of Homer, was reputed to have Homer's works at hand throughout his campaigns in Asia, as the thirteenth-century bishop of Thessalonike, the learned Eustathios, had noted in his commentaries to Homer.[97] Perhaps the mere comparison of the sultan to the Macedonian king would have evoked the notion of the conqueror-student of literature and would have encouraged such speculation among humanists. In addition, as we have observed, Mehmed had a genuine interest in Alexander,[98] with whom he may have been familiar through other oriental and medieval tales and romances, such as the *Iskendername* by Ahmedi (who had been a member of the Porte of Sultan Murad II). Kritoboulos states that when Mehmed visited Athens on the occasion of its formal annexation to the Porte (August 1459), he took time to tour the antiquities, in which he showed great interest.[99] Finally, Aeneas Silvius's letter to Nicholas of Cusa also makes reference to Alexander the Great's visit to Troy and to the supposed tomb of Achilles:[100] *senserat haec Alexander Macedo, qui cum in Sigeo sepulchrum vidisset Achillis. O fortunate, inquit, adolescens, qui tuae virtutis praeconem Homerum inveneris,* "Alexander the Macedonian felt this way, when he saw the tomb of Achilles in Sigeum. He said: 'O young man, you were fortunate to find Homer to be the singer of your excellence!'"

This notion is also linked to the humanistic idealistic view that the Turkish sultan was a modern avenger of ancient injustices and that Constantinople's fate had been dictated by the atrocities that had been committed by the Achaean Greeks upon Troy and the Trojans in the Bronze Age.[101] In the imagery of the modern Trojan/Turk avenging the fate of Troy, Filippo da Rimini, the Venetian Chancellor at Corfu, compiled an early account of the fall of Constantinople by the end of that year and incorporated his composition in a letter he sent to Francesco Barbaro.[102] Da Rimini portrays Mehmed II employing vengeance as his motive for the siege and sack of Constantinople.[103]

It is quite possible that Mehmed eventually took advantage of this Trojan fiction, as there are hints in our Greek sources that he may have used the Trojan-Turk equation to his benefit. The humanistic tale that began with the comparison of the sultan to Alexander and then moved on to attract Troy and other similar powerful images from antiquity must have reached the Levant and may have even enjoyed a limited circulation within the Porte. At least by the time Mehmed's Greek biographer, Kritoboulos, wrote, it seems that the sultan had availed himself of such humanistic comparisons and had presented himself as the just avenger of the sack of Troy, duplicating the actions of Alexander the Great, by visiting the tomb of Achilles, exactly as the Macedonian king had been reputed to have done.[104]

3 Religious propaganda and military strategy

While a large part of Isidore's propaganda seems to have been addressed to Italian humanists (as should be expected given the large circle of humanists in Candia and friends in Italy), the cardinal did not divorce himself from his ecclesiastical position and in some ways his propaganda is also interspersed with themes that address his more conservative Christian colleagues. In this mode, Isidore puts on the robe of an old-fashioned crusader and addresses the Ottoman conquest of Constantinople in religious overtones that would be more familiar to readers who had not yet been baptized into the humanistic sphere. In his letter to Bessarion, Isidore only makes mention of the atrocities committed during the sack with special emphasis on the fate of ecclesiastical objects, but he does not address the need for future crusades and maintains a discreet distance from ecclesiastical eschatology.[105] While Isidore preserves the historian's role and the humanistic reference in his letter to the pope,[106] as Nicholas V was a recognized humanist with considerable interest in ancient Greek texts, at the conclusion of his letter Isidore does evoke a biblical atmosphere with his citation of the fall of Jerusalem and the role of Nebuchadnezzar. In the concluding sentence, he indicates that he is formulating a plan, which, no doubt, would have included a call for a crusade to counter the Islamic threat presented by the Ottoman Turks.[107]

As should be expected, the letter he wrote to all "the faithful in Christ" opens with a biblical allusion:[108] *"audite haec omnes gentes, auribus percipite omnes qui habitatis terram," David propheta ait in sui praefatione psalmi*, "'hear, all nations. All who inhabit the earth listen,' David the Prophet asserted in his preface to the Psalms." In contrast to the factual information encountered in his historical accounts, this letter proceeds through themes which characterized Mehmed II as the precursor of the Antichrist[109] with links to the prophet Mohammed, and points out the sultan's presumed plans for world domination, emphasizing his alleged aversion toward Christianity. In other letters he describes Mehmed II as "Satan's son"[110] and "Beelzebub,"[111] while he also retains his humanistic comparisons of the sultan as a new Alexander of Macedon (but omits Xerxes). In a letter to Francesco Foscari, the Doge of Venice, Isidore, as an ecclesiastic, associates the army of Mehmed with the devil:[112] *intravit itaque nequam ille canis cum suo damnabili exercitu Satanae in sanctam illam civitatem tanquam leo rugens*, "that dog with his cursed Satanic army entered that holy city as if he were a roaring lion." Then to indicate the sultan's aversion towards all Christians, Isidore adds a personal thought with an original observation, to which he returns in other religious polemics:[113]

> *Ille . . . et maxime ferro et suppliciis christianos macerat et affligit, volens totaliter nomen Christi de terra delere; tantum enim alit odium et abhominationem et iracundiam contra Christianos, quod, cum ipse inspexerit suis oculis christianum, existimans se maxime deturpatum fore et sordidatum, proprios oculos abluit et abstergi.*
>
> That man . . . attacks and butchers Christians with sword and torture, in his will to wipe out the name of Christ irrevocably from the earth. Such hatred, abhorrence, and wrath does he nourish against Christians; he believes that he has been so defiled and polluted when he personally sees a Christian that he washes and purges his eyes.

The same thought reappears in his letter to the city of Bologna:[114] *hic Beelzebub tamquam Christi flagellum et abominatio s<a>eculi tanta iniquitate, tanta immanitate tantaque impietate odit Christianos, ut terreat, dum videt Christianum, contamina<vi>sse proprios oculos, et lavat se a macula*, "this Beelzebub [*sc.* Mehmed II], as if he were a scourge of Christ and an eternal abomination, hates Christians with such injustice,[115] such savagery, and such disrespect, that, after he has laid eyes upon a Christian, he fears that he has been contaminated and washes his eyes to remove the stain." He includes the very same observation in his letter to the pope:[116] *tantum enim habet odium et abhominationem in eos, ut cum oculis Christianos perspexit, proprios oculos abluit et abstergit, quasi visione sua foedatus sit*, "to look upon a Christian he considers an abomination and he subsequently washes and cleanses his eyes to rid himself of the pollution."

That is Isidore's personal contribution to his otherwise standard descriptions of the monstrosity of the "infidel" sultan.

These characterizations can be summarized as follows, as they are standard and can be matched by similar sentiments expressed by others, who were either survivors or had been informed about the propaganda that had been initiated soon after the fall:[117]

1   In the di Bertipaglia Latin translation (of the 6th of July), Isidore describes the sultan as follows: *Teucrorum rabido principe et christiani nominis acerrimo*

prosecutor, "the mad prince of the Turks and the most energetic prosecutor of Christians"; and again:[118] *huius perfidi tyrannicam potentiam et innatam superbiam . . . sua barbara saevitia comminatur christianum nomen radicitus extirpare,* "a disloyal man with tyrannical power and native arrogance . . . who threatens with his barbaric savagery to eradicate totally the Christians."

2   In the Lianoro Latin translation of Isidore's letter to Bessarion (the 6th of July), beyond the comparison of Mehmed to Xerxes with his bridge and his impression that the sultan listened daily to accounts of the deeds of Alexander the Great, there is nothing derogatory about the nature of the character of the sultan. Perhaps we should go so far as to suggest that Isidore, at a certain level, felt some admiration for the military accomplishments of the sultan. In his role as a historian, Isidore refrains from using derogatory terms that belong to the genre of propaganda.

3   In his letter addressed to all Christians, Isidore uses very strong terminology to describe Mehmed II:[119]

> *praecursor veri Antichristi, Turcorum princeps et dominus, servus autem tot daemoniorum, quot vitiorum, cujus nomine est Mahumet, inimicus crucis Christi, haeres rei et nominis illius primi pseudoprophetae, et latoris legis spurcissimae Agarenorum, filius Satanae omnium flagitiosissimus; qui furiis invectus et insania, sanguinem Christianorum sine intermissione sitit; nec exstingui valet eius sitis post eorum innumeras caede.*
>
> He is the precursor of the true Antichrist this prince and lord of the Turks. Indeed, he is the servant of countless demons and vices. His name is Mehmed and he is the enemy of Christ's cross. He is the heir and the namesake of the pseudo-prophet Mohammed and honors the most foul laws of the sons of Hagar [Muslims]. He is the most obscene son of Satan, who, driven by fury and madness, thirsts, without restraint, for Christian blood. Nothing can satisfy this thirst except countless acts of slaughter.

In the next paragraph, Mehmed is *hic nefandus tyrannus nominibus blasphemiae plenus,* "this criminal tyrant is full of all the names of blasphemy."[120] Towards the conclusion of this letter, Isidore returns to the "enemy of Christendom" theme:[121] *illis atrocissimis rebus non contentus callidissimus et cruentissimus Mahometus, Christicolarum summus inimicus,* "with these extreme atrocities he was not satisfied, this most bloody and most fervent Mehmed, the greatest enemy of Christians." He concludes by referring to the sultan and his armies as *ipsum Satanam cum satellitibus suis,* "Satan himself with his accomplices."[122]

4   In his formal letter to the pope, the cardinal exhibits restraint and produces a factual account of the siege. We have already encountered the few references to Mehmed in this letter.[123]

5   We have also discussed the references that are included in Isidore's letter to the Venetian Doge, Francesco Foscari.[124]

6   Isidore's personal letter to Cardinal Domenico Capranica contains no references to Mehmed II. It simply expresses Isidore's depressive state over the fall and speaks of the terror that has seized the Aegean world and the Levant. At the very end of the letter, Isidore provides a reference to a certain "Fra Giovanni,"[125] who presumably carried his letter to Capranica. Is it plausible that Fra Giovanni was the personal emissary of Isidore, responsible for carrying all the letters of Isidore to Italy from Candia? Henry of Soemmern tells us that Capranica had accumulated many letters of Isidore. Could they have been copied from the originals brought by Fra Giovanni? The statement of Henry is as follows:[126]

>   <alia [sc. epistula] domini cardinalis> Ruthenis, qui de hac re unam papae, aliam domino cardinali Firmano [Capranica]; tertia<m>que patens erat omnibus Christifidelibus. Et ex duabus aliis scriptis domino Firmano (quorum unam scripsit ipse agens, familiaris et domesticus dicti cardinali Rutheni, aliam vicarius ordinis minorum provinciae Candiae). Quarum omnium copias habeo, ex copiis domini Firmani,
>
>   Another [sc. letter] was written by the lord Cardinal of Ruthenia [Isidore], who sent one report to the pope and another to the lord cardinal Firmano [Capranica], while another letter of his was addressed to faithful Christians. There were also other letters sent to the cardinal. One he wrote himself, another was written by a close friend of the Cardinal of Ruthenia, and a third at Candia by the vicar of the Order of the Minorites. I have copies of all of them, from the copies that belong to the Firmano cardinal.

7   The letter of Isidore to the city of Florence is identical in content and phraseology to the cardinal's letter to the city of Bologna.[127] Again here, as in his letter to all Christians,[128] Isidore refers to Mehmed as "the precursor of the Antichrist," and as "a dog with his cursed army of Satan ... roaring like a lion."[129]

The objective of the cardinal in all these descriptions of the character of Mehmed is to arouse anger and indignation among all Christians against the sultan, so that a reaction can take place against his recent conquests. The cardinal used themes that would have been familiar to his Christian audiences, in addition to his pleas, in classical terms, to western humanists. By contrast, he mentions his escape and his unexpected survival again in Christian imagery, seeking to evoke pity and describe his awe at the divine powers that delivered him from evil. In the di Bertipaglia translation he describes himself as grieving and suggests that a divine miracle delivered him from the evil to make him a living eyewitness to the event.[130] He repeats similar statements to Bessarion,[131] and further suggests that he will give a detailed account of his adventures upon his return to Italy.[132] In his letter to Bologna, he again characterizes his survival and escape as a miracle.[133] He employs biblical allusions in his letter to all

Christians and compares his salvation from the "infidel hands" to the delivery of Jonah from the belly of the whale.[134] At the same time, while he attempts to arouse anger against the sultan, he also seeks from Christians pity for himself.

From indignation and pity the cardinal moves on evoke sorrow for the fate of Constantinople and its inhabitants. He furnishes a list of the atrocities that were committed by the conquering army, concentrating on the desecration of religious establishments and on the fate of the Christian inhabitants. Thus di Bertipaglia becomes the voice of the cardinal and expresses his impressions on the sack, as furnished by the cardinal:[135]

> *Quotquot ea die et sequentibus fuerunt crudeliter occisi, quot captivi! Quot violatae virgins Ecclesiae divino cultu dedicatae, quot honestae mulieres effectae adulteratae! Quot filii a parentibus separati et quot in eorum alvis crudeliter occisi! Quot magnificae domus infinitis opibus spoliatae, quot derobatae et desolatae ecclesiae, quot profanata altaria, quot destituta monasteria, quot sanctorum corpora vituperabiliter spretiata, quot venerandae reliquiae pedibus conculcatae! Denique quot manifestae et detestandae iniuriae summo Deo et christianae religioni ab eisdem canibus perfidi Mahometi sectatoribus impudenter illatae!*

On that day and during the following days so many were cruelly slaughtered, so many were taken into captivity! So many virgins who had dedicated themselves to the rituals of the Church were violated; so many respectable women were raped! So many sons were separated from their parents and so many were butchered while they were in their parents' embraces! How many magnificent buildings were plundered and lost their countless wealth! How many churches were robbed and looted! How many altars were desecrated! How many monasteries were pillaged! How many bodies of saints were viciously scorned! How many reverend relics were trampled under foot! In short, how many detestable insults were shamelessly expressed to our Highest God and to the Christian religion by those dogs who follow the infidel Mohammed!

In the letter to Bessarion, Isidore is extremely graphic in his description of the atrocities committed during the sack, expounding on information supplied in his report that was Latinized by di Bertipaglia.[136] He is more restrained in his official report to Pope Nicholas V, and couches his information totally within the biblical sphere.[137] As should be expected, he returns to more graphic terms in his letter addressed to all Christians, and treats the atrocities *in extenso*,[138] dealing with the indignities that monks and nuns suffered and the separations of parents from children, wives from husbands. He seems especially distressed when he witnessed the upper classes suffering the same fate as the lower, without distinction or respect for individuals of the higher social orders. He then recounts the fate of icons and sacred images, concentrates on the pillage, and concludes that the city of Constantine had been turned into a den of thieves.[139] He devotes special attention to the fate of Santa Sophia and to the Islamic prayers that followed the enslavement and slaughter of those individuals who in vain had sought sanctuary in the ecclesiastical structure and its neighborhood, including himself.[140]

Similar sentiments, in less sensational tones, are expressed in other public letters that he anticipated would be recited to large audiences. Thus in his letters to the Doge of Venice, to Bologna, and to Florence Isidore provides the following details, in almost identical language:[141]

> *Intravit itaque nequam ille canis cum suo damnabili exercitu Satanae in sanctam illam civitatem tanquam leo rugens. Multos necavit et suis bonis spoliavit. Multos captitavit, quam plures pueros et in denegationem fidei Christianae mirabiliter denegavit. Tradidit filios a matrum complexibus et dulcis osculis et matres a filiis privavit clamoribus fletuum usque ad caelum emissis. Virgines monachas Deo dicatas et alias virgines servitio Dei perseverates impio scelere violavit. Admiranda templa Dei decore pretiosa et tanta nobilitate et magnificentia praeclara, in quibus sacra mysteria venerabantur, reduxit in speluncam latronum et synagogas <perditi Mahumeth[142]>. Et cum magno vel maximo opprobrio Christianae religionis iconas[143] Virginis et omnium sanctorum, sacrosancta signacula passionis Iesu Christi cum ceteris reliquiis sanctorum hinc inde dispersit. . . . Quid detestabilius, quid crudelius? Plangant et fundant lacrimas cum amaritudine hi qui Christiani sunt. Et iterum plangant captivitatem huius memorandae et pretiosissimae urbis et crudelissimam eius obsidionem. . . . Caelum ululat, terra clamat, sol obscuratus est tam nefando scelere et mihi mente cogitanti iam defecit anima mea.*

So that dog [*sc.* Mehmed II] entered that sacred city with his cursed satanic army, roaring like a lion. He put many to death and deprived them of their property. He took many prisoners, especially very many boys and forced them to give up their Christian faith. He took away sons from the embraces of their mothers and deprived them of the sweet kisses of their mothers, as their wailing rose up to heaven. Virgin nuns, dedicated to God, and other virgins in the service of God were violated in crimes that knew no respect. The wonderful churches of God, famous for their expensive decorations and nobility, in which the sacred mysteries had taken place, he reduced them to caves of robbers and synagogues [mosques] of the cursed Mohammed. In his great, indeed the greatest, contempt for the Christian religion, he scattered all over the place icons of the Virgin and all saints together with the sacred relics of the passions of our Lord, Jesus Christ, as well as the relics of saints. . . . What can be more detestable, more cruel? All Christians pour out tears and weep with bitterness. They lament the enslavement of that memorable most precious city and its most cruel siege. Heaven weeps, the earth groans, and the sun is darkened by that heinous crime. My soul now fails me as I think over it.

Once he has expressed indignation over the fate of Constantinople, indignation over the fate of its inhabitants, and indignation over the character of the sultan, Isidore rings the alarm bell and plays the part of a prophet, predicting the future designs of the sultan for world domination. He also concentrates on the preparations of the sultan to make his move westward. His earliest warning comes in his letter (Latinized by di Bertipaglia) to the pope:[144]

> *Ceterum, intellige, beatissime pater, et considera huius perfidi tyrannicam potentiam et innatam superbiam, qui non obstante quod glorietur se genus et nomen Graecorum delevisse, sua barbara saevitia comminatur omne christianum nomen radicitus extirpare et tuam Romanam urbem et imperii christianorum sedem vi et armis sibi in breve subiugare. Verumtamen sicut de hac inopinata immanis adversarii victoria non est christiana potentia timendum nec dubitandum, ita ad faciendum debitas provisiones non est ullo modo tardandum; nam in casu isto tam arduo, tam periculoso et tam gravi, mora posset faciliter valde esse nociva.*

> Please understand, most blessed father, and take into account that infidel's tyrannical power and innate arrogance. He glorifies himself and says that he destroyed the nation and the name of the Greeks with no one standing in his way. His barbaric savagery suggests threateningly that he intends to wipe out totally the Christian name and to bring, with force and arms, under his yoke your Roman city and the capital of the Christian Empire. It cannot be doubted, but there is cause to fear. There is no Christian power to obstruct this huge foe from sudden victory. You must make due provisions, as this is no time to delay. This is a hard, dangerous, and serious undertaking. Any delay is going to avail him and it will be disastrous.

Similar sentiments, with specific instances, are to be found in Isidore's letter to all Christians. He suggests that the enemy is already *ante portas*:[145]

> *Haec igitur sunt quae hactenus a Turcis exacta contra Christianos sunt; ea vero quae de cetero contra eos excogitat, quis poterit enarrare? Primo enim triremes centum septuaginta inter parvas et magnas praeparavit et ad Mare Aegaeum misit ad insulas Cycladas causa suo imperio ea subiugandi. Deinde praeparat se cum infinto exercitu ad tres urbes solidas et potentes prope Danubium sitas transmigrare et eas expugnare et devastare, videlicet unam cum Peristeri nuncupamus, aliam Fendorabium, aliam vero Bellestadium; et sic proponit totam transcurrere Hungariam eamque perdere et delere, ut neminem habeat retro se imperatorem, quoniam in Italiam anno futuro transmigrare decrevit, unde iam anno praesenti haec omnia agere introducit et proponit. Itaque praeparat et praeparare conatur galeas parvas et magnas trecentas, naves magnas viginti et ultra, pedestrium et equestrium exercitum ultra trecenta milia. Et sic a Durrachio transire ad Brundicium disponit. Haec omnia non solum agere disponit, verum incipit facere.*

> These are the actions of the Turks against the Christians thus far. How can one enumerate his future intentions? To begin with, he has prepared one hundred and seventy small and large triremes and has directed them to the Aegean towards the islands of the Cyclades, which are to be subjected to his authority. Secondly, he is equipping a countless army to move on, to conquer, and to devastate three fortified cities near the Danube: one we name Peristeri, the second Fendorabium [Siderovia, that is, Smederevo],

and the third Belgrade. Thus, he proposes to devastate, plunder, and wipe out Hungary, which will never have another emperor. He has decided to move into Italy the following year. Already this current year he has introduced these plans and intends to follow through. And so he is equipping three hundred small and large galleys under preparation, twenty or more large ships, and an army of more than three hundred thousand. And so he has decided to move across to Brindisi from Durrazo. All these are not just plans; he has already advanced to their implementation.

In his letter to Bologna, he rings the general alarm bell, without providing any new information about the current activities or the planned activities of the sultan against specific territories.[146] In his letter to Florence, again he avoids the specific intended actions of the sultan and only talks in terms of generalities. He appears to be paraphrasing his statements within the Bologna letter.[147]

Thus far the cardinal is relying on generating powerful emotions among his readers and fostering indignation and pity for the fate of the conquered, which he then hopes will translate into anger and will lead to such emotionalism as to seek revenge and retaliation. He is goading the West to launch another crusading expedition to the east, in order to stop the sultan's plans for world domination, to prevent him from expanding into the west, into central Europe and into Italy. In the process, Isidore is hoping for the liberation of Constantinople. Thus he joins the universal feeling in the West for the formation of a crusade, in which Constantinople would replace the old goal of recovering Jerusalem. He is explicit about the necessity of a crusade that he feels should materialize as soon as possible.[148] In the di Bertipaglia letter he urges the pontiff to take action:[149]

> *Excita ergo potentiam tuam, sanctissime patrum, . . . insiste, exhortare, iube, manda, impera christianissimo et illustrissimo Romanorum invictissimo imperatori, christiani nominis et fidei caput, Sanctictatis tuae primario defensori, et aliis omnibus regibus et principibus christianis, ut celeriter cum omni necessario apparatus tam terrestri qua marino ad bellum se praeparent.*
>
> Most holy of fathers: summon your power, insist, exhort, order, command, and direct the all-invincible, most illustrious, and most Christian emperor [the Holy Roman Emperor], the head of Christianity and the faith, and the primary defender of your Holiness, and all the other kings and princes of the Christians, to prepare themselves swiftly for war with the necessary expedition, armies and navies.

Isidore employs similar tones in his letter of the 16th of July to Nicholas V and urges the pope to prepare Christendom for war.[150] He concludes this letter by stating that he is preparing to return to Italy in the near future in order to delineate his plans for future action against the Turks.[151]

Similar are his fragments of advice to the other authorities. To his political overlord, Doge Foscari, Isidore presents a more scholarly argument, which recalls the era of Fredrick Barbarossa and Isidore urges, with that historical example, Venice to take up arms. Wisely, Isidore avoids any references to the triumph of Venice, when it sacked Constantinople during the Fourth Crusade in 1204.[152] In the letter to the pope, he adds that he is prepared to explain his future plan of action against the Turks and that he will do so in person, as soon as he returns and has an audience with the doge:[153]

> *quae mihi reservo coram tua Celsitudine viva voce referre, neque aestate neque hieme quiescendum est, . . . Et ad haec conficienda potentia multorum regum et principum in primisque favor et iuvamen domini summi Pontificis, ut spero, promptum erit atque paratum per ea quae in mentem meam veniunt. Sed Dominatio vestra esse debet origo et caput huius magnae rei.*

I would like the opportunity to address these matters openly in person with your Highness. Neither summer nor winter must delay us. . . . I do hope that the combined strength of kings and princes, with a kind eye and help from the Highest Pontiff, our lord, will be prompt and we will be ready. Such matters come to my mind. Your lordship must be the font and primary mover of such a great undertaking.

He makes the same argument in his letter to Bologna (and with the exact same terminology encountered in his letter to Florence as well), using religious terms, but, in this case, Isidore avoids reciting historical precedents:[154]

> *Credo enim nec ambigo, quod reductis regibus et principibus Christianis ad unionem pro exaltatione sanctae crucis et nominis sacratissimi Iesu, nedum potentia, quam habet ille impiissimus Teucer, sed ter tantum potentiae, non poterit prevalere contra nos. Eia, ergo, Christianissima com<m>unitas, intuere opprobrium Christianitatis nec velis obmittere, quod hic perfidus canis tam ignominiose tamque superbe et arroganter audeat subvertere Christi fideles et gloriari in sua malitia. Sed velis sumere arma potentia cum aliis regibus et principibus mundi, quibus huiusmodi notitia data est, contra hunc perfidum hostem et extirpare eum de terra viventium, non dubitans in fide Christi Iesu, quod nos reducet ad amplam victoriam contra iniquissimum hostem.*

I have no doubt and I am convinced that, once the Christian kings and princes have united themselves and have taken up the sacred cross, the power of that most ungodly Turk will not prevail over us, even if it were three times greater. And so most of the Christian community reckons the shame that has been heaped upon Christianity and persist, since that infidel dog dares to attack with disrespect, with arrogance, and with conceit the Christians and dares to glorify himself in his wickedness. Be willing to take up strong arms and in concert with other kings wipe him out of the realm of the living, maintaining our faith in Jesus Christ, who will lead us to victory against this most unjust enemy.

Clearly by the middle of July, while on Crete, the cardinal has moved beyond the stages of grief, of sorrow, and of self-pity. He no longer dwells upon his wounds; he is on the road to recovery and is ready to continue the fight. He has found the strength to begin formulating plans against his enemy, the sultan of the Turks.[155] He does not explain his future war strategy in his letters; he certainly had some plans in mind. It became fashionable in Europe at this time for many individuals, from all sectors, to advance future plans for a crusade to liberate Constantinople.[156] None of those plans ever came to fruition or to the organization stage. This failure must have disappointed the cardinal. The earliest recorded proposal for a crusade to the east, however, seems to have originated in the private sector. In an appendix to Tetaldi's account of the fall,[157] someone (probably not Tetaldi himself) advised a coordinated effort by land and sea: a fleet to be manned by Aragonese, Venetians, Genoese, and Florentines that would block the Dardanelles in order to prevent Turkish reinforcements from crossing the straits into Europe. An expeditionary force of Bohemians, Hungarians, Poles, and Wallachians, under the command of the legendary hero, John Corvinus Hunyadi, would move southward from the Balkans to threaten Adrianople (Edirne). At the same time, an Italian army would advance through Albania, enlisting the help of the famous warlord, George Kastriotes Scanderbeg, for this march. The author of this pamphlet that became embedded in Tetaldi's eyewitness account of the fall of Constantinople further believes that during this campaign the lord of Karamania in Anatolia would threaten the eastern provinces of the Ottoman sultan, who would thus be forced to fight on two fronts at once.

There were numerous other proposals, as the recovery of Constantinople from this point onward became the primary goal of numerous projected crusades and assumed the sentimental role that Jerusalem had played in a previous age. Yet none of these ambitious plans ever came to fruition. The age of launching crusades to the east was over. It gradually became clear to the Greeks that, despite strong rhetoric, Europe was not in any position to recover Constantinople and could no longer force the Turks back into Anatolia. In theory, however, the nostalgic notion of a crusade to dislodge the infidel from European soil lingered; and in the West Constantinople assumed, in this late era, the significance that Jerusalem had enjoyed in past centuries. Meanwhile, as these impractical campaigns were being meticulously planned and advertised, the Greeks in the Balkans and the Aegean eagerly awaited the arrival of European liberators. The attitude of Venice, a city that had contributed much to the defense of the Byzantine capital, was more realistic than these well-intentioned, but impractical, thought; characteristic were Philip the Good's romantic theatrics that came to nothing.[158] Early in the summer of 1454, Venice quietly concluded a mutually satisfactory peace treaty with the Porte. This treaty confirmed, in fact, the pact that had been negotiated with the sultan in 1451. Bartolommeo Marcello became the new Venetian *bailo* in Ottoman Constantinople and remained in this post until 1456 when Lorenzo Vitturi replaced him.[159]

While Italy had expressed sympathy and had advanced aggressive moral support to the vanishing enclaves of the Byzantine Greeks against their Oriental foe, actual military and economic aid came belatedly and in minute quantities.

Clearly, the West had been deceived by its hope that the alarming situation would correct itself. Even when it came to the defense of Constantinople, which had been mainly supervised by the Venetian residents of Constantinople and the Genoese mercenaries of the Byzantine emperor, aid to the beleaguered city never came in any substantial form. The Venetian armada, put together and equipped explicitly for the relief of the imperial city, made its way through the Aegean in a so painfully slow and in a so unconcerned manner that it reached the vicinity of the city well after the sack. The disaster that made Constantinople the capital of the Ottoman sultan ignited outcries in the West. Petitions were circulated and were directed to ecclesiastical leaders and secular lords, demanding the formation of a crusade to recover the ancient city. But no actual attempts were made, in spite of the widespread anguish expressed in Christendom. By the mid-summer of 1453, even the Venetians, who had forfeited much property, who had sustained heavy casualties during the siege and sack, and who had lost prominent members of numerous noble families in the wave of executions that followed the disaster, initiated intense negotiations with the conqueror to recover some remnants of their previous privileges that they had enjoyed under the Byzantine emperor. A peace treaty between the *Serenissima* and the Porte was indeed ratified as early as 18 April 1454. Nevertheless, the loss of Constantinople radically altered the situation and the West formulated plans for her recovery. Humanists disseminated various military projects, which were never seriously embraced by the secular powers and never advanced beyond the planning stage. Indeed it was seen as a fight for survival, a war between conflicting ideologies competing to eliminate established ways of life through aggressive military encounters.[160]

Isidore, as a humanist and an ecclesiastic, played a leading role in this intellectual movement by ringing the alarm bells. It should be emphasized that the letters we have examined, which are still available to us, may not present the complete picture. It is likely that Isidore wrote additional letters that have not survived. Is it possible that he had not corresponded with Francesco Filelfo, for instance, with whom he had had numerous contacts in the past (and more would follow upon Isidore's return to Italy)? After all, Filelfo had relatives by marriage in Constantinople, who had been captured in the sack,[161] and he would have been interested in the cardinal's personal impressions and information about them. Did Isidore neglect to write to Guarino, his old friend and contact? Moreover, even the letters that have survived are not direct products of the cardinal's pen. As we have observed, they were translated and paraphrased from the cardinal's original Greek prose. What became of these original Greek compositions? Is it possible that Isidore did not bring them in his files from Candia when he returned to Italy? This seems improbable. He must have kept the originals and perhaps even copies were left in Crete. They have not been transmitted to us or perhaps they are still interspersed with other medieval documents, awaiting discovery by a future archival researcher.

In the meantime, we can only consult the translations. Even if they are exact and accurate translations, the Latinized form of these accounts tell us

270 *Cretan interlude*

little about Isidore's sophisticated Attic style. We know that Isidore could write respectable Attic prose. In doing so, he had many ancient examples in his arsenal of knowledge. Is it possible that he received some of his inspiration for these polemics from the Athenian orator Demosthenes and his harangues about the Macedonian King Philip II and his threat to Athens in the fourth century BC?[162] Could Demosthenes's *Philippics* be the original inspiration for Isidore? We cannot answer this question because we do not have Isidore's original Greek text, which would perhaps have indicated and demonstrated his literary debt through verbal echoes and various imitations of Demosthenes's prose. The likelihood remains that Isidore could have availed himself of Demosthenes through his thorough classical knowledge and command of Attic prose, especially when he addressed Italian humanists.

Notes

1 Barbaro does not mention Sgouros in the exodus. On Barbaro's description, cf. *SF*, pp. 10, 11 and nn. 36–39. But Sgouros's ship was clearly a member of the flotilla, because he arrived in Crete along with Hyalinas and Philomates; and so it is recorded by the scribe at Ankarathos (cf. next note): ἔτ<ε>ι αυνγ´, ἰουνίου κθ´, ἡμέρα ϛ[η], ἦλθαν ἀπὸ τὴν Κωνσταντινούπολιν καράβια τρία Κρητικά, τοῦ Σγούρου, τοῦ Ὑαλινᾶ, καὶ τοῦ Φιλομάτου. Perhaps this is a lapse in the memory of the otherwise reliable Barbaro, who knew that Sgouros had participated in the siege, e.g., 20 [not in *CC* 1]: el Guro [Sgouros] de Candia de botte 700.

2 *Maius* 3.8: ἐγκρατεῖς πάντων ἐγένοντο [sc. οἱ Τοῦρκοι], ἄνευ δὲ τῶν πύργων τῶν λεγομένων Βασιλείου Λέοντος καὶ Ἀλεξίου, ἐν οἷς ἑστήκεσαν οἱ ναῦται ἐκεῖνοι οἱ ἐκ τῆς Κρήτης. αὐτοὶ γὰρ γενναίως ἐμάχοντο μέχρι καὶ τῆς ἕκτης καὶ ἑβδόμης ὥρας. This derivative text goes on to state that the sultan was so impressed with the spirit of the Cretan crews that he allowed them to depart to their ships unharmed, under a truce. No such incident is mentioned in the surviving eyewitness literature and we would give much to know whether this information is authentic or invented. It is not impossible that the writer has preserved some historical details. On this incident, on the authenticity of the passage, and on a possible identification of the towers mentioned by Pseudo-Sphrantzes, cf. *SF*, pp. 468–470.

3 The text of this note was first published in G.M. Arabatzoglou, *Φώτειος Βιβλιοθήκη, ἤτοι Ἐπίσημα καὶ Ἰδιωτικὰ Ἔγγραφα καὶ Ἄλλα Μνημεῖα Σχετικὰ πρὸς τὴν Ἱστορίαν τοῦ Οἰκουμενικοῦ Πατριαρχείου* 1 (Constantinople, 1933), no. 3 (p. 108). The note was republished, with a short discussion, by R. Browning, "A Note on the Capture of Constantinople in 1453," *Byz* 22 (1952): pp. 379–387; and with Italian translation in *TIePN*, p. 214. This note has been discussed in *SF*, p. 110 n. 62.

4 The magnitude of the disaster deeply affected and terrified the Christian inhabitants of the Aegean. One of the earliest citations of this situation is encountered in a letter of the 5th of July (*die quinta Julii in loco Sancti Francisci Candiae*); written by Fra Girolamo (*frater Jeronimus de Florentia, vicarius provinciae Candiae indignus Ordinis Minorum*), the letter is addressed to Cardinal Domenico Capranica (*Reverendissimo in Christo patri et domino, domino de Capranica, miseratione divina sancta sanctae Romanae Ecclesiae cardinali et protectori piisimo*). Aside for the inaccuracies and inevitable exaggerations, Fra Girolamo's letter may have been partially inspired by the information that refugees had brought to Crete and was eventually enriched by the authoritative reports supplied by Cardinal Isidore himself. Cf. *CC* 2: 34:

> Et mala malis addenda, Peram olim Januensium civitatem propinquam subegit [sc. Mehmed II], mcenia <delevit> et breviter suis Turcis inhabitare eam fecit; et, quod est gravius, civitates

et loca omnia Maris Minoris iam videntur esse suae potestati subiecta, totus denique Oriens ac Christianis inhabitatus perdidisse videtur omnem spem et fiduciam.
   This letter has been published in its entirety in *CC* 2: 32–40.
5 Cf. *SF*, p. 11 nn. 36–39. On Grioni, cf. *ibid.*, ch. 11: "Some Defenders and Non-Combatants," p. 664, no. 95.
6 Barbaro 58–59 [*CC* 1: 36].
7 Latin text in S.P. Lampros, "Μονῳδίαι καὶ Θρῆνοι ἐπὶ τῇ Ἁλώσει τῆς Κωνσταντινουπόλεως," *NH* 5 (1908): pp. 263–265 [improved text in *CC* 2: 12–17, with Italian translation].
8 *Supra*, n. 3, for editions. We have retained the original spellings with their numerous errors. A document listing the names of a number of noble refugees who reached Crete on the galley of Zorzi Doria is included in the ms. *Miscellanea Gregolin-Archivio di Stato di Venezia* [= *No. 27: Misc. Gregolin: Testamenti*]; its text was published by K.D. Mertzios, "Περὶ Παλαιολόγων καὶ Ἄλλων Εὐγενῶν Κωνσταντινουπολιτῶν," in *Γέρας Ἀντωνίου Κεραμοπούλλου* (Athens, 1953), pp. 355–372; and *idem*, "Περὶ τῶν ἐκ Κωνσταντινουπόλεως Διαφυγόντων τὸ 1453 Παλαιολόγων καὶ Ἀποβιβασθέντων εἰς Κρήτην," in *Actes du XIIe Congrès International d'Etudes Byzantines*, Ochride, 10–16 Septembre 1961, 2 (Belgrade, 1964), pp. 171–176, no. 36: *Miscellanea Gregolin-Archivio di Stato di Venezia* [= *No. 27 Miscellanea gregolin: Testamenti*]. This document contains a list of nobles aboard the galley of Zorzi Doria who had landed in Crete. It exists in three versions: an Italian rendition based on a Greek original in the archives of Corfu and two Italian renderings published by Mertzios, "Περὶ τῶν ἐκ Κωνσταντινουπόλεως Διαφυγόντων," pp. 170–177. Cf. Nicol, *The Byzantine Family of Kantakouzenos*, p. 194 n. 6. A Greek version of the list can be found in a note by E.G. Protopsaltes, *Ἅλωσις τῆς Κωνσταντινουπόλεως* (Athens, *sine anno*) [= a modern Greek translation of G. Schlumberger, G. *La Siège, la prise et le sac de Constantinople en 1453* (Paris, 1915; repr. 1935)], pp. 284–285 n. 14. Preceding the list, the following note can be read:

   Copia tratta dal originale dal Archivio della Canea Karte 134 tradotta dal greco. Catalogo fatto dal pudentissimo e generoso messer Tomaso Celsi dignissimo Provedidor della nobile armata delli Illustrissimi Veneti per tutti li infelici gentil huomini che fugirono dalla miserabile Costantinopoli doppo la di lei schivitu, i quali venero con le loro famiglie nell'isola di Scio con li galioni del principe Doria genovese ed il predetto generoso Celsi la condusse nella nostra citta della Canea e di poi parte andarono dal beatissimo Papa parte di Corfu parte restarono nelle citta dell'isola di Candia et il presente Catalogo fu fatto l'anno 1453 per comando del predetto domini Proveditore giusta l'autorita veutali dall' Illustrissimo Senato perche fosse dato mantenimento, il tutto scritto per mano di me Bartalameo Floriano publico Tabulario li 29 Maggio 1453.

9 These captains were, of course, known to Barbaro; he refers to them in his narrative as "Filamati" and "el Galina" [Philomates and Hyalenas, respectively], 64 [*CC* 1: 37]. For the documents dealing with their adventures after their escape from the Byzantine capital, cf. *RdD* 3, nos. 2950 and 3026. The Hyalenas family continued to make its home in Crete, until the fall of this island to the Turks; the survivors then migrated to Corfu. Cf. S.P. Lampros, "Κατάλογος τῶν Κρητικῶν Οἴκων Κερκύρας," *NH* 10 (1913): pp. 449–456, esp. 451: the "Gialinà" family is included among the *nobili della città di Candia*, but, it is noted, they ultimately stem from Constantinople.
10 This is evident in the cardinal's letter, which he dictated in Crete. It is dated the 6th of July 1453 and is addressed to Bessarion: *Ysidorus cardinalis in Creta die sexta iulii anno domini MoCCCCoLIIIo*; for the full text of the letter, cf. Hofmann, "Ein Brief des Kardinals Isidor von Kiew an Kardinal Bessarion," pp. 405–414 [*CC* 1: 64–80]. The same date is provided in Isidore's letter, which was translated from the Greek into Latin by Pasio di Bertipaglia: *Ex Candida insulae Cretae pridie Nonas Julii MCCCCLIII*; cf. *CC* 1: 64. Isidore's letter to Florence is dated the 7th of July: *Data VII iulii M CCCC LVIII* [*sic*]; cf. Hofmann, "Quellen zu Isidor von Kiew als Kardinal und Patriarch," p. 148. It

272 *Cretan interlude*

may be concluded that Isidore had reached Crete by 6 July. For a new edition of the di Bertipaglia report, cf. *infra*, n. 14.
11 Perhaps a recitation of the siege and fall also took place in Venice after the arrival of the fleeing galleys. Cf. *SF*, pp. 22–24 and nn. 75–78.
12 The text of Balbo's lamentation, *A Hebrew Lament on the Fall of Constantinople*, is quoted in S. Bowman, *The Jews of Byzantium 1204–1453* (University of Alabama, 1985), Excursus D; for the Hebrew text and English translation, cf. pp. 341–344, and pp. 156, 178, 183,184, 187 n. 40, wherein Bowman further discusses the impact of the fall among the Jews of the Aegean. Quite different was the reaction of the Jews of Spain; cf. D.S. Cirac Estopañan, *Byzancio y España. La caida del imperio byzantino y los Españoles* (Barcelona, 1954), p. 92:

> en un proceso del Santo Oficio de la Inquisición, instruído alrededor del año 1480 en Castilla la Nueva, se testificaba que los judíos de Castilla habían celebrado con gran júbilo la conquista de Constantinopla por el Gran Turco, a quien consideraban como el Mesías, que vendría también a conquistar España y echar de ella a los cristianos.

13 *Chronicles of London*, ed. C.L. Kingsford (Oxford, 1905), p. 164.
14 It is contained in only one *quattrocento* manuscript, *Ven. Marc. lat. 496* (1688), fols. 330ʳ–331ʳ. Selections from this letter (with Italian translation) have been published in *CC* 1: 58–64. The entire text was recently published in a reliable and useful edition, with Italian translation, by L. Silvano, "Per l'epistolario di Isidoro di Kiev: La lettera a papa Niccolò V de 6 luglio 1453," *Medioevo greco* 13 (2013): pp. 241–258.
15 While the letter to Bessarion and the letter to the pope have historical significance, there is one additional communication composed by Isidore in later times that returns to this theme. Thus his letter of the 22nd of February 1455 (*data Romae die XXII Februarii MCCCL° quinto*) to Philip the Good, the duke of Burgundy, was composed after a certain amount of time had passed since the events of the fall. It provides no new information, except Isidore's personal testimony that numerous Genoese volunteers from Pera had assisted in the defense. Evidently the cardinal was trying to correct the widespread impression that the Genoese from Pera had not assisted in the defense of Constantinople, an impression that probably had been reinforced by the withdrawal of Giustiniani and his forces from the walls at a critical moment during the last battle of 29 May:

> nec deerant nobis Ianuenses, qui omni conatu Urbem ipsam tutati sunt, et quamquam simulatu cum Teucro viverent hocque fieret statuto consilio, tamen noctu clam ad nos eos quos valebant ac poterant viros et sic subsidia mittebant frequentique senatu imperatorio aderant.

This letter was published in its entirety, with Italian translation, in an editio princeps, in *CC* 1: 106–110.
16 It was first published by Hofmann, "Ein Brief des Kardinals Isidor von Kiew an Kardinal Bessarion," pp. 405–414, who fails to mention that this is only a translation from a Greek original. The Latin translation survives in three manuscripts: one (from the *quattrocento*) that is housed in Florence, *Riccard. lat. 660* (M II 19), fols. 55ʳ–61ʳ; the second, also from the *quattrocento*, is found in Bologna, *Bibl. Univ. lat. B 52*, fols. 40ʳ–42ᵛ; and the third (from the sixteenth century) is in Padua, *Bibl. Sem. lat. 126*, fols. 33ʳ–36ʳ. The most important of the three manuscripts appears to be the Bolognese *codex*, which is probably the autograph of Lianoro, since it notes that it is a humanistic exercise. The complete Latin text of this note is published in *CC* 1: 53. Selections of the Latin text with Italian translation are printed in *CC* 1: 64–80, with unfortunate omission of passages that contain important information. For the Latin text with the first English translation and further discussion, cf. *supra*, ch. 5, sec. 3.
17 A.G. Welykyi, "Duae Epistulae Cardinalis Isidori Ineditae," *Analecta Ordinis Sancti Basilii*. Записки чина Св. Василий Великого, ser. 3, 1 (1950): pp. 289–291; the exact words of Isidore (or of his translator/redactor, as Isidore had never mastered Latin) were finally published in the selections of *CC* 1. The text (in its edited and abbreviated form) has been published a number of times, including the edition of Lonicer of 1578 (followed

by N. Reusner in 1597, by *PG* 159: cols. 953–956, and by *MHH* 21: 687–702; selections with Italian translation in *CC* 1: 80–90). This was probably the best-known letter by Isidore and survives in eight manuscripts of the fifteenth century and one of the seventeenth.
18 *Quattrocento* mss: *Haegens Bibl. Reg. lat. 71 E. 62*, fols. 3^v–6^v; *Mediol. Bibl. Braid. lat. AE XII 40*, fols. 53^r–54^r; *Mediol. Trivult. lat. N 641*, 27^v–31^v; *Monac. lat. Clm. 4149*, fols. 309^v–312^r; *Monac. lat. Clm. 4689*, fols. 142^r–143^v; Paris. *Nouv. Acquis., lat. 546*, fols. 167^r–169^r; Paris. *Bibl. Nat. lat. 3127*, fols. 19^{2v}–19^{4v}; *Vat. Barb. lat. 2682* [xxxiii, 202], 58^r–59^r. A ninth manuscript, *Monac. lat. Clm. 4143*, fols. 91^r–94^r, dates from the seventeenth century.
19 It was first published by *NE* 2: 522–524, but this edition seems to be an inaccurate transcription containing numerous errors. It is published in its entirety, with Italian translation, in *CC* 1: 90–100, and exists in two surviving *codices* from the fifteenth century: *Mediol. Bibl. Braid. lat. AE XII 40*, fols. 54^v–55^v; and Paris. *Nouv. Acquis., lat. 546*, fols. 169^r–170^v. For the Latin text with the first English translation and further discussion, cf. *supra*, ch. 5, sec. 3.
20 It was first published by Welykyi, "Duae Epistulae Cardinalis Isidori Ineditae," pp. 286–289, along with Letter III, and it exhibits the same problems of transcription. Much better, in terms of the text, are the selections in *CC* 1: 100–106; the text derives from a single manuscript of the *quattrocento*: *Vat. Barb. lat. 2682*, fols. 56^v–58^r. We understand that Professor Luigi Silvano is preparing a new edition of Isidore's letter to Foscari, on the basis of three manuscripts, of which two were unknown to former editors.
21 *CC* 2: 498.
22 It was published in *NE* 2: 518, 519; and with Italian translation in *TIePN*, pp. 12–15.
23 It was published by Hofmann, "Quellen zu Isidor von Kiew als Kardinal und Patriarch," pp. 143–157. Selections, with Italian translations, have been printed in *TIePN*, pp. 16–21.
24 It was published by W. Röll, "Ein zweiter Brief Isidors von Kiew über die Eroberung Konstantinopels," *BZ* 69 (1976): pp. 13–16.
25 *CC* 1: 72:

> *Aliud iterum mirabilius est machinatus, quod et Xerxes quondam fecisse memoratur: pontem siquidem construxit et fabricavit maximum a mari Sanct<a>e Galatin<a>e usque ad m<o>enia Cynegi, quod duplo maius est spatium quam illius Hellespontiaci olim pontis a Xerxe fabricati, per quem non modo pedites verum etiam equites multi simul traducebantur.*

26 *Ibid.*, p. 96: *Deinde pontem super mare, qui usque ad hodiernum diem manet, construxit: habet enim distantiam de terra firma in Constantinopoli per miliare unum et tertium.*
27 Cf. *supra*, ch. 5, n. 65. Tetaldi also notes this bridge in Caput VIII: *Similiter et pontem mira ingeniositate fabricati fecit de vasis, afferibus, trabibus et plancis, mille habentem passus in longitudine et septem in latitudine, ut sui ad nostros pertingere possint super mare ex transverso ambulantes et civitatis muris appropriquantes.* The equivalent passage in the French rendition of Tetaldi, ch. VI, reads as follows: "& un pont de barques que les Chrestiens avoient fait pour aller de Constantinople à Peyre pour s'entre-secourir." Also, cf. Tetaldi, ch. XIV: "Le dit Sengampsa fist un chastel de bois si hault & si grant, qu'il seignourissoit le mur, . . . & plusieurs instruments de bois, desquels il povoit estre sans estre blechié: & si l'y avoit tours de bois tres-haultes, grandes & ligieress."
28 *PG* 159: col. 931 (*CC* 1: 138; the text within < > is omitted by *CC* 1):

> *Proinde hoc ingenio non contentus Theucrus aliud quoque, quo nos terreret magis, construxit, pontem videlicet longitudinis stadiorum circiter triginta, ex ripa urbi opposita maris qui sinum scinderet, vasis vinariis colligatis, subconstructis confixisque lignis, quo exercitus decurreret ad murum prope urbis iuxta fanum, <imitatus Xerxis potentiam, qui ex Asia in Thraciam Bosphoro exercitum traduxit>.*

29 Fol. 315:

> *Non contento perho de queso inzegno, el Turcho per altro modo cercho spauentarne. Et fece construir uno ponte longo 30 stadij sono miglia . . . dal mare fino alla ripa de la terra, fatta la*

274   Cretan interlude

> zatra fermata sopra le botte ligate per diuider el porto, per lo qual ponte exercito poteua correr apresso el muro de la cita, apresso la giesia, imitando la potentia di Xerse el quale de Natolia in Grecia tradusse lo suo exercito per lo stretto de Hellesponto.

30 P. 98:

> Ma non essendo il Turco contento di questo insegno, ne fabricò un'altro per metterli in maggior terrore, cioè vn ponte di lungheza di trenta stadi dalla riua opposita de la città, il qual fendendo l'acqua del mare, si soseneua fu botti da vino ritenute, & incatenate di sotto con traui, per lo quale essercito, se ne venisse, al muro vicino alla Città; imitando la potenza di Serse, il qual traghettò l'essercito dall'Asia nella Thracia per Bosforo.

31 17:

> Τότε έκάμανε μία τζάταρα ἢ σκάλα ἢ ταράτζα ξύλινη οἱ Τοῦρκοι, μακρέα τέσσαρες χιλιάδες ὀργυιὲς καὶ ϖλατέα ϖεντακόσες ὀργυιές, καὶ τὴν ἐκαρφώσανε καλὰ ἀϖάνω εἰς τὴν θάλασσα καὶ τὴν ἐτραβήξανε κοντὰ εἰς τὰ τειχία τῆς Πόλης καὶ ἐβάλανε ἀϖάνω εἰς τὸ αὐτὸ ϖοῦντε ϖολλοὺς Τούρκους καὶ ἐϖολεμούσανε, διατὶ ἀϖὸ κάτω τοῦ αὐτοῦ ϖόντε ἔβαλε ϖολλὰ βουτζία ἄδεια καὶ τὴν ἐκράτειε ἀϖάνω.

32 On this famous elaboration of the *Minus* into the notorious *Maius*, cf. *SF*, pp. 139–191. Is it possible that the musings of Pseudo-Sphrantzes were inspired by reference to Xerxes in connection with the bridge, which he read in his prototype? Cf. *Maius* 3.53:

> ἐγὼ δὲ λογίζομαι· τῷ Καίσαρι Αὐγούστῳ ἐμιμήσατο, ἡνίκα μετὰ τοῦ Ἀντωνίου καὶ Κλεοϖάτρας ἐμάχετο, ὃς διὰ τὸν σάλον τῆς θαλάσσης τοὺς ἐναντίους ἀνέμους οὐκ ἠδυνήθη ϖεριοδεῦσαι κύκλωθεν τῆς νήσου τοῦ Πέλοϖος καὶ ἐλθὼν διὰ τοῦ Ἰσθμοῦ, τὰς νῆας σύρας ἔτι, ϖρὸς ἑῴαν τῆς Ἑλλάδος θαλάσσης, ταχέως ἐν τῇ Ἀσίᾳ ᾤδευεν. ἢ τῷ Νικήτᾳ τῷ ϖατρικίῳ, ὅτε αὐτὸς ἐκ τῆς Ἑλλαδικῆς θαλάσσης τὰς τριήρεις ἐν τῇ δυτικῇ ϖεράσας διὰ τοῦ Ἰσθμοῦ τοὺς Κρῆτας ἐν τῇ Μεθώνῃ καὶ Πύλῳ ἐτροϖώσατο.

33 Pusculo's model was Vergil and, consequently, conscious classical references abound. Four manuscripts exist that must be consulted, compared, and collated before a useful edition becomes available to the modern scholar; cf. Philippides, "The Fall of Constantinople 1453: Bishop Leonardo Giustiniani and His Italian Followers," p. 207 n. 59. On Pusculo, cf. P. Guerrini, "Un umanista bagnolese prigioniero dei Turchi a Costantinopoli e a Rodi," *Brixia sacra* 6 (1915): pp. 261–271; V. Zabughin, "Ubertino Pusculo da Brescia e la sua 'Constantinopolis'," *Roma e l'Oriente* 5 (1915): pp. 26–50; Paulova, pp. 210–212; *SF*, ch. 1: II.A.7 (pp. 31, 32).

34 Pusculo 4.536–544 (pp. 71, 72) [omitted in the selections presented in *CC* 1]:

> atque vna consternere Pontum / Ponte superstructo; et cuneos transmittere siccis / Ipsi urbi pedibus tumidum super aequor et undas. / Xerxem fama canit quondam stravisse frementem / Hellespontiacum pontum, et junxisse rejunctam / Ponte Asiam Europa, siccis atque agmina plantis / Innumera ex Asia Europae immisisse.

35 In time Capranica wrote and published (in printed form with the house of the brothers Antonio and Raphael de Vulterris) an epitaph for Bessarion, titled: *Oratio in funere Bessarionis Cardinalis habita*, first published in 1472, and reprinted in 1480. On Angelo Capranica, cf. M. Miglio, *Dizionario Biografico degli Italiani*, 19: pp. 161–162.

36 Philippides, *Mehmed II the Conqueror*, ch. 4:

> Hanc totam seriem rei gestae collegi fideliter ex diversis epistolis scriptis ad diversos de ista materia. Quarum una scripta est domin<i>o Venetorum per dominum Iacobum Lauredanum, generalem capitaneum eorum super mare; alia per ducem Venetorum scripta est domino papae tribusque aliis cardinalibus; <alia domini cardinalis> Ruthenis, qui de hac re unam papae, aliam domino cardinali Firmano; tertia<m>que palens erat omnibus Christifidelibus. Et ex duabus aliis scriptis domino Firmano (quorum unam scripsit ipse agens, familiaris et

domesticus dicti cardinalis Rutheni, aliam vicarius ordinis minorum provinciae Candiae). Quarum omnium copias habeo, ex copiis domini Firmani.

37 Di Bregantini, 1: 225–447; the text was based on a transcription of the *Codex Marc. lat. XII 73* (4381) (c. 1470 in the hand of Cristoforo Regazzoli) that had been made by Gervasi.

38 Ellissen, Appendix, pp. 12–83, who reprinted di Bregantini's text. Slim selections, which are, nevertheless, based on all of the manuscripts, with Italian translation, are published in *CC* 1: 204–214 (without an *apparatus criticus*). Unfortunately, these are only selections and the entire text has never been printed. In addition to the *codex* in Venice (*supra*, n. 37), the following manuscripts exist: *Bergom. Bibl. Civ. lat. G.V. 21* (c. 1465 in the hand of Giovanni Francesco, *barbitonsor*); *Parmens. Bibl. Palat. lat. 1583* (c. 1470); *Bellun. Bibl. Semin. Gregor. lat. 25*; and *Patav. Bibl. Semn. lat. 125*.

39 Van Millingen, *Byzantine Constantinople*, pp. 104–108, who consistently misnumbers John VIII, labeling him as John VII.

40 The historical significance, unusual in a rhetorical showpiece of this genre, of this anonymous Ἐγκώμιον εἰς τὸν Αὐτοκράτορα [Ἰωάννην τὸν Παλαιολόγον], *ΠκΠ* 3: 292–308, was noted by Bogiatzides. The passage discussed here appears in 3: 296 (quoted and discussed *supra*, ch. 5, n. 14).

41 *Ibid.*, 3: 296.

42 *Ibid.*, 3: 132–199. The true authorship of this panegyric was unknown to Lampros, but was convincingly established by Mercati, *Scritti d'Isidoro*, pp. 6, 7.

43 *Ibid.*, 3: 136 (quoted and discussed *supra*, ch. 5, n. 14).

44 Bibliothèque Nationale de France, Départment des Manuscrits, Paris, *Supplément grec 309*; cf. Evans, no. 1 (p. 26); this *codex* evinces a masterpiece of Greek portraiture, in addition to the Greek text copied by Isidore. The most recent edition of this significant text is by Chrysostomides. The discovery of a "new" text by the hand of Manuel Chrysoloras has also furnished evidence to correct older scholarly notions about Manuel's speech. Patrinelis and Sophianos, esp. pp. 44–48, emend the established scholarly view that this text was delivered to Manuel Chrysoloras by Ioannes Chrysoloras during the latter's trip to Italy in 1410. It is now convincingly demonstrated, with new evidence, that this is an erroneous view. The text could not have been delivered prior to the spring of 1413. In addition, it now becomes evident that Isidore delivered the text orally at a memorial service in the absence of its author, the emperor, sometime in 1415/1416 and not in 1409, as it had been previously supposed by scholars. Cf. our discussion, *supra*, ch. 1, text with nn. 49–68.

45 Patrinelis, "Ἕλληνες Κωδικογράφοι," esp. p. 87: "Ἰσίδωρος Καρδινάλιος (δρᾷ 1409–1464)."

46 His interests in astrology are also demonstrated in his early Greek correspondence, as we have seen, *supra*, ch. 1. In his first letter, Isidore requests horoscopes as a personal favor. In a second communication he repeats the same request. In addition, he was actively involved with manuscripts of an "astrological" nature, such as the series of astronomical tables extracted from Ptolemy, in *Vat. 214*, fol. 69. He as well copied *Vat. 1698*, fols. 73–106ʳ, with the *incipit*: ὁ ζωδιακὸς κύκλος λοξὸς κεῖται. He additionally copied fols. 225ᵛ–128ᵛ, a work related to Ptolemy with the explicit: ἡ πρόγνωσις διχῶς νοεῖται. αἱ μὲν σύνοδοι τῶν δύο ἀστέρων γίγνονται κα΄. For Isidore's considerable astrological and astronomical interests as reflected in his own *codices* and in those that he copied himself, cf. Mercati, *Scritti d'Isidoro*, esp. ch. 3. His astrological interests are indicated in his letter to Bessarion, wherein he states that the sultan launched his general attack on the morning of 29 May, in consultation with his "Persian" astrologers; cf. *CC* 1: 74: *habet* [*sc.* Mehmed II] *diligentissimos astrologos persas, quorum consiliis ac iudicio fretus summa quaeque ac maxima sese consecuturum sperat.* Isidore's statement should not be easily dismissed. Turkish sources confirm this superstitious trait in the sultan's character; Inalcik, "Istanbul: An Islamic City," pp. 249–271, esp. p. 250, documents the sultan's reliance on the supernatural.

47 Vat. 1698.
48 Vatic. Barb. 127; and Vatic. Chisianus F159.
49 Vatic. Urb. 110, fols. 3–13 and 119ʳ–122ʳ.
50 The pertinent text of the oracle has been published by Zakythinos, "Μανουὴλ Β΄ ὁ Παλαιολόγος," pp. 45–69. The text of this oracle has recently been printed in T.E. Gregory, *Isthmia 5: The Hexamilion and the Fortress* (Princeton, 1993) ch. 3: "Testimonia," no. 15 (pp. 20–21), with limited commentary.
51 Extracts from Bessarion's letter were first published by S.P. Lampros, "Τὰ Τείχη τοῦ Ἰσθμοῦ κατὰ τοὺς Μέσους Αἰῶνας," *NH* 2 (1905): pp. 477–479, who edited and published the entire text of this letter in "Ὑπόμνημα τοῦ Καρδιναλίου Βησσαρίωνος εἰς Κωνσταντῖνον τὸν Παλαιολόγον," *NH* 3 (1906): pp. 12–50 (Greek text: pp. 15–27); Lampros published this letter once more in *ΠκΠ* 4 (Athens, 1930; repr. 1972): 32–45.
52 Lampros, " Τὰ Τείχη τοῦ Ἰσθμοῦ," pp. 478, 479.
53 The precise date of the oracle's composition is the subject of a scholarly disagreement. Lampros, "Τὰ Τείχη τοῦ Ἰσθμοῦ," pp. 435–489; and *idem*, "Προσθήκη εἰς τὰ περὶ τῶν Τειχῶν τοῦ Ἰσθμοῦ τῆς Κορίνθου κατὰ τοὺς Μέσους Αἰῶνας," *NH* 4 (1907): pp. 20–26), believes that it was composed c. 1443 in connection with Constantine's building project, but E.W. Bodnar, "The Isthmian Fortifications in Oracular Prophecy," *American Journal of Archaeology* 64 (1960): pp. 165–171, attempts to show that most of the oracle existed earlier and was probably carved on the walls of the Hexamilion at the Isthmus of Corinth. His evidence derives from a number of statements in the journal of Cyriacus of Ancona. This matter, thus far, has not been conclusively settled and Father Bodnar, when he wrote his article, was unaware of the existence of Isidore's explication on this oracle or of his introduction to the text of the oracle. On the date of Constantine's reinforcement of the Hexamilion walls at the Isthmus, cf. P.A. Clement, "The Date of the Hexamilion," in *Essays in Memory of Basil Laourdas* (Thessalonike, 1977), pp. 159–164. A systematic investigation of the remains of the medieval fortifications at the Hexamilion can be found in Gregory, *Isthmia 5*, with detailed topographical maps and excellent photographic documentation.
54 In general, cf. N.A. Bees, "Περὶ τοῦ Ἱστορημένου Χρησμολογίου τῆς Κρατικῆς Βιβλιοθήκης τοῦ Βερολίνου (*Codex Graecus* fol. 62–297) καὶ τοῦ Θρύλου τοῦ Μαρμαρωμένου Βασιλιᾶ," *Byzantinische-Neugriechische Jahrbücher* 13–14 (1936/37): pp. 203–244^αλς΄.
55 Lampros, "Τὰ Τείχη τοῦ Ἰσθμοῦ," pp. 472–480, discusses the various manuscripts which record this popular prophecy.
56 On this scholar and student of George Gemistos Plethon, cf. Philippides, "Herodian 2.4.1," pp. 295–297.
57 It is this version that has been studied by Zakythinos, "Μανουὴλ Β΄ ὁ Παλαιολόγος."
58 ἥξει δὲ καὐτοῖς χαλκόπους ἐρινὺς πολύπους καὶ πολύχειρ καὶ καταβαλεῖ μένος τούτων, ὅταν κόνις πίτυν δέξηται καὶ πίτυς λύθρον, τότε κρατερὸς γενήσεται περίβολος Ἰσθμοῦ.
59 This work of Isidore (included in the *Codex Vat. gr. 1852*, fols. 105–106) has never been edited nor published in its entirety. Isidore addressed his analysis of the Pythian oracle to a "lady who loves literature." It has been supposed that she was Cleopa Malatesta, the wife of Theodoros II, the despot of the Morea. It is also supposed that she had earlier requested from Isidore an exegesis of the popular oracle. Cleopa, however, had died by 1433 (*ODB* 3: 2041 [s.v. Theodore II Palaiologos]) and she was probably not the recipient. Another noble lady must have been intended, who remains to be identified.
60 It is interesting to note in passing that Isidore enjoyed playing the part of an exegete, as early on in his youth he appears to have assumed this role. When he began one of his letters, he playfully declares that he was "neither a bad prophet nor an inferior soothsayer." A.W. Ziegler, "Die restlichen vier unveröffentlichten Briefe Isidors von Kijev," *OCP* 18 (1952): p. 142 (Letter 8): οὐκ ἄρα ἦν ἐγὼ μάντις πονηρὸς οὐδέ τις φαῦλος εἰκαστής.
61 The cardinal's interest in *Perserei* goes back a long way. Early on in his youth he had sent a copy of Xenophon's *Cyropaedeia* to Guarino. In later times, after his escape from

Constantinople, Isidore continued to exhibit interest in the ancient Persians, with his readings of Herodotus and Xenophon, whose works he had borrowed from the Vatican Library. This is noted in Mercati, *Scritti d'Isidoro*, p. 80 no. 3: *Item alter liber in papiro, parvus, vocatus Hyrodotus* [Herodotus] *hystoricus*; (no. 15): *item alter liber mediocris forme in papiro, vocatus Opus Zenofontis* [*Xenophontis*] *de disciplina Persarum*; and (no. 23): *item alter liber in papiro medie forme, vocatus Xenofontis* [*Xenophontis*] *philosophi de sapientia Cyri illustrissimi regis Persarum*. In addition, in one of his youthful letters he provides the following *incipit* (A.W. Ziegler, "Vier bisher nicht veröffentlichte griechische Briefe Isidors von Kijev," *BZ* 44 [1951]: pp. 575 [Letter 2]): τῷ μὲν οὖν βασιλεῖ τῶν Περσῶν Ἀρταξέρξῃ σφόδρα καραθύμιον ἐδόκει, ἄν τις αὐτῷ δῶρα προσάγων; for the context, cf. *supra*, ch. 1, text with n. 113. Thus, it can be demonstrated that he had an active interest in the ἠθοποιία pertaining to the Great King of old. Isidore was also a talented calligrapher and the surviving specimens from his hand display high quality; cf. Ziegler, "Isidore de Kiev, apôtre de l'Union Florentine," p. 406:

> C'était un amateur de calligraphie, et plusieurs de ses écrits sont de chefs-d'œuvre de cet art. Les traits de son écriture, bien que minutieux, sont si réguliers et si tranquilles, si exacts et si clair, qu'on peut déduire de ceux-ci les traits correspondants de son caractère. Légèreté, superficialité et incnstance lui sont étrangères.

62 The first scholar to take note of this comparison is F. Babinger, "Mehemed II., der Eroberer, und Italien," *Byz* 21 (1951): pp. 127–170 [= "Maometto II, il Conquistatore, e l'Italia," *Rivista storica italiana* 63 (1951): pp. 469–505, with some additions and corrections], who reserved a few observations with regard to the humanistic comparisons of Mehmed to Alexander and to other personalities of the ancient world. Babinger's investigation, however, is dated and rather superficial on this specific point, since he was extremely limited by the few sources available to him, as numerous testimonies had not yet been edited or printed, but remained only in unavailable manuscript form. Thus Babinger lacked the letters of Isidore, neglected the testimony of Leonardo, chose to include the later florid text of di Montaldo (which comes at the end of a long tradition, whose origins we are examining here), and was further limited by the prevalent, albeit erroneous, notion of his day that Cyriacus of Ancona was the western scholar who daily read the classics to the sultan; see *supra*, nn. 61 and 62. In addition, see F. Babinger, "Maometto il Conquistatore e gli umanisti d'Italia," in Pertusi, *Venezia e l'Oriente*, pp. 433–449.

63 *Supra*, n. 4.

64 *CC* 1: 86–88. For the Latin text with translation, cf. *infra*, text with n. 146. The information contained in this letter is not quite accurate. Isidore claims that Pera had been razed. The walls were indeed dismantled, but the sultan, through his representative Zaganos, had granted an *aman-name* to the Genoese. For the Greek and Italian text of this document, see Philippides, *Mehmed II the Conqueror*, Appendix 2. Even texts that supply neither classical allusions nor comparisons of the sultan to Alexander voice similar fears, as for instance the letter composed by Lomellino, the *podestà* of the Genoese colony of Pera, which had already received an *aman-name* from the sultan. Obviously disturbed by the fate of Constantinople and upset over the unknown fate of his own relatives who had been captured by Mehmed's troops, Lomellino sent an emotional letter to the authorities of Genoa, in which he expressed similar fears and suggests that the sultan is about to march on Rome (*CC* 1: 48): *Concludendo, de captione Constantinopolis tantam insolentiam cepit, que videtur se facturum in brevi dominum totius orbis, et large dicit non transibunt anni duo que intendit venire usque Romam.*

65 Lauro Quirini was in Crete in July 1453, and had conversed with Isidore concerning the events of the siege. He himself so states in a letter (*TIePN*, p. 74): *ut a reverendissimo cardinali Rutheno accepi*.

66 *CC* 2: 14. Dotti's letter was first published in its entirety (with some errors) by Lampros, "Μονῳδίαι καὶ Θρῆνοι," pp. 263–265. A better text, with Italian translation, has now been published in *CC* 2: 12–18. Independently, the Knights of Saint John from Rhodes

also addressed a letter dictated on the 31st of June 1453 (*datum Rodi, in nostro Conventu, die ultimo mensis Junii, anno 1453*) to the margrave of Bradenburg:

> *Magnus Teucer* [Mehmed II Fatih] . . . *exaltavit namque cor suum et gloriatur se magni Alexandri Macedonis gesta aequiparaturum vel superaturum. Minatur etiam quod Alexander numquam se ad Ytaliam et partes occiduas armis et potentia sua penetravit se experiturum an sibi fortuna faveat, quemadmodum per haec orientalia expertus est.*

A short extract from this letter appears in *NE* 3: 520, 521; a longer version, with Italian translation in *TIePN*, pp. 54–57. The classical interests of the knights of Rhodes are well documented. Even later, when Rhodes was under siege by the troops of Mehmed II, the defender and historian of the siege, Guillaume Caoursin, composed during the siege his famous work, describing the operations in a style that would have been of interest to humanists. For a new edition of Caoursin's text, with English translation and commentary, cf. Philippides, *Mehmed II the Conqueror*, ch. 8.

67 *Supra*, ch. 5, for the text and its translation.
68 *CC* 1: 78. This statement of Isidore suggests that Mehmed II was fluent in numerous languages. In fact this erroneous impression prevailed in the west. For an investigation into this topic and for doubts with regard to the exaggerated views expressed during the Renaissance about Mehmed II's linguistic abilities, cf. C.G. Patrinelis, "Mehmed II the Conqueror and his Presumed Knowledge of Greek and Latin," *Viator: Medieval and Renaissance Studies* 2 (1971): pp. 349–355.
69 Hofmann, "Quellen zur Isidor als Kardinal und Patriarch," pp. 143–157: *Nam numquam Nero crudelissimus, numquam Thyestes, qui prioprios filios edendos patri trad<d>idit . . . regem Alexandrum admirandum Macedonem cum minore potentia subiuga<viss>e totum orbem, et hunc, qui iam imperiale regnum Constantinopolis obtinuit et habet innumerabilem exercitum non posse totum orbem submittere.* The learned cardinal perhaps overlooked the first part of the myth, in which Thyestes had been the victim of his brother Atreus's actions. Cf. the account in *supra*, ch. 5, n. 58. It is more likely that the allusion here is to the eventual murder of Atreus by Thyestes and Aegisthus, as related in Apollodorus, Epitome 2.14. The "cruel" murder of Atreus by Thyestes is illustrated in detail on a two-handled amphora by the Darius Painter, housed in the Museum of Fine Arts, Boston (1991.437), that dates to 340–330 BC.
70 *CC* 1: 100–106. *CC* 1 presents selections from the epistle. There is a complete edition, which, however, includes errors in transcription. Cf. Welykyi, "Duae Epistulae Cardinalis Isidori Ineditae," pp. 286–289.
71 *TIePN*, p. 80.
72 *Ibid*. In Isidore's letter to the doge Nero is described as follows (Welykyi, "Duae epistolae," p. 288): *Nam nunquam Nero crudelissimus, nunquam Thyestes, qui proprios filios edendos patri tradidit, nunquam alius Neronior auditus est tantam crudelitatem committere.* Identical is his statement to the city of Florence (Hofmann, "Quellen zu Isidor als Kardinal und Patriarch," p. 254).
73 *TIePN*, p. 86:

> *Gentilitas ait Scipionem gloriam tantarum rerum fortitudine comparasse, Gneum Pompeium benivolentia, Iulium Caesarem fortuna, Alexandrum Macedonem audacia laborumque tolerantia. . . . Et quis, quaeso, triumphus Romanorum huic tam iusto, tam glorioso comparari poterit? Pauline Aemilii an M. Macelli, an Publii Scipionis, an Gnaei Pompeii?*

74 Leonardo is placed squarely within the humanistic sphere by Cyriacus of Ancona, who had met him, as he notes in a letter of 1444; cf. Bodnar with Foss, letter 6, pp. 15–27: *Vidimus et inter praeclaros eo loco viros Leonardum, venerandum religione ac divinarum et humanarum litterarum peritissimum hominem, quocum multis cum nobilibus splendido in symposio fuimus.* Cyriacus mentions Leonardo once again in a letter of the 27th of August 1444, which was probably written in Constantinople (Bodnar and Foss, Letter 15 [pp. 84–86]): *hodie . . . reverendissimum patrem Leonardum, Lesbeum pontificem, ad hanc urbem adventatem hylaritate revisimus.*

75 *PG* 159: col. 937 (not in *CC* 1): *Fortunam, inquit* [*sc.* Mehmed II], *tentare licebit. An Macedonis potentia mea maior fuit, cui orbis minore cum exercuit paruit?* Is it a coincidence that Cardinal Isidore uses a very similar phrase, *regem Alexandrum admirandum Macedonem cum minori potentia subiuga<vi>sse totum orbem*, in his correspondence? This common phrase and shared sentiment may represent an echo of the actual conversations between the cardinal and his friend during the siege.
76 Fol. 319: *Per queste tal suasion fatte piu animoso el Signor disse: temptemo la fortuna nostra, utrum la mia potentia sia magior de quella d Alexandro macedonico, al qual cum minor exercito del mio tutto el mondo obedite.*
77 *Maius* 3.7.8:

> ἀπεκρίθη οὖν ὁ ἀμηρᾶς [emir, that is, sultan] καὶ εἶπε: . . . ἵνα καὶ ἡμεῖς τὰ νῦν τὴν τύχην γνωρίσωμεν, εἰ ἀρεστὸν αὐτῇ ἐστι καὶ βοηθήσῃ ἡμῖν ὡς καὶ ἑτέροις πολλοῖς. στεῖλον οὖν ἐπὶ τὸν Γαλατᾶν φυλακήν τινα, ἵνα μὴ λαθραίως ἐξ αὐτοῦ περάσωσι καὶ τῇ πόλει βοηθήσωσιν.

78 *Codex Barberinus 111* 24: Τότε εἶπε ὁ σουλτάνος ὅτι νὰ μὴν σταθοῦνε, μόνε νὰ πολεμοῦσι, καὶ εἶπε, ὅτι: τάχα νὰ εἶχε περισσότερη δύναμι ὁ Ἀλέξανδρος ὁ Μακεδὼν ἀπὸ ἐμένα, ὁπου ἐπῆρε ὅλον τὸν κόσμον; Λοιπὸν θέλω νὰ πολεμῶ καὶ νὰ δοκιμάζω τὴν τύχην.
79 For extensive source discussions and scholarly interpretations of the term "Janissary," cf. *supra*, ch. 5, n. 60.
80 *CC* 1: 128–130. There is an echo of Leonardo's usage of this term in the secondary text of Tignosi da Foligno, who employs "Myrmidones" in a more accurate context. He assigns them to Achilles and not to Alexander; *TIePN*, pp. 108–110: *Tria sunt quae non modo interritos sed audacissimos ferunt hostes: primum ab oppidanis omnino desperatum subsidium, secundum defensorum paucitas, tertium ipsorum multitudo quae excreverat <ita> ut Achillis Mirmidones viderentur*. On this author and his account, cf. *infra*, text with n. 92.
81 Fol. 314:

> *cum trecento millia combattenti, et atorno la citade fermo i pauioni, militi piu de cauallo che pedoni, fra li qual pedoni li piu audaci erano deputadi a custodia del Signor, et de la sua porta, li qual da picoli insuxo Christiani, ouer fioli de Christiani son fatti Turchi dicti Janizari, come i Mirmidoni apresso i Macedonici, et sono 15000.*

82 This point is discussed, with the relevant texts, in Philippides, *Mehmed II the Conqueror*, ch. 1.
83 *CC* 2: 132. Selections from Sekoundinos's text in *CC* 2: 128–140; and in *NE* 3: 316–323. Both editions contain long extracts, but not the complete text of the speech. The complete text (with inaccuracies, as it is based on inferior manuscripts) is found only in V.V. Makušev, ed., *Monumenta historica Slavorum Meridiolanum vicinorumque populorum* 1 (Warsaw, 1874), pp. 295–306.
84 Tetaldi 23 (Philippides, *Mehmed II the Conqueror*, pp. 208–210). We possess very few facts about this individual who wrote an eyewitness account of the siege and fall of Constantinople. Even his very name appears to be in doubt, as it is spelled variously. Thus his Christian name appears as Giacomo, Jacopo, or Jacques, while versions of his last name include Tetaldi, Edaldy, Tetardi, Tedardi, Detaldi, and Tedaldi. The manuscript tradition of his account is also confused. His text has come down to us in a French and in a Latin version. The French text is contained in the following manuscripts: *Paris. fr. 2691*, fols. 264–271 (incorporated in the Chronique of Jean Chartier); *Paris. fr. 15217*, fols. 67ᵛ–72ᵛ; *Paris. fr. 6487*, fols. 18–21; *Cambrai 1114*, fols. 28–30; and *Bruxell. fr. 19684*, fols. 253–256 (as part of an anonymous chronicle). It has been argued persuasively that our French text represents the amalgam of two different traditions, as the Cambrai manuscript bears little relationship to the other five French versions. The manuscripts of Tetaldi have been studied by M-L. Concasty, "Les 'Informations' de Jacques Tedaldi sur le siège et la prise de Constantinople," *Byz* 24 (1954): pp. 95–110, but the conclusions are rather speculative, as it has been stressed by Setton in *PaL* 2: 111, 112 n. 9. Concasty's article, nevertheless,

remains the only modern scholarly study of Tetaldi. That the Latin version is earlier than the French text has been argued in Philippides, *Mehmed II the Conqueror*, ch. 5. The parallel passage (ch. 22) in the French version is not quite equivalent and it resurrects the notion of cruelty associated with Nero, which we have encountered in Isidore's letters:

> On trouve par ceulx qui les fuis du Turc ont cogneu ses condicions & sa puissance, qui est de l'âge de ving-trois à vingt-quatre ans, plus cruel que Neron, se delectant à respandre sang humain, courageux & ardant de seignourer & converser tout le monde: voire plus qu'Alexandre, ne Cesar, ne aultre vaillant qui ait esté allegué qu'il a plus grande puissance & seignourie que nul d'eulx n'avoit: & tousjours faisoit lire leur histoire, demande où & comment est posé Venise, combien loing de terre ferme, & comme on y puet entrer par mer & par terre. Et tient legier luy seroit faire ung grant pont durant de Margara à Venise: pour poivoir passer ses gens d'armes. Pareillement deman e de Romme où elle est assise, & du duc de Milan, & de ses vaillans: & d'autres choses que de guerre ne parle.

85 It was first published in M. Sensi, "Niccolò Tignosi da Foligno. L'opera e il pensiero," *Annali della Facoltà di Lettere e filosofia dell'Università degli Studi di Perugia* 9 (1971/1972): pp. 423–431; its pertinent sections have been reprinted, with Italian translation, in *TIePN*, pp. 102–121. Tignosi's account is not widely known and has not been used in modern scholarship. Its information deserves a fresh look and evaluation. On Tignosi, see now N. Bisaha, *Creating East and West* (Philadelphia, 2004), pp. 87, 88 and 126–128.

86 *TIePN*, p. 102: *a quodam Pisaurense, qui toto bello Constantinopolitano affuit et in conflictus fine latuit in caverna per dies aliquot*. For an evaluation of this work, see *SF*, ch. 1, no. B7, p. 37. Tignosi's information is probably authentic, for many other survivors attempted to hide in hollows and caverns. See, for example, Barbaro 55 (*CC* 1: 34): *Ma i nostri marcadanti che scapolò queli si se scoxe in le caverne soto tera; passada il furia, queli si fo trovadi da Turchi, e tuti si fo prexi e poi vendudi per schiavi*. Exactly where these caverns were located is not specified, but it is possible that the huge water cisterns of Constantinople are meant. A number of them, such as the cisterns of Aetius or Aspar in the vicinity of the critical sector, were easily accessible to those defenders who may have been seeking shelter, once they had abandoned their posts on the fortifications around the palace of Blakhernai or the Kaligaria Gate.

87 *TIePN*, p. 108.

88 On the numerous followers of Leonardo in Italian, Greek, and Latin, see *SF*, pp. 14–26.

89 Languschi-Dolfin fol. 313:

> El Signor Maumetho gran Turco . . . aspirante a gloria quanto Alexandro Macedonico, ogni di; se fa lezer historie romane, et de altri da uno compagno di Chiriaco d'Ancona, et da uno altro Italo, da questi se fa lezer Laertio, Herodoto, Livio, Quinto Curtio, Cronice de i papi, de imperatori, de re di Franza, de Longobardi.

90 It should be noted that Cyriacus of Ancona, the father of Greek epigraphy, if not of classical archaeology, could not have been in the Porte at that time, even though Languschi-Dolfin seems, *prima facie*, to state so. Cyriacus had died earlier, in 1452, at Cremona in Italy, as the Trotti ms. 373, fol. 41, of the Ambrosian Library in Milan, makes clear: *Kiriacus Anconitanus Cremone moritur anno Domini McCCCL secundo*, "Cyriacus from Ancona died at Cremona in 1452 AD." The confusion occurs because of a misreading in the Languschi-Dolfin manuscript. The manuscript abbreviation *d* was incorrectly read as *detto*, while the true reading has recently been shown to be *di*. On this point, see J. Raby, "Cyriacus of Ancona and the Sultan Mehmed II," *JWarb* 43 (1980): pp. 242–246; Mitchell and Bodnar, *Vita Viri Clarissimi et Famosissimi Kyriaci Anconitani*, p. 19 n. 2; and C.G. Patrinelis, "Κυριακὸς ὁ Ἀγκωνίτης: Ἡ Δῆθεν Ὑπηρεσία του εἰς τὴν Αὐλὴν τοῦ Σουλτάνου τοῦ Πορθητοῦ καὶ ὁ Χρόνος τοῦ Θανάτου Αὐτοῦ," Ἐπετηρὶς Ἑταιρείας Βυζαντινῶν Σπουδῶν 16 (1968): pp. 152–160. The death of Cyriacus was also mourned by Biondo Flavio (cf. now the excellent edition and translation by J. A. White, *Biondo*

Flavio: Italy Illuminated, The I Tatti Renaissance Library 20 [Cambridge, MA, 2005], 1: IV.5.15 (pp. 260, 261): *cum nuper amiserit* [*sc*.Ancona] *Ciriacum, qui monumenta investigando vetustissima mortuos, ut dicere erat solitus, vivorum memoriae restituebat.*

91 Fol. 313: *El fratello fece occider in Andrinopoli, acio non hauesse compagno in signoria, Cesare et Haniballe dice che fono citadini, Alexandro fiol dil re Macedonia ando in Asia cum minor potentia.*

92 Cf. *infra*, n. 97, for the comments of Eustathios, who relates an account that became widely known among classical scholars in the late Middle Ages.

93 The entire letter is published in *Aeneae Sylvii Piccolominei Senensis, qui post adeptum pontificatum Pius eius nominis secundus appellatus est, opera quae extant omnia, nunc denum post corruptissimas aeditiones summa diligentia castigata et in unum corpus redacta, quorum elenchum versa pagella indicabit* (Basel, *sine anno* [1560?]; repr. 1967): pp. 678–689 and esp. 683.

94 Adamo di Montaldo titles his account: *De Constantinopolitano excidio ad nobilissimum iuvenem Melladucam Cicadam*. It was published by P.A. Dethier, C. Desimoni, and C. Hopf, "Della Conquista di Costantinopoli per Maometto II nel MCCCCLIII," *Atti della Società Ligure di Storia Patria* 10 (1874): pp. 289–354; selections of his text, with Italian translation, were also published in *TIePN*, pp. 188–209. The original editors were under the erroneous impression that the composition had been written soon after 1453, but before 1456. Modern scholarship has corrected the error: Di Montaldo wrote his account in the 1470s, as is evident in internal evidence of the narrative. Cf. *SF*, p. 46; and *TIePN*, pp. 188, 189.

95 Di Montaldo, chs. 5, 6 (pp. 329–330) (not in *TIePN*).

96 Ch. 50 (p. 349; not in *TIePN*):

> *Alexandrum enijm regis Philippi filium, tot regum atque imperatorum novimus parva cum manu victorias adeptum esse. Qui se admisso seniorum consilio desistere coeptis maluisset, non Alexandri Magni, caeterorum trgum et ducum nomen tanta de se laudet usurpasset. Hannibalem Africanum praeclarum in armis ducem, aequatis cum populo Romano viribus in plurimum victorem, quis ignorant, nisi Scipio in senatu Romanos salute jam desperantes conterruisset, urbem sibi atque imperium vendicasse.*

97 *Eustathii Archiepiscopi Thessalonicensis Commentarii*, Προοίμιον, 1: καὶ μαρτυρεῖ ὁ μέγας Ἀλέξανδρος, κειμήλιον εἴτε καὶ ἐφόδιον καὶ ἐν αὐταῖς μάχαις τὴν ὁμηρικὴν βίβλον ἐπαγόμενος, καὶ τὴν κεφαλήν, ὅτε ὕπνου δέοι, ἐπαναπαύων αὐτῇ. The picture of a prince interested in history and literature was of course a well-known *topos* among the humanists of the period. See, e.g., the comments of Biondo Flavio in his *Praefatio* to his *Italia Illustrata* (1, IV.6.27): *Clarissimi etiam plerique senatores, consularesque viri, et nonnulli gloriosissimi principes, qui bellis artibus res gesserunt aeterna dignas memoria, delectati sunt historia.*

98 *MCT*, p. 500: "It can hardly be doubted that Mehmed knew of these works in his earlier youth."

99 3.9.4:

> ἀφικνεῖται διὰ Μεγάρων ἐς τὰς Ἀθήνας. κατεῖχε γὰρ αὐτὸν ἔρως σφοδρὸς τῆς πόλεως ταύτης καὶ φρονήσεως τῶν ἐνταῦθα προγεγονότων ἀνδρῶν καὶ τῆς ἄλλης ἀνδρείας καὶ ἀρετῆς καὶ τῶν πολλῶν καὶ θαυμαστῶν ἔργων, ὧν ἐν τοῖς κατ' αὐτοῖς καιροῖς ἐπεδείξαντο καὶ πρὸς Ἕλληνας καὶ πρὸς βαρβάρους ἀγωνιζόμενοι. καὶ ἐπεθύμει ἰδεῖν τε καὶ ἱστορῆσαι τήν τε πόλιν αὐτὴν τούς τε τόπους οἷς οἱ ἄνδρες ἐκεῖνοι ἐπολιτεύοντο... καὶ εἶδε καὶ ἐθαύμασε καὶ ἐπήνεσε καὶ μάλιστά γε δὴ τὴν ἀκρόπολιν ἀναβὰς ἐς αὐτὴν ἀπό τε τῶν ἐρειπίων καὶ τῶν λειψάνων ὡς σοφός τε καὶ φιλέλλην καὶ μέγας βασιλεὺς τὰ ἀρχαῖα καὶ ἄρτια στοχαζόμενος.

As a result of his visit, the Athenians were granted notable privileges: "Mehmed treated the Athenians with generosity and granted the wishes they presented to him. He confirmed the liberties... already conferred on them" (*MCT*, p. 160). Mehmed's own notes in his exercise books on learning and writing Greek reveal a sophisticated hand and a calligraphy that could easily be the envy of any humanist. On the literary interests of

Mehmed's court, see J. Raby, "Mehmed the Conqueror's Greek Scriptorium," *DOP* 37 (1983): pp. 15–34.

100 *Aeneae Sylvii Piccolominei Senensis* 683.

101 M. Philippides, "History Repeats Itself: Ancient Troy and Renaissance Istanbul," in S. Atasoy, ed. *550th Anniversary of the Istanbul University. International Byzantine and Ottoman Symposium (XVth Century) 30–31 May 2003* (Istanbul, 2004), pp. 41–68; Bisaha, pp. 87 ff.; and *SF*, pp. 193–204.

102 Filippo da Rimini, "Epistola ad Franciscum Barbarum, virum inclitum, procuratorem Sancti Marci dignissimum [Excidium Constantinopolitanae urbis]," in P.A. Déthier and C. Hopf, eds., *Monumenta Hungariae Historica, ser. Scriptores (Második osztály Irok)*, 22.1 (*Sine loco* [Galata?/Pera?], *sine anno* [1872?/1875?]), pp. 656–682. Da Rimini was well-read in classical literature and was a sophisticated author himself. A. Pertusi, ed., "La lettera di Filippo da Rimini, cancelliere di Corfù, a Francisco Barbaro e i primi documenti occidentali sulla caduta di Costantinopoli (1453)," in Μνημόσυνον Σοφίας Ἀντωνιάδη, Βιβλιοθήκη τοῦ Ἑλληνικοῦ Ἰνστιτούτου Βενετίας Βυζαντινῶν καὶ Μεταβυζαντινῶν Σπουδῶν 6 (Venice, 1974), p. 151, remarks: "Il nostro autore è molto letterato: una uso stile ricercato, una forma molto elaborata e talvolta non rifugge da espressioni baroccheggianti. Vuol mostrare che ha letto attentamente i suoi autori latini arcaici e classici, e quindi mescola parole archaiche." Perhaps we should note that da Rimini was one of the acknowledged sources of Languschi-Dolfin, who mentions the chancellor by name (fol. 313):

> *Adoncha lo excidio de Costantinopoli descriuo come la cosa e passada tracta la historia da quelli autori che quella hanno scripto, come hano uisto, imperoche altramente le cose uiste, et altramente le udite se scriueno. Le qual cose ornatamente fono desripte dal R.do vescouo de Mettelino* [Leonardo] *che era in la fameija del Cardinal Sabino* [Cardinal Isidore] *legato mandato per la union de Greci lo qual romaxe preson in Constantinopoli, et fu recaptado, et fu etiam descripto da Filippo da Rimano cancellier a Corfù.*

Da Rimini consistently refers to Mehmed II as "the Trojan." The following few citations will suffice: *profectus Tros Constantinopolim obsidet illucente die invehitur Tros in urbem; quo diro spectaculo motus Tros gestiens ad circumfusos*. Within his Trojan fantasies, da Rimini also includes an allusion to the famous Wooden Horse of the Bronze Age, to which he compares the fortress of Rumeli Hisar that Mehmed II built prior to his siege: *miseri Thraces hostimentum Troiani equi eam fabricatam adpellare poterant; qua erecta Constantinopolis praeter modum exterrita*.

103 Independently, Lauro Quirini expresses similar statements with regard to the devastation (*TIePN*, p. 74): *Mihi animo consideranti vetus Troiae excidium, Carthaginis infelicem eversionem, miseram Ierusalem captivitatem, Saguntinam cladem multarumque praeterea nobilissarum urbium evasionem, nulla videtur neque foedior, neque crudelior, neque miserior fuisse. Quanto enim Urbs nobilior ceteris erat, tanto infelicior casus*. It is understandable why a repetition of antiquity would appeal to humanists. Laonikos Khalkokondyles, who had numerous contacts with humanists in Italy, was also aware of this humanistic construct of Turk/Trojan and the sack of Constantinople as an act of revenge for the fate of Bronze Age Ilium/Troy; see Khalkokondyles (Kadellis's edition, with English translation) 8.30 (pp. 206, 207) [= E. Darkó, ed., *Laonici Chalcocandylae Historiarum Demonstrationes* 2 (Budapest, 1923): 166–167]:

> δοκεῖ δὲ ἡ ξυμφορὰ αὕτη μεγίστη τῶν κατὰ τὴν οἰκουμένην γενομένων ὑπερβαλέσθαι τῷ πάθει, καὶ τῇ τῶν Ἰλίου παραπλησίαν γεγονέναι, δίκην γενέσθαι τοῦ Ἰλίου ὑπὸ τῶν βαρβάρων τοῖς Ἕλλησι πασσυδὶ ἀπολουμένοις ... τὴν τίσιν ἀφῖχθαι τοῖς Ἕλλησι τῆς πάλαι ποτὲ γενομένης Ἰλίου ξυμφορᾶς.

104 R. Reinsch, ed., *Critobuli Imbriote Historiae*, CFHB 22 (Berlin and New York, 1983), IV.11.5:

> καὶ ἀφικόμενος ἐς τὸ Ἴλιον κατεθεᾶτο τά τε τὰ ἐρείπια τοιούτου καὶ τὰ ἴχνη τῆς ... Τροίας καὶ τὸ μέγεθος καὶ τὴν θέσιν καὶ τὴν ἄλλην τῆς χώρας

ἐπιτηδειότητα... προσέτι δὲ καὶ τῶν ἡρώων τοὺς τάφους ἱστόρει, Ἀχιλλέως τέ φημι καὶ Αἴαντος καὶ τῶν ἄλλων, καὶ ἐπῄνεσε καὶ ἐμακάρισεν τούτους τῆς μνήμης καὶ τῶν ἔργων καὶ ὅτι ἔτυχον ἐπαινέτου Ὁμήρου τοῦ ποιητοῦ. ὅτε λέγεται καὶ μικρὸν συγκινήσας τὴν κεφαλὴν εἰπεῖν. ἐμὲ τῆς πόλεως ταύτης καὶ τῶν αὐτῆς οἰκητόρων ἐν τοσούτοις περιόδοις ἐτῶν ἐκδικητὴν ἐταμιεύετο ὁ θεός. ἐχειρωσάμην γὰρ τοὺς τούτων ἐχθροὺς καὶ τὰς πόλεις αὐτῶν ἐπόρθησα καὶ Μυσῶν λείαν τὰ τούτων πεποίημαι. Ἕλληνες γὰρ ἦσαν καὶ Μακεδόνες καὶ Θετταλοὶ καὶ Πελοποννήσιοι οἱ ταύτην πάλαι πορθήσαντες, ὧν οἱ ἀπόγονοι τοσούτοις ἐς ὕστερον περιόδοις ἐνιαυτῶν νῦν ἐμοὶ τὴν δίκην ἀπέτισαν διά τε τὴν τότε ἐς τοὺς Ἀσιανοὺς ἡμᾶς καὶ πολλάκις γενομένην ἐς ὕστερον ὕβριν αὐτῶν.

105 For the Latin text with the first English translation of this early and historically significant epistle and for further discussion, cf. *supra*, ch. 5, sec. 3; for the present context, cf. par. 15.
106 This letter (2) is also quoted and translated, *supra*, ch. 5, sec. 3; for the present context, cf. par. 6:

> *Cuius captivitas omnes ab initio saeculi captivitates superat et excedit: Hierosolymorum ab Nabugodonosor<e> rege pauca equidem et parva fuit respectu tantae et tam magnae; ipsius quidem pecuniae ablatae sunt, populus autem non fuit pedibus et manibus colligatus, sed simul congregatus ad Babyloniam transductus est; et sacra eorum no abrepta, non conculcata, sed Assyriorum rex ea in aedibus suis cum reverentia observabat. Similiter et comparatio nulla in aliam civitatem potest fieri, quae huic potest adaequari.*

107 *Ego autem veniam cito ad vos, Deo dante, animam et corpus exponere pro fide Christiana et statu Christianorum; tunc etiam narrabo, exponens modos destructionis infidelium.*
108 *CC* 1: 80. The *PG* 159: cols. 953–956, version of this letter omits the attribution to David and only states: *Audite, omnes gentes, audite et auribus percipite, qui habitatis orbem* (p. 953). We should remember that the *PG* version is only an abstract made by Antonino (Antoninus), the archbishop of Florence, who, in his *Chronicon seu opus historiarum* (Nürnberg, 1484), part III, ch. 13, states: *Haec in substantia sunt in litteris praedictis, etsi aliqualiter verba immutata.* This statement of the archbishop is omitted in this edition of Isidore's letter. Cf. *SF*, ch. 1, no. II.5.iii (p. 28).
109 *CC* 1: 82: *Notum omnibus sit, domini mei et fidelissimi christiani, quoniam iam prope est Antichristi praecursor, Turchorum princeps et dominus, cuius nomen est Machometa, qui illius primi ac principis haeresis, sed ut potius et varius dicatur impietatis est heres.* The precursor of the Antichrist citation reappears in Isidore's letter to the community of Florence (*TIePN*, p. 16): *ab illo precursore Antichristi teucro Ma<h>umeth*.
110 In the *PG* 159: col. 953, version (that is, the abstract by Archbishop Antonino, cf. *supra*, n. 108): *Turcorum princeps et dominus, servus autem tot daemoniorum, quot vitiorum, cuius nomine es Mahumet, inimicus crucis Christi, here rei et nominis illius primi pseudoprophetae, et latoris legis spurcissimae Hagarenorum, filius Satanae omnium flagitosissimus.*
111 Thus in his letter to the community of Bologna he calls the sultan "Beelzebub" (Röll, pp. 13–16): *hic Beelzebub tamquam Christi flagellum et abominatio s<A>eculi ... iniquitate, ... immanitate ... impietate odit Christianos.*
112 In addition, Isidore, in his letter to the pope, states plainly that the sultan is the instrument of the devil (*CC* 1: 92–94): *Machometa hic iuvenis, Turchorum dominus, magnus amira nuncupatus ... crudelior et magis tyrannicus est et maiorem habet potentiam et ultitudinem exercitus, abundabili militia constra Christianos dyabolum in eo ipso suscipiens fremuit et fremit.*
113 *Ibid.*, 82–84. Isidore repeats the same assessment, that Mehmed wishes to wipe out the name of Christ, in his letter that was rendered into Latin by di Bertipaglia (Silvano, p. 250): *sua barbara saevitia comminatur omne Christianum nomen radicitus excerpere.*
114 Röll, pp. 13–16. In the same letter, he provides a variation: *ille canis cum suo damnabile exercitu Satan<A>e in sacram illam civitatem tamquam leo rugiens.* Isidore's letters to Florence and Bologna are almost identical in the information they present and in their Latin phraseology.

115 In his letter to the doge, Isidore insists upon the injustices of the sultan, whom he labels *hostem iniquissimum* (*CC* 1: 104). In the same letter (*CC* 1: 102), Isidore further characterizes Mehmed II as *perfidus inimicus christianorum*.
116 *Supra*, ch. 5, sec. 3; and *CC* 1:94.
117 For manuscripts, editions, and translations of Isidore's letters, cf. *SF*, ch. 1, II.5 (pp. 26–31).
118 We follow the Silvano edition of the manuscript, which reads *tyrannicam* and *extirpare*. The readings in the selections offered by *CC* 1: 62 differ: *terrenam* ("earthly") and *excerpere* ("wipe out"), respectively.
119 This is the text of the Antonino abstract, as printed in *PG* 159: col. 953. The text of Isidore's actual letter differs; cf. *CC* 1: 82: *Antichristi praecursor, Turchorum princeps et dominus, cuius nomen est Machometa, qui illius primi ac principis haeresis, sed ut potius et veracius dicatur impietatis est heres, qui multo magis nequam est quam ille primus.*
120 Again the text belongs to Antonino's abstract. *CC* 1 omits this section of the letter, while the edition by Welykyi, "Duae Epistulae," pp. 285–291, does not present a text that duplicates or suggests the characterization in Antonino's abstract. The differences among the existing manuscripts and the abstract suggest that Antonino perhaps had another copy of this letter before him, whose text apparently differed from our transmitted text.
121 Again the text belongs to Antonino's abstract and is not reflected in *CC* 1 or in the edition of Welykyi.
122 *PG* 159: col. 956; the reference is not encountered in the text of *CC* 1 or in the edition of Welykyi.
123 *Supra*, text with nn. 106 and 107.
124 *Supra*, text with n. 112.
125 *TIePN*, p. 14: *Latorem privatum fratrem Johannem dignetur Dominatio vestra reverendissima benigne eum videre et amplecti, quem omnipotens Deus felicem et incolumem conservet etc.*
126 Philippides, *Mehmed II the Conqueror*, pp. 128, 129.
127 The letter to Florence is edited in its entirety by Hofmann, "Quellen zu Isidore von Kiew als Kardinal und Patriarch," pp. 43–157 (text: pp. 152–154). The letter to Bologna is edited in Röll, pp. 13–16.
128 *Supra*, nn. 108–113.
129 Bologna: *ab illo precursore Antichristi, Teucro Maumeth . . . ille canis cum suo damnabilie exercitu Satanae . . . tamquam leo rugens*. Florence: *ab illo iniquissimo precursore Antichristi, Teucro Machometh . . . ille canis cum suo damnabili exercitu Satanae*. The "lion" simile is omitted in the Bologna letter.
130 Silvano, p. 250 (identical text in *CC* 12: 64): *dolens Isidorus . . . qui huius crudelissimi excidii verissimus testis sum et impiorum manus nutu divino miserabiliter evasi*. At the end of this letter he repeats his personal grief: *Ego denique dolens Isidorus.*
131 *CC* 1: 66: *me Deus, opinor, servare voluit, ut reliquas tales ac tantas infortunatissimae illius urbis adversitates conspiciam.*
132 *CC* 1: 78: *Quomodo autem impias manus effugerim, brevi cognosces cum in Italiam pervenero: perdisces enim tunc omnia.* In addition, cf. *supra*, ch. 5, sec. 3, letter 1.
133 Röll, p. 15: *Testis ego sum qui vidi, qui pr<A>eda Teucri factus fueram et mirabile sic Deo volente ab ira sceleratissimi pr<A>edonis evasi.* Isidore repeats the same statement verbatim in an almost identical letter to Florence; cf. Hofmann, "Quellen zu Isidor von Kiew als Kardinal und Patriarch," p. 147. The cardinal paraphrases slightly in his letter to the Doge of Venice, Francesco Foscari, Welykyi edition (not included in the selections of *CC* 1), p. 290: *Testis ego sum, qui vidi, qui praeda Teucri factorum fueram et miserabiliter, sic Deo volente, ab ira eius sceleratissimi praedonis evasi.*
134 *CC* 1: 84: *de manibus impiorum me Deus eripuit, ut Jonam ab utero ceti.* The Antonino abstract paraphrases (*PG* 159: col. 955): *de manibus eorum me eripuerit Deus, ut Jonam de ventre ceti.*

135 Silvano, p. 248. This passage is not among the selections offered in *CC* 1. Of course, lamentations over the fate of Constantinople eventually become a genre and are commonplace in the histories that were produced in the fifteenth and sixteenth centuries, as well as in popular songs and demotic literature. In this example, Isidore has produced some of the earliest. In general, cf. Andromache Karanika, "Messengers, Angels, and Laments for the Fall of Constantinople," in M.B. Bacharova, D. Dutch, and A. Suter, eds. *The Fall of Cities in the Mediterranean: Commemoration in Literature, Folk-Songs, and Liturgy* (Cambridge, 2016), pp. 226–252.
136 For the Latin text with English translation, cf. *supra*, ch. 5, sec. 3, letter 1, esp. par. 15.
137 For the Latin text with English translation, cf. *supra*, ch. 5, sec. 3, letter 2, esp. par. 6.
138 These are precisely the sections of the *epistula* that were not published in *CC* 1. They are to be found in Welykyi, "Duae Epistulae":

> *cum permissione Dei Constantinopolitana urbs capta est, aliquos habitatorum denegavit, aliquos pedibus et manibus ligavit, et per collum ligatos extra urbem deiecit, dico, tam nobiles quam populares, tam monachos quam monachas consecratosque autem aliosque simplices populares; et feminas virtute praeditas et nobilitate vitupera<vi>sse et indecorate detractas et nonullis iniuriis refertas ac si meretrices depostubulae institutae essent detrahebat, credens opprobriosas ac inhoneste eas vituperans absque misericordia et compassione; et alia et tanta contra eas peragens. . . . Adulescentulos vero pueros et puellas a parentibus segregabat et divisim eos vendebat. Infantes tam masculos quam feminas communia suis parentibus perdebat; matres suis filiis privabantur, uxores autem suis viris, et viri ab uxoribus misere plorantibus et linguentibus liquebantur, qui et quae disiuncti et ad partes Orientis deducti vendebantur per totam Europam. Patres orbati sunt filiis et filii patribus, quorum lacrimas, ullula plena doloribus quis unquam tam compos mente ac lingue posset explicare quibus fundebantur, dum segregabant sorores vero cum sororibus amplexis oscula conferebant, heu!, heu!, nobis dicentes, quae nostrum alteram videbit et verbis assuetis fruetur dulcibus et iocundis. Illi enim et ille qui paulum principes fuerunt servis suis deteriores effecti sunt; famuli et subiecti cogebant nonnullos esse Teucri nefarii. Negatores fidei Christianae de adolescent<ium> numero numero a decimo infra fieri, et suae neglectae despectae et inregulatae fidei adoratores arcebant esse. His tamen paucis de omnibus, de tantarum rerum numero vobis censeo satisfieri.*

139 Again and only in Welykyi, *ibid*.:

> *Secundo iniurias quas tulerunt versus sacra templa sacratissimae gloriosae virginis Mariae et aliorum sanctorum, contra imagines et reliquias eorum, versus sacratissimas passionis imagines Domini nostri Iesu Christi ineffabiles ignominias et verba detestanda, quibus usi sunt in sacra evangelia eius et in libros sanctorum et in exornationem templorum, et in sacra altaria tam Latina quam Graeca, et in sacras atque divinas cruces, et omnia denique honorabilia et venerabilia apud Christianos sunt. Quis unquam absque maxima suspiratione, lacrimarum et cordis luctu et manuum tremore discurrere poterit illud nomen propheticum verbum illico est consummatum in ipsa expugnationis die, dicens, venerunt reges in hereditatem tuam, deturpaverunt templum sanctum tuum, sed potius templa sancta tua. Urbem namque Constantini speluncam latronum nefariorum et locum sordidum, impiorum habitationem et residentiam malefactorum omnium constituerunt.*

140 *Ibid.*, p. 290:

> *Mox enim in templum eximium et praeclarae Sanctae Sophiae ingressi sunt et sanctissimas imagines sanctorum et sanctarum omnes pedibus conculcaverunt, deturpaverunt, et dirrumperunt. Super quos onne genus vituperii, opprobrii desordita<ve>runt. Similia his et in sacra plebe, hoc est paramenta, egerunt. Haec eadem acta sunt et in sacratissimis flammibus. Eorum qui in sacra altaria ascendentes et assalientes vociferando iubilabant et sic Mahometum impium hymnis et laudibus extollebant et, ut virtutem et maximum omnium prophetarum prophetam et destructorem fidei Christianae omnibus intimabant, inter maxima enim illi Teucrorum nefarii ascribunt templi regimen eiusdem famosae Sanctae Sophiae, ascenderunt et crucem Christi eius cacumini infixam deiecerunt.*

141 The letter to Bologna is edited in Röll, pp. 13–16. The letter to Doge Foscari was first published by Welykyi, "Duae Epistulae," pp. 286–289. Professor Luigi Silvano is currently preparing a new edition of Isidore's letter to Foscari, on the basis of three manuscripts, two of which were unknown to former editors.

142 The phrase *perditi Mahumeth* is taken from similar phraseology in his letter to Florence; the ms. reads: *praedicti Magni*.

143 The ms. reads *anconas*, but *iconas* can be restored from the Florence text.

144 Silvano, "Per l'epistolario di Isidoro di Kiev," pp. 240–250.

145 Welykyi, "Duae Epistulae," p. 290. The Antonino abstract, *PG* 159: col. 956, reads as follows:

> *Expugnata Constantinopoli illis atrocissimis rebus non cententus callidissimus et cruentissimus Mahometus, Christicolarum summus inimicus ad ulteriora se extendit e triremes inter magnas et parvas iam centum septuaginta praeparavit et ad Mare Aegaeum misit ad insulas Cycladas sibi subiciendis. Exinde se praparat cum infinito exercitu ad tre surbes notabiles et potentes prope Danubium sitas transmigrare easque expugnare: unam quam Periston nucupamus, alteram Forabium, tertiam Bellogradum, intendens post totam percurrere Hungariam eamque spoliare, devastare, conterere, ut neminem retro se dimitat impedire ad alia loca profisci volentem. Quin etiam ad Italiam quam citius transmigrare contendit praeparaew quoque conatur galeas magnas et parvas trecentas navesque magnas viginti, pedestrium et equestrium exercitum ultra centum millia et sic a Durrhachio Brundusium transire contendit, quae civitas sita est in regno Apuliae.*

It is not known how the cardinal obtained this faulty intelligence. These are probably his own inferences and cannot be supported by any real intelligence information. In fact, the armies of Mehmed did not threaten Italy until much later, until the year preceding the sultan's death, when an expedition landed in Apuleia and occupied Otranto (1480). Using Otranto as a base, the Turks launched raids as far as Lecce, Brindisi, and Taranto. The duke of Calabria, Alfonso, joined forces with his father, King Ferrante of Naples, and with the support of the pope to begin a campaign against the invaders. In October 1480 the Turkish expeditionary force was compelled to withdraw within the walls of Otranto, while its commander returned to Constantinople to ask for reinforcements. After Mehmed II's death in 1481 the Ottoman garrison departed Otranto. But by the time of this *razzia*, Isidore had been dead for over ten years. For the attempt of the Ottomans to establish a base for the future conquest of Italy in 1481, cf. E. Fossati, "Dal luglio 1480 al 16 aprile 1481: l'opera di Milano," *Archivio storico lombardo* 36 (1909): pp. 1–71; G. Panarco, "In terra d'Otranto dopo l'inasione turchesca," *Rivista storica salentina* 7 (1913): pp. 35–56; P. Coco, *La Guerra contro i Turchi in Otranto. Fatti e persone, 1480–1481* (Lecce, 1945); A. Bombaci, "Venezia e la impressa turca di Otranto," *Rivista storica italiana* 56 (1954): pp. 159–203; and *MCT*, pp. 390–396.

146 Röll, pp. 15, 16:

> *His ergo omnibus accensus et illectus dulcedine tam magn<A>e atque epulentis pr<A>ed<A>e, volens sequi fortunatos cursus su<A>e victori<A>e, non est dubitandum, quod totis spiritibus vigilare volet ad res magnas peragendas contra Christianos. Et si quies aliqua conceditur sibi in hoc principio et permittetur ampliare potentiam, teneat pro certo Vestra Magnificentia omnesque Christifideles, quod non desinet vexare mundum, donec Deus velit eum disperdere. Credo enim nec ambigo, quod inductis regibus et principibus Christianis ad unionem pro ex<s>ultatione sanct<A>e Crucis et nominis sacratissimi Jesu, nedum potentia, quam habet ille impiissimus Teucer, sed ter tantum potenti<A>e, non poterit prevalere contra nos.*

147 Hofmann, "Quellen zu Isidor von Kiew als Kardinal und Patriarch," p. 148:

> *Magni est certe animi, mal<a>e mentis, appetitus insatiabilis, proclivis ad qu<a>eque pessima; habet potentiam magnam, obedientiam apparatus, maximos et bellicosos et pecuniarum copiam; eis ergo omnibus accensus et illectus dulcedine tam magn<a>e et opulentis pr<a>ed<a>e, volens sequi fortunatos cursus su<a>e victori<a>e, non est dubitandum, quod totis spiritibus*

vigilare volet ad res magnas peragendas contra Christianos. Et si quies aliqua sibi concedetur in hoc principio et permittetur ampliare potentiam, teneat pro certo Vestra Magnificentia omnesque Christi fideles, quod non desinet vexare mundum, donec velit Deus eum disperdere. Credo enim nec ambigo, quod reductis regibus et principibus Christianis ad unionem pro ex<s>ultatione sanct<a>e crucis et nominis sacratissimi Jesu, nedum potentia, quam habet ille impiissimus Teucer, sed ter tantum potenti<a>e, non poterit prevalere contra nos.

148 Isidore emphasizes the need for immediate action in his letter to Capranica:

Sed Constantinopolis iam extincta est eodemque die etiam Latinorum civitas Pera. Ad haec nonnullae equidem plures aliae civitates aut partes septentrionales, <quae> tam Graeciae <quam> Europae sunt, ruina maxima imminentur, Mytilena scilicet, Chius, Rhodus, Lemnus, Livorus [Lerus?], Euboea ceteraeque plures. Ob quam causam scribo ad suam Beatitudinem sacrumque collegium ut tut<el>am diligentiamque adhibeant ad resistendum, quam citius possit fieri contra infideles Christi ne, si tardabitur, videant eos in Italia, quemadmodum ipsi Turci cogitant atque deliberant.

According to *CC* 2: 498, this letter was written on the 6th of July. *TIePN*, p. 13 n. 1, clarifies and states: *questa lettera, come pure l'altra seguente benchè scritta forse un giorno prima dell'altra, venne anch'essa affidata a quel fra Giovanni che si apprestava a salpare con una piccola nave verso l'Italia.* There is no date in the ms., if our text is complete. For the text, cf. *TIePN*, pp. 12–15.

149 Silvano, p. 250 [same text in *CC* 1: 62].
150 *CC* 1: 98–100:

Quapropter deprecor, exoro atque adhortor vestram Beatitudinem ut cito fiat aliqua providentia superinde, exinde omnem modum et industriam Beatitudo vestra teneat ad propugnandum et occurendum et conterendum huiusmodi novi Mahometi malignum propositum; quod equidem fiet, Domino disponente, si vestra Beatitudo curabit et festinabit in Italiam pacem fieri; quae cum Domino fiet, ut etiam alio consequatur bona quae Deus et vestra Beatitudo exoptat.

151 Ibid., p. 100: *Ego autem veniam cito ad vos, Deo dante, animam et corpus exponere pro fide Christiana et statu Christianorum; tunc etiam narrabo, exponens modos destructionis infidelium.*
152 Welykyi, "Duae Epistulae," pp. 290, 291:

Credo, non ambigo, quod inductis regibus et princibus Christianis ad unionem et exultationem sanctae crucis et nominis sanctissimi Iesu, nedum potentia quam habet ille impiissimus Teucer, sed omnium infidelium potentia non poterit praevalere contra nos. Sed inter omnes mundi potentias nullam video tam apte tamque benigne tamque ample et abundante assicurare posse subsidia debita pro opportunitate tantae rei quam excellentissimam Dominationem vestram. Considero namque mecum victorias <vestras> paratas trans mare, considero potentiam illam sacrae Dominationis <vestrae>, considero illam magnificentissimam urbem vestram manibus Dei fabricatam altamque mundi monarchiam; video pietatem, video religionem, magnanimitatem ad omnes res; nullus pavor, nulla inimicorum potentia nullaque maior impensa vos tenuerit pro exaltatione nominis et status vestri, sed (quod horum maius est) pro reddendo pacem universali ecclesiae, quot labores, <quot> pericula subistis! Non passa est illa gloriosa Dominatio quo ecclesia Dei et beatissimi eius pastores sub aliqua potentia paterentur opprobrium. Et de hoc adduco verum testem illum potentem Federicum Barbarossa<m> qui facturus persecutor capitalissimus beatissimi Papae Alexandri, et inde quaeritans pro sumendo vindictam non passa est illa sacra dominatio, gerens fidei zelum in pectore, quod beatissimus ille pastor ob fidei catholicae tumultum indebitas poenas lueret. Itaque sua forti potentia irruens contra illum imperatorem eum devicit et sic rediit salvum illum antistitem beatissimum et pastorem qui postmodum conculcata superbia et imperiis imperat; et hanc victoriam adeptam designat pictura illa memoranda in novo praetorio illius Almae civitatis mirabiliter descripta. Etiam descripta victoria et c<h>ronica illius imperatoris nefarii Federici praedicti in quodam libro nomine Florita, in quo quidem gesta omnia mundi sunt inserta. Itaque tot naves, quot galeae vestra Dominatio propria sua virtute armatas tenuit illa Alma praefata civitats pro tenendo securius et paccatum *mare a piratis, ut non damnificent Christianis. Haec omnibus nota sunt, non egent memoria; omittam alia multa quae mundus totus novit. Sed solum dicam quibus modis, quo impulsu Dominatio illa solita est parare ornatus maritimos contra perfidum genus Teucrorum et quot eorum trucidavit et quot eorum destruxit, et quot eorum captitavit, et quot eorum galeas et fustas diversimode cepit et disperdidit; testes illi Teucri sunt, qui multa damna passi sunt. Nunc vero vestra Dominatio patietur quod pro tanta magna iniquitate, quae quae toto mundo damnabilis est, tanta quoque ignominia et <tanto> periculo fidei Christianae, contra honorem Dei, non exponantur vires omnes ad submittendum hostem, non cogitari, non credi potest? Quis ergo et hoc in tempore dubitare poterit quod vestra Christianissima Dominatio his subsecutis tot malis in opprobrium Christianae religionis tollerare possit, non sumere vindictam? Quis etiam credere potest, vestra Dominatio, quod hic perfidus inimicus Christianorum et tuae dominatinis dominari debeat hunc Levantem? Mi<ni>me me certe extitit nemo <qui> aliud credere potest.*

153 *Ibid.*
154 Hofmann, "Quellen zu Isidor von Kiew als Kardinal und Patriarch," p. 148.
155 His bellicose attitude is already present in his earliest letter, cf. *supra*, n. 156. In this communication, Isidore provides specifics about the materiel needs for the upcoming war: *Et licet auditum est multas habere galeas et magnum exercitum.*
156 The most detailed account can be found in R. Schwobel, *The Shadow of the Crescent: The Renaissance Image of the Turk (1453–1517)* (Nieuwkoop, 1967), pp. 5–10.
157 On Tetaldi (and bibliography), cf. Philippides, *Mehmed II the Conqueror*, pp. 21–26. For the Latin text and an English translation of this account (including Tetaldi's "appendix" that explicates the planned crusade), cf. pp. 136–217.
158 Thus on 24 February 1454, Philip the Good of Burgundy and his knights of the Golden Fleece took, in a melodramatic ceremony, the so-called "Oath of the Pheasant" and pledged to wage holy war against the Turks. On the duke of Burgundy and his interest in Constantinople, cf. Y. Lacaze, "Politique 'méditeranéenne' et projets de croisade chez Philippe le Bon: De la chute de Byzance à la victoire chrétienne de Belgrade (mai 1453–juillet 1456," *Annales de Bourgogne* 61 (1969): pp. 5–42, 81–132; A. Grunzweig, "Philippe le Bon et Constantinople," *Byz* 24 (1954): pp. 47–61; and R. Vaughan, *Philip the Good: The Apogee of Burgundy* (London, 1970). The court of Burgundy exhibited a very strong interest in Constantinople at this time. Cf., e.g., the beautiful *Lamentatio Sanctae Matris Ecclesiae Constantinopolitanae* composed by Guillaume Dufay (ca. 1400–1474) [= B. Becherini, "Due canzoni di Dufay del codice Fiorentino 2794," *La Bibliofilia* 43 (1941): pp. 124–127]. An Italian translation of the French/Latin text of this poem appears in *CC* 2: 318; or the fascinating miniature of ms. *Paris. fr. 9087*, fol. 207ᵛ, in the Bibliothèque Nationale at Paris, which depicts the siege of 1453. It was prepared specifically for the duke, in connection with the fifteenth-century Burgundian traveler, Bertrandon de la Brocquière. Its depiction of the city is topographically accurate, in general terms, but the buildings and the fortifications are given western form and style. Discussion of this miniature in *MP*, p. 549.
159 Marcello was accompanied by a Porte official when he returned to Venice after completing the initial negotiations in Constantinople; for other individuals who assisted Marcello in his mission, cf. *MCT*, pp. 111 and 112. For the treaty itself, cf. *RdD* 3: 186 ff. Also, cf. *PaL* 2: 140.
160 For this conflict and the humanistic attempt to create a proper, classical context for the siege and sack, cf. among others the admirable investigations by M. Meserve, *Empires of Islam in Renaissance Historical Thought* (Cambridge, MA, and London, 2008); N. Bisaha, *Creating East and West: Renaissance Humanists and the Ottoman Turks* (Philadelphia, 2004); and, more recently, the admirable, detailed synthesis of J. Schiel, *Mongolesturm und Fall Konstantinopels: Dominikanische Erzählungen im diachronen Vergleich*, Europa im Mittelalter 19 (Berlin, 2011), who treats the religious reaction to the Christian losses in the Levant (including a detailed analysis of Leonardo's narrative). Schiel, however, devotes

only three or four sentences to Isidore, and, consequently, the analysis presented in this chapter is the only study of the writings of Isidore's Cretan sojourn in existence.

161 Francesco Filelfo writes of his captive relatives in a letter to the physician Pierre Tomasi; cf. the entire letter in E. Legrand, *Cent-dix lettres grecques de François Filelfe publiées intégralement pour la première fois d'après le Codex Trivulzianus 873 avec traduction, notes et commentaires* (Paris, 1892), p. 66:

> *non solum quod et socrum mihi carissimam Manfredinam Auriam* [the daughter of the famous teacher Manuel Chrysoloras], *nobilissimam et prudentissimam feminam, ac duas eius et socii mei Johannis Chrysolorae, praestantissimi equites aurati et erudissimi vici, filias, meorum quatuor filiorum materteras, in obscuram servitutem a barbaris et teterrimis Turcis actas audio, sed eo magis quod ea urbe etiam matre sum usus et altrice educatricique iuventae studiorum meorum.*

In addition, cf. his letter to Leodisio Cribelli (p. 66); the letter to André of Ferrara (p. 67); the letter (in Greek) to his son Giovanni Mario (p. 69); and the letter to Ludovico of Mantua (p. 69). In desperation the Philhellene Filelfo wrote a fawning ode to Mehmed II (under the heading Μαομὲτ τῷ μέγα<->αὐθέντῃ καὶ μέγα<->ἀμυρᾷ τῶν Τούρκων), in the hope of obtaining freedom for his relatives (*ibid.*, Ode n. 11 [p. 211; fol. 41ʳ of the ms.]).

162 Comparing the sultan to ancient potentates became a *topos* in humanistic circles in Italy. Francesco Filelfo's son, Giovanni Mario, in his epic poem, *Amyris*, compares the sultan to several famous men from antiquity, including Philip II of Macedon; cf. Philippides, *Mehmed II the Conqueror*, p. 5.

7 Il Cardinal Greco Vecchio
The last years

Cardinal Isidore left the haven of Crete, presumably when he had somehow recovered from his adventures, in late summer or early fall of 1453 and returned to Italy. Apparently, he felt concerned and isolated on the island, as he indicates in one of his letters; he wrote to Capranica in July of that year and expressed his anxiety, because he had received no reply(ies) to his letter(s).[1] What is certain is that Isidore had not reached Italy by 11 September, when Henry of Soemmern produced a summary of Isidore's adventures.[2] Henry states, however, that Isidore was expected to arrive in Rome within the next eight days.[3] As we should suppose, given the ties between Crete and Venice, Isidore first arrived in Venice and then hurriedly[4] departed for Rome. Leonardo Benvoglienti mentions Isidore's arrival in Venice, and his swift departure for Rome in one of his letters from late November 1453.[5] Once Isidore arrived in Rome, he must have been the first authoritative eyewitness to give an accurate and detailed account of the fall of Constantinople and he must have received a memorable reception at the Vatican, especially since the general impression prevailed that he had perished during the sack.[6] This general view also suggests that perhaps his letters had not been received, as he himself feared, or that their contents had not been widely known. Details are lacking from this point on, for we have no letters issued by his pen until 1455, when the last letter of this series appears.[7] It is improbable that, once he came to Italy, Isidore had not continued his propaganda project. In fact, he must have written a large number of letters to numerous acquaintances – friends, humanists, and Greek émigrés. These letters are missing and apparently have not survived, but it is unthinkable that Isidore did not correspond with others, such as Francesco Filelfo, whose relatives by marriage (members of the family of Manuel Chrysoloras) had been enslaved.[8] Filelfo would have wished at the very least to learn from Isidore what had actually happened and what possible information he may have on his enslaved relatives. Yet no correspondences survive (or have been found) and this remains an unfortunate circumstance, as additional letters perhaps would increase our knowledge of the events. It is certain that at this point in time Isidore was still on good terms with Filelfo and their correspondence continued into the future, but no letters from Isidore to Filelfo have survived or so it seems at this present writing.

The last surviving letter of Isidore with regard to the fall of Constantinople is his epistle to the duke of Burgundy, dated the 22nd of February 1455, *Data Romae die XXII Februarii MCCCCL° quinto*.[9] While this letter provides no new information to what the cardinal had earlier written in Crete, it does address the point of the official position of Genoa during the siege, a matter that was of concern to the Genoese and to their colony at Pera.[10] Disturbing rumors of treasonable activities had surfaced since the fall of Constantinople that the Genoese of Pera had sided with Mehmed II and the Ottoman army.[11] During the siege Pera had officially remained neutral, but its actual status contained ambiguities, as the colony supplied food and other goods to the Ottoman army. Yet some of its citizens had volunteered and assisted in the defense of the imperial city. Pera's *podestà*, Angelo Giovanni Lomellino,[12] had received instructions from Genoa to avoid direct confrontation with the Ottoman forces. Nevertheless, the position of Pera was precarious and Lomellino faced numerous challenges[13] in his efforts to maintain the independence of the colony. Immediately after the conquest of Constantinople, Pera was granted an *aman-name* by the sultan, who severely restricted Pera's former privileges. The *aman-name* was signed by Mehmed II's lieutenant, Zaganos.[14] Numerous complaints were voiced after the siege and became axiomatic, for the Ottoman army had received substantial help from westerners and specifically from the Genoese Perenses, whose ambiguous role was to assist both the emperor and sultan. These charges are echoed in numerous secondary narratives.[15] Thus the Genoese were partly blamed for the fall, because Pera had remained officially neutral during the siege and because Giustiniani had withdrawn from his position at the walls in the course of the last battle.[16] While early on, as we have seen,[17] Isidore did not wish to speak of these charges and of the warlord's untimely departure, he vigorously defends in this letter the Genoese Perenses, seeking perhaps to put an end to the circulating bad press. Moreover, we should recall that Isidore was probably ransomed by the Perenses, who then managed for a few days to conceal him in their colony, while the sultan was still searching for him and had put a price on his head.[18] Isidore in his letter to the duke[19] thus paid his debt to his saviors and publically acknowledged their assistance. In this manner he absolved the Genoese of misconduct. In no uncertain terms Isidore states that the Genoese Perenses were on the side of Constantinople and suffered for their actions after the fall:[20]

> *Nam cum pauci essemus, diu rem bellicam, quoad valuimus, gessimus, nec deerant nobis Ianuenses, qui omni conatu Urbem ipsam tutati sunt, et quamquam simulatu cum Teucro viverent hocque fieret statuto consilio, tamen noctu clam ad nos eos quos valebant ac poterant viros et sic subsidia mittebant frequentique senatu imperatorio aderant aliisque cum nationibus reipublicae tutandae consultabant. Et aliquis est qui ipsis improperet eorum culpa et defectu eam Urbem in deditione devenisse Teucrorum, salva eorum pace, non consentaneum audietur, quia, cum in eodemnet ut periculo et discrimine laborarent, non debebant sui discriminis esse patratores. Nam capta Constantinopoli eamet hora et Pera in potestatem pervenit Teucrorum, destructis moenibus et rem ipsorum penitus deletam ac labefactam. Ego, qui praesens*

eram, possum verum de omnibus perhibere testimonium; nam cum viriliter et strenue se gesserint, non dignum et improperentur, equidem loca illa omnia in potestatem et iugum pervenerunt Teucrorum, potissime Chium et Mitilene sub tribute iam constituta.

Indeed we were few but, as long as we possessed strength, we fought on. We were supported in this by the Genoese, who exerted every effort to defend the City itself, and, in spite of their pretended official position with the Turk, they dispatched to us, secretly under the cover of darkness, both aid and men who were strong enough and able. They often participated in the councils of the emperor for the defense of the state. I will not agree with anyone who charges them with blame and improper behavior, as if the City fell to the Turks because they maintained peace with them. After all, they did their best under the dangerous circumstances and they should not be under any suspicion. The moment that Constantinople fell, Pera also came into the possession of the Turks. Pera's walls were demolished and the entire situation was shaken and was changed, as it came into their hands. I was present and I can truthfully testify on every aspect. Since they acted with honor and strength, it is improper for them to come under suspicion. All of their places came under the yoke and the jurisdiction of the Turks. Chios and Lesbos have already been reduced to tributary status.

This is the strongest defense ever produced for the Genoese and it comes from the pen of Isidore.

Once he had reached the safety of Italy, Isidore assumed ecclesiastical duties, but he continued to work on behalf of the liberation of the east from the Ottoman yoke. As we have seen, he already participated in the congress convened by Pope Nicholas V immediately upon his return. He must have grown depressed as time passed by and nothing definite could be accomplished, but he nevertheless pursued his efforts to organize a crusade to retake Constantinople. He became further disappointed when plans for a crusade seemed to have evaporated with the death of Pope Nicholas V on 25 March 1455.[21] In his last years, Nicholas V had exerted himself to organize a crusade, but with his passing all plans dissolved, as Pius II notes in his *Memoirs*.[22] He further provides a brief assessment of Nicholas V and of his achievements, which, he observes, were marred by the fall of Constantinople.[23]

The conclave for the election of the next pope followed and Isidore took time at that moment from his efforts to promote a crusade to the east. As his Latin was never passable, he most probably followed the lead of his friend, Cardinal Bessarion, who also translated for him.[24] In addition, Bessarion was initially favored to become the successor to Nicholas V.[25] Bessarion, however, was passed over. There seems to have emerged a campaign within the Vatican against Greek clerics and refugees. This drive grew with time and various notable Greek émigrés fell victim to the anti-Hellenic wave, including Isidore, as we will have occasion to note. This is the first unambiguously recorded instance, in which Bessarion is attacked precisely because of his Greek roots. The French cardinal of Avignon, Alain de Coëtivy (1403–1472), launched this campaign against the candidacy of Bessarion by openly expressing anti-Greek sentiments. He pointed out that Bessarion (and we should probably add Isidore as well)[26] had retained his beard and had not been wearing a tonsure. The French cardinal stresses that the Latin Church had no need of a Greek pope; moreover, he questioned Bessarion's sincerity in accepting the Latin doctrine.[27] Needless to say, these sentiments and western prejudices were also broadly directed at all Greek émigré prelates.

Thus Bessarion's candidacy failed. Instead, the least likely candidate,[28] Alfonso Borgia, the cardinal of Santi Quattro Coronati and a learned lawyer, though advanced in age, was elected on 28 April 1455, taking the unlikely name of Calixtus III to the surprise of everyone.[29] From our point of view, it is of interest to note that one of his first acts was to continue the propaganda for a crusade that had been initiated by his predecessor. The new pope issued indulgences and summons to prepare for the upcoming crusade.[30] Undoubtedly, Isidore must have supported the papal effort with his own propaganda and drew upon his personal experiences and adventures in the Levant. We discover that under Calixtus, Isidore was granted a house in Rome: *qu<a>edam domus sita iuxta ecclesiam beat<a>e Mari<ae> in Via lata de Urbe*,[31] "a certain house situated next to the Church of Blessed Mary on the Via Lata of the City."[32] We are unaware of any earlier rewards to Isidore during the reign of Nicholas V. Perhaps we can infer that this modest house was Isidore's compensation for his efforts on behalf of the Vatican before and during the siege and for his activities in support of Calixtus III's projected crusade, but we have no further details.

With the acquisition of a house, Isidore then was confronted with the responsibility to organize his household personnel and his retinue. This was an expensive proposition, one that thus far he may have avoided. His stay in Crete and his return may have attracted impoverished individuals from Greece and Rome, who would offer various services to the cardinal. Perhaps, related to these needs, the pope extended the cardinal's revenues by assigning him canonries in the churches on Cyprus (1 May 1456), Nicosia and Paphos, as well as the archdeaconry of Nicosia.[33] While we have no information on how Isidore managed his financial responsibilities or what exactly his expenses were, we may form a general comparative idea, when we consider the following known facts that would confront Bessarion at a later date. When Bessarion took upon himself the role of protector of the three young children of the impoverished despot of the Morea, Thomas Palaiologos, the brother of the last emperor of Constantinople, he set rules in writing for the expenses to be incurred in the household of the princes and also cited specific conditions. The letter may be authentic, by the hand of Bessarion,[34] but there are reasons to make it suspect and dictate caution,[35] as after all we may be encountering yet another forgery by the hand of the notorious Makarios Melissourgos-Melissenos.[36] In any case, we do form an impression of what the expenses of a noble household under the protection of the pope may have been, either in the 1460s (if indeed the letter is actually composed by Bessarion's hand; it is dated and signed as ἐκ

Ῥώμης. Αὐγούστου θ´ αυξε´ ἔτους. Ὁ Βησσαρίων καρδινάλις καὶ πατριάρχης Κωνσταντινουπόλεως,[37] "from Rome, August 7, 1465. Bessarion, Cardinal and Patriarch of Constantinople") or in the 1560s–1580s (if it is a forgery). There is a section in the letter, which addresses the question of finances:[38]

> ὁ ἁγιώτατος πάπας διὰ παρακλήσεως τινων καὶ οἰκείας καλοθελείας καὶ καλοκαγαθίας ἔταξε νὰ δίδῃ κάθε μῆνα τὰ αὐθεντόπουλα δουκάτα τριακόσια, ὥσπερ ἔδιδε καὶ τῷ ἁγίῳ δεσπότῃ καὶ πατρὶ αὐτῶν.
> Θέλει καὶ ὁρίζει ὁ πάπας. . . .
> Τὰ μὲν διακόσια κατὰ μῆναν νὰ εἶναι διὰ τὰ τρία ἀδέλφια . . . νὰ ἐξοδιάζωνται εἰς τροφὴν ἐκείνων καὶ ἀνθρώπων ὑποχειρίων μικρῶν ἓξ ἢ ἑπτά . . . καὶ εἰς ἀγορὰν καὶ τροφὴν ἀλόγων τεσσάρων . . . καὶ εἰς ῥῶγαν τῶν αὐτῶν ὑποχειρίων καὶ εἰς ἐνδύματα τῶν αὐθεντοπούλων . . . καὶ κάτου νὰ περισσεύῃ καὶ τίποτες . . . διὰ νὰ βοηθηθῶσι κάτου εἰς τὴν ἀσθένειάν τους ἢ εἰς ἄλλην ἀνάγκην. . . .
> Τὰ δὲ λοιπὰ ἑκατὸν δουκάτα τὸν μῆνα, ἤγουν χίλια διακόσια τὸν χρόνον, νὰ ἐξοδιάζωνται ἒς τινας ἄρχοντας καὶ καλὰ πρόσωπα, ὁποῦ νὰ εἶναι κοντὰ των, νὰ δουλεύουν καὶ νὰ τὰ συντροφιάζουν καὶ νὰ τὰ φυλάττουν.
> Ἀκούσας δὲ ὁ ἁγιώτατος πάπας τὸ πόσοι ἄνθρωποι εἶναι αὐτοῦ, ὑπερεθαύμασε καταγιγνώσκων μας, διότι ἐὰν εἰς τὸν μακαρισμένον ἐκεῖνον τὸν τοιοῦτον ἄνθρωπον ἐθαύμαζον πῶς εἶχεν ἐδῶ τόσους καὶ ἐκατηγόρουν τον, ὅτι εἰς τὴν ξενετείαν νὰ τρέφῃ τόσους μὲ ξένα δουκάτα καὶ ξένας ἐλπίδας, τόσῳ μᾶλλον τώρα, ὁποῦ ἦλθον καὶ ἄλλοι πλειότεροι, παρὰ ὁποῦ ἦσαν ἐδῶ, καταγιγνώσκονταί των καὶ κατηγοροῦσί των, καὶ μάλιστα εἰς αὐθεντόπουλα νέα καὶ ὀρφανά, ὁποῦ οὔτε ἀξίωμα, οὔτε ὄνομα, οὔτε φήμην ἔχουσιν.

Due to the requests of some friends, as well as out of his good will and nobility, the most holy pope promised monthly to grant three hundred ducats to the princes,[39] the exact sum that he had granted to their father, the saintly despot [Thomas Palaiologos].

So the pope wishes and decrees:

1. Two hundred ducats out of the monthly grant be reserved for the three siblings . . . to be spent for their food supplies and for that of their small retinue of six or seven servants . . . for the purchase and feeding supplies of four horses . . . for the salaries of the servants . . . and for the clothes of the princes . . . with the hope that the entire sum is not exhausted so that they can help someone in sickness or in some other necessity. . . .

2. The remaining one hundred ducats per month (or twelve hundred *per annum*) should be distributed among the lords or persons of good character who are in the retinue of the princes, as their obedient companions and guardians.

The most holy pope has heard that too many people are in attendance there. He was amazed at our behavior. Many others had been amazed and had even found fault with us, as they looked upon the huge number of dependents of the late despot [Thomas Palaiologos] and had expressed astonishment that he supported them with ducats that were not his own, counting on help from strangers. The case is even worse now, as more people have arrived (since, after all there had been fewer in the past). As this fact becomes known, blame is assigned and it is likely to fall upon the young, orphaned princes, who possess no lordships, no well-known title, and no fame.

Isidore may have encountered some financial hardship in properly maintaining his new house and his retinue. Soon, however, after the acquisition of the house, his revenues were increased, for, on 17 September 1457, he was granted additional incomes, when he assumed full rights over of the village Prino in Euboea, which had been under the jurisdiction of the patriarchal church of Khalkis/Negroponte.[40] On 5 September of the following year he was appointed archbishop of Corfu, and on 9 November he was granted the Church of Santa Agatha in Rome.[41] Thus his finances appear to have improved considerably, allowing him to reach a measure of financial stability.

Isidore returned to Venice at the beginning of 1456, where he became involved in a legal proceeding to ensure himself of funds, perhaps needed, given his own financial circumstances that had mounted up after he was granted a house. Thus Isidore brought formal charges against the Venetian nobleman, Bernardo Dandolo, who had managed the possessions of the Latin Patriarch of Constantinople, those that Isidore had acquired when Pope Nicholas V appointed him to the post in 1452.[42] Apparently, Dandolo had been misappropriating most of the funds that for the previous three years should have legally gone to Isidore. The Venetian Senate did in fact find Dandolo guilty on 4 June 1456, and transferred 1,255 ducats to Isidore,[43] who, with this sum in hand, anticipated an amelioration of the present state of his finances.[44] A more important privilege was also granted to Isidore by Venice at this time (18 June 1456), but was never implemented. His experiences, his services, and his efforts on behalf of the church are cited, and on this basis, Isidore and the Greek community of Venice received the right to worship, *greco ritu*, in a church to be built in "a suitable place."[45]

Such honors and privileges, building up around Isidore, certainly attracted attention, but the cardinal also encountered detractors. One can already notice the anti-Greek propaganda operating and accelerating against prominent refugees from the Levant, especially since Italian humanists also disliked the pope. Calixtus III (even though he was a noted humanist himself) had distressed numerous humanists, who viewed the reign of his predecessor as a lost "golden age." Early on Calixtus's policies alienated the humanists, who then undertook a campaign against him, producing malicious rumors, in which Isidore was also implicated. Thus an interesting accusation was made by Bishop Vespasiano da Bistici:[46]

> *Entrato adunque Callisto nel pontificato, e vedendo tanta copia di degni libri, dove n'erano cinquecento coperti di chermesì e forniti d'ariento; giunto dove era tanta*

copia di libri, si cominciò a maravigliare, corne quello che non era uso a vedere se non letture in carta di bambagia e ricollette; . . . e canonista sanza altra dottrina . . . egli disse queste parole: vedi in che egl'ha consumato la robba della Chiesa di Dio. E cominciò a gittare via i libri greci, e dononne al Cardinale Ruteno parecchie centinaja di volumi. Seno il Cardinale tanto vecchio, ch'era alquanto alienato della mente, quegli libri vennono in mano de' famigli, . . . e venderono parte per carlini quelli che erano costati fiorini.

When Calixtus became pope and saw such abundance of precious books – five hundred bound in crimson velvet with silver enforcement, he was greatly amazed, as he was accustomed to see books sewn in linen. He was a jurist without further education . . . he said the following words: "See how the treasure of the Church of God has been spent!" Then he began to give away the Greek books. He gave many hundreds of volumes to the Ruthenian cardinal [Isidore]. The cardinal was very old, and he was deprived of his senses, these books fell into the hands of his retinue, . . . and what had cost florins to acquire now sold for pennies.

Who were those members of Isidore's retinue? They are not identified. That Isidore had household servants is not to be doubted, as there is indirect evidence to suggest that he, like his friend Bessarion, had surrounded himself with Greek scholars, copyists, and refugees who had fled the Greek world under Ottoman rule and had sought better conditions in the west. Most of the refugees naturally gravitated towards Bessarion, but Isidore must have attracted his share of them, who may have found employment in his household. The only evidence that there was a circle of them employed by Isidore can be supported by a statement of the Greek cleric, Theodoros Agallianos,[47] who had survived the siege and sack and had become a member of the Greek Patriarchate during the reign of Mehmed II, after the patriarchate's reconstitution in the days following the conquest of Constantinople. In one of his writings, Agallianos expressed anger against his enemies within the patriarchate, who had accused him of improper priestly conduct. One of his main enemies was George Galesiotes, a *megas skeuophylax* of Patriarch Gennadios II (George Scholarios). George's brother, Andronikos Galesiotes, we are told, left Constantinople and sought better circumstances in Italy. Andronikos Galesiotes, Agallianos states, sought employment in the household of "the cardinal":[48]

ἧκεν οὐπώποτε καὶ Μανουὴλ Χριστώνυμος ἐξ Ἀδριανουπόλεως. ὃς ἦλθε μὲν καὶ ἐπὶ τοῦ ἁγιωτάτου πατριάρχου κὺρ Γενναδίου ἅμ' Ἀνδρονίκῳ τῷ Γαλησιώτῃ, τῷ τοῦ μεγάλου σκευοφύλακος αὐταδέλφῳ, μὴ ἔχοντος δὲ τοῦ πατριάρχου τούτων χρείαν πάλιν ὑπέστρεψαν. καὶ ὁ μὲν τὴν ἐς Ἰταλίαν ἐστείλατο καὶ ἐν τοῖς παρασίτοις τάττεται τοῦ καρδιναλίου.

At some point Manuel Christonymos came from Adrianople. He had also come earlier in the reign of the most holy patriarch, Lord Gennadios [II, that is, George Scholarios] together with Andronikos Galesiotes, the brother of the *megas skeuophylax*, but as the patriarch had no need for their services, they went back. And he [the brother, that is, Andronikos Galesiotes], went to Italy and found employment among the dependents[49] of the cardinal [Isidore?].

Agallianos does not state the name of the cardinal. Could it be that by his reference to "the cardinal" he meant Isidore? Or is it a reference to Bessarion? Galesiotes may have sought the assistance of either cardinal or perhaps both, even in succession.[50] If the allusion is to Isidore, then this is our only reference to the possible members of the cardinal's household.

Much "bad press" targeted Isidore, but the malicious gossip ultimately focused on Calixtus III,[51] who was reputed to be no friend to humanists. Isidore, who had been rewarded by the pope, became one of the victims. It is interesting to note that Vespasiano links Isidore to Calixtus III; it seems puzzling because Isidore was a close friend of Bessarion and Vespasiano had been in the service of Bessarion. In the eyes of numerous humanists in Italy, Isidore may have not been considered a true humanist, precisely because he had never mastered Latin but had labored exclusively on Greek literature. Lacking facility in Latin, Isidore could not have associated himself with the literary gatherings of the Italian humanists, who spoke fluent Latin, and when he did so, he must have been in need of a translator, unless the proceedings were conducted in Attic Greek. This groundless accusation by Vespasiano must originate in prejudice; after all, he draws a major distinction: no Latin books were to be given to Isidore (who, the implication is, would be unable to read them), but only Greek *codices*. Perhaps here we may see traces of the anti-Greek propaganda that was directed at Isidore, as Bessarion's reputation was beyond anyone's reach; Isidore was the easier target; other accusations concerning books from the Vatican Library were also voiced and involved an acquaintance of Isidore, the humanist Francesco Filelfo, who, as we have seen, had Greek relatives by marriage.[52] Moreover, there is no suggestion in the record that Isidore had become senile at this time; again this extraordinary charge from Vespasiano probably has its origins in the malicious gossip of Italians who could not understand Isidore's Greek and probably concluded that he was making no sense.

Filelfo may have been a partner of Vespasiano in spreading bad press on the jurist pope.[53] Filelfo, in this negative portrayal of the pope, brought Cardinal Isidore as well into the picture. We first hear of a problem that Filelfo was facing, as he was missing a rare manuscript of Plutarch's *Parallel Lives* that belonged to him, which Nicholas V had borrowed. After the death of Nicholas V Filelfo's manuscript disappeared and the humanist became desperate to recover it. Filelfo's letter of December 1457[54] to Bessarion explains the intriguing problem:[55]

Λαμπουγνῖνος Βιράγος ὁ καὶ μεδιολανεὺς φίλος ἐμοῦ ἐκ πολλοῦ ὢν τυγχάνει. οὗτος οὖν, κατὰ νόμον φιλίας, τοῖς ἡμετέροις ὡς καὶ ἰδίοις ἐχρῆτο ἅπασιν. ἔχων τοίνυν παρ' ἑαυτῷ σύμπασαν τὴν ἐμὴν κατὰ Πλούταρχον πραγματείαν ἱστορικήν, ἤγουν τὰ λεγόμενα Παράλληλα, βιβλίον τι ἀξιόλογον, ἐδάνεισε τοῦτο, ὡς αὐτὸς λέγει, τῷ ἄκρῳ ἐκείνῳ καὶ σοφωτάτῳ ἀρχιερεῖ Νικολάῳ. ἀποθανόντος δὲ τούτου, συναπέθανεν αὐτῷ, ὡς δοκεῖ, καὶ τὸ ἐμὸν βιβλίον. οὐδεὶς γὰρ οἶδε τἀληθὲς περὶ τούτου. δέομαι γοῦν τῆς σῆς ἱερᾶς κεφαλῆς ἵνα γράψῃς μοι τὸ ὂν περὶ τοῦ τοιούτου βιβλίου.

Lampugnino Birago,[56] who also is from Milan, happens to be an old friend of mine, and who took advantage of all our close ties and of the rules of friendship. He was holding my entire historical work by Plutarch, that is, the so-called *Parallel [Lives]*, which is a book of great worth. He loaned this, as he himself states, to that wonderful and wisest pope, Nicholas [V]. When the latter died, my book, as it seems, died also. No one knows the truth about it. I beg your holiness to write to me and tell me the actual circumstances that befell this worthy book.

Filelfo pursued his search with a letter to Aeneas Sylvius Piccolomini (soon to be Pope Pius II), in which he mentions Isidore, whom he seems to blame for appropriating his precious manuscript:[57]

Audio codicem illum etiam post obitum summi pontificis Nicolai quinti visum esse apud cardinalem Ruthenum. Modo quod in re verum sit non ignoramus, facile futurum spero ut nobilissimus codex ille ad dominum redeat aut pace aut bello, quam vis bello pacem anteponam.

I hear that after the death of Pope Nicholas V that manuscript had been seen at the house of the Ruthenian cardinal [Isidore]. I may not doubt the truth of this and I hope that in the future that excellent manuscript will be returned to its owner either peacefully or with a fight (even though I would prefer peace over a fight).

It is interesting to note that Filelfo did not mention Isidore to Bessarion at all, or his intention to fight for the possession of the Plutarch *codex*. Perhaps he did not wish to alienate Bessarion or Isidore, the two close friends. On the same day he repeated his request to Bessarion, again without making any mention of Isidore, and begged for news, as he wished to discover whether his manuscript existed or had been irretrievably lost.[58] Apparently, Bessarion wrote back, even though his letter does not survive, and simply stated that the manuscript had to be in the Vatican Library, as one can gather from the next letter that Filelfo wrote to Bessarion, thanking him profusely and hinting that a friend of his, a lawyer, can serve as an intermediary. Is this reference to a lawyer a veiled threat directed towards Isidore, since Filelfo was aware that Bessarion would pass it on to his close friend? The pertinent section reads as follows:[59]

Redittae mihi sunt hodierno hoc hodie perhumane atque benignae litterae tuae quibus quod scire desiderabam non obscure intellexi. Itaque habeo tibi gratias immortales . . . reliquum est mihi quid ea in re faciendum sit consulas vel epistola, vel nuncio. Nuncium vero alium velim neminem quam prudentissimum iurisconsultum Othonem Carretum. . . . Is enim quod abs te acceperit, mihi quam primum significabit. Praetera, si quid certius habendum iudicas, id quod mihi quoque videri, debet, habes archidiaconum datarium, quum τῇ βιβλιοθήκῃ *praeest, ut audio, rem omnem poterit quam primum optimeque inquirere.*

On this very day I received your most kind, most caring letter, and I have the clear answer I desired. And so I will be in your debt forever ... now you must advise me how to proceed either by letter or by messenger. I could not wish for a better messenger than the most discreet lawyer Otto da Carreto.... He will tell me what you think as soon as he hears from you. Besides, if you think that there should be further assurances, I will agree. You have the services of the arch-deacon in charge, who presides over the library, as I hear, and he can look into the inquiry in a most reliable way as soon as possible.

The librarian, it appears, carried out a search, but he could not locate the *codex* that belonged to Filelfo.[60] So it appears that the *codex* was no longer in the Vatican Library. Could Isidore have acquired Filelfo's volume? It seems likely that this work had been, after all, lost. It was not to be found among the manuscripts that Isidore was copying or was perusing,[61] which were eventually returned to the library after his death.[62]

Filelfo was not happy and proved relentless in his fruitless search for his precious manuscript.[63] As late as 1458 he was still pursuing the trail. He wrote a polite letter to Bessarion (dated: Μεδιολανόθεν, τῇ πρὸ καλενδῶν ἀπριλίου δεκάτη ἡμέρᾳ, ἔτει ͵αυνη [the 14th of March 1458]), in which he thanks him for his help but emphasizes that he is still searching and expresses his deep disappointment:[64]

Φραγκῖσκος ὁ Φιλέλφος Βησσαρίωνι, τῷ νικαεῖ καρδιναλίῳ, χαίρειν, ἔτι καὶ νῦν δέομαί σου, πάτερ αἰδεσιμώτατε, ἵνα διὰ τὴν φιλοφροσύνην σου πρὸς ἐμὲ καὶ διὰ τὴν σὴν θείαν μεγαλοψυχίαν ἴδῃς πάσῃ σπουδῇ ὅπερ καὶ πρότερον ἄρτι ἐπέστειλά σοι περὶ τῶν ἐμῶν κατὰ Πλούταρχον Παραλλήλων. πρᾶγμα ποιήσεις ἡμῖν ὡς ἥδιστον γράψας περὶ τούτων τἀληθὲς πρὸς τὴν αὐτῶν ἀνάκτησιν. οὐ γὰρ δύναμαι οὐ βαρέως φέρειν τοιούτου πλούτου πρὸς βαρβάρους ἐπιβολήν. ἔρρωσο.

Greetings from Francesco Filelfo to the Nicene cardinal. I still beg you, most reverend father, and depend on your kind sentiments and innate generosity to exert, with the greatest care, your effort on behalf of this matter that I wrote you previously concerning my Plutarch's *Parallel* [*Lives*]. You would give me the greatest pleasure by writing to me the truth in regard to my repossession. I can only bear heavily the loss of such a treasure to barbarians. Farewell.

Indeed that is a polite letter, which, again, fails to mention Isidore. Is, however, the reference to "barbarians" to be understood as "uneducated," in which case Filelfo may be alluding to the servants in Isidore's retinue and household? Is this statement deriving from Vespasiano's statement *libri vennono in mano de' famigli*?[65] In time a compromise was achieved. While Filelfo never found his *codex*, through the intervention and mediation of Cardinal Bessarion, Pope Pius II pacified Filelfo and had a copy of the *Parallel Lives* produced from the Vatican Library, which was then forwarded to the humanist. Filelfo was overjoyed and thanked both Bessarion and the pope.[66]

In the entire long episode what is lacking on the part of Filelfo is any mention of Isidore, whom he did not wish to alienate. Yet is it possible that in his relentless search Filelfo failed to write directly to Isidore? Is it possible that there was some correspondence between them? Are we confronting another gap in our knowledge, since we have no surviving correspondence between the two individuals? In time Filelfo composed, as we will see,[67] an ode in honor of Isidore. Was this an attempt on his part to restore relations that may have soured during his quest for locating his Plutarch manuscript?

The year 1458 was eventful for Isidore. He perhaps even initiated[68] some changes for his Slavic charges, dividing his jurisdiction into two separate components under two metropolitans. This complex division brought about the creation of an ecclesiastical "Superior Russia" theoretically concentrated at Moscow, and an "Inferior Russia" centered about Kiev.[69] Isidore retained the Ruthenian dioceses in Poland and Lithuania, and held at least for the moment, the 21st of July 1458, the nominal title that he had had for the previous six years – "the Titular Metropolitan for Kiev and of All Rus'," while Iona still retained the same title, *sans* titular, with the approval of the Muscovite Synod. But Isidore soon relinquished the title when, on the 3rd of September 1458, Pope Pius II (after the death of Calixtus) formally appointed Gregory, the old companion of Isidore, to the Kievan metropolitan seat.[70] Gregory was ordained "according to the traditional Greek rites"[71] to this office by Gregory III Mammas, the refugee Orthodox and now Uniate Patriarch of Constantinople, who was resident in Rome. Gregory departed for Kiev the 17th of January 1459.[72] This apparently was the last time the two friends, Isidore and Gregory, saw each other.

The few Muscovite annals laconically address the appointment of Gregory to the Kievan seat. *The Muscovite Annalistic Code at the End of the Fifteenth Century* relates:[73]

Сидор же злаго яду насытився никако же отрыгнути могы и ни мала времени пождати не стерпѣ, срама ради обличенниа своего о злыхъ си ересех латынскых, еже дѣлаше, и тмою своего безвѣриа ополкъся, нощию безъдвернемъ ишедъ, татьством бѣгуется и со ученником своим и с черньцом Григорьемъ и злыя латынскыя ереси изнесоша.

Isidore, satiated with malevolent venom, and by no means could he dismiss it, neither in a small span of time nor tolerate, for he shamed his convictions with the maliciousness of the Latin heresy that had taken place. And he clothed himself in this impiety, proceeding day and night through the treeless. As a thief, having borne the evil Latin heresy, he fled with his student and with the Black Gregory.

However, for the year 1471, въ лѣто 6979 – e, *The Annalistic Code for the Year 1497* relates concerning the successors of Gregory on the Kievan metropolitan seat, but makes no reference to the events of 1458:[74] и архиепископа от них не ставливали себѣ, іако же бы нынѣ ставити хотите от Григорна, называщем митрополитом Русн, а оученик той Сидоров, сущен латынни, "and they [the Uniates] did not ordain one of their own archbishop, since they now desired to elevate Gregory, denominated the Metropolitan of Rus', a disciple of that Isidore who was a Latin." The annal further adds:[75] и архиепископа вели нам поставити своему митрополиту Григорни, "and they ordered us to elevate their own Metropolitan Gregory archbishop." On the other hand, *The Book of Degrees of Tsarist Relationships* states:[76]

Лышавъ же, іако злаго Исидора алѣйшій ученикъ и развратникъ, свышереченный Григоріе, пріиде отъ Рима въ Литву и нарицаетъ себе митрополитомъ Кіевскимъ и всеа Русін, поставленіе имѣя отъ Цареградскаго патріарха, отступника православныя вѣры Григорія же, единоименна себе, и начатъ поминати въ первыхъ папу Римьскаго и прочее свою ересь обна]и. . . . Запрещ летъ же преосвященный митрополитъ Іона, дабы никто же не пріобщалася ни во ученіи ни въ службѣ развратнику Григорію, ученику Исидорову.

Having been deprived, since the most renowned student of the evil and pernicious Isidore, the previously named Gregory, came from Rome to Lithuania and was nominated the Metropolitan of Kiev and of all Rus'. Having been ordained by the patriarch of Constantinople [Mammas], Gregory was an apostate to the Orthodox faith and himself univocal. He began to speak of the first Roman pope and henceforth revealed his heresy. . . . He was enjoined by the most reverend Metropolitan Iona, so that no one would associate either with the teaching or the service of the seducer Gregory, the student of Isidore.

According to *The Book of Degrees*, the grand prince of Moscow stipulated to his subjects:[77] Не возможьно, братіе, сице тому быти, еже вдатися намъ кралю и архіепископа пост–авити отъ его называющагося митрополита Григорія, латыніанина суща, иже есть ученикъ сущаго латыніанина, суемысленаго Исидора, "it is not possible, brothers, that this could be that we are given a king and by him an elevated archbishop, who is designated Metropolitan Gregory. Being a Latin, he is a student of the named extant Latinizer, the falsifier Isidore." Two decades later the vitriolic language condemning Isidore continued in the Muscovite annals. This scorn was transferred to his close companion and disciple, Gregory, and he bore the stigmata of his teacher. However, the role of Gregory in the 1460s is shrouded in questions. Did he remain a loyal Uniate, or had he reverted to Greek Orthodoxy and its teachings? This is a subject that will require further study.

At the beginning of August 1458, Pope Calixtus fell ill and died. Cardinal Isidore almost certainly assisted the cardinals in the funeral rites.[78] Ten days later the conclave for the election of the next pope followed and both Greek cardinals participated. Again politics prevailed and once more the Greek cardinals were involved in the issues. At this proceeding Bessarion (and presumably Isidore) supported the candidacy of Guillaume d'Estouteville of Rouen (c. 1412–1483), as is stated by Pius II:[79] *Aderant Vilhelmo certi ex cardinalibus: duo greci, Genuensis, Sancti Sixti, Avinionensis, Columnensis, Papiensis, et vicecancellarius,* "the firm supporters of Guillaume were the following cardinals:[80] the two Greeks, Genoa, San Sisto, Avignon, Colonna, Pavia, and the Vice Chancellor." They met under peculiar circumstances, which compelled Pius to complain bitterly and humorously, and dub them "the latrine contingent of cardinals":[81]

> *Convenere apud latrinas plerique cardinales, eoque loco quam abdito et secretiori pacti inter se sunt quonam modo Vilhelmum pontificem eligerent, scriptisque et iuramentis se astrinxerunt. Quibus ille confisus mox sacerdotia, magistratus et official promisit, ac provincias partitus est. Dignus locus, in quo talis pontifex eligeretur! Nam foedas coniurationes ubi convenientius ineas, quam in latrinis?*
> Many cardinals assembled in the latrines, as in this secret and private place they could elect Guillaume pope. They formed a party bound by written pledges and oaths. That man was convinced that he would soon be chosen and promised honors and positions and divided the provinces among them. That was a worthy place to elect such a pope! What would have been a more convenient place for filthy bargains than the latrines?

The expected machinations followed[82] and there were more questionable activities. The latrine contingent can be characterized as the non-Italian party, consisting of cardinals who were not from Italy. There was a reaction by the Italian cardinals. They were led by the cardinal of San Marco, who was motivated by patriotic fervor to reveal the conspiracy of the latrine contingent.[83] His efforts identified Aeneas Sylvius as the individual to become the likely Italian candidate for the papacy. After mass, the cardinals began the scrutiny and the appropriate vessel to receive the secret ballots was set up with three cardinals, including Isidore, in charge to ensure that no irregularities would occur:[84] *Itum est deinde ad rem divinam, qua peractas, scrutinium incoeperet. Calix autem aureus in ara positus est, et tres cardinals eum observare – Rutenus episcopus, Rhotomagensis presbyter et Columnensis diaconus – inspicientes ne qua fraus intercederet,* "then they turned to ritual. After its completion, the scrutiny began. A golden chalice was place on the altar and three cardinals were placed in charge to ensure the absence of fraud: The Ruthenian bishop [Isidore], the presbyter of Rouen, and the deacon Colonna." When it became evident that Aeneas Sylvius was about to prevail, Isidore and his ally, the cardinal of San Sisto, Juan de Torquemada, attempted to deny a quorum, thus putting off the decision by retreating to the latrines; but their attempt failed:[85] *Iam prope erat, ut Aeneam pontificem videre viderentur. Quod verentes aliqui e loco abiere, ut eius diei fortunam eluderent. Hi fuere Ruthenus et Sancti Sixti cardinales, necessitate causati corporis, sed cum nulli eos sequerentur, mox rediere,* "now it became evident that Aeneas would become pope. Fearing this event, some decided to cheat what fate had decided for that day and withdrew from chamber. These were: the Ruthenian [Isidore] and San Sisto [Juan de Torquemada], who excused themselves citing bodily needs. When no one else followed, they soon returned."

Eventually Aeneas Sylvius was elected and took the name of Pius II. Bessarion was the first to congratulate him and, as Pius II notes, Bessarion was the spokesman on behalf of the party that had earlier tried to elect Guillaume d'Estouteville. At the very end of the process, Bessarion tried to make amends for his latrine behavior and that of his allies, who were mostly comprised of non-Italian cardinals.[86] In the future Pius II did not hold a grudge against either Bessarion or Isidore. Bessarion was a noted humanist like the pope himself.[87] In the diplomatic sphere Pius extensively used Bessarion's efforts, while Isidore faithfully and actively supported the pope's plans for the formation of a crusade to the east, unlike most of the pope's cardinals.

A major project during Pius II's reign was the proposed crusade to the east, which was accelerated by the arrival of disconcerting news regarding the status of the Morea and its conquest by the Turks.[88] Early on, Pius had decided to make war upon the Turks after a debate he held with his cardinals, in which Isidore must have played an important role, perhaps through a translator. Pius notes that he faced opposition from his cardinals;[89] although he does not mention Isidore, Pius must have made effective use of Isidore and of his personal knowledge that he had accumulated during the siege of Constantinople. Once he had obtained, with difficulty, the grudging support of his cardinals, the pope publicly announced his plan:[90]

> *Ibi [sc. Curiae] pontifex, quod diu tectum fuerat, propositum suum publicavit. Quantas in Christianos Turchi clades intulissent, quibus modis evangelicam evertere legem molirentur, exposuit; nihil sibi acerbius esse quam intueri Christianae gentis ruinam; sacratissimae religionis se curam gerere; statuisse occurrere hostium conatibus; at cum id absque auxilio Christianorum regum perficere non posset, habere consilium aut in Utino aut in Mantua decrevisse, ut eorum ibi sententias audiret quorum opem imploraturus esset.*
>
> There [at the papal court] the pope publically announced his proposal that for such a long time had been dear to him. He elucidated the great destructions that the Turks had inflicted upon the Christians and how they were exerting themselves to overturn the laws of the Gospels. For himself nothing was more bitter than to behold the destruction of a Christian nation. His duty was to care for the most sacred religion. So he decided to oppose the plans of the enemy, but he could not accomplish his goal without the help of Christian kings and so he decided to convene a congress either in Udine or in Mantua to hear the opinions of those, whose material help he was about to beg.

Surely, we would not be in error if we detected themes and argumentation in the pope's oration, which had been propagated earlier by Isidore in his epistolography. As we have previously observed, on 5 September 1458 Isidore had been appointed archbishop of Corfu, and on 9 November 1458 Pius had granted to him the Church of Santa Agatha in Rome.[91] Were these grants and awards Isidore's rewards for assisting the pope with his plan and speech?

The first setback and disappointment to the crusade came early on. Pius wanted to hold his congress in Udine but the Venetians, who did not wish to irritate their allies, the Turks, objected to the congress in Udine and Pius was forced to move it to Mantua. He reserved harsh words for the Venetians:[92]

> *Veneti vero, qui per legatos multa Romae adversus Turchos pontifici promiserant, electionem Utini pro conventu Christianorum celebrando respuerunt, ut qui Turchorum, animos quibus foedere coniuncti essent, irritare vererentur; nam cum Constantinopolim Mahumetes occupasset, diffisi suis viribus Veneti et aliorum auxilia desperantes pacem cum Turchis . . . fecere. Sic Turchis obligata civitas more plebis, quae nihil generosum cum periculo audit, pontificem maximum in suis oppidis excipere recusavit, non tam Christianam amans religionerm, quam Turchos timens. Quod cum Pio nuntiatum esset, quamvis dolens tantam inesse potenti populo ignaviam, plenus tamen animo et in Salvatorte Christo spem habens, reiecta Utini mentione, epistolis ad reges missis per quas eos Mantuam evocavit.*

Yet the Venetians (who had made promises to the pope through their envoys at Rome) rejected the selection of Udine for the congress of the Christians, because they feared that they would irritate the Turks, with whom they had concluded a pact. After Mehmed occupied Constantinople, the Venetians no longer had confidence in their own strength and feared that they would receive no help from the kings of the Christians. They made peace with the Turks. . . . So their state was committed and in the manner of mobs who do not dare any noble act in the face of danger, Venice refused to receive the pope in its territories, for they feared the Turks more than they loved the Christian religion. When their attitude was announced to Pius, he grieved over such laziness that controlled the behavior of a powerful nation. Nevertheless, placing his hopes and his soul in Christ the Savior, he gave up the selection of Udine and had letters sent to the kings, in which he summoned them to Mantua.

The pope reached Mantua after a long journey from the 20th of January[93] or the 26th[94] to the 27th of May,[95] which took him through many Italian cities.[96] It was a harsh winter and numerous cardinals, with his permission, were left behind in Rome. They were either too weak or too ill to accompany him in his retinue.[97] Perhaps some had feigned illness, as their hearts were not fully committed to launching a crusade. Eventually, they found their way to Mantua and Isidore was among them.[98] The majority of the cardinals, and numerous secular powers, remained uncommitted to the pope's crusade. Nevertheless, it was evident that something had to be done, for the Ottoman armies of Mehmed II had begun the conquest of the Morea, which was being governed ineptly by the surviving brothers, Thomas and Demetrios, of the last emperor of Constantinople.[99] Thomas was active in ringing the alarm bell, but he was also careful not to ask for what was needed, since he feared that the Italians would be unwilling to commit a large expeditionary force to come to his aid. Thus his ambassadors requested a few hundred warriors, who, they claimed, would be a sufficient force to rout the invading Turks.[100] Bessarion was in agreement,[101] but the pope was reserved and had his doubts about the outcome of such a limited expedition. Once more, on this occasion, Pius II demonstrates that he was aware of the antiquity of the Morea and of its importance in ancient literature.[102]

It is evident from our sources that the vast majority of the cardinals took advantage of the congress to enjoy themselves in every way possible except in the organization of Pius's crusade. Their attitude becomes clear in Mantua's archival sources, which recorded the materials that the cardinals imported for their comfort and enjoyment. The major item of the cardinals' list consisted of wine.[103] By contrast, Isidore imported from Verona and Brescia large quantities of weapons: catapults, spingards, bombards, and axes, and even personally went to Ancona to assemble a small fleet. In his letter from Ancona to Marquis Ludovico Gonzaga of Mantua (the 31st of May 1460) Isidore states that he was ready and willing to take his ship to the Morea, but that he was prevented from doing so because of the actions of Genoese and Catalan pirates in the Adriatic.[104]

In these activities Isidore may have been inspired by the actions of Bianca, the duchess of Milan, who had personally paid for the expenses of 100 of the 300 mercenaries[105] dispatched to the Morea to assist Thomas Palaiologos in his ineffectual resistance against the Turks. The pope praised her zeal but did not think much of the expedition (yet he did not oppose the plan, for it was dear to Bessarion),[106] because it included only a small company. He was not certain that it could achieve much, as it did not, and in fact was disbanded soon after its arrival in the Morea:[107]

Cuncti Mantuam ad pontificis pedes se contulere, egregie armata robusta iuventus. Ianonus Cremonensis his praefuit, quid Blanca delegit, pedestrium copiarum non ignotus doctor; aliis Dotha Senensis, propter civilis discordias patria extorris ... apud Anconam ingressi mare felici vento in Peloponnesum navigare, ubi comiter a Graecis excepti Patracensem urbem primo congres expugnavere. Verum dum alia quaedam summa contentione oppugnant oppida, seu virtutis aemulatione seu praedae cupiditate inter se dissidentes incepta reliquere, dispersique milites in diversa cum dedecore abierunt. Infaustum rebus gerendis omen!

All the young men came to Mantua to kneel before the pope. They were strong and beautifully armed. Giannone of Cremona, a warlord with experience commanding infantry, led Bianca's contribution; the rest were commanded by Dotha of Siena, an exile from his homeland, through civil strife ... at Ancona they embarked and reached the Morea with a favorable wind. The Greeks politely received them[108] and in one assault they took Patras. Next, either because they vied with each other in courage, or because they conceived greed for booty, they quarreled among themselves and scattered widely in shame. Not a good omen for what had to be done!

In Mantua Isidore, Pius II, and Bessarion must have met in person their old acquaintance Francesco Filelfo, who had been included in the retinue of the Milanese contingent, in the capacity of an orator and an ambassador, *ex officio*, of Francesco Sforza.[109] Filelfo was probably attempting to ameliorate his relations with Isidore, after the incident that involved his lost manuscript of Plutarch. Thus it must have been at this time that Filelfo put together a poem, which he dedicated to Isidore. The poem reads as follows:[110]

Ἰσιδώρῳ τῷ τε καρδιναλίῳ καὶ
Κωνσταντινουπόλεως πατριάρχῃ

To Cardinal Isidore and Patriarch of Constantinople

Μοῦσα, δὴν ὀκνεῖς λίαν Ἰσιδώρῳ

πατρὶ πανθείῳ γλυκεροῖς ἀείδειν
σοῦ διὰ γλώττης μέλεσιν, θεάων
Πιερίων πρώτη.

Muse,[111] chief among the Pierian goddesses,[112]
you have long delayed to sing sweet tunes sweet tunes of yours,
for the all-holy Father Isidore.

οὗτος ἐν πρώτοις ἅγιος πεφύκει

καὶ σοφὸς πρῶτος νοερᾷ μαθήσει.

οὗτος ἐν πάσαις ἀρεταῖς ὡς ἄστρον
ἔξοχα λάμπει.

Since birth he has been exceptionally saintly
and is a foremost scholar in intellectual pursuits
in all virtues he shines like a brilliant star.

Τοῦτον ὑψίστου θρόνος εὐσεβοῦντα

ναοῦ ἐν τόσαις ταραχαῖς κακούργων

κἀσεβῶν ἀνδρῶν μόνον αὐτὸς ἕξει
ἀρχιερῆα.

In so many upheavals caused by lawless
and impious men,[113] only this pious,
high priest will be enthroned in the highest church.[114]

Ἑλλάς, ἐκ τούτου θεός ὦ μεγίστη,

ἵλεως σαυτῇ πατρὸς ὡς ταχίστως
ἔσσεται. θάρσει. δολεροῖς πεσεῖται
Τοῦρκος ἐν ὅπλοις.

Greatest Greece: through this father
God will show mercy to you in the nearest future; have courage;
the Turk will fall in a treacherous war.

Οὗτος ὦ Θωμᾶ βασιλεῦ, ἀμύντωρ

πράγμασι τοῖς σοῖς πολὺ φῶς
παρέξει.
ἔστι γὰρ θεία κατὰ πᾶν φρονήσει
φαίδιμος ἔργον.

Emperor Thomas:[115] God as your defender
will supply abundant light for you

in every labor one can be glorious through Divine Providence.

Ὦ Νέας Ῥώμης κλέος ἠδὲ σῶτερ,	Glory and Savior of New Rome![116]
ὦ τῆς ἀρχαίας φάος, ἠδὲ μούνη ἐλπὶς ἀνθρώποις ἰταλοῖς. ὦ πάσης Δέσποτα γαίης	Light of Old Rome and sole hope of the Italians! Lord of all land!
σοὶ θεός, ὦ Θωμᾶ, πάνυ ἐξ ὀλύμπου δεξιὸς λάμπει. ὅτι θεῖος ἤδη σεῖο τὰς πράξεις ἱερεὺς ἀρίστοις δείκνυσι πᾶσιν.	Thomas: The god from Olympus favorably shines on you;[117] already the divine priest shows your deeds To all best men.
Εὐσεβὴς γὰρ παῖς Μανουὴλ ἐκείνου, πάντας ὃς ζῶντας βασιλεῖς ἐνίκα τῷ νόου φέγγει ἀρετῆς τε κάλλει ἄξιος ἦσθα.	You are the pious son of the famed Manuel,[118] the victor over all living kings in brightness of mind and beauty of virtue. You are his worthy son.
Μοῦνον ἀνθρώπων σε λέγει ἁπάντων οὗτος, ὃν σύμπας βασιλῆα κόσμος προσλαβὼν Χριστῷ κατὰ τῶν μαχούντων κοίρανον ἄξει.	This entire assembly[119] addresses you as appropriate king among men and will accept you as its leading lord to fight, in Christ, against the enemy.
Ταῦτα δὴ θείῳ πατρὶ Ἰσιδώρῳ εἰπέ, τὸν πῖλον κεφαλῇ φοροῦντι, ὦ θεά, πυρρόν λέγε πᾶν ταχίστη τῷ πατριάρχῃ.	Goddess:[120] say these words to the holy Father Isidore, who wears the red hat:[121] as soon as possible say Everything to the patriarch.
Πρὸς δὲ τούτοις παρ' ἐμεῖο λέξον ὅσσα συντείνεις πρὸς ἐμὰς κελεύσεις. εἶτα μὴ ὄκνει πάλιν εἰς τὸν οἶκον ὤκιον ἥξειν.	In addition, also state for my part my suggestions your recommendations. Finally, ensure that he will return to his home as soon as possible.

This is indeed a strange poem and one wonders whether its subject is Isidore or Thomas, as Filelfo seems to be addressing Thomas and only accords Isidore a place that the epic poets of antiquity would assign to a seer. The position of Isidore in relation to Thomas is analogous to the seer Kalkhas in relation to Agamemnon in the *Iliad*. The humanist would have been aware of such comparisons.

Is it possible that Filelfo was aware of some family ties between the cardinal and the despot of the Morea? Was Isidore a member of the imperial family? Or is Filelfo alluding in this poem to the efforts of Isidore to buy armament to be sent to Greece on the ships that he was outfitting at Ancona?

By the fall of 1460 Thomas Palaiologos realized that the fall of the Morea was irrevocable and he left his despotate for Italy, with a short stop at Corfu. He deposited his family in the relative safety of Corfu and then arrived in Ancona on 16 November 1460.[122] He had, no doubt, planned for a permanent stay in Italy, receiving a pension from the pope, for whom he brought a gift: the reputed head of Saint Andrew from Patras.[123] Sphrantzes evidently disapproved of the despot's actions, for he furnishes dry comments on this adventure:[124]

> ὁ δὲ δεσπότης Θωμᾶς φθάσας εἰς τὸν Ἀγκῶνα καὶ ἀπ' ἐκεῖ εἰς τὴν Ῥώμην οὐδὲν ἄλλο κατώρθωσεν, εἰ μὴ ὅτι δέδωκε τῷ πάπα Πίῳ τὴν τοῦ ἁγίου ἀποστόλου καὶ πρωτοκλήτου Ἀνδρέου κάραν κἀκεῖνος πρὸς αὐτὸν τὸ μόλις νὰ ζῇ μὲ τοὺς αὐτοῦ αὐτὴν καὶ μόνην τὴν ἀναγκαίαν τροφήν.
>
> Lord Thomas, the despot, reached Ancona and went to Rome, but was unable to accomplish anything with Pope Pius, but to present him with the head of Saint Andrew, the first of the disciples. The pope granted him a pension that was barely sufficient for his sustenance and that of his companions.[125]

Once in Rome, with the papal *curia* in session, Thomas must have met with Cardinal Isidore, although we have no information on such a possible meeting. We may even speculate that Isidore may have encouraged the despot to surrender his relic to the pope.[126] In addition to the pension, Thomas was also honored with the award of the class *rosa aurea* (golden rose) by the pope on 15 March 1461.[127]

Finally, Isidore's active life of incessant traveling and war took its toll. In 1461 he suffered an "apoplexy," which nowadays is designated a stroke. At least this is the information we receive from a text that may have been written either by Alessio, the bishop of Chiusi, or by Pope Pius II.[128] The text addresses the formal reception of the head of Saint Andrew, an occasion that provided the opportunity for the last public appearance of Isidore. Alessio states that it was in the previous year that Isidore suffered the stroke: *anno qui praecesserat proximus percusserat apoplexis Isidorum episcopum Sabinensem, sanctae Romanae ecclesiae Cardinalem, natione Graeco ex Peloponneso, qui olim Rosanis, boreali genti, praefuerat,* "in the course of the last year Isidore suffered apoplexy; he was the bishop of the Sabines and a cardinal of the Holy Roman Church. By origin he was a Greek from the Peloponnese and long ago he had been in charge of the Rus', a northern nation." Alessio adds some additional observations on the consequences of the stroke: *cui [Isidoro] et si sermonem ademit, intellectum tamen non abstulit,* "even if it took away his power of speech, his mind had not been affected." His strength must have failed him and his mobility must have also suffered, for Alessio adds that he was confined to bed at his home, *manebat hic domi languens.*[129]

The ceremony and the celebrations for the *translatio* of the relic took two days and were elaborate.[130] The festivities were accompanied by speeches pronounced by Bessarion and Pius II.[131] What is of interest here is that the procession could be seen or was heard by Isidore as it passed through his neighborhood on the Via Lata/Flaminia.[132] Alessio devotes one paragraph to the reaction of the stricken Isidore:[133]

> *cui et si sermonem ademit, intellectum tamen non abstulit. Manebat hic domi languens, qui ubi transeuntem ante suas aedes sacrum verticem conspicatus est, nullo pacto retineri potuit, quin sequeretur sanctas reliquias. Venit igitur suis pedibus in basilicam beati Petri, et ingressus ferreas craticulas quae sancta sanctorum cingunt et maius altare custodiunt accedens. Pontificem signis ac nutibus indicavit se cupere divinum Apostoli verticem osculari. Impetrata venia, flexis genibus cum multis singultibus et lacrimis et maxima reverentia desiderio suo fecit satis. Et tanquam voti copos exultavit, domumque laetus redijt; nam quasi patriae suae conditorem vidisset; ita sibi ipsi complacuit, et longe iocundior visus et venerandus senex abire.*

The stroke took away his power of speech, but his mind was not affected. He remained at home, withering away. But when he saw the holy head passing by in front of his house, there was no way that he could be stopped from following the sacred relic. On foot he took himself to the basilica of Saint Peter. He entered and approached the iron fence that surrounds the holiest area and the major altar. By signs and gestures he indicated to the pontiff that he wished to kiss the head of the divine Apostle. Permission was granted and he did so with the greatest reverence, amidst sighs and tears. Once he had achieved his wish, he was delighted and returned in joy to his home. It was as if he had seen the founder of his own homeland. So pleased was the venerable elderly man that for a long time after his departure he seemed more content than usual.

We do not have additional information on the last days of Isidore. The cardinal probably took care to prepare his final will and testament. We infer that there had been a testament, for Bessarion inherited some of Isidore's possessions, as he states in his own testament.[134] Beyond that, the only remaining record is the formal note of death. He passed away on Wednesday, 27 April 1463:[135] *Obitus d. Cardinalis Ruteni: Anno a nativitate Domini MCCCCLXIII, die vero Mercurii XXVII mensis Aprilis, reverendissimus Christo pater dominus Cardinalis Rutenus appellatus Ysidorus Rome diem suum clausit extremum. Eius anima in pace requiescat,* "the passing of the Lord cardinal of Russia and most reverend father called Isidore, who spent his last day in Rome: Wednesday, the 27th of April, the 1463rd year since the nativity of our Lord. May his soul rest in peace."

Cardinal Isidore was buried with a great deal of pomp, ceremony, and mourning in the crypts of Saint Peter's. The *Notitia, Purpura docta, Monachii 1714,* is the only source that we are aware of to note the place of burial of Carinal Isidore. It records:[136] *Tandem anno 1463, die 27 Aprilis naturae debitum Romae exsolvit, magno omiunm luctu post obitum conditus ad Sanctum Petrum in Vaticano,* "finally, he paid his debt to nature in Rome on the 27th of April, in the year 1463, and was buried with universal mourning in Saint Peter's in the Vatican."

There remain serious gaps in our knowledge about Isidore's activities in Italy during his last years. We sadly lack personal details of his daily activities and of his ecclesiastical duties. In addition, we know very little about the management of his household and the state of his personal finances. Who were the members of his household staff? Did he have assistance in his copying activities? Was there a minor *scriptorium* associated with him? Did he participate in Bessarion's famous intellectual gatherings attended by Italian humanists on a regular basis, in which antiquarian themes were discussed and the Greek language, in its ancient Attic form (with modern Greek pronunciation, as Erasmus's restored pronunciation of ancient Greek was still off in the future) was used? Who assisted Isidore in translating his Greek into Italian/Latin, or both, in written compositions and in oral communications? Of greater concern are the serious gaps that we encounter in his correspondence. Numerous letters of his may still be buried in various archives and await discovery. Others may be irrevocably lost. Private correspondence in the *quattrocento* suffered and numerous private epistles were lost, as can be easily documented. Filelfo in his later years had lost many of his own letters and desperately tried to collect them from various sources, from his friends, or even attempted to recreate them, in his desire to publish his own epistolography.[137] What, then, was the fate of the majority of Isidore's letters?

Notes

1 This letter is to be found in *TIePN*, pp. 13–15, with Italian translation. Once more, Isidore must have availed himself of a translator, as this letter survives in Latin; the Greek original, if it existed instead of Isidore dictating in Greek to a competent bilingual in Greek and Latin translator, is lost. The cardinal's concerns are expressed at the very beginning of this epistle and he states his suspicion that his previous letters failed to reach their destination:

> Saepe necnon [*TIePN*: nencnon, a misprint] ad Dominationem vestram reverendissimam [Capranica, even though in the title Firmano is erroneously mentioned]: Copia litterae missae per dominum cardinalem Richerum <sc. Ruthenum> ad dominum cardinalem Firmanum scripsi et nullam hucusque responsionem accepi, et nescio si litterae meae ad Dominationem vestram reverendissimam pervenerunt, sive eius responsivae ad me (non) accesserunt, sive forte exceptis meis (non) respondissetis; quam ob rem et nunc iterum scribo rem lacrimarum calamitatumque [*TIePN*: calamitarumque, surely in error] plenam, quemadmodum Constantinopolis, quae antea felicissima excellentissimaque urbs fuerat, nunc vero infelicissima <et> miserrima a Turcis capta – proh dolor! – fuit.

Isidore probably means that the earlier letter he sent was Letter VI (without a date, but probably written on the 6th of July) to Cardinal Domenico Capranica. This correspondence records generalities and cites the impact of the fall in the Aegean world; cf. *supra*, ch. 6, nn. 21 and 22.

2 At the conclusion of his account, Henry records the following date: *Raptim, ex Urbe Romana, XI^a Septembris, per magistrum Henricum de Zomern*. On this letter, cf. *supra*, ch. 5, n. 95; cf. Philippides, *Mehmed the Conqueror*, p. 130.

3 *Ibid.*, p. 128: *qui infra octo dies Romae exspectatur*.

4 Isidore probably did not wish to lose any time, as Pope Nicholas V had convened a congress in Rome to discuss measures against the Turkish threat. The congress lasted from November 1453 to March 1454. If indeed participation in the congress fueled Isidore's haste, he eventually must have been extremely disappointed, for the congress failed to produce positive results. Cf. *PaL* 2: 156 (with previous scholarship cited in n. 57). Given his reports in his correspondence from Crete, Isidore was probably burning with desire to make his testimony to the congress; at least that is how we understand the letter of Benvoglienti, who begins Isidore's report with the following statement (*CC* 2: 109): *Ò visitato la sua Rev.ma S[ignoria] et da quela ò molto inteso de le cose di là. Et quale dela grandissima potentiate inmanissima crudeltà de Turcho contra de christiani*. A list follows, which is similar, if not identical, to the cardinal's propaganda themes that we have encountered in his epistolography from Crete; cf. *supra* ch. 6.

5 Selections from this letter of the 2nd of November 1453 (*in Vinegia, adì 22 de novembre 1453*) in *CC* 2: 108–111; cf., e.g., *CC* 2: 109: *Qua novissamente è venuto el Rev.mo Cardinale di Rossia* [Isidore], *grecho scampato dela fortuna di Costantinopoli.... E presto si dee partire per esser a Roma al papa*. L. Pastor, *The History of the Popes from the Close of the Middle Ages* 2 (London, 1949), p. 287, states that Isidore came in the company of envoys from Rhodes and Cyprus and with Franciscans from Bologna who had been ransomed from Constantinople. Pastor cites a statement of Niccola della Tuccia (cf. *TIePN*, p. 98: *Di novembre gionse in Roma l'imbasciatore del re di Cipri... Un'altra imbasciata gionse... per parte del gran mastro di Rodi*), but della Tuccia has presented nothing about Isidore. Pastor is also mistaken when he states (p. 288) that Isidore made his "escape, first at the Peloponnesus, and thence to Venice." Unless Isidore's ship from Crete made a stop in the Morea during the trip from Crete to Venice, Isidore was not in the Morea at this time. Without documentation, *PaL* 2: 147, also states that Isidore reached the Morea after his Cretan stay.

6 That is stated in Benvoglienti's report of November 1453; cf. *CC* 2: 109:

> *Qua novissamente è venuto el Rev.mo Cardinale di Rossia* [Isidore], *grecho scampato dela fortuna di Costantinopoli, del quale pu[bli]camente si disse essere morto. È stato da questa I[llustre] S[ignoria] gratamente ricevuto et bene veduto, et la venuta sua l'è stata grata et accepta.*

7 Other letters may still exist, unidentified and undetected, in state archives. Thus there exists a letter of the 31st of May 1460 that Isidore addressed to Marquis L. Gonzaga, in the *Archivio di Stato, Mantua, Archivio Gonzaga, b. 840*, c. 420^r, which remains in manuscript form and has neither been edited nor published. Cf. D. S. Chambers, *Popes, Cardinals and War: The Military Church in Renaissance and Early Modern Europe* (London and New York, 2006), p. 200 n. 76.

8 As late as January–February 1454, Filelfo had not received any news about his enslaved relatives, as he mentions in his letter to the physician Pierre Tomasi; cf. Legrand, p. 66; and *supra*, ch. 5, n. 161. In addition, cf. Filelfo's letter of 1465 to Leodisio Cribelli, in which he recalls that he even wrote a letter and ode to Mehmed II (Legrand, p. 66) in his efforts to redeem his relatives:

> *Nec illud vitio dandum et quod ad Mahometum, tyrannum amyramque* [emir] *Turcorum, et epistolam olim et carmen dederim, et id quidem non inscio sapientissimo et innocentissimo principe meo Francesco Sphortia, qui, cum vellet aliquid explorare de apparatus insidiisque Turcorum in christianos, audiretque honestissimam feminam, socrum meam, Manfredinam, uxorem illius splendissimi Chrysolorae, et ipsam et duas filias ex praeda et direptione Constantinopolitana captivas servire apud illam barbariam, permisit ut, illorum redimendarum obtentu, duo quidam iuvenes callidi et ad rem strenui, nomine meo et cum meis item letteris, proficiscentur ad Mahometum.*

His seventy-two-line ode in Greek to Mehmed survives (cf. *ibid.*, p. 211; also published, with Italian translation, in *TIePN*, pp. 266–269). In the hopes of redeeming his relatives,

Filelfo also composed a fawning letter to Mehmed II on the 14th of March 1454; for the Greek text, cf. *ibid.*, no. 32 (pp. 63, 64, with valuable commentary, pp. 64–68).
9 Edited and published, with Italian translation, in an *editio princeps* in *CC* 2: 106–111.
10 This Genoese colony was a separate entity and Genoa had been granted this possession a long time ago by Emperor Michael VIII Palaiologos in the treaty of Nymphaion (1261). Genoese merchants had been extended the privilege of establishing themselves in a suburb of Constantinople and enjoyed the right of trading, free of duty, throughout the ports of the Greek empire.
11 Of course, other groups were also accused and individuals of all cases and from numerous ethnic groups were also suspected of being traitors. For exhaustive analysis, cf. Philippides: "Rumors of Treason."
12 On Lomellino, cf. E. Daleggio d'Alessio, "Lists des potestats de la colonie génoise de Péra (Galata), des prieurs et sous-prieurs de la Magnifica Communità," *REB* 27 (1969): pp. 151–157; for the complaint, cf. *CC* 1: 41; and G. Olgiati, "Angelo Giovanni Lomellino: Attività politica e mercantile e dell'ultimo podestà de Pera," *Storia dei Genovesi* 9 (1989): pp. 129–161. In addition, cf. *SF*, pp. 13, 14.
13 The responsibilities, dangers, and challenges took an emotional toll on Lomellino, as it is evident from the tone of his official report to Genoa; for his report, cf. S. de Sacy, ed., "Pièces diplomatiques tirée des Archives République de Gênnes," *Notices et extraits des manuscrits de la Bibliothéque du Roi* 11 (1827): pp. 74–79; Belgrano, no. 149, pp. 229–233; N. Iorga, ed., "Notes et extraits pour servir à l'histoire des croisades au XVe siècle," *Revue de l'Orient latin* 8 (1900/1901): pp. 105–108; English translation: Melville-Jones, pp. 131–135; and improved text with Italian translation in *CC* 1: 42–51.
14 The *aman-name* has come down to us in several versions: in Greek (which must have been the closest to the original Ottoman document, since Greek was the official diplomatic language of the Porte), and in Italian, which is a translation of the Greek rendition. Both Greek and Italian texts were published by S.P. Lampros, "Ἡ Ἑλληνικὴ ὡς Ἐπίσημος Γλῶσσα τῶν Σουλτάνων," *NH* 5 (1908): pp. 40–79, esp. 66–72. The Greek text was published once more (based on ms. 2817 of the Eggerton Collection in the British Museum): E. Dallegio d'Alesio, "Le text grec du traité conclu par les génois de Galata avec Mehmet II le Ier Juin 1453," *Hellenika* 11 (1939): pp. 115–124; and has been translated into English by Melville-Jones, Appendix, pp. 136, 137. The text of Languschi-Dolfin also includes the Italian version, pp. 34–36 (fol. 322) under the title: *come el gran Turco fece un priuilegio a Genoesi per hauerli data Pera*. The authenticity of the Greek version of the *aman-name* was challenged in the nineteenth century by Paspates, Πολιορκία καὶ Ἅλωσις τῆς Κωνσταντινουπόλεως, but in 1908 Lampros argued in favor of its authenticity. The publication of the document in the British Museum has finally dispelled any doubts as to the authenticity of the *aman-name* and further demonstrates the authenticity of Languschi-Dolfin's text. For a new edition of the Greek and Italian texts, cf. Philippides, *Mehmed the Conqueror*, Appendix 3, pp. 347–360.
15 Cf., e.g., Doukas 38.5:

> οἱ γὰρ τοῦ Γαλατᾶ [Pera] ἐνενόουν, ὡς καθὰ καὶ ἐν ἑτέροις χρόνοις, ἡ Πόλις καταπολεμηθεῖσα παρὰ τῶν γονέων αὐτοῦ [of Mehmed II, that is of Bayezid I Yıldırım and Murad II] οὐδὲν ὠνήσαντο ἀπελθόντες ἄπρακτοι, οἱ δὲ τοῦ Γαλατᾶ [Pera] σὺν ἐκείνοις φιλίαν δεικνύντες, τοὺς μὲν Πολίτας ἐδίδοσαν τὴν παρ' αὐτοῖς ἐξερχομένην βοήθειαν, οὕτω θαρροῦντες γενέσθαι καὶ ἐν τῷ καιρῷ τούτου, ὡς πλάνον μὲν τὴν φιλίαν ὑπώπτευον, τῇ δὲ Πόλει τὰ εἰκότα συνεμάχοντο κρυφίως.

In 38.16 Doukas becomes more explicit:

> ὁ δὲ Ἰουστινιανὸς Ἰωάννης γενναίως ἐμάχετο σὺν πᾶσι τοῖς ὑπ' αὐτὸν καὶ τοῖς τοῦ παλατίου, ἔχοντες ἐκ τοῦ Γαλατᾶ [Pera] μέρος οὐκ ὀλίγον ἀνδρῶν ἐνόπλων. καὶ γὰρ ἦσαν αὐτοὶ δεικνύντες ἀγάπην καὶ ἐξερχόμενοι διῆγον ἐν τῷ κάμπῳ τοῦ φωσάτου ἀφόβως καὶ τὰ ζητούμενα χρειώδη ἐδίδοσαν ἀφθόνως τῷ τυράννῳ

[sultan] καὶ ἔλαιον διὰ τὰς σκευὰς καὶ ἄλλο, εἴ τι αἰτοῦντες οἱ Τοῦρκοι ἐφαίνοντο. τοῖς δὲ Ῥωμαίοις [Greeks], κρύφα καὶ διὰ τῆς νυκτὸς διαβαίνοντες, τὴν ἡμέραν πᾶσαν συμμαχοῦντες ἦσαν. τῇ δὲ ἐπιούσῃ νυκτὶ ἐναλλαττόμενοι, ἄλλοι ἐν τῇ Πόλει καὶ αὐτοὶ ἐν τοῖς οἴκοις καὶ τῷ φωσάτῳ διέτριβον διὰ τὸ λανθάνειν τοὺς Τούρκους.

16 Such is statement in Isidore's letter to Bessarion (for the context, cf. *supra*, ch. 5, sec. 3, letter 1, par. 12 for Latin text and English translation) of the 6th of July 1453: *Erat autem imperatore illo ductor quidam nomine Iohannes Iustinianus, quem multi incusant primam fuisse causam tantae captivitatis et excidii: sed omitamus.* Is it possible that Isidore also felt somewhat responsible if indeed, as we have suggested (*supra*, ch. 4, text with nn. 48 and 49) he was instrumental in recruiting Giustiniani for the defense of Constantinople? Apart from the Venetians, who took great delight in charging the Genoese with cowardice and misconduct (cf., e.g., Barbaro 29 [*CC* 1: 19]: *i Zenovexi de Pera, nemigi de la fede cristiana*), accusations in Western Europe persisted. A statement of Leonardo, an eyewitness and a Genoese, may have aided the augmentation of this "bad press"; cf. *PG* 159: col. 933 [*CC* 1: 134, 135]:

> *Agebant interea Galatae, sive Perenses, quamquam prudentius, ne in Propontide castrum struxisset Theucrus, sollicitam providendi curam nunc armorum nunc militum, clanculo tamen, ne hosti, qui pacem cum eis simulabat, innotuisset. . . . Sic simulata illa pax urbi at tempus profuit. . . . O Genuenses iam quammodo cicurati! Sileo, ne de meis loquar, quos externi cum veritate diiucant.*

While Leonardo states that the Genoese failed to declare publicly war on the Turks, he also hastens to add they also contributed to the defense. It is easy to see how his statement may have subsequently been misconstrued. The difficult position of the Perenses is also noted by Doukas 38.5, who also expresses his own views on this matter; cf. his text quoted *supra*, n. 15.

17 *Supra*, n. 16.
18 Cf. Khalkokondyles, with an English translation, in the Kaldellis edition, Book 8.24 (pp. 198, 199): ἑάλω καὶ Ἰσίδωρος καρδινάλιος Σαβίνων, . . . εἰ μὲν αὐτὸν ἔγνω βασιλεὺς [sultan], . . . οὐκ ἀνίει διαφυγεῖν. νῦν δὲ οἰόμενος αὐτὸν τεθνάναι οὐκ ἐποιεῖτο λόγον οὐδένα. In addition, cf. *supra*, ch. 5, text with n. 101; and the *Notitia* on Isidore (*Purpura Docta, Monachi 1714*, 3, p. 105, as quoted in *PG* 159: col. 952), which translates this passage into Latin as follows: *Si rex Turcarum virum hunc novisset, videlicet quod cardinalis esset, certe eum interfecisset; cum eum inter caeteros occisum putaret, nullam ejus rationem habebat.* The same document (*PG* 159: cols. 951, 952) states that the conquerors searched for Isidore, but the latter had managed to escape because he had shaved his chin and was dressed in the western manner, in the purple robes of a cardinal, which he later discarded by dressing a corpse. It was then assumed that the corpse was that of Isidore:

> *siquidem ab insenquentibus victoribus captus [sc. Isidorus], et quis esset ob rasum mentum vestemque peregrinam non agnitus, nihilominus in servitutem abductus est. Interea cadaver, quod purpuratum Ecclesiae senatorem ex injecta Isidori veste mentiebatur, qui desideratorum numerum inibant, ac corpora passim jacentis explorabant, ingenti elati gaudio repererunt, et ejusdem praecisum caput roseo contectum pileo hastae infigunt; ac clamante praecone, "illud esse caput cardinalis Rutheni," per captae civitatis compita viasque multa cum irrisione circumferunt.*

The same story is repeated in a brief sentence by Pius II, who undoubtedly had also spoken with Isidore. Cf. *Pii Secundi Pontificis Maximi De Captione Urbis Constantinopolis Tractatulus* [text and English translation in Philippides, *Mehmed the Conqueror*, pp. 94–119, esp. 116, 117]: *Isidorus cardinalis in eo tumultu captus, cum veste mutata non fuisset cognitus.* The passage from the *Commentariorum* is repeated by Stefano Magno, "Extraits des Annales de Magno relatifs à la prise de Constantinople par les Turcs," *NE* 3: 295–301): *Disse Pio papa Isidoro cardinale, mutado lo habito, non conosciuto, fù preso con delli altri presoni.* It appears that this account may have originated with Isidore. However, we should note that in his early propaganda and initial letters from Crete to Bessarion and Nicholas V, Isidore never mentioned this tale. Could it be that he elaborated his experiences, with the passage of time, so that he eventually produced a more engaging story of his escape?

19 On the duke of Burgundy, cf. *supra*, ch. 6, n. 158. For depictions of this event, cf. Concasty, planche II, facing p. 101; and J. Bradbury, *The Medieval Siege* (Woodbridge, 1992), p. 221. A color reproduction of the same miniature, of inferior quality, can be found in H.W. Koch, *Medieval Warfare* (London, 1978), p. 214. The best color reproduction appears in P. Sherrard, *Byzantium*, Great Ages of Man, A History of the World's Cultures (New York, 1966), p. 160. A miniature, also depicting the siege, is reproduced in black and white in Concasty, planche I, facing p. 100.

20 *CC* 1: 108.

21 This much is stated by Pius II in his *Commentariorum/Memoirs*; cf. M. Meserve and M. Simonetta, eds. *Pius II Commentaries*, The I Tatti Renaissance Library 12, 1 (Cambridge, MA and London 2003): I.28.2 (pp. 136–138, with English translation):

> *nec Iohannes Capistranus defuit assiduis praedicationibus populum contra Turchos ad arma excitans . . . ecce mors Nicolai Quinti renuntiatur pontificis maximi, quae telam longo iam tempore ordiri coeptam uno momento interrupit, vanasque hominum cogitationes ostendit et inanes auras. . . . Non placuit divinae pietati per id tempus excidi Turchorum imperium.*

22 *Ibid.*, I.28.3 (pp. 138, 139, with English translation): *arteficis doloribus universum corpus invadentibus extinguitur, et cum eo ingentia in Turchos coepta corruerunt.*

23 *Ibid.*, I.28.3 (pp. 138–142, with English translation): *Sederat Nicolaus in Beati Petri solio annos circiter octo . . . doctrina et animi excellens. . . . Celebravit annum Iubilaeum. . . . Urbis official magnifice instauravit . . . cardinals creavit septem . . . clarus felixque fuit, verum Constantinopolitana clade infelix, quae in suum incidens pontificatum nomini eius foedam inussit notham.*

24 Other than the letter from Crete, there is no other surviving correspondence that can document the close friendship between the two cardinals. Their close ties, nevertheless, can be inferred from the will and testament of Bessarion, which was composed after the death of Isidore and is entitled: *Dispositio testamentaria qua card. Bessarion varia sua bona sacello S. Eugeniae in basilica XII Apostolorum donat, ac in eo monumentum sibi poni praecipit, PG* 161: pp. lxxvii–lxxxi, and was dated Friday, the 17th of February 1464 (*PG* 161: p. lxxvii: *in nomine Domini. Amen. Anno a nativitate ejusdem millesimo quadrigentesimo sexagesimo quarto, indict. XII, die vero Veneris 17 mensis Februari, pontificatus Summi in Christo Patris et domini nostri D. Pii, divina providentia papae II anno sexto*). In his will, Bessarion directs the Franciscan monks of the Church of the Twelve Apostles in Rome (*PG* 161: p. lxxvii: *religiosos viros fratres et conventum ordinis S. Francisci in eadem ecclesia SS. Apostolorum*), to commemorate in their daily services the name of Isidore, among others; cf. *PG* 161: p. lxxviii: *pro mortuis post mortem meum, Isidori et Dorothei episcoporum; item Theodori et Theodorae, et Michaelis, ac aliorum quos in intentione mea habeo.* Again the will of Bessarion also cites Isidore a number of times, as Isidore had apparently left an inheritance to Bessarion: cf. *PG* 161: pp. lxxviii–lxxx:

> *Item dono . . . et quoddam aliud nigrum [sc. pavonatzium] de damascino, emptum ab haereditate R<everendissim>i Do<min>i cardinalis Rutheni bonae mem<oriae> . . . item unum missale magnum, emptum ab haereditatem D<omini> cardinalis Rutheni praedicti . . . ac breviarium magnum, emptum ab haereditate R<everendissim>i Do<min>i cardinalis Rutheni piae mem<oriae>.*

25 That Bessarion was the favored candidate is emphasized by Pius II in his *Memoirs* I.28 (pp. 140–142):

> *Scrutinioque semel atque iterum in cassum peracto, collocuti sunt inter se aliqui extra locum scrutinii, Bessarionemque cardinalem Nicenum eligere decreverunt, quod is omnium aptior ad rem republicam gubernandam videretur; conveniebatque numerus in eum sufficiens, nec dubium*

Il Cardinal Greco Vecchio: the last years 315

videbatur quin sequenti scrutinio pontifex a duabus partibus eligeretur; iamque ad eum supplicationes deferebantur.

There is no doubt that the most fervent partisan of Bessarion was Isidore.

26 The fact that Isidore had retained his beard in the Greek ecclesiastical manner can be inferred from a statement in the *Notitia* to the effect that he was saved from certain death during the sack of Constantinople precisely because he took care to disguise himself by shaving his beard; cf. *PG* 159: cols. 951, 952: *et quis esset ob rasum mentum . . . non agnitus*. Also cf. our comments, *supra*, ch. 5, text with n. 103.

27 Pius II, *Commentariorum* I.28.5 (pp. 140, 141, with English translation):

> *Quod ubi ad alios alterius factionis delatum est, Alanus cardinalis Avinionensis nunc istum nunc illum circuiens: "Ergo," inquit, "Ecclesiae Latinae Graecum pontificem dabimus, et in capite libri neophitum collocabimus? Nondum barbam rasit Bessarion, et nostrum caput erit? Et quid scimus, an vera est eius conversio? Heri et nudiustertius Romanae fidem Ecclesiae imougnavit, et quoniam hodie conversus est, magister erit noster et doctor exercitus? En paupertas Ecclesiae Latinae, quae virum non repperit summo apostolatu dignum, nisi ad Graecos recurrat! Sed agite, patres, quod libet. Ego et qui mihi credent in Graecum praesulem numquam consentiemus!"*

No doubt, the words that Pius II places in the mouth of the cardinal of Avignon must reflect the (concealed?) anti-Greek sentiments of others and soon such views would become the general opinion in Italy, as wave after wave of Greek refugees landed there to avoid the Ottoman occupation of their homes.

28 *Ibid.*, I. 28.7 (pp. 140–142, with English translation): *duae partes consensere de quo minor erat expectatio populi.*

29 *Ibid.*, I. 28.7 (pp. 142, 143, with English translation): *Is fuit Alfonsus, cardinalis Sanctorum Quattuor Coronatorum, natione Hispanus, ex civitate Valencia, scientia iuris eminentissimus et multarum rerum experientia praeditus, verum senior gravis ac prope modum decrepitus.*

30 *Ibid.*, I. 28.8 (pp. 142, 143, with English translation):

> *Alfonso in Petri cathedra constituto, Callisto Tertio nomen est inditum; qui mox votum vivit adversus impios Turchos omnia sese studia conversurum. Nec moratus bellum eis indixit, in quo militantibus peccata dimisit, ac legatos in Galliam et in Hungariam ad congregandos exercitus direxit.*

31 The document dated to 1455 neither specifies the month nor the day of the month: *Vat. Reg. 439*, fols. 140^r, 141^v. Cf. *PaL* 2: 4, n. 5.

32 The Via Lata, which is the ancient Via Flaminia, is accessed through the Porta del Popolo and is now known as the Via del Corso.

33 *Vat. Reg. 44*, fols. 262^r–263^v, as quoted in *PaL* 2: 4, n. 5. For some possible evidence on members of Isidore's household, cf. *infra*, text with nn. 47–50.

34 The letter is included in the *Chronicon Maius* of Pseudo-Sphrantzes, and can be found in the authoritative edition of the *Maius* by Grecu. The letter was supposedly written by Bessarion, cf. pp. 556–563. In addition, Lampros (basing his edition on his privately owned seventeenth-century manuscript of the *Maius*) published this letter twice: "Τρεῖς Ἐπιστολαὶ τοῦ Καρδηναλίου Βησσαρίωνος ἐν τῇ Δημώδει Γλώσσῃ," *NH* 5 (1908): pp. 19–39 (esp. 20–28); and again in *ΠκΠ* 4: 283–291. It is also found (with Latin translation) in *PG* 161: cols. 677–686.

35 At the very least, the style and the language of the letter do not reflect the normal educated and cultivated idiom of the learned cardinal; the language is atrocious by Attic standards, but this defect is usually dismissed by simply pointing out that the letter was composed in the spoken idiom. For this view, cf., e.g., Kyrou, p. 223, who simply states that the "language" of the letter is "extremely interesting": Μᾶς ἔχει διασωθῇ [*sc.* τὸ γράμμα] ὁλόκληρον, εἶναι τὸ μόνον ποὺ γνωρίζομεν ἀπὸ τὸν κάλαμον τοῦ Βησσαρίωνος, γραμμένον εἰς τὴν καθομιλουμένην Ἑλληνικὴν τῆς ἐποχῆς καὶ

παρουσιάζει ἐξαιρετικὸν ἐνδιαφέρον. Kyrou is in error; there are other letters by Bessarion in the same "style" (but also remain under suspicion, since they too were "deposited" in Spain, where Melissourgos-Melissenos was busy producing forgeries). Lampros was also uneasy about the idiom in which Bessarion's letter was written, as he commented (in his first edition of the letter [*NH* 5 (1908): 23]): ἀναλογιζόμενοι, ὅτι ὁ ἄλλως πολυγραφώτατος Βησσαρίων ἐποιεῖτο πάντοτε χρῆσιν τῆς ἀρχαϊζούσης ἑλληνικῆς δὲν ἔπρεπεν ἀταλαιπώρως καὶ ἄνευ εἰδικωτέρας ἐξετάσεως νὰ παραδεχθῶμεν, ὅτι τὴν ἐπιστολὴν ταύτην ἔγραψε ὁ καρδινάλιος κατ' ἐξαίρεσιν ἐν τῇ δημώδει. Lampros goes on to point out that there are linguistic parallels between this letter and the style of the *Maius*, even though Lampros was unaware that the *Maius* was an elaboration by Melissourgos-Melissenos. Thus we are justified in retaining reservations about the letter's authenticity and further believe that J. Meursius was closer to the truth when, in the sixteenth century, he castigated the language of this letter as *graecobarbara* (cf. the later edition of his minor works, *Opuscula* 7 [Florence, 1746]: p. 341). We must reserve the notion that this letter supposedly attributed to Bessarion may, after all, be another forgery by Melissourgos. On the *graecobarbara*, the spoken and uneducated idiom of the fifteenth and sixteenth centuries and its connotations, cf. H. Eideneier, "Ἕνας Γερμανός Εὐαγγελικός Παπάς στην Πόλη το 1573–1578," in E. Motos Guirao and M. Morfakidis Filactós, eds. *Constantinopla. 550 años de su caída. Κωνσταντινούπολη. 550 Χρόνια ἀπό την Ἅλωση*, 3: *Constantinopla Otomana*. Οθωμανική Κωνσταντινούπολη (Granada, 2006), pp. 313–317.

36 On this industrious forger and his various prolific activities, cf. *SF*, ch. 3 (pp. 139–191), which cites and examines all previous scholarship on the subject. It has become abundantly clear that any manuscript that was produced or has been in any way linked to this forger and his associates, such as the copyist John Santamaura, must be re-examined by modern scholarship.

37 *ΠκΠ* 4: 291. This letter also appears, with Latin translation, in *PG* 161: cols. 677–686, under the title: *Ad Paedagogum liberorum Thomae despotae*.

38 *ΠκΠ* 4: 284, 285; *PG* 161: cols. 679, 680, with the following Latin translation:

> Scito autem, sanctissimum papam, amicorum quorumdam auctoritate et sua ipsius benevolentia commotum, statuisse, principibus mensibus singulis nummos aureos trecentos pendere, quos hucusque beato despotae pendebat. Vult autem et decrevit sanctissimus papa ut ducenti nummi singulis mensibus aequaliter distribuantur tribus fratribus, ut impendantur ad alendos ipsos et sex septemve singulorum ministros; ad emendos et alendos quatuor minimum equos, ad ministrorum stipendia et principum vestimenta . . . et de cujusvis portione aliquantulum comparcior, ut habeant, quo utantur, si forte in morbum vel alias angustias inciderint. . . . Reliqui autem centum nummi aurei singulorum mensium, vel mille et ducenti totius anni, impendantur in stipendia ptocerum aliquot et hominum elegantium, qui cum principibus vivant et eos custodian. Certior autem factus sanctissimus papa, quot huc advenerint, miratus est et subirascitur. Si enim beatae memoriae principem, talem virum mirati sunt et vituperarunt, quod tot huc ministros adduxisset, quos pecunia et liberalitate aliena sustentaturus esset, quando magis nunc, cum alii plures huc immigrarint, principibus praesertim pueris et orbis succensendum est, qui nec dignitate, nec titulis, nec fama nobiles sunt!

39 The amount is incorrect, as the despot received 500 ducats per month (cf. *infra*, n. 118). Could this citation of the wrong amount of the pension lend further support to the view that this "document" is not genuine but a forgery from the hand of Makarios Melissourgos-Melissenos, or is "Bessarion" here alluding to the pope's contribution, without counting the additional ducats supplied by the cardinals? Thomas Palaiologos was generous with his rather large retinue of noblemen, among whom he distributed his papal pension. Cf. Harris, *Greek Emigres in the West*, pp. 111, 112. The princes alluded to are Andreas and Manuel. Andreas spent his life in Italy and received "bad press," which was part of the increasing anti-Greek, anti-refugee propaganda in Italy. His contemporaries and subsequent scholars have not viewed Andreas kindly, but have seen in him a devious man who squandered the pension granted to him by the pope. Andreas

associated himself with a woman of low class and sold his rights to the Greek throne a number of times (the first occasion was in 1494 to Charles VIII of France for a payment of 4,300 ducats), before he died destitute. Recent scholarship has demonstrated that most of this sad picture originates with the anti-Greek propaganda and bias encountered in the Vatican and in Rome, and in the old-fashioned policies that Andreas pursued in order to motivate a crusade to liberate Greek lands from the Turks; cf. J.P. Harris, "A Worthless Prince? Andreas Palaeologus in Rome – 1464–1502," *OCP* 61 (1995), pp. 537–554; and *idem*, *Greek Emigres in the West*, pp. 113–117. Thus the new rehabilitated picture of Andreas presents a typical member of the Palaiologan family, who perpetuated the policies of Manuel II, John VIII, and Constantine XI. Andreas's ultimate goal was to gain military aid in Europe against the Turks in the Balkans. His sister, Zoë–Sophia, was raised a Catholic under the supervision of Cardinal Bessarion, but reverted to Orthodoxy upon her marriage to the grand prince, Ivan III of Moscow. Moreover, Andreas's brother, Manuel, who was also brought up in Italy, became so disgusted with the financial problems that he encountered in Italy that he defected to Constantinople, placed himself under the authority of the reigning sultan, Mehmed II Fatih, and was granted a comfortable pension by the Porte; cf. the patriarchal chronicle, Ἔκθεσις Χρονικὴ 48:

τοῦ γὰρ δεσπότου κῦρ Θωμᾶ ... ὑπῆρχον δύο υἱοί. ὁ νεώτερος οὖν υἱὸς αὐτοῦ Μανουὴλ ἀποδράσας ἐκ Ῥώμης ἦλθεν ἐν Κωνσταντινουπόλει, πλανήσαντες αὐτὸν ὅ τε Μαγκαφᾶς καὶ Κόντος καὶ Νικόλαος, ὄντες οἰκεῖοι αὐτοῦ ... ἀπατήσαντες οὖν αὐτὸν ἔφερον ἐν τῇ Πόλει ὅθεν ὁ αὐθέντης [Mehmed II] χαριέντως αὐτὸν ὑποδεξάμενος, δέδωκεν αὐτῷ χώρας εἰς διατροφὴν τὸ Σιρέτζιον καὶ τὸ Ἀμπελίτζιον καὶ ἕτερα χωρία δύο, καὶ ρόγαν ἐξέχως ἀνὰ ἄστρα ἑκατὸν καθ᾽ ἡμέραν, δοὺς αὐτῷ καὶ δούλας δύο. ἐποίησε δὲ ἐξ αὐτῶν δύο υἱούς. καὶ τὸν μὲν ὠνόμασεν Ἰωάννην Παλαιολόγον τὸν δὲ ἕτερον Ἀνδρέαν, ἔχει δὲ καλῶς μετὰ τιμῆς καὶ ἀρχόντων οὐκ ὀλίγων ὄντων μετ᾽ αὐτοῦ. ἀλλ᾽ οὖν δέδωκε καὶ αὐτὸς τὸ κοινὸν χρέος ταφεὶς ἐν τῇ χώρᾳ τοῦ Σιρετζίου ἐντὸς τοῦ ναοῦ ... ὡς ἐν ὀλίγῳ μετὰ τοῦ ἀποθανεῖν τὸν πατέρα αὐτῶν, βασιλεύσας ὁ Σουλτὰν Σελίμης ἔλαβεν Ἀνδρέαν τὸν ὕστερον υἱὸν αὐτοῦ καὶ ἔβαλεν ἐν τῷ σαραγίῳ ποιήσας αὐτὸν Ἰσμαηλίτην, ὀνομάσας αὐτὸν Μεχεμέτην. ὁ δὲ ἕτερος υἱὸς αὐτοῦ ὁ Ἰωάννης περιπεσὼν ἐν νόσῳ ἀνιάτῳ ἐτελεύτησεν ταφεὶς ἐν τῇ Παμμακαρίστῳ.

In addition, cf. Harris, *Greek Emigres in the West*, p. 113 n. 140; based on archival material, Harris pinpoints the departure of Manuel from Rome to Constantinople on 15 April 1476.

40 *Vat. Reg. 449*, fols. 216ᵛ–217ᵛ, which *PaL*, p. 4 n. 5, describes as an "interesting document."
41 *Archivio di Stato, Venice, Reg. Vat. 468*, fols. 25 and 320; cf. *PaL*, p. 4 n. 5. Some of his new acquisitions are also enumerated in the *Notitia* (*Purpura Docta, Monachi 1714*, p. 3; p. 105, as cited in *PG* 159: col. 952): *Ubi [Romae] a Nicolao V Pont. Max. multis muneribus in vicem laborum donatus [sc. Isidorus], trino sensim episcopatu, nimirum Sabinensi, Corphiensi, ac Nicasiensi, anctus est.* The following year, Pope Calixtus III further increased his ecclesiastical responsibilities with additional jurisdictions, and apparently an increase in his personal revenues. On these, cf. *Documenta Pontificum Romanorum Historiam Ucrainae Illustrantia (1075–1953)*, 1: *1075–1700*, ed. A.G. Welykyi, Analecta OSBM, series II, section III (Rome, 1953), docs. 80 [*Archivio di Stato, Venice, Reg. Vat. 452*, fols. 70ᵛ–72]: *Romae, 18. IV. 1458, Conceditur Isidor Cardinali Praepositura in dioecesi Cathaniensi ad sublevanda onera expesarum* (pp. 140, 141); and 81 [*Archivio di Stato, Venice, Reg. Vat. 452*, fols. 71ᵛ–72]: *Romae, 18. IV. 1458, Episcopo Cartaginesi aliisque datur facultas introducendi Cardinalem Isidorum in possessionem Praepositurae sibi concessae* (p. 142). Then his successor, Pius II issued one appointment and an announcement of his resignation as Archbishop of Corfu, *ibid.*, docs. 90 [*Archivio di Stato, Venice, Reg. Vat. 468*, fol. 320ʳ, 320ᵛ]: *Romae, 9. XI. 1458, Isidoro Cardinali datur in commendam ecclesia S. Agathae in Urbe* (pp. 154–155); and 95 [*Archivio di Stato, Venice, Reg. Vat. 470*, fol. 145ᵛ]: *Senis, 15. III. 1459, Resignatio Ecclesiae Corphiensis ex parte Isidori, Metropolitae Kioviensis, et Cardinalis Sabiensis* (pp. 158, 159). Unfortunately, we were unable to locate the original document appointing him to the latter position.

318   *Il Cardinal Greco Vecchio: the last years*

42 Hofmann, "Papst Kallixt III," pp. 218, 219 n. 19.
43 The decision is recorded in *Archivio di Stato, Senato Secreta, Cap. 20*, 6.95ᵛ; and in *Archivio di Stato, Senato Terra, reg. 4*, fols. 6ᵛ–7ᵛ. A summary of the decision in Pierling, 1: 83, who, however, erroneously cites the amount as 1,145 ducats; cf. M.I. Manoussakas, "Ἡ Πρώτη Ἄδεια (1456) τῆς Βενετικῆς Γερουσίας γιὰ τὸν Ναὸ τῶν Ἑλλήνων τῆς Βενετίας καὶ ὁ Καρδινάλιος Ἰσίδωρος," *Θησαυρίσματα* 1 (1962): pp. 109–118, esp. 115.
44 *Ibid.*, p. 117.
45 Pertinent discussion in *ibid.*, esp. pp. 113 ff. The document reads as follows: fol. 9ᵛ:

> Die XVIIJ Junij [MCCCCLVJ]
>   Sapientes omnes terre firme.
>   Cum in hoc proximo aduentu suo Venetias Reverendissimus dominus Isidorus, episcopus Sabinensis ac Cardinalis Russiensis, maximam instantiam dominio nostro fecerit, ut prouidere dignaretur, quod Greci orthodoxi et Catholice fidei habere possent aliquam ecclesiam in hac vrbe Venetiarum eisque liceret in ea diuina mysteria et diuina officia Greco ritu celebrare, ut in hac generis et nationis sue calamitate non uideantur omnino derelicti atque reiecti. Et Revertendus Pater dominus Patriarcha Venetiarum exponi Dominio nostro fecerit habuisset superinde breue quondam a Summo Pontifice, per quod sibi mandatus de inuenienda dicta ecclesia, in qua grece Greci persbiterj diuina official celebrare possint. Et eius d. Patriarche paternitas capiat jussis Romani Pontificis ponere, in quantum intelligat et cognoscat, hoc fere gratum dominio nostro, presertim cum sibi de re honesta agi uideatur.

> fol. 10ʳ:

> Vadit pars, quod, consideratis jussis Romani Pontificis ac equisitionibus prefati Reverendissimi domini Cardinalis, tantopere rem hanc considerantes, ut magna multitude Grecorum, que in hac Ciuitate commoratur et catholice sub obedientia Sancte Romane Ecclesie uidit, defectu ecclesie non patiatur incommoditatem divinorum officiorum suorum, cui domino Cardinali honestum est complacere, in re presertim ista pia, et a Summo Pontifice tentopere Reuerendo domino Patriarche injuncta, azuctoritate huius Consilij plena facultas tradatur prelibato somino Patriarche Venetiarum, ut habeat curam inueniendi aliquam ecclesiam dictid Grecis in loco idoneo et oportuno, in qua, sine turbatione alicuius persone, possint celebrare official sua, pout paternitate sue uidebitur conuenire. Verum in casu quo, facta diligenti inquisition, dicta ecclesia non inueniretur, eligatur locus aliquis per paternitatem suam in regione aliqua ciuitatis habili et idonea, ubi edificare liceat dictis Grecis ecclesiam et in ea Greco ritu celebrare official sua. Ita tamen quod cum domino proprietatis dicti loci prius concords remaneant.
>   de parte   53
>   Ser Zacharias Vallaresso
>   Consiliarius
>   Vult quod eis non prouideatur de aliqua ecclesia latina, sed tamen de loco idoneo prouideatur eis per Reuerendum d. Patriarcham, ubi suis expensis hedificare possint uanm ecclesiam, qui locus et forma ipsius hedificationis placeat nostro dominio.
>   de parte   45–37   non sinceri   5
>   de non   7–4

46 A. Mai, ed., *Spicilegium Romanum* 1: *Virorum Illustrium. CIII. qui Saeculo XV. extiterunt Vitae Auctore Coaevo Vespasiano Florentino* (Rome, 1839), pp. 284, 285. Another translation (without the original Italian text) can be found in Pastor, 2: 334. Given the last statement quoted here, could it be that somehow Vespasiano was aware of the financial troubles that could have confronted Isidore?
47 Agallianos's surviving writings qualify as an autobiography and provide us with crucial information about the affairs of the patriarchate under Mehmed II. On his literary output, cf. M. Angold, "Theodore Agallianos: The Last Byzantine Autobiography," in *Constantinople. 550 años de su caida*, 1: *Constantinopla Bizantina. Βυζαντινή Κωνσταντινούπολη*, pp. 35–44.

48 This statement is included in a speech by Agallianos, titled: Περὶ τῶν κατὰ Αὐτὸν ἢ κατὰ τῶν κατ' Αὐτοῦ and designated as Λόγος Α΄ in Patrinelis, ed., Ὁ Θεόδωρος Ἀγαλλιανός, fol. 9ᵛ (p. 100).
49 The word ϖαρασίτοις used by Agallianos may not imply the negative connotations the word had acquired in antiquity, through the stock comedy figure of the "parasite." Here it probably means "dependent servants/members of entourage-retinue."
50 Thus Angold, for instance, tacitly assumes that Galesiotes applied the term to Isidore; cf. "Theodore Agallianos," p. 40: "the latter [Andronikos Galesiotes] went off to seek his fortune in the West in the entourage of Cardinal Isidore." Not much is known about Andronikos and he does not receive a reference in Harris, *Greek Emigres in the West*. His name was corrupted in Italy to the Italicized form "Gallinoto" and he is known to have been a copyist of manuscripts and a teacher in Sicily as late as 1467. His death is recorded to have taken place on 12 December 1467. Cf. Patrinellis, Ὁ Θεόδωρος Ἀγαλλιανός, pp. 62, 63 n. 313. In his speeches Agallianos does not refer by name either to Bessarion or to Isidore; thus his reference to "the cardinal" remains obscure. Given the fact that Bessarion was famous and that he employed an army of copyists and refugees, it is perhaps more expected to assume that Agallianos meant that Galesiotes sought employment with Bessarion and then we may infer that Galesiotes perhaps moved on to his second choice, Isidore. On the other hand, Agallianos had personal dealings with Isidore in 1452–1453, when he had opposed the cardinal's efforts to enforce the union in Constantinople; they both presented arguments against each other's position in court and in official gatherings; cf. *supra*, ch. 4, text with nn. 111–113. Perhaps it was also natural, then, for Agallianos to refer to Isidore, his personal opponent, as simply "the cardinal," as most anti-unionist propaganda did not wish to dignify him by name and rather contemptuously referred to him as "the cardinal." There can be no objective resolution to this problem: either cardinal may have been meant on this occasion. Given the fact that Isidore and Bessarion were close friends, there is also the possibility that they "shared" the services of their employees, so Galesiotes may have served both of them at different times, as the occasion dictated.
51 That Calixtus III had been targeted by humanists and that the charges of Vespasiano do not amount to serious criticism was also noted by the editor of Vespasiano, Cardinal Angelo Mai, who comments (*Spicilegium Romanum* 1: 284 n. 1):

> Sembra che queste discorso di Vespasiano, o più tosto del suo relatore, non abbia fondamenti nell verità; imperocchè gli Assemani nella storia della biblioteca vaticana premessa al tomo I. del catalogo de' mss. p. XXI. dopo le munificenze di Nicolò V. in comperar libri, così parlano di papa Callisto: *Callistus III. Decessorem Nicolaum aemulatus, ut colligeret a barbaris litterarum monumenta, quae Nicolai inquisitores latuerant, quadraginta aureorum milia, tam egregia in re expensa, lucrum existimavit.*

The defense of the pope against these charges of Vespasiano was taken up in detail by Pastor, 2: 334–337, who adds (p. 336): "If he bestowed only two [*sc.* books] on King Alfonso, his intimate friend, we may rest assured that he cannot have given hundreds to Cardinal Isidore.... Thus this oft-repeated tale proves for the most part legendary." In addition, cf. Mercati, p. 61.
52 *Supra*, n. 8.
53 As has been astutely grasped by Pastor, 2: 334: "One of these [*sc.* calumnies] was that propagated by Filelfo and Vespasiano da Bistici, which accused Calixtus of dispersing the Vatican Library."
54 Μεδιολανόθεν, τῇ ιδ΄ ἡμέρᾳ ϖρὸ ἰανουαρίου καλενδῶν [on the fourteenth day before the kalends of January [= the 14th of December], ἔτει ͵αυνζ΄.
55 Legrand, no. 51 (p. 95; with French translation, pp. 95, 96).
56 Lampo Birago was a humanist who wrote one of the early treatises on a projected crusade to recover Constantinople and offered it to Pope Nicholas V; it is titled: *Ad Nicolaum*

320   *Il Cardinal Greco Vecchio: the last years*

   Quintum pontificem maximum Lampi Biragi Strategicon adverse Turcos. For selections from Birago's Latin text, with Italian translation, and for secondary scholarship, cf. *CC* 2: 112–125.
57 Legrand, p. 96. It is interesting to note here that Filelfo sometimes writes his letters to Bessarion in Greek and on other occasions in Latin. Perhaps the letters he wrote in Greek contain material that Filelfo did not wish to become known to others; after all, not everyone could read Greek with ease. He produces one statement to support this contention in his letter of the 12th of August 1458, to Bessarion, in which he asks the cardinal to reply to him in Greek so that few people could understand the contents (*ibid.*, no. 56, pp. 102, 103, with French translation): καὶ γράψον ἐμοὶ ὡς τάχιστα καὶ γράψον δι' ἑλληνικῶν γραμμάτων ἵνα μὴ εὐθὺς ἡ ἐμὴ διάνοια ἔνδηλος γένηται τοῖς πολλοῖς.
58 *Ibid.*, p. 96: *Nec est aliud quicquam quod tantopere in praesentia abs te cupiam quam ut me facias certiorem quid de codico meo sentias, num spei quicquid sit reliquum, an perierit omnino.*
59 *Ibid.*, p. 96. Da Carreto was the ambassador from Milan (the residence of Filelfo) to the court of Rome. The deacon/librarian was Cosimo de Monteserrato.
60 What the search revealed was that there were manuscripts containing Plutarch's work, but they were not the exceptional manuscript that belonged to Filelfo. Cf. Legrand, pp. 96, 97:

   On trouve en réalité dans cette partie de l'inventaire deux manuscrits de Pluraque, mais la description sommaire des ces volumes indique suffisamment qu'aucun d'eux n'est le nobilissimus codex recherché par Filelfe. On le reconnaît sans peine, au contraire, dans la mention suivante: Item unum volume magnum de pergameno copertum corio rubeo et intitulatur PLUTARCHI PARALLELA.

61 Isidore had been associated, as a copyist or as a user, with the following manuscripts in Rome: *Vatic. 175*, fols. 79^v–80^v (a treatise on astronomy); *Vatic. 210*, fols. 3–7 (a poem on an astrolabe); *Vat. 289*, fols. 24–27 (a treatise on medicine); *Vatic. 776* (*olim 812*), fols. 153–196 (Isidore's own poetic lines on Saint Demetrius); *Vatic. 830* (*olim 546*), fols. 90–105 (a treatise on dogma); *Vatic. 1698* (a number of ancient works: Heliodorus, Pseudo-Ptolemy, Polybius, and a treatise on astrology); *Vatic. Barber. 127b* (Lycides, Paul of Aegina, Ptolemy, a treatise on astrology, Hippocrates, Galen, and medical treatises); and *Vatic. Urb. 110*, fols. 3–13, and 119^r–122^r (Philostratus). On these scholarly and copying activities of Isidore, cf. Patrinelis, "Ἕλληνες Κωδικογράφοι τῶν Χρόνων τῆς Ἀναγεννήσεως" pp. 63–124, esp. p. 83 on Isidore. For more information, cf. Mercati, *passim.*
62 *Ibid.*, ch. 3: *Isidoro Bibliofilo pretesa dissipazzione dei codici papacy a lui prestati.* On pp. 61–102, he examines all manuscripts owned by Isidore and concludes that the accusations of Vespasiano were, after all, malicious rumors, as we should expect. Isidore had purchased all the manuscripts that were eventually deposited in the library after his death.
63 The ultimate fate of this manuscript still remains in doubt, as it has not been identified. What is certain is that the Plutarch *codex* was not among the possessions of Isidore cataloged after his death. For an examination of all his privately owned manuscripts, which do not include Filelfo's *codex*, cf. Mercati, ch. 3.
64 Legrand, no. 55, p. 102 (with French translation).
65 *Supra*, n. 45, for the entire passage. On Filelfo, and especially his period of employment in Milan, cf. Diana M. Robin, *Filelfo in Milan: Writings 1451–1457* (Princeton, 1991), who discusses Filelfo's souring relations with his former pupil, Pius II: pp. 116–121.
66 Filelfo wrote to Bessarion (Legrand, *Cent-dix lettres grecques des François Filelfe*, p. 98): *Vix dici queat, quam gratus mihi, quamque periucundus fuerit nuncius tuus de recuperate Plutarcho; quem quum amiseram, me a summon pontifice Pio secundo, tuo interventu, dono accipere in non mediocrem felicitates partem mihi ascribo.* He also thanked Pius II (*ibid.*): *quantam mihi quamque singularem voluptatem attulisti nobilissimo ipso Plutarchi codice.* Legrand adds, p. 98:

   Filelfe se rendit à Rome pour remercier le pape, qui lui avait accordé un pension de deux cent ducats. Il y arriva le 12 janvier 1459, et revint à Milan au mois de février suivant, rapportant sadoute avec lui son manuscrit de Plutarque.

Filelfo was always sensitive about "lost" books that supposedly belonged to him.This was not the only time that he voiced concern over the appropriation of one of his books. After he had spent seven years in Constantinople studying Greek and acquiring *codices*, Filelfo returned to Italy in 1427 and immediately accused the Venetian Leonardo Giustiniani, who had often sponsored him and had supplied funds for him, of appropriating his collection of rare manuscripts of ancient Greek texts, which he had shipped to him for safe-keeping. The incident again resulted in numerous letters of accusations by the two parties. On this incident and the accusations of theft exchanged between Filelfo and Giustiniani, cf. Robin, pp. 22–29.

67 *Infra*, text with nn. 110–118.
68 That Isidore inspired the changes is a supposition made in *CF*, p. 395.
69 O. Halecki, "The Ecclesiastical Separation of Kiev from Moscow in 1458," *Studien zur älteren Geschichte Osteuropas*, Wiener Archiv für Geschichte des Slawentums und Osteuropas II, 1 (1956): 19, 20, suggests that

> the idea of dividing the vast area subject to the Metropolitan of Kiev and all Russia was not entirely new. That idea appeared almost immediately when at the end of the thirteenth century one of these metropolitans transferred his residence from Kiev to the new colonial Russia in the Volga region.

Further, he develops the role of Isidore in the preparation of the papal bulls of 1458 and suggests (p. 21 f.), that Isidore motivated the use of the terminology of two Russias, accepting this geographical/ecclesiastical and perhaps ethnographic division as a fait accompli.

70 The severance of the ecclesiastical seat of Kiev from that of Moscow proved equally disturbing for the Ruthenians. The first concrete attempt to mollify the issue came in 1466, when Casimir, the king of Poland, sought to have Gregory recognized as the metropolitan of Kiev by the patriarch of Constantinople, Dionysius I (1466–1471 and 1488–1490). An understanding was finally arrived at in 1470, and thus Constantinople approved of the ecclesiastical division, but only after much rancor and distrust between Constantinople, Moscow, Poland, and Lithuania. On this subject, cf. Halecki, *From Florence to Brest*, p. 97; A.E. Presniakov, *The Formation of the Great Russian State: A Study of Russian History in the Thirteenth to Fifteenth Centuries*, trans. A.E. Moorhouse (Chicago, 1970; repr. Gulf Breeze, FL, 1993), p. 364; and Vernadsky, *Russia at the Dawn of the Modern Age*, pp. 33 and 48. Gregory apparently in 1466 promised to adhere to Orthodoxy, paving the way for his recognition by the patriarch of Constantinople. There was sincere doubt among the high Muscovite clergy that Gregory was to be believed and, therefore, Moscow never acknowledged him as the metropolitan of Kiev.

71 Cf. Welykyj, *Documenta Pontificum Romanorum*, doc. 83 (pp. 147, 148): *Romae, 3.IX.1458. Pius II Regem Poloniae Casimirum hortatur ne aliquem se in Ecclesiam Metropolotanam Kioviensem intromittere sinat, sed ut Gregorium ad hanc Sedem electrum defendat*. The specific passage (p. 147), reads: *sicut canonice electus archiepiscopus et secundum grecos ritus a venerabili frater nostro Gregorio patriarcha constantinopolitano ordinatus*. For the provisional nomination of Gregory, cf. *ibid*., doc. 82 (pp. 146, 147) (*Archivio di Stato, Venice, Vat. Reg. 468*, fol. 155ᵛ–156ᵛ): *Romae, 3.IX. 1458. Bulla provisionis Ecclesiae Metropolitanae Kioviensis in persona Gregorii et nova circumscriptio eiusdem provinciae ecclesiasticae*.

72 On these matters, cf. *CF*, p. 395; and Halecki, "The Ecclesiastical Separation of Kiev from Moscow," pp. 19–32. On the activities of Gregory in the 1460s, cf. *idem, From Florence to Brest*, esp. pp. 91–100.

73 ПСРЛ 25: 259.
74 *Ibid*., 28: 122. An identical statement appears in *The Annalistic Code for the Year 1518, ibid.*, pp. 291, 292.
75 *Ibid*., p. 123. The entries on pp. 124, 125, and 142, add nothing of significance and repeat the information furnished in the initial statement. Identical repetition is to be noted in *The Annalisitic Code for the Year 1518, ibid.*, pp. 293, 294.
76 *Ibid*., 21/2: 511, 512.
77 *Ibid*., p. 531.

322   *Il Cardinal Greco Vecchio: the last years*

78 The death of the pope is briefly reported by Pius II; cf. *Commentariorum* I.35.6 (pp. 176, 177, with English translation): *pontifex maximus . . . aegritudinem incidit ex qua mortuus est. . . . Obiit autem VIII Idus Augusti anno Salvatoris Christi quadrigensimo qunquagesimo octavo supra millesimum. Cardinales pro more egregias ei exequias fecere.*

79 *Ibid.*, I.36.9 (pp. 182, 183, with English translation). Cf. Harris, *Greek Emigres in the West*, p. 105 n. 99:

> Both Bessarion and Isidore had used a variety of tricks to promote their candidate, the French Cardinal d'Estouteville, in the conclave of 1458. They left the room on a pretended call of nature to disrupt the proceedings and physically prevented a cardinal who wished to cast a contrary vote from rising.

80 They are identified in *Commentariorum*, p. 399 n. 142, as Bessarion, Isidore, Juan de Torquemada, Alain de Coëtivy, Prospero Colonna, Giovanni da Castiglione, and Rodrigo Borgia. It is interesting to note that Bessarion was on the same side as Alain de Coëtivy; the latter had used ethnic slurs, prejudice, and anti-Greek statements to torpedo the candidacy of Bessarion for the papal throne at the previous conclave, as we have seen (*supra*, text with n. 27).

81 *Ibid.*, I.36.8 (pp. 182, 183, with English translation).

82 Noted in excruciating detail by Pius II, *ibid.*, I.36.10–26 (pp. 182–196, with English translation).

83 *Ibid.*, I.36.21 (pp. 190, 191, with English translation): *Petrus autem cardinalis Sancti Marci, cum accepisset Gallorum coniurationem, . . . commotus amore patriae simul ac odio quo Rhotomagensem* [Rouen] *prosequebatur, circuire Italos cardinales, hortari, monere, ne patriam relinquerent . . . cunctos Italos congregavit; exposuitque coniurationem in latrinis factam.*

84 *Ibid.*, I.36.20 (pp. 190, 191, with English translation).

85 *Ibid.*, I.36.25 (pp. 194–197, with English translation).

86 *Ibid.*, I.36.27 (pp. 196, 197, with English translation): *Ibique Bessarion cardinalis Nicenus suo et eorum nomine qui Rhotomagensem* [of Rouen, that is, Guillaume] *faverant.*

87 Pope Pius notes the celebrations upon his election in Rome and he adds the following, typically humanistic, comment on Christian festivities (*ibid.*, I.36. 32, pp. 200, 201, with English translation):

> *Et cum essent armata civitas* [Rome], *nec quisquam in alio quam in ferro vederetur habere fiduciam, mox ut certior factus est populus Aeneae* [of Pius II] *pontificatum obvenisse, deposita arma, adeoque mutata Urbis* [of Rome] *facies ut quae paulo ante Martis, e vestigio non dicam Veneris, Troiani quondam Aeneae matris, sed Pacis et Quietis civitas effecta sit, ubique laeta atque secura.*

88 The overall theme of the status of the papacy under Pius II is beyond the scope of this present work. We will only treat those events that concern Cardinal Isidore. For the history of Pope Pius II's reign, besides his own works, the interested reader may consult the following sources, among others: Pastor, vols. 2 and 3; *PaL* 2; G. Voigt, *Enea Silvio de' Piccolomini als Papst Pius der Zweite und sein Zeitalter*, 3 vols. (Berlin, 1856–1863); J. Helmrath, "Pius II und die Türken," in G. Guthmüller and W. Kühlmann, eds. *Europa und die Türken in der Renaissance* (Tübingen, 2000), pp. 79–138; and the large number of works cited in R. Ceserani, "Rassegna bibliografica di studi piccolominiani," *Giornale storico de la letteratura italiana* 141 (1964): pp. 265–281. Pius's crusade was doomed for the very beginning, because of the incessant wars in Italy, of the apathy and self-interest of Venice, which did not wish to be embroiled in another war with the Porte, and of the indifference of Germany, France, and Burgundy.

89 *Commentariorum* II.4.4–5 (pp. 214, 215, with English translation): *Diu res agitate est in consilio cum cardinalibus, quorum etsi multi adversarentur (quibus res presents abunde suppetebant, et placebat otium in Urbe) vicit tamen praesulis constantia, et in eius sententiam itum est.*

90 *Ibid.*, II.2.4.4–5 (pp. 214, 215, with English translation).

91 *Supra*, n. 41, for the text of the document.

92 *Commentariorum* II.16.1 and 3 (pp. 266, 267, with English translation). Pius, by the title of this chapter, expresses his disapproval of Venice, as he dubs the treaty "shameful": *Venetorum turpe foedus cum Turchis*.
93 *Ibid.*, II.10.1 (pp. 244, 245, with English translation): *ad XIII kalendas Februarias*.
94 *PaL* 2: 204 suggests that Pius left Rome on 2 January; for this date *PaL* 2 is relying on a register in the *Archivo Vaticana, Arm. 39*, tom., fol. 28ᵛ, which states: *Die XXII Ian. MCCCCLVIIII dominus Pius recessit de urbe [Roma]*. This register of Pius's journey provides the following information in translation (the original Latin text is to be found in *PaL* 2: 204 n. 16): 26 January: arrival in Spoleto; 1 February: arrival in Perugia; 1 February: departure from Perugia; 24 February: arrival in Siena; 23 April: departure from Siena; 25 April: arrival in Florence; 5 May: departure from Florence; 9 May: arrival in Bologna; 16 May: departure from Bologna; 17 May: arrival in Ferrara; 25 May: departure from Ferrara; and 27 May: arrival in Mantua.
95 *Commentariorum* II. 44.1 (pp. 372, 373, with English translation): *sexto Kalendas Iunii*. The Vatican register (cf. *supra*, n. 86) agrees: *Die XXVII Mai 1459 intravit Mantuam*.
96 Pius provides all details of his itinerary, with long digressions into the history and politics of each city that he visited. Cf. *ibid.*, II.10–44 (pp. 244–372, with English translation). In addition, G.B. Manucci, "Il viaggio di Pio II da Roma a Mantova," *Bolletino senese di storia patria*, n.s., 12 (1941): pp. 62–65.
97 The six cardinals who accompanied him are listed in *Commentariorum* II. 10.2 (pp. 244–246, with English translation); notable is the absence of Isidore, who must have been given dispensation to remain behind and to await improved weather conditions in the following spring:

> *sex cardinals delecti sunt, qui papae servirent iter agenti: Vilhelmus Rhotomagensis* [Rouen], *e regia stirpe natus; Alanus Avinionensis, nobilis Brito; Philippus Bononiensis, Nicolai pontificis quondam frater; Petrus Sancti Marci; Proper Columnensis; Rhodericus vicecancellarius, qui Romanorum pontificum nepotes fuerint: Eugenii, Martini, Callisti. Cardinales reliqui, ex quis nonnulli valitudinarii fuerunt, iussi sunt Romae manere, aut mitius veris tempus expectare, ac tum pone sequi.*

This passage is confirmed by the archives of Mantua; cf. D.S. Chambers and R. Signorini, "Notizie di storia mantovana (1328–1462) nel ms. Harleian 3462 della British Library," *Civiltà mantovana*, n.s., 18 (1987): pp. 31–68, esp. p. 38 (quoting fol. 271ᵛ [247ᵛ]):

> *Dell'anno 1459, a dì 27 di Maggio [sic ma leggi 22 (h. 18 ca)] entrò papa Pio* [II] *in Mantua con sei cardinali, facendose portar in una sedia fin la chiesa di S. Petro, dove sua Sanctità dette la benediction al populo.*

Another document, presenting essentially the same information but with further details, is also quoted in the accompanying n. 68 (pp. 55, 56). In the same fol. (*ibid.*, p. 38), the provisions that the marquis of Mantua supplied to his visiting cardinals are cited:

> *(e presentò* [that is, *il signor marchese*] *a caduan cardinal le infrascipte robbe): sachi 10 di farina; sachi 20 di biava da cavallo; carra 3 di vino; vittelli 4; forme 4 di formazo; para 6 di caponi; para 12 di polastri e galline; torze 10; livre 2 di candele; livre 3 di pegnocata dorata; live 3 di mandole confette; livre 3 di coriandoli; livre 32 di ànesi; stara di sale 5.*

The pope received larger provisions (*ibid.*):

> *(il signor marchese present le infrascripte cose al papa): sacchi 100 di farina; sacchi 100di orzo; carra 20 di vino; cara 50 di legna; carra 50 di feno; manzi 5, vivi; vittelli 15; forme 16 di formazo; para 40 di caponi; para 100 di polastri; torze 50 di cera biancha; livre 50 di candele di cera biancha; livre 12 di pegnochata [confettura di pinochi e zucchero] adorata; livre 12 di cinamon confetto; livre 12 di mandole confetti; livre 12 di coriandoli; livre 12 d'ànesi confetti; stara 25 di sale.*

324 *Il Cardinal Greco Vecchio: the last years*

98 The Mantuan archives (*ibid.*, fol. 218ʳ [248ʳ] [pp. 38, 39]) supply the following note, which includes a citation for Isidore ("the old Greek cardinal"), with notes about the quarters for the cardinals (which in the cases of Isidore and Bessarion seem to have been reversed); names within brackets are supplied by the editors of the archival notes:

> *Gli reverendissimi cardinali che erano a Mantua cum papa Pio* [II] *allogiorno come di sotta si contiene:*
>   *Rhotomagensis* [Guglielmo di Estouteville], *in casa del conte Christoforo Torrello;*
>   *il cardinal greco vecchio* [Isidoro di Kiev], *in casa di madonna Agata Torrelli* [*sic ma leggi, in casa Forlengo*];
>   *"S. Marco"* [Pietro Barbo], *in casa di Bartholome' di Gorno;*
>   *il "Vicecancellero"* [Rodrigo Lanzol-Borgia], *in casa di messer Benedicto di Strozi;*
>   *il cardinal di Bologna* [Filippo Calandrini], *summo penintentier, in casa di messer Guido da Gonzaga, protonotario;*
>   *il cardinal Colona* [Prospero Colonna], *in casa di signor Alexandro* [Gonzaga];
>   *il "Patriarca"* [Ludovico Scarampi Mezzarota], *in casa di messer Zo. Francesco di Uberti;*
>   *"Santi Quatro"* [Ludovico Giovanni Mila], *in casa di Antonio di Grosi;*
>   *il cardinale Edunensis* [Giovanni Rolin], *in casa di Matteo di Corradi;*
>   *"S. Sixto"* [Giovanni Torquemada], *in casa di Philippino di Grosi;*
>   *il cardinal di Avegnone* [Alano de Coëtivy], *in casa di Georgio da Gonzaga;*
>   *il cardinale Zamorensis* [Giovanni Mella], *in casa di Zanibaldo* [da Brolo];
>   *"S. Netasia"* [Giacomo Tebaldi], *in casa di Zanfrancisco di Grosi;*
>   *il cardinal Greco giovene* [Bessarione da Trebisonda], *in casa di Folegi* [*sic ma leggi, di Agata Torelli*];
>   *"S. Petro in vincula"* [Niccolò da Cusa], *in vescovato.*

Another manuscript cited by Chambers and Signorini, pp. 56, 57 n. 69, furnishes the same information about the quarters of the cardinals, with paraphrases; thus in the case of Isidore it states: *el cardenal Rotenno, greco, monacho, in caxa fu de Pol de Folengi.*

99 The conquest of the Morea by the Turks is beyond the scope of this study; a fresh look into the events by modern scholarship is still needed. Primary sources on the conquest of the Morea include the detailed accounts of the *Minus* (and of the derivative *Maius*), Kritoboulos, Khalkokondyles, and Doukas. In addition, cf. the analysis and the documents cited in *PaL* 2: pp. 219–228.

100 *Commentariorum* III.3.1, 2 (pp. 10–13 with English translation): *legati Thomae despoti Moreae praesulem accedunt . . . nec magno exercitu opus esset dixit* [*sc.* Thoma]: *Italorum parvam manum sufficere ad eiciendos peninsula Turchos.*

101 Thus Bessarion states in an important letter (cf. *PaL* 2: 209: "His letter . . . is a very important document"; it is analyzed in detail in *ibid.*, 2: 209, 210). The Latin text of this letter can be found in *ΠκΠ* 4: 255–258; in this letter Bessarion includes the following statement that is in agreement with the petition of the Moreot ambassadors, *ibid.*, 4: 252: *et quia necesse est ut hoc cito fiat, melius est habere quigentos vel CCCC. vel etiam CCC. in tempore, quam multa millia tarde.*

102 Thus he cites Agamemnon, Helen, Menelaos, and Nestor, the Trojan War, and the Olympic Games; cf. *Commentariorum* III.3.1 (pp. 10, 11 with English translation): *Hic* [*sc.* at the Morea] *nobilis Corinthus fuit et Elis, ludorum* [Olympic Games] *memoria insignis; et vetus Lacedaemon, Agamenonis et Menelai sedes, qui rapinam Helenae vindicantes Ilion delevere; et vetustiores Argi et Nestorea Pylos.*

103 D.S. Chambers, "Spese del sioggiorno di Papa Pio II a Mantua," in A. Calzona, *et al.*, eds. *Il Sogno di Pio II e il viaggio da Roma a Mantova* (Città di Castello, 2003), pp. 391–402; and *idem*, *Popes, Cardinals and War*, p. 70. Chambers has based his conclusions on material in the *Archivo di Stato, Mantua, Fondo Portioli, b. 13*, "Libro Giornale, 1459," cc. 61ᵛ, 66ʳ, 83ʳ, and 88ʳ. For the lack of enthusiasm among the cardinals, cf. Pastor, 3: 62 ff.

104 This letter remains unpublished but it is located in the *Archivio di Stato, Mantua, Archivio Gonzaga: b. 840*, c. 410ʳ, which Chambers has consulted and produced an abstract of the materiel acquired by Isidore; apparently, in this letter Isidore expresses his intentions to go personally to war; cf. Chambers, *Popes, Cardinals and War*, pp. 70 and 200 n. 76. It is hoped that this letter, thus far unknown, of Isidore will find an editor in the near future. Perhaps there is more information to be distilled from the Mantuan Archives on the activities of Isidore in these matters. It should be stated, nevertheless, that, following the example of other cardinals, Isidore also imported wine, in addition to weapons; cf. Chambers, "Spese del sioggiorno," p. 395: "No dimeno l'altro [that is, in addition to Bessarion] benefeciario del sussidio, il cardinal 'Isidore Ruthensis' o Isidoro da Kiev, chiamato 'Cardinalis Grechus' – da non confondere con Bessarione che era sempre chiamato 'Nicenus' – importo un carico di vino il 29 novembre." Chambers supports this statement from documents in the archives of Mantua (p. 395 n. 11).

105 *Commentariorum* III. 3.3 (with English translation, pp. 12, 13): *placuit trecentos illuc* [to the Morea] *pedites mittere. Blanca Mediolanensium dux centum suo aere conduxit. Pius reliquos.*

106 *Commentariorum*, III. 3.3 (with English translation, pp. 12, 13): *Quamvis non probaret* [*sc.* Pius] *coeptis ingentibus tam debile fundamentum apponi, Bessarioni noluit denegare, cui ea res cordi erat.* The pleasure of Bessarion for the activation of this minor band of warriors is evident in his correspondence; cf. his letter of 1459 (*ΠκΠ* 3: 257):

> Crucesignatos . . . Sanctissimus D.N. parabit navim in Ancona, per quam transfretabunt. Opportet autem quod sintviri boni habentes arma aliqua, et habentes exspensas pro uno anno, videlicet L vel LX ducatos aut de suo aute de eleemosyna aliorum, quibus daretis indulgentiam plenariam tam euntibus personaliter, quam conferentibus expensas pro euntibus . . . et quia necesse est ut hoc cito fiat, melius est habere quingentos vel CCCC. Vel etiam CCC. in tempore, quam multa millia tarde . . . sufficit habere usque ad D. vel CCCC. Verl etiam CCC. ad minus, dummodo sint fulciti armis et expensis et mittatis eos usque asd Anconam, et ibi erit navis parata ex parte D. N. quae conducet eos.

107 *Commentariorum* III. 3.3 (with English translation, pp. 12–14). The same information is repeated in the *Annales Minorum* 13: 116 (as quoted in *ΠκΠ* 4: κζ′ v); the two texts are related, as it is obvious by the shared phraseology and the identical lexical items:

> Brevi trecentos expeditos milites ilel conscripsit, e quibus centumcentum Blanca Mediolanensis Ducissa, illo suadente, suo aere conduxit. Cuncti Mantuam ad Pontificis pedes se contulere; egregie armata et robusta iuventus. Jannonus Cremonensis pedestrium copiarumnon ignarus ducotr, illis quos Blanca delegit, praefectus; aliis Dotha Senesis propter civiles discordias patria extorris . . . apud Anconam navem conscedentes, felici cursu Peloponnesum appulerunt, ubi comiter a graecis excepti, Patracensem urbem primo congress expugnaverunt. Verum dum alia quaedam summa contentione oppugnant oppida, seu virtutis aemulatione seu praedae cupiditate inter se dissidentes incepta reliquere, dispersique milites in diversa cum dedecore abierunt.

108 For the gratitude of the Greeks, cf. S.P. Lampros, "Κωνσταντῖνος Παλαιολόγος Γραίτζας: ὁ Ἀμύντωρ τοῦ Σαλμενικοῦ," *NH* 11 (1914): pp. 260–288, esp. 284–288. Graitzas, one of the Greek warlords campaigning against the invading Turks in the Morea, wrote a letter to the duchess of Milan, in which he expresses his gratitude for the assistance that he has received by the leader of her troops; cf. *ibid.*, pp. 260, 261, for the complete text, from which we quote the following selection, with the document's infelicities in orthography, as they appear in the original document's *graecobarbara* style (p. 260):

> ϖανυψιλωτάτῃ [sic], ϖανεκλαμϖροτάτῃ, ϖανευτυχεστάτῃ, ἐμοὶ δὲ ἁγία κυρία δούκαινα τῆς ἐκλαμϖροτάτης Μεδιολάνης . . . τῷ ϖανταγάθῳ θεῷ δέομαι, ἵνα δωρήσηται τῇ ἐκλαμϖρότητί σου τῷ ἐλέει αὐτοῦ καὶ ἐν τῷ νῦν αἰῶνι καὶ ἐν τῷ μέλλοντι . . . τολμῶν ἀναφέρω ὅϖως ἡ ἐκλαμϖρότης σου ἠθέλες μάθη [sic] . . . καὶ τοῦ καϖετάνου οὗ ἐϖρόσταξε ἡ ἐκλαμϖρότης σου καὶ ἦλθεν εἰς βοήθειαν τῶν Χριστιανῶν . . . ἤγουν τοῦ κὺρ Τζουὰν Τασκρέμα [Giannone de Cremona].

326 *Il Cardinal Greco Vecchio: the last years*

There is supposedly an Italian translation of this letter by Filelfo in the archives of Mantua, but Lampros proved unable to locate it during his examination (cf. *ibid.*, p. 261).
109 Robin, p. 118. Filelfo also spoke publicly in the congress and his speech is summarized by Pius II. The pope praised Filelfo in humanistic terms, even invoking the Muse, as Filelfo himself had done in his own poetry (cf. the opening four lines of his ode to Isidore); cf. *Commentariorum* III. 20. 2–3 (with English translation, pp. 80, 81):

> *Franciscum Philelphum, satyrum scriptorem, insignem poetam Latinis ac Graecis litteris ornatu, qui suam causam oraret, interposuit* [*sc.* the duke of Milan]. *Is aliqua de Francisci deque pontificis laude locutus multa de Turchis, plura de Graecis dixit, et quam necessaria esset in Turchos expedition, et quantum Franciscus eam probaret, et quanta promitteret Christianis auxilia, exposuit. Quo auditu laudavit pontifex magnificis verbis orationem Philelphi, eumque Musam Atticam appellavit.*

110 The only edition of the Greek text is published in Legrand, pp. 208–210. The ode consists of eleven stanzas. Each stanza consists of four lines: three anapestic tetrameters, perhaps to suggest a military march: 4 (xx--), with the alternate --, and a concluding Adonian, that is, a dactyl followed by a spondee (- xx--). The word order of the ode betrays a composer who is more at home with Latin poetry than Greek, as we should expect. There is no scholarly study of this poem.
111 The invocation of the Muse suggests ancient epic poetry, with which both Filelfo and Isidore were familiar. The entire poem is a mixture of humanistic elements deriving from ancient literature, with a few remarks to include Christianity, a normal feature in the humanistic literature of the period. Pope Pius II also indulged in such hybrid pagan-Christian notions (*supra*, n. 79, where Venus is mentioned in a Christian context).
112 The Pierian Muses are a *topos* in ancient literature, with which humanists would have been familiar; cf., e.g., among many others, Theocritus's Thyrsis, who repeats, throughout the poem, the line, ἄρχετε βουκολικᾶς, Μοῖσαι φίλαι, ἄρχετε ἀοιδᾶς; Moskhos's *Funeral Song of Bion*: ἄρχετε Σικελικαί, τῷ πένθεος ἄρχετε, Μοῖσαι. Closer to classical antiquity, in addition to Homer, is the invocation to the Muse(s) that is standard in Homeric hymns. Specifically, the "Pierian Muses" were invoked by Hesiod in the opening of his *Works and Days*: Μοῦσαι Πιερίηθεν ἀοιδῆσιν κλείουσαι, δεῦτε. "Muse" in Renaissance humanism signifies "ancient literature"; cf. Pius's praise on Filelfo, who, in the pope's opinion, is well versed in "the Attic Muse" (*supra*, n. 109).
113 An allusion to the Turks, traditionally styled in Greek literature of the period as ἀσεβεῖς/"impious" to be contrasted here with Isidore who is εὐσεβὴς/pious.
114 Probably a convoluted allusion to Isidore as the pope's legate and as the Latin Patriarch of Constantinople in 1452–1453. Thus the church mentioned here is Santa Sophia in Constantinople.
115 Filelfo shifts his emphasis to Thomas Palaiologos, the despot of the Morea, who through his own ineptitude and the treasonous behavior of his brother Demetrios, was about to lose his despotate to the Ottoman Turks. From this point on in the poem Thomas seems to occupy the mind of Filelfo and Isidore plays a secondary part in the ode.
116 "New Rome"/*Roma Nova*, or "Second Rome," was the formal appellation of Constantinople and a similar epithet will eventually apply to Moscow, which would be known as the "Third Rome," especially after the marriage of Thomas Palaiologos's daughter, Zoë/Sophia, to the grand prince Ivan III.
117 There is no problem here with invoking a pagan god, Zeus/Jupiter; cf. Pius's own citation of ancient gods quoted in *supra*, n. 86; humanists, even clerics, were no longer averse to invoking the pagan gods.
118 Emperor Manuel II Palaiologos, whose vast achievements in literature and travels in defense of Constantinople have earned him the honorific title of being a Greek Marcus Aurelius; cf. *MP*, ch. 7, pp. 395–443 and esp. 449. Filelfo may have even met Manuel II during his stay in Constantinople in his youth, when he was studying Greek under Manuel Chrysoloras, a close friend and associate of the emperor; cf. *supra*, ch. 1, text

with n. 29. Is there a reason why Filelfo is linking Thomas, Manuel, and Isidore? Was Filelfo aware of the existence of a family relationship among these individuals?
119 Is this a reference to the congress in Mantua?
120 That is, the Muse.
121 This is an allusion to Isidore being a cardinal.
122 Sphrantzes, *Minus* 41.1–5:

> τοῦ δεσπότου [*sc.* Θωμᾶ] . . . πανοικὶ ἐλθόντος εἰς τοὺς Κορφούς . . . τῇ ις΄ τοῦ Νοεμβρίου τοῦ αὐτοῦ ἔτους [= 6969 *anno mundi* in the Greek notation, that is, 1460 AD] ἐμβὰς εἰς ἓν τῶν Κορφιατικῶν καραβοπούλων ὁ δεσπότης κῦρ Θωμᾶς μετὰ καὶ τῶν πλειόνων ἀρχόντων αὐτοῦ διέβη εἰς τὸν Ἀγκῶνα, ἵνα ἀπ᾽ ἐκεῖσε εἴς τε τὸν πάπαν καὶ τὸν δούκαν Μιλάνας καὶ ἀλλαχοῦ ἀπέλθῃ, εἰς τοὺς Κορφοὺς καταλείψας τήν τε βασίλισσαν καὶ τὰ παιδία αὐτοῦ καί τινας τῶν ἀρχόντων.

123 The body of Saint Andrew had been placed in the Church of the Holy Apostles in Constantinople, but in the hunt for relics after the sack of the imperial capital by the crusaders of 1204, Cardinal Pietro Capuano took the remains to Amalfi. By 1208 these relics had been deposited in Amalfi's Church of Saint Andrew. Capuano's relics lacked the head, which long ago had been brought to Patras in the Morea. In Patras the head was kept in the Church of Saint Andrew by the Sea. On this topic, cf. Comte P. Riant, *Exuviae sacrae Constantinopolitanae* 105 (Geneva, 1877), p. cv ff.; and the detailed study of Lampros, "Ἡ ἐκ Πατρῶν," pp. 33–112.

124 *Minus* 42.8. The same information is also furnished in the fifteenth-century work of the Greco-Venetian Theodoro Spandounis/Spandugnino/Spandugino, who claimed a relationship to the Kantakouzenos family: "De la origine degli imperatori Ottomani ordini de la corte, forma del guerreggiare loro religione rito, et ostume de la nations," in C.N. Sathas, ed., *Μνημεῖα Ἑλληνικῆς Ἱστορίας: Documents inédits relatifs à l'histoire de la Grèce au moyen Âge*, 9 (Paris, 1890; repr. Athens, 1972), pp. 135–261 (the original edition was published in Florence, in 1551; p. 42 treats these events):

> Onde veggendo homaso che Maometto occupaua ogni cosa, no uolle aspettare il furor di quello, ma ibarcato chef u a Patras con on uento se ne nauicò a Roma: et portò con esso la testa di Santo Andrea Apostolo, la qual il donò a Pio II pontefiche.

For an English translation of this early study in ethnography, cf. D.M. Nicol, *Theodore Spandounes: On the Origin of the Ottoman Emperors* (Cambridge, 1997).

125 If the letter by Bessarion, quoted and discussed (*supra*, n. 35), is genuine, the pope's pension to Thomas amounted to 200 ducats per month: δουκάτα τριακόσια, ὥσπερ ἐδίδε καὶ τῷ ἁγίῳ δεσπότῃ. The amount cited by Bessarion does not seem to be correct (unless Bessarion is overlooking the added sum by the cardinals). Thomas received 300 ducats per month from the pope, to which the cardinals added another 200; cf. *PaL* 2: 228. Venice also added another 500 ducats (cf. Lampros, "Ἡ ἐκ Πατρῶν," p. 37 and n. 4). That the pope supplied 300 ducats is also stated by Bartolomeo Bonatto, the Mantuan ambassador to Rome, in a letter of the 9th of March 1461. Bonatto also supplies a description of Thomas (cf. Pastor, 3: 403 [Appendix, no. 43]):

> el dispota de la Morea qual certo e un bel homo et ha uno uno bello et graue aspect et bon modi et molto signorili; po havere da cinquant sei anni. Havea in dosso una turcha de zambeloto negro cum uno capello biancho peloso fodrato de cetanino; velutato negro cum una cerata intorno.

For an English translation and discussion of this section of Bonatto's letter, cf. *PaL* 2: 228, and n. 101. For another translation of this passage and further discussion, cf. Harris, *Greek Emigres in the West*, pp. 111, 112.

126 Relics played an important role in the conduct of diplomacy and state relations, and Thomas was not the only individual to take advantage of his possession of valuable relics. In 1462, a year after the surrender of the head of Saint Andrew, the Venetians brought with fanfare from Aigina the head of Saint George. Cf. Stefano Magno, in

Hopf, *Chroniques Gréco-romanes*, pp. 179–209, esp. 202 (fol. 152ᵛ for the year 1462): *Ex Aigina insula fù tolto la testa del glorioso martire et cavalier S. Zorzi; quod quidem caput Venetias ductum ibique magnifice sepultum est.* The Porte did as well in its relations and diplomatic negotiations with the West. In the reign of Bayezid II in 1484, the sultan donated the right hand of Saint John to the Grand Master of the Knights of Saint John in Rhodes. Another event of 1492 is related by Spandugnino, *De la origine* (Sathas edition, 171):

> et piu per gratificarsi Baiasit con Innocentio octavo Pontefice maximo, li mandò a donare per il suo Capizi bassà Mustapha, che fu poi bassà grande, el ferro della lanza che feri il costato del Salvator nostro Jesu Christo, la spongia, la canna et molte altre reliquie, che sultan Mehemet tenea queste con gran riverentia et honore.

Spandugnino is guilty of exaggeration. The only attested relic to have been received in Italy at this time was the reputed lance of Longinus, which was acquired from Ottoman Constantinople and was paraded in procession throughout the streets of Rome; cf. S.P. Lampros, "Ἑλληνικὰ Γράμματα τοῦ Σουλτάνου Βαγιαζὴτ Β΄," *NH* 5 (1908): pp. 155–189, esp. 177. The relics that were in Constantinople before the Turkish conquest were of great interest to Russian pilgrims; they reverently speak of them in their accounts of their journeys. Cf. the collected testimonies in Majeska, *passim*.

127 Lampros, "Ἡ ἐκ Πατρῶν," p. 38.
128 There has been a long scholarly debate over the true authorship of this account. The text has been transmitted in manuscript form under the title: *Andreis: Incipit Andreis id est Hystoria de receptione capitis Sancti Andreae* (in *Vat. cod. 5667*, fols. 19ᵛ–40ᵛ; and in *cod. Regin. 1995*, fols. 349ᵛ–366ʳ that also is to be found in the Vatican Library). It is also included in Pius's *Memoirs*, Book VIII. There exists a letter by Francesco Piccolomini, which states that this account's author and editor was Alessio, the bishop of Chiusi. This letter has been published by Lampros, "Ἡ ἐκ Πατρῶν," p. 45 n. 2, in which we encounter the following statement: *adiecta etiam Andreide Domini Alessij episcopi Clusini.* On this complicated matter, cf. *PaL* 2: 229 n. 103: "The strange fact is that in the letter... [Francesco Piccolomini] seems to say that the Andreis had been (should we say?) written, edited, or prepared by Alessio de' Cesari, bishop of Chiusi (1438–1462) and archbishop of Benevento (d. 31 July, 1464)." While the question of authorship remains unresolved, we will have to await the opinion of the present editors and translators of Pius II's *Commentariorum*, since the *Andreis* is included in Pius's *Memoirs*, Book VIII (which is in preparation). The *Andreis* definitely exhibits the style and the lexical preferences of Pius. Who then is the true author of the *Andreis*?
129 Similar information is also supplied by Bonatto in his letter of the 1st of May 1461, in which he states that the health of Isidore had become questionable and that it had seriously affected his ability to communicate; cf. Chambers, *Popes, Cardinals and War*, p. 200 n. 76 (citing as evidence the *Archivio di Stato, Mantua, Archivio Gonzaga, b. 841*, c. 62ʳ).
130 Pope Paul VI returned the head of Saint Andrew to Patras in 1964. The relic was deposited in the Church of Saint Andrew (the largest church in Greece) on 24 September 1964.
131 The description of the translation by Alessio is divided into forty-one long paragraphs (or thirty-two printed pages in Lampros's edition).
132 On Isidore's house and the neighborhood, cf. *supra*, n. 32.
133 Para. 30 (p. 103) in Lampros's edition.
134 *Supra*, n. 24 for the evidence.
135 *Acta Consistorialia* in *Arch. Segr. Vaticano, Arm. XXI, tom. 52*, fol. 64ʳ; cf. *PaL* 2: 4.5. The information and date of the 27th of April 1463 are further confirmed in Cardinal Francesco Gonzaga's report; cf. Chambers, *Popes, Cardinals and War*, p. 200 n. 76 (citing archival evidence: *Archivio di Stato, Mantua, Archivio Gonzaga, b. 842*, c. 3ʳ).
136 *PG* 159: col. 952.
137 Cf. the discussion on this topic in Robin, pp. 11–13.

8 Conclusions
Damnatio memoriae?

Cardinal Isidore received a great deal of bad press among the Orthodox Greeks and Muscovite Rus', and among the Catholics in Italy, as he was a recipient of anti-Greek sentiment in Italy that seems to have been on the rise in the last years of his life. An exception within the western bad press is provided in far off Spain, which had not yet received large numbers of refugees from Greece and had not yet experienced or formulated anti-Greek sentiments that were already encountered in Italy. Very few refugees, actual defenders of Constantinople, found their way to Spain after the fall in their endless search to obtain monetary aid to ransom their relatives from the Turks.[1] In time, more refugees looked westward to Spain and eventually arrived in large numbers, especially in the sixteenth century, when Spain and the Holy Roman Empire were fighting the Ottomans in the Mediterranean.[2] In the early period, after 1453, there is at least one chronicle written in Spain in which Isidore is treated with justice and the facts are accurately reported. Its author is Alfonso Fernándes de Palentia (also known as Alonso de Palencia) (1422–1493),[3] who wrote a work entitled: *Gesta Hispaniensia ex Annalibus suorum dierum colligentis* (also cited as *Décadas*), in which he devotes a section to the siege of Constantinople. Alfonso had studied with Bessarion, with George Trapezountios ["of Trebizond"], and with John Laskaris, and received a thorough humanistic education while he resided in Italy.[4] Eventually, he concluded in his *Décadas*[5] that Constantinople had been abandoned by the West, which thus failed to pay attention to the monumental crisis, as western Christianity disregarded the Greek emperor's pleas for relief.[6] Alfonso then mentions Cardinal Isidore,[7] whom he praises as an exception to the general trend. In Alfonso's view, Isidore exerted serious efforts and did his utmost on behalf of the defense of Constantinople:

> *innumeraque commituntur ab infidelibus flagitia sceleratissima in contumeliam Christianae religionis, neglectae potius ab iis qui mollibus induti laesciuiaeque dediti deriserant infoelicissimas legationes. Quorum particeps non fuit Isidorus cardinalis Rutenus, qui quanta potuit pecunia collecta ad succurendum Constantinopolim profectus captusque in expugnatione urbis id periculum diuino auxilio effugit.*
>
> The infidels [Turks] committed multiple sacrilegious and criminal acts of disrespect against the Christian religion, which had been abandoned

by those who had devoted themselves to luxury and had made fun of the [Greek emperor's] envoys. Yet we have to make one exception that stood out from the midst: Cardinal Isidore of Ruthenia amassed as many funds as he could for the defense of Constantinople. He went there and was captured during the sack, and by a divine miracle he was able to escape the danger.

The westerners, who personally knew the cardinal, thought highly of him. That is how Bishop Leonardo felt and he made his sentiments known in his narrative, which highly praises Isidore. Leonardo had attached himself to the cardinal's retinue from the moment that they had encountered each other on Chios, while Isidore was recruiting mercenaries for the defense of Constantinople.[8] He further praises his efforts to enforce and to celebrate church union in a hostile environment.[9] Leonardo emphasizes the important role that Isidore played in the defense before and during the siege, when he strengthened and reinforced at his own expense the ruined fortifications in his sector, in sharp contrast to the attitude of the native Greeks who did not seem to be engaged actively and selflessly in the defense of their own homeland.[10] Leonardo further highlights the advising role of Isidore in the high command and the fact that he was assigned a sector of the fortifications to guard.[11] After citing the repairs that Isidore made in his sector, Leonardo apparently was unaware of what happened to Isidore during the sack. He does not return to him in his narrative, which was finished by 16 August.[12] It is apparent that Leonardo was uninformed of Isidore's adventures during and after the sack. Barbaro also speaks favorably and respectfully of Isidore, whom he cites in his narrative as *el gardenal de Rosìa*, and on one occasion he even adds the title "magnificent" to his normal formula:[13] *del Reverendissimo magnifico monsignor miser lo gardenal*. Similarly, in the preserved sections of his brief *relazione* on the fall of Constantinople, the consul of Ancona, Benvenuto, addresses Isidore with respect, after he could not ascertain his fate during the sack.[14]

From the Greek perspective, the comments and evaluations of Isidore are mixed and for the main part are delineated along religious lines. Among the Greek supporters of church union and the Greek Catholics, Doukas reserves praise for the cardinal, but overlooks his activities on behalf of the defense of Constantinople. Rather, he emphasizes Isidore's scholarly role, together with that of Bessarion, in the Council of Ferrara-Florence:[15] ὁ Βησσαρίων Νικαίας καὶ ὁ Ῥωσσίας Ἰσίδωρος. οὗτοι δὲ ἦσαν οἱ λογιώτεροι τῶν ἀρχιερέων, "there was Bessarion [the bishop] of Nicaea and Isidore [the metropolitan] of Russia. These two individuals were the most scholarly of the [Greek] high priests [in the Council]." Doukas returns to the same theme later in his narrative and mentions Isidore with respect:[16] ἔστειλε δὲ ὁ πάπας τὸν καδδηνάλιον Πολωνίας, τόν ποτε ἀρχιεπίσκοπον Ῥωσίας Ἰσίδωρον, ἄνδρα συνετὸν καὶ σώφρονα καὶ πεπαιδευμένον ἐν δόγμασιν ὀρθοῖς, Ῥωμαῖον τὸ γένος καὶ αὐτὸν ἕνα τῆς ἐν Φλωρεντίᾳ συνόδου ὑπάρχοντα πατέρα τίμιον, "the pope sent Isidore, the

Cardinal of Poland [sic], who had once served as the archbishop of Rus'. He had a good mind, held the right views, and had been educated in correct dogmas. He was a Roman [Greek] by ethnicity, and he was one of the most valued fathers in the Council of Florence."

The views of Doukas seem to be echoed in a later patriarchal chronicle from Constantinople, in which the scholarly character of the Greek delegation is emphasized. Isidore is included:[17]

διεμηνύσατο οὖν ὁ βασιλεὺς τοῖς ἀρχιερεῦσι πᾶσιν Ἀνατολῆς τε καὶ Δύσεως, ὁμοίως καὶ τοὺς μετέχοντας ἐν λόγοις, καὶ ἦλθον ἅπαντες ἐν Κωνσταντινουπόλει. ὅ τε Τραπεζοῦντος ἔχων καὶ τὸν φιλόσοφον Ἀμηρούτζην, ὁ Νικαίας Βησσαρίων, ὁ Ῥωσσίας, καὶ ὁ φιλόσοφος Γεμιστός, καὶ ἄλλοι ἐκ τῶν ἀρχιερέων οὐκ ὀλίγοι.

So the emperor summoned all hierarchs of the east and west and similarly, the educated people. They all came to Constantinople: the [metropolitan of] Trebizond in the company of the philosopher Ameroutzes [Amoiroutzes], Bessarion of Nicaea, [the metropolitan] of Russia [Isidore], the philosopher Gemistos [Plethon], and many other hierarchs.

The same chronicle returns to Isidore and Bessarion and tries to isolate both cardinals from the "scandals" that were wrecking the church, claiming that it was the scandals that followed the Council of Ferrara-Florence that forced them to retreat to Italy, as it also forced the absence of a patriarch in Constantinople. At the end of the statement the author indicates that he did not approve of their "apostasy":[18]

μὴ ὄντος δὲ πατριάρχου οὐδεὶς ἠθέλησε γενέσθαι ἕνεκεν τῶν σκανδάλων. ὁ Νικαίας δὲ Βησσαρίων ὁμοίως καὶ ὁ Ῥωσσίας ἔμειναν ἐν τῇ Ῥώμῃ. ὁ γὰρ Βησσαρίων ἦν πολὺς ἐν τῷ λέγειν καὶ ἄκρος φιλόσοφος. γέγονε καὶ γαρδινάλιος ἔχων τιμὴν καὶ δόξαν οὐ τὴν τυχοῦσαν. ἠγάπησε γὰρ τὴν δόξαν τῶν ἀνθρώπων ἢ τοῦ Θεοῦ.

No one wished to be appointed to the vacant post of patriarch, because of the scandals. Bessarion of Nicaea and similarly the [metropolitan] of Russia remained in Rome. Bessarion was a good speaker and a first rate philosopher; he even became cardinal and enjoyed honor and considerable glory; for he had fallen in love with the glory of men rather than that of God.

Syropoulos, who had personally observed Isidore act on behalf of church union during the Council of 1438–1439, and who seems to have disapproved of Isidore's career in the Catholic Church, expresses disdain for Isidore's office as a cardinal of the Catholic Church, but at the same time voices high praise for him and for his activities before his Catholic "conversion":[19] τὸν τότε τιμιώτατον ἐν ἱερομονάχοις καὶ καθηγούμενον τῆς σεβασμίας μονῆς τοῦ ἁγίου Δημητρίου κῦρ Ἰσίδωρον, τὸν μετὰ ταῦτα Ῥωσίας γεγονότα καὶ ἐς ὕστερον πρὸς τὸ τοῦ καρδηναλίου ὑψωθέντα βάραθρον, "Lord Isidore, who at that time was a most honorable individual among the hieromonks and the abbot of the respected monastery of Saint Demetrios, who later became [the metropolitan] of Rus' and even later was elevated to the abyss of a cardinal." Otherwise, the implacable champion of Orthodoxy, Theodoros Agallianos, speaks of the debates that took place in the city and the vain efforts of Isidore to convert the Greeks to Catholicism prior to the siege, but he produced no negative comments about Isidore. No personal animosity toward him is detected in his writings.

Similarly, Sphrantzes, a supporter of church union and an officer of the Catholic court of Constantinople, expressed serious reservations in his chronicle:[20] ἤθελα γὰρ νὰ εἶχε γενεῖν καλῶς ἑνώσει τῶν ἐκκλησιῶν καὶ νά με ἔλειπεν ὁ εἷς τῶν ὀφθαλμῶν μου, "I wish that the union of the churches had come about properly, even if it had cost me one of my own eyes." Knowingly, he avoids dogmatic debates:[21]

> τὰ τῆς ἐκκλησίας δόγματα, ταῦτα γὰρ παρ' ἄλλοις ἐδόθησαν κρίνεσθαι. ἐμοὶ δ' ἀρκεῖ ἡ πατρική μου διαδοχὴ τῆς πίστεως, καὶ ὅτι οὐδέποτε παρά τινος τῶν τοῦ μέρους ἐκείνου ἤκουσα, ὅτι τὸ ἡμῶν κακόν, ἀλλὰ καλὸν καὶ ἀρχαῖον, καὶ τὸ ἐκείνων οὐ κακόν, ἀλλὰ καλόν.
>
> The dogmas of the church ... there are others to pronounce judgment on such matters. For my part, my ancestral inheritance of our faith is sufficient. Never have I heard anyone from the other side say that our form of worship is incorrect, on the contrary they maintain that it was ancient and proper; similarly, their form of worship is not incorrect but proper.

Sphrantzes further takes the opportunity to reveal his views, which seem to produce a diplomatic compromise.[22] He assigns the siege and fall of Constantinople directly to the fact that the Council of Ferrara-Florence convened and resulted in a church union.[23]

After his liberation from Ottoman captivity, Sphrantzes became a dependent of the despot of the Morea and unsuccessfully sought employment in the household of Cardinal Bessarion.[24] In his authentic work, the *Minus*, he reserves space to note his own failed efforts to support Isidore's elevation to the patriarchal throne of Constantinople in 1452. As he wished to become Isidore's intermediary,[25] he adds neither positive nor negative comments about him.[26] His insertion of Isidore into his narrative allows Sphrantzes to include his own personal opinions on the Council of Ferrara-Florence. This affords him the opportunity to interrupt the annalistic genre so he can provide us with his own personal and private views on religion and on the late foreign policies of the Byzantine imperial court. In the process, the diplomat produces some of the sharpest impressions of a courtier and the most memorable and celebrated passages of his composition. It is at this point in his narrative that Sphrantzes reflects on the long-term foreign policy of the late imperial court of Constantinople, thus providing his own interpretations. Sphrantzes draws a major

Conclusions: damnatio memoriae? 333

distinction between the policies of Manuel II and those of his son and successor John VIII:[27]

καὶ ἀκούσατε λόγους ἀληθεῖς, τὴν αὐτοαλήθειαν ϖροβαλουμένου μου μάρτυρα. εἶϖεν ὁ ἀοίδιμος βασιλεὺς [Μανουὴλ] ϖρὸς τὸν υἱὸν αὐτοῦ, τὸν βασιλέα κὺρ Ἰωάννην, μόνος ϖρὸς μόνον, ἱσταμένου καὶ ἐμοῦ μόνου ἔμϖροσθεν αὐτῶν, ἐμϖεσόντος τοῦ λόγου ϖερὶ τῆς συνόδου ... λοιϖὸν ϖερὶ τῆς συνόδου, μελέτα μὲν αὐτὸ καὶ ἀνακάτωνε, καὶ μάλισθ᾽ ὅταν ἔχῃς χρείαν τινὰ φοβῆσαι τοὺς ἀσεβεῖς. τὸ δὲ νὰ ϖοιήσῃς αὐτήν, μηδὲ ἐϖιχειρισθῇς αὐτὸ τούτου δὲ ἀδύνατον ὄντος σχεδόν, φοβοῦμαι μὴ καὶ χεῖρον σχίσμα γεγένηται. καὶ ἰδοὺ ἀϖεσκεϖάσθημεν εἰς τοὺς ἀσεβεῖς.

Listen now to the true account, as I call on the very truth to be my witness. Our memorable emperor [Manuel II] had spoken in my presence the following words concerning the synod to his son Lord John [VIII], our emperor. No one else was there:"... Well, then, as far as this synod is concerned, continue to study and plan it, especially when you need to frighten the impious [Turks]. But do not bring it about.... As this is impossible to achieve, I fear that a worse schism may develop and we will have nothing to protect us from the impious [Turks]."

John VIII's reaction was ominous, as far as Sphrantzes is concerned, as the young emperor said nothing and departed from his aged father's side in silence, which led Manuel II to comment to Sphrantzes, a sharp evaluation of the young confident emperor:[28]

τοῦ δὲ βασιλέως, ὡς ἔδοξε, μὴ δεξαμένου τὸν λόγον τοῦ ϖατρὸς αὐτοῦ, μηδὲν εἰϖών, ἀναστὰς ἀϖῆλθε. καὶ μικρὸν σύννους γεγονὼς ὁ μακαρίτης καὶ ἀοίδιμος ϖατὴρ αὐτοῦ, ἐμβλέψας ϖρὸς ἐμὲ ὁρίζει "ὁ βασιλεὺς ὁ υἱός μου ἔνι μὲν ἁρμοδίως βασιλεῖ, οὐ τοῦ ϖαρόντος δὲ καιροῦ. βλέπει γὰρ καὶ φρονεῖ μεγάλα καὶ τοιαῦτα, οἷα οἱ καροὶ ἔχρηζον τῆς εὐημερίας τῶν ϖρογόνων ἡμῶν. ἄμη, σήμερον, ὡσὰν ϖαρακολουθοῦσιν εἰς ἡμᾶς τὰ ϖροστάγματα, οὐ βασιλέα θέλει ἡ ἡμῶν ἀρχή, ἀλλ᾽ οἰκονόμον. καὶ φοβοῦμαι, μήϖοτε ἐκ τῶν ἐνθυμημάτων καὶ ἐϖιχειρημάτων αὐτοῦ γένηται χαλασμὸς τοῦ ὁσϖιτίου τούτου."

It seemed that the emperor disagreed with his father. He said nothing, but got up and left. His memorable late father grew thoughtful, looked at me, and said: "My son the emperor is fitted to be an emperor, but not at the present moment. For he has great visions and plans, but ones that were needed in the good old days of our ancestors. Today, as our affairs consume our attention, the empire needs not an emperor but an administrator. And I fear that his ideas and actions will bring about the downfall of our house."

Sphrantzes, with sadness, concludes that the "synod" (Council of Ferrara-Florence) should have not taken place:[29] καὶ ἰδοὺ ἐκμαρτυρία τοῦ ὡς μὴ ὤφελε γενέσθαι τὴν σύνοδον, "indeed, this is sufficient proof that the synod should not have taken place."

Thus Sphrantzes has nothing negative to say about Isidore, except that he became his advocate at the court and his references in the narrative afford him the opportunity to state his own views about the Council of Ferrara-Florence and its consequences. For Sphrantzes the union and by implication the actions of Isidore on behalf of church union brought about the end of his own world. The Greeks clearly disapproved and may have been even offended by the Catholicism of Isidore, whom, nevertheless, they respected as an individual and had high regard for his education. Unlike Isidore's Slavic flock, the Greeks never employed personal animus against the cardinal. Consequently, their ambiguous position reinforced the tendency to avoid mention of him and perhaps assisted in the relegation of Isidore to a fate akin to a *damnatio memoriae*.[30]

The Patriarchate under Sultan Mehmed II Fatih[31] never cites Isidore's role during the Council of Ferrara-Florence and his celebration of the church union during his stay in Constantinople. Even when the official act of the Greek rejection of the decisions taken at the council was officially formulated, the role of the Greek cardinals, Isidore and Bessarion, is never noted and the distinguished clerics are passed over in silence. In addition, the Constantinopolitan celebration of the union in Santa Sophia on the 12th of December 1452 is also passed over in silence in this official document of 1483–1484. The patriarchal formulation of the formal rejection of Florence has survived in numerous copies and one of them is probably the original text as it was originally written;[32] copies of the "decree" also exist. The document states that a "patriarchal ecumenical synod"[33] assembled and drafted the contents in the period of 1 September 1483 to 31 August 1484. This is long after Ferrara-Florence[34] and after the sack of Constantinople, but the Patriarchate took time to get reorganized and reestablish itself under Ottoman rule.[35] Finally, the hierarchs felt strong enough to reject formally the church union that had been declared in Florence and had been celebrated in Constantinople. The document itself never mentions by name the participants in Ferrara-Florence nor does it comment upon them in their participation of the celebration of church union in Constantinople. Yet, the contents demonstrate that the document had in mind the principal Greek priests, Bessarion and Isidore, who had accepted the union in Florence.

Thus the document cites the Council of Ferrara-Florence in a negative light and at the outset expresses its faith in the original Nicene Creed, takes pleasure in citing the procession of the Holy Spirit from the Father alone, without any reference to the later Latin addition of *filioque*.[36] The document's first reference to the Council of Ferrara-Florence seeks to link the council's conclusions to the devil and to heresies:

ἀλλ' οὐδ' οὕτως ἔγνωκεν ἐφησυχάσαι ὁ τῆς κακίας ἐφευρετής, ἀλλὰ διὰ προσχήματος οἰκουμενικῆς δῆθεν συνόδου, ἥτις ἐν Φλωρεντίᾳ, οὐ πρὸ πολλοῦ, τῆς Ἰταλίας συνέστη, αὖθις τὴν εἰρημένην καὶ προαπoιχομένην αἵρεσιν καὶ ἄλλ' ἄττα ἀλλόκοτα ἀνανεώσασθαι οὐκ ἠμέλησεν. ὅθεν ἔκτοτε ἐς δεῦρο λοιπόν, τῆς ἐκκλησίας οὕτως ταραττομένης καὶ κυμαινομένης διὰ τὸ παραδέξασθαι πολλοὺς τῶν ἡμετέρων τῆς ἐκκλησίας τροφίμων τὰς τοιαύτας αἱρέσεις καὶ σπουδάζειν ἀπεναντίας τοῦ θείου θελήματος ταύτας κατέχειν, ἡ ἁγία αὕτη καὶ οἰκουμενικὴ τῶν ἀρχιερέων καὶ πατριαρχῶν σύνοδος διὰ τοῦ παρόντος αὐτῆς ὅρου ἔγνωκε δεῖν τὰ κακῶς τε καὶ ἀπερισκέπτως ἐν τῇ Φλωρεντίᾳ συνοδικῶς πραχθέντα καὶ δογματισθέντα, ὡς δόγματα νόθα καὶ τῆς καθολικῆς ἐκκλησίας ἀλλότρια, ταῦτα καταστρέψαι.

Yet the inventor of evil [devil][37] failed to acquiesce and in the pretext of a supposedly ecumenical Council, which took place in Italy's Florence some time ago, did not neglect to renew the aforementioned heresy and sanctioned further innovations. And so until the present time, the Church was thrown into confusion and wavered in a storm because many of the nourishing dogmas of our Church, which oppose God's will, were imposed. Therefore, this holy and ecumenical synod consisting of hierarchs and patriarchs, declares, through its formal decision, that the proceedings and the declarations of the Council of [Ferrara-]Florence, were concluded improperly and thoughtlessly, as they were false dogmas foreign to the Catholic[38] Church and must be rejected.

This brief and unsophisticated declaration of the Patriarchate, which concentrates on the differences and the ritual without treating the more profound theological differences and the finer points that western theology, with its emphasis on logical argumentation and scholastically minute analysis of all statements, had raised during the Ferrara-Florence proceedings, condemns both the achievements of church union and, by implication, the Greek hierarchs who had worked on behalf of the union. The text concludes in the following manner:[39]

ἔτι δὲ καὶ διὰ τοῦ παρόντος συνοδικοῦ τόμου καὶ τὴν ἐν Φλωρεντίᾳ συστᾶσαν ἀνατρέπομεν σύνοδον καὶ ἅπερ ὁ ἐκδοθεὶς ὑπ' αὐτῆς ὅρος περιέχει κεφάλαια καὶ ἀργὴν καὶ ἀνενέργητον ἀποφαινόμεθα ἀπὸ τοῦδε[40] ταύτην εἶναι, καὶ ὡς μηδὲ τὸ κατ' ἀρχὰς[41] ὅλως συστᾶσαν ἡγούμεθα καὶ ἔχομεν, ὡς ἀσύμφωνα δογματίσασαν καὶ πολέμια ταῖς πρὸ αὐτῆς ἁγίαις ὀκτὼ καὶ οἰκουμενικαῖς συνόδοις περί τε τοῦ ζητήματος τῆς ἐκπορεύσεως τοῦ ἁγίου πνεύματος καὶ τῶν λοιπῶν. ἔτι δὲ καὶ τὴν δι' ἀζύμων θυσίαν ἀποστρεφόμεθα καὶ τὰ λοιπά, ἅπερ ἐν τῇ Φλωρεντίᾳ ἐστέρχθη καὶ τῷ ἐκεῖ γενομένῳ ὅρῳ ἐμπεριέχεται, καθὼς προειρήκαμεν, συμφωνοῦντες ἐν ἅπασι δόγμασί τε καὶ ἔθεσιν ἐκκλησίας, ἐγγράφοις τε καὶ ἀγράφοις, ταῖς προλεχθείσαις ἁγίαις καὶ οἰκουμενικαῖς συνόδοις. καὶ εἰς τὸν αἰῶνα τὸν ἅπαντα τὰ δογματισθέντα ὑπ' αὐτῶν καὶ παρ' ἡμῶν ἐν τῷ παρόντι τόμῳ συμφώνως φυλάττεσθαι καὶ ἀπαραποίητα καὶ ἀσάλευτα καὶ βουλόμεθα καὶ εὐχόμεθα, σκέπῃ καὶ βοηθείᾳ τῆς ἁγίας ἀκτίστου καὶ ὁμοουσίου τριάδος, τοῦ ἑνὸς τῶν ὅλων δεσποτῶν τε καὶ Θεοῦ, ὅτι αὐτῷ πρέπει ἡ δόξα, ἡ τιμὴ καὶ ἡ μεγαλοπρέπεια εἰς τοὺς ἀτελευτήτους αἰῶνας. ἀμήν.

336 *Conclusions:* damnatio memoriae?

In addition, through the present document, we overturn both the Council that took place in [Ferrara-]Florence and all chapters that are included in its decree, and declare that the Council is null and invalid from this point on. It is our opinion and belief that the Council had not been properly assembled, since the dogmas that it produced run contrary to, and do not agree with, the eight holy synods that preceded the Council, especially in regard to the subject of the procession of the Holy Spirit [*filioque*] and the remaining matters. Moreover, we reject the sacrifice of the unleavened bread and the remaining matters that were decided and were included in the decree that was issued in Florence, as we mentioned. We agree and accept all the dogmas and customs of the Church, written and unwritten, as they have been settled in the aforementioned holy ecumenical synods. We wish and pray, under the protection of God and through divine help, that everything that they have sanctioned in dogma and by us in the present document, is guarded and remains firm and unchanged for all eternity, under the protection and help from the Holy Trinity, which is the true and of the same essence as that of God, the Lord of all. His is the glory, the honor, and the magnificence for eternity. Amen.

In the *corpus* of surviving documents of the early Patriarchate under the Ottoman sultans, mention of the Greek rejection of the Council of Ferrara-Florence is made only once, when Patriarch Nephon II (his reign lasted from the end of 1486 to the beginning of 1488) announced his elevation to the patriarchal throne to the Patriarch of Alexandria. In this letter, Nephon II reminds his colleague of the official Greek rejection of the union. Otherwise, this document deals with other official business, with charges that had been brought against the Patriarch of Jerusalem. Nephon II felt compelled to remind the Patriarch of Alexandria of the official rejection. This is puzzling. Were there any problems in accepting this document? Since this letter was directed to someone who had already accepted the rejection, is there a hint of possible problems in accepting the formal decision of the Patriarchate of Constantinople? The pertinent section of the letter reads as follows:[42]

> ἔτι τε ἀνατρέπομεν ὡς καὶ πρότερον τὴν ἐν Φλωρεντίᾳ ἐκείνην λατινικὴν σύνοδον καὶ ὅσα κακῶς ἔστερξεν ἐκείνη, ἀπ' ἐναντίας τῆς διδασκαλίας τοῦ εὐαγγελίου καὶ τῶν ἁγίων συνόδων καὶ ὡς μηδὲ τὸ κατ' ἀρχὰς συστῆναι λογιζόμεθα ταύτην, καθὼς ἐδέξω πρότερον καὶ τὰ κακὰ τῆς συνόδου ταύτης συνοδικὰ γράμματα, εἰς ἅπερ καὶ ἡ σὴ ἁγιότης συνεψηφίσω διὰ τοῦ σοῦ τοποτηρητοῦ, τότε μὲν Σμύρνης, νῦν δὲ Ἐφέσου κὺρ Δανιήλ.

We further declare, as we did earlier, that the Latin synod in [Ferrara-]Florence was invalid, as it made the wrong decisions, contrary to the teachings of the Gospel and of the holy synods, and we conclude that it had not been made up properly, a decision that you yourself embraced earlier. Your Holiness further voted, through your representative Lord Daniel (who was then [the metropolitan] of Smyrna and is currently [the metropolitan] of Ephesus), that the letters of that synod were improper.

More vocal and more personal attacks against Isidore are the sentiments of his Slavic flock, which remained fiercely Orthodox, in spite of the cardinal's efforts to bring the Muscovite and Kievan Church back into the fold during the Council of Ferrara-Florence. In Muscovite literature, as we have seen,[43] Isidore is equated with the devil himself. Contemporary citations about Isidore in Slavic lands remain negative, but are not disrespectful, and he is seen as a difficult personality, whose motives were puzzling and alien to his flock. The following phrase is a typical comment:[44] Сидоръ злочестивый, "the impious Isidore." After Isidore departed Moscow, the "bad press" continued, even when Isidore's associate, Gregory, was appointed to the Kievan seat, and the cardinal was described[45] as "poisonous," "impious," and a "thief of the night, a Latin heretic who fled with his student Gregory." Another text[46] characterizes him as a "most renowned student of evil." Moreover, elsewhere[47] he is described as a "falsifier," суемысленаго Исидора. A summary of his ministry describes him in dark colors.[48]

There exist no detailed descriptions of Isidore and no character portraits in the surviving literature. None of those who closely worked with him have left us surviving accounts of his personality. One would give much to know how Gregory, Isidore's assistant during Isidore's Muscovite period, regarded the cardinal. Yet, nothing survives in the record. One would like to know as well what Cardinal Bessarion thought of him. What we can actually state safely is that Isidore was a peculiar personality who seems to cross what appear to be the firm borders in the *quattrocento*. Often he fails to confine himself within one grouping. He was a humanist, but he was limited to the Greek world, and never achieved competence in Latin, thus limiting him in the Latin world. He was a priest, but he was a fighting priest and a warrior. He traveled extensively, perhaps as much or even more than Emperor Manuel II or John VIII. Although a priest and initially an Orthodox prelate, he did not hesitate to cross the line and enthusiastically embrace Catholicism, when circumstances dictated this form of action. His motives for doing so are not clear. Did he really believe that Orthodoxy had gone astray? He was not well versed in the Latin Fathers of the church, thus he could not read them fluently. Was his motivation dictated by the policies of the Constantinopolitan court and Emperor John VIII, who was determined to bring about church union in order to save Constantinople from the Ottoman Turks? Isidore seems to have been selected by the Greek emperor precisely because the emperor could rely on Isidore to support his plans, based on the cold facts of the day and on *Realpolitik*. With the objective of bringing the Muscovites into union with Rome, Isidore seems to have been selected by the imperial court, with the acquiescence of the patriarchate, to head the Slavic Church, contrary to the native desires of the Muscovite Rus' who sought to appoint their own metropolitan.

In addition, Isidore was an indefatigable traveler in an era when extended journeys were not the norm. He belongs to the late Byzantine generation of travelers, who, for one reason or another (and more often to attract western allies against the Turkish threat), made never-ending journeys. Prior to him, Manuel II Palaiologos had been compelled to visit France and London in an endless search for aid (Spring 1400–Spring 1403).[49] Since the days of Constantine the Great, no emperor of Constantinople had traveled as extensively. Manuel II's son, John VIII Palaiologos, had also traveled to Hungary and Italy.[50] These emperors had also dispatched to the West a number of delegations. But Isidore, one of the latter, went even farther. His early journeys brought him to the Morea (1414–1417);[51] a passage on a ship accidentally and unexpectedly brought him to Sicily (1429);[52] and the next decade brought him as a representative of the Greek Church to Basle (1433).[53] His appointment to Muscovy brought him to Moscow (1437–1438) and beyond, for he then went to Ferrara and Florence (1438–1439).[54] From Italy, Isidore returned to Moscow (1441), was arrested by the secular authorities but escaped by September 1441, traveled to Tver (where he was arrested once more), and proceeded to Lithuania; from there an extended journey brought him to Rome.[55] In 1450, Isidore on a papal mission traveled briefly to Constantinople and then returned to Rome.[56] In the Spring of 1452, Pope Nicholas V dispatched Isidore, as his legate, to Constantinople to enforce and to celebrate the union. Isidore took his time and made a long trip, making stops at Naples and Chios, so that he could gather some mercenary reinforcements for the defense of the city.[57] Following the sack of Constantinople he fled to Bursa, moved on to Chios, and finally reached Candia on Crete (Summer 1453).[58] Thus his later years brought him back to Constantinople, Asia Minor, and the Levant, his last long journey, and then he returned to Italy in the fall of 1453.

This record alone demonstrates his incredible stamina at a time when few people were able to travel so extensively. In addition to his travels, Isidore was an active scholar of ancient Greek, a notable historian, a theologian within the *Realpolitik* of the Constantinopolitan court. He remained an active prelate, whose work involved him with the Greek patriarchate, with the metropolitanate of Kiev and all Rus', and with the Vatican. In addition to this, he was an able diplomat and served in the role of papal legate. Moreover, he was an active warrior and warlord, and even a prolific propagandist. Until his very last years Isidore worked on behalf of Greek liberty. Patriotism seems to have been his primary motivation.

Isidore also was a bridge between the two versions of Christianity: the Orthodox and the Catholic. While he began life as an Orthodox and even advanced to the position of metropolitan, the highest office of the Muscovite Orthodox Church, Isidore went on to accept and even to enforce church union and concluded his life as a Catholic cardinal. The following is a list of the known positions held by Isidore at different times in his life:[59]

1   Abbot of the Monastery Saint Demetrios in Constantinople (until 1437);
2   Metropolitan of Kiev and all Rus' (1437–1442);
3   Cardinal and priest (1442–1458);

4   Cardinal and Bishop of Sabina (1451–1463);
5   Latin Patriarch (titular) of Constantinople (1452–1453; 1459–1463);
6   Latin Archbishop of Nicosia (Cyprus) (1456–1458);
7   Latin Archbishop of Kiev and all Rus' (1458–1463).

Thus Isidore within his lifetime held a number of prestigious positions in the Orthodox and the Catholic churches. In fact, he seems to have held more positions than his more famous friend, Cardinal Bessarion.[60] Thus Isidore's career appears exceptional, given the fact that he had achieved these prominent positions in both churches. Yet as we have seen he was more than a cleric with high standing in both churches. He carried out diplomatic missions (e.g., to Constantinople as a diplomat and mediator between the Venetians and the Greek court before and during the siege of 1453), and even assumed the duties of a warlord during the actual siege and oversaw the defense of a sector of the walls. We are faced with a very active career that can be best described as stellar.

Along with Bessarion, Isidore did his utmost at Ferrara and Florence to have the Orthodox representatives accept the union. In many ways he was the right hand of Emperor John in urging the Greeks to adopt this position. Yet his actions at Florence and his acceptance of the Latin view earned him the enmity of his flock. In Florence his actions went contrary to the instructions he had received from the authorities in Moscow. After his return he became the devil incarnate for his Slavic flock, which continued to heap abuse upon him long after his death. The Greeks were not as explicit and chose to pass over him in silence and disregarded his activities in 1452, when he attempted again, probably for the secular salvation and on behalf of Greek independence, to enforce the Catholic position in the Greek capital. His role as an active defender of the city in 1453 was overlooked by the Greeks and by Greek historians in subsequent centuries. Posterity has been much kinder to the scholarly Bessarion. Today there exists a minor street in Athens named in Bessarion's honor.[61] Isidore was never honored in a similar manner, and there is no street named after him, even though his actions were those of an active and perhaps even heroic patriot who fought in the defense of Constantinople in his personal efforts to preserve the freedom of the city. Bessarion played a different role, as he concentrated his efforts and energy on the survival of ancient and medieval Greek culture and literature through the formation of a collection and the preservation of manuscripts and texts, in the hope that this action would initiate an educational process that would eventually result in the rebirth of the Greek nation.[62]

Once Isidore returned to Italy from his adventures in the Levant, he encountered snide remarks and he was never fully accepted by the Vatican as a true Catholic, in spite of the positions of honor that he was granted by various popes. His role remained ambiguous. He stood out as a Greek and perhaps his conversion to Catholicism and his appearance with a bearded face remained under suspicion. He was even accused of being senile by some Italians.[63]

Thus Isidore remains an enigmatic personality. Who was the true Isidore? The only aspect of his personality that can be ascertained is that he was a patriot. His actions shortly before, during, and after the sack of Constantinople admirably demonstrate this aspect of his personality. There may be questions about his true religiosity but there can be no doubt about his patriotism. Perhaps his religious beliefs were subordinated to his main objective throughout his life: the survival of Constantinople. He did his best to see that his goal was realized but he must have been extremely affected when the city fell. His disappointment must have reached a nadir when he subsequently realized that the papal efforts on behalf of the liberation of Greece were insufficient and were doomed. Posterity has not been kind to Isidore, as his efforts have been neglected and his actual role as a defender of Constantinople has been largely overlooked and has been forgotten. Isidore's close friend, Cardinal Bessarion, with his towering intellectual personality, may have unwittingly lessened the contributions of Isidore, who remained in the background of Italian humanism during the early Renaissance.

Yet in many ways, perhaps because Isidore was a man of the church, many of his views were firmly grounded in the thought of the Middle Ages and in his propaganda he used terms and plans that were still firmly rooted in the European concept of the crusade, which was becoming obsolete. Moreover, he never achieved the next level of national consciousness that characterizes the thought of George Gemistos Plethon and his pupil Laonikos Khalkokondyles, who seem to have moved beyond the medieval concept of what a Byzantine-Roman-Christian was and come close to our concept of Neo-Hellenism, anticipating the formation of the modern Greek nation that would emerge four centuries later.[64] However, Isidore probably would have agreed and would have expressed similar sentiments with the vision of Laonikos, who predicted the formation of the Greek nation at the beginning of his work with the following words:[65]

> μὴ δὲ ἐκεῖνό γε πάνυ ἐκφαύλως ἔχον ἡμῖν, ὡς Ἑλληνικῇ φωνῇ ταῦτα διέξιμεν, ἐπεὶ ἥ γε τῶν Ἑλλήνων φωνὴ πολλαχῇ ἀνὰ τὴν οἰκουμένην διέσπαρται καὶ συχναῖς ἐκαταμέμεικται. καὶ κλέος μὲν αὐτῇ μέγα τὸ παραυτίκα μεῖζον δὲ καὶ ἐς αὖθις, ὁπότε δὴ ἀνὰ βασιλείαν οὐ φαύλην Ἕλλην τε αὐτὸς βασιλεὺς καὶ ἐξ αὐτοῦ ἐσόμενοι βασιλεῖς, οἱ δὴ καὶ οἱ τῶν Ἑλλήνων παῖδες ξυλλεγόμενοι κατὰ τὰ σφῶν ἔθιμα ὡς ἥδιστα μὲν σφίσιν αὐτοῖς, τοῖς δὲ ἄλλοις ὡς κράτιστα πολιτεύοιντο.

> It is not that I am being perverse in writing my history in the Greek language, since the Greek language has been dispersed in so many places throughout the world and has already been mixed with many other languages. Already its prestige is great and will further be enhanced in the future, when a Hellene king and his dynasty will lord over a Hellenic kingdom, in which the descendants of the Hellenes will also gather and will mightily exercise those political rights that are most agreeable to their own ancestral customs.

Isidore was not a Renaissance man. Unlike Khalkokondyles, he could not divorce himself from the classics and produce a history of his times with neutral feelings towards religion.[66] After all, he was an ecclesiastic. In addition, unlike Bessarion, Isidore was not a philosopher and he did not contribute to the burning scholarly debates among humanists of that time, such as on a delineation of the differences between Plato and Aristotle. He concentrated on two patriotic goals: securing the salvation of Constantinople and, after its fall and occupation, its liberation. He should have been declared a national hero for all his efforts on behalf of his fatherland; yet religious attitudes and the unmitigated fanaticism of his age stood in the way. In the cold light of the day, after the passage of more than five centuries since Isidore's time, we find no quarrel with the brief *laudatio* of Isidore's activities, as it is simply and eloquently stated in the *Notitia*:[67]

> *Erat autem Isidorus cardinalis vir undecunque doctissimus, theologus Graecorum insignis, in divinis Scripturis apprime versatus, ingenio subtilis et acer, in dicendo nervosus et gravis.... Dictus alicubi facundus Graecorum doctor, et gentis decus.*

Cardinal Isidore was a thoroughly learned man, a notable Greek, extremely well versed in the Sacred Scriptures. He had a subtle genius and he was clever, while his oratorical style was energetic and serious.... Elsewhere he has been called a prolific Greek scholar. He was the glory of his nation.

Notes

1 J. Harris, *Greek Emigres in the West 1400–1520* (Camberley, Surrey, 1995), pp. 19–20, cites documentation for two refugees: John Alexander, who had lost an arm during the siege, and John Aralli (Raoul/Rhalles?), both having made their way to Aragon in their quest for alms.

2 Western scholarship has not as yet thoroughly examined the arrival and the establishment of Greek refugees in Spain, although at least one individual from Crete, Domenikos Theotokopoulos (the famed "el Greco") is well known, because of his success as a notable painter of the Renaissance. Others were also there; cf. our brief comments in *SF*, pp. 155–157. There is evidence to suggest that there were Greeks among the Spanish conquistadores in the New World. Within the original small band of Don Hernan Cortés, the eventual Marqués del Valle de Oaxaca, which landed in Mexico in 1519, there were Greeks who then participated in his *conquista* of the "Aztecs." The Greeks were known among Cortés's group; having written their memoirs of those days, some of the *conquistadores* mention the Greeks by their ethnicity. Cf., e.g., the account of Fray Francisco [Alonso] de Aguilar and a participant in the conquest of Mexico, entitled: *Relación breve de la conquista de la Nueva España* (8th ed., Mexico, 1980), who mentions in the second *Jornada* of his work the ethnic composition of Cortés's band. Cf. Patricia de Fuentes, *The Conquistadors: First-person Accounts of the Conquest of Mexico* (New York, 1963), p. 137: "There were also Venetians, Greeks, Sicilians, Italians, Biscaians, Montanese, Asturians, Portuguese, Andalusians and Estremenians." A decade later the *conquistador* of Peru, Don Francisco Pizarro, included in his staff a chief of artillery named Pedro da Candia (Petros Kretikos) and a company of sixteen Greeks. Pedro was eventually executed by Pizarro's associate, Diego Almagro. There exists no detailed scholarly study on this enigmatic figure, Pedro da Candia, and of his Greek band of conquistadores in Peru. The only work is that of P. Kontoglou, *Φημισμένοι Άντρες καὶ Λησμονημένοι* (Athens, 1942), pp. 31–44, which suffers from an absence of scholarly citations. On the Greeks in Spain, some fundamental research has been carried out in the two studies of

Khasiotes, *Μακάριος, Θεόδωρος καὶ Νικηφόρος οἱ Μελισσηνοὶ (Μελισσουργοί)*; and *Οἱ Ἕλληνες στὶς Παραμονὲς τῆς Ναυμαχίας τῆς Ναυπάκτου: Ἐκκλήσεις, Ἐπαναστατικὲς Κινήσεις καὶ Ἐξεγέρσεις στὴν Ἑλληνικὴ Χερσόνησο ἀπὸ τὶς Παραμονὲς ὡς τὸ Τέλος τοῦ Κυπριακοῦ Πολέμου (1568–1571)* (Thessalonike, 1970), but a great deal of research into Spanish archives remains to be done.

3 On this chronicler, cf., among others, J. Durán Barceló, "Bibliografía de Alfonso de Palencia," *Boletin Bibliográfico dela Associación Hispánica de Literatura Medieval* 9 (1955): pp. 289–341; R.B. Tate, "The Civic Humanism of Alfonso de Palencia," *Renaissance and Modern Studies* 5 (1979): pp. 25–44; and idem, "La sociedad castellana en la obra de Alfonso de Palencia," *Actas del III Coloquio de Historia Medieval Andaluza* (1983), pp. 5–23.

4 For Alfonso, his humanism, and his Greek teachers in Italy, cf., among others, G. Morocho Gayo, "Constantinopla: historia y rétorica en los cronistas Alonso de Palencia y Pedro de Valenica," *Biblioteca des Autores Españoles* 257 (Madrid, 1904), pp. 9–27; and C. Real Torres, "La presencia de Grecia en el humanismo castellano. Relaciones entre Oriente y Occidente: la influencia bizantina en el humanismo castellano," in I. Garcia Galvez, ed. *Grecia y la tradición clásica* 2 (La Laguna-Tenerife, 2002), pp. 627–640.

5 The Latin text of Alfonso's *Décadas* has been published by R.B. Tate and J. Lawrence, *Alfonso de Palencia, Gesta Hispaniensia ex annalibus suorum diebus collecta*, 2 vols. (Madrid 1998–1999).

6 The section of the *Décadas* that refers to the conquest of Constantinople is not well known and has received very little scholarly attention. It was only recently recovered by M. Morfakidis, who printed and discusses it; cf. M. Morfakidis, "Ἡ Ἅλωση τῆς Κωνσταντινούπολης στο Χρονικό του Alonso de Palencia," in E. Motos Guirao and M. Morfakidis Filactós, eds. *Constantinopla. 550 años de su caída, Κωνσταντινούπολη. 550 Χρόνια ἀπό την Ἅλωση,* 2: *La Caída. Ἡ Ἅλωση* (Granada, 2006), pp. 53, 54 (the Latin text of Alfonso with modern Greek translation: pp. 62–69). Morfakidis also points out (p. 53 n. 3) that Pertusi should have included Alfonso's text in *CC* 2. Also cf. J. López del Toro, *Cuarta Década de Alonso de Palencia* (Madrid, 1971).

7 Alfonso was in the service of Bessarion in Florence, together with Vespasiano da Bistici, until his return to Spain. In Rome he studied with George Trapezountios. Alfonso's coworker, da Bistici, was also familiar with Isidore and he may have contributed, perhaps unwittingly, to the "bad press" that had been accumulating around the Greek cardinal, as he was involved in the quest of Filelfo to retrieve his Plutarch manuscript (cf. *supra*, ch. 7, text with nn. 56–73). Is it possible that, through the mediation of Bessarion, Alfonso had corresponded or even had met Cardinal Isidore (perhaps after his return from Candia)? There is no definitive evidence to suggest that Isidore had corresponded with Alfonso or that the two humanists personally knew each other and that the two humanists had even encountered one another. Nevertheless, Alfonso had numerous interactions with Greek humanists in Italy, who taught him ancient Greek. He became very proficient in the ancient language and was able to translate into Spanish the *Parallel Lives* of Plutarch in 1491 and the following year the work of Flavius Josephus; cf. Morfakidis, "Ἡ Ἅλωση," p. 54 n. 15.

8 *CC* 1: 124–126: *Cum igitur reverendissimus pater, dominus cardinalis Sabinensis* [Isidore], . . . *in eius famulatum me ex Chio vocasset, egi summa cum animi mei diligentia, ut fidem . . . defensarem.* Barbaro also speaks of the arrival of Isidore and further specifies the aid that he brought with him; cf. *CC* 1: 10:

> *l'azonse una nave che vigna da Zenova, de Zenovexi, de portada portare de cantara trenta sie millia con el gardenal de Rosìa* [Isidore], *che manda el papa per dover far la union, e dusse con si homeni 200 fra scopetieri e balestrieri per secorso de questa zitade de Costantinopoli.*

Benvenuto also mentions the substantial aid that Isidore brought to Constantinople; cf. *TIePN*, p. 5: *Item quod erant tantum homines ad custodiendum menias cum reverendissimo domino cardinali* [Isidore] *7000.*

9 *Ibid.*, pp. 126–128: *actum est industria et probitate praefatis cardinalis* [Isidore], *ut sancta unio . . . firmaretur celebrareturque.* Barbaro speaks of the celebration of the union and also

Conclusions: damnatio memoriae?   343

cites Isidore; cf. *CC* 1: 11: *fo fatto la union . . . en etiam ve jera el reverendo gardenal de Rosìa* [Isidore].
10 *Ibid.* p. 146: *Sed o Graecorum impietatem, o patriae direptores, o avaros! . . . A paucis nihilominus quaedam ultronea oblation facta est. Cardinalis* [Isidore] *hercle omne stadium habuit in ferenda ope, in reparandis turribus et muro.* Later in his narrative, Leonardo makes it clear that it was the Anemades towers that were repaired through the cardinal's personal funds; cf. *CC* 1: 150: *turres, quas Anemadas vacant impensis cardinalis* [Isidore] *reparatas*. On these towers, cf. *SF*, p. 355. In shaper contrast, Greek contractors enriched themselves to the detriment of the walls, a fact that was noted by Leonardo; cf., e.g., the case of the contractor Manuel Iagaris and his associate, Neophytus of Rhodes, discussed in *SF*, pp. 305, 306.
11 *Ibid.*, p. 150: *Cardinalis* [Isidore], *a consilio nunquam absens, Sancti Demetrii regionem ad mare defensabat*. Benvenuto also speaks of Isidore's active military role in the defense; cf. *TIePN*, 4: *quod stabat super murum ad custodiam*. The fact that Isidore played an important part in the councils charged with the preparation of the defenses, as he mediated between Greeks and Venetians, is also emphasized by Barbaro; cf. *CC* 1: 10:

> *fo praticado de retignir le galìe grosse de marcavo per conservation de Costantinopoli, e quest pratica fo fatta in la giexia de Santa Sofia, e lì ve iera l'imperador, el gardenal de Rosìa* [Isidore], *el vescovo de Metelin* [Leonardo], *e tuti i baroni del imperador, e tuti marcadanti de la nation*.

12 *Ibid.*, p. 170: *Data Chii, XVI die Augusti, 1453*. Since the two ecclesiastics became such good friends during the siege, is it possible that they never again were in touch with each other after Isidore's return to Italy? Is it probable that they never corresponded thereafter? Or are we to assume, once again, that our knowledge about such events is so imperfect precisely because most of the correspondence of Isidore has disappeared or remains to be retrieved in the various archives? The lost corpus may have included letters that the two prelates exchanged with each other.
13 Barbaro 7 (not in *CC* 1).
14 *TIePN*, p. 4: *Item quod de reverendissimo domino cardinali* [Isidore] *nichil scit det*[*er*]*minate, nisi quod stabat super murum ad custodiam*.
15 Doukas 31.3.
16 *Ibid.*, 36.1.
17 Ἔκθεσις Χρονικὴ 12 (p. 32).
18 *Ibid.*, 16 (p. 34).
19 II.22 (p. 126). Syropoulos elsewhere indicates that he was aware of the cardinal's learning and educational background, and occasionally he even praises him, even though he also disapproves of his support of the church union at Ferrara and Florence. Isidore's main role in the disputations of the Council consists of mediating between the Greek emperor and the various factions of the court and Latin prelates; cf. Syropoulos VIII.7 (p. 398); VIII.21 (p. 408); and VIII.27 (p. 414). In addition, cf. *supra*, ch. 3, *passim*. The educational background of Isidore receives favorable mention even in Muscovite accounts, in which Isidore is not seen in a favorable light. Thus the early sixteenth-century *Patriarchal or Nikon Annal* records the following impression of Isidore's arrival, ПСРЛ 12: 23: "In the Spring on the Tuesday of Bright Week, after the Great day [Resurrection or Easter Sunday], Metropolitan Isidore, a Greek, came to Moscow for the metropolitanate from Tsargrad, from the Patriarch Joseph. [He was] a speaker of many languages and learned."
20 *Minus* 23.4.
21 *Ibid.*, 23.2.
22 *Ibid.*, 23.3, in which he produces a parable, "the way to Santa Sophia," to illustrate his views. His narrative at this point emulates a biblical and ecclesiastical style:

> καὶ νὰ εἴπω, ὡς ἐν παραδείγματι, ὅτι τὴν Μέσην ὁδὸν τῆς Πόλεως, τὴν πλατείαν καὶ εὐρύχωρον, διέρχομαι πολλοὺς χρόνους μετά τινων, δι' ἧς ἐκαταντῶμεν εἰς τὴν Ἁγίαν Σοφίαν. εἶτα μετά τινας καιροὺς εὑρέθη παρά τινων καὶ ἄλλη ὁδὸς καταντῶσα, καὶ αὕτη, ἐκεῖ καὶ νά με παροτρύνωσιν, ὅτι "ἐλθὲ καὶ διὰ τῆς ὁδοῦ

ταύτης ἧς εὕρομεν. καὶ γάρ, εἰ καὶ ἔστιν αὕτη, ὁπού ἀπέρχῃ, καλὴ καὶ ἀρχαία καὶ ἡμῖν ἀρχῆθεν σὺν ἡμῖν γνωστὴ καὶ διερχομένη, ἀλλὰ καὶ αὕτη, ἣν εὕρομεν νῦν, καλή ἐστιν." ἐγὼ δὲ νὰ ἀκούω παρὰ μὲν τῶν, ὅτι καλή ἐστι, παρὰ δὲ τῶν, ὅτι οὐ καλή, διὰ τί νὰ μηδὲν εἴπω. "μετ᾽ εἰρήνης καὶ ἀγάπης ἀπέρχεσθε καλῶς εἰς τὴν Ἁγίαν Σοφίαν, ὁπόθεν βούλεσθε. ἐγὼ δὲ πάλιν θέλω διέρχεσθαι διὰ τῆς ὁδοῦ, ἣν καὶ μεθ᾽ ἡμῶν πολύν τινα χρόνον διηρχόμην καὶ καλὴν αὐτὴν καὶ παρ᾽ ὑμῶν καὶ τῶν προγόνων μου μαρτυρουμένην καὶ διερχομένην."

This approach is clearly a studied, if not a tortured (as Sphrantzes deeply in his heart was Orthodox), reaction of an imperial functionary who struggled to find a compromise and an accommodation that would satisfy both irreconcilable sides. For the extreme reaction of the general population of Constantinople, cf. the numerous incidents recounted by Doukas in his narrative, 36.1–7.

23 *Minus* 23. 4: καὶ αὕτη ἡ τῆς συνόδου δουλεία αἰτία μία καὶ πρώτη καὶ μεγάλη εἰς τὸ νὰ γένηται ἡ κατὰ τῆς Πόλεως τῶν ἀσεβῶν [Turks] ἔφοδος καὶ ἀπὸ ταύτην πάλιν ἡ πολιορκία καὶ ἡ αἰχμαλωσία καὶ τοιαύτη καὶ τοσαύτη συμφορὰ ἡμῶν.

24 *Ibid.*, 43.1–2:

κἀγὼ ἀναγκασθεὶς ὑπὸ τῆς ἐνδείας ἀπριλίῳ ιη^η ἐξῆλθον καὶ ἀπῆλθον εἰς τὸν Ἀγκῶνα τῇ ιζ^η μαΐου. Καὶ τῇ α^η πάλιν ἰουνίου ἐξελθόντος μου, ἀπῆλθον διὰ τῆς ὁδοῦ τοῦ Βιτέλμου, ἐπεὶ κἀκεῖσε εἰς τὰ θέρμα εὑρίσκεσθαι τὸν καρδινάλιν [*sc.* Bessarion] μεμαθήκαμεν ... ἐξελθόντες ἀπεσώθημεν ἐνταῦθα εἰς τοὺς Κορυφοὺς τῇ ε^η τοῦ σεπτεμβρίου μηνὸς τοῦ οε$^ου$ ἔτους [1466].

25 *Ibid.*, 36.5: εὑρεθέντος γὰρ καὶ τοῦ καρδιναλίου Ῥωσσίας [Isidore] εἰς τὴν Πόλιν, μέσος ἐγὼ παρ᾽ αὐτοῦ γέγονα ... ἵνα γένηται πατριάρχης καὶ τὰ καὶ τὰ γένωνται παρ᾽ αὐτοῦ καὶ τοῦ τότε πάπα, ἢ κἂν ἐκ δευτέρου νὰ μνημονευθῇ ὁ πάπας.

26 The expressed religious beliefs of Sphrantzes were ambiguous, at best; cf. *supra*, n. 22. As a court official he had to accept the union of Florence but later on, after the fall of Constantinople and the conquest of the Morea, while he was a refugee on Corfu, he reverted to Orthodoxy and before he died, in accordance to the Orthodox-Byzantine tradition, both he and his wife took monastic vows. Cf. *Minus* 45.3: τοῦ αὐτοῦ δηλονότι ουου ἔτους [1468] ... τῶν κοσμικῶν φορεμάτων ἡμῶν διαλυθέντων, ἐρασοφορέσαμεν τῇ αη τοῦ αὐγούστου μηνὸς καὶ ἀντὶ Γεωργίου Γρηγόριος, ἀντὶ δὲ Ἑλένης Εὐπραξία ὠνομάσθημεν, διδόντες πρῶτον τὴν εἰς Θεὸν τῆς πίστεως ὁμολογίαν ἡμῶν. As an indication of his Orthodox faith, Sphrantzes cites a variation of the Orthodox Nicene creed, which does not include the Catholic *filioque* phrase.

27 *Ibid.*, 23.5, 6.
28 *Ibid.*, 23.7.
29 *Ibid.*, 23.12.
30 Sphrantzes, who knew Isidore and had acted on his behalf, urging the emperor to elevate him to the patriarchal throne of Constantinople, fails to mention the cardinal's death, even though he notes the later death and the burial place of Bessarion. Yet, he makes no statement of Isidore's passing. On Bessarion, cf. *Minus* 46.11: περὶ δὲ τὸ φθινόπωρον τοῦ παου ἔτους [1472] ... ὁ καρδινάλις κῦρ Βησσαρίων ... τῇ ιε^η νοεμβρίου ἀπέθανε ... μετὰ τιμῆς ὅτι πλείστης ἔθαψαν αὐτὸν εἰς τὸν ναὸν τῶν Ἁγίων Ἀποστόλων, ἔνθα δὴ ... τὸν τάφον αὐτοῦ προητοίμασεν πλησίον τοῦ τάφου τῆς ἁγίας ὁσιομάρτυρος Εὐγενείας.

31 On the Patriarchate's reconstitution after the Ottoman conquest of Constantinople, and on its relations and financial obligations toward the Porte, cf. now T. Papademetriou, *Render unto the Sultan: Power, Authority, and the Greek Orthodox Church in the Early Ottoman Centuries* (Oxford, 2015).

32 The original document, in its entirety, has been recently published by M. Paize-Apostolopoulou and D.G. Apostolopoulos, *Ἐπίσημα Κείμενα τοῦ Πατριαρχείου Κωνσταντινουπόλεως: Τὰ Σωζόμενα ἀπὸ τὴν Περίοδο 1454–1498* (Athens, 2011), no.

26 (pp. 183–190). This original document is incorporated in the "Νόμιμον τῆς Μεγάλης Ἐκκλησίας," ms. 12, fol. 194ʳ–195ᵛ, in the Diocese of Samos and Ikaria. A copy also exists in the Moscow ms. 3554 (*Vlad. 242*), fols. 81ᵛ–84ᵛ. Cf. Archimandrite Vladimir, *Систематическое Описаніе Рукописей Московской Синодальной (Патриаршей) Библиотеки* [*A Systematic Description of the Muscovite Synodal (Patriarchal) Manuscripts*] 1: *Рукописи Греческія* [*Greek Manuscripts*] (Moscow 1894), pp. 320–322. In addition, cf. D.G. Apostolopoulos, *Ὁ "Ἱερὸς Κῶδιξ" τοῦ Πατριαρχείου Κωνσταντινουπόλεως στὸ Β´ Μισὸ τοῦ ΙΕ´ Αἰώνα, Τὰ Μόνα Γνωστὰ Σπαράγματα* (Athens, 1999), no. 6, pp. 124–129, which again includes the text of the "decree"; in the same study Apostolopoulos supplies a facsimile of the Samos ms. 12, fols. 194ʳ–195ᵛ (pp. 29–31).

33 The term appears a number of times in the document. In the beginning the "ecumenical synod" is self-defined as ἡ ἁγία μεγάλη καὶ οἰκουμενικὴ αὕτη σύνοδος, taking place ἐν τῷ θείῳ καὶ πανσέπτῳ ναῷ τῆς ὑπεραγίας Θεοτόκου τῆς Παμμακαρίστου, in the reigns of two patriarchs: Maximos III (Spring, 1476–3 April 1482); and Symeon I (April 1482–Fall of 1486, his third reign): τοῦ τε ἀοιδίμου ἐκείνου τοῦ ἤδη προαποιχουμένου, κυροῦ Μαξίμου καὶ τοῦ νῦν τοὺς οἴακας τῆς καθολικῆς [= Orthodox] Ἐκκλησίας ἰθύνοντος κυροῦ Συμεών. The "ecumenical synod" is cited once more in the conclusion of the document: ὑπεγράφη ὁ παρὼν ἱερὸς τόμος καὶ ἐβεβαιώθη ὑπὸ τῶν τὴν ἁγίαν ταύτην καὶ οἰκουμενικὴν σύνοδον ἀναπληρούντων. One hundred and fourteen signatures follow (with two lines remaining blank). The signing hierarchs are from the Greek world. Notably absent are the participation of and signatures of the metropolitans (or their representatives) from Muscovite Rus' and Iberia (Georgia), who had participated in the Council of Ferrara-Florence. Armenia is also absent.

34 Yet the text tries to overlook the intervening long period by stating that the Council of Ferrara-Florence, which it describes as "the supposed ecumenical synod" (οἰκουμενικῆς δῆθεν συνόδου), took place recently, p. 186: διὰ προσχήματος οἰκουμενικῆς δῆθεν συνόδου, ἥτις ἐν Φλωρεντίᾳ, οὐ πρὸ πολλοῦ, τῆς Ἰταλίας συνέστη.

35 The Patriarchate was first reestablished in the dilapidated Church of the Holy Apostles, but the patriarch was forced to move and that church became the Fatih Camii, which eventually included the grave/*türbe* of Sultan Mehmed II Fatih. On these events, cf. *SF*, p. 28, and esp. n. 260. At the time of the conversion the Patriarchate moved to the Monastery of the Pammakaristos, where "the patriarchal ecumenical synod" assembled.

36 P. 184 (with our restorations to the abbreviations and few editorial changes):

πιστεύομεν εἰς ἕνα Θεόν, πατέρα παντοκράτορα, ποιητὴν οὐρανοῦ καὶ γῆς, ὁρατῶν τε πάντων καὶ ἀοράτων καὶ εἰς ἕνα Κύριον, Ἰησοῦν Χριστόν, τὸν υἱὸν τοῦ Θεοῦ τὸν μονογενῆ, τὸν ἐκ τοῦ πατρὸς γεννηθέντα πρὸ πάντων τῶν αἰώνων, φῶς ἐκ φωτός, τὸν ἀληθινὸν ἐκ Θεοῦ ἀληθινοῦ, γεννηθέντα, οὐ ποιηθέντα, ὁμοούσιον τῷ πατρὶ δι' οὗ τὰ πάντα ἐγένετο, τὸν δι' ἡμᾶς τοὺς ἀνθρώπους καὶ διὰ τὴν ἡμετέραν σωτηρίαν κατελθόντα ἐκ τῶν οὐρανῶν καὶ σαρκωθέντα ἐκ πνεύματος ἁγίου καὶ Μαρίας τῆς Παρθένου καὶ ἐνανθρωπήσαντα, σταυρωθέντα τε ὑπὲρ ἡμῶν ἐπὶ Ποντίου Πιλάτου καὶ παθόντα καὶ ταφέντα καὶ ἀναστάντα τῇ τρίτῃ ἡμέρᾳ κατὰ τὰς γραφὰς καὶ ἀνελθόντα εἰς τοὺς οὐρανούς, καὶ καθεζόμενον ἐκ δεξιῶν τοῦ πατρός, καὶ πάλιν ἐρχόμενον μετὰ δόξης κρῖναι ζῶντας καὶ νεκρούς, οὗ τῆς βασιλείας οὐκ ἔσται τέλος. καὶ εἰς τὸ πνεῦμα τὸ ἅγιον, τὸ κύριον, τὸ ζωοποιόν, τὸ ἐκ τοῦ πατρὸς ἐκπορευόμενον, τὸ σὺν πατρὶ καὶ υἱῷ συμπροσκυνούμενον καὶ συνδοξαζόμενον, τὸ λαλῆσαν διὰ τῶν προφητῶν. εἰς μίαν, ἁγίαν, καθολικὴν καὶ ἀποστολικὴν ἐκκλησίαν ὁμολογοῦμεν ἓν βάπτισμα εἰς ἄφεσιν ἁμαρτιῶν, προδοκῶμεν ἀνάστασιν νεκρῶν καὶ ζωὴν τοῦ μέλλοντος αἰῶνος. ἀμήν.

37 The same definition of the devil as the inventor of evil, who sows dissension and discord within the church, was also mentioned and was utilized by Isidore himself in his address to the Council of Basle, entitled: *Πρὸς τὴν ἐν Βασιλείᾳ Σύνοδον*, quoted and translated, *supra*, ch. 2; in par. 3, Isidore explains the schism in terms of the work of the devil: ἀλλ' ἐς

τοσοῦτον ὁ τῆς κακίας ὥπλισεν ἀμφοτέρους κατ᾽ ἀμφοτέρων ἄρχων καὶ δημιουργὸς [devil], ὡς καὶ λόγοις κατ᾽ ἀλλήλων ὁπλίζεσθαι καὶ ἀκροβολίζειν ἄμφω τὰ μέρη καὶ πρὸς ἄλληλα.

38 The term "Catholic" employed by the Orthodox does not mean "Roman Catholic," but "universal."
39 P. 187. In numerous ways, the letter that was dispatched by the Muscovite court and Church to the Greek emperor, following the return of Isidore to Moscow after the Council of Ferrara-Florence, is more sophisticated and raises more significant question than the Greek text in its rejection of church union. For the Muscovite letter to Emperor John VIII, text and translation, cf. *supra*, ch. 3, text with n. 76.
40 In the document as one word: ἀπotοῦδε.
41 In the document as one word: καταρχάς.
42 Paize-Apostolopoulou and Apostolopoulos, Ἐπίσημα Κείμενα, no. 32 (pp. 215–219); our quotation: p. 217.
43 *Supra*, ch. 3, *passim*.
44 For the context, cf. *supra*, ch. 3, n. 64. Perhaps it should be noted that the equivalent term in Greek, ἀσεβής, was restricted to Muslims, Turks, that is, non-Christians in general, and derogatorily denotes "infidel."
45 ПСРЛ 25: 259.
46 *Ibid.*, 21/2: 511, 512.
47 *Ibid.*, p. 531.
48 *Ibid.*, 21/2: ch. 19, pp. 506, 507.
49 The emperor's journey to the West has been studied in detail by modern scholars. Cf., among others, D.M. Nicol, "A Byzantine Emperor in England: Manuel II's Visit to London in 1400–1401," *University of Birmingham Historical Journal* 12 (1971): pp. 104–225; *MP*, pp. 167–199; S. Runciman, *The Fall of Constantinople 1453* (Cambridge, 1965), p. 13 (with the valid criticism of Barker in *MP*, p. 166 n. 75); Cirac Estopañan, pp. 52–66; G. Schlumberger, "Un Empereur de Byzance à Paris et à Londres," in *idem, Byzance et Croisades. Pages médiévales* (Paris, 1927), pp. 87–147; A.A. Vasiliev, "Путешествие Визнтийского Императора Мануила Палеолога по Западной Европе (1399–1403 г.)," *Журнал Мнинстерства Народнаго Просвещения*, n.s., 39 (1912): pp. 41–78 and 260–304.
50 With the exception of his visit to Venice, Ferrara, and Florence, the other journeys of John VIII are not well known and have not been studied in detail, unlike the journeys of his peripatetic father, Manuel II. In November 1423, John VIII, in search of aid, visited Hungary and Italy; cf. *Minus* 12.3: καὶ τῇ ιε$^\text{η}$ τοῦ νοεμβρίου τοῦ λβ$^\text{ου}$ ἔτους διέβη ὁ βασιλεὺς κὺρ Ἰωάννης εἰς τὴν Ἰταλίαν καὶ Οὑγγαρίαν. He returned at the end of October of the following year (*Minus* 13.1: καὶ εἰς τὸ τέλος τοῦ ὀκτωβρίου μηνὸς τοῦ λγ$^\text{ου}$ ἔτους ἐπανῆλθε).
51 For the chronology of this early trip, cf. *supra*, ch. 1.
52 For this trip and Isidore's own account, cf. *supra*, ch. 1, text and translation with n. 120.
53 For this journey and Isidore's active participation in the Council, cf. *supra*, ch. 2.
54 *Supra*, ch. 3, *passim*.
55 *Supra*, ch. 3, text with nn. 69–75.
56 *Supra*, ch. 4.
57 *Ibid*.
58 *Supra*, ch. 5.
59 There are other possibilities to extend Isidore's *cursus honorum* further, but they are based on a number of assumptions and argumentation; cf. *supra*, ch. 2, n. 10, for the available evidence.
60 Bessarion held the following positions: metropolitan of Nicaea (1437–1439); cardinal and priest (1439–1449); cardinal and bishop of Sabina (1439?); cardinal and bishop of Tusculum (1449–1468); Latin Patriarch (titular) of Constantinople (1463–1472), after the death of Isidore.

Conclusions: damnatio memoriae?   347

61 Bessarion continues to be attacked by zealous Orthodox detractors. Cf., e.g., the biography of Scholarios-Gennadios II by Zeses, Γεννάδιος Β΄ Σχολάριος; and *supra*, p. 126 n. 61.
62 Bessarion employed an army of minor humanists in his efforts to amass a serious collection of manuscripts from antiquity and the Middle Ages. Among his agents and copyists, for whom he provided the best paper available, were Greek clerics such as Presbyter Ioannes Rhosos from Crete and the monk Kosmas, who always signed the copies of his work for Bessarion with the following *explicit*: Κοσμᾶς ἀνάξιος ἱερομόναχος ἀρετῆς πάσης ξένος, and further added that he copied the work προστάγματι καὶ ἀναλώμασι Βησσαρίωνος δεσπότου. Other copyists employed by Bessarion include well-known figures such as the humanist Michael Apostoles and Ioannes Plousiadenos who copied Herodotus, Xenophon, and Thucydides for Bessarion; Plousiadenos was rewarded through the efforts of Bessarion and became the bishop of Methone in the Morea. Bessarion also employed western humanists from Italy and Germany. One of Bessarion's personal searches in monastery libraries resulted in the discovery of an ancient manuscript that had been lost for centuries: the *Codex Hydruntinus* from Otranto in Calabria, which contained the epic poem by Quintus Smyrnaeus, narrating the events that took place in the Trojan War after the death of Hector and thus summarizes the contents of the lost ancient Trojan Cycle which continued the plot line of Homer's *Iliad*; cf. *SF*, p. 206. Eventually Bessarion willed his notable collection of manuscripts to Venice; his collection eventually formed the original nucleus of the Marciana Library. Bessarion's notable library contained 746 *codices*, of which 486 *codices* were in Greek. Thus his collection almost complements the personal library of Pope Nicholas V, which contained 824 *codices*. Cf. Kyrou, 2: 158–162, on Bessarion's library and his donation to Venice, which established the Marciana in 1475, but proper space was not allotted to Bessarion's collection until 1515; even then the new building program postponed a permanent assigned location, which finally took place in 1574.
63 Cf., e.g., the statement of Vespasiano da Bisticci, cited and discussed *supra*, ch. 7, text with n. 46.
64 For the latest synthesis on the thorny scholarly problem over the actual ethnicity of the Byzantines, cf. A. Kaldellis, *A New Herodotus: Laonikos Khalkokondyles on the Ottoman Empire, the Fall of Byzantium, and the Emergence of the West*, Supplements to the Dumbarton Oaks Medieval Library 33–34 (Washington, DC, 2014), pp. 207–236.
65 Khalkokondyles I.2 (pp. 2, 3 in Kaldellis's edition, with another English translation).
66 Khalkokondyles produced a work that is void of religious animus, an achievement for his time; cf. A. Kaldellis, *A New Herodotus*, p. x: "[Khalkokondyles] has no discernable religious bias, an amazing feat of the fifteenth century."
67 *Notitia, Purpura Docta, Monachii 1714*, part III: 105, in *PG* 159: col. 952.

Appendix

Isidore the historian

As we discussed earlier (*supra*, ch. 2, text with nn. 114 and 115), Isidore in his youth, while he was a resident of the Morea, took up his pen and composed a very long *Panegyric* in honor of Manuel II and John VIII. This oratorical piece is historically important, for it treats some major events of that period. Some of his information is not duplicated elsewhere and is not reported by other authors. Perhaps Isidore had been an eyewitness to some of those events or he took advantage of knowledgeable informants who had been eyewitnesses.

Within this oratorical text, belonging to the genre of panegyrics, a genre that was popular in the late Palaiologan era, there is great deal of history embedded. Isidore comes close, in numerous sections, to demonstrating his skills as a historian. He has preserved for us an account of the military campaigns of the imperial family in the Morea during the late 1420s. As we have previously observed, S.P. Lampros edited and published Isidore's text in *ΠκΠ* 3: 132–221. After his death, Bogiatzides continued the editorial work on *ΠκΠ*. The long text was published under the title: Ἀνωνύμου Πανηγυρικὸς εἰς Μανουὴλ Β΄ καὶ Ἰωάννην Η΄ τοὺς Παλαιολόγους, *ΠκΠ* 3: 132–199.

This speech clearly displays Isidore's superior classical education. It contains substantial references to antiquity and is composed in an admirable ancient Greek style, even though Bogiatzides unjustly criticized its language. We wonder whether Bogiatzides (cf., e.g., p. γ΄ of the introduction: μετ' οὐκ ὀλίγων αὐτοῦ τοῦ συγγραφέως σολοικισμῶν καὶ βαρβαρισμῶν) would have expressed this criticism if he had known that it had been composed by Isidore. The manuscript does not contain the author's name in the *incipit*, which was only added by a later hand:

> *In Constantinopolitatum Imp. Et Constantinopolim ipsam encomion panegyricum; in quo praeter cetera, quod Imperator Constantinopoli a Turcis periclitante, ipse ad petenda ab Italis et Germanis auxilia profect. Suscep.*

The work was eventually attributed to Isidore by Mercati, pp. 2 ff.

Bogiatzides, however, realized the exceptional importance of this work, e.g., p. γ΄ of the introduction: ϖολυτιμοτάτου δὲ διὰ τὰς ϖεριεχομένας ἱστορικὰς εἰδήσεις ἀγνώστους ἀλλαχόθεν. He recognized that it is more than a speech, for it provides us with precious historical information on the events of the period that is embedded in the rhetorical text. In addition to the battle of Ekhinades and the treaty that followed, which was sealed with the marriage of Constantine XI, the son of Manuel II, to the daughter of Tocco, it is the only Greek text that addresses in detail the long voyage of Manuel II to the West during the blockade of Constantinople by Bayezid I, thus providing us in a narrative form a detailed Greek view of the emperor's journey abroad. It is unfortunate that modern scholarship has largely overlooked the precious historical details furnished by Isidore in this *encomium*.

Isidore's speech is as long as Manuel's *Funeral Oration* for his brother. Isidore's *Panegyric* is contained in the Lampros edition. The very length of the speech prohibits us from reproducing the full text, which approaches three hundred pages. We have therefore selected the historically important passages that deal with the period in question. We reproduce Lampros's and Bogiatzides's text, but we have divided it into sections and paragraphs for easier reference and comprehension. We have thus included the late reign of Manuel II, the blockade of Constantinople by Emir Bayezid I, and the lesser-known campaign of the Palaiologoi in the Morea against the Latin lords. We have also supplied, in notes, a modest commentary with secondary literature on the events covered by Isidore.

Thus we have seen Isidore as the composer of an account of a perilous voyage to Sicily, as a theologian with his Basle speech, as a reporter of the siege operations of the siege of Constantinople in 1453 in his epistolographies to his friend Cardinal Bessarion and to Pope Nicholas V, and as a propagandist from Crete, urging Christians to organize a crusade and to liberate Constantinople. In the following instance, we see Isidore in the guise of young historian treating events that took place during his sojourn in the Morea.

Selections from Isidore's *Panegyric* to Manuel II and John VIII

[pp. 158–166]

I Πολιορκία τῆς Πόλεως ὑπὸ Παγιαζήτου

1 ὡς γὰρ κεκίνητο Παγιαζίτης ἐκεῖνος, ὃν ἐκάλουν Ἀστραπὴν [Yıldırım], τῇ τε τῆς τύχης φορᾷ καὶ τῷ θράσει τῇ τε τῶν προγεγονότων καὶ προκατειργασμένων αὐτῷ τε καὶ τοῖς προγόνοις τῶν ἐθνῶν ὑποταγῇ καὶ δυναστείᾳ, θρασὺς καὶ βάρβαρος ἀνὴρ καὶ τῷ πλήθει τοῦ στρατοῦ καὶ τῷ πλούτῳ καὶ τῇ τοῦ σφετέρου γένους πολυανδρίᾳ, βρέμων ὅλως καί τι δεινὸν καὶ μανικὸν πνέων κατὰ ὁσίου, ταυτὸν δ᾽ εἰπεῖν κατὰ τῆς εὐσεβείας καὶ τοῦ θεοῦ χωρεῖ. ᾤετο γὰρ ἐκεῖνον καταγωνισάμενος πάντα χωρῆσαι κατὰ ῥοῦν αὐτῷ, οὐδενὸς ἐμποδῶν, οὐδ᾽ ἐσομένου τοῦ κωλύοντος, ἀλλὰ καὶ τὸ διάδημα ἑαυτῷ περιθεῖναι καὶ τὴν ἐλευθέραν ἀεὶ καὶ βασιλίδα [Constantinople] δούλην

ἐσχηκέναι ῥᾳδίως τῶν πόλεων καὶ οὐδένα οἱ τῶν ὑφ᾽ ἡλίῳ πάντων τὴν ἐκείνου διαπεφευγέναι σαγήνην. καὶ μὴν οὐχ οὕτω μὲν ᾤετο οὐκ ἐπεχείρει δέ. οὐδ᾽ αὖ ἐγχειρῶν, ἧττον τῆς προσούσης αὐτῷ δυνάμεως ἥπτετο, οὐδ᾽ ἁπτόμενος πάσης ἐνεδίδου καὶ ποτέ, ἀλλ᾽ ὅλος ἄτρεπτος, ἀτεράμων ὅλος, ἀμαλακτότερος τῶν κερασβόλων ἐνέμεινε κυάμων, ἕως οὗ κακὸς κακῶς τὸ ζῆν ἐξέτισεν. ἀλλ᾽ ἀναμεινάτω γε μὴν τὸ περὶ τούτου τέλος.

2 ἔτι δ᾽ ἄγων καὶ φέρων τὰ Ῥωμαίων [Greeks] καὶ εἰς στενὸν καθυποβάλλων αὐτὰ κομιδῇ, συσφίγξας καὶ συγκλείσας πανταχόθεν ἐπολιόρκει τὴν πόλιν, πειρώμενος μηχανῇ τῇ πάσῃ καταβαλεῖν καὶ κρατῆσαι ταύτης. ὁ ἀγχίνους ὁ πολύς, ὁ συνετός, ὁ μέγας ἐκεῖνος [Manuel II] οὐδὲν ἀγεννές, οὐδὲν ταπεινὸν πρὸς τὴν ὕβριν ἐκείνην τὴν τοσαύτην τῆς τύχης ἀποβλέψας, οὐδέ τι φαῦλον καὶ μικρὸν ἐννοήσας, ἀλλὰ πανταχόθεν περιαγαγὼν ἑαυτὸν καὶ περιαθροίσας οἷά τις κυβερνήτης ἄριστος χειμαζομένης ἔτι τῆς νεὼς καὶ σχεδὸν εἰπεῖν διαλυομένης, τοῦ πελάγους τῶν πραγμάτων ἀφυβρίζοντος τῷ κλύδωνι καὶ σάλῳ καὶ τῇ καταιγίδι τῶν ἐθνικῶν πνευμάτων, κατὰ νοῦν βαλόμενος κινεῖ τὰς ἑσπερίας δυνάμεις πάσας καὶ ἀντιπερίστησι τὸν ἀγῶνα τῷ βαρβάρῳ, οὐ τὸν περὶ ψυχῆς μόνον, ἀλλὰ καλῶς βουλευσάμενος κινεῖ Κελτῶν κινεῖ Γαλατῶν [French]. ἦσαν ἐκεῖ καὶ Ἰβήρων ἑσπερίων [Spaniards], οἶμαι, γένη. καὶ Γερμανῶν τὸν βασιλέα μεθ᾽ ὅσης ἂν εἴποι τις τῆς περὶ αὐτὸν δυνάμεως. τοῦτο τὸ βούλευμα ὑπὲρ τὰ Κύρου καὶ Δαρείου, ὑπὲρ τὰ Φιλίππου καὶ Ἀλεξάνδρου. καὶ οὓς ἄρχοντας ἐκεῖνοι μόλις ἦγον, ὧν οὐκ ἄρχων ἦν ὁ βασιλεύς, ἐκείνους ἔπεισε γράμμασι καὶ πρεσβείαις τὸν πρὸς τοὺς βαρβάρους ἀνελέσθαι πόλεμον. καὶ διήνεγκον ἂν καὶ συνεπέραναν ὥσπερ ἐβούλοντο, εἰ ταῖς εἰσηγήσεσιν ἐχρῶντο διὰ τέλους καὶ ταῖς παραινέσεσιν ἐκείνου, ἃς ὑπετίθει τούτοις καλῶς καὶ λέγων καὶ ποιῶν καὶ παρασκευαζόμενος ἐκείνοις χρῆσθαι τοῖς τοῦ πολέμου τακτικοῖς.

3 ἀλλὰ ἐκεῖνοι θαρρήσαντες σφῶν τῇ εὐανδρίᾳ, τῇ πολυανδρείᾳ, τοῖς ὅπλοις, τοῖς χρήμασι, τοῖς τῶν ἵππων καταφράκτοις, διαβαλόντες τὸν Ἴστρον [the Danube], περὶ τὴν ἐκεῖσε πόλιν τὴν Νικόπολιν, τοῖς βαρβάροις συρρήγνυνται, καί, φθόρον δράσαντες πολύν, ἀτακτότερον ἐπεξιόντες καὶ περιεκδραμόντες, μᾶλλον οὐδὲ τακτικῶς συστάντες τρέπονταί τινα τροπὴν νεανικὴν καὶ κατάπτυστον. καὶ τί μὲν ἔπαθον, τί δὲ ἐγένοντο Ἴστρου προχοαὶ καὶ τὰ παρίστρια τοῦτ᾽ ἴσασι πεδία! ἑάλωσαν δὲ καὶ πολλοὶ Γαλατῶν τῶν εὐγενῶν, οἳ καὶ πρῶτοι τοῖς βαρβάροις συνέπεσον, καὶ μετὰ μικρὸν οὐκ ὀλίγοι τῶν ἄλλων καὶ τὸ στρατόπεδον ἅπαν. ὁ δ᾽ ἐκείνων βασιλεύς, ὥσπερ ὑπότρομος ὑπεκφυγών, ἐνέβη ταῖς ναυσίν. ἐφώρμων γὰρ ἐκεῖσε τριήρεις ῥωμαϊκαί τε καὶ βασιλικαί. καὶ παρὰ τὴν μεγάλην κατῆρε πόλιν, καὶ ὁ χθὲς καὶ πρὸ μικροῦ ὑψηλὸς καὶ γαῦρος καὶ μετέωρος, ὅλος ταπεινὸς εὐθύς, ὅλος συνεσταλμένος, πανταχόθεν συνεπτυγμένος, πανταχόθεν συμπεπιλημένος, πολλὰ ἑαυτῷ, τοῖς ἑτέροις τῶν ἀρχόντων, τοῖς παραδυναστεύουσιν αὐτῷ, πολλὰ μεμψάμενος τοῖς στρατηγοῖς, ὑποθήκας μὴ δεξαμένοις μηδὲ παραινέσεις τοῦ φρονιμωτάτου βασιλέως, μηδὲ κατὰ νοῦν βαλομένοις, πῶς δεῖ τῷ πολέμῳ χρῆσθαι καὶ τοῖς τακτικοῖς. ἔγνω δὲ μάλιστα τὸ γένος οἷόν ἐστι Ῥωμαίων καὶ ὁ ἐκείνων ἐξηγούμενος ἡλίκος, τῇ τοσαύτῃ τῶν βαρβάρων ἀντιταττόμενος τύχῃ καὶ δυνάμει καὶ τοσούτῳ τῷ πλήθει, περιρρεομένων

πανταχόθεν καὶ περικυκλουμένων καὶ τοσοῦτον χρόνον ἀνθισταμένων πρὸς αὐτούς.

4 ἀλλὰ τὰ μὲν πράγματα τότ᾽ ἴσως ἔδοξε καὶ τοῖς εὖ φρονοῦσιν αὐτοῖς, προσδοκίας ἐπέκεινα πάσης, καὶ οὐδὲν ἐλπίσιν ἦν τοῖς Ῥωμαίοις ὅ,τι καὶ δράσειαν βουλεύεσθαι. ἀλλ᾽ ἐκεῖνος ἔδειξεν ὁ καιρὸς ὅσον εἷς ἀνὴρ χρῆμα καὶ ὅσον ἐστὶν εὐβουλία μετὰ δικαιοσύνης ἅμα καὶ ἀρετῆς, καί, κατεπτηχότων πάντων τῷ δέει καὶ σχεδὸν προτεθνηξάντων τοῖς προσδοκωμένοις τῶν δεινῶν. οὐκέτι γὰρ ὑφεώρων, ἀλλὰ καθεώρων σαφῶς τὰ πράγματα εἰς ἐσχάτην ἀπορίαν ἥκοντα καὶ ᾐωρημένα, καὶ πάντας ἦν ὁρᾶν τὸ καθ᾽ ἑαυτὸν ἕκαστον σκοποῦντα ποῦ γῆς ἂν ἐξερευνησάμενος εὕροι μυχοὺς καὶ καταδὺ τὸν κατακλυσμὸν ἐκεῖνον καὶ τὴν βίαν ἀποδράσειεν, ἀλλ᾽ ἡ φρόνησις ἡλίκον, ἀλλ᾽ ἡ πρὸς θεὸν πίστις καὶ εὐσέβεια μέγα τι χρῆμα καὶ πάντα κατ᾽ αὐτὸν δυνατὰ τῷ πιστεύοντι.

5 συνεπισκεψάμενος τοίνυν καὶ συνεωρακὼς τὰ μὲν κατ᾽ ἤπειρον πάντ᾽ ἀπερρυηκότα καὶ πεφθαρμένα, ἔχει δ᾽ ἔτι ἀκμὴν ἡ θάλαττα καὶ δύναμίν τινα, καί, ταύτης εἰ κρατεῖν ξυμβαίη, ξυμβαίη ἂν καὶ τὴν ἀπὸ τῶν βαρβάρων ἐκφυγεῖν πανωλεθρίαν, συμμάχους ὑποποιησάμενος πάντας ὅσοι θαλάττης σχεδὸν ἥπτοντο, πάντες δ᾽ ἦσαν οὗτοι οἱ πρὸς ἑσπέραν ἀπὸ τοῦ Αἰγαίου μέχρι Ἡρακλείων στηλῶν [Straits of Gibraltar] καθήκοντες, νησιώτιδες καὶ πάραλοι πόλεις θαλασσοκρατοῦσαι τηνικαῦτα, καὶ τούτους μᾶλλον ἢ τοὺς ἀρχομένους ἑτέροις πείσας, εἶχε παρὰ τῇ πόλει συνεχεῖς τοὺς ἀποστόλους πέμποντας, τοῦτο μὲν εἰς φυλακήν, τοῦτο δ᾽ εἰς τὴν τῶν ἐπιτηδείων κατακομιδήν, τοῦτο δ᾽ εἰς ἄμυναν τῶν πολεμίων. ἔγνω τοιγαροῦν κατὰ ῥοῦν ἔτι τῶν πραγμάτων τοῖς βαρβάροις φερομένων, πάλιν διεγεῖραι τὰς ἑσπερίας καὶ ἠπειρωτικὰς δυνάμεις, κἀκεῖνον εἶναι τούτων στρατηγὸν καὶ σώματι καὶ ψυχῇ, μᾶλλον δ᾽ εἰπεῖν τοῖς ἐκείνων οἰκειότερον σώμασιν αὐτὸν ἐνθεῖναι ψυχήν. τῇ γὰρ πάντων ἐκείνων ῥώμῃ ὥσπερ τινὸς ἐντεθείσης ψυχῆς τῆς ἐκείνου φρονήσεως ἢ καί τινος ὀξύτητος ξίφους καὶ ἀκμῆς, συνεπιτιθεμένων ἐκείνων τῷ παντὶ τοῦ σώματος βάρει καὶ βάθει, σὺν θεῷ δ᾽ εἰρήσθω, δι᾽ οὗ καὶ πάντα ἐκεῖνος ἐνήργει, τί ὧν ἐβούλετο οὐκ ἐπέπρακτο ἢ τί ὧν ἔδει παρέδραμε, τί τῶν ἐφετῶν, τί τῶν ἐπωφελῶν οὐκ ἐγίγνετ᾽ ἄν;

6 ὅθεν καὶ καλεῖ τὸν ἀδελφιδοῦν αὐτῷ καὶ βασιλέα [John VII Palaiologos], ἄνδρα τῷ θεῷ προσῳκειωμένον τὰ μάλιστα καὶ πάσῃ κεκοσμημένον ἀρετῇ, ὥς ἔδειξεν ὁ μετὰ ταῦτα χρόνος, καὶ τοῦτον εἰσάγει παρὰ τὴν πόλιν, πολιοῦχον καὶ φύλακα μετὰ θεὸν καὶ βασιλέα καταλιπών. τῶν γάρ τοι φιλτάτων ὁ νῦν εὐφημούμενος αὐτῷ βασιλεὺς νεαρὰν ἔτι κομιδῇ καὶ ἡλικίαν ἦγεν ἁπαλήν, κἂν τὸ φρόνημα πολιὸν ἐδείκνυ καὶ σεμνόν, προδεικνύων, ὥσπερ τὰ εὐγενῆ τῶν δένδρων τοῖς τῶν κλάδων ἁπαλοῖς καὶ τοῖς ἄνθεσι τοὺς ἐσομένους καρπούς.

II Μανουὴλ ἐν Ἑσπερίᾳ καὶ ὁ Τεμίρης

1 καὶ τοίνυν ἄρας ἐκεῖθεν στόλῳ παμπληθεῖ, ὃν ἐκόμισεν αὐτῷ Γαλάτης ἀνὴρ τῶν εὖ γεγονότων, Μανεσκάλος [Jean le Meingre, Maréchal Boucicaut] ἐκεῖνος, καὶ τὰ μέγιστα δυνάμενος παρὰ βασιλεῖ τῷ Γαλατῶν [Charles VI],

ἦκεν εἰς Πελοπόννησον, ἦκεν εἰς Μονεμβασίαν, πόλιν τῆς Πελοποννήσου τὴν ἐρυμνοτάτην. ᾤκει παρ' αὐτῇ δεσπότης ἐκεῖνος ὁ καλὸς καὶ τοῦ γενναίου βασιλέως ἀδελφὸς [Theodoros I Palaiologos], οὗ τὸ γένος καὶ τὴν φύσιν μόνον, ἀλλὰ καὶ τὸν τρόπον καὶ τὴν προαίρεσιν καὶ διὰ πάντων ἀδελφὰ φρονῶν καὶ οὔτε ἐκεῖνον ἑτέρου τινὸς ἀδελφοῦ τυγχάνειν, ὅτι μὴ τούτου, οὔτε τοῦτον ἐχρῆν ἄλλον ἄγειν ἀδελφὸν καὶ βασιλέα καὶ μήτ' ἐκεῖνον ἑτέρῳ παρακεχωρηκέναι τὴν φύσιν μετ' ἐκεῖνον εἶναι, οὔτε τοῦτον αὖ ἕτερον πρὸ τούτου τιμᾶν. καὶ παραθεὶς αὐτῷ βασιλείαν καὶ τὰ φίλτατα, ὅλῳ ποδὶ ἀναχωρεῖ παρὰ τὴν ἑσπέραν.

2 καὶ γίγνεται τοῖς ἰδοῦσιν ὁ βασιλεὺς θαῦμα, καὶ δέχονται τοῦτον οἱ ἐκεῖσε βασιλεῖς καὶ ἄρχοντες καὶ πᾶσα ἡ ἑσπέρα ὥσπερ βασιλέα σφῶν, καὶ τιμῶσι καὶ δοξάζουσιν ὡσπερεί τιν' ἀπ' οὐρανοῦ φανέντα. καὶ διαβάλλει μέχρι Ἀλουίωνος [Albion/England]. χρόνος οὐκ ὀλίγος ἐν τῷ μεταξύ, καὶ κινεῖ θεὸς μάστιγα [Timur/Tamburlaine] κατὰ τῆς μάστιγος [Bayezid I] καὶ πατάσσει τὸν πατάξαι καὶ συντρῖψαι τοὺς αὐχένας Ῥωμαίων κατεπαιρόμενον, καὶ κακοποιῷ κολάζει δυνάμει περσικῇ [Mongol] τὴν τῶν Τούρκων φθαρτικὴν καὶ ἀφανιστικήν. καὶ ὅπως τοῦτο συνέβη πᾶς ἄν τις ἀκούων καὶ θαυμάζοι.

3 ἔτι γὰρ παρὰ τὴν πόλιν καὶ τὰ οἰκεῖα τελῶν ὁ αὐτοκράτωρ τὴν τῶν βαρβάρων φθορὰν καὶ πανωλεθρίαν, τοῦτο δ' ἐστὶν εἰπεῖν τῶν Ῥωμαίων καὶ παντὸς ἐλευθερίαν χριστιανικοῦ γένους φέρων ἐν νῷ οὐδὲν ὅ,τι καὶ μὴ διενοεῖτο ὅσα χρὴ καὶ διανοεῖσθαι ἄνδρα συνέσει καὶ σοφίᾳ καὶ εὐψυχίᾳ τηνικαῦτα καιροῦ πάντων ὑπερκείμενον, πρεσβείᾳ τινί, τῷ τοῦ κρείττονος δὲ μᾶλλον προνοίας ἔργον τοῦτο εἰλικρινέστατον, οἷα δὴ τὰ παλαιὰ ἐκεῖνα τῶν θαυμάτων. κινεῖ τὸν Τεμίρην ἐκεῖνον [Timur/Tamburlaine] καὶ καθοπλίζει καὶ διερεθίζει τοῦ Παγιαζίτη. ἦρχε δὲ τηνικαῦτα Περσίδος ἐκεῖνος καὶ Μηδικῆς, Ὑρκανίων τε καὶ Βακτρίων καὶ πολλῶν ἑτέρων γενῶν τῶν καὶ ἐς Καυκάσια ὄρη ἀνηκόντων καὶ ὁρμᾷ δυνάμεσι πολλαῖς καὶ πάσαις ἱππικαῖς, καὶ περίπου τὴν τῶν Γαλατῶν Ἄγκυραν συντρίψας αὐτὸν καὶ κατατροπωσάμενος αὐτοῖς παισίν, αὐταῖς δυνάμεσι πάσαις, αἱρεῖ τὸν ἀγέρωχον ἐκεῖνον καὶ ὑψαύχενα καὶ ἀλαζόνα τύραννον καὶ τοῦτον αἰχμάλωτον ἄγει καὶ σιδήροις δεσμεῖ καὶ κλοιοῖς τὸ δουλικὸν ἀνδράποδον ὑποβάλλει καὶ ζωγρίαν ἕλκει τὸν πρὸ μικροῦ φυσῶντα καὶ καταπιεῖν καὶ λαφύξαι πᾶσαν ὠρυόμενον τὴν οἰκουμένην.

4 καὶ δείκνυται θέαμα ἐλεεινόν, θαυμάτων πάντων ἐλεεινότερον, καὶ ἡμερωτέρων ἀνθρώπων ὀφθαλμοῖς οἶκτος καὶ ἔλεος, καί τις ἂν καὶ δάκρυον προὔχυσε τοῦ σκληροῦ καὶ ἀκαμποῦς τὴν ἄστατον τύχην καὶ ἀδόκητον ἐκείνῳ μεταβολὴν θαυμάσας, ὡς οἷα τὰ ἀνθρώπινα. ἀληθῶς γὰρ οὐδὲν τῆς τύχης μόνιμον, οὐδὲν διαρκές. τὰ ἐκείνης οὐδὲν ἀποδέοντα πάντα σκιᾶς ἢ ὀνείρων, καὶ ὅπου ἂν αὕτη μὴ παρῇ μετ' ἀρετῆς, τῷ μὲν ἑνὶ τοῖν ποδοῖν ἐπὶ σφαίρας, θατέρῳ δ' ἐπὶ ξυροῦ τὴν βάσιν ἔχει, ὥσπερ δὴ καὶ τῷ ἀνθρώπῳ ἐκείνῳ.

5 αὐθωρὸν γὰρ ἥλω μὲν αὐτός, ἥλω δὲ φιλτάτων τινά, ἥλωσαν αἱ τούτου σύζυγοι. εἶδεν αὐτὰς δουλικὸν ἠμφιεσμένας καὶ οἰνοχοούσας δαιτυμόσι παρ' ἄλλοις. ἥλω καὶ κατέθραυσται καὶ προσούδισται πᾶν αὐτῷ τὸ στράτευμα πληροῦν εἰς μυριάδας ὅ,τι πλείστας χρημάτων ἀμυθήτων καὶ παντοδαπῶν

θημωνίαι, πόλεις ἀριθμῷ τάχα δὴ μηδ᾽ ὑποτίπτουσαι, ἐπαρχίαι πᾶσαι. αὗται δ᾽ εἰσὶν ἀπὸ τῆς Σινωπέων μέχρι Κιλίκων. καὶ πᾶσα ἡ ἐντὸς ταυρικῶν ὀρέων μέχρι θαλάττης καθήκουσα καὶ περιγραφομένη γῆ ἐξ ἐφόδου μιᾶς τεμιρικῆς, ὥσπερ ἀπό τινος φορᾶς ὑδάτων κατακλυσμοῦ, κατεκλύσθη, καὶ ὑπέσυρε πᾶσαν αὐτὴν καὶ κατηνδραποδίσατο μηδὲ τῶν ἀλόγων ἐκεῖνος φεισάμενος. καὶ γίνονται τῷ βασιλεῖ καὶ Ῥωμαίοις οἱ τὸ πῦρ ἐκείνου πνέοντες παῖδες ἱκέται καὶ ὑπήκοοι.

6 κἀντεῦθεν ὁ βασιλεὺς ἐκεῖνος λαμπρῶς ἀνάγεται τῆς ἑσπέρας καὶ τῶν οἰκητόρων ἐξιόντες οἱ εὐδαίμονες καὶ ὅσοι τῆς συγκλήτου καὶ βασιλεὺς αὐτὸς μετὰ λαμπρᾶς τινος ἀπαντῶσι τῆς ὑποδοχῆς, οἱ μὲν κατὰ Πελοπόννησον, οἱ πολλοὶ δὲ καὶ βασιλεὺς κατὰ τὸν Ἑλλήσποντον. καὶ ὥσπερ τινὰ δεξάμενοι καὶ ἰδόντες ἀσμένως ἄλλον ἥλιον ἀπὸ δυσμῶν ἀπανήκοντα καὶ ἑορτάσαντες ἡδίω πασῶν ἑορτήν, τὸν βασίλειον ἀπολαβόντα θρόνον ἐκθειάζοντες προσεκύνουν ἅπαντες, τῇ μητρὶ τοῦ θεοῦ τὰ εἰσητήριά τε τελοῦντες καὶ ἀποβατήρια, μᾶλλον δὲ καὶ ἐλευθερωτήρια, πληρέστατά τε διαρκέστατα. καὶ πόλεις εὐθὺς ἀπολαμβάνει πολλάς, τὰς μὲν Θρακικάς, τὰς δὲ Θετταλικάς, καὶ φόρου ὑποτελεῖς τῶν βαρβάρων οὐκ ὀλίγοι γίγνονται. καὶ μετὰ μικρὸν διευθετεῖ τοὺς ἡγεμόνας αὐτῶν, καί, συμπιπτόντων ἀλλήλοις περὶ τῆς ἡγεμονίας καὶ ἀρχῆς καὶ συγκρουόντων καὶ τοῦ μὲν νικῶντος, τοῦ δ᾽ ἡττωμένου καὶ παρ᾽ ἐκεῖνον ἀεὶ προσπεφευγότος τοῦ ἥττονος, πλὴν ἑνὸς τῶν πάντων. ἐξ δ᾽ ἐτέλουν. οὐδεὶς αὐτῷ τὸν αὐχένα μὴ καθυποκλίνας οὐκ ἦν.

7 καὶ τό γε δὴ πολλοῦ θαύματος ἄξιον, ὅτι μετὰ τοσαύτην πολυετίαν, ἐκείνου δὴ τοῦ μὴ καθυποκύψαντος υἱὸς ἱκέτης [Mehmed I] ἥκει προσφυγὼν ἄρτι παρὰ τὸν νῦν εὐφημούμενον θειότατον αὐτοκράτορα, ὥσπερ ἀποπληρῶν τὴν τοῦ πατρὸς ἀπόδρασιν. ἀλλὰ μὴν τόν γε δὴ νεώτερον ἐκείνων ῥόδον ἔδειξε ἐξ ἀκανθῶν καὶ ἐξ ἀσεβῶν εὐσεβῆ. παρ᾽ ἑαυτῷ γὰρ κατέχων ἐρρύθμιζε καὶ τὴν εὐσέβειαν ἐδίδασκε καὶ τὴν τοσαύτης σειρᾶς τῆς ἀσεβείας βλάστην εὐσεβῆ καὶ καρποφόρον τῷ θεῷ παρέπεμψε. τῶν δ᾽ ἄλλων οὐδεὶς τῶν προσιόντων ὅτι μὴ τὴν νικῶσαν ἐλάμβανε, τάχιστα καθυπείκων ἐκείνῳ καὶ συνδεδεμένος, ἕως οὗ τοῖς ὅρκοις ἦν καὶ ταῖς συνθήκαις ἐμμένων. ἀλλ᾽ οὐδεὶς οὐκ ἦν ὃς διὰ τέλους εὐτυχῶν μὴ πονηρὸς καὶ ἀχάριστος. καὶ γὰρ τί ἄλλο ἢ λυκιδεῖς ἦσαν ἅπαντες, οἳ καὶ κακοὶ κακῶς ὑπ᾽ ἀλλήλων ἀπώλλυντο;

III Μανουὴλ Β΄ καὶ ἐπαρχίαι

1 οὕτω θεὸς τοῖς αὐτοῦ τὰς τῶν καλῶν ἀποδίδωσιν ἀμοιβάς, καὶ οὕτω ἐξοικονομῶν ὁ βασιλεὺς ἐκεῖνος ἐν τῷ μεταξὺ τὰ κατ᾽ ἐκείνους νῦν ἧκεν εἰς Πελοπόννησον τὰ ἐκείνης εὖ θήσων, τοῦ φίλου καὶ ἀδελφοῦ [Theodoros I] τῶν ὧδε ἀπάραντος καὶ πρὸς ἀμείνω πορείαν μεταστάντος καὶ ἀνταλλαξαμένου τῆς ἐπικήρου ταύτης τὴν μετέωρον ἐκείνην καὶ ἀμετάπτωτον. ὃν καὶ πενθήσας ἀξίως κατεκόσμησε λόγοις ἐπιταφίοις γενναίοις πάνυ καὶ δεξιοῖς. καὶ παρὰ τοσούτοις διαπεφοίτηκεν ἡ ἐκείνου δόξα παρ᾽ ὅσοις οἱ λόγοι, παρὰ τοσούτοις δὲ οἱ λόγοι παρ᾽ ὅσοις τὸ φρονεῖν καὶ λέγειν, παρὰ τοσούτοις δὲ καὶ οὗτοι παρ᾽ ὅσοις ἐστὶν ἐφετὸν τὸ μανθάνειν καὶ ἀκούειν. τοῦτο δ᾽ ἐστὶ σχεδὸν παρὰ πᾶσιν ἀνθρώποις.

2 νῦν δὲ εἰς Θεσσαλονίκην τοῦ ἀδελφιδοῦ καὶ βασιλέως μετατεθειμένου καὶ τὸ γεῶδες ἀποδόντος τῇ κοινῇ τροφῷ τῇδε καὶ μητρὶ καὶ λῆξιν ἐπειλημμένου ἀγήρῳ καὶ διὰ τῆς ἐπιγείου καὶ ἐφημέρου τῆσδε τῆς ἀειθαλοῦς καὶ ἀειζώου κληρονομήσαντος βασιλείας καὶ δόξαν τοῖς ἐντυγχάνουσι καταλείψαντος τῷ σχήματι ἔργου καὶ λόγου παντὸς ἀείμνηστον, κἀκείνην τοίνυν καλῶς καὶ προσηκόντως ἐξοικονομησάμενος καὶ στηρίξας τὴν πόλιν ἐκείνην εὖ καὶ ὡς ἔδει, τὴν βασιλίδα καταλαμβάνει καὶ τὰ μὲν φιλοσοφεῖ λόγοις καὶ συγγράμασι εὖ πεφυκόσι, τὰ δὲ κυβερνᾷ καὶ διιθύνει τὴν πολιτικὴν καὶ βασίλειον ἀρχὴν καὶ πάντα συνίστησι τῇ πόλει, τὰ μὲν πρὸς ἀσφάλειαν, ὅσα ὁ μακρὸς χρόνος κατήρειψε, τὰ δὲ πρὸς κάλλος, ὅσα πέφυκε τέρπειν τὰ ὄμματα. καὶ νῦν μὲν ὁμιλεῖ φιλοσόφων καὶ ῥητόρων χοροῖς, νῦν δὲ δικαστὰς καθίστησι καὶ νομοθετεῖ πῶς δεῖ χρῆσθαι νόμοις καὶ δικαστικῇ, καὶ δογμάτων τοῖς προϊσταμένοις κοινωνεῖ, μᾶλλον δὲ καὶ τούτους ἐκεῖνα διδάσκει καὶ πᾶσι γίγνεται στάθμη τις καὶ κανὼν ἀκριβέστατος.

3 καὶ τάδε μὲν ὅσα χρώμενος αὐτῷ οἷόν τινι παραψυχῇ καὶ θυμηδίᾳ καὶ ἀνέσει ψυχῆς. ὅσα δὲ πρὸς θεὸν ἀνάγει καὶ ψυχὴν καθαίρει καὶ νοῦν κατακοσμεῖ καὶ ὡς ἦν ἐκείνῳ πρὸ παντὸς ἡ πρὸς τὸ κρεῖττον θεωρία καὶ ἀνάβασις ἐκεῖνος οἶδε μᾶλλον ἢ εἴ τις κατ' ἐκεῖνον. τὸ γὰρ σπουδαζόμενον καὶ μέχρι τέλους ἐφετὸν τοῦτ' ἦν αὐτῷ προσοικειοῦσθαι, καθ' ὅσον ἐφικτὸν ἀνθρώπῳ, θεῷ. οὐ μὴν ἀλλ' ἐπεὶ καὶ τὸ κοινὸν αὐτὸν ἀπησχόλει τῶν πραγμάτων καὶ πρὸς ἐπίδοσιν ἀεὶ τοῦ γένους ἑώρα. βασιλεὺς γὰρ ἦν καὶ βασιλεύειν ἔκρινε τὸν μὴ τούτου φροντίζοντα μηδαμῶς, τὴν μὲν πόλιν καὶ τὴν ἀρχὴν τῷ νέῳ βασιλεῖ καὶ υἱεῖ [John VIII] παραθείς, μᾶλλον δ' αὐτὸν ἀναθεὶς ἅμ' ἐκείνοις θεῷ, ᾧ καὶ ἐπεποίθει καὶ δι' οὗ πάντα ἔπραττεν ἄρας, παρὰ τὴν νῆσον γίγνεται Θάσον, καὶ πολιορκήσας ταύτην, τῇ τῶν Ῥωμαίων ἐπανέσωσε ἡγεμονίᾳ, καὶ Θετταλῶν εὐθὺς καταλαμβάνει τὴν μητρόπολιν.

4 καὶ ταύτην εὖ διαθεὶς ἀνὰ τὴν Πέλοπος ἧκεν εὐθύς, καί, Κεγχρεαῖς προσορμίσας καὶ Κορίνθου ἐπιβὰς τειχίζει Πελοποννήσου πάντα τὸν ἰσθμὸν [the Hexamilion], καὶ ἀνίστησι τὸν περίβολον θᾶττον ἤπερ ᾤοντο πάντες, γίγνεται μόνον οὐ τοῖς ἰδοῦσι καινόν, ἀλλὰ καὶ τοῖς ἀκούσασι πᾶσι. καὶ τὴν Πέλοπος καταστησάμενος πᾶσαν, τυραννίδος ἐπειλημμένους ἐξελὼν τινας, ταύτην ἐπιτρέπει τῷ μετὰ βασιλέα τελοῦντι τῶν υἱέων [Theodoros II], καὶ ταύτης ἄρχοντα καὶ φροντιστὴν ἀναδείκνυσιν. οὗτός ἐστιν ὁ πορφύρας θαλλός, δεσπότης ὁ κλεινός, οὐχ ἧττον ἀρετῆς ἤπερ ἐπειλημμένος ἀρχῆς.

5 ἐπανῆκε μὴν ἀνὰ τὴν Κωνσταντίνου καὶ χρίει τὸν καὶ πρὸ τοῦδε προσήκοντα τῇ βασιλείᾳ βασιλέα [John VIII], καὶ τὴν ἡγεμονίαν τῷ δὲ παρατίθεται καὶ ἀρχήν. καὶ συνευδοκοῦσι πάντες αὐτοῖς ἑκόντες τὴν αὐτοκράτορα καὶ βασίλειον ἀρχήν. ἡ γὰρ ἑκατέρων ἀεὶ ἰσογονία θατέρῳ μὲν παρέχει βασιλεύειν ἀσφαλῶς, τῷ δὲ λοιπῷ ἐρίζειν μηδ' ἀμφιβάλλειν μηδέν, ἄρχεσθαι δὲ ὑπείκειν διὰ παντὸς πεφυκότι τοῦ χρόνου. γίνεται δ' ἀμφοῖν ὁ μακρὸς καθαπερεὶ φύσις χρόνος. ᾗ καὶ μηδ' ἄν τι λέγειν ἢ φιλονικεῖν ἔξεστί τινι τῶν πάντων, ἀλλ' εἴκειν αὐτοῖς πάντα ἑκόντι, τῇ φύσει δουλεύοντας μετ' ἀρετῆς, ταὐτὸν δ' εἰπεῖν νόμοις τισὶ καὶ θεσμοῖς φυσικοῖς ὥσπερ ἄλλο τι χρέος ἀναγκαῖον καὶ ἀπαραίτητον.

IV Ἰωάννης Η΄ καὶ Παγιαζίτου ἀδελφός

[pp. 173–221]

1 ... αὐτοκράτωρ [John VIII] πρῶτον καθ᾽ ἑαυτὸν ἐκστρατεύει καὶ παρὰ τὴν Θετταλῶν παραγίγνεται μητρόπολιν [Thessalonike], καὶ ὑποδέχονται λαμπρῶς καὶ προσκυνοῦσι πάντες, καὶ πεῖραν ἐκείνου πρῶτοι λαμβάνουσι τῆς φύσεως ἀρίστην καὶ θαυμάζουσιν αὐτήν. περιεστοιχομένης γὰρ ὑπὸ πλήθους βαρβαρικοῦ [Turkish troops] τῆς πόλεως ἐκείνης, πᾶν ἐξαίφνης φανεὶς ἔλυσεν αὐτῆς τὸ δεινόν. τοῦ γὰρ ἡγεμόνος [Mehmed I] τῶν βαρβάρων ἀδελφὸς [Mustafa "the pretender"] προσφυγὼν τῇ πόλει ταραχὴν καὶ ζημίαν οὐκ ὀλίγην ἀνὰ πᾶσαν ἔσπειρε τὴν ἀρχὴν ἐκείνων. φύσει γὰρ τὸ βάρβαρον ἐκεῖνο γένος καὶ τὸν αὐτάδελφον ἔχθιστον ἡγεῖται καὶ πολέμιον, πρὸς τὴν ἡγεμονίαν καὶ ἀρχὴν ἀφορῶν, οὐδενὸς ἀνταλλαττόμενον ἐκείνην. ἀλλ᾽ ἀφειδοῦν καὶ τῆς τῶν σφῶν αὐτῶν ὑπὲρ αὐτῆς ζωῆς. οὕτω τοιγαροῦν τεταραγμένων ὄντων καὶ μετεώρων πάντων βαρβάρων τὰς γνώμας, τοῦ μὲν μείζονος καὶ ἄρχοντος ὑφ᾽ αὑτῷ πᾶσαν ὑπεζωσμένου διοίκησιν τῆς ἀρχῆς καὶ τὴν πόλιν ἐκείνην ἁρπάσειν ἀπειλοῦντος εἰ μὴ ἔκδοτον οἱ πολῖται τὸν αὐτόμολον καὶ πρὸς τιμωρίαν δοῖεν αὐτῷ, ἐκείνου δὲ δεομένου τὸν ἱκέτην μὴ καταπροδοῦναι σφᾶς, ὁ θειότατος οὗτος, ὥσπερ εἴρηται, βασιλεὺς φανεὶς τὸ μὲν φρόνημα τοῦ βαρβάρου κατεστόρεσε τοῖς δὲ πολίταις ἔλυσεν εὐθὺς ἐκείνοις τὰ δεινὰ καὶ τὸν προσφυγόντα τῇ πόλει σῶν ἐκεῖθεν ἐκβαλὼν παρὰ τὴν νῆσον στέλλει Λῆμνον. μάστιγα τηρῶν κατ᾽ ἐκείνου καί τιν᾽ ἴσως ἔφεδρον, εἰ νεωτερίσας καὶ τύχοι τὰς σπονδὰς λυσάμενος. οὕτως βουλευσάμενος καὶ πράξας εὖ καὶ τὰ περὶ τὴν πόλιν ἐκείνην πάντα καὶ αὐτὴν εὖ διαθείς, τοῦ ἀδελφοῦ [Andronikos Palaiologos, the despot of Thessalonike], τῆς γνώμης ἐξαρτᾷ, ἐς δεσπότου τελοῦντος ἀξίωμα, καὶ τὴν ἀρχὴν ἐκείνης ἀνατίθησιν αὐτῷ, καὶ πρὸ τούτου τήνδ᾽ ἐμπεπιστευμένῳ καὶ ἄρχοντι.

V Ἰωάννης Η΄ ἐν Πελοποννήσῳ

1 ἄρας τοίνυν ἐκεῖθεν, πάντων οἰομένων ἐς τὴν βασιλίδα [Constantinople] παλιννοστῆσαι, πρύμναν ἐξαίφνης κρουσάμενος, καταλαμβάνει τὴν Πέλοπος μηδὲ τῶν ἐν τέλει τί καὶ δρᾶσαι βούλεται γινωσκόντων. ἀποβάντος τοίνυν, πᾶσαν ἀγείρας τὴν Πέλοπος, ἀπαντᾷ μετά τινος λαμπρᾶς τῆς πομπῆς ὁ μετ᾽ ἐκεῖνον ἀδελφὸς αὐτῷ ὁ δεσπότης ὁ λαμπρὸς [Theodoros II], ὃν τῆς πορφύρας ἔμπροσθεν ὁ λόγος φθάσας ἔδειξε θαλλόν. ὃς ἄρχων καὶ δεσπόζων τῆς Πελοποννήσου καὶ πρῶτος αὐτός, ὥσπερ ἔθος, τὸν βασιλέα προσκυνήσας, πάντα γίνεται τούτῳ· παῖς, ἀδελφός, φίλος, σύμβουλος, καὶ στρατηγὸς ὧν ἂν δέοι, καὶ ὅποι περ ἂν ἀπελθεῖν καλευσθείη ὠκύτερος ἐδείκνυτο καὶ πτερωτοῦ καὶ συνεργάζεται τούτῳ πᾶν ὅπερ ᾤετο πρὸς ἐπίδοσιν εἶναι τῆς βασιλείας καὶ αὔξησιν.

2 ἔτη γὰρ οὐδ᾽ εὑρεῖν ὅσα καὶ ῥάδιον, τὴν Μεσσηνίων, τὴν Ἠλείων, καὶ σχεδὸν πᾶσαν τὴν Ἀχαιῶν ἰταλικαὶ δυνάμεις καὶ μεγάλαι κατεῖχον, πάλαι πᾶσαν Πελοπόννησον κατακρατήσασαι καὶ καταδουλώσασαι. ἀλλὰ τῶν μὲν

ἄλλων ἐξῶσαν Ἰταλοὺς οἱ πάλαι βασιλεῖς καὶ πρόγονοι τοῦ νῦν εὐφημένου μερῶν. ἐκείνων δὲ συχνοὺς ἦσαν ἄρχοντες τοὺς χρόνους, μηδενὸς αὐτοῖς ἐμποδὼν γιγνομένου, ἀλλ᾽ ὡσπερεί τινος κλήρου πατρῴου τὴν ἑλληνίδα νεμομένοις γῆν. τοῦτο βαλόμενος εἰς νοῦν καὶ καλῶς συνεωρακὼς καὶ τὰς δυνάμεις συναθροίσας, τὴν Μεσσηνίαν οὐδὲ ὅλου τοῦ μηνὸς ἐντὸς παρεστήσατο πᾶσαν, φρούρια καὶ πόλεις ἔχουσαν ἐγγύς που τριάκοντα, οὐδενὸς ἐκείνων ἀποδρᾶναι δυνηθένος οὐδὲ τῶν ἐρυμνοτάτων κἂν ταῖς ἀκρωρίαις ἀνῳκοδομημένων. ἑάλωσαν δὲ καὶ αὐτῷ τινες τῶν Ἡλείων πόλεις, ἃς κάμψαντι τὸν αὐχένα τῷ κατάρχοντι πάλαι τούτων Ἰταλῷ, τούτῳ δὴ τῷ πρίγκηπι, παρῆκε χρῆσθαι ταύταις αὐτῷ. εἶξε δὲ μετὰ χρόνον καὶ πολλὴν τὴν πολιορκίαν πόλις καλὴ [Glarentza/Clarence/Kyllene] τῶν Ἀχαιῶν ἐν καλῷ τῆς Ἀχαιίδος παρὰ τῷ Κρισαίῳ κειμένη κόλπῳ. κοινῇ τάδε κατεπραξάτην αὐταδέλφω τὼ δύο τούτω, καὶ τοῦ τάττοντος ὥσπερ ὁ βασίλειος ἑταίρει θεσμός, τοῦ δ᾽ ἐκτελοῦντος τὰ ῥᾷστα καὶ σὺν ἡδονῇ τὸ προστατόμενον.

[...]

3 ...ἐπείπερ εἶδεν ἐκεῖνα Πελοπόννησος, ἀπολαμβάνουσα τὴν πάτριον καὶ ῥωμαϊκὴν ἐλευθερίαν, παρέπεμψε εὐφημοῦσα μετὰ κρότων καὶ λαμπρῶν τῶν ἐπαίνων νικητὴν καὶ τροπαιοῦχον καὶ σωτῆρα καὶ ῥύστην ἀποκαλοῦσα, καὶ εἴ τι που καὶ περιλέλειπται καλῶς εὐχομένη, τούτῳ συγκατειργάσθαι τοῖς ἄλλοις καὶ ταῦτα καὶ μηδὲν ἔτι περιλελεῖφθαι ταύτης τῆς βασιλικῆς ἐπικρατείας ἐκτός. οὕτω καὶ φρονοῦσα καὶ δοξάζουσα καὶ γεραίρουσα κοινῇ προπέμπει πᾶσα μέχρι Κεγχρεῶν καὶ θαλάττης τὸν φιλόπονον καὶ φιλορρώμαιον βασιλέα.

VI Πολιορκία Κωνσταντινουπόλεως ὑπὸ Μουρὰτ Β

1 ...χρόνος τοιγαροῦν παρερρυήκει συχνὸς καὶ συνέχοντος ἔτι τῷ πατρὶ καὶ βασιλεῖ τὴν ὅλην ἀρχὴν καὶ προστασίαν καὶ συνόντος ἐκείνῳ διὰ παντός, καὶ φερομένων εὖ τῶν πραγμάτων Ῥωμαίοις, λαῖλαψ ἐγείρεται καὶ καταιγὶς ἐθνική, ταράσσουσα πᾶσαν γῆν ῥωμαΐδα καὶ συνέχουσα καὶ ἐς στενὸν ἄγουσα κομιδῇ, καταπιεῖν ὠρυομένην καὶ λαφύξαι τὸν περιούσιον τοῦ θεοῦ λαόν. καὶ κινεῖται γένος ἅπαν τουρκικὸν καὶ περσικὸν ὅσον ἐντὸς ταυρικῶν ἐς Ἀσίαν ὀρῶν, καὶ κατατρέχει τῆς πόλεως, καὶ χάρακα πήγνυται καὶ συμβάλλει καὶ πολιορκεῖ μετὰ πολλῆς τῆς ῥύμης καὶ σφοδρᾶς καὶ ὑπορύσσει καὶ κριοὺς καὶ ἑλεπόλεις καὶ πάσας ἐπάγει κατὰ τῶν τειχέων προσβολὰς καὶ μηχανάς, οὐδὲ παρεῖσα τῶν ὅσ᾽ ἀνθρώπου διάνοια πέφυκεν ἐπινοεῖν, οὔθ᾽ ἐμφανῆ, οὔθ᾽ ὅσα τῷ ἀφανεῖ καὶ πανούργῳ συγκατακεκρύφαται. ἀλλ᾽ οὔτε γαλήνη καὶ νηνεμία τὸν ἄριστον κυβερνήτην, οὔτε νοσημάτων τὰ κοῦφα καὶ ὁμαλὰ τὸν πεπειραμένον Ἀσκληπιάδην, οὔτε πραγμάτων ἠρεμία καὶ κατάστασις τὸν περιεσκεμμένον καὶ γενναῖον πόρρω φρονήσεως ἥκοντα δείκνυσιν ἄρχοντα... ὅθεν καὶ ἡ βίαιος ἐκείνη τοῦ κατακλυσμοῦ φορὰ λαμπρότερον καὶ τεχνικώτερον ἔδειξε, βασιλεῦ ἄριστε, σὲ τῶν πολλὰ καὶ μεγάλα τρόπαια καὶ νίκας πηξάντων καὶ παρεσχηκότων τοῖς ἰδίοις... οὐ γὰρ μόνον ἀνήνυτα τὸ βαρβαρικὸν ἐκεῖνο στράτευμα καθ᾽ ἡμῶν ἐπεχείρησεν, ἀλλὰ καὶ παθόντες ἔφθησαν πλείω μᾶλλον ἢ δράσαντες, καὶ ἦν ἐκεῖνο ἰδεῖν ἐν ταῖς προσβολαῖς

καὶ τοῖς ἀγῶσι καὶ τῇ ῥώμῃ καὶ ἀκμῇ τοῦ πολέμου νῦν μὲν ὡπλισμένον καὶ ἱππεύοντα καὶ μεταξὺ διιόντα τοῖν τειχέοιν, ἔργ᾽ Ἄρεως ἐπιδεικνύμενον, νῦν δ᾽ ὅλας νύκτας περιπολοῦντα τὸν περίβολον πάντα καὶ τοὺς ἐπὶ τῶν ἐπάλξεων παραθαρρύνοντα καὶ τῶν πύργων διεγείροντα καὶ ἀφυπνίζοντας πάντας ἐς φυλακὴν ἀκριβῆ καὶ μάχας καὶ τὴν ἐνυάλιον σάλπιγγα θᾶττον ἐφορμῶντας ἢ πρὸς χοροὺς τινας καὶ θαλίας καὶ ᾄσματα ὑμέναια καὶ ἑορτὰς καὶ θυμηδίας οὕτως εὐψύχους, οὔτε καρτερικοὺς περὶ τὰ δεινὰ πάντας, οὕτως ὁμόσε βαρβάροις ἐπιέναι παρέθηξε καὶ παρώτρυνε ... ἀλλὰ μήν, πολλοὺς ἀποβαλλόντες οἱ βάρβαροι τῷ πολέμῳ ἐκείνῳ τέλος ἀπειπόντες ἀπιόντες ᾤχοντο, μάτην ὥσπερ λύκος, τὸ τοῦ λόγου, χανόντες.

2 ... καὶ ἐπεὶ τῆς μὲν πόλεως ἀπανίστανται καὶ διασκεδάζονται, αὐτὴ δ᾽ οὐδὲν ἧττον συνεῖχε καὶ ἐπίεζεν ἡ τῶν ἀναγκαίων ἔνδεια πάντων, περικεκλεισμένην πανταχόθεν καὶ στενοχωρουμένην, διανοεῖται μεῖζον τι καὶ τῆς σπουδῆς μόνον καὶ προθυμίας ἄξιον αὐτοῦ, καὶ χωρεῖ παρὰ τὴν Ἑσπέραν καὶ δυνάσταις ὁμιλεῖ καὶ βασιλεῦσιν Ἰταλῶν, Γερμανῶν, καί τινων ἄλλων ἐθνῶν, καὶ θαυμάζεται τοῦ πατρὸς οὐχ ἧττον, καὶ τιμᾶται παρ᾽ ἐκείνων ὥσπερ αὐτῶν βασιλεὺς καὶ φιλεῖται, τὰς αὐτῶν δυνάμεις οὐχ ὡς κινήσων, ἀλλ᾽ ὡς παρέξων, ἄλλο ἐκείνοις αὐτός. οὕτω καὶ πρὸς ταῦτ᾽ εὖ πως κέκρατο, ἄριστος ἐν πᾶσι φαινόμενος καὶ κατὰ τὸ ὁμηρικὸν ἔπος "βασιλεύς τ᾽ ἀγαθὸς κρατερός τ᾽ αἰχμητής."

3 ταῦτα τοίνυν ἐννοῶν ὁ τῶν Τούρκων ἡγεμὼν [Sultan Murad II] (ἀμηρᾶν [emir] ἐκεῖνοι τοῦτον ἀπὸ τοῦ σχήματος λέγουσι) σπένδεται τῷ βασιλεῖ καὶ τοῖς πολίταις. ἔτι γὰρ ἔμπνους ἦν [Manuel II], ἐπὶ κλίνης κείμενος, νοσήματι παλαιῶν ὀλεθρίῳ καὶ δεινῷ καὶ πρὸς ἐκφορὰν ἀφορῶν ὁ μὴ θανάτου καὶ σοροῦ, ἀλλ᾽ ἀθανασίας καὶ φωτὸς ἐπάξιος. καὶ σπένδεται δὴ σκεπτόμενος ἐπανελθεῖν ἀπὸ τῆς Ἑσπέρας καὶ τὸν κρατοῦντα, μηδὲν κατ᾽ ἐκείνου τῶν Ἑσπερίων κινήσοντα δυνάμεων. δέος γὰρ ἐκείνῳ μέτριον οὐχ ὑπῆν, ὁρῶντι μηδενὸς ἀπολειπόμενον τῶν ὅσα πέφυκε κινεῖν καὶ παραθήγειν οὐχ ὅτι γε τοὺς σπουδαίους καὶ προθύμους, ἀλλὰ καὶ ἐπανιὼν οὕτως εὗρεν ἐκεῖνον κατεπτηχότ᾽ ἴσως καὶ κατειλημμένον τοῖς ὅρκοις καὶ καλῶς καὶ ἀσφαλῶς ἐμπεπεδημένον, ὥστε δὴ καὶ τῆς σήμερον ἄχρι, μηδενὸς τῶν ὀμωμένων αὐτῷ παραβεβαμένου, ἀλλ᾽ οὕτως ἀπρὶξ ἐχομένων τῶν σπονδῶν, ὡς δοκεῖ ἐκεῖνον δεόμενον ἡμῶν, ἀλλ᾽ οὐχὶ τούτου γε ἡμᾶς.

VII Ἡ Ναυμαχία

1 ἔστι Κάρουλος γένος Ἰταλός, ὀξὺς καὶ δραστήριος ἀνήρ, τὰ μέγιστα πεπονθὼς πρὸς τῶν βασιλέων εὖ καὶ τιμηθεὶς ἀξίαν οὐ τὴν τυχοῦσαν, ἀλλὰ καὶ ἐς δεσπότου φθάσας ἀξίωμα, τὴν προγονικὴν τῶν νήσων προκατάρχων τὴν ἀρχήν. νησιῶτις γάρ. ἡ δ᾽ ἐστὶν Ἰθάκη, Ζάκυνθος, Λευκὰς καὶ Κεφαλληνία. συγκατέλαβε παρὰ μικρὸν τὴν ἀπ᾽ Αἰτωλῶν μέχρι Θεσπρωτῶν καὶ Μολοττῶν, ἣ τῆς Ἠπείρου μέρος, οὐ ξύμπασα, ἀλλὰ καὶ τῆς Ἀχαΐας τελεῖ. ὅσον ἀπ᾽ Ἀχελῴου μέχρις Εὐήνου διήκει ποταμοῦ. πάσης δὲ ἐκείνης τὰ μὲν ἐπὶ θάλατταν χωρία Ἕλληνες ᾤκουν, τὰ δ᾽ ἀνωτέρω καὶ πρὸς μεσόγαιαν βάρβαροι καὶ πάλαι καὶ νῦν, οὓς ἐκβαλών, τοῦτο μὲν ἀπάτῃ, τοῦτο δὲ δόλῳ,

ἔστι δ' οἷς καὶ βίαν ἐπαγαγών, ἄρχει συμπάσης, ἐν ᾗ τὸ παλαιὸν τοσάδε διανενέμητο τὰ γένη, Αἰτωλῶν, Ἀκαρνάνων, Ἀμφιλόχων, Κασσιοπαίων, Δολόπων, Ἀμπρακιωτῶν, Ἀθαμάνων, Θεσπρωτῶν, Μολοττῶν καὶ Χαόνων τῶν καὶ ἀνηκόντων ἐς Ἀκροκεραύνια ὄρη. ταῦτα γένη παλαιὰ καὶ πολλά, εὐανδροῦντα καὶ πολυαδροῦντα τὸ πάλαι, νῦν ἀπορίᾳ μεγάλῃ κατείληπται καὶ τοὔνομα προσαπολωλὸς ἕκαστόν ἐστι. χρόνος γὰρ ὁ μακρὸς λήθην καταχέει πάντων μακράν. καὶ τανῦν ᾤκισται σποράδην ἐκείνη καὶ κατὰ μικρὸν ὑπ' Ἀλβανῶν, γένους ἰλλυρικοῦ ξύμπασα καὶ κωμηδόν. νομαδικὸν γὰρ τὸ γένος, καὶ λυπρόβιον, οὐ πόλεσιν, οὐ φρουρίοις, οὐ κώμαις οὐκ ἀγροῖς, οὐκ ἀμπελῶσιν, ἀλλ' ὄρεσι χαῖρον καὶ πεδιάσιν. αἱ δὲ πόλεις καθαρὸν ἔτι σώζουσι τὸ ἑλληνικὸν γένος, ὧν δύο ἐστὸν ἄρτι προκαθεζομένῳ, Ἀμπρακία μὲν τῷ παρ' αὐτῆς ἐπωνύμῳ κόλπῳ, ἀνωτέρω κειμένη τοῦ μυχοῦ. ᾤκισται δὲ παρὰ Γόλγου τοῦ Κυψέλου ... ἡ δ' ἑτέρα πρὸς τῇ Ἀχερουσίᾳ λίμνῃ νέον, οὐ πάνυ νέον οἰκισθεῖσα πρός τινος Ἰωάννου καὶ τὴν ἐκείνου φέρουσαν τανῦν ἐπωνυμίαν. τάχα δ' ἂν εἴη αὕτη Ἔφυρα Θεσπρωτῶν ἡ πόλις ἡ ὅ,τι ταύτης ἐγγυτέρω κειμένη πάλαι. ταῦτα τοίνυν προσκτησάμενος ὠνεῖται παρὰ Λιβερίου καί τινα Πελοποννήσου πόλιν, ἣ Κυλλήνη τὸ παλαιόν, οἶμαι, ἐλέγετο καὶ ἦν Ἠλείων ἐπίνειον, ἐξ ὅτου δὲ παρ' Ἰταλῶν ἑάλω Πελοπόννησος εἰς σχῆμα μείζονος παρ' αὐτῶν ἀνεγήγερται πόλεως, τῷ μακρῷ κατεργασθείσης χρόνῳ καὶ μηδ' ἴχνος σχεδὸν τηνικαῦτα φερούσῃ, Κλαρέντζης παρ' αὐτῶν μετονομασθείσης. τὰ μὲν οὖν μεταξὺ πάντα παρίημι, ἔργον ἱστορίας καὶ συγγραφῆς τυγχάνοντα. ἐκείνης τοίνυν, ὥσπερ εἴρηται, κρατήσας συμπεριλαμβάνει καὶ τὴν ἀπὸ τῶν ἐκβολῶν διήκουσαν Ἀλφειοῦ μέχρις Ἀχελῴου ποταμοῦ πᾶσαν, πρὸς ᾧπερ Δύμη πάλαι πόλις ἀχαϊκή, καὶ πᾶσαν Ἦλιν κοίλην ἀνήκουσαν ὡς πρὸς μεσόγαιαν τῆς Πελοποννήσου καὶ ὅσ' ἀνήκει πρὸς τῷ ὄρει Φολόης πάνθ' ὑφ' ἑαυτῷ πεποίηκε, τὰ μὲν πείσας, τὰ δὲ καὶ βιασάμενος Κεντηρίωνα [Centurione] τὸν πρίγκηπα, παρ' οὗ φθάσας ἔδειξεν ὁ λόγος ἀφελόμενον τὸν αὐτοκράτορα τὰς πόλεις Μεσσηνίων καὶ τὰ λοιπά.

2 ταῦτα τοίνυν ἔχων πάντα καὶ μὴ βουλόμενος ἠρεμεῖν, ἀλλ' ἀχαρίστων περὶ τοὺς εὐεργέτας, μεσοῦντος ἤδη τοῦ χειμῶνος, τρίτου ἔτους ἤδη παρερρυηκότος, τὰς ἀγέλας ἀφαιρεῖται τῶν ἐν Πελοποννήσῳ πάσας Ἰλλυριῶν, παμπόλλας μὲν ἵππων, παμπόλλας δὲ βοῶν, πλείστας προβάτων, πλείστας συῶν. ἔνσπονδος γὰρ ὤν, παρασπονδήσας εὐθύς, πάσας ὑφεῖλεν ἐκείνας, ἐπιτηδείου τοῦ τῆς Ἤλιδος ὄντος χωρίου, καὶ μᾶλλον διὰ τὴν τῶν ἀνθρώπων ἐρημίαν. συχνὴ γὰρ κατέλαβε πρὸ ἐτῶν αὐτὴν ἱκανῶν ἀπορία. χειμάζειν εὐμαρῶς τὰ ζῷα καὶ χόρτον ἱκανὸν φέροντος καὶ ἀλεεινοτέρου ὄντος καὶ ὡς παραλίου καὶ ἀπὸ τῆς ἐπωνυμίας κοίλου τοῦ χωρίου φαινομένου. πρὸς ἐκεῖνον τοίνυν τὰς δυνάμεις συναγαγόντες, περιεκάθησαν πηξάμενοι χάρακα, τὴν παράλιον καὶ προκαθεζομένην πόλιν ἄρτι τῶν Ἠλείων πολιορκοῦντες, ἀπὸ μὲν τῆς ἠπείρου τὰς πεζικὰς συναγαγόμενοι δυνάμεις, ἀπὸ δὲ θαλάττης ταῖς τριήρεσι περικυκλώσαντες. ταῦτα μαθὼν καὶ δείσας ὁ Κάρουλος στόλον ἀθροίζει τὸν μὲν ἀπὸ τῶν νήσων, τὸν δ' ἀπὸ τῆς Ἠπείρου, καί τινας προσκαλεσάμενος Μασσαλιωτῶν, ἐκπέμπει, στρατηγὸν ἕνα τῶν υἱῶν αὐτοῦ, ᾧ Τόρνος, ἐπιστήσας, ὄνομα.

3 ἐκπέμπει δὲ καὶ βασιλεὺς τὰς τριήρεις, ἀναδείξας ἄρχοντα καὶ στρατηγὸν καὶ ὑποθεὶς αὐτῷ πάνθ' ὅσα πρὸς ἀσφάλειαν πρῶτον καὶ σύστασιν καθορᾷ τῶν ἰδίων, Λεοντάριον τὸν καλόν, εἶτα καὶ τὴν νίκην καὶ τὴν συμπλοκὴν ὡς δεῖ καταπραχθῆναι. ἄραντες οὖν πρὸς ταῖς Ἐχινάσιν ἐντυγχάνουσι ταῖς ἐναντίοις νήσοις [καὶ] σημείων ἀρθέντων παιανί[σαντ]ες καὶ ταῖς μὲν σάλπιγξι ἠχή[σαντ]ες τοῖς δὲ ῥόπτροις καὶ τοῖς κυμβάλοις περι[δουπ]ήσαντες βύθιόν τι καὶ [. . .]ῶδες, καὶ τούτοις ὁρμῇ τινι καὶ τεχνήματι θάρσους ἐμβαλόντες καὶ ἀναρρήξαντές τινων παρεξειρεσίας συνέτριψαν, φόνον ἐργασάμενοι τῶν ἐναντίων οὐκ ὀλίγον, τόξοις τὰ πρῶτα καὶ ἀκροβολισμοῖς χρώμενοι, εἶτα δόρασι καὶ κοντοῖς καὶ καταπέλταις, ἐγγυτέρω γεγονότες, ὥσπερ τινὸς πεζομαχίας συνισταμένης. καὶ τὰς μὲν αὐτάνδρους εἷλον τῶν νεῶν, τὰς δ' ἐς ἀπορίαν κατέστησαν ἐσχάτην, ἔσω ὑποχωρῆσαι πρὸς φυγήν. ἑάλω δ' ἂν καὶ ἡ στρατηγὶς παρὰ μικρὸν αὐτῷ, τῶν ἐπὶ τοῦ καταστρώματος στρατιωτῶν τῶν πλείστων πεσόντων. τῶν δὲ περιλειπομένων ἀσπίδας ῥίψαντές τινες καὶ δόρατα βασιλέα εὐφήμουν, καὶ σφᾶς αὐτοὺς κατωνόμαζον δούλους, πρὸς ἱκεσίαν τραπέντες. οἱ δ' ἐρέται ἐς τὰ κοῖλα τῆς νεὼς ἀπερρυήκεισαν. σχεδὸν δ' ἥλω, εἰ μὴ τύχη τις ἐκώλυσε παρεμπεσοῦσα. οἰομένων γὰρ ἤδη οὐχ οἵαν τε οὖσαν ὅλως ἀντέχειν καὶ πρὸς ἄλλας τρεπομένων. ἀπερρυήκει γὰρ τοῦ δεσμοῦ. καὶ τῆς τοῦ καμπύλου σιδηρᾶς ἐκείνης ἐπανακάμψαντος ἀγκύρας, δι' ἧς καὶ συνείχετο. ἀπερρήγνυτο γάρ. καὶ περίπλουν τῆς στρατηγίδος ποιῆσαι βουλομένης, ὑπὸ δὲ ὄγκου καὶ βρίθους βραδεῖαν τὴν ἀναστροφὴν καὶ ἀντεπεξέλασιν ποιούσης, ἐξαίφνης ὑπέδρα, τὰ ἱστία χαλάσασα, πνεῦμα τι ἐγερθὲν πελάγιον καὶ σφοδρότερον ἐμπεσὸν τὴν ὀθόνην ὑπεκόλπου, τῇ φυγῇ τὴν ἐλευθερίαν αὐτῆς χαρισάμενον. ἢ καὶ διωκομένη προσώκειλε τῇ Λευκαδίων, ἀποδράσει τὴν σωτηρίαν ὑφελομένη. ἥλωσαν τοίνυν ἄνδρες πεντήκοντα μὲν πρὸς τοῖς ἑκατόν, καὶ τούτων πολλοὶ τῶν εὖ γεγονότων, ἐν οἷς καὶ ἀδελφιδοῦς Καρούλου δεσπότου. πεσόντες δὲ καὶ τετρωμένοι τῶν ἀποφυγόντων ἦσαν οἱ πλείους.

4 οἱ δ' ἡμέτεροι τὴν ἄδακρυν σχεδὸν εἰργάσαντο νίκην. τοῦτο τὸ τρόπαιον κατέσεισε τὴν ἐκείνου ψυχήν. τοῦτο καθεῖλε τὸ φρόνημα τῶν ἀνθισταμένων. τοῦτο πᾶσαν ὑπέσυρεν ἐκείνῳ τὴν προσδοκίαν καὶ ὑπεχάλασε. τοῦθ' ἡμῖν ἀπέδωκεν Ἤλιδος ἁπάσας πόλεις, καὶ φίλον ἀντὶ δυσμενοῦς, συγγενῆ δ' ἀντ' ἀλλοτρίουμ καὶ ξύμμαχον πεποίηκεν ἀντὶ πολεμίου. καὶ πόλεμον ἐκεῖνος καὶ ὅπλα διεκφυγὼν ἐνέτυχε θαλίᾳ καὶ πανηγύρει, τὸν αὐτάδελφον αὐτοκράτορος τοῦ θειοτάτου γαμβρὸν εὑρηκὼς δεσπότην τὸν καλὸν καὶ γενναῖον, οὗ τὰ πλεονεκτήματα πολλῶν δεῖται τῶν ἐγκωμίων.

English translation of selections from Isidore's *Panegyric* to Manuel II and John VIII

[pp. 158–166]

I The blockade of Bayezid I Yıldırım

1 That legendary man, Bayezid,[1] whom they used to call "Lightning" [*Yıldırım*], mobilized, under the influence of the [wheel of] Fortune's turn and the boldness he had inherited from his ancestors and from his own deeds that had brought other nations under his sway and dynasty. This barbarian was encouraged by the multitude of his army, by his wealth, and by the large numbers of his race's men and, consumed by roars and madness, was blustering against holiness, against piety; so he then marched against God. He was under the impression that he would overwhelm Him totally and everything else would then flow into his lap, as no one could stand in his way and no one could check him. He thought that he would assume the [imperial] crown, that he would easily turn the free Queen of Cities [Constantinople] into a slave, and that no one in the universe would escape from his hunting net.[2] Had he not thought so, he would not have made the attempt. But he did try with all his might and never hesitated. He remained entirely resolved, without fear, and became harder than horny game pawns all his life. He had an evil life and an evil death. Let his death wait for the time being.

2 Busy with attacks against the Romans [Greeks], he completely surrounded them in every way. He completed and tightened his noose around the City, as he began his siege, in which he employed every engine conceivable in order to destroy and conquer her. But that extremely wise, prudent, and great man [Manuel II] neglected none of his duties during that insult that the City had received from Fortune. He did not overlook even the slightest and most humble device in his plan. He took himself everywhere and amassed all the necessities that a most capable captain would put together, when his ship was still facing a storm and indeed she was about to break up, so to speak, as the boiling waves of the sea came under the influence of a mighty gale and a raging wind that the gentile nations had roused. His mind urged him to mobilize all western powers and he resisted the barbarian in this struggle, which was not just for his own survival but also for that of his nation, of his power, and of his empire. He came up with a good plan and he mobilized the western nations of the Kelts, the Gauls [French], and the Iberians [Spaniards], I believe, as well the king of the Germans and his entire might. His plan of action surpassed those of Cyrus, Darius, Philip [II of Macedon], and Alexander [the Great]. The emperor's letters and embassies tried to persuade those independent lords to take up arms against the barbarians [Turks]. Had they made use of the emperor's good and useful tactical and strategic suggestions that he had extended and had kept on sending to them until the very end, there would have been a different outcome and they would have achieved their goals.

3 They were emboldened by their own numbers, by their armament, by their wealth, and by their cataphract cavalry [knights]. They crossed the Ister [the Danube], and broke through in the vicinity of the neighboring city of Nicopolis, attacked the barbarians [Turks], killed many, and then pressed on in chaos and in a loose formation. Their lines were no longer standing in order and they were put to an unprecedented and abominable flight.[3] What they suffered and what became of them is best known to the mouth of the Ister and its surrounding fields! Many noble Gauls [Frenchmen] were captured,[4] as they were the first to engage the barbarians [Turks] and, soon afterwards, many of the others and their entire camp were taken. Their king fled in terror and embarked on the ships, as Roman [Greek] and imperial triremes [galleys] had been standing by the shore. And he sailed to the large city [Constantinople]. The day before and in the recent past he had been haughty and proud. Now he had lost all his airs and was all meekness and self-effacing to himself and to all other lords and associates. He blamed his generals, who failed to take into account and overlooked the advice of the wise emperor [Manuel II], who had recommended strategy and tactics for the upcoming battle. He knew the character of the Roman [Greek] nation and the sound advice of the emperor, who had fought and resisted the fortune, the power, and the huge number of the barbarians [Turks], who had poured in from every side and had surrounded them.

4 At that time the situation seemed desperate and hopeless,[5] even to the best minds. The Romans [Greeks] had no hope of accomplishing their wishes. Yet time demonstrated how important a single man can be and what marvels can be achieved through good counsel, justice, and virtue, even though everyone else had been frightened to death and expected nothing short of a catastrophe. They no longer suspected, but had actually seen the situation deteriorate to its nadir and to total disintegration. As the saying goes, everything was on "a razor's edge" or, more appropriately, "hanging by a thread," as each man searched to find shelter anywhere and wait out that deluge and violence. Good counsel may be significant, yet faith in God and piety are of the utmost importance. All can be achieved if one has faith.

5 He concluded in a review of the situation that on land there was nothing left to be done. The sea, however, offered a solution and powerful means. If he happened to have control over it, he could escape utter destruction at the hands of the barbarians [Turks], and then proceed to form alliances with all those who control the sea. Such thalassocratic powers were to be found in the west, from the Aegean Sea to the Pillars of Hercules [the Straits of Gibraltar], distributed over islands and maritime cities. They and their lords had to be persuaded. From the vicinity of the City [Constantinople], he had already dispatched numerous emissaries asking for military aid and for the shipment of necessities so that he could defend himself against the enemy. He was well aware that circumstances were favoring the barbarians [Turks] and he knew that, once more, he had to awaken the western land powers and that he had to be their physical and mental general, who would inspire them with his courage. His acumen, his way of thinking, and his sharp sword would contribute to their strength, and

they would commit to war all their body and soul (and, let be said, it would be accomplished with God's help). With this premise he was working out all details. What did he fail to do in his actions, what necessity, what command, what service did he overlook?

6 So he summoned his nephew and emperor [John VII Palaiologos],[6] who in the passage of time revealed himself to be an especially devout and virtuous man. He brought him to the City [Constantinople] and left him there in charge, as the emperor, to be her guardian after God. This acclaimed emperor was still rather young, but he displayed a solemn mind that usually comes with advanced years. In a similar way, noble trees display their future fruit with tender blossoms that grow on branches.

II Manuel's Voyage to the west, Timur's invasion, and the Ottoman interregnum

1 He took advantage of the numerous fleet that the famous noble, Manescal [Jean le Meingre, Maréchal Boucicaut],[7] from Gaul [France], who was very powerful at the court of the king of the Gauls [Charles VI], that he had brought for him, and went to the well-fortified city of Monemvasia in the Peloponnese. Nearby lived the emperor's good brother and despot [Theodoros I Palaiologos], who through family ties, nature, character, and choice, had always been a good brother, better than [the others] whom the emperor could not have asked for, nor could he have held any one else in higher esteem. He handed him the imperial authority and his closest relatives and he departed to the west.[8]

2 Those who saw the emperor considered the experience a miracle. The local kings and lords and the entire west gave him a reception fit for their own kings. They honored and glorified him as if Heaven had sent him. He went as far as Albion [England]. Some time passed by and God set in motion a scourge [Timur/Tamburlaine] against the scourge [Bayezid I] in order to destroy the would-be destroyer who had claimed that he would crush the necks of the Romans [Greeks]. The malevolent Persian [Mongol] power chastened the destructive man and vanquished the might of the Turks. How this came about will be surprising to hear.[9]

3 While the emperor was still home in the City and was attempting to stop the destruction and obliteration brought upon the Romans [Greeks] and upon all free Christian nations by the barbarians [Turks], he focused his mind on such matters that any wise and brave man would in such upheavals and came up with a measure that was more significant than foresight itself, as a true miracle of old times. Through an embassy he mobilized, armed, and incited that famous Timur against Bayezid. He was the lord of Persia, of Media, of Hyrcania, of Bactria, and of many other nations around the Caucasian Mountains. He moved his numerous forces and all his cavalry to attack, rout, and obliterate him [Bayezid], his sons, and his entire army around Galatian Ankara. He captured that arrogant, conceited, and haughty tyrant and led his prisoner,

bound in iron manacles and fetters, away.[10] He dragged away his captive; it was only recently that the latter had been loudly bragging that he would swallow and devour the entire world.

4 It was a pitiable spectacle, more so than any other that even made our people feel pity and sorrow. Some people even shed tears over the cruel, unbending, and unstable nature of Fortune, admiring how his circumstances had been turned upside down and how unpredictable the state of human affairs is. Truly Fortune is so changeable and so fleeting! Fortune offers shadows and dreams and wherever she may be without the support of virtue, one would find himself standing with one leg on a ball and the other on a razor. That is what happened to that man.

5 He, some of his sons, and his wives were captured at that time. He saw his wives, in slave dress, pouring wine for others participating in feasts. His entire army, numbering to unprecedented tens of thousands, was broken up and was dashed to the ground, and so were his heaps of indescribable riches, his countless cities, and all his provinces that stretched from Sinope to as far as Cilicia. Timur overwhelmed the entire land, stretching from the Taurus Mountains to the sea in one invasion; it was as if his realm had been inundated in a deluge. He took it over and enslaved it, sparing none, not even horses. His [Bayezid's] sons, who earlier had been breathing fire, then became suppliants and subjects of the emperor and the Romans.[11]

6 Then the emperor [Manuel II] made his triumphal return from the west and was gloriously received by all who came out of their houses to meet him: the wealthy, the senators, and the emperor himself [John VII]. Many had already received him in the Peloponnese, but the vast majority welcomed the emperor by the Hellespont. They looked upon him with joy as if he were another sun returned from the west and were entertained in an unsurpassed festival. All worshipped him and prostrated themselves before him as he ascended the imperial throne; they put together a festival for his return and gave thanks to the Mother of God; it could have been our longest lasting and fullest festival of liberation. Without delay he received many cities, some in Thrace, some in Thessaly, and many of the barbarians [Turks] became his tax-paying subjects.[12] Soon thereafter, he issued an order upon their lords, who had been fighting in a civil war to assume control of their lordship and its leaderships. As one won an upper hand and another was defeated, the losers, with one exception, fled to him [Manuel II] at all times; they were six in all. There was not a single one who refused to bow before him.[13]

7 It was indeed a miracle that after so many years, the only son of Bayezid [Mehmed I] who had not bowed, came as a suppliant to the celebrated most divine emperor, as if he had been fulfilling his father's instructions. The emperor demonstrated that the youngest son [of Bayezid] was the one pious man out of a group of impious men, like a rose blossoming from thorns. He restrained him with his supervision, taught him piety, and made him into a virtuous, fruit-bearing shoot for God, in spite of the impiety of his dynasty. Not one of the

other sons looked for anything other than victory but he, by swiftly listening to him and forming a bond, proved true to his oaths and observed the treaties. The fact that he met with good fortune was due to his demonstrated gratitude and absence of wickedness. All the others were evil, like wolves, and they came to a bad end that they inflicted upon one another.[14]

III Manuel II and his provinces

1 In this way God rewarded him for his good works and in the meantime the emperor took stock of his situation and traveled to the Peloponnese [Morea] to straighten out the local situation; at that time his dear brother [Theodoros I] departed from the earth and made his way towards better conditions by exchanging our mortal life for the heavenly and unchangeable life. He mourned for him and pronounced a worthy, appropriate eulogy.[15] His glory reached all those who received the speech, the wise and the learned, as well as those who wish to hear and learn. That is to say, almost all of humanity.

2 Then his nephew and emperor [John VII] who had been transferred to Thessalonike paid the earthly debt to our common nurse and mother, and moved on to immortality.[16] After our earthly ephemeral existence, he inherited the ageless and ever-lasting kingdom. Through his memorable actions and deeds he was survived by his glory that he had earned justly and fittingly when he protected our famous City dutifully and capably. Manuel took over the imperial city and played the part of the philosopher by composing speeches and well-written essays. He governed well and directed his political and imperial authority for the benefit of the City, overseeing its protection. He also repaired all structures that had collapsed with the passage of time, as he took note of esthetics, creating a delight to eyes. He held conversations with groups of philosophers and orators. He appointed judges and instructed them in the proper use of laws and in adjudication. He passed on to them the primary doctrines, or even better, he instructed them himself so that a universal balance and accurate laws were established.

3 He was able to utilize all his talents and he did so in comfort, joy, and relaxation. He always looked to God for the purification of his soul and his mental wellbeing, and he surpassed all in spirituality. He always studied thoroughly and brought to completion, with God's help, his projects, as far as it was humanly possible. He was always concerned about the commonwealth and the expansion of his nation. He was our emperor and he thought that an emperor should have such concerns; and so he transferred the City and the empire to a new emperor, his son [John VIII], and entrusted him and the empire to God, as he had accomplished everything through Him. So he moved on to Thasos and, after a siege, it reverted to the empire of the Romans [Greeks]; without further delay, he next moved to the metropolis of the Thessalians [Thessalonike].[17]

4 He settled its affairs and then moved straight to the Peloponnese. He landed at Kenkhreai, moved to Corinth, and fortified the entire isthmus of the Peloponnese [the Hexamilion of the Morea]. He erected the walls with such

unprecedented speed that it became a marvel to behold and hear.[18] He corrected the affairs of the Peloponnese,[19] placed some individuals in charge, and then appointed one of his sons [Theodoros II], who was next in the succession after the emperor [John VIII], to be its caretaker and lord. He was the glorious, born-in-the-purple, despot, whose virtue matched that of his brother, who had been chosen emperor [John VIII].

5 He returned to Constantinople and anointed the emperor [John VIII], to whom earlier he had entrusted the empire and the throne. All willingly and joyfully agreed that he should be emperor and should assume charge of the imperial authority. As they were equal in birth, one man should be the secure emperor, and the other should neither quarrel nor appear ambivalent but should naturally obey and be advised throughout his life. Nature accorded to both of them a long life. Among the naturally virtuous, there should be no quarrels but only willing cooperation, that is, they should operate as necessity demands, under laws and natural constrictions.

IV *John VIII and the pretender Mustafa*

1 ... the emperor [John VIII] first went on an expedition and came to the metropolis of the Thessalians [Thessalonike]. He encountered a splendid reception and all bowed before him. They were the first to experience and admire his virtuous character. The city was under blockade by a barbarian horde [the Ottoman army], but his sudden, unexpected arrival delivered the city from a terrible situation. The brother [Mustafa, the "pretender"][20] of the lord [Mehmed I] of the barbarians [Turks] had fled to the city and had sown considerable confusion and danger throughout their realm. By nature that barbarian race [Turks] considers even a brother a serious enemy, when it comes down to their lordship and realm, and the antagonism is resolved by elimination often. And so the situation had been confused and seemed uncertain, as far as the intentions of the barbarians [Turks] were concerned. The senior man in power [Mehmed I], who controlled the administration of the realm, was threatening to seize that city [Thessalonike] unless the citizens handed over the defector to him for punishment. The suppliant-defector, however, begged them not to hand him over. As has been stated, the most divine emperor [John VIII] came and soothed the anger of the barbarian [Mehmed I], delivered the citizens from a difficult situation, and sent the refugee to Lemnos,[21] away from the city. He threatened him with physical harm and even impalement, if he happened to revolt and to violate the terms of the treaty. That was his good decision that brought the city back to normal, and appointed his brother [Andronikos Palaiologos] despot of Thessalonike. He gave him authority over the city, as he had even earlier entrusted it to his leadership.

V *John VIII in the Peloponnese*

1 He departed and everyone was under the impression that he was on his way to the Queen of cities [Constantinople]; unexpectedly, he reversed his course and went to the land of Pelops [Morea]. Those in authority did not know what

his plans were.[22] He disembarked and summoned all inhabitants of the land of Pelops to a gathering. His junior brother, the eldest of the remaining princes, the illustrious despot [Theodoros II], born-in-the purple, as I relayed earlier, met him in a glorious procession. He was the lord and despot of the Peloponnese [Morea]. He was the first to arrive and to bow before the emperor, in accordance with the established ritual, and he became his most capable right hand in everything: son, brother, friend, councilor, and general as the circumstances demanded. He proceeded to his appointed destinations faster than a bird and he cooperated with him [John VIII] in everything that pertained to the benefit and enlargement of the empire.

2 It would be difficult to discover exactly when the mighty Italian powers had taken over and enslaved almost all the lands of the Achaeans, of the Messenians, and of the Elians, and the entire Peloponnese. Yet the emperors of long ago, the ancestors of our emperor, whose name I am celebrating now, had managed to evict some of the Italians from some areas. The latter had ruled those places for many years, as no one had stood in their way and they controlled the Greek land as if they had inherited it from their fathers. The emperor thought about this situation and made provisions. He gathered his forces and established himself in Messenia, which contains almost thirty castles and cities. No one was able to escape, not even those who were in possession of mighty castles built on summits.[23] He seized some of the cities of the Elians, who long ago had submitted to an Italian lord, the predecessor of the current prince,[24] who was allowed to make use of them. Later, after a long siege, a beautiful city [Kyllene/Glarentza/Clarence] of the Achaeans, situated in an attractive part of Achaea by the Gulf of Krisa, yielded to him. The two brothers accomplished everything together; one was in command, as the imperial rule declares, and the other one was glad to follow his orders with pleasure.

[...]

3 ... the Peloponnese witnessed these events, as it reclaimed her ancestral Roman [Greek] liberation. The land sent him [John VIII] away with loud applause and praises, calling him "victor, trophy winner, savior, and defender." Countless blessings were bestowed upon him and the wish was expressed that no part of the territory should remain outside of the empire. With such thoughts, praises, and crowns of glory, the indefatigable and Philhellenic emperor proceeded through the entire Peloponnese to Kenkhreai and the sea.

VI *The Siege of Constantinople by Murad II*

1 ... considerable time passed; he [John VIII] cooperated with his father in the administration and protected the empire; in fact, the circumstances were favoring the Romans [Greeks], when a tornado and a barbarian tempest arose to unsettle and shake the entire Roman [Greek] realm, threatening to devour and swallow God's people. All Turkish and Persian nations within the Taurus Mountains in Asia were mobilized and attacked the City.[25] They dug a trench, attacked, and began a mighty and powerful siege, utilizing mines, siege engines,

battering rams, and artillery in their assaults against the walls. No engine that human ingenuity can, or ever will, devise had been neglected, not even those that are invisible and remain concealed by treacherous minds.[26] Generally speaking, fair weather or tranquility will never reveal an excellent captain. Superficial illness and good constitution will not indicate an experienced follower of Asklepios [a physician]. And normal and routine circumstances will not expose an excellent lord who has gone beyond the call of duty.... So, most virtuous emperor, the violent deluge demonstrated your illustrious skills, as you amassed numerous great trophies and victories for your people ... the barbarian army achieved nothing with its operations against us but, on the contrary, suffered extended destruction in its vain attempts. What one remembers from the assaults and the struggle during the most intense part of the siege was our emperor: he was in armor, on his horse, galloping in the space between the two lines of walls,[27] and patrolling the entire *peribolos*.[28] He encouraged the men behind the battlements; he awakened those stationed on towers; and he urged them to remain extremely vigilant. In one word: he turned them into men of Ares who took up arms and responded to the war trumpet more willingly than to invitations to dances, entertainment, weddings, festivals, and celebrations. He urged them on and fortified them to endure suffering at the hands of the barbarians [Turks]. Indeed, the barbarians [Turks] lost so many of their men in that war that they finally withdrew and departed like wolves with unsatisfied jaws, as the saying goes.

2 ... they [the Turks] left the neighborhood of the city and dispersed, but the City was still under pressure as it lacked all necessities. He [John VIII] came up with a major policy worthy of his concern and industry. He departed for the West[29] and held talks with the lords and kings of the Italians, of the Germans, and of some other nations. He was admired as much as his father [Manuel II], and was honored cordially by them as if he were their own king. His purpose was not to inspire them to mobilize their forces but to make himself available to them. And so his purpose in these matters prevailed. He excelled in everything and proved himself, as Homer's saying goes, "a good, mighty, and spear-bearing king."

3 The lord of the Turks [Sultan Murad] (whose title they themselves cite as "emir") realized what was occurring, so he concluded a treaty with the king [emperor, that is, Manuel II] and with the citizens [of Constantinople]. For he [Manuel II] was still alive, although bedridden, wrestling with a mortal and terrible illness, in anticipation not so much of death and of a funeral but of immortality, since he was worthy to enter the light. So he concluded a truce, as he was awaiting the man in charge to return from the West, who had failed to mobilize the western powers. He was terribly apprehensive, as he had employed all appropriate arguments to mobilize them, all willing and important lords, and urge them on. Upon his return he discovered that he [Manuel II], weak that he was, had managed to secure a sworn treaty, which is still in effect in our own days, as no terms have been violated thus far, but has steadily remained in effect in such a way that he [Sultan Murad], and not we, appears to have asked for it.

VII The campaign against Carlo Tocco and the sea battle at the Ekhinades [Curzolari] Islands

1 Carlo, the Italian, was an impetuous and energetic individual, who was honored greatly by our emperors and was even elevated to the rank of despot. He was an islander who ruled over the islands that he had inherited: Ithaka, Zakynthos, Leukas, and Kephalonia. He almost seized the entire area that stretches from Aetolia to Thesprotia and Molossia (a part of Epeiros as big as a section of Achaea), from the River Achelous to the River Evenos. Greeks used to inhabit all the shore regions; nowadays, as in the past, barbarians are encountered in the upper and inland regions. He removed them through deception and persuasion (that is, he employed a trick), and with force he took over the entire area, which in antiquity was inhabited by Aetolians, Akarnanians, Amphilochians, Kassiopians, Dolopians, Amprakiots, Athamans, Thesprotians, Molottians, and the Chaonian natives of the Akrokeraunian Mountains. There were many populous brave tribes in antiquity but nowadays the area is deserted and their names have been forgotten, as time has consigned them to Lethe. Nowadays one encounters scattered small groups of Albanians, descendants of the Illyrians. Their tribes are nomadic, leading a wretched life. They have no cities, no citadels, no towns, no fields, and no vineyards. They delight in mountains and in valleys. Cities have managed to retain their Hellenic purity. Two of them are situated in this area: one is Amprakia by the gulf named after it, lying on the upper curve; it was founded by Golgos, the son of Kypselos. . . . Controlling these regions, he [Carlo] bought from Liverios [Oliveri], a city in the Peloponnese, which was called Kyllene in antiquity, I believe, when it served as the port of Elis. After the Peloponnese fell into the hands of the Italians, a major city was erected but hardly any trace of it survives with the passage of time. They renamed it Clarence [Glarentza]. I will omit the intervening events, as they deserve their own historical account and exposition. He took over and assumed control of that city and included it in his territory; his entire area stretched from the mouth of the Alpheios River to the Achelous River, towards the ancient Achaean city of Dyme, and the entire valley of Elis in the middle of the Peloponnese, in addition to the regions of Pholoe. Some of these areas came under his jurisdiction by persuasion; others he extracted from Prince Centurione, whom, as my speech has already indicated, the emperor deprived of his Messenian cities and the other regions.

2 While he was in control of all these places and having no wish to remain quiet, he [Tocco] showed ingratitude to his benefactors. Three years had passed and it was already the middle of the winter. He seized all the herds of the Peloponnesian Illyrians [Albanians]. There were many horses, many oxen, numerous sheep, and a multitude of pigs. Even though he had accepted a treaty, he did not hesitate to violate its terms and he appropriated all those herds. That region of Elis had been suited for husbandry, as it lay depopulated for the most part, since it has been deprived of resources many years ago. So animals could winter there, as it was by the sea and, as it is obvious from its environment, it is a valley

growing enough products for animals. So they gathered their forces against him and began a regular siege of the city of the Elians with a ditch. They assembled their infantry on land and also performed an encircling maneuver with their triremes [galleys]. Carlo learned of the developments and became apprehensive; so he assembled his fleet from the islands and from Epeiros, while he also summoned some ships from Massalia [Marseilles] and appointed one of his sons, Tornos [Turno], commander in chief.

3 The emperor placed, as lord and admiral over his triremes, Leontarios, a good man, whom he advised as to the safe course of action that was to be taken in order to win a victory in the ensuing engagement. Then the ships set sail. Once they were in the vicinity of the Ekhinades Islands, they raised their standards, sang the *paean*, and sounded the trumpets . . . they made a courageous and daring attack. They broke the oars of the enemy ships and put many opponents to death. At first they used bows and missiles; then, once they drew near, they used spears, lances, and catapults. This engagement took on the appearance of a pitched battle on land. Some ships they captured with their crews and others they pressed so hard that they had no choice but to flee. Their flagship came very close to being captured by our admiral himself, as most soldiers on her deck had perished. Those few still alive lowered their shields and spears and acknowledged the emperor, adding in supplication that they were his servants. The rowers in the hold of the ship broke away. She would have been captured, if chance had not intervened. Under the impression that she could not hold out any longer, they turned their attention to the other ships. She broke loose from her rope and from her crooked anchor, and started drifting. As the flagship sailed on and was making her way slowly on account of her size and mass, suddenly she fled. They lowered the sails. With a sea breeze suddenly rising, her main sail became full and she found her way to freedom. Under pursuit, she made it to Leukas and to safety. One hundred and fifty of their men were captured; many of them were notable individuals. Among them was the son of Despot Carlo's sister. Many fell and most of those who managed to get away were wounded.

4 Our side enjoyed an almost tearless victory. This victory made his soul tremble and the morale of their defenders fell to a low point. All his expectations were frustrated and vanished. That victory restored to our side all the cities of Elis and, moreover, turned him from an enemy into a friend, from a stranger into a relative, and from an opponent into an ally. He abandoned war and weapons and came to a marriage feast and a celebration, as he became the father-in-law of our emperor's brother [Constantine XI Palaiologos], the brave and noble despot, whose superior traits are in need of many other *encomia*.

Notes

1 On Bayezid I, cf. the old, but still useful, work of Gibbons; *MP*, pp. 112 ff.; Shaw, 1: ch. 3; S.W. Reinert, "The Palaologoi, Yildirim Bayezid and Constantinople: June 1389– March 1391," *Τὸ Ἑλληνικόν: Studies in Honor of Speros Vryonis, Jr. 1: Hellenic Antiquity and*

Byzantium, eds. J.S. Langdon, S.W. Reinert, Jelisaveta Stanojevich Allen, C. P. Ioannides (New Rochelle, 1993), pp. 289–367. Cf. G. Ostrogorsky, "Byzance état tributaire de l'empire turc," *Zbornik Radova Vizantijloškog Instituta, Srpska Akademija Nauka* 5 (1958): pp. 49–58. For the territorial limits of the late medieval Greek state, cf. A.E. Bakalopulos [Vacalopoulos], "Les limits de l'empire byzantine depuis la fin du XIVe siècle jusqu'à sa chute," *BZ* 55 (1962): pp. 55–65; also cf. *idem.*, *Origins of the Greek Nation*, ch. 5. In addition, cf. now Nevra Necipoğlu, *Byzantium between the Ottomans and the Latins: Politics and Society in the Late Empire* (Cambridge, 2009), pp. 30 ff.

2 The beginning and duration of this siege present serious chronological difficulties; cf. the discussion in *MP*, Appendix X: "The Beginning and Duration of Bayazid's Siege of Constantinople," pp. 479–482. P. Gautier, "Action de graces de Démetrius Chrysoloras," *REB* 19 (1961): pp. 347, has demonstrated that the capital was already under siege by 1394. On the other hand, *FC*, pp. 39, 40, cites the year 1396 for the beginning of the siege; and Stacton, p. 114, cites the year 1397, after the battle of Nicopolis. *MP*, p. 481, concludes that the blockade began early in the summer of 1394. A short chronicle is explicit with regard to the duration of the siege, even though it errs in regard to the actual year of the commencement of hostilities; cf. *CBB* 1: 7.25 (p. 70): κατὰ δὲ τὸ ‚ςϙγ´ ἔτος, μηνὶ ἰουνίῳ, ἐκίνησε κατ᾽ αὐτοῦ ὁ ἀσεβὴς τῶν Τούρκων, ὁ προρρηθεὶς Παγιαζίτης, μάχην βαρυτάτην. ἣν καὶ ἐκράτησεν ἰσχυρῶς ἐπὶ χρόνοις ἔγγιστα η´ ἕως ἐλθὼν ὁ Τεμίρμπεης ἐξ Ἀνατολῶν. In addition, cf. *ibid.*, 1: 22.26 (p. 184): Παϊαζίτης ὁ σουλτάν, ὁ λεγόμενος Ἠλταρίμ, οἷον ἀστραπῆ, κυριεύσας καὶ πορθήσας κόσμους ἀπέκλεισε καὶ τὴν Κωνσταντινούπολιν χρόνους θ´, ὡς γενέσθαι τὸ μουζούρι, τὸ σιτάρι, ἄσπρα ρ´, καὶ οὐχ εὑρίσκετο. Another entry may, in fact, be alluding to a skirmish outside the walls, which resulted in serious devastation (*ibid.*, 1: 70.8 [p. 544]): ἐπολέμησεν τὴν Κωνσταντινούπολιν ὁ σουλτὰν Παγιαζίτης . . . καὶ ἐχάλασεν ὅλα τὰ ἔξω κτίσματα, περιβόλια καὶ δένδρη. The period 1394–1402 for the duration of the blockade has been accepted by D. Bernicolas-Hatzopoulos, "Le premier siège de Constantinople par les Ottomans (1394–1402)," Ph.D. dissertation, Université de Montréal, 1980; also cf. *idem*, "The First Siege of Constantinople by the Ottomans (1394–1402) and Its Repercussions on the Civilian Population of the City," *Byzantine Studies/Etudes Byzantines* 10 (1983): pp. 39–51. Cf. now, *idem*, *Le premier siège de Constantinople par les Ottomans, 1394–1402* (Montreal, 1995) [= modern Greek translation by the author, with additions: *Ἡ Πρώτη Πολιορκία τῆς Κωνσταντινουπόλεως ἀπὸ τοὺς Ὀθωμανοὺς (1304–1402)* (Athens, *sine anno*)].

3 On the crusade of Nikopolis and its effects on Constantinople, cf. A.S. Atiya, *The Crusade in the Later Middle Ages* (London, 1938), pp. 435–462; *idem*, *The Crusade of Nicopolis* (London, 1934), esp. chs. 4–6; R. Rosetti, "Note on the Battle of Nicopolis," *The Slavonic Review* 15 (1936/37): pp. 629–638; H.L. Savage, "Enguerrand de Coucy VII and the Campaign of Nicopolis," *Speculum* 14 (1939): pp. 423–442; C.L. Tipton, "The English at Nicopolis," *Speculum* 37 (1962): pp. 528–540; *PaL* 1: 341–369; *MP*, pp. 128–138; *LCB*, p. 319; Geanakoplos, "Byzantium and the Crusades," 3: ch. 3, esp. pp. 81–85; and B.W. Tuchman, *A Distant Mirror: The Calamitous Fourteenth Century* (New York, 1978), the last three chapters. In the corpus of the short chronicles this campaign and battle receive one laconic entry, *CBB* 3: 71a.9 (p. 159): ὅταν ἐτζάκισαν οἱ Τοῦρκοι τὸν Συμιχὰμ κράλην εἰς τὴν Νικόπολιν. Contrary to what is often stated, that the objective of this campaign was to save Constantinople, *PaL* 1: 342 ff., and Geanakoplos, "Byzantium and the Crusades," pp. 81 ff., have demonstrated that the primary goal of the expedition was the defense of the northern Balkans and of Hungary. The relief of Constantinople was only a secondary, if not incidental, goal of this campaign. For a very brief summary of the crusade, cf. Bradbury, p. 217. For the repercussions of this crusade in the Ottoman state, cf. Necipoğlu, pp. 150 ff.

4 The slaughter of western prisoners is well documented: about 3,000 individuals were massacred. Years after the event Sigismund speaks of it in one of his letters; for a pertinent

extract, cf. *PaL* 1: 355 n. 131. Another famous participant, Johann Schiltberger, has also left us an account of this battle. Cf. his *Reisebuch*, V. Langmantel, ed. (Tübingen, 1855), pp. 3–5. Bayezid's most notable prisoners were spared, because of the ransom that they would fetch. For the fate of Bayezid's prisoners after the battle, cf. *PaL* 1: 355–369 (with references to primary sources and documents). Even by a conservative estimate the courts of Europe experienced great difficulty in scraping together the enormous amount of ransom demanded for the release of the captives. Even the negotiations proceeded at a slow pace.

5 Probably it was shortly after the Christian disaster at Nicopolis that Manuel wrote a letter, whose concluding paragraph reveals the emperor's utter despair. For the letter, cf. Dennis, *The Letters of Manuel II*, no. 31, pp. 80–86; this letter is also translated in *MP*, pp. 133–137. Sigismund, who escaped from the battlefield, reached Constantinople and conferred with Manuel. While there, Sigismund wrote another important letter; for its text and translation, cf. *MP*, Appendix 11, pp. 482–485. The rout of the European armies had perhaps brought the Greek emperor to the point of resignation, for at this moment he seems to have gone so far as to propose the cession of Constantinople to Venice. The *Sapientes*, however, wisely declined his generous offer.

6 For Manuel's rival, John VII, cf. E. Zachariadou, "John VII (Alias Andronicus) Palaeologus," *DOP* 31 (1977): pp. 339–342 [repr. in *idem, Romania and the Turks, c. 1300–c. 1500* (London, 1985), Essay 9].

7 For the heroic Jean le Meingre, Maréchal Boucicaut, whose career became inseparably bound with the affairs of the Levant in the next decade, cf. *PaL* 1: ch. 15; and *MP*, pp. 166 ff. A contemporaneous biography can be found in the *Livre des faicts du bon messire Jean le Maingre, dit Bouciquaut, Maréschal de France et Gouverneur de Jennes*, J. Buchon, ed., in J. de Froissart, *Les Chroniques*, 3 (Paris, 1835), pp. xxx ff. and 563–603. Boucicaut appears to have been instrumental in bringing about the reconciliation between Manuel II and John VII; without his mediation, Manuel could not have left his capital, in spite of the presence of a French contingent. Boucicaut seems to have realized that his modest force would not achieve much against Bayezid. He and Manuel (with help from the Knights Hospitallers) campaigned and took Riva, a castle on the Bosphoros held by the Turks. Boucicaut also raided and harassed the Turkish forces in the neighborhood of the Greek capital, but he could not force Bayezid to raise the siege. Cf. *Livre des faicts*, pp. xxxiii–xxxiv, and 607; *MP*, pp. 200, 207, and 219 (with n. 28). Earlier John VII may have attempted to sell his rights to the throne of Constantinople to Charles VI of France; cf. the document summarized in *RKOR*: no. 3194 (p. 74); also cf. P. Wirth, "Zum Geschichtsbild Kaiser Johannes VII. Palaiologos," *Byz* 35 (1965): pp. 592–594, who attaches less importance to this machination. Boucicaut's mediation resulted in this temporary reconciliation and John VII was appointed regent. Upon Manuel's return, it was further stipulated that John VII would be granted Thessalonike. On John VII, cf. *PLP* 9: no. 21480 (pp. 92, 93).

8 Years later Manuel expressed his own personal feelings about this mission in his *Funeral Speech*, the Ἐπιτάφιος for his dead brother, Theodoros I of the Morea. The pertinent passages are translated into English in *MP*, pp. 168, 169. Modern scholars have studied the emperor's journey to the west in detail. Cf., among others, Nicol, "A Byzantine Emperor in England," pp. 104–225; *MP*, pp. 167–199; *FC*, p. 13 (with the valid criticism by Barker in *MP*, p. 166 n. 75); Schlumberger, "Un Empereur de Byzance à Paris et à Londres," pp. 87–147; and B. de Xivrey, "Mémoire sur la vie et les ouvrages de l'empereur Manuel Paléologue," *Mémoires de l'Institut de France: Académie des inscriptions et belles-lettres* 19.1 (1853): pp. 1–201.

9 On Timur-i-lenk and Bayezid, cf. Gibbons, esp. pp. 243–254; Pears, ch. 7; and Rollof, pp. 244–262. On the Mongols, in general, cf. R. Grousset, *L'Empire de steppes: Attila, Gengis Khan, Tamerlan* (Paris, 1939), esp. pp. 528–533; D. Morgan, *The Mongols* (London, 1987); Maria-Matilda Alexandrescu-Dersca Bulgari, *La Campagne de Timur en Anatolie (1402)*

372 *Appendix*

(rev. ed., London, 1977); Hookham; and B.F. Manz, *The Rise and Rule of Tamerlane*, Cambridge Studies in Islamic Civilization (Cambridge, 1989). Eastern and Greek sources are listed in *MP*, p. 216 n. 20; and *PaL* 1: 376.

10 On the actual battle, cf. Shaw, 1: 35, who further supplies (p. 307) modern Turkish literature on this subject, and a bibliography. The battle was fought on 27/28 July 1402, the Mongol "Year of the Horse," and lasted fourteen hours. The most readable account of it is provided in Hookham, ch. 14. The numerous entries in Greek chronicles indicate that the defeat of Bayezid by the Mongols impressed the Greeks deeply. In addition, cf. *CBB* 1: 29.4 (p. 214); 36.11 (p. 292); 38.5 (p. 304); 42.3 (p. 321); 49.10 (p. 352); 53.9 (p. 380); 54.9 (p. 389); 69.60 (p. 538); 75.1 (p. 570); 94A.2 (p. 630); 95.1 (p. 634); and 114.2 (p. 683). *Ibid.*, 1: 49.10 (p. 352), bears the evident stamp of an eyewitness, who must have seen the survivors and refugees from this battle pouring into Constantinople in their search for safety. On this battle, cf. K.-P. Matschke, *Die Schlacht bei Ankara und das Schicksal von Byzanz: Studien zur spätbyzantinischen Geschichte zwischen 1402 und 1422* (Weimar, 1981).

11 Bayezid died at Ak Shehir on the 9th of March 1403. His death may have been caused by apoplexy (Gibbons, p. 259), but suicide cannot be ruled out (*LCB*, p. 329). At least that is the tale that Spandugnino (Spandounis) had heard, p. 148:

> Et vedendo Ildrim Baiasit la maglie in tanto opprobrio et vergogna, dolendosi della perversa fortuna, et volendosi amazzar se stesso, et non travondo coltello o altro expediente, percosse tanto con la testa in quella gabbia che era di ferro che amazzò miserabilmente.

It remains a fact, however, that Timur sent his most competent physicians, including his own personal doctor, to attend the captive emir (Hookham, p. 273). Bayezid's remains were buried with all honors in Prousa. In addition, cf. Codex Barberinus Graecus 111, 2 n. 47. The subsequent campaign of Timur after Ankara is treated in *CBB* 1: 12.11a, 11b, 11c, 11d, 11e, and 11f (pp. 112 and 113). Years later Syropoulos recalled that Bayezid's death had been predicted by the appearance of a "smoking star" (comet?), XI.20: ἀνεμιμνησκόμεθα δὲ καὶ τοῦ μεγάλου ἄστρου τοῦ καπνίζοντος ἐπὶ πλεῖστον πρὸ τῆς ἁλώσεως καὶ τοῦ θανάτου τοῦ Παγιαζίτου ἀμηρᾶ ὅπως προεδήλωσε τὸν θάνατον ἐκείνου.

12 While Manuel was still away, John VII negotiated a treaty with Suleyman Çelebi, the first successor of Bayezid I, in February 1403. This treaty was co-signed by Venice, Genoa, the duchy of Naxos, the Knights of Saint John on Rhodes, and John VII. There is an extensive secondary literature on this treaty; cf. the discussion in *MP*, pp. 218–238; also cf. *LCB*, p. 335; and *PaL* 1: 377, 378. The Latin-Italian text of this treaty can be found in G.T. Dennis, "The Byzantine-Turkish Treaty of 1403," *OCP* 33 (1967): pp. 72–88 [= Byzantium, Essay 6]. In addition, cf. Elizabeth A. Zachariadou, "Süleiman Çelebi in Rumili and the Ottoman Chronicles," *Der Islam* 60/62 (1983): pp. 268–297.

13 The flavor of the rapid succession of events and the excitement that the Greek court must have experienced is further indicated in a brief summary by Sphrantzes that includes many events that occurred over a number of years, *Minus* 3.

14 The gratitude of Mehmed I to the Greek emperor is emphasized by other sources also; cf., e.g., Doukas 20.1.

15 Manuel's Ἐπιτάφιος is discussed *supra*, ch. 1, text with nn. 42 ff. Prior to his death, Theodoros I took monastic vows and received the name Theodoretos; cf. *MP*, p. 272 n. 126. For the date of his death, cf. Mompherratos, p. 29; R.-J. Loenertz, "Pour l'histoire du Péloponnèse au XIVe siècle," *REB* 1 (1943): p. 156; Zakythinos, *Le despotat grec de Morée*, pp. 164–165; and *LCB*, p. 338. Theodoros I was buried in the monastery of the Brontokhion; his tomb may have displayed the following inscription: ὁ αὐτάδελφος τοῦ κραταιοῦ καὶ ἁγίου ἡμῶν αὐθέντου καὶ βασιλέως διὰ τοῦ ἀγγελικοῦ σχήματος μετονομασθεὶς Θεοδώρητος μοναχός. It is not absolutely certain however that this inscription marked his grave, as it has also been assigned to the tomb of Theodoros II; cf.

the brief discussion in Zakythinos, *Le despotat grec de Morée*, p. 165 n. 1; also cf. G. Millet, "Portraits byzantins," *Revue de l'art chrétien* 41 (1911): pp. 447–449. Although the exact date of his death remains in dispute, Venetian documents [*RdD* 2: 1269, 1282] make it clear that Theodoros I died sometime between May and July of 1407.

16 He died in September 1408.

17 Sphrantzes summarizes the same events, *Minus* 3.

18 It should be added that most of the work carried out by Manuel consisted of reconditioning the existing ruins of the wall that had been erected by Justinian I. Manuel did not build fortifications *in extenso*. Within one month 153 towers were erected. Remains of Manuel's project are still visible in the area southeast of the modern Corinth Canal. For the chronology of Manuel's trip in general, cf. J.W. Barker, "On the Chronology of the Activities of Manuel II Palaeologus in the Morea in 1415," *BZ* 55 (1962): pp. 39–55. During the renovations, according to Sphrantzes, who also emphasizes the haste with which this defensive line was brought to completion, an inscription dating from the reign of Justinian I was discovered; cf. *Minus* 4.2. The inscription [IG IV: 204; it is also included in N.A. Bees, *Die griechisch-christlichen Inschriften des Peloponnes* (Athens, 1941), no. 1, 1–4] is quoted in Sphrantzes's text; it is also cited in a Paris manuscript, *Codex 1278*, fol. 172. There are problems in the interpretation of the inscription's text, complicated by faulty grammar and spelling; cf. Gregory, *Isthmia 5*: 12–14, who, in Plate 1a, also supplies a black and white photograph of it. In 1883 the inscription was rediscovered and was removed for storage; it is currently housed in the Corinth Museum. The inscription seems to postdate 548 (the year of Theodora's death), since the empress is not mentioned. On this subject, cf. S.P. Lampros, "Σημειώματα περὶ Ἀρχαίων Ἑλληνικῶν Ἐπιγραφῶν ἐν Μεσαιωνικοῖς Κώδιξι καὶ Χειρογράφοις Συλλογαῖς Ἑσπερίων Λογίων," *NH* 1 (1904): pp. 257–279, esp. 268 ff. All sources (with modern scholarship and commentary) dealing with the renovations of the Hexamilion in the *quattrocento* are conveniently gathered by Gregory, *Isthmia 5*: ch. 3: "The Testimonia," pp. 11–27. For a general discussion concerning the various walls that had been erected in the area over the ages, cf. Lampros, "Τὰ Τείχη τοῦ Ἰσθμοῦ τῆς Κορίνθου," pp. 435–489; J.R. Wiseman, "A Trans-Isthmian Fortification Wall," *Hesperia* 32 (1963): 248–275; Bodnar, "The Isthmian Fortifications," pp. 165–171; R.L. Hohlfelder, "Trans-Isthmian Walls in the Age of Justinian," *Greek, Roman, and Byzantine Studies* 18 (1977): pp. 173–179; and T.E. Gregory, "The Late Roman Wall at Corinth," *Archaeology* 35 (1982): pp. 14–21. For a study of the area in question, cf. M.S. Kordoses, *Συμβολὴ στὴν Ἱστορία καὶ Τοπογραφία τῆς Περιοχῆς Κορίνθου στοὺς Μέσους Χρόνους* [*Βιβλιοθήκη Ἱστορικῶν Μελετῶν 159*] (Athens, 1981). For a thorough analysis of the Hexamilion from the perspective of a modern archaeologist, cf. now Gregory, *Isthmia 5*.

19 Cf. the statement of Demetrios Chrysoloras in *ΠκΠ* 3: 242, 243. A later text, *Codex Barberinus Graecus 111*, 5.2., of the early seventeenth century, also alludes to these events in one paragraph and further adds the realistic observation that the Peloponnesian rebels had good reason to be alarmed because Manuel enjoyed Mehmed I's friendship.

20 This man was yet another pretender to the Ottoman throne, claiming to be another son of Bayezid. The Porte refused to acknowledge Mustafa's claim and regarded him as a pretender. Furthermore, Mustafa failed to win popular support among the Turks. After his campaign to take over Rumeli collapsed, Mustafa and his associate, Juneid, fled to Thessalonike. Mehmed I demanded the surrender of the pretender from Demetrios Laskaris Leontaris, the senior administrator in the city, who governed in the name of Prince Andronikos. On Mustafa, cf. *MP*, pp. 340–342. Mustafa's claim has not been substantiated; he may, or may not, have been a true son of Bayezid. He was eventually apprehended and executed by Mehmed I's successor, Murad II. Doukas seems to believe that Mustafa was indeed the son of Bayezid; cf., e.g., 22.2. In order to invalidate Mustafa's claim, Sultan Murad II had him publicly executed, thus denying him the right of being privately strangled with a bowstring, which was the normal and privileged way of

dispatching true members of the Osmanli dynasty. The Codex Barberinus Graecus 111, 5.5, further states that there had been a Mustafa, an actual son of Bayezid, who, however, had died before the appearance of this pretender.
21 *MP*, p. 342. Mehmed I agreed to pay 300,000 aspers annually for the maintenance of his rival. John VIII supervised the resettlement of Mustafa; cf. *RKOR*: 3361. For a reasonable reconstruction of these events (accepted by *MP*, p. 343 n. 83), cf. N. Iorga, *Geschichte des osmanischen Reiches*, 1 (Gotha, 1900): 374. Sphrantzes treats the entire incident in one paragraph, *Minus* 4.4, but he is our only surce to state that John VIII sent the pretender to Mistra and not to Lemnos. The *Codex Barberinus Graecus 111*, 5.5, claims that Mustafa was sent to Μυτιλήνη. This is probably a copyist's error in the transmission of this chronicle. The Italian name for Lemnos at this time was "Stalimene" (a corruption of the phrase στὴ Λῆμνο) and a change from "Stalimene" to "Mytilene" cannot be ruled out.
22 Our sources for this campaign consist mainly of the *Panegyric* by Isidore and a chronicle from Cephalonia. On the latter chronicle, cf. G. Schirò, "Manuele II Palaeologo incorona Carlo Tocco despota di Gianina," *Byz* 29/30 (1959/1960): pp. 209–230; and *PaL* 2: 10–12.
23 The Venetians became alarmed at the activities of the Greek princes and dispatched a steady stream of official complaints to the brothers and especially to Manuel in Constantinople. It is perhaps reasonable to assume that at this time they sought to create a rift between Manuel and his two sons. Cf. *PaL* 2: 10–12. John moved against the Latin principality of Achaea and its prince, Zaccaria Centurione, and then even invaded Venetian territories. His raids brought a number of loud protests from Venice to the court of Constantinople, and were presented by the Venetian *bailo* himself, Fantino Viaro.
24 The two brothers, John VIII and Theodoros II, cooperated in this operation. During Manuel's previous visit, Zaccaria Centurione, the Latin prince of Achaea, had accepted the Greek emperor as his overlord. After John's arrival, hostilities broke out anew between the Greeks and Centurione. Within one year John seized Androusa, the key city in the province of Messenia. This expedition took him into Messenia and he was able to pursue Centurione into Elis; then the Latin prince sought safety within the walls of Glarentza.
25 A detailed description of this last unsuccessful Ottoman siege of Constantinople of 1422 is provided by Ioannes Kananos, an eyewitness author. The Greek text of this account can be found in its entirety in the CSHB corpus (the volume containing the *Maius* by Pseudo-Sphrantzes: Bonn, 1838) [= *PG* 156: cols. 61–81]. For another edition of Kananos (with Italian translation), cf. E. Pinto, ed., *L'assedio di Costantinopoli* (Messina, 1977). The most recent edition, with English translation, is by A.M. Cuomo, *Ioannis Canani de Constantinopolitana Obsidione Relatio*, Byzantinische Archiv 30 (Boston and Berlin, 2016). Kananos was obviously an eyewitness and composed his account while the unexpected victory and the events of the siege were still fresh in his mind. His text begins with a quotation from the Biblical Apocrypha (Tobit 12) and, after a short introduction, continues to present a straightforward, highly readable account of the operations and of the general assault. Also cf. *MP*, pp. 359–366. In addition, cf. the brief comments on the siege by M.C. Bartusis, *The Late Byzantine Army: Arms and Society, 1204–1453* (Philadelphia, 1992), p. 117.
26 P. Contamine, *War in the Middle Ages* (Oxford, 1984), pp. 200–207. The most recent and most comprehensive account on the role of siege engines and cannons can be found in Bradbury, pp. 241–296. For Turkish weapons and artillery in the *quattrocento*, cf. A. Williams, "Ottoman Military Technology: the Metallurgy of Turkish Armor," and K. De Vries, "Gunpowder Weapons at the Siege of Constantinople, 1453," in Y. Lev, ed., *War and Society in the Eastern Mediterranean, 7th–15th Centuries*, The Medieval Mediterranean. Peoples, Economies and Cultures, 400–1453, 9 (Leiden, New York and Cologne, 1997), respectively, pp. 363–399 and 343–363; M. Philippides, "Urban's Bombard(s),

Gunpowder, and the Siege of Constantinople (1453)," *Byzantine Studies/Etudes Byzantines*, n.s., 4 (1999): pp. 1–67; and *SF*, pp. 413–425.

27 Kananos uses similar phraseology and relates that John VIII "mounted his horse in full armor as he ought, came out of the Gate of Saint Romanos, and made his stand there in the vicinity of the Gate"; cf. the Bekker edition, pp. 461, 462. This was the vulnerable sector, as it would be again in 1453. Kananos emphasizes the vulnerability of the area. Of further importance are the comments of Kananos with regard to the moat of Constantinople, as we hear very little about it in other sources. For the topography of this sector, near the modern neighborhood of Sulu Kule, cf. *SF*, pp. 338–342.

28 On the formidable fortifications of Constantinople and on the various issues and problems involving the topography, cf. the investigation in *SF*, ch. 5, pp. 297–359.

29 On 15 November 1423, John VIII set out, leaving behind as regent his brother Constantine XI, who was elevated to the rank of despot; cf. *Minus* 12.3. The departure of John VIII is mentioned in *CBB* 1: 13.10 (p. 117), which furnishes an alternate date for his departure; *CBB* 1: 34.2 (p. 266), mistakenly states that John went to attend a synod. Syropoulos states that John's objective was to secure aid from Hungary, but his narrative contains a *lacuna* at this point, 2.12. He visited Venice and Milan and then went on to confer with Sigismund of Hungary; on Sigismund and John VIII, cf. *CF*, p. 39; G. Beckmann, *Der Kampf Kaiser Sigismunds gegen die werdende Weltmacht der Osmanen, 1392–1437. Eine historische Grundlegung* (Gotha, 1902), p. 97; and G. Moravcsik, "Византийские Императори их Посли в Г. Буда," *Acta Historica Academiae Scientiarum Hungaricae* 8 (1961): pp. 239–256.

Bibliography

1 Manuscripts

Arch. Segr. Vaticano, Arm. XXI
Arch. Segr. Vaticana, Arm. XXXI
Archiv. Segr. Reg. Vat. 398
Archivio di Stato, Mantua, Archivio Gonzaga, b. 840
Archivio di Stato, Mantua, Archivio Gonzaga, b. 841
Archivio di Stato, Mantua, Archivio Gonzaga, b. 842
Archivio di Stato, Mantua, Fondo Portioli, b. 13
Archivio di Stato, Venice, Reg. Vat. 452
Archivio di Stato, Venice, Reg. Vat. 468
Archivio di Stato, Venice, Reg. Vat. 469
Archivio di Stato, Venice, Reg. Vat. 470
Archivio di Stato, Venice, Reg. Vat. 498
Archivio di Stato, Venice, Senato Mar. R. 4
Archivio di Stato, Venice, Sen. Secr. T 19
Archivio antico dell'Università di Padova. Acta Collegii Aristarum no. 309
Archivio di Stato di Venezia, Gregolin Archivo No. 36 (= Miscellanea gregolin No. 27. Testamenti)
Archivo Vaticana, Arm. 39
Bellun. Bibl. Semin. Gregor. lat. 25
Bergom. Bibl. Civ. lat G. V. 21
Bibliothèque National de France, ms. fr. 9087
Bibliothèque National de France, Départment des Manuscrits, ms. 817
Bibliothèque National de France, Départment des Manuscrits, Supplément Grec 309
Bologna, *Codex Bibl. Univ. lat. B 52*
British Museum. Eggerton Collection, *ms. 2817*
Bruxell fr. 19684
Cambrai 1114
Codex Barberinus Graecus 111
Codex Bonn. Univ. lat. B 52, busta 22
Codex Marc. 496
Codex Marc. lat. XII 73 (4381)
Codex Monac. gr. 157
Codex Monac. gr. 186
Codex Palat. 597
Codex Regin. 1995

Codex Scorial gr. 14 (R-I-14)
Codex Strozzi 33
Codex Vat. 4137
Codex Vat. gr. 133
Codex Vat. gr. 706
Codex Vat. gr. 807
Codex Vat. gr. 914
Codex Vat. gr. 1018
Codex Vat. gr. 1152
Codex Vat. gr. 1823
Codex Vat. gr. 1852
Codex Vat. gr. 1858
Codex Vat. gr. 1896
Codex Vat. gr. 1904
Codex Vat. sl. 14
Flor. Riccard. lat. 660 (M II 19)
ГИМ No. 284
Haegens Bibl. Reg. lat. 71 E. 62
Mazurin Collection, Moscow, *Codex No. 1530*
Mediol. Bibl. Braid. lat. AE XII 40
Mediol. Trivult. lat. N 641
Meteora, *Metamorphosis 154*
Misc. Gregolin-Archivio di Stato di Venezia (= No. 27, Misc. Gregolin: Testament)
Monac. lat. Clm. 4143
Monac. lat. Clm. 4689
Moscow, *ms. 3554 (Vlad. 242)*
Musée du Louvre, Paris, Ivories A 53
Oxford Bodleian 87 ms.
Padua, *Bibl. Sem. lat. 126*
Palatino gr. 226
Paris. *Bibl. Nat. lat. 3127*
Paris. *Codex 1278*
Paris. fr. 2691
Paris. fr. 6487
Paris. fr. 15217
Paris. Nouv. Acquis., lat. 546,
Parmens. Bibl. Papalt. lat. 1583
Patav. Bibl. Semn. lat. 125
Reg. Vat. 44
Reg. Vat. 439
Reg. Vat. 449
Samos, ms. 12
Trotti ms. 373, Ambrosian Library
Vat. 214
Vat. 289
Vat. 1698
Vat. Barb. 127
Vat. Barb. lat. 2682
Vat. cod. 5667

Vat. gr. 133
Vat. gr. 776
Vat. gr. Codex 1852
Vat. Reg. 44
Vat. Reg. 365
Vat. Reg. 439
Vat. Reg. 468
Vat. Reg. 470
Vat. sl. 12
Vat. 175
Vat. 210
Vat. 776 (olim 812)
Vat. 830 (olim 546)
Vat. 1698
Vatic. Barber. 127b
Vat. Chisianus F139
Vat. Urb. 110
Ven. Marc. lat. 496

2 Collection of sources

Acta et diplomata graeca medii aevi sacra et profana. F. Miklosich and J. Müller, eds. Vol. 2. Vienna, 1860.
Acta Slavica Concilii Florentini. Narrationes et Documenta. J. Krajcar, SJ, ed. Concilium Florentinum. Documenta et Scriptores. Series A, vol. 11. Rome, 1976.
Акты Историческіе. Vol. 1. St. Petersburg, 1841.
Analecta Byzantino-Russica. W. Regel, ed. Petropoli. St. Petersburg, 1891.
Analekten der mittel- und neugriechischen Literatur. A.S. Ellissen, ed. Vol. 3. Leipzig, 1857.
Andreas de Santacroce, Advocatus Consistorialis. Acta Latina Concilii Florentini. G. Hofmann, SJ, ed. Concilium Florentinum. Documenta et Scriptores. Series B, Vol. 6. Rome, 1955.
Byzantine Monastic Foundation Documents: A Complete Translation of the Surviving Founders' Typika and Testaments. J. Thomas and Angela Constantinidis Hero, eds. 5 vols. Dumbarton Oaks Studies 35. Washington, DC, 2000.
Die byzantinischen Kleinchroniken, Chronica Byzantina Breviora. P. Schreiner, ed. 3 vols. Corpus Fontium Historiae Byzantinae 22/1, 22/2, and 22/3. Vienna, 1975–1979.
La Caduta di Costantinopoli. Vol. 1: *Le Testimonianze dei Contemporanei.* Vol. 2: *L'Eco nel Mondo.* A. Pertusi, ed. Verona, 1976.
Catalogus codicum manu scriptorium Bibliotheca Monacensis, Vol. 2/Part 4: *Codices Graecos 181–265 Continens / Katalog der griechischen Handschriften der Bayerischen Staatsbibliothek München,* Vol. 4: *Codices graeci Monacenses 181–265.* Kerstin Hajdú, ed. Wiesbaden, 2012.
Cent-dix lettres grecques des François Filelfe publiées intégralment pour la première fois d'après le codex Trivulzianus 873 avec traduction, notes et commentaires par É. Legrand. É. Legrand, ed. Publications de l'Ecole des langues orientales vivantes, 3rd series. Vol. 12. Paris, 1892.
Corpus Christianorum, Continuatio Mediaevalis LXII, Apologiae duae: Gazechni epistola ad Walcherum; Burchardi, ut videtur, Abbatis Bellevallis Apologia de Barbis. R.B.C. Huygens. Turnholt, 1985.
Decrees of the Ecumenical Councils. Vol. 1: *Nicaea I to Lateran V.* N. P. Tanner, ed. Washington, DC, 1990.

Documenta Pontificum Romanorum Historiam Ucrainae Illustrantia (1075–1953). Vol. I: 1075– 1700. A.G. Welykyj, ed. Analecta OSBM, series II, section III. Rome, 1953.

Ἐπίσημα Κείμενα τοῦ Πατριαρχείου Κωνσταντινουπόλεως: Τὰ Σωζόμενα ἀπὸ τὴν Περίοδο *1454–1498.* M. Paize-Apostolopoulou and D.G. Apostolopoulos, eds. Athens, 2011.

Epistolae Pontificiae ad Concilium Florentinum Spectantes. Part 1: *Epistolae Pontificiae de rebus anto Concilium Florentinum Gestis (1418–1438).* Part 2: *Epistolae Pontificiae de Rebus in Concilio Florentino Annis 1438–1439 Gestis.* Part 3: *Epistolae Pontificiae de Ultimis Actis Concilii Florentini Annis 1440–1445 et de Rebus post Concilium Gestis Annis 1446–1453.* G. Hofmann, ed. Concilium Florentinum. Documenta et Scriptores. Series A. Rome, 1940–1946.

I Libri Commemoriali. R. Predelli, ed. 8 vols. Venice, 1876–1924.

Ioannes de Torquemada O.P., Cardinalis Sancti Sixti. Apparatus super Decretum Florentinum Unionis Graecorum. E. Candal, SJ, ed. Concilium Florentinum. Documenta et Scriptores. Series B, Vol. 2/Part 1. Rome, 1942.

Mehmed II the Conqueror and the Fall of the Franco-Byzantine Levant to the Ottoman Turks: Some Western Views and Testimonies. M. Philippides, ed. Medieval and Renaissance Texts and Studies 302. Tempe, 2007.

Μνημεῖα Ἑλληνικῆς Ἱστορίας: *Documents inédits relatifs à l'histoire de la Grèce au moyen Âge.* C.N. Sathas, ed. Vol. 9. Paris, 1890; repr. Athens, 1972.

Monumenta conciliorum generalium seculi decimi quinti. Concilium Basileense, scriptorum. F. Palacký, E. von Birk, K. and K.W. Hieronimus, eds. Vols. 1–4. Vienna and Basil, 1857–1935.

Monumenta Hungariae Historica. Ser. Scriptores (Második osztály Irok), 21/1–2; 22/1–2. P.A. Déthier and K. (C.) Hopf, eds. Sine loco (Galata/Pera? or Budapest?), sine anno (1872?/1875?).

Notes et Extraits pour servir à l'histoire des Croisades au XVe Siècle. N. Iorga (Jorga), ed. 8 vols. Paris and Bucharest, 1899–1902, 1916.

Oratio Dogmatica de Unione. E. Candal, SJ, ed. Concilium Florentinum. Documenta et Scriptores. Series B, 7/1. Rome, 1958.

Orientalium Documenta Minora. G. Hofmann, ed. Concilium Florentinum. Documenta et Scriptores. Series A, 3/fasc. 3. Rome, 1953.

Ouevres complètes de Gennade Scholarios. L. Petit, X.A. Sidéridès and M. Jugie, eds. 4 vols. Paris, 1930–1935.

Παλαιολόγεια καὶ Πελοποννησιακά. S.P. Lampros, ed. 4 vols. Athens, 1912–1930; repr. 1972.

Patrologia Cursus Completus. Series Graeco-Latina. J.-P. Migne, ed. Vols. 159 and 161. Paris, 1866.

Pius II Commentaries. Margaret Meserve and M. Simonetta, eds. The I Tatti Renaissance Library 12. Vol. 2. Cambridge, MA and London, 2003.

Полное Собраніе Русскихъ Лѣтописей. Vol. 1. St. Petersburg, 1846.

Quae supersunt Actorum Graecorum Concilii Florentini, necnon descriptionis cuiusdam eiusdem. J. Gill, ed. 2 parts. Concilium Florentinum. Documenta et Scriptores, ser. B, Vol. 5, fasc. 1–2. Rome, 1953.

Recensionem codicum graecorum continens. H.O. Coxe, comp. Catalogi codicum manuscriptorum bibliothecae Bodleianae, pars 1. Oxford, 1853.

Regesten der Kaiserurkunden des oströmischen Reiches. F. Dölger, ed. Vol. 5. Munich and Berlin, 1965.

Régestes des deliberations du Sénat de Venise concernant la Romanie. F. Thiriet, ed. Vol. 3. Paris, 1961.

Sacrorum Conciliorum Nova, et Amplissima Collectio, in qua præter ea, quæ Phil. Labbeus, et Gabr. Cossartius . . . . J.D. Mansi, ed. Vols. 30 and 31. Venice, 1792–1793.

Scritti d'Isidoro il Cardinale Ruteno e Codici a lui Appartenuti che si Conservano nella Biblioteca Apostolica Vaticana. G. Mercati, ed. Studi e testi 46. Rome, 1926.

380 Bibliography

The Siege of Constantinople 1453: Seven Contemporary Accounts. J.R. Melville Jones. Amsterdam, 1972.

Систематическое Описанiе Рукописй Московской Синодалной (Патриаршей) Библиотеки. Vol. 1: *Рукописи Греческiя.* Archimandrite Vladimir, compiler. Moscow, 1894.

Social and Political Thought in Byzantium. From Justinian I to the Last Palaeologus. Passages from Byzantine Writers and Documents. E. Barker, trans. Oxford, 1957.

Spicilegium Romanum. Vol. 1: *Virorum Illustrium. CIII. qui Saeculo XV. extiterunt Vitae Auctore Coaevo Vespasiano Florentino.* A. Mai, ed. Rome, 1839.

Studi storici Concilio di Ferenze. Con documenti inediti o nuovamente dati all luce sui manoscritti di Firenze e di Roma. Part 1: *Antededenti del Concilio.* E. Cecconi, ed. Florence, 1869.

Testi Inediti e Poco Noti sulla Caduta di Costantinopoli. A. Pertusi, ed. Il Mondo Medievale. Studi di Storia e Storiographia: Sezione di Storia Bizantina e Slava 4 (*edizione postuma a cura di A. Carile*). Bologna, 1983.

3 Individual sources

Agallianos, Theodoros. *Ὁ Θεόδωρος Ἀγαλλιανὸς Ταυτιζόμενος ϖρὸς τὸν Θεοφάνην Μηδείας καὶ οἱ Ἀνέκδοτοι Λόγοι του. Μία Νέα Ἱστορικὴ Πηγὴ ϖερὶ τοῦ Πατριαρχείου Κωνσταντινουϖόλεως κατὰ τοὺς Πρώτους μετὰ τὴν Ἅλωσιν Χρόνους.* C.G. Patrinelis, ed. Athens, 1966.

———. *Τοῦ Τιμιωτάτου Δικαιοφύλακος τῆς Μεγάλης Ἐκκλησίας Κυρίου Θεοδώρου τοῦ Ἀγαλλιανοῦ Ἀνασκευὴ τοῦ ὑϖὲρ τῆς Δόξης Λατίνων Βιβλίου Ἰωάννου τοῦ Ἀργυροϖούλου.* S.P. Lampros, ed. *Ἀργυροϖούλεια: Ἰωάννου Ἀργυροϖούλου Λόγοι, Πραγματεῖαι, Ἐϖιστολαί, Προσφωνήματα, Ἀϖαντήσεις καὶ Ἐϖιστολαὶ ϖρὸς Αὐτὸν καὶ τὸν Υἱὸν Ἰσαάκιον. Ἐϖιστολαὶ καὶ Ἀϖοφάσεις ϖερὶ Αὐτῶν. Προτάσσεται Εἰσαγωγὴ ϖερὶ Ἰωάννου Ἀργυροϖούλου, τῆς Οἰκογενείας Αὐτοῦ καὶ τῶν Ἀργυροϖούλων καθ' Ὅλου.* Athens, 1910. Pp. 234–303.

Anonymous. *Χρονικὸν ϖερὶ τῶν Τούρκων Σουλτάνων (κατὰ τὸν Βαρβ. Ἑλληνικὸν Κώδικα 111).* G.T. Zoras, ed. Athens, 1958.

Ἡ Ἅλωσις τῆς Κωνσταντινουϖόλεως καὶ ἡ Βασιλεία Μωάμεθ Β' τοῦ Κατακτητοῦ (κατὰ τὸν Ἀνέκδοτον Ἑλληνικὸν Βαρβερινὸν Κώδικα 111 τῆς Βατικανῆς Βιβλιοθήκης). G.T. Zoras, ed. Athens, 1952.

English translation: Philippides, M. *Byzantium, Europe, and the Early Ottoman Sultans 1373–1513: An Anonymous Greek Chronicle of the Seventeenth Century* (*Codex Barberinus Graecus 111*). Late Byzantine and Ottoman Studies 4. New Rochelle, 1990.

———. *Ἐγκώμιον εἰς τὸν Αὐτοκράτορα [Ἰωάννην τὸν Παλαιολόγον], Παλαιολόγεια καὶ Πελοϖοννησιακά,* Vol. 3. S.P. Lampros, ed. with I.K. Bogiatzides. Athens, 1926; repr. 1972. Pp. 292–308.

———. *Ἔκθεσις Χρονική: Ecthesis Chronica and Chronicon Athenarum.* S.P. Lampros, ed. London, 1902.

Philippides, M. ed. and trans. *Emperors, Patriarchs and Sultans of Constantinople, 1373–1513: An Anonymous Greek Chronicle of the Sixteenth Century.* Brookline, MA, 1990.

———. *Ὁ "Ἱερὸς Κῶδιξ" τοῦ Πατριαρχείου Κωνσταντινουϖόλεως στὸ Β' Μισὸ τοῦ ΙΕ' Αἰώνα, Τὰ Μόνα Γνωστὰ Σϖαράγματα.* D.G. Apostolopoulos, ed. Athens, 1999.

Antonino (Antoninus), Archbishop of Florence. *Chronicon seu opus historiarum.* Nürnberg, 1484.

Argyropoulos, Ioannes. Ἀργυροπούλεια: Ἰωάννου Ἀργυροπούλου Λόγοι, Πραγματεῖαι, Ἐπιστολαί, Προσφωνήματα, Ἀπαντήσεις καὶ Ἐπιστολαὶ πρὸς Αὐτὸν καὶ τὸν Υἱὸν Ἰσαάκιον. Ἐπιστολαὶ καὶ Ἀποφάσεις περὶ Αὐτῶν. Προτάσσεται Εἰσαγωγὴ περὶ Ἰωάννου Ἀργυροπούλου, τῆς Οἰκογενείας Αὐτοῦ καὶ τῶν Ἀργυροπούλων καθ᾽ Ὅλου. S.P. Lampros, ed. Athens, 1910.

———. Τῷ Λαμπροτάτῳ καὶ Περιφανεστάτῳ Μεγάλῳ Δουκὶ Ἰωάννης διδάσκαλος ὁ Ἀργυρόπουλος Συνοπτικώτατον περὶ τῆς τοῦ Ἁγίου Πνεύματος Ἐκπορεύσεως, ἐν ᾧ καὶ Ἀνάπτυξις τοῦ Ὅρου τοῦ ἐν Φλωρεντίᾳ Γεγενημένου. Ἀργυροπούλεια: Ἰωάννου Ἀργυροπούλου Λόγοι, Πραγματεῖαι, Ἐπιστολαί, Προσφωνήματα, Ἀπαντήσεις καὶ Ἐπιστολαὶ πρὸς Αὐτὸν καὶ τὸν Υἱὸν Ἰσαάκιον. Ἐπιστολαὶ καὶ Ἀποφάσεις περὶ Αὐτῶν. Προτάσσεται Εἰσαγωγὴ περὶ Ἰωάννου Ἀργυροπούλου, τῆς Οἰκογενείας Αὐτοῦ καὶ τῶν Ἀργυροπούλων καθ᾽ Ὅλου. S.P. Lampros, ed. Athens, 1910. Pp. 107–128.

———. Ἰωάννου τοῦ Ἀργυροπούλου τοῦ Κριτοῦ τοῦ Δημοσίου τῆς Κωνσταντινουπόλεως εἰς τὸν Μακαριώτατον Πάπαν Κὺρ Νικόλαον. Ἀργυροπούλεια: Ἰωάννου Ἀργυροπούλου Λόγοι, Πραγματεῖαι, Ἐπιστολαί, Προσφωνήματα, Ἀπαντήσεις καὶ Ἐπιστολαὶ πρὸς Αὐτὸν καὶ τὸν Υἱὸν Ἰσαάκιον. Ἐπιστολαὶ καὶ Ἀποφάσεις περὶ Αὐτῶν. Προτάσσεται Εἰσαγωγὴ περὶ Ἰωάννου Ἀργυροπούλου, τῆς Οἰκογενείας Αὐτοῦ καὶ τῶν Ἀργυροπούλων καθ᾽ Ὅλου. S.P. Lampros, ed. Athens, 1910. Pp. 129–141.

Barbaro, Nicolò. *Giornale dell' assedio di Costantinopoli 1453 di Nicolò Barbaro P.V. correddato di note e documenti*. E. Cornet, ed. Vienna, 1856.

La Caduta di Costantinopoli. A. Pertusi, ed. Vol. 1: *Le Testimonianze dei Contemporanei*. Verona, 1976. Pp. 8–38 (selections with improved text).

English Translation: [Melville] Jones, J.R. *Nicolò Barbaro: Diary of the Siege of Constantinople*. Jericho, 1969.

Modern Greek Translation: V.A. Lappa, *Η Πόλις Ἑάλω: Το Χρονικό τῆς Πολιορκίας και της Ἀλώσης τῆς Πόλης*. Athens, 1991. Pp. 93–213.

Benedeto, Archishop. *Leonardi Chiensis De Lesbo a Turcis capta epistola Pio papae II missa ex. cod. ms. Ticinensis*. C. Hopf, ed. Regimonti, 1866.

Chroniques Gréco-Romanes Inédites ou peu connues publiées avec notes et tables généalogiques. C. Hopf, ed. Paris, 1873; repr. Brussels, 1966. Pp. 359–366.

Bessarion, Cardinal. Funeral oration by Bishop Angelo Capranica of Fermo. *Oratio in funere Bessarionis Cardinalis habita*. Rome, 1472; repr. Rome, 1480.

Brant, S. *Decreta & acta Consilii basiliensis* . . . . Bound with *Acta scitu dignissima docteq[ue] concinnata Constantiensis consilii celebratissimi* . . . . Basel, 1499.

Caoursin, Guillaume. *Guglielmi Caorsici* [sic] *Rhodiorum vicecancellarii obsidionis Rhodiae urbis descriptio*. Rome, 1480–1481.

Mehmed II the Conqueror and the Fall of the Franco-Byzantine Levant to the Ottoman Turks: Some Western Views and Testimonies. M. Philippides, ed. and trans. Medieval and Renaissance Texts and Studies 302. Tempe, Arizona, 2007. Pp. 261–315.

Castellana dalla, Jacopo. Perdita di Negroponte. In *Mehmed II the Conqueror and the Fall of the Franco-Byzantine Levant to the Ottoman Turks: Some Western Views and Testimonies*. M. Philippides, ed. and trans. Medieval and Renaissance Texts and Studies 302. Tempe, Arizona, 2007. Pp. 249–261.

Corpus Christianorum, Continuatio Mediaevalis LXII, Apologia duae: Gozechni epistola ad Walcherum; Burchardi, ut videtur, Abbatis Believallis Apologia de Barbis. R.B.C. Huygens, ed. Turnholt, 1985.

Cyriacus of Ancona. *Cyriac of Ancona: Later Travels*. E.W. Bodnar, SJ, ed. and trans with C. Foss. The I Tatti Renaissance Library 10. Cambridge, MA, 2003.

Da Rimini, Filippo. "Epistola ad Franciscum Barbarum, virum inclitum, procuratorem Sancti Marci dignissimum [Excidium Constantinopolitanae urbis]". In P.A. Déthier and C. Hopf, eds. *Monumenta Hungariae Historica. Ser. Scriptores (Második osztály Irok)*.Vol. 22.1. *Sine loco.* Galata/Pera? *sine anno* (1872?/1875?). Pp. 656–682.

"La lettera di Filippo da Rimini, cancelliere di Corfù, a Francesco Barbaro e i primi documenti occidentali sulla caduta di Costantinopoli (1453)." In A. Pertusi, ed. *Μνημόσυνον Σοφίας Ἀντωνιάδη*. Βιβλιοθήκη τοῦ Ἑλληνικοῦ Ἰνστιτούτου Βενετίας Βυζαντινῶν καὶ Μεταβυζαντινῶν Σπουδῶν 6.Venice, 1974. Pp. 120–157.

Selections with Italian translation: *Testi Inediti e Poco Noti sulla Caduta di Costantinopoli.* A. Pertusi, ed. Il Mondo Medievale. Studi di Storia e Storiographia: Sezione di Storia Bizantina e Slava 4 (*edizione postuma a cura di A. Carile*). Bologna, 1983. Pp. 127–141.

De Aguilar, Francisco [Alonso], Fray. *Relación breve de la conquista de la Nuena España.* 8th ed., Mexico, 1980.

De Bertipaglia, Pasius. *Epistola composita per ser Pasium de Bertipalia notarium ad instantiam reverendissimi domini domini Isidori cardinalis Sabiniensis.* In *La Caduta di Costantinopoli*, vol 2: *L'Eco nel Mondo.* A. Pertusi, ed.Verona, 1976. Pp. 60–64.

De Xivrey, Berger. "Mémoire sur la vie et les ouvrages de l'empereur Manuel Paléologue." In *Mémoires de l'Institut de France: Académie des inscriptions et belles-lettres* 19.1 (Paris, 1853). Pp. 1–201.

Di Montaldo, Adamo. "*De Constantinopolitano excidio ad nobilissimum iuvenem Melladucam Cicadam.*" In P. A. Déthier, C. Desimoni and C. Hopf. "Della Conquita di Costantinopoli per Maometto II nel MCCCCLIII." *Atti della Società Ligure di Storia Patria* 10 (1874). Pp. 289–354.

Dotti, Paolo. "Μονῳδίαι καὶ Θρῆνοι ἐπὶ τῇ Ἁλώσει τῆς Κωνσταντινουπόλεως." S.P. Lampros, ed. *Νέος Ἑλληνομνήμων* 5 (1908). Pp. 263–265.

*Notes et Extraits pour servir à l'histoire des Croisades au XV*ᵉ *Siècle.* N. Iorga (Jorga), ed.Vol. 2. Paris and Bucharest, 1899. Pp. 513–514 (extracts only).

With Italian translation, in *La Caduta di Costantinopoli.* A. Pertusi, ed.Vol. 2: *L'Eco nel Mondo.* Verona, 1976. Pp. 12–17.

Doukas [Michael?]. *Ducae Michaelis Ducae nepotis historia Byzantina.* I. Bekker, ed. Corpus Scriptorum Historiae Byzantinae. Bonn, 1834.

*Historia Turco-Byzantina.*V. Grecu, ed. Bucharest, 1858.

Μιχαὴλ Δούκα, Βυζαντινοτουρκικὴ Ἱστορία. B. Karales, with translation into Modern Greek. Κείμενα Βυζαντινῆς Ἱστοριογραφίας 7. Athens, 1997.

English Translation: *Decline and Fall of Byzantium to the Ottoman Turks, An Annotated Translation of "Historia Turco-Byzantina."* H. Magoulias, trans. Detroit, 1975.

Eparkhos, Thomas and Diplovatatzes, Joseph. *Aviso. Notes et Extraits pour servir à l'histoire des Croisades au XV*ᵉ *Siècle.* N. Iorga (Jorga), ed.Vol. 2. Paris and Bucharest, 1899. Pp. 514–518. Italian translation (without the original German text): *La Caduta di Costantinopoli.* A. Pertusi, ed.Vol. 1: *Le Testimonianze dei Contemporanei.*Verona, 1976. Pp. 234–239.

Giustiniani, Hieronimo and Argenti, Philip P. eds. *Hieronimo Giustiniani's History of Chios.* Cambridge, 1943.

Giustiniani, Leonardo. "*Epistula.*" In D.P. Lonicer, ed. *D. Philippi Loniceri Chronica Turcica.* Vol. 2. *Francofurti ad Moenum* [Frankfurt am Main], 1578. Pp. 84–102.

Epistula. J.-P. Migne ed. *Patrologia graeca.*Vol. 159. Paris, 1866. Cols. 923–953.

Epistula. P.A. Déthier and K. (C.) Hopf, eds. *Monumenta Hungariae Historica. Ser. Scriptores (Második osztály Irok)*, 21/1–2; 22/1–2. *Sine loco* (Galata/Pera? or Budapest?), *sine anno* (1872?/1875?). Pp. 333–616.

Epistola reverendissimi in Christo patris et domini domini Leonardi Ordinis Praedicatorum, archiepiscopi Mitileni, sacrarum litterarum professoris, ad beatissimum dominum nostrum Nicolaum papam quintum [*De urbis Constantinopolis captivitate*]. L.T. Belgrano, ed. In "Prima Serie di Documenti Riguardanti la Colonia di Pera." *Atti della Società Ligure di Storia Patria* 13 (1877), no. 150. Pp. 233–257.

De Urbis Constantinopoleos Jactura Captivitateque. I.I. Sreznevskii, ed. *Повѣсть о Цареградъ.* Saint Petersburg, 1855. Pp. 50–68.
Selections (with improved text and Italian translation): *La Caduta di Costantinopoli.* A. Pertusi, ed. Vol. 1: *Le Testimonianze dei Contemporanei.* Verona, 1976. Pp. 124–171.
English translation: Melville Jones, J.R. *The Siege of Constantinople 1453: Seven Contemporary Accounts.* Amsterdam, 1972. Pp. 11–42.
Henry [Heinrich] of Soemmern. "Codice diplomatico delle colonie Tauro-Liguri durante la signoria dell'Ufficio di S. Giorgio (MCCCLIII–MCCCCLXXV)." A. Vigna, ed. *Atti della Società Ligure di Storia Patria* 6 (1868). Pp. 19–21.
Notes et Extraits pour servir à l'histoire des Croisades au XVe Siècle. N. Iorga (Jorga), ed. Vol. 3. Paris and Bucharest, 1902. Pp. 307–315.
Selections with Italian translation: *La Caduta di Costantinopoli.* A. Pertusi, ed. Vol. 2: *L'Eco nel Mondo.* Verona, 1976. Pp. 82–96.
Text and English trans. M. Philippides, *Mehmed II the Conqueror and the Fall of the Franco-Byzantine Levant to the Ottoman Turks: Some Western Views and Testimonies.* Medieval and Renaissance Texts and Studies 302. Tempe, Arizona, 2007. Pp. 121–133.
Iona, Metropolitan. "Новонайденная Духовная Граммота Митрополита Ионану." In A. I. Pliguzov, et al., eds. *Рускии Феолальный Архив XIV-первой трети XVI в.* Vol. 3. Moscow, 1988. Pp. 640–654.
Isidore, Cardinal. *Isidorus Arch. Kioviensis et Totius Russiae. Sermones inter Concilium Florentinum Conscripti.* G. Hofmann, E. Candal and Cardinal Julian Cesarini, eds. Concilium Florentinum. Documenta et Scriptores. Series A, Vol. 10/Part 1. Rome, 1971.
Epistolae Isidori Hieromonachi (postea Metropolitae Kijoviensis). W. Regel, ed. *Analecta Byzantino-Russica.* Petropoli, 1851. Pp. 59–71.
Epistola composita per Pasium de Bertipalia notarium ad instantiam reverendissimi domini Isidori cardinalis Sabiniensis. La Caduta di Costantinopoli. A. Pertusi, ed. Vol. 1: *Le Testimonianze dei Contemporanei.* Verona, 1976. Pp. 58–64 (selections with Italian translation).
Epistola reverendissimi patris domini Isidori cardinalis Ruteni scripta ad reverendissimum dominum Bisarionem episcopum Tusculanum ac cardinalem Nicenum Bononiaeque legatum. In "Ein Brief des Kardinals Isidor von Kiew an Kardinal Bessarion." G. Hofmann, ed. *Orientalia Christiana Periodica* 14 (1948). Pp. 405–414.
Ziegler, A.W. "Die restlichen vier unveröffentlichten Briefe Isidores von Kijev." *Orientalia Christinia Periodica* 18 (1952). Pp. 135–142.
———. "Vier bisher nicht veröffentlichte griechische Briefe." *Byzantinische Zeitschrift* 44 (1951). Pp. 570–577. Selections with Italian translation: *La Caduta di Costantinopoli.* A. Pertusi, ed. Vol. 1: *Le Testimonianze dei Contemporanei.* Verona, 1976. Pp. 64–80.
Universis et singulis Christi fidelibus. In "Duae Epistulae Cardinalis Isidori Ineditae." A.G. Welykyi, ed. *Analecta Ordinis Sancti Basilii* [*Записки Чина Св. Василий Вликого*], ser. 3, 1 (1950). Pp. 289–291.
———. *Patrologia Cursus Completus. Series Graeco-Latina.* J.-P. Migne, ed. Vol. 159. Paris, 1867. Cols. 953–956.
———. *Monumenta Hungariae Historica.* P.A. Déthier and C. Hopf, eds. Vol. 21/1. *Sine loco* [Galata/Pera? or Budapest?], *sine anno* [1872/1875?]. Pp. 687–702.
———. Selections with Italian translation: *La Caduta di Costantinopoli.* A. Pertusi, ed. Vol. 1: *Le Testimonianze dei Contemporanei.* Verona, 1976. Pp. 80–90.
Letter to the Pope: *Notes et Extraits pour servir à l'histoire des Croisades au XVe Siècle.* N. Iorga (Jorga), ed. Vol. 2. Paris and Bucharest, 1899. Pp. 522–524.
Selections with Italian translation: *La Caduta di Costantinopoli.* A. Pertusi, ed. Vol. 1: *Le Testimonianze dei Contemporanei.* Verona, 1976. Pp. 90–100.

Letter to Doge Foscari: "Duae Epistulae Cardinalis Isidori Ineditae." A. G. Welykyi, ed. *Analecta Ordinis Sancti Basilii* [Записки Чина Св. Василий Великого], ser. 3, 1 (1950). Pp. 286–289. Selections with Italian translation: *La Caduta di Costantinopoli*. A. Pertusi, ed. Vol. 1: *Le Testimonianze dei Contemporanei*. Verona, 1976. Pp. 100–106.

Letter to Capranica. *Notes et Extraits pour servir à l'histoire des Croisades au XV⁽ Siècle*. N. Iorga (Jorga), ed. Vol. 2. Paris and Bucharest, 1899. Pp. 518–519. With Italian translation: *Testi Inediti e Poco Noti sulla Caduta di Costantinopoli*. A. Pertusi, ed. Il Mondo Medievale. Studi di Storia e Storiographia: Sezione di Storia Bizantina e Slava 4 (*edizione postuma a cura di A. Carile*). Bologna, 1983. Pp. 12–15.

Magnificis dominis prioribus palatii et communitatis Florentinorum. "Quellen zu Isidor von Kiew als Kardinal und Patriarch." In G. Hofmann, ed. *Orientalia Christiana Periodica* 18 (1952). Pp. 143–157. Selections with Italian translation: *Testi Inediti e Poco Noti sulla Caduta di Costantinopoli*. A. Pertusi, ed. Il Mondo Medievale. Studi di Storia e Storiographia: Sezione di Storia Bizantina e Slava 4 (*edizione postuma a cura di A. Carile*). Bologna, 1983. Pp. 16–21.

Letter to Philip the Good. With Italian translation: *La Caduta di Costantinopoli*. A. Pertusi, ed. Vol. 1: *Le Testimonianze dei Contemporanei*. Verona, 1976. Pp. 106–110.

Travel account. "Anónimo ruso sobre et viaje de Isidoro de Kíev al Concilio de Florencia." Bádenas de la Peña, P. and A. L. Encinas Moral. *Erytheia* 35 (2014). Pp. 251–299.

"Хождение Митрополита Исидора на Флорентійскій Соборъ." In J. Krajcar, ed. *Acta Slavica Concilii Florentini. Narrationes et Documenta*. Concilium Florentinum. Documenta et Scriptores. Series A, Vol. 11. Rome, 1976.

Библиотека Лутературы Древней Руси. D. S. Likhachev, *et al*., eds. Vol. 6. St. Petersburg, 1999. Pp. 464–487.

"Reisebericht eines unbekannten Russen (1437–1440)." In G. Stökl, ed. *Europe im XV Jahrhundert von byzantinern Gesehen*. Graz, Vienna and Cologne, 1954. Pp. 151–189.

Iustiniani, M. "*Vita Leonardi*." In *Caroli Pogii de nobilitate liber disceptatorius et Leonardi Chiensis de vera nobilitate contra Poggium tractactus apologeticus*. Abelini, 1657. Cols. 43–48.

Ivani (da Sarzana), Antonio. *Expugnatio Constantinopolitana ad illustrem dominum Federicum Montisferetri Urbini ac Durantis comitem*. Published as *Anonymi historiola quae inscribitur Constantinopolitanae civitatis expugnatio conscripta a 1459 p. Chr. e cod. chart. Bibl. Templi Cathedr. Strengnes*. In *Monumenta Hungariae Historica*. P. A. Déthier and C. Hopf, eds. Vol. 21.1. Sine loco [Galata/Pera? or Budapest?], sine anno [1872/1875?]. Pp. 71–94.

Selections with Italian translation: *Testi Inediti e Poco Noti sulla Caduta di Costantinopoli*. A. Pertusi, ed. Il Mondo Medievale. Studi di Storia e Storiographia: Sezione di Storia Bizantina e Slava 4 (*edizione postuma a cura di A. Carile*). Bologna, 1983. Pp. 146–165.

Kananos, Ioannes. "Διήγησις περὶ τοῦ ἐν Κωνσταντινουπόλει Γεγονότος Πολέμου. Ioannes Canani de Constantinopoli anno 1422 oppugnata narratio." In I. Bekker, ed. *Georgius Phrantzes. Ioannes Cananus. Ioannes Anagnostes*. Corpus Scriptorum Historiae Byzantinae. Bonn, 1838. Pp. 457–479 [= *Patrologia Graeca*, Vol. 156. Cols. 151–166, with Latin translation by Leo Allatius].

"Sulla Διήγησις di Giovanni Cananos." M. E. Colonna, ed. and trans. into Italian. *Università di Napoli, Annali della Facoltà di lettere e filosofie* 7 (1957). Pp. 151–166.

L'assedio di Costantinopoli. E. Pinto, ed. Messina, 1977.

Ioannis Canani de Constantinopolitana Obsidione Relatio. A. M. Cuomo ed. and trans. Byzantinische Archiv 30. Boston and Berlin, 2016.

Khalkokondyles, Laonikos [Nikolaos]. *Laonici Chalcocandylae Atheniensis Historiarum Libri Decem*. I. Bekker, ed. Corpus Scriptorum Historiae Byzantinae, Book 1. Bonn, 1843 [= *Patrologia Graeca*, vol. 159. Cols. 13–556, with Latin translation].

Laonici Chalcocandylae Historiarum Demonstrationes. E. Darkó, ed. Vol. 2. Budapest, 1923.

Laonikos Chalkokondyles. *A Translation and Commentary of the "Demostrations of Histories (Books I-III)."* N. Nicoloudis. Historical Monographs 16. Athens, 1996.
The Histories. A. Kaldellis, trans. Dumbarton Oaks Medieval Library 33–34. 2 vols. Cambridge, MA, 2014.
Der Russland-Exkurs des Laonikos Chalkokondyles. N. Ditten. Berliner Byzantinistische Arbeiten Band 39. Berlin, 1968.
Khrysoloras (Chrysoloras), Manuel. *Manuel Chrysoloras and His Discourse Addressed to the Emperor Manuel II Palaeologus. Μανουὴλ Χρυσολωρᾶ Λόγος πρὸς τὸν Αὐτοκράτορα Μανουὴλ Β΄.* C.G. Patrinelis and D.Z. Sofianos, eds. Athens, 2001.
Kritoboulos, Michael Hermodorus. *Κριτόβουλος: Βίος τοῦ Μωάμεθ Β΄. Monumenta Hungariae Historica. Ser. Scriptores (Második osztály Irok).* P.A. Déthier, ed. Vol. 21.1. *Sine loco* [Galata/Pera? or Budapest?], *sine anno* [1872?/1875?]. Pp. 1–346.
"De rebus gestis Muhammetis II." In C. Müller, ed. *Fragmenta Historicorum Graecorum.* Vol. 5. Paris, 1870. Pp. 40–160. Vol. 6. Paris, 1883. Pp. 52–164.
Critobul din Imbros din domnia lui Mahomed al II-lea anii 1451–1467. V. Grecu, ed. (with Rumanian translation). Scriptores Byzantini 4. Bucharest, 1963.
Critobuli Imbriotae Historiae. D.R. Reinsch, ed. Corpus Fontium Historiae Byzantinae 22. Berlin and New York, 1983.
English translation: *Kritovoulos. A History of Mehmed the Conqueror.* C.T. Riggs. Princeton, 1954; repr. 1970.
La Caduta di Costantinopoli. A. Pertusi, ed. Vol. 2: *L'Eco nel Mondo.* Verona, 1976. Pp. 230–251 (selections with Italian translation).
Languschi, Giacomo (Dolfin, Zorzi). *Excidio e presa di Constantinopoli nell' anno 1453.* In "Die Eroberung Constantinopels im Jahre 1453 auf einer venetianischen Chronik." G.M. Thomas, ed. *Sitzungsberichte der köngl. bayer. Akademie der Wissenschaften, philos.-hist. Klasse.* Band 2. Munich, 1866. Pp. 1–38.
Testi Inediti e Poco Noti sulla Caduta di Costantinopoli. A. Pertusi and A. Carile, eds. Il Mondo Medievale. Studi di Storia e Storiographia: Sezione di Storia Bizantina e Slava 4 (*edizione postuma a cura di A. Carile*). Bologna, 1983. Pp. 169–180 (selections).
Lomellino, Angelo Giovanni. "Pièces diplomatiques tirée des Archives République de Gênnes." S. de Sacy, ed. *Notices et extraits des manuscripts de la Bibliothéque du Roi* 11 (1827). Pp. 74–79.
"Prima serie di documenti riguardanti la colonia di Pera." L.T. Belgrano, ed. *Atti della Società Ligure di Storia Patria* 13 (1877), no. 149. Pp. 229–233.
"Notes et extraits pour servir à l'histoire des croisades au XVe siècle." N. Iorga, ed. *Revue de l'Orient latin* 8 (1900/1901). Pp. 105–108.
English translation: *The Siege of Constantinople 1453: Seven Contemporary Accounts.* J.R. Melville Jones, trans. Amsterdam, 1972. Pp. 131–135.
La Caduta di Costantinopoli. A. Pertusi, ed. Vol. 1: *Le Testimonianze dei Contemporanei.* Verona, 1976. Pp. 42–51 (improved text with Italian translation).
Lonicer, P. *Chronicorum Turcicorum.* Vol. 1. Frankfurt am Main, 1584.
Manuel II Palaiologos. *Προθεωρία εἰς τὸν Λόγον τοῦ Βασιλέως Μανουὴλ Παλαιολόγου Ἐπιτάφιον εἰς τὸν Ἀδελφὸν Θεόδωρον. Manuel II Palaeologus: Funeral Oration on His Brother Theodore.* Corpus Fontium Historiae Byzantinae 26. J. Chrystostomides, ed. Thessalonike, 1985.
The Letters of Manuel II Palaeologus. G.T. Dennis, ed. and trans. Corpus Fontium Historiae Byzantinae 8. Washington, DC, 1977.
Maréschal, Jean le Maingre, di Bouciqaut. *Livre des faicts du bon messiere Jean le Maingre, dit Bouciqaut, Maréschal de France et Gouverneur de Jennes.* J. Buchon, ed. In J. de Froissart. *Les Chroniques.* Vol. 3. Paris, 1835. Pp. 563–603.

Melissourgos-Melissenos, Makarios. *Chronicon Minus. Georgios Sphrantzes, Memorii 1401–1477. În anexa Pseudo-Phrantzes. Macarie Melissenos Cronica, 1258–1481.*V. Grecu, ed. and trans. into Roumanian. Scriptores Byzantini 5. Bucharest, 1966.

Georgius Phrantzes. Ioannes Cananus. Ioannes Anagnostes. Corpus Scriptorum Historiae Byzantinae. I. Bekker, ed. Bonn, 1838. Pp. 3–479.

English translation of siege section: Philippides, M. *The Fall of the Byzantine Empire. A Chronicle by George Sphrantzes, 1401–1477.* Amherst, 1980.

"Μονῳδίαι καὶ Θρῆνοι ἐπὶ τῇ Ἁλώσει τῆς Κωνσταντινουπόλεως." S.P. Lampros, ed. *Νέος Ἑλληνομνήμων* 5 (1908). Pp. 263–265.

Московский Льтонисный Сводъ Конча XV Вѣка. Полное Собранʼе Русскихъ Льтопсей 25. Moscow-Leningrad, 1949.

Nestor-Iskander [Iskinder]. *Повѣсть о Царьградѣ.* I. Sreznevky, ed. St. Petersburg, 1855.

Сказание о Царьградѣ по Древнимъ Рукописиамъ. V. Iakovlev, ed. St. Petersburg, 1868. Pp. 56–116.

Повѣсть о Царьградѣ (его Оснований и Взятли Турками в 1453 Году), Нестора Искандера XV Вѣка. Archimandrite Leonid, ed. *Pamqtniki Drevnej Pis; mnenosti i Iskusstva.* St. Petersburg, 1888.

The Tale of Constantinople (Of Its Origin and Capture by the Turks in the Year 1453) by Nestor-Iskander (From the Early Sixteenth-Century Manuscript of the Troitse-Sergieva Lavra, No. 773). W.K. Hanak and M. Philippides, eds. and trans. into English. New Rochelle, Athens and Moscow, 1998.

Ἡ Πολιορκία καί Ἅλωση τῆς Πόλης. Τό Ρωσικό Χρονικό τοῦ Νέστορα Ἰσκεντέρη. M. Alexandropoulos, trans. into Modern Greek. Athens, 1978.

Anonymous Moscovita. P.A. Déthier, trans. into French. In *Monumenta Hungariae Historica. Ser. Scriptores (Második osztály Irok).* Vol. 21.1. Sine loco, sine anno. Pp. 1047–1122.

Bericht über die Eroberung Konstantinopels nach der Nikon-Chronik übersezt und erläutert. M. Braun and M. Schneider, trans. Leipzig, 1943.

Piccolomini, Aenea Silvio. *Aeneae Sylvii Piccolominei Senensis, qui post adeptum pontificatum Pius eius nominis secundus appellatus est, opera quae extant omnia, nunc demum post corruptissimas aeditiones summa diligientia castigata et in unum corpus redacta, quorum elenchum versa pagella indicabit.* Basel, *sine anno* (1560?); repr. 1967.

Pusculo, Ubertino. *Constantinopolis libri IV.* In G. Bregantini, ed. *Miscellanea di varie operette.* Vol. 1. Venice, 1740.

Analekten der mittel-und neugriechischen Literatur. A.S. Ellissen, ed. Vol. 3. Leipzig, 1857, Appendix. Pp. 12–83.

Selections with improved text and Italian translation: *La Caduta di Costantinopoli.* Vol. 1: *Le Testimonianze dei Contemporanei.* Vol. 2: *L'Eco nel Mondo.* A. Pertusi, ed. Verona, 1976. Pp. 200–213.

Quae supersunt Actorum Graecorum Concilii Florentini, necnon descriptionis cuiusdam eiusdem. J. Gill, ed. Concilium Florentinum Documenta et Scriptores. Editum Consilio et Impensis Pontificii Instituti Orientalium Studiorum. Series B, Vol. 5, fasc. 1. Rome, 1953.

Quirini, Lauro. *Epistola ad beatissimum Nicolaum V pontificem maximum.* "Le Epistole Storiche di Lauro Quirini sulla Caduta di Costantinopoli e la Potenza dei Turchi." A. Pertusi. ed. *Lauro Quirini Umanista.* Studi e Testi a cura di P.O. Kristeller, K. Krauter, A. Pertusi, G. Ravegnani and C. Seno. Florence, 1977.

Selections with some Italian translations: *Testi Inediti e Poco Noti sulla Caduta di Costantinopoli.* A. Pertusi, ed. Il Mondo Medievale. Studi di Storia e Storiographia: Sezione di Storia Bizantina e Slava 4 (*edizione postuma a cura di A. Carile*). Bologna, 1983. Pp. 62–94.

Rizzardo, Giacomo. *Caso ruinoso della cittade di Negroponte inteso per mi Iacomo Rizzardo scrivan dello spectabil uomo Messer Lorenzo Contarini Suoracomito di una galia grossa di Flandra.* In

Mehmed II the Conqueror and the Fall of the Franco-Byzantine Levant to the Ottoman Turks: Some Western Views and Testimonies. Medieval and Renaissance Texts and Studies 302. M. Philippides, ed. and trans. Tempe and Arizona, 2007. Pp. 219–249.

Scalamonti, Francesco. Vita Viri Clarissimi et Famosissimi Kyriaci Anconitani by Francesco Scalamonti. C. Mitchell and E.W. Bodnar, SJ, eds. Transactions of the American Philosophical Society 86.4. Philadelphia, 1996.

Sansovino, Francesco. Historia universale dell'origine et imperio de Turchi: nella quale si contengono la origine, l'usanze, i costumi, cose religiose come mondani de Turchi: oltre ciò vi sono tutte le guerre cher di tempo sono state fatted a quella natione cominciando da Othomano primo Re di questa dente fino al moderno Selim con le vite ditu tutti I principi da casa Othomana. Venice, 1564, 1568, 1571.

Schiltberger, Johann. Reisebuch. V. Langmantel, ed. Tübingen, 1855.

Scholarius, Georgios [Gennadius II]. "Πρὸς τὸν Βασιλέα [Κωνσταντῖνον τὸν Παλαιολόγον] Ἀπολογητικός." In S.P. Lampros, ed. Παλαιολόγεια καὶ Πελοποννησιακά. Vol. 2. Athens, 1912–1924; repr. 1972. Pp. 89–105.

———. "Τῷ Βασιλεῖ Κωνσταντίνῳ [Ἐγράφη ὅτε Ἀνεχώρησε τοῦ Παλατίου καὶ τῆς Μονῆς τοῦ Παντοκράτορος]." In S.P. Lampros, ed. Παλαιολόγεια καὶ Πελοποννησιακά. Vol. 2. Athens, 1924; repr. 1972. Pp. 105–119.

———. "Τῷ Βασιλεῖ Κωνσταντίνῳ [Τοῦτο Ἐστάλη τοῖς Ἐκκλησιαστικοῖς . . .]." In S.P. Lampros, ed. Παλαιολόγεια καὶ Πελοποννησιακά. Vol. 2. Athens, 1924. Pp. 122–128.

———. Τοῦ Αὐτοῦ [Γενναδίου τοῦ Σχολαρίου] περὶ τῶν Ἀγγέλλων πρὸς τὴν τοῦ Ἀργυροπούλου Γνώμην Ἀντιφερόμενον. Ἀργυροπούλεια: Ἰωάννου Ἀργυροπούλου Λόγοι, Πραγματεῖαι, Ἐπιστολαί, Προσφωνήματα, Ἀπαντήσεις καὶ Ἐπιστολαὶ πρὸς Αὐτὸν καὶ τὸν Υἱὸν Ἰσαάκιον. Ἐπιστολαὶ καὶ Ἀποφάσεις περὶ Αὐτῶν. Προτάσσεται Εἰσαγωγὴ περὶ Ἰωάννου Ἀργυροπούλου, τῆς Οἰκογενείας Αὐτοῦ καὶ τῶν Ἀργυροπούλων καθ' Ὅλου. S.P. Lampros, ed. Athens, 1910. Pp. ρ´– ρκε´.

———. Oeuvres complètes de Gennade Scolarios. L. Petit, X.A. Sidéridès and M. Jugie, eds. 8 vols. Paris, 1928–1936.

Sekoundinos, Nikolaos. "De Familia Othomanorum Epitome ad Aeneam Senarum Episcopum." In M. Philippides, ed. and trans. Mehmed II the Conqueror and the Fall of the Franco-Byzantine Levant to the Ottoman Turks: Some Western Views and Testimonies. Medieval and Renaissance Texts and Studies 302. Tempe, Arizona, 2007. Pp. 55–93.

———. Ad serenissimum principem et invictissimum regem Alfonsum Nicolai Sagundini oratio. Monumenta historica Slavorum Meridiolanum vicinorumque populorum. V.V. Makušev, ed. Vol. 1. Warsaw, 1874. Pp. 295–306.

Selections: Notes et Extraits pour servir à l'histoire des Croisades au XVe Siècle. N. Iorga (Jorga), ed. Vol. 3. Paris and Bucharest, 1902. Pp. 316–323.

Selections with Italian translation: La Caduta di Costantinopoli. A. Pertusi, ed. Vol. 1: Le Testimonianze dei Contemporanei. Verona, 1976. Pp. 128–140.

Simeon of Suzdal. Acta Slavica Concilii Florentini. Narrationis et Documenta. J. Krajcar, ed. Concilium Florentinum Documenta et Scriptores. Series A, 9. Rome, 1976.

Sphrantzes, Georgios. Georgios Sphrantzes, Memorii 1401–1477. În anexa Pseudo-Phrantzes: Macarie Melissenos Cronica, 1258–1481. V. Grecu, ed. and trans. into Roumanian. Scriptores Byzantini 5. Bucharest, 1966.

A Contemporary Greek Source for the Siege of Constantinople 1453: The Sphrantzes Chronicle. M. Carroll, trans. Amsterdam, 1985.

The Fall of the Byzantine Empire. A Chronicle by George Sphrantzes 1401–1477. M. Philippides, trans. Amherst, 1980.

Georgii Sphrantze Chronicon. R. Maisano, ed. and trans. into Italian. Corpus Fontium Historiae Byzantinae 29. Rome, 1990.

Syropoulos, Sylvestros [Sylvester]. *Les "Mémoires" du Grand Ecclésiarque de l'Eglise Constantinople de Sylvestre Syropoulos sur le concile de Florence (1438–1439)*.V. Laurent, ed. and trans. into French. Concilium Florentinum. Documenta et Scriptorum. Series B, vol. 9. Paris, 1971.

The Syropoulos Project. The Memoirs of Sylvester Syropoulos. Section 4. Centre for Byzantine, Ottoman and Modern Greek Studies. IAA. University of Birmingham, 2008. Electronic Study.

Vera historia unionis non verae inter graecos et latinos, sive Concilii Florentini narration. R. Creyghton, trans. into Latin. Hague, 1660.

Tetaldi, Giacomo. *Informations envoyées, tant par Francisco de Franc, à très reverend pere en Dieu monseigneur le cardinal d'Avignon, que par Jehan Blanchin & Jacques Edaldy marchant Florentin, de la prise de Constantinople par l'empereur Turc le xxix. jour de May MCCCCLIII, à laquelle ledit Jacques estoit personnellement*, E. Martène and U. Durand, eds. In *Thesaurus novus anecdotorum*.Vol. 1: *Tomus primus complectens regum ac principum aliorumque virorum illustrium epistolas et diplomata benè multa*. Paris, 1717. Cols. 1819–1826.

Veterum scriptorum et monumentorum historicorum, dogmaticorum, moralium amplissima collectio. E. Martène and U. Durand, eds.Vol. 5. Paris, 1729. Pp. 785–800.

Mehmed II the Conqueror and the Fall of the Franco-Byzantine Levant to the Ottoman Turks: Some Western Views and Testimonies. Medieval and Renaissance Texts and Studies 302. M. Philippides, ed. and trans.Tempe, Arizona, 2007. Pp. 133–216.

The Siege of Constantinople 1453: Seven Contemporary Accounts. English Translation of the French Version, J.R. Melville Jones. Amsterdam, 1972. Pp. 1–10.

Tignosi (da Foligno), Nicolò. *Expugnatio Constantinopolitana*. In "Niccolò Tignosi da Foligno. L'opera e il pensiero." M. Sensi, ed. *Annali della Facoltà di Lettere e filosofia dell'Università degli Studi di Perugia* 9 (1971/1972). Pp. 423–431.

Selections with Italian translation: *Testi Inediti e Poco Noti sulla Caduta di Costantinopoli*. A. Pertusi, ed. Il Mondo Medievale. Studi di Storia e Storiographia: Sezione di Storia Bizantina e Slava 4 (*edizione postuma a cura di A. Carile*). Bologna, 1983. Pp. 102–121.

4 Modern works

Alberigo, G., ed. *Christian Unity: The Council of Ferrara-Florence 1438/39–1989*. Bibliotheca Ephemeridum Theologicarum Lovaniensium 97. Leuven, 1991.

Alexandrescu-Dersca Bulgari, Maria-Matilda. "L'action diplomatique et militaire de Venise pour la defense de Constantinople (1453)." *Revue roumaine d'histoire* 13 (1974). Pp. 247–267.

———. *La Campagne de Timur en Anatolie (1402)*. Rev. ed., London, 1977.

Angold, M. *The Fall of Constantinople to the Ottomans: Context and Consequences*. Harlow, 2012.

———. "Theodore Agallianos: The Last Byzantine Autobiography." In *Constantinopla. 550 años de su caída*, Κωνσταντινούπολη. 550 Χρόνια από την Άλωση.Vol. 1: Βυζαντινή Κωνσταντινούπολη. Granada, 2006. Pp. 35–44.

Antoniadi, E. M. Έκφρασις τῆς Ἁγίας Σοφίας. 3 vols. Athens, 1907–1909; repr. in 4 vols., Athens, 1983.

Arabatzoglou, G. M. Φώτειος Βιβλιοθήκη, ἤτοι Ἐπίσημα καὶ Ἰδιωτικὰ Ἔγγραφα καὶ Ἄλλα Μνημεῖα Σχετικὰ πρὸς τὴν Ἱστορίαν τοῦ Οἰκουμενικοῦ Πατριαρχείου 1. Constantinople, 1933.

Atiya, A. S. *The Crusade in the Later Middle Ages*. London, 1938.

———. *The Crusade of Nicopolis*. London, 1934.

Babinger, F. "Maometto il Conquistatore e gli umanisti d'Italia." In A. Pertusi, ed. *Venezia e l'Oriente fra tardo Medioevo e Rinascimento*. Civiltà Europa e Civiltà Veneziana, Aspetti e Problemi 4. Venice, 1966. Pp. 433–449.

———. "Mehemed II., der Eroberer, and Italien." *Byzantion* 21 (1951). Pp. 127–170. With some additions and corrections, repr. under the title of "Maometto II, il Conquistatore e l'Italia." *Rivista storica italiana* 63 (1951). Pp. 469–505.

———. *Mehmed the Conqueror and His Times*. R. Manheim, trans. and W.C. Hickman, ed. Bollingen Series 96. Princeton, 1978.

———. "Nikolaos Sagountinos, ein griechisch-venedischer Humanist des 15. Jhdts." In *Χαριστήριον εἰς Ἀναστάσιον Ὀρλάνδον*. Vol. 1. Athens, 1965. Pp. 198–212.

Baker, G. *The Walls of Constantinople*. London, 1910; repr. New York, 1975.

Balard, M. and A. Ducellier, eds. *Migrations et Diasporas Méditerrannéenes (X*^{e}*–XVI*^{e} *siècles)*. Actes du colloque des Conques (Octobre 1990). Série Byzantina Sorbonensia 19. Paris, 2002

Baloglou, C. P. *Γενεαλογία τῶν Παλαιολόγων: 1259–1453*. Athens, 2007.

Bandini, A. M. *De Bessarionis vita, rebus gestis, scriptis commentariis*. Rome, 1777.

Barker, J. W. "On the Chronology of the Activities of Manuel II Palaeologus in the Morea in 1415." *Byzantinische Zeitschrift* 55 (1962). Pp. 39–55.

———. *Manuel II Palaeologus (1391–1425): A Study in Late Byzantine Statesmanship*. New Brunswick, 1969.

Bartusis, M. C. "The Kavallarioi of Byzantium." *Speculum* 63 (1988). Pp. 343–350.

———. *The Late Byzantine Army: Arms and Society, 1204–1453*. Philadelphia, 1992.

Barzos, C. *Ἡ Γενεαλογία τῶν Κομνηνῶν* 1. Κέντρον Βυζαντινῶν Ἐρευνῶν. Βυζαντινὰ Κείμενα καὶ Μελέται 20α 6. Thessalonike, 1984.

Baxandall, M. "Guarino, Pisanello and Manuel Chrysololoras." *Journal of the Warburg and Courtauld Institutes* 28 (1965). Pp. 183–204.

Beaton, R. and Charlotte Roueché, eds. *The Making of Byzantine History: Studies Dedicated to Donald M. Nicol on His Seventieth Birthday*. London, 1993.

Becherini, B. "Due canzoni di Dufay del codice Florentino 2794." *La Bibliofilia* 43 (1941). Pp. 124–127.

Beckmann, G. *Der Kampf Kaiser Sigismunds gegen die werdende Weltmacht der Osmanen, 1392–1437. Eine historische Grundlegung*. Gotha, 1902.

Bees, N. A. *Die griechisch-christlichen Inschriften des Peloponnes*. Athens, 1941.

———. "Περὶ τοῦ Ἱστορημένου Χρησμολογίου τῆς Κρατικῆς Βιβλιοθήκης τοῦ Βερολίνου (*Codex Graecus*, fol. 62–297) καὶ τοῦ Θρύλου τοῦ ᾿Μαρμαρωμένου Βασιλιᾶ᾿." *Byzantinische-Neugriechische Jahrbücher* 13–14 (1936/1937). Pp. 203–244$^{α-λς'}$.

Belgrano, L. T., ed. "Prima serie di documenti riguardanti la colonia di Pera." *Atti della Società Ligure di Storia Patria* 13 (1877), no. 149. Pp. 229–233.

Belting, H. *Das illuminierte Buch in der spätbyzantinischen Gesellschaft*. Heidelberg, 1970.

Bendall, S. "The Coinage of Constantine XI." *Revue Numismatique* (*VI*^{e} *série*) 33 (1991). Pp. 134–142, with plates XIII–XVII.

Bernicolas-Hatzopoulos, D. "The First Siege of Constantinople by the Ottomans (1394–1402) and Its Repercussions on the Civilian Population of the City." *Byzantine Studies/Etudes Byzantines* 10 (1983). Pp. 39–51.

———. "Le premier siège de Constantinople par les Ottomans (1394–1402)." Ph.D. dissertation. Université de Montréal. Montreal, 1980.

———. *Le premier siège de Constantinople par les Ottomans, 1394–1402*. Montreal, 1995.

———. *Ἡ Πρώτη Πολιορκία τῆς Κωνσταντινουπόλεως ἀπὸ τοὺς Ὀθωμανοὺς (1304–1402)*. Athens, *sine anno*.

Bilderbach, D. L. "The Membership of the Council of Basle." Unpublished doctoral dissertation. Seattle, The University of Washington, 1966.

Bisaha, N. *Creating East and West: Renaissance Humanists and the Ottoman Turks*. Philadelphia, 2004.

Black, A. "Popes and Councils." In *The New Cambridge Medieval History. Vol. 7: c. 1415– c. 1500*. C. Allmand, ed. Cambridge, 1998. Ch. 3.

Blanchet, Marie-Hélène. "L'église byzantine à la suite de l'Union de Florence (1439–1445). De la contestation à la scission." In *Byzantinische Forschungen* 29 [= *VIIIe Symposion Byzantinon. L'Eglise dans le monde byzantine de la IVe croisade (1204) à la chute de Constantinople (1453)*]. Strasbourg, 7, 8 et 9 novembre 2002), 2007. Pp. 79–123.

———. "Le reaction byzantine à l'Union de Florence (1439): Le discours antiromain de la Synaxe des orthodoxies." In *idem* and Gabriel Frédéric, eds. *Réduire le schisme? Ecclésiologies et politiques de l'Union entre Orient et Occident (XIIIe–XVIIIe siècle)*. Centre de Recherche d'Histoire et Civilisation de Byzance, Monographies, 39. Paris, 2013. Pp. 181–196.

———. ed. *Théodore Agallianos. Dialogue avec un moine contre les Latins (1442)*. Byzantina Sorbonensia 27. Paris, 2013.

Bodnar, E. W. "The Isthmian Fortifications in Oracular Prophecy." *American Journal of Archaeology* 64 (1960). Pp. 165–171.

Bogiatzides, I. K. "Τὸ Ζήτημα τῆς Στέψεως Κωνσταντίνου τοῦ Παλαιολόγου." *Λαογραφία* 2 (1923). Pp. 449–456.

Bombaci, A. "Venezie e la impressa turca di Otranto." *Rivista storica italiana* 56 (1954). Pp. 159–203.

Bordier, H. *Description des peintures et autres ornaments contenus dans les manuscripts grecs de la Bibliothèque nationale*. Paris, 1883.

Bowman, S. *The Jews of Byzantium 1204–1453*. University of Alabama, 1985.

Bradbury, J. *The Medieval Siege*. Woodbridge, 1992.

Browning, R. "A Note on the Capture of Constantinople in 1453." *Byzantion* 22 (1952). Pp. 379–387.

Buchon, J., ed. *Livre des faicts du bon messier Jean le Maingre, dit Bouciqaut, Maréschal de France et Gouverneur de Jennes*. In J. de Froissart, ed. *Les Chroniques*. Vol. 3. Paris, 1835. Pp. xxx ff. and 563–603.

Buckley, J. M. "Diplomatic Background of Byzantine Support for the Papacy at Ferrara-Florence, 1438–1439." Unpublished doctoral dissertation. George Washington University, 1970.

Byzantinos, S. D. *Ἡ Κωνσταντινούπολις, ἢ Περιγραφὴ Τοπογραφικὴ Ἀρχαιολογικὴ καὶ Ἱστορικὴ τῆς Περιωνύμου Ταύτης Μεγαλοπόλεως*. Vol. 1. Athens, 1851.

Caciolli, Lidia. "Codici di Giovanni Aurispa e di Ambrogio Traversari negli anni de Concilio di Firenze." In P. Viti, ed. *Firenze e il Concilio del 1439. Convegno di Studi Firenze, 29 novembre-2 dicembre 1989*. Biblioteca Storica Toscana 29. Vol. 2. Florence, 1994. Pp. 559–647.

Cammelli, G. *I dotti bizantini et le origini dell'umanismo*. Vol. 1: *Manuele Crisolora*. Florence, 1941.

Carroll (Klopf), Margaret G. "Constantine XI Palaeologus: Some Problems of Image." In Ann Moffatt, ed. *Maistor: Classical, Byzantine and Renaissance Studies for Robert Browning*. Canberra, 1984. Pp. 329–343.

Ceserani, R. "Rassegna bibliografica di studi piccolominiani." *Giornale storico de la letteratura italiana* 141 (1964). Pp. 265–281.

Chacón (Ciaconi), A., et al. *Vitae et res gestae pontificum romanorum et S.R.E. Cardinalium ab initio nascentis ecclesiae usque ad Urbanum VIII*. Vol. 1. Rome, 1630.

Chambers, D. S. *Popes, Cardinals and War: The Military Church in Renaissance and Early Modern Europe*. London and New York, 2006.

———. "Spese del sioggiorno di Papa Pio II a Mantua." In A. Calzona, et al., eds. *Il Sogno di Pio II e il viaggio da Roma a Mantova*. Città di Castello, 2003. Pp. 391–402.

Chambers, D. S. and Signorini, R. "Notizie di storia mantovana (1328–1462) nel ms. Harleian 3462 della British Library." *Civiltà mantovano*, n.s., 18 (1987). Pp. 31–68.

Charanis, P. "Coronation and Its Constitutional Significance in the Later Roman Empire." *Byzantion* 15 (1940/1941). Pp. 49–66.
Cheetham, N. *Mediaeval Greece*. New Haven and London, 1981.
Cherniavsky, M. "The Reception of the Council of Florence in Moscow." *Church History* 24/4 (1955). Pp. 347–359.
Christophilopoulou, Aikaterine. "Ἐκλογή, Ἀναγόρευσις καὶ Στέψις τοῦ Βυζαντινοῦ Αὐτοκράτορος." *Πραγματεῖαι τῆς Ἀκαδημίας Ἀθηνῶν* 22 (1956). Pp. 199–201.
———. "Περὶ τὸ Πρόβλημα τῆς Ἀναδείξεως τοῦ Βυζαντινοῦ Αὐτοκράτορος." *Ἐπιστημονικὴ Ἐπετηρὶς τῆς Φιλοσοφικῆς Σχολῆς τοῦ Πανεπιστημίου Ἀθηνῶν* 13 (1962/1963). Pp. 393–399.
Cirac Estopañan, D. S. *Bizancio y España. La Union, Manuel Paléologo y sus recuerdos en España*. Barcelona, 1953.
Clement, P. A. "The Date of the Hexamilion." In *Essays in Memory of Basil Laourdas*. Thessaloniki, 1977. Pp. 159–164.
Coco, P. *La Guerra contro i Turchi in Otranto. Fatti e persone, 1480–1481*. Lecce, 1945.
Concasty, M-L. "Les 'Informations' de Jacques Tedaldi sur le siege et la prise de Constantinople." *Byzantion* 24 (1954). Pp. 95–110.
Contamine, P. *War in the Middle Ages*. Oxford, 1984.
Cortesi, Mariarosa. "La letteratura Cristiana tra i libri di Niccolò Cusano." In M. Cortesi, ed. *Padri Greci e Latini a Confronto (Secoli XIII–XV). Atti del Convegno di studi della Società Internazionale per lo Studio del Medioevo Latino (SISMEL). Cerrosa del Galluzzo Firenze, 19–20 ottobre 2001*. Florence, 2004. Pp. 113–132.
Crane, H., trans. and annotations. *The Garden of the Mosques: Hafiz Hüseyin Al-Ayvansaryí's Guide to the Muslim Monuments of Ottoman Istanbul*. Leiden, Boston and Cologne, 2000.
Daleggio d'Alessio, E. "Le text grec du traité conclu par les génois de Galata avec Mehmet II le Ier Juin 1453." *Hellenika* 11 (1939). Pp. 115–124.
———. "Lists des potestats de la colonie génoise de Péra (Galata), des prieurs et sous-prieurs de la Magnifica Communità." *Revue des études byzantines* 27 (1969). Pp. 151–157.
Darrouzès, J. *Recherches sur les ΟΦΦΙΚΙΑ de l'Eglise byzantine*. Paris, 1970.
Davies, M. C. "An Enigma and a Phantom: Giovanni Aretino and Giacomo Languschi." *Humanistica Lovaniensia* 37 (1988). Pp. 1–29.
De Fuentes, Patricia. *The Conquistadors: First Person Accounts of the Conquest of Mexico*. New York, 1963.
DeVries, J. *Heroic Song and Heroic Legend*. Oxford, 1963.
DeVries, K. "Gunpowder Weapons at the Siege of Constantinople, 1453." In Y. Lev, ed. *War and Society in the Eastern Mediterranean, 7th–15th Centuries*. The Medieval Mediterranean: Peoples, Economies and Cultures, 400–1453. Vol. 9. Leiden, NewYork and Cologne, 1997. Pp. 343–362.
Dennis, G. T. "The Byzantine-Turkish Treaty of 1403." *Orientalia Christiana Periodica* 33 (1967). Pp. 72–88.
———. *Byzantium and the Franks*. London, 1982.
Detorakis, T. E. "Ἡ Πανώλης ἐν Κρήτῃ. Συμβολὴ εἰς τὴν Ἱστορίαν τῶν Ἐπιδημιῶν τῆς Νήσου." *Ἐπιστημονικὴ Ἐπετηρὶς τῆς Φιλοσοφικῆς Σχολῆς τοῦ Πανεπιστημίου Ἀθηνῶν* 21, ser. 2 (1970). Pp. 118–136.
Di Branco, M. "Da Ferrara a Firenze. Gli itinerari delle delegazioni conciliari (Gennaio-Febbraio 1439) e le visite di Eugenio IV e GiovanniVIII a Pistoria." *Rendiconti* 19 (2008). Pp. 727–745.
Djuriç, I. *Il crepuscolo di Bizanzio. I tempi di Giovanni VIII Paleologo (1392–1448)*. Rome, 1995.

Du Cange, C. du Fresne. *Historia Byzantina: Constantinopolis Christiana, seu Descriptio Urbis – Constantinopolitanae*. Paris, 1680.
Ducellier, A. and T. Ganchou. *Les élites urbaines au Moyen Age*. Paris, 1997.
Duda, B. *Joannis Stoikoviç de Ragusio OP doctrina de cognoscibilitate Ecclesiae*. Rome, 1958.
Dujãev, I. "La conquête turque et la prise de Constantinople dans la littérature slave de l'époque." *Medioevo Byzantinoslavo* 3 (1971). Pp. 412–446.
———. "Un fragment des Notitiae Episcopatuum Russiae Copié par Isidore Ruthenus." *Зборник Радова Внзантолошког Института* 11 (1968). Pp. 235–240.
Durán Barceló, J. "Bibliografia de Alfonso de Palencia." *Boletin Bibliográfico dela Associación Hispánica de Literatura Medieval* 9 (1955). Pp. 289–341.
Dvornik, F. *Byzantine Missions Among the Slavs: SS. Constantine-Cyril and Methodius*. Rutgers Byzantine Series. New Brunswick, 1970.
———. *The Photian Schism: History and Legend*. Cambridge, 1948; repr. 1970.
Eideneier, H. "Ένας Γερμανός Ευαγγελικός Παπάς στην Πόλη το 1573–1578." In M. Guirao and and M. Filactós, eds. *550 años de su caida. Κωνσταντινούπολη, 550 Χρόνια από την Άλωση*. Vol. 3: *Constantinopla Otomana. Οθωμανική Κωνσταντινούπολη*. E. Granada, 2006. Pp. 313–317.
Elia, E. "Un restauro erudite: Isidoro di Kiev e il codice Peyron 11 della Biblioteca Nazionale Universitaria di Torino." *Medioevo Greco. Rivista di storia e filologia bizantina* 12 (2012). Pp. 71–85.
Emellos, S. D. "Ὁ Κωνσταντῖνος Παλαιολόγος καὶ τὸ Ξύλινο Σπαθί του." In *Θρυλούμενα γιὰ τὴν Ἄλωση καὶ τὴν Ἐθνικὴ Ἀποκατάσταση*. Athens, 1991. Pp. 50–59.
Estangüi Gómez, R. *Byzance face aux Ottomans. Exercice du pouvoir et contrôle du territoire sous les derniers Paléologues (milieu XIVe–milieu XVe siècle)*. Byzantina Sorbonensia 28. Paris, 2014.
Evans, G. R. "The Council of Florence and the Problem of Ecclesiastical Identity." In G. Alberigo, ed. *Christian Unity: The Council of Ferrara-Florence 1438/39–1989*. Bibliotheca Ephemeridum Theologicarum Lovaniensium 97. Leuvan, 1991. Pp. 177–185.
Evans, Helen C., ed. *Byzantium: Faith and Power (1261–1557)*. New York, New Haven and London, 2004.
Filaret, Archbishop of Chernigov. *Исторія Русской Церкви. Періодъ Тремей, отъ раздѣленія Митрополій до Учрежденія Патріаршетва. (1410–1588 Г.)*. Vol. 3. 4th ed., Chernigov, 1862.
Fine, J.V.A., Jr. *The Late Medieval Balkans: A Critical Survey from the Late Twelfth Century to the Ottoman Conquest*. Ann Arbor, 1987.
Fonkich, B. L. "Греческие Писцы эпохи Возрожения. [Part] 3." *Византийский Временник* 42 (1981). Pp. 124–128.
Fonkich, B. L. and Poljakov, F. B. "Ein unbekanntes Autograph des Metropoliten Isidoros von Kiev." *Byzantinische Zeitschrift* 82 (1989). Pp. 96–101.
Foss, C. and Winfield, D. *Byzantine Fortifications: An Introduction*. Muckleneuk and Pretoria, 1985.
Fossati, E. "Dal luglio 1480 al 16 aprile 1481: l'opera di Milano." *Archivio storico Lombardo* 36 (1909). Pp. 1–71.
Freeley, J. and Çakmak, A. S. *Byzantine Monuments of Istanbul*. Cambridge, 2004.
Frommann, T. *Kritische Beiträge zur Geschichte der Florentiner Kircheneinigung*. Balle, 1872.
Ganchou, T. "Géôrgios Scholarios, 'Secrétaire' du Patriarche Unioniste Grègorios III Mammas? Le Mystère Résolu." In *Le Patriarcat Œcuménique de Constantinople aux XIVe–XVIe siècles: Rupture et Continuité. Actes du colloque international Rome, 5–6–7 décembre 2005*. Dossiers Byzantins 7. Paris, 2007. Pp. 117–194.

———. "Le rachat des Notaras après la chute de Constantinople ou les relations 'étrangères' de l'élite byzantine au XVe siècle." In M. Balard and A. Ducellier, eds. *Migrations et Diasporas Méditerrannéenes (X^e–XVIe siècles). Actes du colloque des Conques (Octobre 1999)*. Série Byzantina Sorbonensia 19. Paris, 2002. Pp. 149–229.

———. "Sur quelques erreurs relatives aux dernier défenseurs grecs de Constantinople en 1453." *Θησαυρίσματα: Περιοδικὸν τοῦ Ἑλληνικοῦ Ἰνστιτούτου Βυζαντινῶν καὶ Μεταβυζαντινῶν Σπουδῶν τῆς Βενετίας* 25 (1995). Pp. 61–82.

Gautier, P. "Action de graces de Démetrius Chrysoloras." *Revue des études byzantines* 19 (1961). Pp. 340–357.

Geanakoplos, D. J. *Byzantine East and Latin West: Two Worlds of Christendom in the Middle Ages and Renaissance: Studies in Ecclesiastical and Cultural History*. Oxford, 1966.

———. "Byzantium and the Crusades, 1354–1453." In K. M. Setton, ed. *A History of the Crusades*. Vol. 3: *The Fourteenth and Fifteenth Centuries*. H. W. Hazard, ed. Madison, 1975. Ch. 3.

———. *Constantinople and the West: Essays on the Late Byzantine (Palaeologan) and Italian Renaissances and the Byzantine and Roman Churches*. Madison, 1989.

———. "The Council of Florence (1438–1439) and the Problem of Union Between the Greek and Latin Churches." *Church History* 24/4 (1955). Pp. 324–346.

———. "Die Konzile von Basel und Florentz (1431–49) als Paradigma für das Studium moderner ökumenischer Konzile aus orthodoxer Perspektive." *Theologische Zeitschrift* 38 (1982). Pp. 330–359.

———. *Greek Scholars in Venice: Studies in the Dissemination of Greek Learning from Byzantium to the West*. Cambridge, 1962; repr. as *Byzantium and the Renaissance*. Hamden, 1972.

———. "The Italian Renaissance and Byzantium: The Career of the Greek Humanist-Professor John Argyropoulos in Florence and Rome (1415–1487)." *Conspectus of History* 1 (1974). Pp. 13–28.

———. "Italian Thought and Learning and the Role of Byzantine Emigré Scholars in Florence, Rome, and Venice: A Reassessment." *Rivista di studi bizantini e slavi* 3 (1984). Pp. 129–157.

———. *Interaction of the "Sibling" Byzantine and Western Cultures in the Middle Ages and Italian Renaissance (330–1600)*. New Haven and London, 1976.

———. "A New Reading of the *Acta*, especially Syropoulos." In G. Alberigo, ed. *Christian Unity: The Council of Ferrara-Florence 1438/39–1989*. Bibliotheca Ephemeridum Theologicarum Lovaniensium 97. Leuven, 1991. Pp. 325–351.

———. "An Orthodox View of the Councils of Basel (1431–49) and of Florence (1438–39) as a Paradigm for the Study of Modern Ecumenical Councils." Repr. of *Greek Orthodox Theological Review* 38 (1982). Pp. 330–359. In D. J. Geanakoplos, ed. *Constantinople and the West: Essays on the Late Byzantine (Palaeologan) and the Byzantine and Roman Churches*. Madison, 1989. Pp. 255–278.

Gennadios, Metropolitan of Heliopolis. " Ὑπῆρξεν ἢ Ὄχι Πατριάρχης Ἀθανάσιος Ὀλίγον πρὸ τῆς Ἁλώσεως." *Ὀρθοδοξία* 18 (1943). Pp. 117–123.

Gibbons, H. A. *The Foundation of the Ottoman Empire: A History of the Osmanlis Up to the Death of Bayezid I (1330–1403)*. New York, 1916.

Gill, J. *Constance et Bâle-Florence*. Paris, 1965.

———. *The Council of Florence*. Cambridge, 1958.

———. "George Scholarius." *Unitas* 12 (1960). Pp. 99–112.

———. "Isidore's Encyclical Letter from Buda." In A. G. Welykyi, ed. *Analecta Ordinis S. Basilii Magni. Miscellanea in Honorem Cardinalis Isidore (1463–1963)*. 4/1–2. Rome, 1963. Pp. 1–8.

———. "Isidoros, Metropolit v. Kiew u. ganz Rußland (1437)." *Lexikon für Theologie und Kirche*. Vol. 5. Freiburg, 1960. Cols. 788, 789.
———. *Personalities of the Council of Florence and Other Essays*. London, 1964.
Golubinsky, E. E. *История Русской Церкви*. Vol. 1. 2nd ed. Moscow, 1901.
Gregory, T. E. *Isthmia 5: The Hexamilion and the Fortress*. Princeton, 1993.
———. "The Late Roman Wall at Corinth." *Archaeology* 35 (1982). Pp. 14–21.
Grousset, R. *L'Empire de steppes: Attila, Gengis Khan, Tamerlan*. Paris, 1939.
Grunsweig, A. "Philippe le Bon et Constantinople." *Byzantion* 24 (1954). Pp. 47–61.
Guerrini, P. "Un umanista bagnolese progioniero dei Turchi a Costantinopoli e a Rodi." *Brixia sacra* 6 (1915). Pp. 261–271.
Guilland, R. "Αἱ πρὸς τὴν Δύσιν Ἐκκλήσεις τοῦ Κωνσταντίνου ΙΑ΄ τοῦ Δράγαση πρὸς Σωτηρίαν τῆς Κωνσταντινουπόλεως." *Ἐπετηρὶς Ἑταρείας Βυζαντινῶν Σπουδῶν* 22 (1952). Pp. 60–74.
———. "Les Appels de Constantin XI Paléologue à Rome et à Venise pour sauveur Constantinople (1452–1453)." *Byzantinoslavica* 14 (1953). Pp. 226–244.
Halecki, O. "The Ecclesiastical Separation of Kiev from Moscow in 1458." In *Studien zur ältern Geschichte Osteuropas* 1 (1956). Wiener Archiv für Geschichte des Slawentums und Osteuropas II. Pp. 19–32.
———. *From Florence to Brest (1439–1596)*. Rome, 1958.
Haller, J. *Concilium Basiliense. Studien und Quellen zur Geschichte des Concils von Basel*. Vols. 1–4. Basil, 1896–1905; repr. Nendeln, 1971.
Hanak, W. K. "Pope Nicholas V and the Aborted Crusade of 1452–1453 to Rescue Constantinople from the Ottoman Turks." *Byzantinoslavica* 65 (2007). Pp. 337–359.
———. "Who Was Nestor-Iskander?" In *Abstracts of Papers, 12th Annual Byzantine Studies Conference*. Bryn Mawr, 1986. P. 15.
Hankins, J. "Cosimo de' Medici and the 'Platonic Academy'." *Journal of the Warburg and Courtauld Institutes* 53 (1990). Pp. 144–162. Repr. and enlarged with appendices in Hankins, J., *Humanism and Platonism in the Italian Renaissance*. Storia e Letteratura. Raccolta di Studi e Testi 220, 2 (Rome, 2004). Pp. 187–217.
———. *Humanism and Platonism in the Italian Renaissance*. Storia e Letteratura. Raccolta di Studi e Testi 215 and 220. 2 vols. Rome, 2003–2004.
———. "Renaissance Crusaders: Humanist Crusade Literature in the Age of Mehmed II." *Dumbarton Oaks Papers* 49 (1995). Pp. 111–209. Repr. and enlarged with appendices in Hankins, J. *Humanism and Platonism in the Italian Renaissance*. Storia e Letteratura. Raccolta di Studi e Testi 215, 1 (Rome, 2003). Pp. 293–424.
Harris, J. P. *Greek Emigres in the West 1400–1520*. Camberley and Surrey, 1995.
———. "A Worthless Prince? Andreas Palaeologus in Rome – 1464–1502." *Orientalia Christiana Periodica* 61 (1995). Pp. 537–554.
Helmrath, J. *Die Basler Konzil. Forschungsstand und Probleme*. Cologne and Vienna, 1987.
———. "Pius II und die Türken." In G. Guthmüller and W. Kühlmann, eds. *Europa und die Türken in der Renaissance*. Tübingen, 2000. Pp. 79–138.
Herre, H. *Concilium Basiliense: Studien und Quellen zur Geschichte von Basel*. Repr. Nendeln, 1971.
———. "Handschriften und Drucke Baser Konzilsakten." In *Deutsche Reichstagsakten unter Kaiser Sigmund*. Part 4/1: 1431–1432. Vol. 10/1. Göttingen, 1957. Pp. xcvi–ci.
Hinterberger, M., ed. *The Language of Byzantine Learned Literature*. Turnhout, 2014.
Hofmann, G. "Die Konzilsarbeit in Ferrara." *Orientalia Christiana Periodica* 3 (1937). Pp. 110–140 and 403–455.
———. "Die Konzilsarbeit in Florence." *Orientalia Christiana Periodica* 4 (1938). Pp. 157–188 and 372–422.

———. "Ein Brief des Kardinals Isidor von Kiew an Kardinal Besaarion." *Orientalia Christiana Periodica* 14 (1948). Pp. 405–414.

———. "Papst Kalixt III, Etscheidet die Frage, ob der lateinischen Patriarch von Konstantinopel eine kirchliche Ernennung in den lateinischen Bistuemern Kretas vornehmen darf." In *Miscellanea Giovanni Mercati*, 3: *Letteratura e Storia Bizantina*. Studi e Testi 123. Vatican City, 1946. Pp. 218–221.

———. "Quellen zu Isidor von Kiew als Kardinal und Patriarch." *Orientalia Christiana Periodica* 18 (1952). Pp. 143–157.

Hofmeister, A. "Von der Trabea triumphalis des römischen Kaisers über das byzantinischen Lorum zur Stola der abendländischen Herrescher. Ein Beispiel für den Wandel von Form und Bedeutung im Lanfe der Jahrhunderts und bei der Überstragun von einem Land in das andere." In P.E. Schramm, ed. *Herrschaftszeichen und Staatssymbolik: Beiträge zu ihrer Geschichte vom dritten bis zum sechzehnten Jahrhundert*. Schriften der Monumenta Germania Historia, Bd. 13. Vol. 1. Stuttgart, 1954. Pp. 25–50.

Hohfelder, R. L. "Trans-Isthmian Walls in the Age of Justinian." *Greek, Roman and Byzantine Studies* 18 (1977). Pp. 173–179.

Hookham, H. *Tamburlaine the Conqueror*. London, 1962.

Hopf, K. *Les Giustiniani dynastes de Chios étude historique*, traduite de l'Allemane par Etienne A. Vlasto. Paris, 1888.

Hunger, H. *Johannes Chortasmenos (ca. 1370–a. 1436/37)*. Wiener byzantinische Studien 7. Vienna, 1967.

Hunger, H. and Wurm, H. "Isidoros von Kiev, Begrüßungsansprachen an Kaiser Sigismund (Ulm, 24. Juni 1434." *Römische Historische Mitteilungen* 38 (1996). Pp. 143–180.

Imber, C. *The Crusade of Varna, 1443–45*. Crusade Texts in Translation 14. Aldershot, 2006.

Inalcik, H. *Essays in Ottoman History*. Istanbul, 1998.

———. *Fatih Devri Üzerinde Tetkiklev ve Vesikalar*. Türk Tarih Kurumu. Ankara, 1954.

———. "Istanbul: An Islamic City." In *Essays in Ottoman History*. Istanbul, 1998. Pp. 49–271.

Iorga (Jorga), N. *Geschichte des osmanischen Reiches*. Vol. 1. Gotha, 1900.

———. ed. "Notes et extraits pour server à l'histoire des croisades au XVe siècle." *Revue de l'Orient latin* 8 (1900/1901). Pp. 105–108.

Iustiniani, M. "Vita Leonardi." In *Caroli Pogii de nobilitate liber disceptatorius et Leonardi Chiensis de vera nobilitate contra Poggium tractatus apolologeticus*. Abelini, 1657. Cols. 43–48.

Jacob, E. *Essays in the Conciliar Epoch*. Manchester, 1953.

Janin, R. *Constantinople byzantine: Développement urbain et répertoire topographique*. Archives de l'Orient Chrétien 4A. 2nd ed., Paris, 1964.

———. *La géographie ecclésiastique de l'empire Byzantin*. Vols. 1: *Le Siège de Constantinople et le patriarcat oecuménique*. Paris, 1969; and Vols. 3: *Les églises et les monasteries*. 2nd ed., Paris, 1969.

———. "Les sanctuaries byzantines des saints militaires." *Echos d'Orient* 33 (1934). Pp. 163–180 and 331–342; and 34 (1935): 56–70.

Kaldellis, A. *A New Herodotus: Laonikos Khalkokondyles on the Ottoman Empire, the Fall of Byzantium, and the Emergence of the West*. Supplements to the Dumbarton Oaks Medieval Library 33–34. Washington, DC, 2014.

Kalligas, Haris. A. *Byzantine Monemvasia: The Sources*. Monemvasia, 1990.

———. *Monemvasia: A Byzantine City State*. London and New York, 2010.

Karanika, Andromache. "Messengers, Angels, and Laments for the Fall of Constantinople." In M. B. Bacharova, D. Dutch and A. Suter eds. *The Fall of Cities in the Mediterranean: Commemoration in Literature, Folk-Songs, and Liturgy*. Cambridge, 2016. Pp. 226–252.

Karpat, K. *An Inquiry into the Social Foundations of Nationalism in the Ottoman State: From Estates to Classes, from Millets to Nations*. Princeton, 1973.

Kazakova, N. A. "Первоначальная Редакция 'Хождения на Флорентйскийй Собор'." *Труды Отдела Древне Русской Литературы* 25: *Памятники Русской Литературы X–XVII вв*. Moscow, 1970. Pp. 60–72.

Khasiotis, I. K. *Οἱ Ἕλληνες στὶς Παραμονὲς τῆς Ναυμαχίας τῆς Ναυπάκτου: Ἐκκλήσεις, Ἐπαναστατικὲς Κινήσεις καὶ Ἐξεγέρσεις στὴν Ἑλληνικὴ Χερσόνησο ἀπὸ τὶς Παραμονὲς ὡς τὸ Τέλος τοῦ Κυπριακοῦ Πολέμου (1568–1571)*. Thessalonike, 1970.

———. *Μακάριος, Θεόδωρος καὶ Νικηφόρος οἱ Μελισσηνοὶ (Μελισσουργοὶ) (16ος-17ος Αἰ.)*. Thessalonike, 1966.

Khatzopoulos, D. *Ἡ Πρώτη Πολιορκία τῆς Κωνσταντινουπόλεως ἀπὸ τοὺς Ὀθωμανοὺς (1394–1402)*. Athens, sine anno.

———. *Le premier siege de Constantinople par les Ottomans, 1394–1402*. Montreal, 1995.

Kingsford, C. L., ed. *Chronicles of London*. Oxford, 1905.

Klosterman, R. A. "Jagaris oder Gagarin? Zur Deutung eines griechischen und russischen Familiennames." *Orientalia Christiana Periodica* 204 (1977). Pp. 221–237.

Koch, H. W. *Medieval Warfare*. London, 1978.

Kolditz, S. *Johannes VIII. Palaiologos und das Konzil von Ferrara-Florenz (1438/39). Das byzantinische Kaisertum im Dialog mit dem Westen*. Monographien zur Geschichte des Mittelalters, Band 60. 2 vols. Stuttgart, 2013–2014.

Kondyli, F., Andriopoulou, V., Panou, E., and Cunningham, M., eds. *Sylvester Syropoulos on Politics and Culture in the Fifteenth-Century Mediterranean. Themes and Problems in the Memoirs, Section IV*. Birmingham Byzantine and Ottoman Studies 16. Farnham, 2014.

Kontoglou, P. *Φημισμένοι Ἄντρες καὶ Λησμονημένοι*. Athens, 1942.

Kordatos, I. *Τὰ Τελευταῖα Χρόνια τῆς Βυζαντινῆς Αὐτοκρατορίας*. Athens, 1931.

Kordoses, M. S. "The Question of Constantine Palaiologos' Coronation." In R. Beaton and Charlotte Roueché, eds. *The Making of Byzantine History: Studies Dedicated to Donald M. Nicol*. London, 1993. Pp. 137–141.

———. *Συμβολὴ στὴν Ἱστορία καὶ Τοπογραφία τῆς Περιοχῆς Κορίνθου στοὺς Μέσους Χρόνους*. Βιβλιοθήκη Ἱστορικῶν Μελετῶν 159. Athens, 1981.

Kougeas, S. "Περὶ τῶν Μελιγκῶν τοῦ Ταϋγέτου ἐξ Ἀφορμῆς Ἀνεκδότου Βυζαντινῆς Ἐπιγραφῆς ἐκ Λακωνίας." *Πραγματεῖαι τῆς Ἀκαδημίας Ἀθηνῶν* 15 (1950). Pp. 29–30.

Krajcar, J., SJ. "Metropolitan Isidore's Journey to the Council of Florence. Some Remarks." *Orientalia Christiana Periodica* 38 (1972). Pp. 367–387.

———. "Simeon of Suzdal's Account of the Council of Florence." *Orientalia Christiana Periodica* 39 (1973). Pp. 103–130.

Kresten, O. *Eine Sammlung von Konzilsakten aus dem Besitze des Kardinals Isidoros von Kiev*. Österreichische Akademie der Wissenschaften. Philosophisch-Historische Klasse Denkschriften, 123. Vienna, 1976.

Kubalik, J. "Jean de Raguse. Son importance pour l'ecclésiologie du XVe siècle." *Revue des Sciences Religieuses* 157 (1967). Pp. 150–167.

Kyrou, A. *Βησσαρίων ὁ Ἕλλην*. 2 vols. Athens, 1947.

Labarte, J. *Le palais de Constantinople et ses abords*. Paris, 1861.

Lacaze, Y. "Politique 'méditeranéenne' et projets de croisade chez Philippe le Bon: De la chute de Byzance à la victoire chrétienne de Belgrade (mai 1453-juillet 1456)." *Annales de Bourgogne* 61 (1969). Pp. 5–42.

Lampros, S. P. "Αἱ Βιβλιοθῆκαι Ἰωάννου Μαρμαρᾶ καὶ Ἰωάννου Δοκειανοῦ καὶ Ἀνώνυμος Ἀναγραφὴ Βιβλίων." *Νέος Ἑλληνομνήμων* 1 (1904). Pp. 295–312.

———. "Δύο Ἀναφοραὶ Μητροπολίτου Μονεμβασίας πρὸς τὸν Πατριάρχην." *Νέος Ἑλληνομνήμων* 12 (1915). Pp. 255–318.

———. "Ἑλληνικὰ Γράμματα τοῦ Σουλτάνου Βαγιαζὴτ Β΄." *Νέος Ἑλληνομνήμων* 5 (1908). Pp. 155–189.

———. "Ἡ Ἑλληνικὴ ὡς Ἐπίσημος Γλῶσσα τῶν Σουλτάνων." *Νέος Ἑλληνομνήμων* 5 (1908). Pp. 40–72.

———. "Τὸ Ἔθος τοῦ Μασχαλισμοῦ παρὰ τοῖς Μανιάταις τῶν Μέσων Αἰώνων." *Νέος Ἑλληνομνήμων* 2 (1905). Pp. 181–186.

———. *Ἱστορία τῆς Ἑλλάδος ἀπὸ τῶν Ἀρχαιοτάτων Χρόνων μέχρι τῆς Ἁλώσεως τῆς Κωνσταντινουπόλεως (1453)*. Vol. 6. Athens, 1908; repr. Athens, 1998.

———. "Κατάλογος τῶν Κρητικῶν Οἴκων Κερκύρας." *Νέος Ἑλληνομνήμων* 10 (1913). Pp. 449–456.

———. "Κωνσταντῖνος Παλαιολόγος Γραίτζας: ὁ Ἀμύντωρ τοῦ Σαλμενικοῦ." *Νέος Ἑλληνομνήμων* 11 (1914). Pp. 284–288.

———. *Λεύκωμα τῶν Βυζαντινῶν Αὐτοκρατόρων*. Athens, 1930.

———. "Μία Ἐπιμνημόσυνος Τελετὴ ἐν Μυστρᾷ." *Σπαρτιατικὸν Ἡμερολόγιον* 11 (1910). Pp. 33–42.

———. "Μονῳδίαι καὶ Θρῆνοι ἐπὶ τῇ Ἁλώσει τῆς Κωνσταντινουπόλεως." *Νέος Ἑλληνομνήμων* 5 (1908). Pp. 263–265.

———. "Ἡ ἐκ Πατρῶν εἰς Ῥώμην Ἀνακομιδὴ τῆς Κάρας τοῦ Ἁγίου Ἀνδρέου." *Νέος Ἑλληνομνήμων* 10 (1913). Pp. 3–112.

———. "Προσθήκη εἰς τὰ περὶ τῶν Τειχῶν τοῦ Ἰσθμοῦ τῆς Κορίνθου κατὰ τοὺς Μέσους Αἰῶνας." *Νέος Ἑλληνομνήμων* 4 (1907). Pp. 20–26.

———. "Σημειώματα περὶ Ἀρχαίων Ἑλληνικῶν Ἐπιγραφῶν ἐν Μεσαιωνικοῖς Κώδιξι καὶ Χειρογράφοις Συλλογαῖς Ἑσπερίων Λογίων." *Νέος Ἑλληνομνήμων* 1 (1904). Pp. 385–411.

———. "Τὰ Τείχη τοῦ Ἰσθμοῦ τῆς Κορίνθου κατὰ τοὺς Μέσους Αἰῶνας." *Νέος Ἑλληνομνήμων* 2 (1905). Pp. 477–479.

———. "Τρεῖς Ἐπιστολαὶ τοῦ Καρδηναλίου Βησσαρίωνος ἐν τῇ Δημώδει Γλώσσῃ." *Νέος Ἑλληνομνήμων* 5 (1908). Pp. 19–39.

———. "Ὑπόμνημα τοῦ Καρδιναλίου Βησσαρίωνος εἰς Κωνσταντῖνον τὸν Παλαιολόγον." *Νέος Ἑλληνομνήμων* 3 (1906). Pp. 12–50.

Lampsides, O. "George Chrysocossis, le médecin, et son oeuvre." *Byzantinische Zeitschrift* 38 (1938). Pp. 312–322.

———. "Γεώργιος ὁ Χρυσοκόκκης ὁ Ἰατρός." *Ἀρχεῖον Πόντου* 24 (1961). Pp. 38–41.

Langlois, V. "Mémoire sur le sabre de Constantine XIV Dracosès, dernier empereur grec de Constantinople." *Revue de l'Orient et de l'Algerie et des Colonies*. Paris, 1858. Pp. 153–165.

———. "Notice sur le sabre de Constantine XIV, dernier empereur de Constantinople, conservé à l'Armeria Reale de Turin." *Revue archéologique* 14 (1857). Pp. 292–294.

Laurent, V. "Isidore de Kiev et la métropol de Monembasie." *Revue des études byzantines* 17 (1959). Pp. 150–157.

———. "Le dernier goveneur byzantine de Constantinople: Démétrius Paléologue Métochitès." *Revue des études byzantines* 15 (1957). Pp. 197–206.

———. "Le Vaticanus latinus 4789. IV. Alliances et filiations des Cantacuzènes au XVe siècle." *Revue des études byzantines* 9 (1951). Pp. 64–105.

Livanos, C. *Greek Tradition and Latin Influence in the Work of George Scholarios*. Piscataway, NJ, 2006.

Loenertz, R-J. "La Société des Frères Pérègrinants, Etude sur l'Orient Dominicain." Vol. 1. Inst. Hist. FF. Praed., Diss. Hist 7. Rome, 1937.

———. "Pour l'histoire du Péloponnèse au XIVe siècle." *Revue des etudes byzantines* 1 (1943). Pp. 152–196.

Loomis, W. T. "Pausanias, Byzantion and the Formation of the Delian League: A Chronological Note." *Historia: Zeitschrift für Alte Geschichte* 39/4 (1990). Pp. 487–492.

López del Toro, J. *Cuarta Década de Alonso de Palencia*. Madrid, 1971.

Luria (Lur'e), J. S. "Fifteenth-Century Chronicles as a Source for the History of the Formation of the Muscovite State." In M.S. Flier and D. Rowland, eds. *Medieval Russian Culture*. California Slavic Studies 19/2. Berkeley, Los Angeles and London, 1994. Pp. 47–56.

Mainstone, R. J. *Hagia Sophia: Architecture, Structure and Liturgy of Justinian's Great Church*. New York, 1988.

Majeska, G. P. *Russian Travelers to Constantinople in the Fourteenth and Fifteenth Centuries*. Dumbarton Oaks Studies 19. Washington, DC, 1984.

Makarii, Archbishop of Kharkov. *Исторія Русской Церкви въ Періодъ Монгольскій*. Vol. 4, book 1. St. Petersburg, 1866.

Malinin, V. *Старецъ Елеазарова Монастыря Филоѳей и его Посланія. Историко-Литературное Изслѣдованіе*. Kiev, 1901.

Maltezou, C. *Ἄννα Παλαιολογίνα Νοταρᾶ: Μιὰ Τραγικὴ Μορφὴ ἀνάμεσα στὸν Βυζαντινὸ καὶ τὸν Νέο Ἑλληνικὸ Κόσμο*. Βιβλιοθήκη Ἑλληνικοῦ Ἰνστιτούτου Βυζαντινῶν καὶ Μεταβυζαντινῶν Σπουδῶν Βενετίας 23. Venice, 2004.

———. *Ὁ Θεσμὸς τοῦ ἐν Κωνσταντινουπόλει Βενετοῦ Βαΐλου (1268–1453)*. Βιβλιοθήκη Σοφίας Ν. Σαριπόλου 6. Athens, 1970.

Manfredini, M. "Inventario dei codici scritti da Isidoro di Kiev." *Studi Classici e Orientali* 46/2 (1997). Pp. 611–624.

Mango, C. A. *Hagia Sophia: A Vision for Empires*. Istanbul, 1997.

Manoussakas, M. I. "Les dernier défenseurs crétois de Constantinople d'après les documents vénitiens." In F. Dölger and H-G. Beck, eds. *Actes des XI. Internationalen Byzantinischen Kongresses*. Munich, 1958. Pp. 331–340.

———. "Ἡ Πρώτη Ἄδεια (1456) τῆς Βενετικῆς Γερουσίας γιὰ τὸ Ναὸ τῶν Ἑλλήνων τῆς Βενετίας καὶ ὁ Καρδινάλιος Ἰσίδωρος." *Θησαυρίσματα: Περιοδικὸν τοῦ Ἑλληνικοῦ Ἰνστιτούτου Βυζαντινῶν καὶ Μεταβυζαντινῶν Σπουδῶν τῆς Βενετίας* 1 (1962). Pp. 109–118.

Manucci, G. B. "Il viaggio di Pio II da Roma a Mantova." *Bolletino senese di storia patria*, n.s., 12 (1941). Pp. 62–65.

Manz, B. F. *The Rise and Rule of Tamerlane*. Cambridge Studies in Islamic Civilization. Cambridge, 1989.

Marinesco [Marinescu], C. "Deux Empereurs byzantins, Manuel II et Jean VIII Paléologue, vus par des artistes occidentaux." *Le Flambeau* 40 (November–December, 1957). Pp. 758–762.

———. "Deux Empereurs byzantins en Occident: Manuel II et Jean Paléologue." In *Comptes rendus de l'Academie des Inscriptions et Belles-Lettres* (January–March, 1957). Paris, 1958. Pp. 23–24.

———. "Le pape Nicolas V (1447–1455) et son attitude envers l'Empire byzantine." In B. D. Filov, ed. *Actes du IVe Congrès international des Etudes byzantines, Sofia, Septembre 1934*. *Известия на Българския Археологически Институтъ*/Bulletin de l'Institut Archéologique Bulgare 9, 1. Sofia, 1935. Pp. 331–342.

———. "Notes sur quelques ambassadeurs byzantins en Occident à la veille de la chute de Constantinople sous les Turcs." *Annuaire de l'Institut de philologie et d'histoire orientales et slaves* 10 (1950). Pp. 426–427.

Mark, R. and Çakmak, A. S. eds. *Hagia Sophia from the Age of Justinian to the Present*. Cambridge, 1992.

Masai, F. *Pléthon et le platonisme de Mistra*. Paris, 1956.

Mastrodemetres, P. D. "Nicolaos Secundinòs a Napoli dopo la caduta di Costantinopoli." *Ἰταλοελληνικά: Rivista di cultura greco-moderna* 2 (1989). Pp. 21–38.

———. *Νικόλαος Σεκουνδινὸς (1402–1464) Βίος καὶ Ἔργον: Συμβολὴ εἰς τὴν Μελέτην τῶν Ἑλλήνων τῆς Διασπορᾶς*. Βιβλιοθήκη Σοφίας Ν. Σαριπόλου 9. Athens, 1970.

Matschke, K.-P. *Die Schlacht bei Ankara und das Schicksal von Byzanz: Studien zur spätbyzantinischen Geschichte zwischen 1402 und 1422*. Weimar, 1981.

———. "The Notaras Family and Its Italian Connections." *Dumbarton Oaks Papers* 9 (= Symposium on Byzantium and the Italians, 13th-15th Centuries) (1995). Pp. 59–72.

———. "Personengeschichte, Familiengeschichte, Socialgeschichte: Die Notaras im späten Byzanz." In L. Balleto, ed. *Oriente e Occidente tra Medioevo et Età Moderna Studi in onore di Geno Pistarino*. Vol. 2. Geneva, 1997. Pp. 718–812.

———. "Leonard von Chios, Gennadios Scholarios, und die 'Collegae' Thomas Pyropulos und Johannes Basilikos vor, während und nach der Eroberung von Konstantinopel durch die Türken." *Βυζαντινά* 21 (2000). Pp. 227–236.

Mavroudi, Maria. "Translations from Greek into Latin and Arabic During the Middle Ages: Searching for the Classical Tradition." *Speculum* 90/1 (2015). Pp. 28–59.

Medlin, W.V. *Moscow and East Rome, A Political Study of Church and State in Muscovite Russia*. Etudes d'histoire économique, politique et social 1. Geneva, 1952.

Medvedev, I. P. *Византийский Гуманисм XIV–XV вв.* Leningrad, 1976.

Mergiali-Falangas, S. "Ἕνας Ἰταλὸς Οὑμανιστὴς καὶ Ἕνας Πελοποννήσιος Δάσκαλος: Σχέσεις Μάρκου Ἀντωνίου Ἀντιμάχου καὶ Ἰωάννου Μόσχου." *Modern Greek Studies Yearbook* 10/11 (1994–1995). Pp. 579–584.

Mertzios, K. D. "Περὶ Παλαιολόγων καὶ Ἄλλων Εὐγενῶν Κωνσταντινουπολιτῶν." In *Γέρας Ἀντωνίου Κεραμοπούλλου. Ἑταιρεία Μακεδονικῶν Σπουδῶν: Ἐπιστημονικαὶ Πραγματεῖαι Σειρὰ Φιλολογικὴ καὶ Θεολογικὴ* 9. Athens, 1953. Pp. 355–372.

———. "Περὶ τῶν ἐκ Κωνσταντινουπόλεως Διαφυγόντων τὸ 1453 Παλαιολόγων καὶ Ἀποβιβασθέντων εἰς Κρήτην." In *Actes du XIIᵉ Congrès International d'Etudes Byzantines, Ochride, 10–16 Septembre 1961*. Vol. 2. Belgrade, 1964. Pp. 170–176.

Meserve, Margaret. *Empires of Islam in Renaissance Historical Thought*. Cambridge, MA and London, 2008.

Meursius, J. *Opuscula*. Vol. 7. Florence, 1746.

Meyendorff, J. *Byzantine Theology: Historical Trends and Doctrinal Themes*. New York, 1979.

———. "Was There Ever a 'Third Rome'? Remarks on the Byzantine Legacy in Russia." In J.J.Yiannias, ed. *The Byzantine Tradition After the Fall of Constantinople*. Charlottesville and London, 1991. Pp. 45–60.

Miglio, M. *Dizionario Biografico degli Italiani*. Vol. 19 (1976). Pp. 161–162.

Mijatovich, Ch. *Constantine Palaeologus. The Last Emperor of the Greeks, 1448–1453. The Conquest of Constantinople by the Turks*. London, 1892.

Miller, W. *Essays on the Latin Orient*. Cambridge, 1921.

Millet, G. "Portraits byzantins." *Revue de l'art chrétien* 41 (1911). Pp. 445–451.

Moffatt, Ann, ed. *Maistor: Classical, Byzantine and Renaissance Studies for Robert Browning*. Canberra, 1984.

Mompherratos, A. G. *Οἱ Παλαιολόγοι ἐν Πελοποννήσῳ*. Athens, 1913.

Monfasani, J. "The Greeks and Renaissance Humanism." In D. Rundle, ed. *Humanism in Fifteenth-Century Europe*. Medium Ævum Monographs 30. Oxford, 2012. Pp. 31–68.

Moravcsik, G. "Византийские Императори их Посли в Г. Буда." *Acta Historica Academiae Scientiarum Hungaricae* 8 (1961). Pp. 239–256.

Mordtmann, A. *Esquisse Topografique de Constantinople*. Lille, 1892.

Morfakidis, M. "Η Άλωση της Κωνσταντινούπολης στο Χρονικό του Alonso de Palencia." In E. Motos Guirao and M. Morfakidis, eds. *Constantinopla. 550 años de su caída, Κωνσταντινούπολη. 550 Χρόνια από την Άλωση.* Vol. 2: *La Caída. Η Άλωση.* Granada, 2006. Pp. 53–74.

Morgan, D. *The Mongols.* London, 1987.

Morocho Gayo, G. "Constatinopla: historia y rétorica en los cronistas Alonso de Palencia y Pedro de Valenica." *Biblioteca des Autores Españoles* 257. Madrid, 1904. Pp. 9–27.

Müller-Wiener, W. *Bildlexikon zur Topographie Istanbuls. Byzantion–Konstantinupolis–Istabul bis zum Beginn des 17. Jahrhunderts.* Tübingen, 1977.

Murray, W. M. "Do Modern Winds Equal Ancient Winds?" *Mediterranean Historical Review* 2 (1987). Pp. 139–167.

Necipoğlu, Nevra. *Byzantium Between the Ottomans and the Latins: Politics and Society in the Late Empire.* Cambridge, 2009.

Nelson, R. S. *Hagia Sophia, 1850–1950: Holy Wisdom Modern Monument.* Chicago and London, 2004.

Nicol, D. M. "A Byzantine Emperor in England: Manuel II's Visit to London in 1400–1401." *University of Birmingham Historical Journal* 12 (1971). Pp. 104–225.

———. *The Byzantine Family of Kantakouzenos (Cantacuzenus) ca. 1100–1460. A Genealogical and Prosopographical Study.* Dumbarton Oaks Studies 11. Washington, DC, 1968.

———. *Byzantium and Venice: A Study in Diplomatic and Cultural Relations.* Cambridge, 1988.

———. *The Immortal Emperor: The Life and Legend of Constantine Palaiologos, Last Emperor of the Romans.* Cambridge, 1992.

———. *The Last Centuries of Byzantium, 1261–1453.* New York, 1972; 2nd ed., Cambridge, 1993.

———. *Theodore Spandounes: On the Origin of the Ottoman Empire.* Cambridge, 1997.

Nusia, Ph. "Ανέκδοτο Κείμενο περί Σκευασίας Μελανιού, Κινναβάρεως Βαρζίου, Καταστατού και Κόλλησις Χαρτιού, (15ος Αι.)." In N. Tsirones, M. Lengas and A. Lazaridou, eds. *Βιβλιοαμφιάστης.* Vol. 3: *Τὸ Βιβλίο στὸ Βυζάντιο. Βυζαντινὴ καὶ Μεταβυζαντινὴ Βιβλιοδεσία. Πρακτικὰ Διεθνοῦς Συνεδρίου. Ἀθήνα 13–16 Ὀκτωβρίου 2005.* Athens, 2008. Pp. 43–62.

Olgiati, G. "Angelo Giovanni Lomellino: Attività politica e mercantile e dell'ultimo podestà de Pera." *Storia dei Genovesi* 9 (1989). Pp. 129–161.

Ostrogorsky, G. "Byzance état tributaire de l'empire turc." *Zbornik Radova Vizantološkog Instituta* 5 (1958). Pp. 49–58.

———. "The Byzantine Empire and the Hierarchical World-Order." *Slavonic and East European Review* 35 (1956). Pp. 1–14.

Ostroumov [Ostroumoff], I. *The History of the Council of Florence.* B. Popov [Popoff], trans. Boston, 1971.

Pagani, Maria Pia. "Il 'perfido' protagonista: Isidoro di Kiev al concilio del 1439." In G. De Rosa and F. Lomastro, eds. *L'età di Kiev e la sua eredità nell'incontro con l'Occidente. Atti del Convegno Vicenza, 11–13 aprile 2002.* Rome, 2003. Pp. 157–180.

Panarko, G. "In terra d'Otranto dopo l'inasione turchesca." *Rivista storica salentina* 7 (1913). Pp. 35–56.

Papadakis, A. "The Byzantines and the Rise of the Papacy: Points for Reflection, 1204–1453." In M. Hinterberger and C. Schabel. eds. *Greeks, Latins, and Intellectual History 1204–1500.* Bibliotheca 11. Leuven, Paris and Walpole, MA, 2011. Pp. 19–42.

———. "Isidore of Kiev." In P. Kazhdan, et al., eds. *The Oxford Dictionary of Byzantium.* Vol. 2. New York and Oxford, 1991. Pp. 1015–1016.

Papademetriou, T. *Render unto the Sultan: Power, Authority, and the Greek Orthodox Church in the Early Ottoman Centuries.* Oxford, 2015.

Papadopoulos [Papadopulos], A. Th. *Versuch einer Geneaologie der Palaiologen, 1259–1453.* Munich, 1938.

Papadrianos, I. A. "Manojlo Palaeolog, Vizantijski poslanik u Serbij 1451." *Zbornik Radova Vizantolo·kog Instituta* 7 [= *Mélanges G. Ostrogorsky 2*] (1954). Pp. 311–315.

Papaioannou, C. "Τὰ Πρακτικὰ τῆς Οὕτω Λεγομένης Ὑστάτης ἐν Ἁγίᾳ Σοφίᾳ Συνόδου καὶ ἡ Ἱστορικὴ Ἀξία Αὐτῶν." *Ἐκκλησιαστικὴ Ἀλήθεια* 15 (1895–1896). Pp. 237–238 and 259–260.

Papoulia, B. *Ursprung und Wesen der "Knabenlese" im osmanischen Reich.* Munich, 1964.

Paspates, A. G. *Βυζαντιναὶ Μελέται Τοπογραφικαὶ καὶ Ἱστορικαί.* Βιβλιοθήκη Ἱστορικῶν Μελετῶν 208. Constantinople, 1877; repr. Athens, 1986.

———. *Πολιορκία καὶ Ἅλωσις τῆς Κωνσταντινουπόλεως ὑπὸ τῶν Ὀθωμανῶν ἐν Ἔτει 1453.* Athens, 1890; repr. 1995.

Pastor, L. *The History of the Popes from the Close of the Middle Ages.* Vol. 2. London, 1949.

Paszkiewicz, H. *The Making of the Russian Nation.* London, 1963.

Patrinelis, C. G. "Ἕλληνες Κωδικογράφοι τῶν Χρόνων τῆς Ἀναγεννήσεως." *Ἐπετηρὶς τοῦ Μεσαιωνικοῦ Ἀρχείου* 8–9 (1958/1959). Pp. 63–124.

———. "Κυριακὸς ὁ Ἀγκωνίτης: Ἡ Δῆθεν Ὑπηρεσία του εἰς τὴν Αὐλὴν τοῦ Σουλτάνου τοῦ Πορθητοῦ καὶ ὁ Χρόνος τοῦ Θανάτου Αὐτοῦ." *Ἐπετηρὶς Ἑταιρείας Βυζαντινῶν Σπουδῶν* 16 (1968). Pp. 152–160.

———. "Mehmed II the Conqueror and His Presumed Knowledge of Greek and Latin." *Viator: Medieval and Renaissance Studies* 2 (1971). Pp. 349–355.

———. "An Unknown Discourse of Chrysoloras Addressed to Manuel II Palaeologus." *Greek, Roman and Byzantine Studies* 13 (1972). Pp. 497–502.

Paulova, M. "L'empire byzantin et les Tchèques avant la chute de Constantinople." *Byzantinoslavica* 14 (1953). Pp. 158–225.

Pavlov, A. S. *Критические Опыты по Ястрии Древнейщей Греко-Руской против Латиням.* St. Peterburg, 1878.

Pears, E. *The Destruction of the Greek Empire and the Story of the Capture of Constantinople by the Turks.* London, New York and Bombay, 1903; repr. New York, 1968.

Pertusi, A., ed. *Venezia e l'Oriente fra Tardo Medioevo e Rinascimento.* Civiltà Europa e Civiltà Veneziana, Aspetti e Problemi 4. Venice, 1966.

Philippides, M. "An Ancient Business Success and a Medieval Failure: Lessons in Ethics from Old Business Approaches and Practices." In G. Prastacos, *et al.*, eds. *Leadership and Management in a Changing World.* Heidelberg, 2012. Pp. 351–365.

———. *Constantine XI Dragaš Palaeologus (1404–1453): The Last Emperor of Byzantium.* Forthcoming.

———. "The Fall of Constantinople: Bishop Leonard and the Greek Accounts." *Greek, Roman and Byzantine Studies* 22 (1981). Pp. 287–300.

———. "The Fall of Constantinople 1453: Bishop Leonardo Giustiniani and His Italian Followers." *Viator: Medieval and Renaissance Studies* 29 (1998). Pp. 189–227.

———. "The Fall of Constantinople 1453: Classical Comparisons and the Circle of Cardinal Isidore." *Viator: Medieval and Renaissance Studies* 38/1 (2007). Pp. 349–383.

———. "Giovanni Guglielmo Longo Giustiniani, the Genoese *Condottiere* of Constantinople in 1453." *Byzantine Studies/Etudes Byzantines*, n. s., 3 (1998). Pp. 13–54.

———. The Historical Value of Nestor-Iskander's *Povest' o Tsar'grade. Abstracts of Papers, 12th Annual Byzantine Studies Conference.* Bryn Mawr, 1986. Pp. 13–15.

———. "History Repeats Itself: Ancient Troy and Renaissance Istanbul." In S. Atasöy, ed. *Istanbul Üniversiteti 550. Yıl Uluśrarası Bizans ve Osmanlı (XV.Yüzyıl), 30–31 Mayıs 2003.* Istanbul, 2004. Pp. 41–69.

———. "Herodian 2.4.1 and Pertinax." *The Classical World* 77 (1984). Pp. 295–297.

———. ed., trans. and annotator. *Mehmed II the Conqueror, and the Fall of the Franco-Byzantine Levant to the Ottoman Turks: Some Western Views and Testimonies.* Medieval and Renaissance Texts and Studies 302. Tempe, 2007.

———. "Rumors of Treason: Intelligence Activities and Clandestine Operations in the Siege of 1453." In Murat Arslan and Turhan Kaçar, eds. *Byzantion'dan Constantinopolis'e Istanbul Kuşatmaları.* Istanbul, 2017. Pp. 403–445.

———. "Tears of the Great Church: The Lamentation of Santa Sophia." *Greek, Roman and Byzantine Studies* 52 (2012). Pp. 715–738.

———. "Venice, Genoa, and John VIII Palaeologus' Renovation of the Fortifications of Constantinople." *Greek, Roman and Byzantine Studies* 56 (2016). Pp. 377–397.

———. "Urban's Bombard(s), Gunpowder, and the Siege of Constantinople (1453)." *Byzantine Studies/Etudes Byzantines*, n.s., 4 (1999). Pp. 1–67.

Philippides, M. and Hanak, W. K. *The Siege and the Fall of Constantinople in 1453: Historiography, Topography, and Military Studies.* Farnham, 2011.

Pierling, P. *La Russie et la Saint-Siège. Etudes diplomatiques.* Paris, 1986.

Podskalsky, G. *Von Photios zu Bessarion. Der Vorrang humanistisch geprägter Theologie in Byzanz und deren bleibende Bedeutung.* Schriften zur Geistesgeschichte des östlichen Europa, Band 25. Wiesbaden, 2003.

Popov, A. N. *Историко-литературный обзор древне-русских полемических сочинений против латинан (XI–XIV в.).* Moscow, 1875; repr. London, 1972.

Presniakov, A. E. *The Formation of the Great Russian State: A Study of Russian History in the Thirteenth to Fifteenth Centuries.* A. E. Moorhouse, trans. Chicago, 1970; repr. Gulf Breeze, FL, 1993.

Protopsaltes, E. G. *Ἅλωσις τῆς Κωνσταντινουπόλεως.* Athens, *sine anno*.

Quétif, J. and Echard, J. *Scriptores Ordinis Praedicatorum.* Vol. 1. Paris, 1729.

Raby, J. "Cyriacus of Ancona and the Sultan Mehmed II." *Journal of the Warburg and Courtauld Institutes* 43 (1980). Pp. 242–246.

———. "Mehmed the Conqueror's Greek *Scriptorium*." *Dumbarton Oaks Papers* 37 (1983). Pp. 15–34.

Ramm, B. Ia. *Папство и Русь в X–XV Веках.* Moscow–Leningrad, 1959.

Real Torres, C. "La presencia de Grecia en el humanism castellano. Relaciones entre Oriente y Occidente: la influencia bizantina en el humanismo castellano." In G. Galvez, ed. *Grecia y la tradición clásica* 2. I. La Laguna-Tenerife, 2002. Pp. 627–640.

Reinert, S. W. "The Palaiologoi, Yildirim Bayezid and Constantinople: June 1389–March 1391." In J.S. Langdon, S.W. Reinert, J.S. Allen, and C.P. Ioannides, eds. *Τὸ Ἑλληνικόν: Studies in Honor of Speros Vryonis, Jr.* Vol. 1: *Hellenic Antiquity and Byzantium.* New Rochelle, 1993. Pp. 289–367.

Riant, P. *Exuviae sacrae Constantinopolitanae* 105. Geneva, 1877.

Robin, Diana M. *Filelfo in Milan: Writings 1451–1477.* Princeton, 1991.

Röll, W. "Ein zweiter Brief Isidors von Kiew über die Eroberung Konstantinopels." *Byzantinische Zeitschrift* 69 (1976). Pp. 13–16.

Roloff, G. "Die Schlacht bei Angora." *Historische Zeitschrift* 161 (1943). Pp. 244–262.

Rosetti, R. "Notes on the Battle of Nicopolis." *The Slavonic Review* 15 (1936/1937). Pp. 629–638.

Runciman, S. *Byzantium and the Renaissance.* Tucson, 1970.

———. *The Fall of Constantinople 1453*. Cambridge, 1965.
———. *The Great Church in Captivity: A Study of the Patriarchate of Constantinople from the Eve of the Turkish Conquest to the Greek War of Independence*. Cambridge, 1968.
———. *The Last Byzantine Renaissance*. Cambridge, 1970.
———. "The Marriages of the Sons of the Emperor Manuel II." In *Rivista di Studi Bizantini e Slavi: Miscellanea Agostino Pertusi*. Vol. 1. Bologna, 1981. Pp. 273–282.
———. *Mistra: The Byzantine Capital of the Peloponnese*. London, 1980.
———. "Rum Milleti: The Orthodox Community under the Ottoman Sultans." In J. J. Yiannias, ed. *The Byzantine Tradition After the Fall of Constantinople*. Charlottesville and London, 1991. Pp. 1–17.
Rundle, D., ed. *Humanism in Fifteenth-Century Europe*. Medium Ævum Monographs 30. Oxford, 2012.
Savage, H. L. "Enguerrand de Coucy VII and the Campaign of Nicopolis." *Speculum* 14 (1939). Pp. 423–444.
Schiel, J. *Mongolesturm und Fall Konstantinopels: Dominikanische Erzählungen im diachronen Vergleich*. Europa im Mittelalter 19. Berlin, 2011.
Schirò, G. "Manuele II Palaeologo incorona Carlo Tocco despota di Gianina." *Byzantion* 29/30 (1959/60). Pp. 209–230.
Schlumberger, G. L. *Byzance et Croisades. Pages médiévales*. Paris, 1927.
———. *Un Empereur de Byzance à Paris et à Londres*. Paris, 1916.
———. *La Siège, la prise et le sac de Constantinople en 1453*. Paris, 1915; repr., Paris, 1935.
Schmitt, O. J., "Kaiserrede und Zeitgeschichte im späten Byzanz ein Panegyrikos Isidors von Kiew aus dem Jahre 1429." *Jahrbuch der österreichischen Byzantinistik* 48 (1998). Pp. 209–242.
Schreiner, P. "Ein byzantinischer Gelehrter zwischen Ost und West. Zur Biographie des Isidor von Kiew und seinem Besuch in Lviv (1436)." *Bollettino della Badia Greca di Grottaferrata* 3/3 (2006). Pp. 215–228.
———. "I teologi bizantini del XIV e XV secolo e i padri della Chiesa, con particolare riguardo alla biblioteca di Isidoro di Kiev." In M. Cortesi, ed. *Padri Greci e Latini a Confronto (Secoli XIII–XV). Atti del Convegno di studi della Società Internazionale per lo Studio del Medioevo Latino (SISMEL). Certosa del Galluzzo Firenze, 19–20 ottobre 2001*. Florence, 2004. Pp. 133–141.
Schwobel, R. *The Shadow of the Crescent: The Renaissance Image of the Turk (1453–1517)*. Nieuwkoop, 1967.
Sensi, M. "Niccolò Tignosi da Foligno. L'opera e il pensiero." *Annali della Facoltà di Lettere e filosofia dell'Università degli Studi di Perugia* 9 (1971/1972). Pp. 423–431.
Senyk, Sophia. "The Patriarchate of Constantinople and the Metropolitans of Rus', 1300–1600." In *Le patriarcat œcuménique de Constantinople aux XIVe–XVIe siècles: rupture et continuité*. Actes du colloque international Rome, 5–6–7 décembre 2005. Dossiers byzantins 7. Paris, 2007. Pp. 91–101.
Serges, M. G. *Γεώργιος Σχολάριος-Γεννάδιος Β΄ ο Πρώτος μετα΄την Άλωση Οικουμενικός Πατριάρχης: Εθνοϊστορική Μελέτη. Μελέτες για τη Βυζαντινή και Μεταβυζαντινή Ιστορία* 3. Athens, *sine anno*.
Setton, K. M. "The Bulgars in the Balkans and the Occupation of Corinth in the Seventh Century." *Speculum* 25 (1950). Pp. 502–543.
———. "The Byzantine Background to the Italian Renaissance." *Proceedings of the American Philosophical Society* 100 (1956). Pp. 1–76.
———. *The Papacy and the Levant (1204–1517)*. Vol. 2: *The Fifteenth Century*. Philadelphia, 1978.

Shaw, S. *History of the Ottoman Empire and Modern Turkey*. Vol. 1: *Empire of the Gazis: The Rise and Fall of the Ottoman Empire, 1280–1808*. Cambridge, 1976.

Shepard, J., ed. *The Cambridge History of the Byzantine Empire c. 500–1492*. Cambridge, 2008.

Sherrard, P. *Byzantium*. Great Ages of Man, A History of World Cultures. New York, 1966.

Ševčenko, I. "Intellectual Repercussions of the Council of Florence." *Church History* 24/4 (1955). Pp. 291–323.

———. "The Palaeologan Renaissance." In W. Treadgold, ed. *Renaissance Before the Renaissance: Cultural Revivals of Late Antiquity and the Middle Ages*. Stanford, 1984. Pp. 144–171.

Siderides, X. A. "Κωνσταντίνου Παλαιολόγου Θάνατος, Τάφος, καὶ Σπάθη." *Ἡ Μελέτη* 2 (1908). Pp. 143–146.

Silvano, L. "Per l'epistolario di Isidoro di Kiev: La lettera a papa Niccolò V de 6 luglio 1453." *Medioevo greco* 13 (2013). Pp. 241–258.

Siniossoglou, N. *Radical Platonism in Byzantium: Illumination and Utopia in Gemistos Plethon*. Cambridge, 2011.

Smirnov, N. A. "Историческое Значение Русской [Повести] Нестора Искендера о Взятий Турками Константинополя 1453." *Византийский Временник* 7 (1953). Pp. 50–71.

Sokolov, P. "Был-ли Московскій Митрополитъ Исидоръ Папскимъ Легатомъ для Мосвы." In *Чтения въ Историческомъ Обществе Нестора-Летопца* 20/2. Kiev, 1908.

Soloviev, S. M. *Исторя Россіи с Древнейшіх Времен*. Vol. 2 (vol. 4). Moscow, 1960.

Sophronios Eustratiades, Metropolitan of Leontopolis. "Ἐκ τοῦ Κώδικος τοῦ Νικολάου Καρατζᾶ." *Ἐκκλησιαστικὸς Φάρος* 6 (1910). Pp. 200–206.

Soteriou, G. A. "Τὸ Λεγόμενον Ξίφος τοῦ Κωνσταντίνου Παλαιολόγου." *Κιβωτὸς* 17/18 (1953). P. 240.

Spatharakis, I. *The Portrait in Byzantine Illuminated Manuscripts*. Leiden, 1976.

Stacton, D. *The World on the Last Day: The Sack of Constantinople by the Turks, May 29, 1453. Its Causes and Consequences*. London, 1965 [= D. Dereksen, *The Crescent and the Cross: The Fall of Byzantium, May 29, 1453*. New York, 1964].

Staikos, C. S. *Χάρτα τῆς Ἑλληνικῆς Τυπογραφίας: Ἡ Ἐκδοτικὴ Δραστηριότητα τῶν Ἑλλήνων καὶ ἡ Συμβολή τους στὴν Πνευματικὰ Ἀναγέννηση τῆς Δύσης*. Vol. 1: *15ος Αἰώνας*. Athens, 1989.

Stieber, J. W. *Pope Eugenius IV, the Council of Basel, and the Secular and Ecclesiastical Authorities in the Empire: The Conflict over Supreme Authority and Power in the Church*. Leiden, 1978.

Syson, L. and Gordon, D. *Pisanello: Painter to the Renaissance Court*. London, 2001.

Tachiaos, A-E. "The Greek Metropolitans of Kievan Rus': An Evaluation of Their Spiritual and Cultural Activity." *Harvard Ukrainian Studies* 12–13 (1988–1989), Pp. 430–445. Repr. in Tachiaos, A-E., *Greeks and Slavs: Cultural, Ecclesiastical and Literary Relations*. Thessalonike, 1997. Pp. 349–364.

———. *Greeks and Slavs: Cultural, Ecclesiastical and Literary Relations*. Thessalonike, 1997.

———. "The Testament of Photius Monembasiotes, Metropolitan of Russia (1408–1431): Byzantine Ideology in XVth-Century Muscovy." *Cyrillomethodianum* 8–9 (1984–1985). Pp. 77–109. Repr. in Tachiaos, A-E., *Greeks and Slavs: Cultural, Ecclesiastical and Literary Relations*. Thessaloniki, 1987. Pp. 365–397.

Talbot, Alice-Mary. "Dokeianos, John." In A.P. Kazhdan, *et al.*, eds. *The Oxford Dictionary of Byzantium*. Vol. 1. New York and Oxford, 1991. P. 645.

———. "Sekoundinos, Nicholas." In A.P. Khazdan, *et al.*, eds. *The Oxford Dictionary of Byzantium*. Vol. 3. New York and Oxford, 1991. P. 1865.

———. "Theodore I Palaiologos." In A.P. Kazhdan, *et al.*, eds. *The Oxford Dictionary of Byzantium*. Vol. 3. New York and Oxford, 1991. P. 2040.

Tate, R. B. "The Civic Humanism of Alfonso de Palencia." *Renaissance and Modern Studies* 5 (1979). Pp. 25–44.

———. "La sociedad castellana en la obra de Alfonso de Palencia." *Actas del III Coloquio de Historia Medieval Andaluza* (1983). Pp. 5–23.

Tate, R. B. and Lawrence, J. *Alfonso de Palencia, Gesta Hispaniensia ex annalibus suorum dierum collecta*. 2 vols. Madrid, 1998–1999.

Teteriatnikov, Natalia B. *Mosaics of Hagia Sophia, Istanbul: The Fossati Restoration and the Work of the Byzantine Institute*. Washington, DC, 1998.

Thomson, I. "Manuel Chrysoloras and the Early Renaissance." *Greek, Roman and Byzantine Studies* 7 (1966). Pp. 63–82.

Tipton, C. L. "The English at Nicopolis." *Speculum* 37 (1962). Pp. 341–369.

Topping, P. "Greek Ms. 1 (The Works of Joannes Dokeianos) of the University of Pennsylvania Library." *The Library Chronicle* 29 (1963). Pp. 1–15.

Trapp, E., *et al.*, eds. *Prosopographische Lexikon der Palaiologenzeit*. Vienna, 1976.

Treadgold, W., ed. *Renaissance before the Renaissance: Cultural Revivals of Late Antiquity and the Middle Ages*. Stanford, 1984.

Tsangadas, P. *The Fortifications and Defense of Constantinople*. East European Monographs 71. Boulder and New York, 1980.

Tsirpanlis, C. N. *Mark Eugenicus and the Council of Florence: A Historical Re-evaluation of His Personality*. New York, 1979.

Tuchman, B. W. *A Distant Mirror: The Calamitous Fourteenth Century*. New York, 1978.

Tyerman, C. "'New Wine in Old Skins'? Crusade Literature and Crusading in the Eastern Mediterranean in Later Middle Ages." In J. Harris, C. Holmes and E. Russell, eds. *Byzantines, Latins, and Turks in the Eastern Mediterranean World After 1150*. Oxford, 2012. Pp. 265–289.

Udal'tsova, Zanaida V. "Борьба Византийских Партий на Флорентийском Соборе и Роль Виссариона Никейского в Закончении Унии." *Византийский Временник* 3 (1949). Pp. 106–132.

Unbegaun, B. "Les relations vieux-russes de la prise de Constantinople." *Revue des études slaves* 9 (1929). Pp. 13–38.

———. *Selected Papers on Russian and Slavonic Philology*. Oxford, 1969.

Uspensky, F. *История Византииский Империи*. Vol. 3. Moscow–Leningrad, 1948.

Vacalopoulos, A. E. *The Greek Nation, 1453–1669: The Cultural and Economic Background of Modern Greek Society*. New Brunswick, 1976.

———. [Bakalopoulos]. "Les limits de l'empire byzantine depuis la fin di XIVe siè jusqu'à sa chute." *Byzantinische Zeitschrift* 55 (1962). Pp. 55–65.

———. *Origins of the Greek Nation: The Byzantine Period, 1204–1461*. New Brunswick, 1970.

Van der Vin, J. P. A. *Travellers to Greece and Constantinople: Ancient Monuments and Old Traditions in Medieval Travellers' Tales*. 2 vols. Leiden, 1980.

Van Millingen, A. *Byzantine Churches in Constantinople: Their History and Architecture*. London, 1912.

———. *Byzantine Constantinople: The Walls of the City and Adjoining Historical Sites*. London, 1899.

Van Nice, R. L. *Saint Sophia in Istanbul: An Architectural Survey*. 2 vols. Washington, DC, 1965 and 1986.

Vasiliev, A. A. "Путешествие Византийского Императора Мануила Палеолога по Западной Европе (1399–1403 г.)." *Журнал Мнинистерства Народнаго Просвещения*, n.s., 39 (1912). Pp. 41–78 and 260–304.

———. "Was Old Russia a Vassal State of Byzantium?" *Speculum* 7 (1932). Pp. 350–360.

Vaughan, R. *Philip the Good: The Apogee of Burgundy*. London, 1970.

Vernadsky, G. *The Mongols and Russia*. A History of Russia 3. New Haven and London, 1959.

———. *Russia at the Dawn of the Modern Age*. A History of Russia 4. New Haven and London, 1959.
Vigna, A. "Codice diplomatico delle colonie Tauro-Liguri durante la signoria dell'Ufficio di S. Giorgio (MCCCCLIII–MCCCCLXXV)." *Atii della Società Ligure di Storia Patria* 6 (1868). Pp. 19–21.
Viti, P., ed. *Firenze e il Concilio del 1439. Convegno di Studi Firenze, 29 novembre-2 decembre 1989*. Biblioteca Storica Toscana 29. 2 vols. Florence, 1994.
Vlasto, A. P. *The Entry of the Slavs into Christendom: An Introduction to the Medieval History of the Slavs*. Cambridge, 1970.
Voigt, G. *Enea Silvio de Piccolomini als Papst Pius der Zweite und sein Zeitalter*. 3 vols. Berlin, 1856–1863.
Von Muralt, E. *Essai de chronographie byzantine, 1057–1453*. St. Petersburg, 1871; repr. 1966.
Vryonis, S. "Isidore Glabas and the Turkish Devshirme." *Speculum* 31 (1956). Pp. 433–443. Repr. in *Byzantium: Its Internal History and Relations with the Muslim World. Collected Studies*. London, 1971. Studies 12 and 13.
———. "Seljuk Gulams and Ottoman Devshirmes." *Der Islam* 41 (1965). Pp. 224–252.
Waugh, W. T. "The Councils of Constance and Basle." In J. B. Bury, et al., eds. *The Cambridge Medieval History*. Vol. 3. Cambridge, 1936. Ch. 1.
Welykyi, A. G., ed. *Analecta Ordinis S. Basilii Magni. Miscellanea in Honorem Cardinalis Isidori (1463–1963)*. Vol. 4 (10), fasc. 1–2. Rome, 1963.
———. "Duae Epistulae Cardinalis Isidori Ineditae." *Analecta Ordinis Sancti Basilii. Записки Чина Св. Василий Великого*. Ser. 3, 1 (1950). Pp. 286–291.
White, J. A. *Biondo Flavio Italy Illuminated*. The I Tatti Renaissance Library 20. Cambridge, MA, 2005.
Williams, A. "Ottoman Military Technology: The Metallurgy of Turkish Armor." In Y. Lev, ed. *War and Society in the Eastern Mediterranean, 7th–15th Centuries*. The Medieval Mediterranean: Peoples, Economies and Cultures, 400–1453. Vol. 9. Leiden, New York and Cologne, 1997. Pp. 363–397.
Wirth, P. "Zum Geschichtsbild Kaiser Johannes VII Palaiologos." *Byzantion* 35 (1965). Pp. 592–600.
Wiseman, J. R. "A Trans-Isthmian Fortification Wall." *Hesperia* 32 (1963). Pp. 248–275.
Woodhouse, C. M. *Gemistos Plethon: The Last of the Hellenes*. Oxford, 1986.
Yiannias, J. J., ed. *The Byzantine Tradition after the Fall of Constantinople*. Charlottesville and London, 1991.
Zabughin, V. "Ubertino Pusculo da Brescia e la sua 'Constantinopolis'." *Roma e l'Oriente* 5 (1915). Pp. 26–50.
Zachariadou, Elizabeth A. "Les 'janissaires' de l'empereur byzantine." In *Studia Turcologica Memoriae Alexii Bombaci Dicata*. Instituto Universitatio Orientale. Seminario di Studi Asiatici 19. Naples, 1982. Pp. 591–597. Repr. in idem, *Romania and the Turks (c. 1300–c. 1500)*. London, 1985. Essay 11.
———. "John VII (Alias Andronicus) Palaeologus." *Dumbarton Oaks Papers* 31 (1977). Pp. 339–342. Repr. in idem, *Romania and the Turks (c. 1300–c.1500)*. London, 1985. Essay 9.
———. "Τὰ Λόγια καὶ ὁ Θάνατος τοῦ Λουκᾶ Νοταρᾶ." In *Ροδωνιά: Τιμὴ στὸν Μ. Ι. Μανούσακα*. Rethymno, 1996. Pp. 135–146.
———. *Romania and the Turks (c.1300–c. 1500)*. London, 1985.
———. "Süleiman Çelebi in Rumili and the Ottoman Chronicles." *Der Islam* 60/62 (1983). Pp. 268–297.
Zakythinos, D. A. *Le despotat grec de Morée (1262–1460)*. Vol. 2: *Vie et institutions*. Athens, 1953.

———. "Μανουὴλ ὁ Β´ καὶ ὁ Καρδινάλιος Ἰσίδωρος ἐν Πελοποννήσῳ." In *Mélanges offerts à Octave et Melpo Merlier à l'occasion du 25ᵉ anniversaire de leur arrivée en Grèce*. Collection de l'Institut Français d'Athènes 94. Athens, 1957. Pp. 45–69.

———. "Τὸ Πρόβλημα τῆς Ἑλληνικῆς Συμβολῆς εἰς τὴν Ἀναγέννησιν." *Ἐπετηρὶς τῆς Φιλοσοφικῆς Σχολῆς τοῦ Πανεπιστημίου Ἀθηνῶν* 5 (1954–1955). Pp. 126–138.

———. *Οἱ Σλάβοι ἐν Ἑλλάδι. Συμβολαὶ εἰς τὴν Ἱστορίαν τοῦ Μεσαιωνικοῦ Ἑλληνισμοῦ*. Athens, 1945.

Zeses, T. N. *Γεννάδιος Β´ Σχολάριος: Βίος-Συγγράμματα-Διδασκαλία*. Ἀνάλεκτα Βλατάδων 30. Thessaloniki, 1980.

Ziegler, A. W. "Die restlichen vier unveröffentlichen Briefs Isidors von Kijev." *Orientalia Christiana Periodica* 18 (1952). Pp. 135–142.

———. *Die Union des Konzils von Florenz in der russischen Kirche*. Das östlichen Christentum 4/5. Würzburg, 1938.

———. "Isidore de Kiev, apôtre de l'Union Florentine." *Irénikon* 13/4 (1936). Pp. 393–410.

———. "Vier bisher nicht veröffentliche griechischen Briefe Isidors von Kijev." *Byzantinische Zeitschrift* 44 (1951). Pp. 570–577.

Index Nominum

Agallianos, Theodoros 140, 141, 148, 149, 179n98, 180n110, 181n113, 181n117, 181n118, 183n133, 296, 297, 318n47, 319n48, 319n49, 319n50, 332
Ahmedi 258
Akakios, bishop of Darkos 180n110
Akakios the Elder 21n6
Albertus, King 98
Alessio [Alexius], Bishop of Chiusi [Clusium] see De' Cesari Alessio [Alexius], Bishop of Chiusi [Clusium]
Alexander, John 341n1
Alfonso, King 124, 319n51
Almagro, Diego 341n1
Ameroutzes [Amoiroutzes] 331
Anastasios 19n1, 74n15, 137, 178n85, 178n88
André of Ferrara 289n161
Andrew, Saint 308, 309, 327n123, 327n126, 328n130
Andrew of Rhodes 92
Anna of Russia 10, 33n79
Antoninus [Antonino], bishop of Florence 283n108, 283n110, 284n119, 284n134, 289n145
Apostoles, Michael 149, 157, 181n120, 184n156, 185n181
Aquinas, Thomas 95
Aralli [Raoul, Ralles], John 341n1
Argyropoulos, Ioannes 32n60, 122, 141, 42, 144, 145, 149, 157, 163n1, 164n2, 181n117, 181n120, 182n124, 183n133, 183n137
Athanasios 19n1, 74n15, 136, 137, 178n88
Aurispa, Giovanni 57, 59, 75n34, 76n36

Babylas, Priest 102
Balsamon 180n110
Barbaro, Francesco 259, 260, 261

Barbaro, Nicolò 130, 151, 154, 162, 163, 169n27, 171n38, 171n40, 178n81, 178n82, 178n3, 178n85, 178n88, 186n199, 187n204, 190, 195, 219, 221n1, 223n3, 223 n.8, 223n9, 223n10, 228n28, 228n29, 229n40, 236n84, 239n106, 241n122, 243, 270 n.1, 271n9, 280n86, 330, 342n8, 342n9, 343n11
Barbaro Marco [il genealogista] 192, 228n28, 229n39
Barbarossa, Frederick 267, 287n152
Barlam of Kolomensk 111
Basil, Saint 94
Basilikos [Basilicus], Ioannes 160, 186n189
Bayezid I Yıldırım, Emir 4, 27n26, 27n27, 28n33, 30n45, 162, 312n15, 349, 360, 362, 363, 370 n.1, 370n2, 371n4, 371n7, 372n10, 372n12, 373n20, 374n20
Bayezid II, Sultan 328n126
Benedetto, archbishop of Mytilene 168n25
Benvenuto, Anconitan Consul 195, 215, 230n41, 237n88, 330, 342n8, 343n11
Benvoglienti, Leonardo 237n94, 237n109, 290, 311n4, 311n6
Bessarion, John, Cardinal 11, 24n18, 26n25, 39, 72n6, 91, 92, 113n1, 122, 126, 129, 166n13, 168n24, 171n45, 172n49, 195, 196, 197, 198, 203, 216, 221n21, 228n30, 232n57, 237n83, 237n89, 238n104, 242n126, 242n135, 245, 246, 247, 249, 250, 253, 259, 261, 262, 263, 271n10, 272n15, 176n51, 292, 293, 294, 296, 297, 298, 299, 300, 302, 303, 305, 306, 309, 310n16, 314n18, 314n24, 314n25, 315n34, 316n35, 316n39, 317n39, 319n50, 320n57, 320n66, 322n79, 322n80, 322n86, 324n98, 324n101, 325n104, 325n106, 325n107, 327n125, 329, 330, 331, 332, 334, 337, 339, 340,

Index Nominum 409

341, 342 n.7, 344n30, 346n60, 347n61, 347n62, 349
Bianca [Blanca], Duchess of Milan 305, 325n107, 325n108
Biondo, Flavio 280n90, 281n97
Birago, Lamp [Lampugnino] 298, 319n56, 320n56
Bocchiardi Brothers 241n125, 242n125
Bonatto, Bartolomeo 327n125, 328n129
Borgia Alfonso *see* Calixtus III [Borgia Alfonso], Pope
Boucicaut *see* Jean le Meingre, Maréchal Boucicaut
Bracciolini, Poggio 127

Calixtus III [Borgia Alfonso], Pope 293, 295, 296, 297, 300, 301, 317n41, 319n51, 319n53, 322n78
Caoursin, Guillaume 278n66
Capistrano [Capistranus], Giovanni [Iohannes, John] 314n21
Capranica, Angelo, bishop of Fermo 249, 274n35, 290
Capranica, Domenico, cardinal 19n1, 127, 246, 249, 270n4, 310n1
Capuano, Pietro, Cardinal 327n123
Casimir, grand duke 119n64
Cataneo, Maurizio 241n125, 242n125
Centurione, Zaccaria 15, 368, 374n23, 374n24
Cesarini, Giuliano, Cardinal 77n57
Charles V, King of France 317n39
Charles VI, King of France 362
Christoforo *see* Garatone, Christoforo
Christonymos, Manuel 296
Chrysoloras, Ioannes 275n44, 289n161
Chrysoloras, Manuel 4, 5, 6, 27n30, 29n41, 30n47, 30n50, 31n52, 32n71, 45, 118n55, 275n44, 289n161, 290, 311n8, 326n118
Chrysostom[os], Ioannes 94
Coëtivy, Alain, Cardinal 293, 315n27, 322n80
Constantine I, the Great 38, 108, 109, 134, 263, 338
Constantine-Cyril, Saint
Contarini, Catarino 187n203
Contarino [Contarini], Giovanni 72n10, 178n90
Cortés, Hernan 341n1
Cribelli, Leodisio 289n161, 311n8
Cusanus [of Cusa], Nicholas 257, 258
Cyriacus of Ancona 127, 128, 233n59, 251, 257, 276n53, 277n62, 278n74, 280n90

Cyril, bishop of Monemvasia 39
Cyril, Hieromonk 180n110

Da Bistici, Vespasiano, Bishop 295, 297, 299, 319n51, 319n53, 320n62, 342n7, 347n63
Da Canale, Nicolò 191, 192, 225n16
Da Candia, pedro [Kretikos, Petros] 341n1
Da Carreto, Otto 298, 299, 320n59
Da Foligno, Tignosi Niccolò 173n51, 222n1, 234n61, 255, 279n80, 280n84, 287n157
Da Monteserrato, Cosimo 320n59
Danaianos of Moldowallachia 180n110
Dandolo, Bernardo 295
Daniel, Metropolitan 336
Da Rimini, Filippo 22n1, 234n61, 259, 282n102
Da Sarzana, Antonio Ivani 124
David, prophet 53, 259, 283n108
De Aguilar, Francisco [Alonso] 341n1
De' Cesari Alessio [Alexius], Bishop of Chiusi [Clusium] 308, 309, 328n131
Dei Guarini, Guarino 5, 6, 9, 10, 11, 12, 13, 31n53, 31n54, 36n113, 269, 276n61
Dei Lianori, Lianoro 167n24, 235n69, 246, 272n16
De la Brocquière, Bertrandon 288n158
De Langasco, Leonardo 193
Della Tuccia, Niccola 311n5
De Palencia, Alfonso Fernándes [Alonso de Palencia] 329, 342n4
De Santacroce, Andreas, Cardinal 92
D'Estouteville, Guillaume, Cardinal 302, 303, 322n79
De Torquemata, Iohannis [Juan], Cardinal 93, 302, 303, 322n80
Di Bertipaglia, Pasio 197, 213, 214, 236n71, 236n82, 237n85, 239n108, 240n114, 242n135, 245, 260, 262, 263, 264, 271n10, 272n10
Diedo, Alvise 243
Di Montaldo, Adamo 227n25, 227n28, 257, 258, 277n62, 281n94, 281n95
Dionysius, Metropolitan 113n1
Dionysius I, Patriarcgh 321n70
Diplovatatzes, Joseph [George] 172n49, 234n62
Dishypatos [Disypatos, Dissipato], Ioannes, Ioannes 43, 65, 77n50, 77n54
Dokeianos, Ioannes 34n92, 149, 166n15, 251
Doldio, Baron 119n64
Dolfin, Dolfin 243

Index Nominum

Dolfin, Zorzi 165n10, 172n49, 196, 222 n.2, 223n2, 226n22, 226n23, 227n28, 228n31, 229n35, 230n43, 213n45, 231n51, 232n51, 233n61, 234n62, 239n106, 241n119, 241n120, 241n121, 249, 255, 257, 280n86, 282n102
Doria, Zorzi 271n8
Dorotheos, Patriarch of Antioch 96, 119n58
Dotti, Paolo 244, 253, 277n65
Doukas [Michael?] 10, 22n9, 130, 136, 138, 146, 17, 148, 150, 151, 156, 158, 159, 161, 165n10, 166n19, 166n20, 167n22, 172n45, 177n78, 179n96, 180n112, 182n127, 182n128, 184n146, 184n159, 186n195, 237n85, 239n108, 312n15, 313n16, 324n99, 330, 331, 372n14
Dufay, Guillaume 288n158

Eparkhos, Thomas 172n49, 234n62
Erasmus 310
Eugenikos [Eugenicus], Mark[os] 91, 113n1, 149
Eugenikos [Eugenikos], Ioannes 149, 184n154
Eugenius IV, Pope 44, 61, 63, 83, 88, 96, 97, 98, 110, 113n1, 119n64, 121n77, 123, 124, 153
Eupraxia, Princess 87
Eustathius, Bishop of Thessalonike 258, 281n92

Ferrante, king of Naples 286n145
Filelfo, Francesco 248, 269, 289n161, 289n161, 289n162, 290, 297, 298, 299, 300, 306, 307, 308, 309, 311n8, 312n8, 319n53, 320n57, 320n59, 320n63, 320n65, 320n66, 321n66, 326n108, 326n109, 326n112, 326n115, 326n118, 327n118, 342n7
Filelfo, Giovanni Mario 289n161, 289n162
Foscari, Francesco, Doge of Venice 192, 232n58, 246, 253, 264, 266, 267, 273n20, 278n72, 284n115, 284n133, 289n141
Frederick III, Holy Roman Emperor 124
Fréron, Symeon 62, 64

Galesiotes, George 296
Galesiotes [Gallinoto], Andronikos 296, 297, 319n50
Garatone, Christoforo 65, 68, 69
Gazes, Demetrios 8
Gazes [Gaza], Theodoros 7, 8, 32n65, 164n10, 165n10

Gennadios II, Patriarch see Scholarios, Georgios [Gennadios II, Patriarch]
George, Saint 327n126
Gerasim, of Perm 81, 111, 114n9
Germanos, Hieromonk 180n110
Gerontios, Hieromonk 180n110
Giovanni, Fra 262, 287n148
Girolamo of Florence, Fra 198, 237n93, 270n4
Giustiniani, Leonardo 14, 25n19, 127, 128, 129, 130, 138, 144, 145, 146, 151, 152, 153, 156, 157, 160, 162, 163, 168n25, 169n28, 170n28, 171n36, 171n38, 171n44, 173n51, 176n72, 176n73, 179n97, 179n102, 184n163, 190, 192, 193, 194, 195, 196, 197, 198, 211, 215, 217, 219, 221 n.1, 222n2, 223n2, 223n5, 223n7, 224n22, 227n28, 229n39, 230n43, 230n45, 231n45, 231n46, 231n48, 231n49, 231n50, 231n51, 232n51, 233n58, 233n59, 233n61, 234n62, 236n77, 236n84, 237n99, 239n106, 241n119, 241n120, 241n121, 243, 249, 250, 254, 255, 257, 273n29, 277n62, 278n74, 280n88, 288n160, 313n16, 330, 343n10, 343n11
Giustiniani Longo, Giovanni Guglielmo 131, 132, 172n49, 173n51, 173n52, 173n54, 173n55, 174n56, 194, 195, 206, 218, 231n43, 232n57, 236n84, 241n122, 243, 277, 291, 312n15, 313n16
Gonzaga, Francesco, Cardinal 328n135
Gonzaga, Ludovico, Marquis of Mantua 305, 311n7
Goudeles [Gredeta], Nikolaos 207, 242n126
Gregory, companion of Isidore 90, 104, 119 n.65, 120n68, 300, 301, 321n70, 321n72, 337
Griffolini [d'Arezzo], Francesco 229n36, 237n95
Grioni, Zaccaria 243
Guarino see Dei Guarini, Guarino

Halil, Pasha 195, 231n49, 231n50, 232n51
Heinrich [Henry] of Soemmern 24n18, 129, 171n35, 172n48, 213, 214, 218, 220, 222n1, 236n75, 237n86, 237n93, 239n105, 241n118, 242n127, 242n131, 242n135, 245, 249, 262, 290, 310n2
Hunyadi, Corvinus, John 268
Hus, Jan 29n41
Hyalinas [Yalinas, Galina], Antonios 243, 244, 270n1, 271n9

Index Nominum 411

Iagaris, Manuel 193, 194, 229n37, 229n39, 230n43, 343n60
Iona [Jonas], bishop of Riazan 69, 78n76, 80, 81, 82, 89, 104, 109, 111, 114n11, 114n12, 115n12, 301
Iova of Saray 111
Isidore, Hieromobk 145, 155
Ivan III, Grand Prince of Moscow 317n39, 326n116

Jean le Meingre, Maréchal Boucicaut 362, 371n7
John, Brother 207
John, Saint 328n126
John of Ragusa 64, 65, 66, 67, 68
Jonah 203, 284n134
Jonas *see* Iona [Jonas], bishop of Riazan
Joseph, Hieromonk 180n110
Joseph, Patriarch of Constantinople 40, 41, 43, 44, 44, 60, 62, 63, 64, 65, 66, 77n50, 82, 83, 88, 109, 114n12, 116n31, 117n37, 120n76, 343n19
Juneid 373n20
Justinian I. 373n18

Kalojan [Kalojohn] *see* Palaiologos, John VIII [Kalojan, Kalojohn]
Kananos, Ioannes 35n96, 374n25, 375n27
Kantakouzenos 68, 159, 160, 186n189
Karystenos, Theodoros 171n44, 204
Khalkokondyles, Demetrios 57
Khalkokondyles, Laonikos [Nikolaos] 15, 29n43, 149, 166n20, 215, 233n60, 238n102, 282n103, 313n18, 324n99, 340
Khortasmenos, Ioannes Ignatios 12, 32n68
Kohen Balbo, Michael ben Shabettai 245, 272n12
Kosmas, Monk 347n62
Kritoboulos 149, 164n10, 172n51, 174n56, 235n68, 258, 259, 282n104, 324n99

Languschi, Giacomo 165n10, 172n49, 196, 222 n.2, 223n2, 226n22, 226n23, 227n28, 228n31, 229n35, 230n43, 213n45, 231n51, 232n51, 233n61, 234n62, 239n106, 241n119, 241n120, 241n121, 249, 255, 257, 280n86, 282n102
Laskaris, Janos 57
Leonardo of Chios *see* Giustiniani, Leonardo
Leontaris, Bryennios, Andronikos 124, 125, 164n10, 166n16, 373n20

Leontaris (Leontarios) Laskaris, Demetrios 15, 37n117, 369
Leunclavius, Joannis 229n32
Lianoro *see* Dei Lianori, Lianoro
Lomellino, Angelo Giovanni, *podestà* 187n203, 218, 219, 240n114, 240n116, 241n125, 277n64, 291, 312n12, 312n13
Ludovico of Mantua 289n161

Magno, Stefano 187n203, 313n18, 327n126
Mai, Angelo, Cardinal 319n51
Makarios, bishop of Nikomedeia 180n110
Malatesta, Cleopa 276n59
Mamas, Gregorios [Gregory] III, Patriarch of Constantinople 73n10, 135, 136, 137, 138, 156, 177n75, 177n76, 189, 210, 300, 301
Manuel, Brother 66
Marcello, Bartolommeo 268, 288n159
Martin V, Pope 43
Matthaios, Confessor 67
Maximos III, Patriarch of Constantinople 345n33
Mehmed I, Sultan 363, 365, 372n13, 373n19, 373n20, 374n20, 374n21
Mehmed II Fatih, Sultan 2, 11, 12, 14, 25n21, 35n96, 125, 137, 149, 151, 158, 159, 160, 163, 169n23, 173n51, 174n56, 186n198, 192, 195, 196, 204, 205, 206, 207, 210, 214, 216, 232n58, 233n58, 233n61, 235n68, 238n95, 238n100, 239n106, 241n117, 241n125, 244, 247, 248, 252, 253, 254, 255, 256, 257, 258, 259, 260, 261, 262, 264, 265, 269, 270n2, 277n62, 277n64, 277n66, 278n68, 279n77, 280n86, 280n90, 281n98, 282n99, 282n102, 283n111, 283n113, 284n115, 284n119, 284n129, 286n142, 286n145, 287n150, 289n161, 291, 296, 304, 311n8, 312n8, 313n18, 317n39, 334, 345n35
Melissourgos Melissenos, Makarios [Pseudo-Sphrantzes] 173n51, 196, 222n2, 226n22, 226n3, 243, 249, 255, 270n2, 274n32, 293, 315n34, 316n35, 316n39, 374n25
Menger [Mencer], Henry [Heinrich] 62, 64, 69, 77n49
Mersaites *see* Seid-Bokari [Mersaites]
Methodios, Saint 12
Metrophane II, Patriarch of Constantinople 120n76

412   Index Nominum

Minotto, Girolamo, *bailo* 163, 187n203, 190, 191, 194, 223n4
Minotto, Paolo 187n203
Minotto, Zorzi 187n203
Mohammed, Prophet *see* Muhammad, Prophet
Morozini [Morexini], Girolamo [Jeruolemo] 243
Moskhos, Ioannes 161, 227n26, 227n27
Muhammad, Prophet [Mohammed, Prophet] 108, 210, 260, 261, 263
Murad II, Sultan 2, 35n96, 77n55, 160, 162, 258, 312n15, 366, 367, 373n20
Mustafa, pretender 365, 373n20, 374n20
Musurus [Mousouros], Markos 57

Neophytos of Rhodes, Hieromonk 140, 143, 155, 180n110, 194, 222n2, 230n43, 343n10
Nephon II, Patriarch of Constantinole 336
Nestor-Iskander 19n1, 40, 74n15, 136, 137, 169n25, 171n44, 178n81, 178n82, 178n83, 178n85, 178n88
Nicholas V, Pope 72n10, 73n10, 124, 129, 135, 153, 156, 164n2, 164n9, 165n10, 165n12, 167n22, 176 n.74, 181n121, 183n135, 189, 197, 198, 207, 210, 213, 222n1, 232n54, 235n76, 236n78, 242n135, 246, 249, 254, 259, 261, 263, 264, 266, 283n112, 292, 293, 295, 297, 298, 311n4, 314n18, 314n23, 319n51, 319n56, 330, 338, 344n24, 347n62, 349
Notaras, Anna 161
Notaras, Loukas 68, 140, 141, 142, 148, 159, 160, 161, 162, 180n112, 181n118, 182n124, 186n196, 192, 194, 195, 207, 210, 213, 225n20, 226n24, 227n28, 230n43, 232n51, 239n108, 242n126

Oliveri 368
Orhan 216, 239n108

Palaiologina, Helene 23n14
Palaiologina, Zoë-Sophia 317n39, 326n116
Palaiologina Kantakouzene, Helena 2, 23n14
Palaiologina Malatesta, Cleopa 23n14
Palaiologos, Andreas 316n39
Palaiologos, Andronikos 365, 374n20
Palaiologos, Demetrios 148, 304, 326n115
Palaiologos, Georgios 25n20
Palaiologos, John V 2
Palaiologos, John VII 364

Palaiologos, John VIII [Kalojan, Kalojohn] 2, 5, 10, 14, 15, 16, 24n15, 24n17, 37n115, 38, 43, 54, 60, 61, 62, 63, 65, 66, 68, 69, 72n7, 77n50, 77n55, 83, 87, 88, 90, 91, 95, 98, 99, 108, 113n1, 114n2, 116n31, 117n37, 120n76, 124, 131, 133, 175n62, 181n120, 191, 224n12, 224n14, 225n14, 250, 252, 275n39, 317n39, 331, 333, 337, 338, 339, 346n39, 346n50, 348, 360, 362, 363, 364, 365, 366, 367, 368, 371n6, 372n12, 374n21, 374n23, 374n24, 375n28, 375n29
Palaiologos, Manuel 16n39
Palaiologos, Manuel II 2, 3, 4, 5, 6, 7, 8, 10, 11, 12, 24n15, 24n17, 26n23, 27n29, 27n31, 27n32, 28n35, 29n42, 29n43, 30n45, 30n47, 31n53, 57, 250, 307, 316n39, 317n39, 326n118, 327n118, 333, 337, 338, 346n49, 346n50, 348, 349, 360, 361, 362, 363, 364, 367, 371n5, 371n7, 371n8, 372n12, 372n14, 372n15, 373n18, 373n19, 374n21
Palaiologos, Michael VIII 312n10
Palaiologos, Theodoros I 2, 3, 5, 6, 7, 8, 23n14, 24n14, 28n35, 29n42, 31n51, 362, 364, 371n8, 372n15, 373n15
Palaiologos, Theodoros II 7, 113, 14, 15, 16, 23n14, 276n59, 365, 366, 373n15, 374n24
Palaiologos, Theophilos 145, 183n138
Palaiologos, Thomas 15, 293, 294, 295, 304, 305, 306, 307, 308, 316n39, 326n115, 327n118, 327n122, 327n125, 332
Palaiologos Dragaš, Constantine XI 2, 14, 15, 37n115, 124, 125, 129, 133, 134, 135, 137, 138, 139, 148, 149, 151, 153, 154, 155, 156, 161, 162, 163, 164n10, 165n10, 166n19, 172n46, 175n40, 176n71, 176n72, 176n73, 178n85, 179n90, 179n92, 179n96, 183n127, 184n142, 184n155, 184n156, 191, 192, 194, 206, 216, 217, 225n21, 244, 250, 251, 269, 276n53, 293, 304, 317n39, 329, 330, 349, 369, 375n29
Palaiologos Graitzas, Constantine 325n108
Palaiologos Metokhites, Demetrios 43, 65, 74n27, 74n30, 77n50, 77n56
Paul VI, Pope 328n130
Peter, Saint 38, 111, 309
Philip the Good, duke of Burgundy 198, 219, 240n114, 268, 272n15, 288n158, 291, 314n19
Philomates, Angelos Demetrios 66

Index Nominum   413

Philomates [Filamati], Antonios 243, 244, 270n1, 271n9
Photios, metropolitan of Kiev 80, 109, 114n4
Photios, Patriarch 38
Piccolomini, Aeneas Sylvius *see* Pius II [Aeneas Sylvius Piccolomini]
Piccolomini, Francesco 328n130
Pisanello 175n62
Pius II [Aeneas Sylvius Piccolomini] 24n15, 168n25, 218, 222n2, 234n61, 238n97, 239n106, 240n113, 242n131, 257, 258, 281n93, 292, 298, 300, 302, 303, 304, 305, 306, 308, 309, 313n18, 314n21, 314n25, 315n27, 320n55, 322n78, 322n82, 322n88, 323n92, 323n74, 323n96, 324n102, 325n106, 326n109, 326n111, 326n112, 326n117, 327n125, 328n128
Pizzaro, Francisco 341n1
Plethon Gemistos, George 6, 11, 26n25, 31n52, 34n92, 39, 7n6, 166n15, 227n26, 276n56, 331, 340
Plousiadenos, John 347n62
Pseudo-Sphrantzes *see* Melissourgo Melissenos, Makarios [Pseudo-Sphrantzes]
Pusculo, Ubertino 21n6, 123, 128, 152, 153, 154, 157, 159, 160, 164n5, 164n6, 165 n.10, 166n19, 120n32, 185n167, 185n172, 185n181, 186n189, 195, 197, 235n67, 249, 274n33, 274n34

Quirini, Lauro 127, 198, 233n61, 236n77, 236n78, 236n79, 253, 254, 277n65, 282n104

Rhosos, Ioannes, Presbyter 347n62
Rizzardo, Giacomo 233n60, 239n106
Rupecremata 93, 94

Salvatoros of Stolpa 102
Samuel, Bishop 234n62
Sanderbeg, Kastriotes, George 268
Sansovino, Francesco 169n25, 196, 222n2, 249, 255
Santacroce, Andreas, Cardinal 118n53
Santamaura, John 316n36
Scholarios, Georgios [Gennadios II, Patriarch] 66, 78n65, 95, 117n41, 118n54, 120n72, 124, 125, 138, 140, 141, 142, 143, 145, 147, 148, 149, 155, 158, 159, 161, 162, 166n13, 166n14, 166n16,

179n98, 179n104, 180n109, 181n115, 181n115, 182n128, 128n129, 183n129, 183n130, 183n133, 184n144, 184n146, 186n189, 186n195, 190, 222n2, 296, 347n61
Seid-Bokhari [Mersaites/*murşid*] 25n96
Sekoundinos, Nikolaos 174n56, 248, 255, 279n88
Sforza, Francesco, Duke of Milan 306, 311n8
Sgouros [Guro, Sguro], [Petros] 243, 244, 270n1
Sigismund of Germany/Hungary 41, 370n4, 371n5
Simeon of Suzdal 103, 116n31, 117n35
Soderini, Nicholas 131
Spandounes [Spanugnino], Theodoro 327n124, 328n126, 372n11, 379n29
Sphrantzes, Georgios 10, 15, 16, 29n42, 40, 132, 137, 138, 142, 149, 156, 167n20, 177n76, 180n112, 183n141, 183n142, 308, 327n122, 332, 333, 334, 344n22, 344n25, 344n26, 344n30, 372n13, 373n17, 373n18, 374n21
Spyrid[i]on, Saint 152
Steven [Stephen] of Novgorod 25n21, 230n42
Stojkovicà, John, of Ragusa 77n47
Suleyman Çelebi 372n12
Svidrigailo, grand duke 80, 81
Symeon I, Patriarch of Constantinople 345n33
Syropoulos, Sylvestros [Silvestros] 40, 41, 62, 64, 65, 67, 72n10, 73n10, 74n23, 74n26, 77n50, 77n58, 78n65, 78n66, 95, 115n15, 117n36, 117n37, 117n42, 118n55, 118n56, 140, 143, 172n46, 179n98, 180n110, 331, 343n19, 372n11, 375n29

Tetaldi, Giacomo 172n49, 173n51, 195, 223n8, 234n61, 234n63, 255, 273n27, 279n84, 280n84, 287n157
Theodosia, Santa 237n85, 244
Theodotos, hieromonk 180n110
Theotokopoulos, Domenikos [el Greco] 341n1
Thomas [Doubting], Saint 64
Tignosi *see* Da Foligno, Tignosi Niccolò
Timur [Timur-i-lenk, Tamerlan, Tamburlain, Tamburlaine] 27n26, 362, 372n9, 372n11
Tocco, Carlo 14, 15, 30n45, 349, 368, 369

414 *Index Nominum*

Tocco, Turnus [Turno, Torno] 15, 30n45, 369
Tomasi, Pierre 289n161, 311n8
Trapezountios ["of Trebizond"], George 181n121, 329, 342n7
Traversari, Ambrogio 31n54, 76n36
Trevixan [Trivixan, Trevizano], Gabriel, Captain General 163, 243

Vasilii [Basil] II Vasili'evich, grand prince of Moscow 2, 79, 80, 82, 83, 84, 85, 86, 88, 97, 103, 114n12, 121n78, 175n70

Vasilii I Dimitrievich, grand prince of Moscow 109, 175n70
Vitturi, Lorenzo 268
Vladimir I 87, 108, 109, 112, 121n77
Vokovt, grand duke 78

Zaganos 240n114, 241n117, 279n64, 291
Zeyrek Mehmed 182n128
Zustignan [Giustiniani], Leonardo of Venice 170n30, 320n66
Zygomalas, Theodosios 228n32

Index Locorum

Acelous, River 368
Achaea 54, 366, 368, 374n23, 374n24
Actium 15
Adrianople [Edirne] 206, 268, 281n91
Aegean [Sea] 126, 128, 134, 243, 244, 246, 247, 253, 262, 264, 268, 269, 270n4, 272n12, 289n145, 310n1
Aetolia 368
Africa 18
Aigina 327n126
Ak Shehir [Şehir] 372n11
Albania 247, 268
Alexandria 173n55, 203, 336
Alpheios, River 15, 368
Amalfi 327n123
Anatolia 268
Ancona 60, 215, 276n53, 277n62, 279n74, 280n86, 281n90, 305, 308, 327n122, 330, 347n24
Ankara 4, 362, 372n11
Ankarathos Monastery 243, 244, 270n1
Antioch 96
Apulia 244, 289n145
Aragon 207, 341n1
Asia 53, 54, 366
Asia Minor 220, 255, 338
Athens 258, 281n99, 339
Athos, Mount 197
Attica 54
Avignon 44, 69, 76n42, 293, 302, 315n27

Balkans 99, 128, 247, 253, 255, 268
Basel [Bâle, Basil, Basel] 1, 23n10, 38, 40, 41, 43, 44, 58, 59, 60, 61, 62, 63, 64, 65, 66, 67, 68, 69, 70, 71n5, 74n30, 74n32, 76n42, 77n47, 77n49, 77n54, 78n76, 78n77, 79, 81, 96, 338, 345n37
Belgrade [Bellogradum] 266, 289n145
Black Sea 10, 130

Boeotia 54
Bohemia 44, 99
Bologna 60, 123, 207, 221n1, 246, 247, 260, 262, 266, 267, 272n16, 283n111, 283n114, 284n129, 284n133, 286n141, 311n5, 323n94
Bosphoros 371n7
Bradenburg 278n65
Brescia 305
Brindisi [Brundusium] 266, 289n145
Brittania 59
Brontokhion, Monastery 372n15
Buda 60, 99
Bulgaria 247
Burgundy 198, 219, 240n114, 272n15, 288n158, 291, 314n19, 322n88
Bursa 339; see also Prousa
Byzantium 3, 95, 248; see also Constantinople

Caffa 130
Cairo 167n20
Calabria 19, 60, 289n145
Candia 19n1, 197, 198, 221, 232n58, 236n75, 243, 244, 245, 248, 253, 254, 259, 262, 338, 341n1, 342n7
Caucasus, Mountai 362
Chelm [Cholm, Kholm] 102, 103
Chios [Chyos, Chius] 14, 54, 127, 130, 131, 132, 176n74, 190, 220, 221, 237n99, 242n133, 242n133, 243, 289n145, 292, 330, 338, 343n11
Chudov, Monastery 102
Cilicia 363
Constance 29n41, 62, 71n2, 75n32
Constantinople 2, 3, 4, 5, 6, 7, 9, 10, 11, 12, 14, 15, 16, 20n4, 24n14, 24n18, 25n21, 27n29, 27n32, 28n33, 28n34, 30n45, 39, 40, 43, 44, 54, 58, 60, 61, 64, 68,

416 *Index Locorum*

69, 70, 72n10, 73n10, 74n10, 75n32, 76n42, 77n50, 79, 80, 81, 88, 101, 102, 113n1, 115n29, 120n76, 121n77, 122, 123, 125, 126, 127, 128, 129, 130, 131, 132, 135, 136, 137, 138, 142, 143, 144, 145, 146, 149, 151, 152, 157, 162, 163, 164n1, 165n10, 166n19, 167n10, 168n74, 169n25, 170n30, 170n31, 170n33, 172n46, 172n49, 173n51, 174n86, 175n70, 176n71, 177n76, 178n83, 178n90, 179n90, 179n92, 183n135, 188n205, 189, 190, 191, 192, 197, 198, 203, 205, 221n1, 223n8, 224n13, 230n41, 230n42, 233n59, 237n91, 237n93, 237n95, 240n114, 241n131, 243, 244, 245, 247, 248, 249, 250, 251, 252, 253, 254, 255, 257, 258, 259, 263, 266, 267, 268, 269, 271n9, 277n61, 277n64, 279n74, 279n84, 280n86, 281n94, 282n102, 285n138, 290, 291, 292, 294, 295, 296, 300, 303, 304, 306, 307, 311n4, 311n5, 312n10, 313n16, 313n18, 315n25, 317n39, 319n56, 320n66, 321n70, 322n70, 323n94, 326n114, 326n116, 326n118, 327n123, 329, 330, 331, 332, 334, 336, 337, 338, 339, 340, 341, 342n6, 343n11, 344n22, 344n30, 344n31, 346n60, 349, 360, 361, 362, 363, 364, 367, 370n23, 371n5, 371n7, 371n8, 372n10, 374n21; *see also* Byzantium and Tsargrad

Constantinople: **Churches, Monasteries:** Holy Apostles [Fatih Camii] 327n122, 345n35; Kharsianites, Monastery 142, 179n104, 180n112, 182n128, 184n146; Nea Ekklesia 66; Pammakaristots, Church 345n33, 345n35; Pantokrator [Zeyrek Camii], Monastery 142, 143, 146, 180n110, 180n112, 182n120, 184n146; Peribleptos, Monastery 180n110; Prodromos 25n20; Saint Basil 180n110, 216, 217; Saint Blaise 20n4; Saint Demetrios [Atik Mustafa Pasha], Monastery 3, 25n21, 39, 76n34, 79, 194, 230n42, 331, 332, 338, 343n11; San Marco 191; Santa [Hagia] Sophia 4, 24n18, 40, 124, 136, 137, 150, 152, 155, 157, 158, 162, 176n71, 178n85, 184n142, 185n168, 194, 203, 206, 211, 214, 218, 219, 220, 221, 236n83, 237n86, 263, 285n140, 326n114, 334, 343n11, 343n22; Santa Theodosia [Gül Camii] 237n85; Studios [Stoudios, Stoudion], Monastery 180n110

Constantinople: **Districts, Buildings, Cisterns, and Quarters:** Academy 142; Aetius Cistern 280n86; Anemades [Aveniades] Towers 193, 229n32, 343n10; Aspar Cistern 289n86; Augoustaion 211, 212; Blakhernai, Palace 193, 280n86; Blankas 225n14; Bosphoros 128; Contoscalion [Kontoskalion] Harbor 25n21, 230n42; Diplokionion 205; Galatas Mount 205; Giudecca 230n42; Golden Horn 3, 20n4, 162, 163, 190, 193, 240n131, 249; [Kral's] Xenon 122, 164n1, 181n120; Mesoteikhion 195, 232n57; Mokios Cistern 20n4; Pera [Galatas] 187n203, 211, 214, 218, 219, 220, 221, 235n68, 240n113, 240n114, 240n116, 241n122, 241n126, 242n131, 242n113, 247, 270n4, 272n15, 277n64, 287n161, 291, 312n10, 312n15, 313n16; Santa Galatina 205; Sulu Kule 375n27; Wall of Herakleios 3, 25n21; Xylalas Palace 140, 143, 146, 179n98, 180n108, 182n128, 183n142, 184n146

Contantinople: Gates: Aya Kapı 237n85; Basilike 224n14; Beautiful 205; Jewish 230n42; Kaligaria 204, 205, 280n86; Kharsia [Edirne Kapı] 217; Pempton [Hücüm Kapı] 131, 194; Saint Romanos [Top Kapı] 194, 206, 217, 375n27; Ventura 204; Xyloporta [Wooden] 193

Corfu 54, 222n1, 259, 271n9, 295, 304, 308, 319n41

Corinth 15, 16, 39, 72n7, 250, 251, 276n50, 364, 373n18

Cremona 280n90, 305

Crete 3, 11, 33n77, 54, 72n10, 126, 131, 140, 170n35, 181n121, 183n135, 196, 198, 203, 207, 208, 214, 221, 233n58, 235n75, 236n78, 237n93, 237n99, 239n109, 242n135, 243, 244, 249, 253, 254, 267, 269, 270n1, 276n4, 271n8, 290, 291, 293, 311n4, 311n5, 311n24, 338, 341n1, 347n62

Croatia 89

Cyclades 54, 264

Cyprus 54, 293, 311n5, 339

Dalmatia 2, 21n6

Danube, River 289n145, 361

Dardanelles 130, 244, 268

Darkos 180n110

Drama 95

Durrazo [Durrachium] 266, 289n145

Index Locorum 417

Egypt 167n20
Ekhinades [Curzolari] 15, 30n45,
  37n115
Elis 15, 368, 374n24
England [Albion] 24n17, 59, 172n49, 362
Ephesus 91, 113n1, 337
Epiros [Epeiros] 15, 54, 368
Euboea 54, 178n90, 243, 289n145, 295
Europe 53, 58, 151, 245, 247, 249, 268,
  313n16, 317n39, 371n4
Evenos, River 368

Ferrara 1, 21n6, 22n9, 23n10, 26n25, 38, 41,
  44, 58, 71n1, 71n5, 73n10, 75n34, 77n44,
  77n44, 77n55, 88, 89, 90, 91, 92, 95, 99,
  101, 102, 112, 115n15, 115n6, 116n29,
  116n31, 117n37, 117n39, 118n53,
  120n76, 121n78, 122, 123, 125, 126, 127,
  136, 140, 144, 153, 164n10, 167n22,
  174n56, 182n124, 248, 289n161, 323n94,
  330, 331, 332, 333, 334, 335, 336, 337,
  339, 342n7, 343n19, 345n33, 345n34,
  346n39
Florence 1, 21n6, 22n9, 23n10, 26n25, 38,
  41, 58, 71n1, 71n5, 73n10, 75n34, 77n44,
  77n55, 88, 89, 90, 91, 92, 93, 95, 98, 99,
  101, 102, 112, 115n15, 116n30, 116n31,
  117n33, 117n37, 117n39, 118n49,
  118n53, 120n76, 122, 123, 125, 131, 135,
  136, 140, 144, 153, 167n22, 174n56,
  182n124, 198, 232n58, 246, 248, 253,
  254, 262, 264, 266, 267, 271n10, 272n16,
  279n73, 283n108, 283n109, 283n114,
  284n127, 289n142, 323n94, 330, 331,
  332, 333, 334, 335, 336, 337, 339, 342n7,
  343n19, 345n33, 345n34, 346n39
Forabium [Siderovia, Smederevo] 264,
  289n145
France 59, 257, 280n86, 322n88, 327n124,
  338, 362; *see also* Galatia, Gallia

Galatia, Gallia 56, 59; *see also* France
Genoa [Zenova] 59, 174n56, 218, 241n122,
  277n64, 291, 302, 312n10, 342n8,
  372n12
Germany 98, 100, 102, 110, 322n88,
  346n60
Gibraltar 361
Glarentza [Clarence, Kyllene] 14, 15, 366,
  368, 374n24
Goza 19
Greece [Graecia] 14, 289n145, 293, 306,
  308, 328n130, 329, 340; *see also* Hellas

Hellas 54
Hellespont 18, 197, 249, 363
Hexamilion 250, 251, 276n53, 364, 373n18
Hungary 60, 89, 98, 247, 266, 289n145,
  338, 346n50, 379n29

Iberia [Georgia] 54
Illyria 54
Ionian Sea 15
Isthmus of Corinth 250, 276n53, 364; *see
  also* Hexamilion
Istria 89
Italy 4, 56, 57, 59, 89, 122, 127, 144, 154,
  169n25, 169n28, 176n74, 207, 241n125,
  245, 249, 253, 259, 262, 266, 268,
  280n90, 287n50, 290, 292, 296, 308,
  309, 316n39, 317n39, 329, 335, 338, 339,
  342n4, 343n11, 346n50, 347n62
Ithaka 368

Jerusalem 56, 203, 211, 259, 266,
  282n103, 336

Kalavryta 34n93
Kallipolis 43
Karaman[ia] 268
Kenkhreai 15, 364, 366
Kephalonia 54, 368
Khalkis *see* Negropontes [Khalkis]
Kiev 1, 39, 69, 79, 87, 91, 96, 99, 100, 102,
  108, 109, 113n1, 115n12, 194, 300,
  321n69, 321n70, 338, 339
Kolosmensk 111
Kontostephanos Monastery 21n6, 22n9,
  24n14
Krisa, Gulf 366
Kyllene *see* Glarentza [Clarence, Kyllene]
Kythera 18

Lampsakos 18
Latvia 100, 102, 110
Lecce 289n145
Lemnos [Stalimene] 174n56, 365, 374n20
Lepanto [Naupaktos] 15, 30n45
Lesbos 54, 127, 128, 168n25,
  169n25, 292
Leucas [Leukas] 54, 368
Levant 126, 132, 192, 253, 288n160, 293,
  295, 338, 339, 371n7
Libya 18
Lithuania 80, 81, 82, 89, 96, 99, 100, 102,
  110, 300, 321n70, 338
Livonia 89, 96

418 *Index Locorum*

London 245, 338
L'vov [L'viv] 113n1

Macedon[ia] 54, 253, 254, 289n162
Maina [Mani, Mane] 72n7
Makronnesos 18
Mantua 303, 304, 305, 306, 323n94, 323n97, 325n108, 326n108, 326n108, 326n119
Marseilles 15, 369
Media 362
Megara 281n99
Melenikos 95
Melite 19
Melos 18
Messenia 366, 374n24
Methone 18, 347n62
Mexico 341n1
Milan 60, 256, 280n90, 298, 320n59, 320n65, 320n66, 325n108, 326n109, 327n122, 326n109, 327n122, 379n29
Mistra 6, 8, 11, 15, 16, 26n25, 28n37, 31n52, 34n93, 39, 194, 374n20
Moldowallachia 54, 180n110
Molossia 368
Monemvasia [Monembasia] 2, 3, 21n6, 22n9, 24n14, 28n37, 39, 72n7, 72n8, 114n4, 362
Morea 2, 4, 5, 6, 7, 9, 11, 12, 13, 14, 15, 24n14, 27n29, 31n52, 34n93, 37n115, 39, 148, 170n71, 250, 293, 304, 305, 308, 311n5, 324n99, 324n102, 325n105, 325n108, 326n115, 327n123, 327n125, 332, 344n25, 347n62, 348, 349, 364, 365; *see also* Peloponnese
Moscow 1, 79, 81, 82, 83, 87, 88, 89, 96, 97, 99, 102, 103, 113n1, 115n15, 115n25, 120n74, 120n76, 121n77, 300, 301, 317n39, 321n70, 337, 338, 339, 343n19, 346n39
Muscovy 2, 70, 96, 101, 116n31
Mysia 54
Mytilene [Metelin, Mytilina, Mitilene] 163, 168n25, 190, 191, 289n145, 292, 343n11, 374n20; *see also* Lesbos

Naples 126, 164n10, 289n145
Naxos 372n12
Negropontes [Khalkis] 72n10, 178n90, 225n16, 233n60, 239n106, 243, 295
Nicaea 39, 86, 113n1, 330, 331, 338, 346n60
Nicopolis 361, 370n2, 370n3, 371n5
Nicosia 39, 293, 339

Nikomedeia 180n110
Novgorod 103, 230n42

Orsanmichele 90

Padua 142, 272n16
Paphos 293, 338
Paris 44
Patras 13, 327n123, 328n130
Pavia 302
Peloponnese [Peloponnesus] 2, 3, 9, 12, 18, 28n37, 54, 250, 251, 308, 311n5, 362, 363, 364, 365, 366, 368; *see also* Morea
Peristeri 264
Perm 111
Persia 14, 36n113, 205, 235n68, 249, 250, 252, 362
Peru 341n1
Perugia 127, 257, 323n94
Phocis 54
Phokaia [Focis] 220, 221, 242n133
Pholoe 368
Poland [Liakhia] 89, 96, 99, 102, 103, 300, 321n70
Prague 29n41, 44
Prino 295
Proikonnesos 18
Prousa [Bursa] 220, 221, 242n133, 372n11

Rhodes 54, 92, 128, 249, 277n65, 278n65, 289n145, 311n5, 328n128, 372n12
Riazan 69, 80, 98, 104, 109, 111
Riva 371n7
Rome 2, 3, 4, 60, 63, 64, 70, 87, 88, 94, 104, 108, 109, 115n26, 122, 124, 127, 129, 135, 164n1, 164n10, 179n101, 189, 203, 204, 210, 214, 226n22, 255, 256, 277n64, 290, 293, 295, 300, 301, 304, 307, 308, 309, 310n3, 311n4, 314n24, 317n39, 320n59, 320n60, 320n66, 326n116, 327n125, 331, 337, 338, 342n7, 344n26, 345n33
Rouen 302
Rumeli 373n20
Rumeli Hisar 210, 282n102
Rus' 1, 39, 40, 54, 69, 70, 79, 80, 81, 85, 86, 87, 88, 89, 91, 96, 97, 99, 100, 101, 102, 103, 109, 110, 112, 120n76, 137, 140, 152, 162, 190, 300, 301, 308, 332, 338, 339, 345n33; *see also* Russia
Russia [Rosia, Rosìa] 3, 113n1, 229n35, 239n120, 309, 321n69, 330, 331, 343n11; *see also* Rus'
Ruthenia 22n9, 214, 262, 330

Sabina 39, 245, 339, 346n60
Sameniko 325n108
Saray 111
Sardis 113n1
Sarmatia 167n20
Savoy 54, 60, 67
Serbia 247
Sicily 16, 319n50, 338
Siena 305, 323n94
Sigrion 18
Sinope 363
Skyros 18
Smyrna 337
Spain 272n12, 329, 341n1, 347n62
Spoleto 323n94
Stolpa 102
Suzdal 103, 116n31, 117n35, 120n72
Syracuse 19

Taranto 289n145
Taurus, Mountain 363, 366
Tenedos 18
Thesprotia 368
Thessalonike 2, 3, 20n4, 21n6, 25n20, 258, 364, 365, 371n7, 373n20
Thrace 54, 123, 363
Tornovo 180n110
Transylvania 247

Trebizond 331
Tsargrad [Constantinople] 81, 83, 87, 343n19
Turin 132, 133
Turkey 128, 132
Tuscany 203, 246
Tusculum 39, 346n60
Tver 120n74, 339

Udine 303, 304
Uspensky [Annunciation], Cathedral 103

Varna 125
Vatican 77n49, 125, 129, 135, 136, 144, 166n19, 167n20, 234n62, 290, 293, 309, 317n39, 338, 339
Venice 4, 59, 98, 99, 164n6, 164n10, 190, 191, 250, 256, 260, 264, 266, 267, 275n38, 288n159, 290, 295, 311n5, 347n62, 371n5, 372n12, 374n23, 379n29
Verona 305
Vienna 60
Volga, River 321n69

Wallachia 54

Zacynthos [Zakynthos] 54, 368

Index Rerum Antiquarum

Achilles 258, 259, 279n80, 283n104
Aegisthus 278n61
Aelius Aristides 12, 57
Aetius 280n86
Agamemnon 307, 324n102
Alexander the Great 196, 207, 233n58,
    233n61, 234n62, 235n68, 253, 254, 255,
    256, 257, 258, 259, 260, 261, 277n62,
    277n64, 278n69, 279n75, 279n76,
    279n80, 281n90, 287n95, 360
Apollo 252
Apollodorus 278n69
Argos 324n102
Arian 254
Aristotle 26n25, 164n3, 341
Artaxerxes, Great King 14, 277n61
Arthur, King 251
Asklepios 367
Aspar 280n86
Assyria 211
Athenaeus 10
Athens 248, 270
Atreus 232, 258, 278n68
Aurelius, Marcus 27n32, 326n118

Babylon 56
Bactria 362

Caesar, Julius 164n3, 281n91
Caligula, Emperor 257
Cambyses 164n3
Carthagae 255
Cassandra 148
Charybdis 164n3
Cicero 12
Cleopatra 249
Corinth 324n102
Croesus 164n3
Curtius, Quintus 257, 280n86
Cyrus 164n3, 360

Darius 360
Delphi 251
Delphic Oracle 250, 252
Demosthenes 12, 31n58, 57, 270

Eleusinian Mysteries 6
Elis 324n102
Eos 164n3
Erinys 251

Gaul 362
Golgos 367
Great King [of Persia] 197, 235n68, 248,
    249, 250, 252, 277n61

Hannibal 257, 281n91, 281n95
Hector 347n62
Helen [of Troy] 324n102
Heliodorus 320n61
Helios 54
Hellas 252
Herakles [Hercules] 164n3, 361
Herodotus 257, 277n61, 280n86, 347n62
Hesiod 164n3, 326n112
Homer 35n107, 164n3, 258, 263n104,
    326n112, 367
Hyrcania 362

Ister 361
Isthmus of Corinth 252

Josephus, Flavius 342n7
Julian, the Apostate 238n104
Julius, Caesar 254, 255

Kalkhas 307
Kypselos 368

Lacedaemon 324n102
Laertius, Diogenes 257, 280n86

Livy 257, 280n86
Longinus 327n127
Lucian 10
Lycides 320n61

Mandane 164n3
Mark Anthony 15
Massalia 369
Menelaos 324n102
Moskhos 326n111
Muse(s) 306, 326n109, 326n111, 426n112, 327n120
Myrmidon[e]s 196, 255, 279n80, 279n81

Nebuchanezzar 211, 259
Nero, Emperor 254, 279n72, 280n94
Nestor 324n102
Niketas, Patrician 249

Octavian [Augustus] 15, 249, 256
Odysseus 12, 164n3
Olympia 251
Olympic Games 7, 324n102

Paul of Aigina 320n61
Paulus, Aemilius 254, 279n73
Pelops 365
Persia 19
Philip II, of Macedon 270, 281n91, 281n95, 360
Philostratus 320n61
Pillars o Hercules 361
Plato 31n58, 341
Plutarch 297, 298, 299, 300, 306, 320n60, 320n63, 320n66, 342n7
Polybius 320n61
Pompey [Pompeius, Gnaeus], the Great 254, 279n73

Priam 248
[Pseudo-] Ptolemy 250, 320n61
Pylos 324n102
Pythia 250, 252

Rome 255

Salamis 248
Samosata 10
Scipio, Publius 254, 279n73, 281n96, 281n97
Scylla 164n3
Sibylla 164n3
Sirens 12
Smyrnaeus, Quintus 347n62
Solon 164n3
Sparta 255

Thebes 203
Theocritus 326n111
Thucydides 347n2
Thyestes [Tiestis] 232n58, 233n58, 234n62, 253, 277n69
Titans 164n3
Trojan Cycle 347n62
Trojan War 324n102
Troy [Ilium] 203, 248, 258, 259, 282n101, 282n103, 283n104, 286n145, 287n148, 288n159

Vergil 154, 248, 274n33

Xenophon 10, 36n118, 276n61, 277n61, 347n2
Xerxes, Great King 14, 196, 197, 234n62, 235n66, 235n67, 235n68, 248, 249, 250, 252, 260, 261, 274n32

Zeus [Jupiter] 32n74, 164n3, 326n117